The Economics of European Integration

Fourth Edition

Richard Baldwin and Charles Wyplosz

**McGraw-Hill
Higher Education**

London Boston Burr Ridge, IL Dubuque, IA Madison, WI New York San Francisco St. Louis
Bangkok Bogotá Caracas Kuala Lumpur Lisbon Madrid Mexico City
Milan Montreal New Delhi Santiago Seoul Singapore Sydney Taipei Toronto

The Economics of European Integration, 4th Edition

Richard Baldwin and Charles Wyplosz

ISBN-13 9780077131722

ISBN-10 007713172X

Mc Graw Hill McGraw-Hill Higher Education

Published by McGraw-Hill Education
Shoppenhangers Road
Maidenhead
Berkshire
SL6 2QL
Telephone: 44 (0) 1628 502 500
Fax: 44 (0) 1628 770 224
Website: www.mcgraw-hill.co.uk

British Library Cataloguing in Publication Data
A catalogue record for this book is available from the British Library

Library of Congress Cataloguing in Publication Data
The Library of Congress data for this book has been applied for from the Library of Congress

Executive Editor: Natalie Jacobs
Commissioning Editor: Rebecca Birtwistle
Production Editor: Alison Davis
Marketing Manager: Vanessa Boddington

Text Design by HL Studios
Cover design by Adam Renvoize
Printed and bound in The UK by Ashford Colour Press Ltd, Gosport, Hants PO13 0FW

ISBN-13 9780077131722
ISBN-10 007713172X

The **McGraw·Hill** Companies

For Sarah, Ted, Julia and Nick - R.B.
In memory of my parents, whose sufferings inspired my yearning for a
Europe at peace, and who taught me the pleasure of learning - C.W.

Brief Table of Contents

Detailed Table of Contents

Preface

In the summer of 2011, our preparation for the fourth edition was thrown off course by the Eurozone crisis – just as the Global Crisis of 2008 interrupted our preparation of the third edition. With hindsight, the strategy we adopted for the Third Edition – highlighting the Eurozone's weak spots – was correct, as the result provided a guide for readers to interpret events that have unfolded in such a spectacular fashion in 2011. In fact, as this edition goes to print (October 2011), the Eurozone crisis it is getting deeper by the day. As we write, a number of commentators even predict disintegration and a breakup of the Eurozone.

Once again, history has presented us with a tough trade-off in addressing events that affect the core of our topic, European integration. On the one hand, a textbook has to take some distance from immediate events. On the other hand, these events are transforming the nature of the European economic landscape. We need to take these events into accounts, even though future events may well turn things in yet another direction. With so much uncertainty, the trade-off is between ignoring how European integration is being transformed on one hand, or addressing them but at the risk of drawing conclusions that subsequent events prove wrong on the other hand. Our response has been to deeply rewrite the macroeconomic chapters, to provide more information on the issues raised by the crisis – e.g. the US subprime mortgage loans or the functioning of financial markets – and to add a new chapter entirely dedicated to the European sovereign debt crisis.

Pedagogy, however, remains our main concern. Following a review of book users, we have decided on two important changes from the Third Edition:

- We have reverted to the traditional ordering of chapters. Parts I presents history and institutions, Parts II and III cover trade and market integration, and Parts IV and V are dedicated to monetary integration.
- We have also restructured the three chapters that used to present the macroeconomic tools, the issue of the choice of an exchange rate regime and the European Monetary System. In order to improve coherence, we merged three chapters into two. By streamlining the exposition[1] and avoiding repetitions, we thus made room for the new chapter on the crisis without making the book longer. We have also streamlined some of the material in the chapters on microeconomic essentials in order to make room for a fuller verbal treatment of the material.

In addition, we made a large number of small editions. It is impossible to list them all. For example, Chapter 1, which reviews the history of economic integration in Europe has been updated to account for the entry into force the Lisbon Treaty. The Lisbon Treaty changes have also been fully integrated into Chapter 2 (Facts, Law and Institutions). In the monetary integration part, we now provide a more detailed treatment of rational expectations and of budget constraints, if only because this is needed to make sense of the crisis.

As before, the goal of this book is to provide an accessible presentation of the facts, theories, policies and controversies that are necessary to understand Europe's economic integration process. Our approach is rooted deeply in economic principles for the simple reason that economic integration has been the vanguard of broader European integration since the 1948 Organization for European Economic Cooperation.

---

[1] particular, we no longer present the IS-LM and AD-AS models, which can be found in most macroeconomic textbooks.

What this book is

This is a textbook for courses on European economic integration. Its emphasis is on economics, covering both the microeconomics and macroeconomics of European integration. Understanding European economic integration, however, requires much more than economics, so the book also covers the essential aspects of European history, institutions, laws, politics and policies.

The book is written at a level that should be accessible to second- and third-year undergraduates in economics as well as advanced undergraduates and graduate students in business and in international affairs, European studies and political science. Some knowledge of economics is needed to absorb all the material with ease – a first-year course in the principles of economics should suffice – but the book is self-contained in that it reviews most essential economics behind the analysis.

What is in this book

The book is organized into five parts: essential background (Part I), the microeconomics of European integration (Part II), microeconomic policies (Part III), the macroeconomic of monetary integration (Part IV) and macroeconomic policies (Part V).

Part I presents the essential background for studying European integration.

- An overview of the post-Second World War historical development of European integration is presented in Chapter 1. The chapter should be useful to all students, even those who are familiar with the main historical events, as this chapter stresses the economic and political economy logic behind the events.
- A concise presentation of the indispensable background information necessary for the study of European integration is presented in Chapter 2. This includes key facts concerning European economies and a brief review of the EU's legal system and principles (fully updated to reflect the Lisbon Treaty changes). Chapter 2 also presents information on the vital EU institutions and the EU's legislative processes as well as the main features of the EU budget.
- Chapter 3 presents an economic framework for thinking about EU institutions. The first part explains how the 'theory of fiscal federalism' can be used to consider the appropriateness of the allocation of powers between EU institutions and EU Member States. The second part explains how economic reasoning – game theory in particular – can be used to analyse EU decision-making procedures for their decision-making efficiency as well as their implications for the distribution of power among EU members. While these are not classic topics in the study of European integration, they are essential to understanding the current challenges facing the EU, such as the 2004 enlargement and the debates around the Lisbon Treaty. This is more relevant than ever as the Eurozone crisis is almost sure to produce a shifting of some competences from the national level to the supranational level – or at the very least, a serious debate over such shifts.

Part II presents the microeconomic aspects of European integration.

- An introduction to the fundamental methods of trade policy analysis is presented in Chapter 4. The chapter introduces basic supply and demand analysis in an open economy, the key economic welfare concepts of consumer and producer surplus, and uses these to study the simple economics of tariff protection.
- An in-depth analysis of European preferential trade liberalization is given in Chapter 5. The focus is on how the formation of a customs union or free trade area affects people, companies and governments inside and outside the integrating nations.
- A thorough study of how the market-expanding aspects of European integration affects the efficiency of European firms is presented in Chapter 6. The main line of reasoning explains how integration in the presence of scale economies and imperfect competition can produce fewer, bigger and more efficient firms facing more effective competition from each other. Again, the ongoing enlargement of the European Union makes this sort of logic more relevant than ever.

- Chapter 7 gives a detailed study of the growth effects of European integration. The emphasis is on the economic logic linking European integration to medium-run and long-run growth effects. Neoclassical and endogenous growth theories are covered to the extent that they help students understand the growth-integration linkages. The basic facts and empirical evidence are also covered.

- Chapter 8 deals with the labour markets. It recalls the basics of labour economics in order to explain unemployment and develop the notion that social requirements may have seriously negative effects in terms of jobs, wages and growth. The chapter uses these insights to study the effects of integration. It deals with many controversial issues such as social dumping and migration, trying hard to stay above the fray by presenting economic analysis as one logic, not the only one.

Part III presents the main microeconomic policies of the EU.

- Chapter 9 looks at the Common Agricultural Policy (CAP), presenting the economics and facts that are essential for understanding its effects. The chapter takes particular care to examine the economic forces behind recent CAP reform in the light of international trade negotiations (the Doha Round), the Eastern enlargement and the reforms that are being discussed for the post-2013 financial period.

- Chapter 10 presents the economics that link European integration to the location of economic activities. This includes a presentation of the main facts on how the location of economic activity has shifted both within and between nations. To organize thinking about these facts – and to understand how EU regional policy might affect it – the chapter presents the location effects of integration in the light of neoclassical theories (Heckscher–Ohlin), as well as the so-called new economic geography. The chapter also presents the main features of the EU's regional policy and considers the implications of the eastern enlargement.

- Chapter 11 covers the basic elements of the EU's competition policy and state aid policy (EU jargon for subsidies). Instead of just describing the policies, the chapter motivates and explains them by introducing the basic economic logic of anticompetitive practices. It has been updated to include several recent cases that illustrate the difficulties of applying simple economics to the complex world of international business.

- Chapter 12 addresses EU trade policy, i.e. its commercial policies with the rest of the world. While trade policy is not as central to the EU as, say, the CAP and cohesion policies are, it is important. The EU is the world's biggest trader, and trade policy is probably the only EU 'foreign policy' that is consistently effective. The chapter covers EU trade policy by presenting the basic facts on EU trade, covering the EU's institutional arrangements as concerns trade policy, and finally summarizing the EU's policies towards its various trade partners. It has been fully updated to reflect changes introduced by the Lisbon Treaty.

Part IV continues the approach of Part II by providing the basic principles behind macroeconomic and monetary integration.

- The principles needed for the macroeconomic analysis are presented in Chapter 13. This chapter presents the macroeconomic theories and tools needed to analyze monetary integration. It organized around three principles: interest rate parity, purchasing power parity, and the impossible trinity that affects the choice of exchange rate regimes.

- The long process of European monetary integration is recounted in Chapter 14. It starts back from ancient times when Europe was a de facto monetary union under the gold standard, reviews the Bretton Wood period when Europe's exchange rates were tied together via the US dollar and then moves to the European Monetary System, past and present. The process of euro adoption is briefly reviewed.

- Chapter 15 presents the optimum currency area theory that helps to understand the main costs and benefits from sharing a common currency. The theory does not provide a black-and- white answer; rather, it develops a set of economic, political and institutional criteria to evaluate the costs and benefits of forming a monetary union. In addition, the costs and benefits may be endogenous. Europe fulfils some criteria but not others, which explains the unending debates on the merits of the European monetary union.

Part V is the counterpart to Part III, as it presents the main macroeconomic policies of the EU.

■ The main features of the European monetary union are laid out in Chapter 16. This includes a description and an analysis of the institutions created by the Maastricht Treaty. It explains the importance attached to price stability and the measures adopted to achieve this objective. The chapter also provides a review of the first decade of the euro until the crisis.

■ Fiscal policy is the last national macroeconomic instrument remaining once national monetary policy has been lost. Chapter 17 looks at the Stability and Growth Pact, designed to deliver enough budgetary discipline not to endanger the overriding price stability objective. Since the first edition of this book, we have underlined the Pact's serious shortcomings, now made plain by the sovereign debt crisis. We emphasize the economic and political difficulties inherent in preserving the last national macroeconomic instrument while ensuring fiscal discipline.

■ Chapter 18 deals with the financial markets. The financial services industry has being transformed by the Single European Act of 1986 and by the adoption of a single currency. The chapter starts with a review of what makes this industry special and then introduces the microeconomics of capital integration. It then looks at the evolution of banks, bond markets and stock markets, discussing the shortcomings in regulation and supervision that have been illustrated during the crisis. The chapter also examines whether the euro is becoming a worldwide currency, alongside the US dollar.

■ Finally, Chapter 19 offers an overview of the Eurozone crisis. It looks at the global crisis that started in the US and its transmission to Europe. The next step, the sovereign crisis, is then described and analyzed, bringing together much of the material presented in earlier chapters. It then looks at short and long term policy responses.

How to use this book

The book is suitable for a one-semester course that aims at covering both the microeconomics and the macroeconomics of European integration. If the course is long enough, the book can be used sequentially for two courses.

Shorter courses may focus on the trade and competition aspects; they can use only Parts I, II and III. Conversely, a course dealing only with the macroeconomic aspects can use Parts IV and V, and finish with labour market issues as covered in Chapter 8 (which does not really require the previous microeconomic material).

Eclectic courses that focus on theory and cover trade, competition and macroeconomics, can use only Chapters 1 to 8 and 16 to 19, or just 4 to 8 and 16 to 19.

Eclectic courses oriented towards policy issues can use, with some additional lecturing if the students are not familiar with basic theory, Chapters 1 and 2, 9 to 12 and 16 to 19. In general, all chapters are self-contained but, inevitably, they often refer to results and facts presented elsewhere.

Each chapter includes self-assessment questions designed to help the students check how well they master the material, and essay questions which can be given as assignments. We also provide additional readings; most of them are easily accessible to undergraduate students though, occasionally, when we did not find adequate references, we point to more advanced material. Students may find some of these readings rewarding.

The fourth edition continues with our tradition of providing many internet links that should allow students and lecturers alike to get the latest information on the EU's many fast-developing areas. We have observed that the internet is an excellent way to stimulate students' interest by bringing classroom teaching to real issues they see every day in the media. The links we provide go well beyond journalist treatments in a way that allows students to realize the usefulness of the basics they have learned from the text.

Guided Tour

Introduction

The members of the European Union are
that is historically unprecedented. In man
federated nations such as Canada and Swi
by a cocktail of economic, political, histo
laws and policies. This chapter presents
features that is essential to the study of E

The chapter starts by detailing the ext
to more institutional issues – EU organiza
legislative process. The chapter then pres
and economic size), which is essential for
The final section covers the Constitution

Introduction

Each part and chapter opens with an introduction which
indicates the ideas and concepts that will be presented
in the following pages.

Figure 1.2 The four-way division of Germany

Maps and Diagrams

These are provided throughout the text to
show geographically the impact of changes in
the EU integration across the continent.

Box 1.3 The European Payments Union (EPU),

Most European nations were bankrupt after 1945,
basis of bilateral agreements, often involving barte
deals. Each month, EPU members added up the de
accounts with other EPU members. These were off
remained with an overall surplus or deficit with resp
was that, since nations no longer owed money to ea
for importing from or exporting to a particular parti
to loosen the web of bilateral trade restrictions that
In its first year, the EPU removed all discriminatory
OEEC membership also fostered overall trade liberal
required members to lower trade barriers progress
During this time intra-European trade boomed, r
(1950–58); imports from North America grew by or

Boxes

Each chapter provides a number of boxes that provide
further examples and explanations of key facts, events
or economic ideas relating to the European Union.

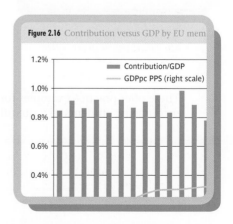

Figure 2.16 Contribution versus GDP by EU mem

Clear presentation

Economic models are clearly presented to aid the
interpretation of economic curves and graphs, with
extra notes and explanations where appropriate.

Table 3.1 Allocation of competencies to the EU

Exclusive	Shared	
Customs union	Exclusive if EU has policy	Nor
Competition policy	Internal Market	R&I
Eurozone monetary policy	Certain social policy	Out poli
Conservation of marine resources	Cohesion policy	Dev coo
Common commercial policy	Agriculture and fisheries	Hur
	Environment	

Tables

Placed throughout the chapters the tables provide relevant statistics and current data about the European Union and its member states.

1.9 Summary

It is impossible to summarize 50 years of European is possible to highlight the main events and lesson integration are concerned.

European integration has always been driven by to prevent another European war to a desire to share democratic nations in central and eastern Europe. Y the means were always economic.

There have been basically three big increase Formation of the customs union from 1958 to 1 intra-EU trade. The Single Market Programme in (although elements are still being implemented barriers and liberalized capital flows within the EU Union melded together the currencies of most EU

Each of these steps towards deeper integration – the Single Market Programme – engendered discrim

Summaries

Placed at the end of each chapter they recap the ideas introduced in the preceding pages and emphasize key findings.

Self-assessment questions

1 Draw a diagram (or diagrams) that graphicall economic integration, along with dates and th sure to discuss explicitly the removal of variou labour and capital.

2 Draw a diagram like Fig. 1.4 that shows the Europe, including all European nations west of

3 Make a list of all the EU treaties (with dates) and of each treaty's major contribution to European

4 Make a list of the dates of the major stages in tl reforms (see europa.eu.int/comm/agriculture/in

5 Make a list of the dates of the major stages in t (see europa.eu.int/comm/regional_policy/index

Self-assessment questions

Useful for testing knowledge of the economic concepts and facts featured in the chapter.

Essay questions

1 What role has the Council of Europe, whic European integration?

2 How important was the USA's role in prom Europe would have formed the EEC, or som creation of the OEEC a condition for aid?

3 Describe the evolution of the various British integration in the 1945 to 1975 period. In tl while Conservatives supported it, but rece think this is so?

4 Provide an explanation for why only six of th list specific reasons for each non-member.

5 Write an essay on the work towards deeper context of the OEEC. Why did this fail?

6 Write an essay on whether Charles de Gaulle

Essay questions

These offer practice examples for exams or assessment, encouraging students to write full answers that explore ideas in more detail.

Further reading: the aficionado's

For a good, general description of the dev
Urwin, D. (1995) *The Community of Euro*

Two books that challenge the traditional are:
Milward, A. (1992) *The European Rescue*
Moravcsik, A. (1998) *The Choice for Eu*
    University Press, Ithaca, NY.

A detailed description of post-war growth
Botting, D. (1985) *From the Ruins of the F*

Further reading, websites and references
All help provide direction for further research around the topics covered in the chapter.

Annex
Where appropriate Annex sections offer further economic explanations, data or background information. The appendices enable further study to complement the chapter, covering more advanced concepts and providing greater detail.

Annex A Chronology from

Year	Date	Event	Explanation
1948	16 April	OEEC	Organization fo (OEEC) establish
1950	9 May	Schuman Plan	French Foreign the establishme Community (EC Monnet's vision 9 May is celebra
1952	1 January	ECSC	The ECSC is est. 2002.
1952	27 May	EDC	'The Six' sign th Defence Comm French Nationa

Online Learning Centre
www.mcgraw-hill.co.uk/textbooks/baldwin

Online
Learning Centre

Students – Helping you to Connect, Learn and Succeed

We understand that studying for your module is not just about reading this textbook. It's also about researching online, revising key terms, preparing for assignments, and passing the exam. The website above provides you with a number of **FREE** resources to help you succeed on your module, including:

- *Self-test quizzes*
- *Web links*
- *'In the News' section*
- *Glossary*

Lecturer support – Helping you to help your students

The Online Learning Centre also offers lecturers adopting this book a range of resources designed to offer:

- **Faster course preparation** – time-saving support for your module
- **High-calibre content to support your students** – resources written by your academic peers, who understand your need for rigorous and reliable content

The materials created specifically for lecturers adopting this textbook include:

- *Chapter Summaries*
- *Learning Objectives*
- *Lecture Outlines*
- *PowerPoint Presentations*
- *Essay Questions and Answers*
- *Key Concepts and Terms*

To request your password to access these resources, contact your McGraw-Hill representative or visit www.mcgraw-hill.co.uk/textbooks/baldwin

Mc Graw Hill create

At McGraw-Hill Education our aim is to help lecturers to find the most suitable content for their needs delivered to their students in the most appropriate way. Our **custom publishing solutions** offer the ideal combination of content delivered in the way which best suits lecturer and students.

Our custom publishing programme offers lecturers the opportunity to select just the chapters or sections of material they wish to deliver to their students from a database called CREATE™ at

www.mcgrawhillcreate.co.uk

CREATE™ contains over two million pages of content from:

- textbooks
- professional books
- case books – Harvard Articles, Insead, Ivey, Darden, Thunderbird and BusinessWeek
- Taking Sides – debate materials

Across the following imprints:

- McGraw-Hill Education
- Open University Press
- Harvard Business Publishing
- US and European material

There is also the option to include additional material authored by lecturers in the custom product – this does not necessarily have to be in English.

We will take care of everything from start to finish in the process of developing and delivering a custom product to ensure that lecturers and students receive exactly the material needed in the most suitable way.

With a **Custom Publishing Solution**, students enjoy the best selection of material deemed to be the most suitable for learning everything they need for their courses – something of real value to support their learning. Teachers are able to use exactly the material they want, in the way they want, to support their teaching on the course.

Please contact **your local McGraw-Hill representative** with any questions or, alternatively, contact Warren Eels **e:** warren_eels@mcgraw-hill.com.

Acknowledgements

Our thanks go to the following reviewers for their comments at various stages in the text's development:

Stephen Dearden, Manchester Metropolitan University
Gerrit Faber, Utrecht University
Nico Groenendijk, University of Twente
Carsten Hefeker, University of Siegen
Peter Holmes, University of Sussex
Matteo Iannizzotto, Durham Business School
Stephen Kinsella, University of Limerick
Wilhelm Kohler, University of Tübingen
John O'Hagan, Trinity College Dublin
Jonathan Perraton, University of Sheffield
Malcolm Sawyer, University of Leeds
Pamela Whisker, Plymouth University
Maurizio Zanardi, Université Libre de Bruxelles

Each new edition lengthens our indebtedness to colleagues, former and present students and editors. It also increases our pleasure when the time has finally come to thank them all. Over the current and previous edition, a number of colleagues have made useful suggestions and caught mistakes. While we alone are responsible for the remaining old and new mistakes, we thank Nigel Allington, Cardiff Business School, Steven Brakman, University of Groningen, Daivd Bywaters, University of Herfordshire, Andreas Cornett, University of Southern Denmark, Norman Dytianquin, University of Maastricht, Fin Olesen, University of Southern Denmark, Tom Verbeke, Ghent University, Jef Cuchelen, Vrije Universiteit Brussel, Rolf Weder, University of Basel.

As always, McGraw-Hill has lined up a first-class team. Natalie Jacobs, now Executive Editor, has once more organized a review of the previous edition and made innumerable suggestions for improvement. Rebecca Birtwistle, who took over as Commissioning Editor, has gently prodded us to deliver and supervised the whole process with firm patience. We also are grateful to Alison Davis, the Production Editor, Annette Abel, the Copy Editor and Ruth Freestone King, the proof-reader – all of whom improve the quality of the text.

Acknowledgements

Our thanks go to the following reviewers for their comments at various stages in the text's development:

Stephen Pearson, Manchester Metropolitan University
Gerard Fahey, Limerick University
... University of Twente
Carsten Hefeker, University of Siegen
Petri Holmes, University of Sussex
Marko Iannixxxko, Durham Business School
Stephen Kinsella, University of Limerick
Wenshu Kohler, University of Tübingen
John G Hagan, Trinity College Dublin
Jonathan Perraton, University of Sheffield
Malcolm Sawyer, University of Leeds
Pamela Wilson, Plymouth University
Manuela Kunz, Université Libre de Bruxelles

Each new edition reunites our indebtedness to colleagues, former and present students and reform. It also increases our pleasure when the time has finally come to thank them all. Over the current and previous editions, a number of colleagues have made useful suggestions and caught mistakes. While we alone are responsible for the remaining old and new mistakes, we thank Nigel Allington, Small Business School, Steven Brakman, University of Groningen, David Bywaters, University of Hertfordshire, Andrea Carmeni, University of Southern Denmark, Norman Brownann, University of Maastricht, Jan Olsson, University of Southern Denmark, Tom Stebeke, Oltoni University, Jef Cochelet, Vigozhetschei Basset, Rolf Weder, University of Basel.

As always, McGraw-Hill has lined up a first-class team. Natalie Jarvis, now Natalie Swart-Elton, has once more organised a review of the previous edition and made innumerable suggestions for improvement. Rebecca Birtwistle, who took over as commissioning editor, has gently prodded us to deliver and supervised the whole process with firm patience. We also are grateful to Alison Davis, the Production Editor, Ambrina Abol, Thoy Ley, Peter and Ruth Freelance King, the proof-readers – all of whom improve the quality of the text.

Every effort has been made to trace and acknowledge ownership of copyright and to clear permission for material reproduced in this book. The publishers will be pleased to make suitable arrangements to clear permission with any copyright holders whom it has not been possible to contact.

Part I

History, Facts and Institutions

Chapter 1

History

> And what is the plight to which Europe has been reduced? . . . over wide areas a vast quivering mass of tormented, hungry, care-worn and bewildered human beings gape at the ruins of their cities and their homes, and scan the dark horizons for the approach of some new peril, tyranny or terror. . . . That is all that Europeans, grouped in so many ancient states and nations . . . have got by tearing each other to pieces and spreading havoc far and wide.
>
> Yet all the while there is a remedy . . . It is to re-create the European Family, or as much of it as we can, and to provide it with a structure under which it can dwell in peace, in safety and in freedom. We must build a kind of United States of Europe.
>
> Winston Churchill Zurich, 19 September 1946

Chapter Contents

Introduction

Understanding Europe's economic integration today requires a good notion of Europe's recent past. This chapter presents the main events of European economic integration in chronological order, stressing, wherever possible, the economic and political economy logic behind the events.

1.1 Early post-war period

In 1945, a family standing almost anywhere in Europe found themselves in a nation which was, or had recently been: (a) ruled by a brutal fascist dictator, (b) occupied by a foreign army or (c) both. As a direct result of these governmental failures, tens of millions of Europeans were dead and Europe's economy lay in ruins. Worse yet, the Second World War was not an isolated historical event. If the parents were middle-aged, it would have been their second experience of colossal death and destruction; the Second World War started just two decades after the cataclysm of the First World War (1914–18). Indeed, the Second World War was the fourth time in 130 years that France and Germany were at the core of increasingly horrifying wars.

1.1.1 A climate for radical change

In 1945, it was plain to all that something was desperately wrong with the way Europe governed itself. Minds were open to radical changes.

It is hard for students born in the 1980s or later to connect emotionally with the misery and hardship that were so commonplace in Europe at the end of the Second World War. Difficult, yet it is essential. One simply cannot understand European integration without comprehending the mindset of Europeans in the late 1940s.

The miracle of the web now allows students to see photos (see Fig. 1.1), watch videos, read original documents and listen to speeches from the time. One of the best sites for all European

Figure 1.1 London 1944 and Dresden 1945

Source: National Maritime Museum, London and German Historical Museum (DHM), Berlin

documents is the Luxembourg-based Centre Virtuel de la Connaissance sur l'Europe. Its excellent and well-organized website is at www.cvce.eu. Also, www.dhm.de/lemo/html/Nachkriegsjahre/ DasEndeAlsAnfang/ provides some powerful photos and videos of Germany's experience.

Table 1.1 shows some figures on the death and destruction in the Second World War. In western Europe, the war killed about 8 million people, with Germans accounting for three-quarters of this total. In central and eastern Europe over 9 million perished, of whom 6.3 million were Poles. The Soviet Union alone lost over 20 million. The fact that much of the killing was deliberate genocide made it even more horrifying (see www.jewishvirtuallibrary.org for information on the Holocaust).

The scale of this devastation is the key to understanding the post-1945 drive for European integration. It may, however, be difficult to imagine the mindset in 1945. To put it in perspective, note that the terrible attacks in the USA on 11 September 2001 resulted in about 3000 deaths. This event radically altered many people's and many governments' perception of the world. To approach the Second World War death toll in western and central Europe, it would have taken two '11 September' attacks on every single day between 1938 and 1945, and this excludes the 20-plus million people who perished in the Union of Soviet Socialist Republics (USSR).

The war also caused enormous economic damage. Figures are difficult to find for central and eastern Europe, but the estimates for western Europe are staggering, as Table 1.1 shows. The war cost Germany and Italy four decades or more of growth and put Austrian and French GDPs back to nineteenth-century levels.

Refugees, hunger and political instability

The economic, political and humanitarian situation in Europe was dire in the years 1945–47, especially in Germany. Food production in 1946 was low and the 1946–47 winter was especially

Table 1.1 Death and destruction in the Second World War

	Death toll	The economic setback: pre-war year when GDP equalled that of 1945
Austria	525,000	1886
Belgium	82,750	1924
Denmark	4,250	1936
Finland	79,000	1938
France	505,750	1891
Germany	6,363,000	1908
Italy	355,500	1909
Netherlands	250,000	1912
Norway	10,250	1937
Sweden	0	(a)
Switzerland	0	(a)
UK	325,000	(a)

(a) GDP grew during the Second World War.

Source: GDP data from Crafts and Toniolo (1996), p. 4; death toll from http://encarta.msn.com

harsh. Hunger was widespread. Food was rationed in most European nations up to the mid-1950s. At times, rations fell to just 900 calories per day in some parts of Germany (2000 calories per day is the standard today). Much of Europe's infrastructure, industry and housing lay in ruins. Many Europeans in these years were dependent on humanitarian aid, in much the same way as people in war-torn African nations are today. The UN Relief and Rehabilitation Administration (UNRRA) spent nearly $4 billion on emergency food and medical aid, helped about 7 million displaced persons return home, and provided camps for about a million refugees who did not want to be repatriated.

Politically, western Europe suffered governmental and constitutional crises. General de Gaulle resigned as president of the provisional government in 1946 over a disagreement on France's new constitution. Italy and Belgium saw bitter internal conflicts over their monarchy. Italy abolished its monarchy in a referendum that involved accusations of communist manipulation. The return of the Belgian king sparked riots. If all this seems like the plot of a B-grade apocalypse movie, you should watch some of the online audiovisual material at www.cvce.eu to see just how real it was. Hunger, riots and refugee camps were commonplace all across western Europe.

1.1.2 The prime question and guiding ideologies

The horror and revulsion arising from this devastation pushed one question to the forefront in the mid-1940s: 'How can Europe avoid another war?' The solutions offered depended on beliefs about the causes of the war; three schools of thought were in evidence:

1 *Germany was to blame.* Guided by this belief, the so-called Morgenthau plan of 1944 proposed to avoid future European war by turning Germany into 'a country primarily agricultural and pastoral in character'. The same thinking guided post-First World War arrangements in Europe. That war was blamed on Germany and the victors were rewarded with territorial gains and financial reparations. The result was a cycle of recovery, resentment and national rivalry that led to the Second World War.

2 *Capitalism was to blame.* Marxism–Leninism blamed capitalism for most of the world's evils, including both world wars. This belief suggested that communism was the solution.

3 *Nationalism was to blame.* The third school blamed the excesses of destructive nationalism for the war. The solution suggested by this belief was tighter integration of all European nations. While calls for a united Europe were heard after the 1914–18 war and during the 1939–45 war, the school's most famous post-war statement was the 1946 'United States of Europe' speech by Winston Churchill (you can listen to it at www.cvce.eu).

School number 3 and the European integration solution ultimately prevailed, but this was far from clear in the late 1940s. Most European nations were either struggling to re-establish their governments and economies or were under direct military occupation. Germany and Austria were divided into US, UK, French and Soviet zones (Fig. 1.2). Soviet troops occupied all of central and eastern Europe. In western Europe, 1945 and 1946 passed with hardly any progress towards the establishment of a post-war architecture. West European governments' limited governance capacities were overloaded by the dismal humanitarian situation.

Things moved more rapidly in the east. The Soviet Union had already begun to implement its vision of a new Europe during the war. Communism was imposed on the previously independent nations of Estonia, Latvia and Lithuania, and by 1948 communist parties had been pushed to power in every Soviet-occupied country. Communists took power in Albania and Yugoslavia, and were gaining strength in Greece.

The notion that capitalism was to blame and would cause yet more suffering was widely held in western Europe. In the parliamentary elections of 1946, communists won 19 per cent of the vote in Italy and 29 per cent in France.

Figure 1.2 The four-way division of Germany

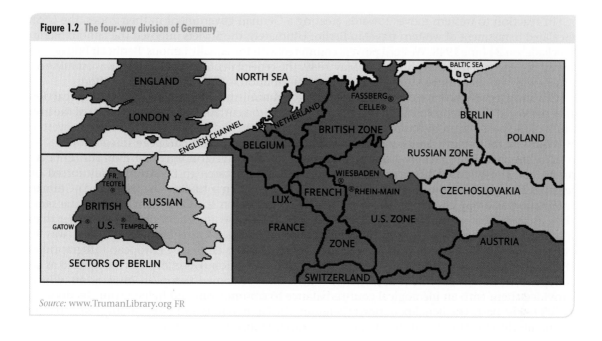

Source: www.TrumanLibrary.org FR

1.1.3 Emergence of a divided Europe: the Cold War

America and Britain categorically rejected the Soviet's world vision. Their wartime alliance with the USSR unravelled and the Allies-versus-Axis confrontation was replaced by an East–West confrontation, called the Cold War. By 1947, the USA and Britain had concluded that an economically strong Germany would be essential to the defence of liberal democracy in western Europe. They merged the UK and US zones into 'Bizonia' (September 1947), and France, which had originally favoured the Morgenthau Plan, added its zone in 1948. Germany drew up a constitution in 1948 under the leadership of Konrad Adenauer (see Box 1.1).

Box 1.1   Konrad Adenauer (1876–1967)

Photo: © European Union 2012

Born to a family of modest means, he rose to become Mayor of Cologne, a post he was stripped of by the Nazis in 1933. He was President of the 1948 Parliamentary Council that drew up Germany's constitution ('Basic Law') before becoming the first Chancellor (i.e. Prime Minister) of Germany – an office he held from 1949 to 1963. Under his leadership, Germany regained its sovereignty, joined the European Economic Community and NATO, and evolved into a cornerstone of western European democracy and economic strength. Adenauer was a key promoter of close Franco-German cooperation and of Germany's social welfare system.

In reaction to western moves towards creating a German government in their zones, the USSR escalated harassment of western travel to Berlin. Ultimately, the Soviets imposed the famous 'Berlin Blockade' on 24 June 1948. Western powers countered with the equally famous 'Berlin air bridge' (see www.cvce.eu for details and photos). In May 1949, the Federal Republic of Germany was established. The new government agreed to make a military contribution to the western defence effort.

Soviet aggressive promotion of their solution (communism for all) triggered a western reaction that narrowed the three solutions down to two with an 'iron curtain' between them. East of the iron curtain, the post-war architecture was based on communism and one-party politics. To the west, it was built on multi-party democracy, the social market economy and European integration.

The merger of the French, US and UK zones was a defining moment in Europe. Tentative and ideologically based support for European integration came to be strongly reinforced by western European nations pursuing their own interests. French leaders saw the Franco-German integration as a way of counterbalancing US–UK influence on the Continent while at the same time assuring that a reindustrialized Germany would become an economic partner rather than a military adversary. The UK and the USA supported European integration as the best way to counter the spread of communism in Europe. German leaders embraced European integration as the surest route to re-establishing Germany as a 'normal' nation (Germany was recognized as an independent nation only in 1955). Italian leaders also welcomed European integration, which provided them with an ideological counterbalance to communism and helped shut the door on Italy's fascist past. The Benelux nations (Belgium, the Netherlands and Luxembourg) were happy about anything that reduced the chances of another Franco-German war.

1.1.4 First steps: the OEEC and EPU

From the perspective of European integration, the most important result of the western European effort to resist communism was the so-called Marshall Plan and the Organization for European Economic Cooperation (OEEC). In reaction to the dire economic conditions in Europe and the attendant threat that communists might come to power in Greece, Italy and France, US Secretary of State (i.e. Foreign Minister) George Marshall announced that the USA would give financial assistance to all European nations 'west of the Urals', if they could agree to a joint programme for economic reconstruction.

Almost immediately, European nations gathered in Paris to study Marshall's proposal (the USSR and the central and eastern European countries eventually withdrew and never received Marshall Plan funds). The conference was intended to determine the amount of aid required and, at US insistence, to create a permanent organization (the OEEC) in which Europeans would cooperate in their mutual economic recovery. A joint programme and organization were duly developed by the Europeans. The US Congress, which was initially reluctant, funded the Marshall Plan in April 1948 after the communist takeover in Czechoslovakia.

The OEEC was established in 1948 with 13 members of the old EU15 (Finland was under Soviet pressure to stay neutral and Spain was under Franco's dictatorship) plus Norway, Iceland, Switzerland, Turkey and the US–UK zone of the Free Territory of Trieste until it was merged with Italy. Germany was still under occupation, but representatives from the Western Zones participated. From 1948 to 1952, Marshall Plan aid amounted to $12 billion, with half of this going to the UK, France and West Germany. The Soviet bloc's counterpart, the Council of Mutual Economic Assistance (CMEA), was set up in 1949.

The OEEC divided American aid among its members (see Box 1.2), but a far more important role, as far as European history is concerned, was the OEEC's mandate to advance European economic integration. It did this by reducing intra-European trade barriers and improving the intra-European system of payments by establishing the European Payments Union (EPU); see Box 1.3.

In 1949, the USA demanded that the OEEC make greater efforts to bring about direct European economic integration, especially intra-OEEC trade liberalization. Up to this point, Marshall Plan money was mainly used to finance European countries' dollar deficits in the EPU. In reaction to US

Box 1.2   The Organization for European Economic Cooperation (OEEC)

The OEEC's members formed the Council of the Organization which ruled on the basis of intergovernmental decision making (unanimity). It was chaired by high-profile figures of the era (Paul-Henri Spaak, Paul van Zeeland, Dirk Strikker, Anthony Eden, Richard Heathcoat Amory). The OEEC's importance waned in 1952 as Marshall Plan aid ended and the focus of American spending shifted to more explicitly military ends in the form of the North Atlantic Treaty Organization (NATO). In 1961, the OEEC was transformed into the Organization for Economic Co-operation and Development (OECD).

Source: This box is based on the OECD's website at www.oecd.org

---

pressure, the OEEC nations agreed to remove quantitative restrictions on private imports. While this had limited scope (at the time, much of intra-European trade was conducted by government-controlled corporations), 60 per cent of private intra-European trade was freed by 1950 thanks to OEEC action, with this figure rising to 89 per cent in 1959. The OEEC's trade liberalization was important in at least two ways:

1 The liberalization fostered a rapid growth of trade and incomes. As the figures in Table 1.2 show, the 1950s were marked by a remarkable increase in GDP and the export of manufactured goods, at least on the Continent.

2 The thinking of policy makers was profoundly affected by the fact that industrial output grew at historically unprecedented rates even as European trade was being liberalized.

Box 1.3   The European Payments Union (EPU), July 1950 to December 1958

Most European nations were bankrupt after 1945, so trade was generally conducted on the basis of bilateral agreements, often involving barter. The EPU multi-lateralized these bilateral deals. Each month, EPU members added up the deficits and surpluses in their bilateral trade accounts with other EPU members. These were offset against each other so that each nation remained with an overall surplus or deficit with respect to the EPU. The great advantage of this was that, since nations no longer owed money to each other directly, the debt-based incentives for importing from or exporting to a particular partner vanished. As a consequence, it was easy to loosen the web of bilateral trade restrictions that had been set up in the early post-war years. In its first year, the EPU removed all discriminatory trade measures among EPU members. EPU/ OEEC membership also fostered overall trade liberalization via its 'Code of Liberalization'. This required members to lower trade barriers progressively by 25 per cent of their initial levels. During this time intra-European trade boomed, more than doubling in the EPU's lifetime (1950–58); imports from North America grew by only 50 per cent. The trade surplus with the US allowed European national central banks to accumulate substantial dollar reserves. This restored their financial stability and fostered trade liberalization by undermining balance-of-payments justifications for import restrictions. By 1958, the financial position of EPU members was strong enough to allow them to restore the convertibility of their currencies (prior to this, the currencies were unconvertible, e.g. it was illegal for private citizens to exchange French francs for dollars or Deutschmarks without government permission).

Source: This box is based largely on Eichengreen and de Macedo (2001)

Table 1.2   Western European trade and output growth in manufactures, 1950–58

	GDP growth (% per annum)	Manufacturing export growth (% per annum)
Germany (West)	7.8	19.7
Italy	5.0	9.2
Netherlands	4.3	11.7
UK	2.0	1.8
France	4.4	3.8

Source: Milward (1992), Table 4.1

The second point was a critical change in policy makers' mindset – one that eventually opened the door to the Treaty of Rome's deep economic liberalization. In the decades following the First World War, especially during the 1930s, economic growth was viewed as a competition between nations. In this competition, trade barriers played a central role as each nation sought to 'save' its market for its own industrialists.

In sharp contrast, the correlation between trade barriers and industrial growth was completely reversed in the 1940s and 1950s. Trade liberalization among west European nations went hand-in-hand with spectacular growth; intra-European imports and exports expanded even more rapidly than output. Europe's leaders came to view European integration as an idea that made as much sense economically as it did politically. As Milward (1992) put it: 'The proposals for trade liberalisation and customs unions that were made fell therefore on to a receptive soil.'

1.1.5 The drive for deeper integration

While the OEEC succeeded in economic terms, some OEEC members found it too limited to bring about the deeper integration that they felt was necessary to avoid future war and restore economic strength. The Cold War lent urgency to this drive. With East–West tensions rising steadily, Germany would not only have to be allowed to regain its industrial might, it would have to rearm in order to counter the threat of Soviet territorial aggression. Since many Europeans, including many Germans, were still uncomfortable with the idea of a Germany that was both economically and militarily strong, integrating Germany into a supranational Europe seemed a natural way forward.

1.2 Two strands of European integration: federalism and intergovernmentalism

While it was clear by the late 1940s that European integration would be the foundation of western Europe's post-war architecture, a serious schism immediately emerged over the role of nation-states. Even today, this schism defines the debate over European integration, so it is worth considering the origins of the two positions.

1 Some Europeans felt that national sovereignty and the nation-state constituted a fragile system prone to warfare. Since time immemorial, European states had been engaged in intermittent struggles for dominance – struggles that typically involved the invasion of other European nations. As industrialization made killing much more 'efficient', the cost of these struggles rose to the point where no one could win. To these thinkers, even democracy was insufficient to prevent

horrifying wars. Hitler, after all, gained his first hold on power through democratic means. To prevent another cycle of recovery and national rivalry that might lead to a third world war, nations should be embedded in a *federalist* structure – a supranational organization embodied with some of the powers that had traditionally been exercised exclusively by nations.

2 Other Europeans, led by Britain, continued to view nation-states as the most effective and most stable form of government. To them, European integration should take the form of closer cooperation – especially closer economic cooperation – conducted strictly on an *intergovernmental* basis, i.e. all power would remain in the hands of national officials and any cooperation would have to be agreed unanimously by all participants.

Not surprisingly, the federalist school was most popular in nations that experienced the greatest failures of governance – failures measured in terms of wartime death and destruction (see Table 1.1). This group included Belgium, the Netherlands, Luxembourg, France, Austria, Germany and Italy.

People from nations whose governments avoided foreign occupation and/or catastrophic loss of life tended to maintain their traditional faith in the nation-state. This included the UK, Denmark, Norway and Iceland as well as the neutrals, Ireland, Sweden and Switzerland. Spain and Portugal remained under fascist dictators until the 1970s.

1.2.1 Two early extremes: Council of Europe and the ECSC

Intergovernmentalism initially dominated the post-war architecture. In part, this was simply a matter of timing.

The only major European nation with a truly effective, democratic government before 1947 was Britain – a firm believer in intergovernmentalism. The first three organizations – the OEEC, the Council of Europe and the Court of Human Rights – followed the intergovernmental tradition. The OEEC was strictly intergovernmental (see Box 1.2), and the 1948 'Congress of Europe' established two intergovernmental structures, the Council of Europe (1949) and the Court of Human Rights (1950), both of which continue to function today and are entirely unrelated to the EU.

The first big federalist step came in 1952 with the Schuman Plan inspired by the 'father of European integration', Jean Monnet, but promoted by French Foreign Minister Robert Schuman (see Box 1.4). Schuman proposed that France and Germany should place their coal and steel sectors under the control of a supranational authority.

This was a radical move at the time. An equivalent move today would be entirely unthinkable. The point is that coal and steel were viewed as the 'commanding heights' of an industrial economy at the time and crucial to a nation's military and industrial strength. Schuman explicitly justified his Plan as a means of rendering future Franco-German wars materially impossible.

Other European nations were invited to join this European Coal and Steel Community (ECSC), and Belgium, Luxembourg, the Netherlands and Italy actually did. This created a group of nations known simply as 'the Six' – a group that has been the driving force behind European integration ever since. See Box 1.5.

Times had changed

By the time the ECSC was in operation, Europe was a very different place from what it had been in 1945. The year was 1952 and Cold War tensions were high and rising. Economically, things continued to get better. As Table 1.3 shows, the Six had managed to get their economies back on track, having experienced miraculous growth.

1.2.2 Federalist track: the Treaty of Rome

The ECSC was a success, not so much in that it solved the thorny problems of Europe's coal and steel sectors, but rather as a training scheme for European integration. It showed that the Six

---

Box 1.4   Robert Schuman (1886–1963) and Jean Monnet (1888–1979)

Born in Luxembourg, Schuman studied and worked in Germany until the end of the First World War. He became French when Alsace-Lorraine reverted to France in 1918. He held several positions in the post-war French governments, including Finance Minister, Premier and Foreign Minister. Schuman provided the political push for the European Coal and Steel Community, which most consider to be the wellspring for the European Union. He was also the first President (1958–60) of the European Parliament.

Jean Monnet, born in Cognac in 1888, was a brilliant organizer and as such helped to organize Allied military supply operations in the First and Second World Wars. Near the end of the Second World War he joined Charles de Gaulle's provisional Free French government, and was responsible for the 'Monnet Plan', which is credited with helping France's post-war industrialization. Monnet was a convinced Europeanist and led the European movement in the 1950s and 1960s. Monnet, who is sometimes called the 'father of European integration', was the intellect behind the idea of the ECSC and the first president of its 'High Authority' (precursor of the European Commission) from 1952 to 1955. He continued to push for the European Economic Community and the European Atomic Energy Community (Euratom). He died in 1979.

T: European Union 2012
Source B: http://www.hdg.de/lemo/html/biografien/MonnetJean/index.html

---

Box 1.5   The European Coal and Steel Community (ECSC)

France and Germany launched the ECSC initiative, inviting other nations to place their coal and steel sectors under its supranational authority. Since coal and steel were considered the backbone of a modern industrial economy at the time, most nations declined. The ECSC's structure submerged the role of nation-states to an extent that seems unimaginable from today's perspective. It still represents the 'high-water mark' of European federalism. Crucial decisions concerning such issues as pricing, trade and production in the then critical coal and steel sectors were placed in the hands of the 'High Authority'. This body, the forerunner of today's European Commission, consisted of officials appointed by the six Member States. The High Authority's decisions, some made by majority voting, were subject to limited control by Member State governments. See Spierenburg and Poidevin (1994) for details on the ECSC. The photo depicts the symbolic opening of the ECSC as a train bearing the flags of the Six crosses a border with coal and steel.

Source: © European Union 2012

Table 1.3 Post-Second World War reconstruction

	Back-on-track year (year GDP attained highest pre-WWII level)	Reconstruction growth (growth rate during reconstruction years, 1945 to back-on-track year)
Austria	1951	15.2%
Belgium	1948	6.0%
Denmark	1946	13.5%
Finland	1945	n.a.
France	1949	19.0%
Germany	1951	13.5%
Italy	1950	11.2%
Netherlands	1947	39.8%
Norway	1946	9.7%

Source: Crafts and Toniolo (1996), p. 4

could cooperate in a federal structure. The Six as a whole, but especially Germany, continued to grow spectacularly, while East–West tensions continued to mount. This combination made German rearmament essential.

In 1955, Germany joined western Europe's main defence organization, the North Atlantic Treaty Organization (NATO), and began to rearm in earnest. This triggered a reaction from the Soviet bloc – the USSR and the central and eastern European nations formed the Warsaw Pact to counter NATO. It also brought back the question of deeper European integration.

By 1955, it had become clear that coal and steel were no longer the 'commanding heights' of Europe's economy in economic or military terms. The ECSC might not be enough to ensure that another Franco-German war remained unthinkable. European leaders turned their minds to broader economic integration. Having failed to move directly to political or military integration (see Box 1.6), the natural way forward was broader economic integration.

Box 1.6 Failed integration, EDC and EPC

Encouraged by the rapid acceptance of the ECSC, federalists pressed ahead with ambitious plans. In the first years of the 1950s, leaders from the Six worked out plans for a supranational organization concerning defence – the European Defence Community (EDC) – as well as for deep political integration – the European Political Community (EPC). This remarkable enthusiasm for supranationality ultimately failed when the French parliament rejected the EDC explicitly, after which EPC plans were dropped.

The ECSC, EDC and EPC proposals were revolutionary by today's standards. When most voters had lived through the traumatic years of the Second World War, radical thinking was mainstream. Today, by contrast, European governments balk at pooling their sovereignty over comparatively trivial issues such as air traffic control.

Source: Distilled from information on www.cvce.eu

A key force behind supranationalism was Jean Monnet who formed a high-powered pressure group – the Action Committee for the United States of Europe – whose membership included leading figures from all the main political parties in each of 'the Six'. The aim was to merge European nation-states into a supranational organization along the lines of the ECSC but much broader in scope.

Foreign Ministers of the Six met in Messina in June 1955 (Fig. 1.3) to start a process that soon led to the signing, on 25 March 1957, of two treaties in Rome: the first created the European Atomic Energy Community (Euratom); the second created the European Economic Community (EEC). Because the EEC eventually became much more important than Euratom, the term 'The Treaty of Rome' is used to refer to the EEC treaty. The Treaty of Rome was quickly ratified by the six national parliaments and the EEC came into existence in January 1958. (The institutions of the ECSC, the EEC and Euratom were merged into the 'European Communities', or EC, in 1965.) The Treaties of Rome were drafted by the Spaak Committee working from July 1955 to April 1956. The British partook in preliminary meetings of the Committee, but dropped out in October 1955. Jean Monnet and others felt the UK was trying to sabotage the Six's federalist initiatives.

The Treaty of Rome committed the Six to extraordinarily deep economic integration. In addition to forming a customs union (removing all tariffs and quotas on intra-EEC trade and adopting a common tariff on imports from non-member nations; Box 1.7), it promised free labour mobility, capital market integration, free trade in services and a range of common policies – some of which were to be implemented by a supranational body. The Treaty also set up a series of supranational institutions such as the European Parliamentary Assembly (forerunner of the European Parliament), the European Court of Justice (see Chapter 2) and most important of all – the European Commission.

1.2.3 Intergovernmental track: from OEEC to EFTA

Formation of the EEC introduced an important new element into European economic integration. Hitherto trade liberalization in Europe had been orchestrated by the OEEC, with nations liberalizing on a non-discriminatory basis.

The EEC would go much further, removing *all* trade barriers, but on a discriminatory, i.e. preferential, basis. Imports from non-member nations would not benefit from the opening.

Figure 1.3 Messina Conference and signing of the Treaty of Rome

Left photo: Conference of Messina – the Foreign Ministers of the Six (left to right: Johan Beyen, Gaetano Martino, Joseph Bech, Antoine Pinay, Walter Hallstein, Paul-Henri Spaak). Right photo: Signing of the Treaties establishing the EEC and Euratom in Rome. *Photos: © European Union 2012*

Box 1.7   Formation of the EEC customs union

The nascent EEC spent much of its first year of life setting up its administrative machinery in Brussels and developing an integration programme. It started with the most concrete part of the Treaty's ambitious integration scheme: the customs union.

According to the Treaty, the elimination of intra-EEC tariffs was to take place in three stages of four years each: January 1958–December 1961, January 1962–December 1965 and January 1966–December 1969. The possibility of a three-year delay was foreseen, so the maximum liberalization period was 15 years. As it turned out, no extra time was needed. Intra-EEC import quotas were abolished ahead of schedule in 1961 and tariffs were zero by July 1968 – a year and a half ahead of schedule.

Why was the EEC able to achieve their ambitious Common Market 18 months early? The formation of the customs union coincided with a period of unprecedented economic prosperity and this largely offset the political and economic costs of liberalization-induced restructuring. Indeed, during this so-called golden age of growth, 1950–73, European unemployment averaged only 2.5 per cent and incomes either doubled, as in France, Belgium and the Netherlands, or tripled, as in Germany and Italy.

The new Common External Tariff (CET) applied by all EEC members was set at the simple arithmetic average of the Six's pre-EEC tariffs. Typically this meant that France and Italy lowered their external tariffs and the Benelux nations raised theirs. Germany's tariffs were approximately at the average to begin with. Under Treaty of Rome rules, the tariff revenue was paid directly to the European Commission. This avoided discussions over a 'fair' division of the revenue (e.g. Dutch authorities collected the CET in Rotterdam even though Rotterdam was the port of entry for many German imports from the USA).

Moreover, the Six were committed to adopting a common tariff against all imports from nonmember nations. The other 11 OEEC members were left on the sidelines.

Fearing the discrimination and marginalization that might occur if they faced the EEC bilaterally, seven of these 'outsiders' reacted by forming their own bloc in 1960, the European Free Trade Association (EFTA), with this move led by the UK (Box 1.8). By the early 1970s, all western European nations had forsaken bilateralism except Ireland, which was in a monetary union with its major trading partner (the UK). Greece and Turkey both applied for associate EEC membership almost as soon as the Treaty of Rome was signed, and Spain signed a preferential trade agreement with the EEC in 1970 (with EFTA in 1979).

Box 1.8   Formation of EFTA

The Stockholm Convention – EFTA's founding document – committed the EFTA nations (EFTAns) to removing tariffs on trade among themselves in tandem with the EEC's schedule and EFTA matched the EEC accelerated tariff-cutting. Importantly, EFTA was a free trade area, not a customs union, so external trade policy did not have to be decided in common. This was important if supranational decision making was to be avoided and it allowed the UK to maintain its preferential tariffs with the Commonwealth. Trade in agricultural goods was excluded from EFTA's liberalization.

1.2.4 Two non-overlapping circles: Common Market and EFTA

The trade liberalization promised by the Treaty of Rome and the Stockholm Convention (EFTA's founding document) rapidly came into effect in the 1960s. By the late 1960s, trade arrangements in western Europe could be described as two non-overlapping circles (Fig. 1.4).

Figure 1.4 Europe of two non-overlapping circles

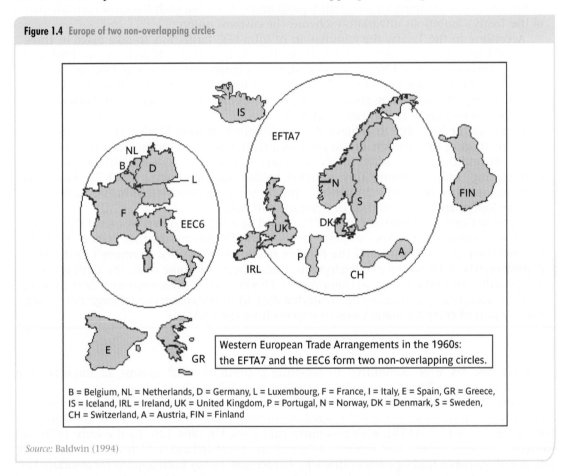

Western European Trade Arrangements in the 1960s: the EFTA7 and the EEC6 form two non-overlapping circles.

B = Belgium, NL = Netherlands, D = Germany, L = Luxembourg, F = France, I = Italy, E = Spain, GR = Greece, IS = Iceland, IRL = Ireland, UK = United Kingdom, P = Portugal, N = Norway, DK = Denmark, S = Sweden, CH = Switzerland, A = Austria, FIN = Finland

Source: Baldwin (1994)

The lowering of intra-EEC trade barriers had an immediate and dramatic impact on trade patterns. During the formation of the customs union (CU), the EEC's share in its own trade rose from about 30 per cent to almost 50 per cent. At the same time, the share of EEC imports coming from six other major European nations remained almost unchanged, falling from 8 to 7 per cent. (More on this in Chapter 5.)

1.3 Evolution to two concentric circles: the domino effect part I

At the beginning of the 1960s, EFTA-based and EEC-based firms had roughly equal access to each others' markets as the preferential tariff cutting had only just begun. As the barriers began to fall within the EEC and within EFTA (but not between the groups), discrimination appeared. This discrimination meant lost profit opportunities for exporters in both groups. Importantly, the relative economic weight and economic performance of the two circles were far from equal. The GDP – and thus the potential market size – of the six EEC nations was more than twice that of the seven EFTA nations and the EEC incomes were growing twice as fast. The EEC club was far more attractive to exporters than the EFTA club. Accordingly, the progressive reduction of within-group barriers generated new political economy forces in favour of EEC enlargement, but how did discriminatory liberalization create these forces for inclusion?

Discriminatory liberalization is studied in depth in Chapter 5, but the idea behind these new political economy forces can be illustrated with an anecdote. Two campers in Yellowstone National Park, who have just settled down in their tent, hear the roar of a hungry Grizzly bear very close by. One camper sits up and starts putting on his running shoes. The other camper says: 'Are you crazy? You can't outrun a bear!' The first camper, who continues tying his laces, replies: 'Oh, I don't have to outrun the bear. I just have to outrun you.' When it comes to outrunning bears and succeeding in business, relative competitiveness is the key to success. A firm is harmed by anything that helps its rivals.

In the case at hand, closer EEC integration diminished the relative competitiveness of non-EEC firms in EEC markets, thereby harming their sales and profits. Of course, the same happened to EEC firms in EFTA, but given the EEC's much greater economic size, pressures on EFTA members to adjust were much greater than those on EEC nations. This effect helps explain why preferential integration among some nations can change the political economy attitudes of excluded nations. This is what Baldwin (1994, 1995) calls the 'domino theory' of regional integration; the preferential lowering of some trade barriers creates new pressures for outsiders to join the trade bloc and as the trade bloc gets bigger, the pressure to join grows. As history would have it, the British government was first to react to the pressure.

1.3.1 First enlargement and EEC–EFTA FTAs

In 1961, the UK applied for EEC membership. There are many reasons for this *volte face*. In the late 1950s, Britain half-expected the EEC to fail just as the EDC and EPC had before it. Moreover,

Figure 1.5 German Chancellor Willy Brandt trying to get the UK into the EEC past the objections of French President Charles de Gaulle

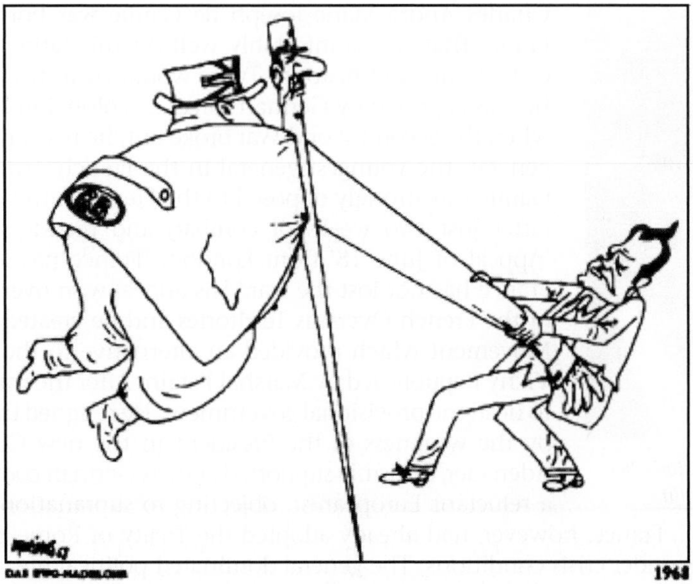

Source: www.cvce.eu

the war's legacy hung heavy in the air; Clement Attlee, former UK Prime Minister, dismissed the EEC as 'six nations, four of whom we had to rescue from the other two'. Once the EEC was up and working well, however, the situation was entirely different. UK industries faced the reality of rising discrimination in Europe's largest and fastest-growing markets. The British government had to react; EFTA was not a substitute for free trade access to the EEC6 markets.

Britain's unilateral decision tipped over more dominoes. If the UK was to jump from EFTA to the EEC, the remaining EFTAns would face discrimination in an even larger market (since the EEC is a customs union, the UK would have had to re-impose tariffs on imports from other EFTAns). This possibility led other nations to change their attitude towards membership. In this case, Ireland, Denmark and Norway quickly followed Britain's unilateral move. The other EFTAns did not apply for political reasons, such as neutrality (Austria, Finland, Sweden and Switzerland), lack of democracy (Portugal), or because they were not heavily dependent on the EEC market (Iceland).

While Germany was broadly in favour of UK membership, France was opposed to it (see Fig. 1.5). In a renowned January 1963 press conference, French President Charles de Gaulle (see Box 1.9) said 'non' to this first enlargement attempt (you can hear it on www.cvce.eu). The four EFTAns reapplied in 1967 and de Gaulle issued another famous 'non', but, after he retired, the applications were reactivated by invitation of the EEC. After many delays, membership for the four was granted in 1973. At that time, Norway's population refused EEC membership in a referendum.

The impending departure of four EFTAns to the EEC was anticipated well in advance and triggered a secondary domino effect. The 1973 EEC enlargement meant a swelling of the EEC markets and a shrinking of the EFTA markets. Firms based in the remaining EFTA states would suffer a disadvantage (compared to their EEC-based rivals) in more markets and enjoy an advantage (over their EEC-based rivals) in fewer markets. Accordingly, EFTA industries pushed their governments to redress this situation. The result was a set of bilateral free trade agreements (FTAs) between each remaining EFTAn and the EEC, which took place when the UK and company acceded to the EEC.

Box 1.9   Charles de Gaulle (1890–1970)

Photo: Deutsches Historisches Museum (DHM), Berlin

Charles André Marie Joseph de Gaulle was born in Lille into a family that was comfortably well off (his father was a professor of literature and history). Twice wounded in the First World War, he was captured by German forces. A colonel in the French Army when the Second World War broke out, he rose rapidly to brigadier general (the youngest general in the French Army at age 49). De Gaulle was strongly opposed to the French surrender in June 1940 (after just two weeks of combat) and broadcast his renowned 'Appeal of June 18' from London: 'France has lost a battle, but France has not lost the war.' His appeal won over leaders in some of the French Overseas Territories and he created the Free French Movement which provided an alternative to the collaborationist Vichy Republic led by Marshal Pétain. After the war, he was elected to head the provisional government. He resigned in 1946, frustrated by the weakness of the President in the new Constitution. Like Adenauer, he firmly supported Franco-German cooperation but was a reluctant Europeanist, objecting to supranational organizations such as the ECSC. France, however, had already adopted the Treaty of Rome before his return to power in 1958 under crisis conditions. The general dominated political life and did much to restore French dignity and power. He resigned in 1969 and died the following year.

Notice that this change of heart does need some explaining. The stance of, say, Sweden towards an FTA with the then EEC was a matter of top-level political calculation. It may seem strange, therefore, that the calculations of Sweden's political elite led them to sign an FTA in 1972 when they had not found it politically optimal to sign one in the preceding decades. The explanation, of course, is that tighter integration among a nation's trade partners (in this case between the UK, Denmark and Ireland and the EEC) alters the economic landscape facing Swedish exporters. This reshaping of the economic landscape gets translated into a new political landscape. Such forces are in operation today. The 2004 enlargement stimulates demand for free trade with nations on the EU25's new eastern border.

By the mid-1970s, trade arrangements in western Europe had evolved into two concentric circles (Fig. 1.6). The outer circle, which encompassed both EFTA and EEC nations, represents a 'virtual' free trade area for industrial products, formed by concatenation of the Treaty of Rome (for intra-EEC trade), EFTA's charter, the Stockholm Convention (for intra-EFTA trade) and individual bilateral FTAs between each EFTA member and the EEC (for EEC–EFTA trade). The inner circle, the EEC, was more deeply integrated.

Figure 1.6 Europe of two concentric circles

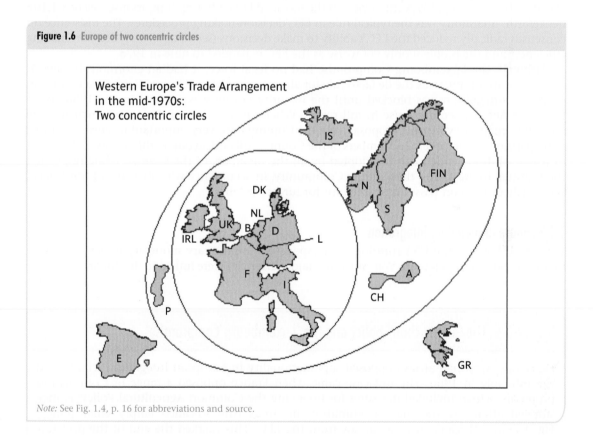

Note: See Fig. 1.4, p. 16 for abbreviations and source.

1.4 Euro-pessimism

Although the customs union was implemented smoothly and ahead of schedule, European integration stagnated soon after its completion. The Community was rocked by a series of political crises in the 1960s soon to be followed by economic shocks in the early 1970s. This created a period known as 'Euro-pessimism' (1973–86).

1.4.1 Political shocks

The spectacularly good economic performance of Europe's economies in the 1950s and 1960s – teamed with the manifest success of European economic integration – went a long way to restoring the confidence of Europeans in their governments' ability to govern (Milward, 1984). So much so that some nations began to regret the promises of deep integration they made in the Treaty of Rome. At the head of this pro-national sovereignty charge was French President Charles de Gaulle.

The issue came to a head as the final stage in the Treaty of Rome's transition period approached (1 January 1966). At this stage the voting procedures in the EEC's key decision-making body, the Council of Ministers, were scheduled to switch to majority voting (see Section 3.3.1).

For de Gaulle, the objectionable part of majority voting was that France might have to accept a majority-backed policy even if France had voted against it. In the end, de Gaulle forced the other EEC members to accept his point of view in the so-called Luxembourg Compromise (see Box 1.10); henceforth, unanimity was the typical rule in EEC decision-making procedures. The insistence on consensus radically reduced the EEC's ability to make decisions (see Chapter 3 on decision-making efficiency) and the problem only got worse as the EEC expanded to nine in 1973.

Although the Luxembourg Compromise had no legal force, it had an enormous impact. It meant that unanimity was the de facto rule for almost everything. Almost all progress on deeper economic integration was blocked until the majority voting was restored in the 1986 Single European Act. The compromise in full reads: 'Where, in the case of decisions which may be taken by a majority vote on a proposal from the Commission, very important interests of one or more partners are at stake, the Members of the Council will endeavour, within a reasonable time, to reach solutions which can be adopted by all the Members of the Council while respecting their mutual interests and those of the Community, in accordance with Article 2 of the Treaty.' See Factsheet 1.3.6 on www.europarl.eu.int for further details.

1.4.2 Failure of monetary integration

The late 1960s saw the USA running an irresponsibly inflationary monetary policy – printing money to pay for the Vietnam War. Since all major currencies were linked to the dollar at the time

---

> **Box 1.10   The 'empty chair' policy and the 'Luxembourg Compromise'**
>
> De Gaulle, who had always opposed supranationality in European integration, challenged the principle in 1966. The test case came when France opposed a range of Commission proposals, which included measures for financing the Common Agricultural Policy. France stopped attending the main Community meetings (the so-called empty chair policy; Fig. 1.7) and threatened to withdraw from the EEC. This marked the end of the post-war climate for radical change, but not the end of the EEC. In exchange for its return to the Council of Ministers, France demanded a political agreement – the Luxembourg Compromise – that de facto overturned the Treaty of Rome's majority voting provisions whenever a Member State announced that it felt that 'very important interests' were at stake. In short, this reversed much of the unlimited supranationality that the Six committed themselves to in the Treaty of Rome just ten years before.

Figure 1.7 *Crise de la chaise vide, 1965*

Photo: © European Union 2012

(via the global fixed exchange rate system called Bretton Woods), US inflation was transmitted into inflation in Europe and elsewhere. This, in turn, led to the gradual breakdown of the global fixed exchange rate system (between 1971 and 1973; see Chapter 10 for details).

Exchange rate stability was widely viewed as a critical factor supporting the rapid post-war growth in trade and international investment and the rising prosperity these brought. It prevented nations from offsetting the market-opening effects of European integration with a competitive devaluation. The EEC searched for ways of restoring intra-European exchange rate stability. It established the Werner Committee which designed a step-by-step plan for European monetary union by 1980. EU leaders adopted the Werner Plan in 1971.

The economic environment for this new European monetary arrangement could not have been worse. Months after it was launched, the Yom Kippur War in the Middle East triggered an Arab oil boycott of western states. The resulting sharp rise in oil prices had a ruinous economic impact on western Europe. Just as inflationary tendencies were heating up from US actions, the oil shock severely dampened economic activity in Europe and all of its global trading partners. Most European nations adopted expansionary monetary and fiscal policies to compensate for the economic downturn and these further fuelled inflation. The result was falling incomes and rising inflation known as 'stagflation'. Just as the world was recovering from the 1973 oil shock, the Iranian Revolution produced a second massive oil price hike in 1979, aggravating stagflation. A debilitating series of exchange rate crises – caused by these massive external shocks – put the Werner Plan on hold for ever. This monetary integration failure was a key feature of Euro-pessimism.

1.4.3 Failure of deeper trade integration
As tariff barriers fell, Europeans erected new trade barriers. These new barriers consisted of detailed technical regulations and standards, which had the effect of fragmenting the European markets.

While these policies, called 'technical barriers to trade' (TBT), undoubtedly inhibited intra-European trade, their announced goal was to protect consumers. EEC leaders had recognized the trade-inhibiting effects of TBTs in the Treaty of Rome (Article 100 requires 'approximation', Euro-speak for harmonization, of national regulations for the 'proper functioning of the common market'). However, as European voters became richer, they demanded tighter regulation of markets and products. The usual machinery of vested-interest politics meant that many of the new standards and regulations tended to protect domestic firms.

The EU first systematically took up the removal of technical barriers in 1969 with its 'General Programme'. This launched what came to be called the 'traditional' or 'old' approach to TBT liberalization. The approach adopted relied on detailed technical regulations for single products or groups of products implemented by unanimously agreed directives. Since unanimity was required, this approach failed. Harmonization proceeded much more slowly than the development of new national barriers. For example, ten years were required to adopt a directive on gas containers made of unalloyed steel and nine and a half years was the average delay for the 15 directives adopted en masse in 1984. In the meantime, Member States were implementing thousands of technical standards and regulations a year.

Stagflation, teamed with the failure of the initiatives for deeper monetary and trade integration, created a gloom over the 'European construction'. Many inside and outside Europe suspected that the ideals that had driven European integration since the late 1940s were dying or dead; the stars, so to speak, were falling off the EU flag (Fig. 1.8).

Yet there were some bright spots in European integration during this period.

1.4.4 Bright spots

Spain, Portugal and Greece all adopted democratic governments, thus rendering them eligible for EEC membership. Greece joined in 1981 followed by the Iberians in 1986. The European Monetary System (EMS) started operation in 1978 and had good success in stabilizing intra-EEC exchange rates. EEC financing was put on a firm footing with two budget treaties (1970 and 1975, see Chapter 2 for details). The institutions of the three communities (ESCS, Euratom and EEC)

Figure 1.8 Euro-pessimism

Source: http://skovgaard.org. © Finn Skovgaard 2001, 2004. Used with permission.

were rationalized by the 1965 Merger Treaty and the EU Parliament was directly elected for the first time in 1979; previously, its members came from the members' national parliaments.

In the USA and Europe, central bankers decided to fight inflation – which had reached double-digit figures in most industrial nations. They did this by inducing a long hard recession. Between 1981 and 1983 growth was negative or only slightly positive in most of Europe. While inflation rates did decline, this was at the cost of a significant increase in unemployment.

Starting in 1984, economic growth recovered. Political attitudes also changed – in particular, a deepened belief in market economics began to spread throughout the industrialized world. US President Reagan and British Prime Minister Thatcher are often cited as vanguards, but even the Socialist French President Mitterrand adopted a much more favourable attitude towards market-based solutions. While there are many causes for this philosophical shift, the fact that highly interventionist policies had failed to prevent ten years of poor economic performance is surely one of the most important.

1.5 Deeper circles and the domino effect part II: the Single Market Programme and the EEA

This favourable economic climate was matched with the arrival of a talented promoter of European integration, Jacques Delors (see Box 1.11). Delors, who was appointed to the Presidency

---

Box 1.11   Jacques Delors (1925–)

Jacques Lucien Jean Delors, born in Paris, held a series of posts in banking and the French government. He was deeply engaged in the trade union movement and a devout Catholic. After a stint in the European Parliament, he became Finance Minister under French President Mitterrand in the early 1980s. Always a committed European integrationist, he was chosen in 1985 to be President of the European Commission, a post he held for two four-year terms. This period was marked by the most important increase in European economic integration since the 1950s; most observers give much credit for this to the savvy and energy of Jacques Delors. The Single European Act, which reinstated majority voting on most economic integration issues, restored the Community's ability to act. This led to a sweeping economic integration effort known as the Single Market Programme, and while this formally ended in 1992, the programme continues to be extended and deepened even today.

Delors was also instrumental in the adoption of the Economic and Monetary Union (EMU), which led to the creation of the euro. Delors' term as Commission President was extended to help the EU to deal with the Danish rejection of the Maastricht Treaty and exchange rate crises of the early 1990s. Among Delors' many other accomplishments, the two multi-year budget deals negotiated while he was President reformed EU financing and redirected EU spending away from agriculture and towards support for disadvantaged regions. His term as President ended in January 1995.

Source: © European Union 2012

of the European Commission in 1985, was devoted to the idea of kick-starting European integration. To this end, he pushed a programme that would complete the internal market. He dubbed this the 'Single Market Programme', although it is known by many names (the Internal Market Programme, the 1992 Programme, Completing the Internal Market, etc.). The plan was framed by Lord Cockfield's 1985 White Paper which listed 300 measures necessary to transform the Common Market into the Single Market. By July 1987, all Member States had adopted the Single European Act, which is the Community legislation that implemented the Single Market measures (along with many other changes).

1.5.1 The Single Market Programme: EC92

In 1985, EU firms enjoyed duty-free access to each other's markets; however, they did not enjoy free trade. Intra-EC trade was shackled by a long list of trade-inhibiting barriers such as differing technical standards and industrial regulations, capital controls, preferential public procurement, administrative and frontier formalities, VAT and excise tax rate differences and differing transport regulations, to mention just a few. Although the vast majority of these policies seem negligible individually, the confluence of their effects served to substantially restrict intra-Community trade.

Indeed, many of these barriers were introduced in the 1970s as European nations increasingly adopted standards and regulations that were aimed at protecting consumers, workers and the environment. The free movement of goods was also restricted by practices of national and local governments such as biased purchasing patterns, exclusive production or service rights, and production subsidies to national champions. Likewise, the free movement of services – which was guaranteed in principle by the Treaty of Rome – was far from being a reality, again largely due to national prudential and safety regulations. Service providers typically were required to possess local certification and the requirements for such certification often varied across nations. Moreover, the certification process was often controlled or influenced by the national service providers who had an economic interest in excluding foreign competitors via this certification process.

The key changes in the Single Market Programme were designed to reinforce the 'four freedoms' (free movement of goods, services, people and capital) promised by the Treaty of Rome. The concrete steps were:

- Goods trade liberalization.
- Streamlining or elimination of border formalities.
- Harmonization of VAT rates within wide bands.
- Liberalization of government procurement.
- Harmonization and mutual recognition of technical standards in production, packaging and marketing.
- Factor trade liberalization.
- Removal of all capital controls.
- Increase in capital market integration.
- Liberalization of cross-border market-entry policies, including mutual recognition of approval by national regulatory agencies.

The Single European Act also implemented important institutional changes. To clear the decision-making log-jam that had held up similar integration initiatives in the 1970s, the programme included a major change in the EU's decision-making procedures. Decisions concerning Single Market issues would be adopted on the basis of majority voting instead of on a basis of unanimity (see Chapter 3 for a discussion of EU decision-making procedures). This change in voting procedures was part of the so-called new approach to TBT liberalization.

Focus on capital mobility

The most novel aspect of the Single Market Programme was its focus on capital mobility; other features can be viewed as deepening or extending integration initiatives already agreed. Some EU members had unilaterally liberalized capital mobility, but substantial pan-EU liberalization came only in the second half of the 1980s with a series of Single Market Programme directives. The opening was completed in 1988 by a directive that ruled out all remaining restrictions on capital movements among EU residents. The definitive system was codified in the Maastricht Treaty.

It is possible to think of this aspect of the Single Market Programme as unleashing a political economy process that eventually led to the euro. Simple macroeconomic logic (explained in Chapter 14) tells us that without capital controls, nations must choose between controlling their exchange rate and controlling their monetary policy. Since exchange rate stability was considered paramount, EU members slaved their monetary policy to exchange rate stabilization in the context of the EMS. But once nations were no longer actively using monetary policy, resistance to centralizing monetary policy decisions in a European central bank was greatly weakened.

1.5.2 The EEA and the fourth enlargement

Since the Single European Act promised much tighter economic integration among EU members, non-EU nations again found themselves threatened by the discriminatory effects of integration in the EU. As in the 1960s and early 1970s, this triggered a domino effect as EFTA firms prompted their governments to offset the discrimination by seeking closer ties to the EU.

In the late 1980s, EFTA governments had decided that they must react to the Single Market. Several considered applying for EU membership (Austria actually did), while others considered bilateral negotiations. Jacques Delors forced the decision in January 1989 by proposing the European Economic Area (EEA) agreement – an agreement that essentially extends the Single Market to EFTA economies (apart from agriculture and the Common External Tariff).

Given the political economy forces described above, it is easy to understand why EFTA nations wanted the EEA. Two aspects of the EEA, however, are extraordinary. First, the EEA is unbalanced in terms of the rights and obligations of EFTA nations when it comes to future EEC legislation. The EEA commits EFTA nations to accepting future EU legislation concerning the Single Market, without any formal input into the formation of these new laws. Second, the EEA created supranationality among the EFTA nations, a feature that they had resisted since the end of the war.

As it turned out, EFTA nations were not happy with the EEA compromises, especially in the post-Cold War environment, where the East–West political division of Europe appeared to have vanished. By the end of the EEA negotiations, Austria, Finland, Sweden, Norway and Switzerland had put in EU membership applications. For them, the EEA was a transitional arrangement. Swiss voters rejected the EEA in December 1992, effectively freezing their EU application. Accession talks with the four EFTAns were successful, so the EEA now consists of the EU27 on one hand, with Norway, Liechtenstein and Iceland on the other (Norway's voters rejected EU membership by referendum and Switzerland has an EEA-like bilateral deal with the EU).

The Single Market, EEA and plans for monetary union were launched while Cold War politics still mattered. They came to fruition in a very different world.

1.6 Communism's creeping failure and spectacular collapse

The division of Europe into communist and capitalist camps was cemented, quite literally, in 1961 by the construction of the Berlin Wall (Fig. 1.9). While living standards were not too dissimilar to begin with, by the 1980s western European living standards far outstripped those in eastern Europe and the USSR. Anyone could plainly see that the West's economic system

Figure 1.9 The Berlin Wall circa 1980

Source: http://community.webshots.com

(free markets and an extensive social welfare system) when teamed up with its political system (multi-party democracy and freedom of the press) provided a far better way of life compared to the east's system of planned economies and one-party rule.

While this 'creeping failure' of communism was apparent to the central and eastern European countries (CEECs), Soviet leaders repeatedly thwarted reform efforts via constant economic pressure and occasional military interventions. By the 1980s, the inadequacy of the Soviet system forced changes inside the USSR itself. The USSR adopted a policy of timid pro-market reforms (*perestroika*) and a policy of openness (*glasnost*), which involved a marked reduction in internal repression and diminished intervention in the affairs of the Soviet republics and Soviet-bloc nations.

As far as European integration was concerned, the Soviet foreign policy changes were critical. Pro-democracy forces in the CEECs, which had been repeatedly put down by military force hereto, found little resistance from Moscow in the late 1980s. The first breach came in June 1989 when the Polish labour movement 'Solidarity' forced the communist government to accept free parliamentary elections (Fig. 1.10). The communists lost and the first democratic government in the Soviet bloc took power. Moscow rapidly established ties with the new Polish government.

Moscow's hands-off approach to the Polish election triggered a chain of events over the next two years that revolutionized European affairs. Pro-reform elements inside the Hungarian communist party pressed for democratic elections, and, more dramatically, Hungary opened its border with Austria. Thousands of East Germans reacted by moving to West Germany via Hungary and Austria. This set off mass protests against communist repression in East Germany which culminated in the opening of the border between East and West Germany.

On 9 November 1989, thousands of West and East Berlin citizens converged on the Berlin Wall with pickaxes and sledgehammers to dismantle that symbol of a divided Europe (Fig. 1.10). By the end of 1989, democratic forces were in control in Poland, Hungary, Czechoslovakia and East Germany. In 1990, East and West Germany formed a unified Germany and three Soviet

Figure 1.10 Solidarity movement and fall of the Wall

Source: Polish Maritime Museum and www.berlin-wall.org

Republics – Estonia, Latvia and Lithuania – declared their independence from the USSR. By the end of 1991, the Soviet Union itself broke up, putting a definitive end to its interference in central and eastern Europe. The European Union reacted swiftly to this geopolitical earthquake by providing emergency aid and loans to the fledgling democracies.

1.6.1 Maastricht Treaty, the euro and German unification

The 'political earthquake' caused by the falling of the wall also yielded substantial changes within the EU. With the Berlin Wall gone, unification of the western and eastern parts of Germany was the natural next step, but a unified Germany would be a behemoth. With 80 million citizens and 30 per cent of Europe's output, Germany would be much larger than France, Britain or Italy. This raised many fears, ranging from a disturbed political balance in the EU to the unlikely, but still scary, spectre of German militarism. Many Europeans, including many Germans, felt that Germany would be best unified in conjunction with a big increase in the forces tying EU members together.

Riding on his success with the Single Market, Jacques Delors seized this historical moment and proposed a radical increase in European economic integration – the formation of a monetary union – a step that he believed would eventually lead to political integration.

The idea was quickly championed by French President François Mitterrand and German Chancellor Helmut Kohl. After extensive negotiations, the EU committed itself to a target of forming a monetary union by 1999 and adopting a single currency by 2002 (see Chapter 17). This commitment was made in the Treaty of Maastricht.

The Maastricht Treaty is covered in depth in Chapter 17, but for the purposes of this chapter it is important to note that the Maastricht Treaty – formally known as the Treaty on European Union – embodied the most profound deepening of European integration since the Treaty of Rome. In addition to committing members to a transfer of national sovereignty over monetary power to a supranational body (the European Central Bank), and abandonment of their national currencies for the euro, the Treaty also:

- created EU citizenship; this included the right to move to and live in any EU state (the Treaty of Rome only guaranteed the right to work in any Member State) and to vote in European and local elections in any Member State;

- locked in the free movement of capital;
- strengthened EU cooperation in non-economic areas, including security and defence policy as well as law enforcement, criminal justice, civil judicial matters, and asylum and immigration policies;
- enshrined the principle of subsidiarity that was meant to control the transfer of responsibilities from Member States to the European Union;
- strengthened the European Parliament's power over EU legislation;
- introduced the 'Social Chapter' which expanded the EU's social dimension by introducing policies on workers' health and safety, workplace conditions, equal pay and the consultation of employees.

The most historic change was of course the commitment to adopt a single currency. As this is covered in Part V of the book in great detail, this chapter deals only with the aspects that are essential to understanding subsequent developments – except those related to the Eurozone crisis which are dealt with at length in Chapter 19.

Maastricht ratification difficulties

EU treaties such as Maastricht have power because they must be part of each Member State's domestic law, i.e. EU treaties must be ratified by each and every member if they are to come into force. In many EU nations, ratification involves a vote by the national parliament, in others, a referendum. The Maastricht Treaty had great difficulties with ratification.

During the negotiations, the British insisted on a formal opt-out from the common currency (the idea was that all other members would have to adopt the euro once they met the criteria) and from the Social Chapter. Even with these provisos, Eurosceptics from his own party nearly brought down British Prime Minister John Major's government during the UK Parliamentary ratification vote. French President François Mitterrand put the Treaty to a referendum expecting a massive 'yes' vote that would bolster the Treaty's prospects (referenda are not mandatory in France), but only 51.4 per cent of the French voted 'yes'. The Treaty was challenged (unsuccessfully) as unconstitutional before Germany's High Court.

More problematic was the fact that Danish voters narrowly rejected the Treaty in a 1992 referendum. After EU leaders agreed to grant Denmark opt-outs on the single currency and defence matters, a second vote on Maastricht was held and the Danes reversed their own veto by voting 'yes'. The Treaty came into force in November 1993.

1.7 Reuniting east and west Europe

Given that almost every other nation in the region had free trade access to the enormous EU market, free trade agreements with the EU were a commercial necessity for the newly free central and eastern European countries (CEECs). Their strategic goal, however, was EU and NATO membership. CEEC leaders felt unsure that the new situation was permanent. If things went wrong in Russia and the iron curtain re-descended, each CEEC wanted to be sure that the curtain would, this time, come down east of its border.

1.7.1 First steps: the Europe Agreements

Each CEEC announced that its goal was to join the EU. The EU, by contrast, was reluctant in the early 1990s. Sidestepping the membership issue, the EU signed Association Agreements (also called Europe Agreements) with Poland, Hungary and Czechoslovakia in 1991. Europe Agreements for other CEECs followed progressively. By 1994, such deals had been signed with Romania, Bulgaria, Albania, Estonia, Latvia and Lithuania. EFTA negotiated similar bilateral agreements in parallel. Some CEECs also signed trade arrangements among themselves, the most important being the 1991 Central European Free Trade Agreement among Czechoslovakia, Hungary and Poland (subsequently extended to Slovenia, Bulgaria and Romania).

The Europe Agreements established bilateral free trade between the EU and each individual CEEC. They committed the EU to removing tariffs and quantitative restrictions on most industrial products by the end of 1994. Substantial EU protection remained for a group of 'sensitive' industrial products, including some textiles, some coal and steel products, and almost all agricultural trade. Beyond the removal of tariffs on most industrial goods, a further goal was to make progress towards 'realizing between them the other economic freedoms on which the Community is based'. The adoption of EU laws and practices (competition policy, harmonized standards, etc.) helped the CEECs establish functioning market economies faster than they could have on their own.

By committing the CEECs to adopt the main elements of EU economic integration and regulation, the Europe Agreements were crucial in guiding these nations' economic transitions from planned to market economies. The goal of EU membership provided an important political anchorage that kept the pro-market reforms on track.

The Europe Agreements stopped short of offering EU membership. This reflected the profound ambivalence that many west Europeans initially felt towards eastern enlargement of the EU. For instance, slow action of the parliaments of EU Member States meant that the Europe Agreements signed with Hungary and Poland in December 1991 entered into force only in February 1994. Most of the hesitation was due to the economic nature of the CEEC. The CEECs were poor, populous and agrarian. Since the EU spends 80 per cent of its budget on farms and poor regions, eastern enlargement was viewed as a threat to special interest groups in the EU15.

1.7.2 Copenhagen to Copenhagen: from 1993 accession criteria to EU membership

The EU officially ended its hesitancy in June 1993. In Copenhagen, the EU's key political body – the European Council – decided the associated CEECs could become EU members. The Council laid out the so-called Copenhagen Criteria for membership. These – which are still applied today – are:

- political stability of institutions that guarantee democracy, the rule of law, human rights and respect for and protection of minorities;
- a functioning market economy capable of dealing with the competitive pressure and market forces within the Union; and
- acceptance of the Community 'acquis' (EU law in its entirety, including all the Treaties and subsequent rules) and the ability to take on the obligations of membership, including adherence to the aims of political, economic and monetary union.

1.8 Preparing for eastern enlargement: a string of new treaties

Once the EU15 leaders confirmed that the CEECs would eventually join, the next order of business was to get EU institutions – which had been designed for six members and were straining to work with 15 – ready for a dozen new members. This started a chain of events that eventually ended in adoption of the Lisbon Treaty in December 2009.

The process began formally in December 1993. A treaty-writing exercise (what the EU calls an Intergovernmental Conference, or IGC) had already been scheduled in the 1992 Maastricht Treaty for 1996. The original purpose was a something of a 'check-up' halfway into the timetable for monetary union. Building on this, the 1993 Brussels European Council added EU institutional reform to its agenda.[1] To prepare the IGC 1996, the EU established a 'Reflection Group' whose job was to study institutional reforms necessary to keep the EU on track after enlargement. In setting up the group, EU leaders explicitly mentioned two issues to be addressed: Council of Minister voting (specifically, weighting of votes and the threshold for qualified majority decisions), and the number of members of the Commission.

The Group's report (the Westendorp Report) presented a consensus on the problems facing an enlarged EU – a clear statement of the 'whys' of EU institutional reform.[2] It also describes a thorough lack of consensus on solutions. This agreement on problems and disagreement on solutions marked the four attempts the EU made over 16 years (Amsterdam, Nice, Constitutional and Lisbon Treaties). Moreover, the disagreements it highlights – big member vs. small members, federalists vs. intergovernmentalists, etc. – are exactly the ones that plagued every step of the decade-long process of reforming EU institutions.

The deep problems that required EU institutional reform concerned the Union's decision-making machinery on the one hand, and the changing nature of the EU's role in the world on the other.

- The decision-making problems are complex (see Chapter 3) but the need for reform is easy to understand. Every student will have observed that taking a group decision – such as rescheduling a workshop or lecture – is fairly easy in a group consisting of a handful or fewer members. It becomes almost impossible when the group gets much beyond a dozen. The same logic applies to the EU decision-making bodies such as the Council of Ministers and the European Commission.

- Changes in EU external policy, by contrast, were forced by external events. The end of the Cold War – and the attendant demise of the two-superpower system – made international politics a much more complex affair, one in which the EU could play a role. Moreover, events in the former Yugoslavia convinced many Europeans that the traditional hands-off approach was no longer justified. Given their modest size, however, effective action would typically require some coordination among at least a subset of EU members.

1.8.1 Amsterdam Treaty: cleaning up the Maastricht Treaty

The 1996 IGC produced the Amsterdam Treaty in 1997. Ambitions for the Amsterdam Treaty were high – the mandate was to agree all the necessary enlargement-related reforms that the Westendorp Report highlighted. By this yardstick, it failed.

The Amsterdam Treaty is best thought of as a tidying up of the Maastricht Treaty. The substantive additions included a more substantial role for the EU in social policy (UK Prime Minister Tony Blair cancelled the British opt-out). The European Parliament powers were modestly boosted, and the notion of flexible integration, so-called closer cooperation, was introduced (see Chapter 2 for details).

---

[1] For a detailed account, see the essay at http://shop.ceps.eu/downfree.php?item_id=1332.

[2] See www.cvce.eu for a copy of the Westendorp Report and all the other reports mentioned in this chapter.

The key enlargement-related reforms were not settled but were still pressing, so EU leaders agreed a list called the 'Amsterdam leftovers'. They also agreed to launch a new IGC in 2000.

1.8.2 Nice Treaty: failed attempt to reform EU institutions

After the year-long preparation of the IGC 2000, EU leaders met in Nice in December 2000 to wrap up a new treaty that was supposed to deal with the Amsterdam leftovers. At four o'clock in the morning after the longest EU summit in history, EU leaders announced political agreement on a new treaty.

The result – the Treaty of Nice – was not a success. The critical Amsterdam leftover issues – the size and composition of the Commission, extension of majority voting in the Council of Ministers and reform of Council voting rules – were not fully solved (see Chapter 3 for details). For example, the chairmanship of then French President Jacques Chirac (France had the chair of the European Council at the time) was heavily criticized by leaders of the European Parliament and the President of the European Commission, Romano Prodi. Indeed, a few days after the Nice Summit, the European Parliament adopted a resolution which accused the governments of having given 'priority to their short-term national interests rather than to EU interests'. Back then, however, the European Parliament did not have the power to block a new Treaty.

Figure 1.11 The Irish 'no' to the Nice Treaty

Note: Sinn Féin opposed the Nice Treaty, but most political parties supported it. Irish voters reversed themselves after EU assurances on military issues.

Photo: www.sinnfein.ie

Nice Treaty ratification difficulties

The Treaty had some trouble with ratification but not nearly as much as the Maastricht Treaty. Only the Irish refused the Nice Treaty in a referendum; Fig. 1.11. Since a new treaty cannot come into force until all EU members have ratified it, the Irish 'no' had to be addressed. The solution was to make a number of political commitments guaranteeing Irish neutrality and to have all 14 other members ratify the Treaty. Irish voters were then asked to vote again; the second time they said 'yes'.

Incomplete reform

EU leaders at the Nice Summit knew that the Treaty did not fully adjust the EU to the new realities of the coming enlargement. In what had become a familiar pattern, part of the final political deal on the Treaty at Nice was an agreement to hold another IGC to complete the reform process. This 'Declaration on the Future of the Union' highlighted four themes:

1 defining a more precise division of powers between the EU and its members;
2 clarifying the status of the Charter of Fundamental Rights proclaimed in Nice;

3 making the Treaties easier to understand without changing their meaning;

4 defining the role of national parliaments in the European institutions.

1.8.3 Eastern enlargement and the Constitutional Treaty

One year after the Nice Summit, the European Council met in the Belgian city of Laeken to adopt the 'Declaration on the Future of the European Union'. This provided an outline for thinking about the new treaty to be written by the IGC in 2004.

In light of the difficult Nice Summit, the Laeken Council also decided on a novel working method. It convened the 'Convention on the Future of Europe', which came to be known as the European Convention, consisting of a large number of men and women representing current and prospective Member States, the national parliaments, the European Parliament and the Commission. The Convention's output was to be the point of departure for the IGC 2004 that would draft the actual treaty (as required by EU law).

As far as its contents are concerned, the 'Laeken Declaration' contains a list of issues that is surprisingly close to that of the 1995 Westendorp Report; 56 questions grouped under the four themes of the Nice Declaration. The Laeken Declaration, however, included two crucial novelties. First, the Declaration implicitly admits that the Nice reforms were insufficient. One question is: 'How we can improve the efficiency of decision-making and the workings of the institutions in a Union of some 30 Member States?' Since this was the main goal of the Nice Treaty, EU leaders essentially admitted that the Nice reforms would not be enough. In effect, it asks the Convention to reform the Nice Treaty reforms even before the Nice reforms had been implemented (most Nice Treaty changes only took effect after 2004). Second, while the Nice Declaration made no mention of a constitution, the word does appear in the Laeken Declaration.

The Laeken Declaration did not instruct the Convention to write a constitution. It included the question: 'The question ultimately arises as to whether this simplification and reorganization might not lead in the long run to the adoption of a constitutional text in the Union. What might the basic features of such a constitution be? The values which the Union cherishes, the fundamental rights and obligations of its citizens, the relationship between Member States in the Union?'

The European Convention, February 2002 to July 2003

The European Convention was run by former French President Valéry Giscard d'Estaing with the assistance of two Vice-Chairmen (see Fig. 1.12). It started slowly and many early observers expected its large size and ill-defined objectives to result in a muddled outcome.

However by mid-2002, President Giscard d'Estaing had redefined the Convention's purpose. The 'Convention on the Future of Europe' was transformed into a constitution-writing convention. The new goal was to present the EU heads of state and government with a fully written constitution. This changed everything. From that point forward, EU members started sending heavyweight politicians in place of low-level representatives. All arguments over the need for a constitution were dropped; discussion turned instead to its content.

The Chairman Valéry Giscard d'Estaing was firmly in charge. The Convention's decision-making procedure involved no voting by representatives and indeed no standard democratic procedure of any kind. The Convention adopted its recommendations by 'consensus', with Giscard d'Estaing defining when a consensus existed. The representatives of the candidate countries participated fully in the debate, but their voices were not allowed to prevent a consensus among representatives of the then 15 members of the EU.

Figure 1.12 The European Convention was run by its presidium

Presidential podium at the plenary session debate on institutional questions, January 2003. From the left, Jean-Luc Dehaene (Vice-Chairman, Belgium), Giuliano Amato (Vice-Chairman, Italy) and Valéry Giscard d'Estaing (Chairman, France).

Source: European Commission

These unusual features of the Convention working method go a long way to explaining the many problems that the Constitutional Treaty was soon to face.

The IGC's failure and the Irish compromise

The process of turning the Convention's draft into an EU treaty (see Fig. 1.13) did not start well. Although the draft was presented in July 2003, the Italian Presidency dithered; Italian Prime Minister Silvio Berlusconi (Italy was Chairman of European Council at the time) convened the IGC only in October 2003. Differences that had been papered over in the Convention emerged immediately – especially the critical Council voting question which had not been openly discussed in the Convention. The deal-breaking issue turned on the fact that new voting rules shifted a great deal of voting power (compared to the Nice Treaty rules) to Germany and away from Spain and Poland (see Chapter 3 for details). The Italian Presidency failed to bridge the differences.

All EU members – including the ten members that joined in January 2004 – agreed that institutional reform was a must, so the Irish government, which took over the EU Presidency from the Italians, made a new attempt to rewrite the European Convention's rejected draft. Skilful diplomacy by the Irish Presidency and a change of government in Spain permitted a grudging and difficult but ultimately unanimous acceptance of a new draft at the June 2004 summit of EU25 leaders. With this high-level political compromise in hand, the IGC completed its work and the Constitution was signed in Rome in October 2004.

Constitutional Treaty ratification difficulties

For a variety of reasons, five EU nations that would normally have ratified the Constitutional Treaty by parliamentary vote opted for referenda: France, the Netherlands, the UK, Luxembourg and Spain. Two of these – France and the Netherlands – turned in 'no' votes in mid-2005 that derailed the whole process.

The French and Dutch 'nos' were quite a different problem for EU leaders from the Danish and Irish 'nos' on the Maastricht and Nice Treaties. Apart from the fact that the Dutch and French were founding members, the number of no-voters was entirely different. In the first Irish poll on the Nice Treaty, less than a million people voted and only 530,000 said 'no'. In the French referendum, 16 of 29 million French voters said 'no' (see Fig. 1.14). Three days later, 4.7 out of 7.6 million Dutch rejected the Treaty. While EU leaders could 'work around' 530,000 Irish no-sayers, it was impossible to ignore over 20 million nos.

In reaction, EU leaders suspended the ratification process and declared a 'period of reflection'.

Figure 1.13 Toast at the Convention's last Plenary Session, 13 June 2003

Source: European Commission

1.8.4 The Lisbon Treaty

Two inadequate reform attempts (Amsterdam and Nice Treaties), a decade of on-and-off negotiations and four rejections by European voters made it clear that EU institutional reform was not easy and not popular with EU voters. Why didn't EU leaders just abandon the project? The answer lies in the factors that had been obvious since the 1993 Westendorp Report. Europe had to reform its institutions if it was to continue functioning effectively and legitimately, and the Nice Treaty reforms were not good enough.

Germany re-launches the institutional reform process

The process was re-launched when Germany took on the rotating EU Presidency in 2007. Guided by forceful German leadership, EU leaders declared the Constitutional Treaty to be dead and agreed on the basic outlines of its replacement – the Reform Treaty, which came to be known as the Lisbon Treaty after the city in which it was signed in December 2007.

As EU leaders had been talking about institutional reform since the mid-1990s and the best they could agree on was already in the Constitutional Treaty, EU leaders included all the main Constitutional Treaty reforms in the Lisbon Treaty but packaged them very differently.

- All the grandiloquent language and gestures to supranationalism were dropped.
- All references to symbols of statehood were jettisoned – the flag, the anthem, the Foreign Ministers and the like.
- The word 'constitution' was banished.

The only federalist token was to merge the term 'European Community' with European Union.

Figure 1.14 Posters for French Constitutional Treaty referendum

Photo: © European Union 2012

Lisbon Treaty ratification difficulties

The idea behind the German repackaging strategy was to avoid referenda in as many nations as possible. By making it more of a technocratic amendment of the existing legal structure, most EU governments felt they would be justified in ratifying the Lisbon Treaty by a vote of the national parliament – the procedure adopted for most Treaties by most members since the very beginning. By and large, it worked. The Irish constitution, however, requires a referendum on any law that changes the relationship between Irish law and EU law. Since the Lisbon Treaty certainly meets this criterion, a vote was held in July 2008. The no-voters won by a solid margin.

To justify holding a new vote, the Irish government obtained three key promises from fellow EU leaders that directly addressed the concerns of certain segments of the Irish electorate. The three were:

- that Irish neutrality would not be questioned or threatened by anything in the Lisbon Treaty;
- that Ireland would continue always to have a European commissioner; and
- Ireland's ban on abortion was not to be questioned or threatened by the Treaty.

With these promises in hand, the Irish reversed their 'no' in October 2009. The Treaty came into effect in December 2009.

The Lisbon Treaty instituted many important changes. These are addressed at length in Chapters 2 and 3.

1.9 Summary

It is impossible to summarize 50 years of European integration in a few paragraphs. But it is possible to highlight the main events and lessons as far as the economics of European integration are concerned.

European integration has always been driven by political factors, ranging from a desire to prevent another European war to a desire to share the fruit of integration with the newly democratic nations in central and eastern Europe. Yet while the goals were always political, the means were always economic.

There have been basically three big increases in European economic integration. Formation of the customs union from 1958 to 1968 eliminated tariffs and quotas on intra-EU trade. The Single Market Programme implemented between 1986 and 1992 (although elements are still being implemented today) eliminated many non-tariff barriers and liberalized capital flows within the EU. Finally, the Economic and Monetary Union melded together the currencies of most EU members.

Each of these steps towards deeper integration – but especially the customs union and the Single Market Programme – engendered discriminatory effects that triggered reactions in the non-member nations. Just as the knocking down of one domino triggers a chain reaction that leads to the fall of all dominoes, the discriminatory effects of EU integration have created a powerful gravitational force that has progressively drawn all but the most reluctant Europeans into the EU. If there is a lesson to draw from this for the future, it is that the 2004 enlargement is likely to greatly magnify the pro-EU membership forces in the nations further east and south.

Self-assessment questions

1 Draw a diagram (or diagrams) that graphically shows the major steps in European economic integration, along with dates and the names of the countries involved. Be sure to discuss explicitly the removal of various barriers to the movement of goods, labour and capital.

2 Draw a diagram like Fig. 1.4 that shows the current state of trade arrangements in Europe, including all European nations west of the Urals.

3 Make a list of all the EU treaties (with dates) and provide a ten-words-or-less explanation of each treaty's major contribution to European integration.

4 Make a list of the dates of the major stages in the Common Agricultural Policy and its reforms (see europa.eu.int/comm/agriculture/index_en.htm for details).

5 Make a list of the dates of the major stages in the EU structural spending programmes (see europa.eu.int/comm/regional_policy/index_en.htm for details).

6 What were the main challenges posed by eastern enlargement of the European Union and how was the Nice Treaty meant to address these challenges?

7 Some European integration experts subscribe to the so-called bicycle theory of integration, which asserts that European integration must continually move forward to prevent it from 'falling over', i.e. breaking down. List a sequence of events from 1958 to 1992 that lends support to the theory.

8 Explain how Cold War politics accelerated European integration in some ways but hindered it in others, such as geographic expansion of the EU.

9 Explain when and by which means the organization that is known as the European Union has changed names since its inception in 1958.

10 Make a table showing the dates of all changes in EU and EFTA membership.

Essay questions

1 What role has the Council of Europe, which is a non-EU institution, played in pan-European integration?

2 How important was the USA's role in promoting European integration? Do you think Europe would have formed the EEC, or something like it, if the USA had not made the creation of the OEEC a condition for aid?

3 Describe the evolution of the various British governments' attitudes towards European integration in the 1945 to 1975 period. In the early years Labour opposed membership while Conservatives supported it, but recently the roles have reversed. Why do you think this is so?

4 Provide an explanation for why only six of the EU15 nations joined in 1957. You should list specific reasons for each non-member.

5 Write an essay on the work towards deeper European integration that was done in the context of the OEEC. Why did this fail?

6 Write an essay on whether Charles de Gaulle promoted or hindered European integration. Chapter 8 of Urwin (1995) is a good place to start.

7 Why did the EPC and EDC plans fail when the ECSC succeeded?

8 Explain why economic integration can promote peace.

9 Explain why some countries organize referenda before ratifying European treaties.

10 In a historical perspective, has the enlargement of the EU made reforms more difficult?

11 What would be the political and economic reasons for Georgia to join the EU?

12 Why was de Gaulle against UK membership of the EEC?

13 Why was it important to the USA for Germany to be economically strong?

14 In a historical perspective, do you think opt-outs facilitate or hinder further integration?

15 What were Churchill's arguments for the creation of the 'United States of Europe'? Listen to or read his 1946 Zurich speech at www.cvce.eu to answer this question. Why did he exclude the UK from this proposed union?

16 Why were the Benelux countries the first in Europe to form a customs union?

17 State which countries you would like to see join the EU in the future and give the reasons why they would want to do so.

18 Would you say it was economic forces that brought democracy throughout Europe?

Further reading: the aficionado's corner

For a good, general description of the development of European integration, see:
Urwin, D. (1995) *The Community of Europe*, Longman, London.

Two books that challenge the traditional view that federalist idealism was important in the development of Europe are:
Milward, A. (1992) *The European Rescue of the Nation-state*, Cambridge University Press, Cambridge.
Moravcsik, A. (1998) *The Choice for Europe: Social Purpose and State Power from Messina to Maastricht*, Cornell University Press, Ithaca, NY.

A detailed description of post-war growth can be found in:
Botting, D. (1985) *From the Ruins of the Reich: Germany 1945–1949*, New American Library, New York.
Crafts, N. and G. Toniolo (1996) *Economic Growth in Europe since 1945*, Cambridge University Press, Cambridge.
Jackson, J. (2003) *The Fall of France*, Oxford University Press, Oxford.
Lamfalussy, A. (1963) *The UK and the Six: An Essay on Economic Growth in Western Europe*, Macmillan, London.
Moravcsik, A. (1998) *The Choice for Europe: Social Purpose and State Power from Messina to Maastricht*, Cornell University Press, Ithaca, NY.
Tsebelis, G. (2005) 'Agenda Setting in the EU Constitution: From the Giscard Plan to the Pros Ratification(?) Document', paper presented at the DOSEI conference, Brussels, http://sitemaker.umich.edu/tsebelis/files/giscardagenda.pdf.

Useful websites

The European Parliament's 'factsheets' provide an excellent, authoritative and succinct coverage of many historical institutions, policies and debates. For example, it has pages on the historical development of the Parliament's role, on historical enlargements, and on every Treaty. See www.europarl.eu.int/factsheets/default_en.htm.

The EU's 'Easy Reading Corner' is not very well organized and the search engine is useless (instead try Google with site:europe.eu.int added to your keyword) but it has a lot of material and will eventually lead you to very detailed information on any topic concerning the EU; many brochures are oversimplified and not much use to students at the level of this textbook. See http://europa.eu.int/comm/publications/index_en.htm.

A good glossary can be found at http://europa.eu.int/abc/eurojargon/index_en.htm.

Details on specific Treaties (including handy summaries) can be found at http://europa.eu.int/abc/treaties_en.htm.

For Marxist–Leninist thinking on capitalism, imperialism and war, see this tract by Leon Trotsky at www.marxists.org/archive/trotsky/works/1939/1939-lenin.htm.

The Truman Library website www.trumanlibrary.org/teacher/berlin.htm is a good source for early post-war background documents online.

The Centre Virtuel de la Connaissance sur l'Europe provides a complete and well-organized website for documents, photos, videos, etc. on virtually every aspect of European integration at www.cvce.eu.

The German Historical Museum (DHM) provides photos and videos of Germany's wartime experience at www.dhm.de/lemo/html/Nachkriegsjahre/DasEndeAlsAnfang/.

References

Baldwin, R. (1994) *Towards an Integrated Europe*, CEPR, London. Freely downloadable from http://heiwww.unige.ch7Baldwin/papers.htm.
Baldwin, R. (1995) 'A domino theory of regionalism', in R. Baldwin, P. Haaparanta and J. Kiander (eds) *Expanding European Regionalism: The EU's New Members*, Cambridge University Press, Cambridge.
Crafts, N. and G. Toniolo (1996) *Economic Growth in Europe since 1945*, Cambridge University Press, Cambridge.
Eichengreen, B. and J.B. de Macedo (2001) 'The European Payments Union: history and implications for the evolution of the International Financial Architecture', in A. Lamfalussy, B. Snoy and J. Wilson (eds) *Fragility of the International Financial System*, P.I.E.-Peter Lang, Brussels.
Milward, A. (1984) *The European Rescue of the Nation-state: 1945–51*, Routledge, London.
Milward, A. (1992) *The European Rescue of the Nation-state*, Cambridge University Press, Cambridge.
Spierenburg, D. and R. Poidevin (1994) *The History of the European Coal and Steel Community*, Weidenfeld & Nicolson, London.
Urwin, D. (1995) *The Community of Europe*, Longman, London.

Annex A Chronology from 1948 to 2007

Year	Date	Event	Explanation
1948	16 April	OEEC	Organization for European Economic Cooperation (OEEC) established.
1950	9 May	Schuman Plan	French Foreign Minister Robert Schuman proposes the establishment of the European Coal and Steel Community (ECSC). Schuman was inspired by Jean Monnet's vision of building Europe step by step. 9 May is celebrated as the Day of Europe.
1952	1 January	ECSC	The ECSC is established for 50 years; expired 23 July 2002.
1952	27 May	EDC	'The Six' sign the Treaty establishing the European Defence Community (EDC). The project fails as the French National Assembly rejects the Treaty in 1954.
1953	9 March	EPC	A plan for the European Political Community (EPC) is published.
1957	25 March	EEC	The Six sign Treaties in Rome establishing the European Economic Community (EEC) and the European Atomic Energy Community (Euratom). EEC begins 1 January 1958.
1959	21 July	EFTA	European Free Trade Association (EFTA) is established by the Stockholm Convention among Austria, Denmark, Norway, Portugal, Sweden, Switzerland and the United Kingdom. EFTA begins 3 May 1960.
1962	1 January	CAP	Common Agricultural Policy starts.
1968	1 July	CU completed	Customs union is completed within the EEC and a common external tariff is established.
1969	1–2 December	Failed monetary integration launched	At the Hague Summit, EC leaders agree to establish a single market, to accelerate integration, and to introduce Economic and Monetary Union (EMU) by 1980.
1972	22 July	EC–EFTA FTAs	Free trade agreements (FTAs) signed with Austria, Iceland, Portugal, Sweden and Switzerland.
1973	1 January	First enlargement	The Six become the Nine as Denmark, Ireland and the UK join the EC. Accession Treaties were signed 1 January 1972. EEC signs free trade agreements with Norway (May) and Finland (October).
1974	9–10 December	European Council formalized	At Paris Summit, EC leaders agree to meet regularly as a European Council.
1978	6–7 July	EMS founded	Bremen European Council establishes the European Monetary System (EMS) and the European currency unit (ECU).

Year	Date	Event	Explanation
1981	1 January	Second enlargement	Greece joins.
1985	14 June	EC92 White Paper	Commission presents the Cockfield White Paper on the completion of the single market (blueprint for economics in Single European Act).
1986	1 January	Third enlargement	Spain and Portugal join.
1986	17, 28 February	Single European Act	Single European Act is signed. Treaty enters into force on 1 July 1987.
1990	1 July	EMU stage 1	First stage of Economic and Monetary Union (EMU) begins.
1990	10 October	Germany unites	Germany is united as the former German Democratic Republic länder join the EEC.
1991		First Europe Agreements	EC signs Europe Agreements with Poland, Hungary and Czechoslovakia; Europe Agreements for other CEECs signed by 1995.
1992	7 February	Maastricht Treaty	Treaty on European Union is signed in Maastricht, creating the EU. Treaty enters into force 1 November 1993 after a difficult ratification process in Denmark.
1992	2 May	EEA	EC and EFTA sign an Agreement establishing the European Economic Area (EEA).
1993	21–22 June	CEECs can join when ready	EU leaders decide CEECs with Europe Agreements can join when they meet the 'Copenhagen criteria'.
1994	1 January	EMU stage 2	The second stage of EMU begins.
1994	9–10 December		Essen European Council agrees strategy on eastern enlargement.
1995	1 January	Fourth enlargement	Austria, Finland and Sweden join the EU.
1997	2 October	Amsterdam Treaty	Treaty of Amsterdam is signed; comes into force 1 May 1999.
1998	1–2 May	The euro	EU leaders decide 11 to join Eurozone (Austria, Belgium, Finland, France, Germany, Ireland, Italy, Luxembourg, the Netherlands, Portugal and Spain).
1998	1 June	ECB	The European Central Bank (ECB) is established.
1999	1 January	EMU stage 3	Euro becomes a currency in its own right; only electronic currency until January 2002.
2000	7–9 December	Nice Treaty	Treaty of Nice is signed; comes into force on 1 February 2003 after a difficult ratification process in Ireland.
2002	1 January	Euro cash	Euro notes and coins circulate.
2002	February	European Convention	Following Laeken Declaration (15 December 2001), the Convention starts; it finishes June 2003.
2003	20 June	Draft Constitution	EU leaders accept the Giscard d'Estaing's draft Constitution as starting point for IGC.

Year	Date	Event	Explanation
2003	October	Constitutional IGC	The IGC begins under Italian Presidency.
2003	13 December	Draft Treaty rejected	European Council fails to adopt the Italian draft of the Treaty; IGC continues.
2004	1 May	Eastern enlargement	Ten new members join (Poland, Hungary, Slovakia, Czech Republic, Slovenia, Estonia, Latvia, Lithuania, Malta and Cyprus).
2004	18 June	Constitutional Treaty signed	EU heads of state and government sign the Constitutional Treaty. Ratification begins.
2005	30 May	French reject Constitution	French referendum on Constitution results in 55% no with 69% participation.
2005	1 June	Dutch reject Constitution	62% of Dutch voters reject Constitution; turnout was 63%.
2005	17 June	Ratification suspended	EU leaders decide to suspend the November 2006 deadline for ratifying the Constitution. Each Member State decides whether to continue ratification process.
2007	1 January		Bulgaria and Romania join the EU. Croatia, the Former Yugoslav Republic of Macedonia and Turkey are also candidates for future membership.
2007	13 December	Treaty of Lisbon	Signed by 27 member countries, the Treaty is planned to be ratified before the end of 2008 but the rejection of the Treaty by the Irish electorate puts it on hiatus.
2007	12 June	Treaty of Lisbon	Irish voters reject the Lisbon Treaty in a referendum.

Note: These chronologies are based on the excellent and succinct chronology on the website of the 1999 Finnish Presidency of the EU (http://presidency..nland../doc/eu/eu_5chro.htm), and the extremely detailed chronology on the European Commission's website (http://europa.eu.int/abc/history/index_en.htm).

Chapter 2

Facts, law, institutions and the budget

> In the infancy of societies, the chiefs of the state shape its institutions; later the institutions shape the chiefs of state.
>
> Baron de Montesquieu

Chapter Contents

Introduction

The members of the European Union are economically and politically integrated to an extent that is historically unprecedented. In many ways, the EU is already more integrated than loosely federated nations such as Canada and Switzerland. This integration is maintained and advanced by a cocktail of economic, political, historical and legal forces shaped by European institutions, laws and policies. This chapter presents the background information on these institutional features that is essential to the study of European economic integration.

The chapter starts by detailing the extent of European economic integration, before turning to more institutional issues – EU organization, EU law, EU institutions and the legislative process. The chapter then presents basic facts on EU members (population, incomes and economic size), which are essential for understanding the subsequent topic, the EU budget.

2.1 Economic integration in the EU

If markets are so integrated, you can't cook a different soup in one corner of the pot.

Andres Sutt, Deputy Governor of the Bank of Estonia,
on why Estonia wanted to join the Eurozone

The extent and nature of EU economic integration cannot be fully understood without reference to the founders' intentions. The post-war architects of Europe had radical goals in mind when they established the European Economic Community with the 1957 Treaty of Rome (which has been re-labelled the 'Treaty on the Functioning of the European Union' by the 2009 Lisbon Treaty).

The Treaty of Rome's main architect, Jean Monnet, headed an influential pan-European group called the Action Committee for the United States of Europe. Having failed with their plans for a European Political Community and a European Defence Community in the early 1950s, they switched to economic integration as the means of achieving their lofty goal (see Chapter 1 for details). This insight is critical to understanding the basic outlines of European economic integration. The various elements were not subjected to individual cost–benefit calculations. The idea was to fuse the six national economies into a unified economic area so as to launch a gradual process that would draw the nations into an ever-closer union.[1] In short, economics was to be the road to the 'finalité politique'.

This section reviews economic integration in today's European Union, organizing the main features according to the logic of a unified economic area.

2.1.1 Treaty of Rome – fountainhead of EU economic integration

The Treaty of Rome was a far-reaching document. It is, in a sense, the bud whose leaves unfolded over 50 years into today's European Union. It laid out virtually every aspect of economic integration that Europe has implemented right up to the 1992 Maastricht Treaty which explicitly added monetary union to EU economic integration. As a bonus, the Treaty of Rome is easy and rewarding to read. Unlike today's efforts – e.g. the Lisbon Treaty – the original Treaty of Rome was written from scratch by highly literate and fairly idealistic politicians and diplomats. Students should at least read the three-page 'PART ONE – Principles' in the original version (available in many

---

[1] A clear statement of this can be found in the so-called Spaak Report, 'Rapport des chefs de délégation aux ministres des Affaires étrangères', Bruxelles, 21 avril 1956, the outcome of the experts group set up by the Messina Conference. See www.cvce.lu.

languages on many web pages, such as www.eurotreaties.com). Box 2.1 reproduces verbatim the first three articles since Article 1 establishes the European Economic Community, Article 2 sets out the main goals, and Article 3 lists the integration initiatives to be undertaken among the original six members.

Box 2.1   Articles 1, 2 and 3 of the Treaty of Rome

ARTICLE 1. By this Treaty, the High Contracting Parties establish among themselves a EUROPEAN ECONOMIC COMMUNITY.

ARTICLE 2. The Community shall have as its task, by establishing a common market and progressively approximating the economic policies of Member States, to promote throughout the Community a harmonious development of economic activities, a continuous and balanced expansion, an increase in stability, an accelerated raising of the standard of living and closer relations between the States belonging to it.

ARTICLE 3. For the purposes set out in Article 2, the activities of the Community shall include, as provided in this Treaty and in accordance with the timetable set out therein:

(a) the elimination, as between Member States, of customs duties and of quantitative restrictions on the import and export of goods, and of all other measures having equivalent effect;

(b) the establishment of a common customs tariff and of a common commercial policy towards third countries;

(c) the abolition, as between Member States, of obstacles to freedom of movement for persons, services and capital;

(d) the adoption of a common policy in the sphere of agriculture;

(e) the adoption of a common policy in the sphere of transport;

(f) the institution of a system ensuring that competition in the common market is not distorted;

(g) the application of procedures by which the economic policies of Member States can be coordinated and disequilibria in their balances of payments remedied;

(h) the approximation of the laws of Member States to the extent required for the proper functioning of the common market;

(i) the creation of a European Social Fund in order to improve employment opportunities for workers and to contribute to the raising of their standard of living;

(j) the establishment of a European Investment Bank to facilitate the economic expansion of the Community by opening up fresh resources;

(k) the association of the overseas countries and territories in order to increase trade and to promote jointly economic and social development.

Note: The Treaty of Rome has been amended and renamed many times since the 1950s (see Box 2.2); the current name, Treaty on the Functioning of the European Union, is so dull that many writers continue to call it the Treaty of Rome.

2.1.2 How to create a unified economic area

The best way to understand European economic integration is not to read the Treaties in detail – it is to think about the founders' goal of an ever-closer union and their thinking on how economic

---

Box 2.2   Treaty or Treaties of Rome?

Study of European integration is plagued by duplicate names. Many authors use the term the Treaty of Rome, others use Treaties of Rome. In fact two Treaties were signed on 25 March 1957 in the Capitol in Rome – The 'Treaty establishing the European Economic Community', which set up the basic economic integration, and another treaty, the 'Treaty establishing the European Atomic Energy Community (Euratom)'.

As the full Treaty names are unwieldy, the abbreviations TEEC (Treaty Establishing the European Community) and Euratom were frequently used. Together they are known as the Treaties of Rome. However, the TEEC turned out to be vastly more important, so 'Treaty of Rome' became the short name for the TEEC.

To complicate things, the 'Treaty establishing the European Economic Community' got renamed as the 'Treaty establishing the European Community', or TEC, by the 1992 Maastricht Treaty. The TEC was then re-labelled by the Lisbon Treaty as the 'Treaty on the Functioning of the European Union' or TFEU.

The Maastricht Treaty, which created the European Union (see Section 2.2 for details), is formally called the 'Treaty on European Union', or TEU. This has never been renamed, but the TEU and TEC were often called 'the Treaties'; now 'the Treaties' refers to the TEU and the TFEU.

---

integration would trigger this. In this light, the Treaty of Rome's intention was to create a unified economic area, i.e. an area where firms and consumers located anywhere in the area would have equal opportunities to sell or buy goods throughout the area, and where owners of labour and capital should be free to employ their resources in any economic activity anywhere in the area.

The plan was that this unified economic area would draw Europeans into ever-closer and ever more intricate economic exchanges and this, in turn, would lead Europeans to embrace ever-closer political cooperation and integration. As history shows, the plan worked (see Chapter 1); Europeans in 2011 are integrated on an economic, political, social and cultural level that would have been almost unimaginable in 1957. Remember, back then, most voters had lived through the German occupation of every other member of the Six.

The steps necessary to establish this unified economic area are presented below, along with references to the relevant articles in the current consolidated version of the Treaty of Rome (formally known as the Treaty establishing the European Community, or TEC for short).

Free trade in goods

The most obvious requirement is to remove trade barriers. Article 3a removes all tariffs and quantitative restrictions among members, thus establishing a free trade area for all goods. Tariffs and quotas, however, are not the only means of discriminating against foreign goods and services. Throughout the ages, governments have proved wonderfully imaginative in developing tariff-like and quota-like barriers against foreign goods and services. To remove such 'non-tariff' barriers, and to prevent new non-tariff barriers from offsetting the tariff liberalization, the Treaty rules out all measures that act like tariffs or quotas.

Common trade policy with the rest of the world

Trade can never be truly free among nations if they do not harmonize their trade policy towards non-members. If members had different external tariffs, trade among the Six would have to be closely controlled to prevent 'trade deflection', i.e. imports from non-members pouring into the area through the member with the lowest external tariff. Since such controls would themselves be barriers to intra-EU trade, Article 3b requires the Six to adopt a 'common commercial policy', in other words, identical restrictions on imports from non-members. With these in place, every member can be sure that any product that is physically inside the European Union has paid the common tariff and met any common restrictions on, for example, health and safety standards. Tariffs are one of the most important restrictions on external trade, so a common commercial policy with respect to tariffs is referred to with the special name 'customs union'.

Ensuring undistorted competition

Even a customs union is not enough to create a unified economic area. Trade liberalization can be offset by public and private measures that operate inside the borders of EU members. For example, French companies might make a deal whereby they buy only from each other. The Treaty therefore calls for a system ensuring that competition in the area is undistorted (in Article 3g). This general principle is fleshed out in a series of articles that: (i) prohibit trade-distorting subsidies to national producers, (ii) create a common competition policy, (iii) harmonize national laws that affect the operation of the common market and (iv) harmonize some national taxes. Why are all of these necessary to ensure undistorted competition?

- **State aid prohibited.** Perhaps the most obvious distortions to competition stem from production subsidies or other forms of government assistance granted to producers located in a particular nation. Such subsidies (called 'state aid' in EU jargon) allow firms to sell their goods cheaper and/or allow uncompetitive firms to stay in business. Both effects put unsubsidized firms in other nations at a disadvantage. Most forms of 'state aid' are prohibited by the Treaty, although a list of exceptions is specified.
- **Anti-competitive behaviour.** Discrimination from a private agreement operating within a Member State – e.g. a cartel or exclusive purchasing deal – can distort competition. The Treaty prohibits any agreement that prevents, restricts or distorts competition in the area.

Box 2.3   What was really signed in Rome on 25 March 1957?

The Treaty of Rome took nine months to write, which seems like lightning speed compared to today's treaty-writing negotiations. Writing and ratifying, however, are quite different things. The particular problem in 1957 was the staunch opposition of Charles de Gaulle to supranationality. De Gaulle was not in power when the Treaty was signed but France was in the midst of a political crisis and many believed that de Gaulle would return to power and kill the European project. In the rush to get the ratification process done under a favourable French government, the signing ceremony in Rome was scheduled even before the agreement was fully fleshed out (e.g. additional Protocols were signed in April 1957). See Fig. 2.1.

As Allan Little, the BBC's World Affairs Correspondent, wrote: 'The treaty – still being argued over and translated into four languages until the last minute – was not printed. The six went ahead with the ceremony anyway.' The source for this remarkable piece of historical trivia is Pierre Pescatore, a former EU Court Judge, who was there on 25 March 1957. He told a BBC programme to mark the 50th anniversary of the event: 'They signed a bundle of blank pages. The first title existed in four languages, and also the protocol at the end. Nobody looked at what was in between.' (You can hear Pescatore's remarks, in French, at www.cvce.lu.)

Figure 2.1 Is the pile on the right just blank paper?

Source: Signature des traités de Rome. Rome: Photothèque Parlement européen

The focus is on restrictive business practices and abuse of a dominant position (see Chapter 14). Restrictive business practices include a host of unfair practices undertaken by private or state-owned firms. For example, the Treaty explicitly outlaws price-fixing agreements, controls on production, marketing, R&D or investment, and allocation of exclusive territories to firms in order to reduce competition. The Treaty also requires government monopolies of a commercial character to avoid discrimination based on the nationality of suppliers or customers.

- **Approximation of laws** (EU jargon for harmonize). Another source of discrimination stems from product standards and regulations since these can have a dramatic impact on competition and indirectly favour national firms. Moreover, since many product standards are highly technical, national firms are typically involved in writing a nation's rules. These firms, quite naturally, advise the government to adopt rules that discriminate in favour of their products.

- **Taxes**. Taxes applied inside Member States can distort competition directly or indirectly by benefiting national firms. On countering this type of discrimination, the Treaty is weak, requiring only that the Commission consider how taxes can be harmonized in the interest of the common market. Of course, if a particular tax provision clearly benefits a well-identified firm or sector within one Member State, then it could be considered as a subsidy and thus directly forbidden.

Unrestricted trade in services

Right from the Treaty of Rome, the principle of freedom of movement of services was embraced, although fleshing this into reality has been hard. Services are provided by people and governments have to regulate the qualifications of service providers (e.g. medical doctors). The problem has been to separate prudential regulation of qualifications from protectionist restrictions.

A recent example comes from an EU Court ruling in October 2011 concerning the broadcasting of Premier League football games. Premier League football charged different prices in various EU nations for the same broadcasts. A British pub owner who bought a Greek decoder and decoder card to save money was prosecuted in Britain for violating the Premier League's restrictions. Appealing to the EU Court, she argued that EU citizens had the right to import services freely. The Court agreed.

Labour and capital market integration

If it works properly, a customs union with undistorted competition allows firms and consumers to buy and sell goods throughout the area without facing discrimination based on nationality. This is sufficient to create a unified economic area as far as the trade in goods is concerned. It is not, however, sufficient to fuse national economies into a unified economic area. Accomplishing this also requires integration of capital and labour markets.

Article 3c extends integration to factor markets by instituting a common employment and investment area. It does this by abolishing barriers to the free movement of workers and capital. The basic principles of labour and capital mobility are elaborated in subsequent articles. For instance, the freedom of movement for workers means the elimination of any form of discrimination based on nationality regarding hiring, firing, pay and working conditions. The Treaty also explicitly allows workers to travel freely in search of work.

As for capital mobility, the Treaty focuses on two types of freedom. The first is the right of any Community firm to set up in another Member State. These 'rights of establishment' are essential to integration in sectors with high 'natural' trade barriers, e.g. in sectors such as insurance and banking, where a physical presence in the local market is critical to doing business. The second type concerns financial capital and here the Treaty goes deep. It states that all restrictions on capital flows (e.g. cross-border investments in stocks and bonds, and direct investment in productive assets by multinationals) shall be abolished. It applies the same to current payments related to capital flows (e.g. the payment of interest and repatriation of profits). Very little capital-market liberalization, however, was undertaken until the 1980s since the Treaty provided an important loophole. It allowed capital market restrictions when capital movements create disturbances in the functioning of a Member State's capital market. Moreover, it did not set a timetable for this liberalization. Capital market liberalization only became a reality 30 years later with the Single European Act and the Maastricht Treaty.

Exchange rate and macroeconomic coordination

Fixed exchanges rates were the norm when the Treaty of Rome was written, and throughout the late 1940s and 1950s nations occasionally found that the level of their fixed exchange rate induced their citizens to purchase a value of foreign products and assets that exceeded foreigners' purchases of domestic goods and assets. Such situations, known as balance-of-payments crises, historically led to many policies – such as tariffs, quotas and competitive devaluations – that would be disruptive in a unified economic area. To avoid such disruptions, the Treaty of Rome called for mechanisms for coordinating members' macroeconomic policies and for fixing balance-of-payments crises. This seed in the Treaty of Rome eventually sprouted into the euro, the Stability Pact and the European Central Bank. See Chapters 17 and 18 for details.

Common policy in agriculture

From a logical point of view, it might seem that a unified economic area could treat trade in agricultural goods the same way as it treats trade in services and manufactured goods. From a political point of view, however, agriculture is very different and the EU has explicitly recognized this right from the beginning.

In the 1950s, Europe's farm sector was far more important economically than it is today. In many European nations, a fifth or more of all workers were employed in the sector. Moreover, national policies in the sector were very important and very different across nations. In reaction to the great economic and social turmoil of the 1920s and 1930s, most

European nations had adopted highly interventionist policies in agriculture. These typically involved price controls teamed with trade barriers (Milward, 1992). Moreover, in the 1950s, the competitiveness of the Six's farm sectors differed massively. French and Dutch farmers were far more competitive than German farmers. If the Six were to form a truly integrated economic area, trade in farm goods would have to be included. However, given sharp differences in farm competitiveness among the Six, free trade would have had massively negative effects on many farmers, although, as usual with free trade, the winners would have won more than the losers would have lost.

These simple facts prevented the writers of the Treaty of Rome from including more than the barest sketch of a common farm policy. They did manage to agree on the goals, general principles and a two-year deadline for establishing the common policy. The Common Agricultural Policy came into effect in 1962 (see Chapter 9).

2.1.3 Omitted integration: social policy and taxes

The Treaty of Rome was enormously ambitious with respect to economic integration, but it was noticeably silent on two politically sensitive areas that might naturally be thought of as subject to the same logic as competition policy. The first was the harmonization of social policies (the set of rules that directly affects labour costs such as wage policies, working hours and conditions, and social benefits). The second was harmonization of tax policy.

Subsequent treaties have pushed social integration further but not anywhere near as deep as economic integration. Harmonization of taxes has advanced only slightly since the 1950s. This section considers the economic and political logic behind these omissions.

Social policy

Social harmonization is very difficult politically for at least two reasons. First, nations – even nations as similar as the original six members of the EEC – held very different opinions on what types of social policies should be dictated by the government. Moreover, social policies very directly and very continuously touch citizens' lives, so these opinions are strongly held; much more strongly, than, for example, opinions on the Common External Tariff or the elimination of intra-EEC quotas. The second reason concerns the difficulty of viewing social harmonization as an exchange of concessions.

With tariffs, all Six lower their tariffs against each other's goods. Although the tariffs might not have been identical to start with, there is a certain balance to the notion that we eliminate our tariffs and they eliminate theirs. With social policy, harmonization tends to be viewed as either an upward harmonization (e.g. all adopt a 35-hour week) or a downward harmonization (e.g. all have to allow stores to open on Sundays). Since social policies in each nation are the outcome of a finely balanced political equilibrium, changes that are 'imposed' by the EU are easy to characterize as undue interference by foreigners, rather than two-way exchange. For instance, it would be hard to view as 'balanced' a demand that Germans allow Sunday shopping in the name of social policy harmonization. The same could be said if France were forbidden from imposing the 35-hour week in the name of European integration.

In addition to social harmonization being significantly more difficult politically, there are economic arguments suggesting that it is not necessary.

The economics: two schools of thought

Does European economic integration demand harmonization of social policies? This question has been the subject of an intense debate for decades. It arose when the Benelux nations formed their customs union in 1947, when the OEEC was established in 1948, when the European Coal and Steel Community was created in 1953 and when the Treaty of Rome was negotiated.

From the very beginning of this debate there have been two schools of thought. One – the harmonize-before-liberalizing school – holds that international differences in wages and social conditions provide an 'unfair' advantage to countries with more laissez-faire social policies. In contrast, the no-need-to-harmonize school argues that wages and social policies are reflections of productivity differences and social preferences – differences that wage adjustments will counter. This school rejects calls for harmonization and notes that, in any case, social policies tend to converge as all nations get richer.

The harmonize-before-you-liberalize school is easier to explain. If nations initially have very different social policies, then lowering trade barriers will give nations with low social standards an unbalanced advantage, assuming that exchange rates and wages do not adjust.

The other school of thought – i.e. the school whose ideas prevailed in the Treaty of Rome – points out that wages do adjust. The economics of this is explained in depth in Chapter 8, but here it is in a nutshell. Roughly speaking, firms hire workers up to the point where the total cost of employing workers equals the value they create for the company. As far as the firm is concerned, it is not important whether the cost of the worker stems from a social policy or from wages paid directly to the worker. Different nations have different productivity levels and this is why wages can differ. Now if one nation has more expensive social policies, the workers in that nation will end up taking home (in the form of wages) a lower share of the value they create for the firm. The reason is that the firm pays the costs of the social policy out of the value that workers themselves create for the firm. In short, French workers in our example would be implicitly trading off lower take-home pay for workplace rules that made their lives better. This line of thinking requires an understanding of how markets work, so it is less easily grasped.

Tax policy

Like social policies, tax policy directly touches the lives of most citizens. This means that a nation's tax policy is the outcome of a hard-fought political compromise between broad groups of citizens, firms and labour unions, all of whom are well informed and fully engaged. Given this, EU leaders have always found it difficult politically to harmonize taxes.

The political difficulties are clear in the drafting of the Treaty of Rome's main mention of tax harmonization, Article 99: 'The Commission shall consider in what way the law of the various Member States concerning turnover taxes, excise duties and other forms of indirect taxation, including compensatory measures applying to exchanges between Member States, can be harmonised in the interest of the Common Market. The Commission shall submit proposals to the Council which shall act by means of a unanimous vote.'

The contrast between this weak language and the muscular language on, say, tariffs is striking. Here is the whole of Article 16 on 'customs duties' (i.e. tariffs): 'Member States shall abolish as between themselves, not later than at the end of the first stage, the customs duties on exportation and charges with equivalent effect.'

The general versus specific distinction

As with social policy, the difficult politics is matched with an economic argument that harmonization is not necessary, at least for broadly applied taxes – such as corporate taxes paid by all firms, taxes taken from workers' salaries (so-called social charges) and income taxes. When it comes to taxes, this logic is known as the general vs. specific distinction.

If a tax applies only to a specific sector, then the idea that national wages difference will adjust to offset national tax rate differences does not hold, so the tax differences may affect competitiveness and thus be viewed as unfair (see Chapter 8 for details). If the tax is applied quite broadly across the economy, then the economic offset-mechanism should be enough. In practice this distinction has guided the Commission's supervision of unfair taxes right from the EU's inception.

2.1.4 Quantifying European economic integration

Research by economic historians permits us to quantify the progress of European economic integration. A careful reading of the timing with which various policies were implemented allows the economic historian to quantify (somewhat subjectively) the extent of integration. The indices developed by two different groups are shown in Fig. 2.2. Although the two indices differ in details, they show that European economic integration has been a 'work in progress' for half a century. The DFFM index, which has finer detail on EU integration, clearly shows the main deepening phases:

- Customs union formation, 1958–68;
- Single Market, 1986–92;
- Economic and Monetary Union (EMU), 1993–2001.

European economic integration stagnated from roughly 1968 to 1986, although the formation of the European Monetary System in reaction to the collapse of the global monetary system in the mid-1970s was significant (see Chapters 1 and 16 for details).

Figure 2.2 Index of European economic integration

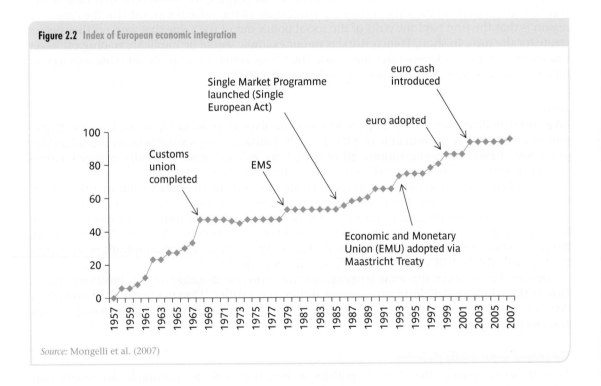

Source: Mongelli et al. (2007)

2.2 EU structure pre- and post-Lisbon

The 2009 Lisbon Treaty simplified the EU's structure. However, a great deal of writing on the EU refers to the old structure – or explains the new structure with reference to the old structure. Thus students have to learn both the old and new systems if they want to be able to follow today's discussion on European integration. Fortunately, they are not too different and understanding the motives behind the old structure makes it easier to understand the motives behind the new structure.

2.2.1 The EU's pre-Lisbon structure

Up to the 1992 Maastricht Treaty (formally, Treaty on European Union, or TEU), things were simple. There was the European Economic Community (EEC) that mattered a lot and a couple of other Communities (Coal and Steel, and Euratom) that did not. The Maastricht Treaty took a big leap forward in economic integration with the monetary union, but it also pushed forward a broadening of European integration ambition. The members, however, were somewhat suspicious that this new broadening might get out of hand if the European Commission and European Court continued to push for an 'ever closer Europe'. To counter this, EU members insisted that the Maastricht Treaty put in place some 'fire breaks'.

More specifically, up to the 1992 Maastricht Treaty, most integration initiative were subject to the Treaty of Rome's supranational decision-making procedures; for example, majority voting on EU laws which implied that any law which passed had to be implemented by all members, even members who voted against it. Moreover, the European Court was the ultimate authority over disputes involving all such laws and the Court's rulings occasionally had the effect of boosting integration (see the Cassis de Dijon case in Chapter 4 for a famous example).

This supranationality created two related problems – an understanding of which provides a logical framework that makes sense of the unusual structure of the EU pre-Lisbon and helps build an understanding of why the Lisbon changes are important.

- The first problem concerned the old schism between federalists and intergovernmentalists (see Chapter 1).

On the one hand, some EU members – the 'vanguard' – wished to spread European integration to areas that were not covered in the original Treaties, such as harmonization of social policies and taxation. On the other hand, another group of members – call them the 'doubters' – worried that supranational decision-making procedures were producing an irresistible increase in the depth and breadth of European integration that forced their citizens to accept more integration than they wanted. Germany is an example of the vanguard and Britain an example of the doubters.

The vanguard called this irresistible increase the 'Community method' while the doubters called it 'creeping competences' ('competence' is the EU jargon for policy areas where EU-level policy takes the lead over Member States' national policies).

To the doubters, a particularly worrisome feature was the EU Court's ability to interpret the Treaty of Rome and subsequent amendments. The Treaty of Rome says that the EU can make laws in areas not mentioned in the Treaty, if the Court rules that doing so is necessary to attain Treaty objectives. The Treaty objectives, however, are extremely far-reaching; the first line of the Treaty of Rome's Preamble says that the members are 'determined to lay the foundations of an ever closer union among the peoples of Europe'. Doubters worried that the Treaty's ambitious objectives combined with the Court's ability to sanction law-making in areas not explicitly mentioned in the Treaties opened the door to essentially unlimited transfers of national sovereignty to the EU level.

- The second problem concerned integration that was taking place outside of the EU's structure due to differences between the vanguard and the doubters.

The Schengen Accord is the classic example (Fig. 2.3). While the free movement of people is an EU goal dating back to 1958, some members (e.g. Britain) held up progress towards passport-free travel. In 1985, five EU members signed an agreement ending controls on their internal frontiers. This was completely outside of the EU's structure and many observers feared that such ad hoc arrangements could undermine the unity of the Single Market and possibly foster tensions among EU members. A more recent example is the 2005 Prüm Treaty on police cooperation, which was signed outside the EU umbrella by seven EU members.

Both problems were addressed by the rather complex structure EU members set up with the Maastricht Treaty.

Figure 2.3 Schengen Accord, deeper integration outside the EU framework

Note: The passport-free travel zone of Schengen includes non-EU nations such as Iceland, Switzerland and Norway, but two EU members are not in it (Britain and Ireland).

Photo: © European Union 1995–2012; Map: Swedish airport services; source of map: http://commons.wikimedia.org/wiki/File:SchengenAgreement_map.svg.

2.2.2 Maastricht and the three pillars as fire breaks

The Maastricht Treaty drew a clear line between supranational and intergovernmental policy areas by creating the 'three-pillar' organizational structure. The deep economic integration – basically the integration in the Treaty of Rome, Single European Act and the monetary union part of the Maastricht Treaty – were placed in the supranational 'first pillar'. The intergovernmental policies – foreign and defence matters (second pillar) and police, justice and other 'home affairs' (third pillar) – are under the European Union 'roof' but were not subject to supranationality in terms of decision making and EU Court rulings (top panel of Fig. 2.4).

The three-pillar structure solved the two problems mentioned above. The clear distinction between supranational and intergovernmental cooperation allowed initiatives like Schengen to be brought under the EU's wing without forcing every member to join. This greatly reduced the

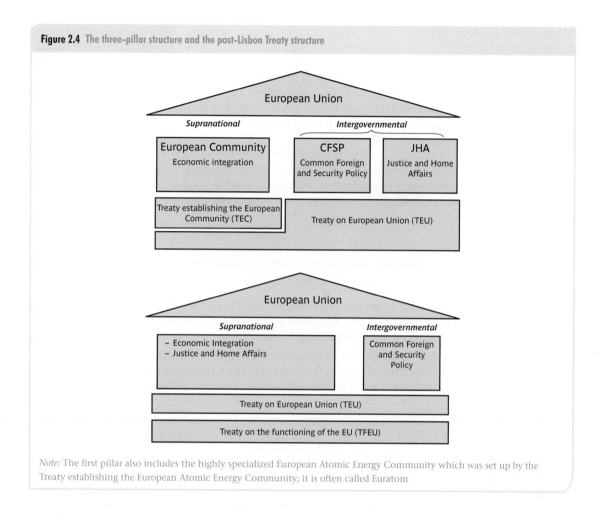

Figure 2.4 The three-pillar structure and the post-Lisbon Treaty structure

Note: The first pillar also includes the highly specialized European Atomic Energy Community which was set up by the Treaty establishing the European Atomic Energy Community; it is often called Euratom

resistance of Britain and other doubters to further discussion of closer integration in areas like police cooperation and foreign policy cooperation.

The key, as far as the doubters were concerned, is that Maastricht put Member States clearly in control in second- and third-pillar areas. There was no possibility of the Court or Commission using their authority to force deeper integration on reluctant members in pursuit of the duties assigned to them by the Treaty of Rome.

As we shall see below, one of the most radical things in the Lisbon Treaty is the de jure removal of the three-pillar structure. However, the basic need that some members have for a fire break against deeper integration in second-pillar issues meant that Lisbon is best understood as merging the third pillar into the first. The new structure (bottom panel of Fig. 2.4) essentially has two pillars – a supranational pillar and an intergovernmental pillar. It is therefore worth learning about the old three-pillar structure in some detail to understand which of today's EU policies are governed by supranationality (see Box 2.4) and which are governed by intergovernmentalism.

Details of the three pillars

The first pillar, which encompassed the vast majority of EU activity, was called the European Community (formerly known as the European Economic Community). It includes the Internal

Market with its four freedoms (free movement of goods, services, workers and capital) and harmonization of members' health, safety and environment regulations and standards, the control of competition subsidies policies, and the big-money common policies (the Common Agricultural Policy and Regional Policy). The legal foundation for all these policies, laws, institutions and practices was the TEC (i.e. the Treaty of Rome as amended by subsequent treaties). The first pillar also includes the Economic and Monetary Union (EMU) and thus comprises the European Central Bank, the single money, and all the attendant rules and procedures. The legal foundations for these are in the Treaty on European Union.

Integration efforts in second- and third-pillar areas were intergovernmental in the sense that such efforts are undertaken by direct negotiation among Member States and any agreement requires unanimity. The powers of the European Commission and Court were greatly limited for second- and third-pillar policies.

Box 2.4   Supranationality in the EU

Supranationality arises in the EU in three main ways:

1 The Commission can propose new laws that are then voted on by the Member States (in the Council of Ministers) and the European Parliament. If passed, these new laws bind every Member State, even those that disagree with them.

2 The Commission has direct executive authority in a limited number of areas – the most prominent being competition policy. For instance, the Commission can block a merger between two EU companies even if their governments support the merger. (See Chapter 14 for details.)

3 The rulings of the European Court of Justice can alter laws, rules and practices in Member States, at least in limited areas. (See the Factortame case discussed in Section 2.3 for an example).

The Maastricht Treaty states that these forms of supranationality continue to apply to first-pillar issues. It also defines quite precisely the limited role of the Commission, Court and Council in the second and third pillars. Reflecting concerns such as the internationalization of crime, international terrorism, human trafficking, etc., EU leaders agreed in the Amsterdam and Nice Treaties to apply first-pillar supranationality to certain Justice and Home Affairs issues.

The second pillar consists of the Common Foreign and Security Policy.

The third pillar comprises Justice and Home Affairs. Much of the EU's third-pillar policy has its origin in the 1985 Schengen Agreement. That agreement gradually removed border controls. To replace police controls that had previously relied upon border checks, Schengen members agreed to tighter cooperation among their police and court systems. In particular, the issue of non-EU citizens required coordination of asylum and immigration policies. Much of this cooperation was transferred to the EU level by the Maastricht Treaty, although Britain famously opted out of Schengen's no-passport control rules (and many other areas). The Maastricht Treaty's introduction of EU citizenship is also usually considered a third-pillar issue.

The 'Europeanization' of today's Europeans forced even the doubters to recognize the need for additional integration on matters like international transfers of pension schemes, divorce procedures and contract law. Since it proved all but impossible to make progress on these concerns without some form of supranational decision making – and since progress on such topics was viewed as important by EU firms and workers – many third-pillar issues were shifted into the first pillar by Amsterdam and Nice Treaty amendments. As part of this, the EU established cooperating agencies such as Europol (police matters), Eurojust (cooperation between national prosecutors) and Frontex (cooperation among border officials). One important and practical element of this is the Schengen Information System, a computer network which helps members fight crime, terrorism and illegal immigration.

The Lisbon Treaty went even further by basically merging the third-pillar issues into the first pillar with all its supranationality.

2.2.3 Post-Lisbon organization: two pillars in a single organization

The three-pillars-and-a-roof organization is replaced (see Fig. 2.4). The Lisbon Treaty abolishes the European Community, replacing the term 'Community' with 'Union' throughout the TEU and TFEU (henceforth 'the amended Treaties' for short). Some writers refer to this as the removal of the pillar structure because there is now just one organization and it has what lawyers call 'legal personality' (it can sign agreements with nations and organizations). See Box 2.5.

From the perspective of European economic integration, a deeper and more insightful way of thinking of the organizational change is as the integration of the third pillar into the first pillar. 'Justice and Home Affairs' (third-pillar) policies – with a few exceptions and wholesale opt-outs for Britain and Poland – are placed under the old first-pillar supranational institutions and practices. New laws in third-pillar areas are made by majority voting instead of unanimity. The Commission has monopoly on the right of initiative (with a few exceptions). The EU Court has jurisdiction and its rulings are supreme to those of national courts. This new pillar includes most internal policies but also some external policies such as trade, aid and humanitarian assistance.

Second-pillar issues – foreign and external security policies – continue to be subject to the intergovernmental procedures and practices. The amended Treaties are explicit on this point:[2]

- 'The common foreign and security policy is subject to specific rules and procedures. It shall be defined and implemented by the European Council and the Council acting unanimously . . .'
- 'The adoption of legislative acts shall be excluded.'
- 'The Court of Justice of the European Union shall not have jurisdiction with respect to these provisions . . .'

In short, the post-Lisbon Treaty EU has a roof and two pillars – one for supranational issues and one for intergovernmental issues.

Box 2.5   EU or EC?

In one of the muddles that make the EU so hard to study, saying 'EU' logically implies all three pillars. However, European Union sounds better than European Community, so the term EU was used almost universally in the media and by politicians even when they were really talking about purely EC (i.e. first-pillar) issues. The only place that the EU/EC distinction really mattered was when it came to European law (see Section 2.3).

Students will be happy to know that the Lisbon Treaty merges the two names. From now on, you can say EU for everything and not be wrong.

---

[2] Students interested in knowing more should read House of Lords (2008). For the Eurosceptic view, see Open European (2008b).

2.3 EU law

One of the most unusual and important things about the EU is its supranational legal system. This is a direct implication of the EU's usual degree of economic integration. Implementing and maintaining a unified economic area requires a legal system of some kind since disputes over interpretation and conflicts among various laws are inevitable.

By the standards of every other international organization in the world, the European legal system is extremely supranational. For example, even the highest courts in EU Member States must defer to decisions by the EU's Court of Justice on matters concerning the interpretation of EU law. The EU is very much like a federal state in this respect. Just as the decisions of lower courts in France, Germany and Italy can be overturned by those nations' supreme courts, the EU's Court of Justice has the ultimate say on questions concerning European law.

Before the Lisbon Treaty, the deep, supranational aspects of EU law only applied to first-pillar issues, i.e. where supranationality was the agreed principle. While the Lisbon Treaty removed the pillars, it did not remove the distinction between areas where EU law's deep supranationality apply and areas where it does not. Now, however, the default option is that it applies to all areas except those areas explicitly excluded.

The topic of EU law is as intricate as it is fascinating. This section presents the barest outlines of the subject, focusing on the elements that are essential for understanding the decision-making process in particular, and the economics of European integration more generally. Note that this section is largely based on the freely downloadable book by Borchandt (2010), *The ABC of European Union Law*, which has been fully updated to reflect Lisbon Treaty changes. This book is the best online introduction to the subject.

2.3.1 'Sources' of EU law

Where did the EU's legal system come from? The legal systems of most democratic nations are based on a constitution. The EU does not have a formal constitution, so where did these principles come from? As is true of so many things in the EU, a complete answer to this question would fill a book or two, but the short answer is easy: the Treaty of Rome created the Court and the Court created the EC legal system.

The Treaty of Rome commits Member States to a series of general economic and political goals, and it transfers important elements of national sovereignty to the European level; for example, after 1958 Member States no longer had the right to control their external trade policy. The Treaty was meant to be a dynamic and adaptive agreement, so it also created ways of making new laws and modifying old ones. Most importantly for the subject at hand, it established a Court to adjudicate the disputes and questions of interpretations that were bound to arise.

The Treaty was not very specific when it came to setting up the legal system. The Treaty establishes the Court of Justice (Fig. 2.5) and states that its general task is to 'ensure observance of law and justice in the interpretation and application of this Treaty' (Article 164 in the original Treaty). It then goes on to define the Court's composition and to assign the Court a few specific tasks.

The Treaty of Rome was also not specific enough to deal with the many issues that came before the Court. The Court reacted to the lack of specificity in the Treaty by creating the Community's legal system via case law. That is to say, it used decisions relating to particular cases to establish general principles of the EC legal system.

EC law is now an enormous mass of laws, rules and practices that has been established by Treaties (primary law), EU laws (secondary law) and decisions of the Court (case law).

Figure 2.5 Working session of the Court of Justice

Source: European Parliament

2.3.2 EU legal system: main principles

Since the EC legal system was not created by any single document, its principles were never been officially proclaimed before the Lisbon Treaty. The 'principles' of EC law were thus general patterns that various jurists have discerned from the thousands of pages of primary, secondary and case law, and different jurists list different principles. Three principles that are always mentioned are 'direct effect', 'primacy of EC law' and 'autonomy' of the EC legal system. These were first established in two landmark cases in 1963 and 1964 (see Box 2.6). These three have been explicitly confirmed in the Lisbon Treaty (see below for details).

'Direct effect'

'Direct effect' is simple to define – it means that Treaty provisions or other forms of EU law such as directives can create rights which EU citizens can rely upon when they go before their domestic courts. This is radical. It means that EC laws must be enforced by Member States' courts, just as if the law had been passed by the national parliament. A good example is the case of a Sabena air stewardess (as they called female flight attendants in the 1970s) who claimed that she was paid less and had to retire earlier than male flight attendants. Although this was not a violation of Belgian law at the time, the EC Court ruled in 1976 that the Treaty of Rome (which provides for equality of pay between the sexes) had the force of law in Belgium, or in legal-ese it had direct effect. The stewardess won the case.

The principle of direct effect is quite unique. For example, when New Zealand ratifies the Kyoto Protocol, it is agreeing to certain obligations, but New Zealand courts ignore these obligations unless they are implemented by a law passed by the New Zealand parliament. Even more unusual is that this 'direct effect' notion applies to EU laws passed by majority voting, e.g. directives. This means that even if a Member State government votes against a particular law, that law automatically has the force of law, so its national courts must treat the EU law as if it were a national law. Importantly, there are complex conditions for a Treaty provision to have direct effect, so not everything in every Treaty is automatically enforceable in Member States.

Box 2.6   Two cases that established the EC legal system

The EC legal system was not explicitly established in any Treaty, so the Court used some early cases to establish three key principles. Since these principles arose in the course of real-world cases, it can be difficult to precisely distinguish among the three principles in the two cases.

Van Gend & Loos v. Netherlands, 1963. In this case, the Dutch company Van Gend & Loos brought an action against its own government for imposing an import duty on a chemical product from Germany which was higher than duties on an earlier shipment; the company claimed that this violated the Treaty of Rome's prohibition on tariff hikes on intra-EC trade. The Dutch court suspended the case and asked the EC Court to clarify. The EC Court ruled that the company could rely on provisions in the Treaties when arguing against the Dutch government before a Dutch court.

Plainly, this case has an element of direct effect and primacy. The Dutch government had one rule – the higher tariff rate – while the Treaty had another (no increase allowed). The EC Court said the Treaty provision trumped the national provision. Moreover, the EC Court said that the Dutch court should consider the Treaty directly rather than, for example, the Dutch Parliament's transposition of the Treaty's principles into Dutch law. In effect, the Court said that the Treaty was Dutch law as far as the Dutch court was to be concerned. This was new, since normally a national court can consider only national law when judging a case.

The European Court also took the opportunity to write down its thoughts on the fundamental nature of the EC legal system. In the Van Gend & Loos v. Netherlands decision, it wrote: 'The Community constitutes a new legal order of international law for the benefit of which the States have limited their sovereign rights, albeit within limited fields, and the subjects of which comprise not only Member States but also their nationals.'

Costa v. ENEL, 1964 decision by the Court of Justice. The next year, the Court expanded its view of the EC legal system in a case involving a dispute over one euro! In 1962, Italy nationalized its electricity grid and grouped it under the National Electricity Board (ENEL in Italian). Mr Flaminio Costa, a shareholder of one nationalized company, felt he had been unjustly deprived of his dividend and so refused to pay his electricity bill for two thousand lira. The non-payment matter came before an arbitration court in Milan but since Mr Costa argued that the nationalization violated EC law, the Milan court asked the European Court to interpret various aspects of the Treaty of Rome.

The Court took the opportunity to go way beyond the question at hand. In its judgment, the Court stated the principle of autonomy and direct effect:

- 'By contrast with ordinary international treaties, the EEC Treaty has created its own legal system which . . . became an integral part of the legal systems of the Member States and which their courts are bound to apply.'
- 'Member States have limited their sovereign rights, albeit within limited fields, and have thus created a body of law which binds both their nationals and themselves.'

Relying on the logic of what the Treaty of Rome implied – at least implicitly – the Court established the principle of primacy:

- '[T]he law stemming from the Treaty, an independent source of law, could not, because of its special and original nature, be overridden by domestic legal provisions, however framed, without being deprived of its character as Community law and without the legal basis of the Community itself being called into question. The transfer by the States from their domestic legal system to the Community legal system of the rights and obligations arising under the Treaty carries with it a permanent limitation of their sovereign rights, against which a subsequent unilateral act incompatible with the concept of the Community cannot prevail.'

The Court's justification was that if EC law were not supreme, the objectives of the Treaty could not be met: 'The executive force of Community law cannot vary from one State to another in deference to subsequent domestic laws, without jeopardising the attainment of the objectives of the Treaty.'

The logical necessity of this principle is straightforward. If laws agreed in Brussels could be ignored in any Member State, the EU would fall into a shambles. Each member would be tempted to implement only the EU laws it liked. This would, for example, make it impossible to create a single market or ensure the free movement of workers.

Primacy of EC law

This principle, which means that Community law has the final say, is not in the Treaty of Rome and indeed appears explicitly for the first time only in the rejected Constitutional Treaty (it is included in the Lisbon Treaty). It was, nonetheless, a principle that had been generally accepted by all EU members even before the Lisbon Treaty. It was repeatedly used to overturn Member State laws.

One classic example of this is the 1991 Factortame case which confirmed the supremacy of EC law over UK law. The UK's Merchant Shipping Act of 1988 had the effect of forbidding a Spanish fishing company called Factortame from fishing in UK waters. Factortame asserted in UK courts that this violated EC law, and asked the UK court to suspend the Merchant Shipping Act until the EC Court could rule on the matter (this often takes a couple of years). Under UK law, no British court can suspend an Act of Parliament. The EC Court ruled that under EC law, which was supreme to UK law, a national court could suspend laws which contravened EC law. Subsequently, the highest UK court did strike down the Merchant Fishing Act.

The logical necessity of this principle is just as clear as that of direct effect. Simplifying for clarity's sake, 'direct effect' says that EC laws are automatically laws in every Member State. Primacy says that when EC law and national, regional or local laws conflict, the EC law is what must be enforced.

Autonomy

Most European nations have several layers of courts – local, regional and national. The lower courts, however, do not exist independently of the higher courts, and often the higher courts depend upon the lower courts (e.g., in some nations, the high court can rule only after the case has been tried at a lower level). The EC legal system, however, is entirely independent of the Member States' legal systems according to the principle of autonomy.

2.4 The 'Big-5' institutions

There are many EU agencies, bodies and committees, but one can achieve a very good understanding of how the EU works by knowing only the 'Big-5'. Using the names in the Lisbon Treaty, these are: the European Council (heads of state and governments), the Council (member nation's ministers, often called by its old names, the Council of Ministers or the Council of the European Union), the European Commission (executive branch of the EU), the European Parliament (directly elected), and the EU Court (appointed judges). (On the other institutions, see Borchandt, 2010.)

2.4.1 The European Council

The European Council is the highest political-level body in the EU. As such, it provides political guidance at the highest level. Most really important EU initiatives and policies are instigated by the European Council. For example, it provides broad guidelines for EU policy and thrashes out the final compromises necessary to conclude the most sensitive aspects of EU business, including reforms of the major EU policies, the EU's multi-year budget plan, treaty changes and the final terms of enlargements. This body is by far the most influential institution because its members are the leaders of their respective nations. Moreover, it takes decisions by consensus, so its decisions have the implicit backing of every EU national leader.

Before the Lisbon Treaty, it was chaired by the head of the nation holding the Presidency of the EU. As the Presidency of the EU rotated every six months among every EU member, and different EU members had different national priorities, the rotating chair of the European Council hindered long-term planning and multi-year efforts.

Lisbon addressed this shortcoming by creating a 'President of the European Council' who chairs the European Council for two and a half years. The President, who cannot simultaneously hold a position in a Member State, is selected by qualified-majority voting in the European Council (i.e. by leaders of EU nations). The President leads preparations for European Council meetings and ensure follow-though on its decisions. He/she also represents the EU at international summits in the area of foreign and security policy. The first President is Herman Van Rompuy (see Box 2.7).

Box 2.7   Herman van Rompuy, first President of the European Council (2009–12)

Once the Lisbon Treaty came into effect in December 2009, EU leaders asked one of their own to become the first long-term President of the European Council – then Belgian Prime Minister Herman Van Rompuy. The life-long politician, with a University degree in economics and a penchant for haiku poetry, espouses modesty and 'quiet determination'.

His key accomplishment as prime minister was to restore calm to his native country after the worst political crisis in his country's 180-year history – the near breakup of Belgium over Flemish demands for more regional autonomy. Given the pressures facing the Eurozone in today's crisis, such talents may be invaluable in helping the EU pull through the turbulence.

In his acceptance speech, he said: 'My whole political life has been about mutual understanding, and I intend to continue on that route.' On what the President's profile should be, he said: 'There is only one profile, one of dialogue, unity and action.'

To date Van Rompuy has been true to his word, working largely behind the scenes to make the European Council's reactions to various events – especially the Eurozone crisis – more effective and expedient.

Photo: © European Union, 1995–2012; http://en.wikipedia.org/wiki/File:Herman_Van_Rompuy_at_the_37th_G8_Summit_in_Deauville_030.jpg

Figure 2.6 European Council group photo, June 2011

Source: http://www.consilium.europa.eu/uedocs/cms_data/docs/pressData/Pics/photoGallery/%7Bac1d6f65-ee8a-4778-b862
-e50382294530%7D.jpg

The European Council consists of the leaders of each EU Member State, the appointed President of the European Council and the President of the European Commission. The High Representative of the Union for Foreign Affairs and Security Policy takes part in its work, but is not a member. It meets at least four times a year, with the most important meetings usually coming in June and December (at the end of each six-month term of the Presidency of the EU). These June and December meetings are important, high-profile media events – the one aspect of the EU that almost every European has seen on television (Fig. 2.6).

The 'Conclusions' and lack of legislative power

The most important decisions of each Presidency are contained in a document, known as the 'Conclusions of the Presidency', which is published at the end of each European Council meeting. Students who want to track the EU's position on a particular topic – be it the need for a constitution or its position on Zimbabwe – will do well to start from the Conclusions. The Council's website posts Conclusions (www.consilium.europa.eu), but since it is poorly organized a direct internet search may be easier.

One peculiarity of the EU is that the most powerful body by far – the European Council – has no formal role in EU law-making. The political decisions made by the European Council are translated into law following the standard legislative procedures (more on this below).

Confusingly, the European Council and the Council (what was called the Council of Ministers or Council of the EU before the Lisbon Treaty) are often both called 'the Council'. Moreover, neither of these Councils should be confused with the Council of Europe, which is an international organization set up in the 1940s and entirely unrelated to the EU.

2.4.2 The Council

The Council – known officially as the Council of the European Union before the Lisbon Treaty and as the Council of Ministers for most of the EU's history – is the EU's main decision-making

Figure 2.7 Meeting of the Council of Ministers in Brussels

Photo: © European Union, 1995–2012.

body (Fig. 2.7). Almost every piece of legislation is subject to its approval. The Council consists of one representative from each EU member. The national representatives must be authorized to commit their governments to Council decisions, so Council members are the government ministers responsible for the relevant area – the finance ministers on budget issues, agriculture ministers on farm issues and so on.

The Council is where the Member States' governments assert their influence directly. Since all EU governments are elected (democracy is a must for membership) and the Council members represent their governments, the Council is the ultimate point of democratic control over the EU actions and law-making. Although the European Parliament is elected directly, very few Europeans know the name of their Member of the European Parliament. European voters do know the name of their Prime Minister – and will hold him or her accountable if something goes seriously wrong in the EU.

The Council has responsibilities in all first-pillar areas. To meet these responsibilities, it has the following powers:

- To pass European laws (jointly with the European Parliament, see Section 2.5).

Most of the laws passed concern measures necessary to implement the Treaties, or simply to keep the EU vital parts running smoothly (the internal market, the Common Agricultural Policy, etc.).

- To coordinate the general economic policies of the Member States in the context of the Economic and Monetary Union (EMU); see Chapter 16 for details.
- To pass final judgement on international agreements between the EU and other countries or international organizations (a power it shares with the European Parliament).
- To approve the EU's budget, jointly with the European Parliament.

In addition to these tasks linked to economic integration, the Council takes the decisions pertaining to Common Foreign and Security Policies (CFSP). To the average European, these are some of the most visible actions of the Council.

Although the Council is a single institution, it follows the somewhat confusing practice of using different names to describe the Council according to the matters being discussed. For example, when the Council addresses EMU matters it is called the Economic and Financial Affairs Council, or 'ECOFIN' to insiders.

Decision-making rules

The Council has two main decision-making rules. On the most important issues – such as Treaty changes, the accession of new members and setting the multi-year budget plan – the Council must decide unanimously. However, on most issues (about 80 per cent of all Council decisions), the Council decides on the basis of a form of majority voting called 'qualified majority voting' (QMV). These rules are extremely important for understanding how Europe works, so they are the subject of extensive analysis in Chapter 3.

Presidency of the EU

One EU Member State at a time holds the Presidency, with this office rotating every six months. The Presidency nation sets the EU basic agenda and chairs all the Council of Ministers meetings except the those dealing with foreign affairs and security policy which are chaired by the High Representative of the Union for Foreign Affairs and Security Policy (more on this position below). There is no EU president per se. For many purposes the Prime Minister of the Presidency nation plays this role, but for other purposes, the role is played by the President of the European Council, or the President of the European Commission. To reduce disruptions arising from the biannual rotation of the Presidency, a three-nation group consisting of the members that are the past, present and future presidents cooperate.

The Council (i.e. Council of Ministers) can easily be confused with the European Council. One way to remember the difference is to note that the European Council is a meeting of the 'bosses' of the Council members, i.e. the Prime Ministers and heads of state (European Council) rather than the relevant Ministers (Council of Ministers).

The High Representative of the Union for Foreign Affairs and Security Policy

This is a new post created by the Lisbon Treaty. Previously, leadership and representation of EU policy on Common Foreign and Security Policy were divided between the Council of Ministers – in the form of the High Representative for Common Foreign and Security Policy (a post occupied very ably by Javier Solana for ten years) – and the European Commission – in the form of the Commissioner for External Relations.

Lisbon merged the two positions so that the new High Representative of the Union for Foreign Affairs and Security Policy (High Representative for short) attends both Council meetings and Commission meetings. Specifically the High Representative chairs the Foreign Affairs Council (the name for the Council when foreign affairs ministers meet) and is a Vice-President of the Commission in charge of foreign affairs. Under the more ambitious plans of the rejected Constitutional Treaty, the post would have been called the EU's foreign minister, and some writers still use that label.

Lisbon also created the European External Action Service to assist the High Representative. This is a new organization; its roles and form are still evolving. Its most obvious manifestation is the EU Delegations (something like an embassy) in about 150 non-EU nations.

The first High Representative, Catherine Ashton, was appointed in 2009 for a five-year term (see Box 2.8).

2.4.3 Commission

The European Commission is best thought of as the executive branch of the EU, but with a twist. It is charged with enforcing the Treaties and with driving forward European integration. Indeed,

Photo: © World Economic Forum

Cathy Ashton was serving as the EU Trade Commissioner when she was elevated to the new post in 2009. Apart from her experience as Trade Commissioner, she had no foreign affairs experience and had held the Trade Commissioner slot only since 2008. Previously, she worked in the Labour government of Tony Blair before being appointed as Leader of the House of Lords. She was made a 'Life Peer' with the title of Baroness in 1999 so that she could join the Blair government (in Britain, all ministers must be members of the elected House of Commons, or appointed House of Lords). She was born to a working-class family with roots in Lancashire coal mining; she was the first person in her family to attend a university.

Ashton has struggled to make a clear mark on EU foreign affairs. At least part of the reason is that she took over a position that merges three full-time jobs (the Council foreign policy representative, the Commission's external relations Commissioner, and chairperson of the External Affairs Council) – all while setting up the European External Action Service and wrestling with EU institutional turf wars.

since the EU's foundation, it has been the main driving force behind deeper and wider European integration – often pushing, pulling and prodding EU Member States towards the goal of an ever-closer union. The body, based in Brussels, has three main roles:

1 to propose legislation to the Council and Parliament;
2 to administer and implement EU policies;
3 to provide surveillance and enforcement of EU law in coordination with the EU Court.

As part of its third role, it is the 'guardian of the Treaties', i.e. the body that is ultimately charged with ensuring that the Treaties are implemented and enforced.

The Commission also represents the EU at some international negotiations, such as those relating to World Trade Organization (WTO) trade talks. The Commission's negotiating stances at such meetings are closely monitored by EU members.

Commissioners and the Commission's composition

The European Commission is made up of one Commissioner from each EU member. This includes the President and two Vice-Presidents. The current Commission President, José Manuel Barroso, is a former Prime Minister of Portugal. Commissioners, including the President of the Commission, are appointed all together and serve for five years. This is why people often refer to each Commission as being the 'Barroso Commission' (Fig. 2.8) or the 'Prodi Commission'. The appointments are made just after European Parliamentary elections and take effect in the January of the following year. The current Commission's term ends in 2014.

The original intention of the Lisbon Treaty was to reduce the number of Commissioners to less than the number of Member States, but a political promise made by EU leaders to Ireland annuls that goal, so there will be one Commissioner per member for the foreseeable future.

Figure 2.8 The Barroso Commission, 2011

Source: © European Union, 1995–2012.

Commissioners are effectively chosen by their own national governments, but the choices are subject to political agreement by other members. The Commission as a whole and the Commission President individually must also be approved by the European Parliament.

Commissioners are not supposed to act as national representatives. They are forbidden from accepting or seeking instruction from their country's government. In practice, Commissioners are generally quite independent of their home governments, but since they have typically held high political office in their home nations, they are naturally sensitive to issues that are of particular concern back home. This ensures that all decisive national sensitivities are heard in Commission deliberations.

The Commission has a great deal of independence in practice and often takes views that differ substantially from the Member States, the Council and the Parliament. However, it is ultimately answerable to the European Parliament since the Parliament can dismiss the Commission as a whole by adopting a motion of censure. Although this has never happened, a censure motion was almost passed in 2005. In 1999 a similar near-censure triggered a sequence of events that ended in mass resignation of the Commission led by President Jacques Santer.

Each politically appointed Commissioner is in charge of a specific area of EU policy. In particular, each runs what can be thought of as the EU equivalent of a national ministry. These 'ministries', called Directorates-General or DGs in EU jargon, employ a relatively modest number of international civil servants. The Commission as a whole employs about 17,000, which is fewer than the number of people who work for the city of Vienna. Just as in national ministries, Commission officials tend to provide most of the expertise necessary to administer and analyse the EU's vastly complex network of policies since the Commissioners themselves are typically generalists.

Legislative powers

The Commission's main law-making duty is to prepare proposals for new EU legislation. These range from a new directive on minimum elevator safety standards to the reform of the Common Agricultural Policy (CAP). Neither the Council nor the Parliament can adopt legislation until the

Commission presents its proposals, except under extraordinary procedures. This monopoly on the 'right to initiate' makes the Commission the gatekeeper of EU integration. It also allows the Commission occasionally to become the driving force behind deeper or broader integration. This was especially true under the two Delors Commissions that served from 1985 to 1994 and pushed forward the Single European Act and the Maastricht Treaty.

Commission proposals are usually based on general guidelines established by the Council of Ministers, the European Council, the Parliament or the Treaties. A proposal is prepared by the relevant Directorate-General in collaboration with other DGs concerned. In exercising this power of initiative, the Commission consults a very broad range of EU actors, including national governments, the European Parliament, national administrations, professional groups and trade union organizations. This complex consultation process is known in EU jargon as 'comitology'.

Executive powers

The Commission is the executive in all of the EU's endeavours, but its power is most obvious in competition policy. Chapter 14 explains in more detail how the Commission has the power to block mergers, to fine corporations for unfair practices and to insist that EU members remove or modify subsidies to their firms. The Commission also has substantial latitude in administering the Common Agricultural Policy, including the right to impose fines on members that violate CAP rules.

One of the key responsibilities of the Commission is to manage the EU budget, subject to supervision by a specialized institution called the EU Court of Auditors. For example, while the Council and Parliament decided the programme-by-programme allocation of funds in the EU's current multi-year budget (Financial Perspective in EU jargon), the Commission basically decides the year-by-year indicative allocation of Structural Funds across members.

Decision making

The Commission decides, in principle, on the basis of a simple majority. The 'in principle' proviso is necessary because the Commission makes almost all of its decision on the basis of consensus. The reason is that the Commission usually has to get its actions approved by the Council and the Parliament. A Commission decision that fails to attract the support of a very substantial majority of the Commissioners will almost surely fail in the Council and/or Parliament.

2.4.4 The European Parliament

The Parliament has two main tasks: sharing legislative powers with the Council of Ministers and the Commission; and overseeing all EU institutions, but especially the Commission. The Parliament, on its own initiative, has also begun to act as the 'conscience' of the EU, for example condemning various nations for human rights violations via non-binding resolutions.

The Lisbon Treaty boosted the power of the Parliament substantially, making it equal to the Council on most types of EU legislation. Especially noteworthy are the Parliament's new powers over the budget (in particular, CAP spending where previously the Parliament had little say, and third-pillar issues involving Justice and Home Affairs). The European Parliament also gets an increased role in Treaty revision, an increased role in the selection of senior EU leaders, and a right of refusal for most international agreements, including trade agreements.

Organization

The European Parliament (EP) has about 750 members who are directly elected by EU citizens in special elections organized in each Member State every five years. The number of Members of European Parliament (MEPs) per nation varies with population, but the number of MEPs per million EU citizens is much higher for small nations than for large. For example, in the 2009–14

Parliament, Luxembourg has six MEPs and Germany has 99, despite the fact that Germany's population is about 160 times that of Luxembourg.

MEPs are supposed to represent their local constituencies, but the Parliament's organization has evolved along classic European political lines rather than along national lines (for details see Noury and Roland, 2002). The EP election campaigns are generally run by each nation's main political parties and MEPs are generally associated with a particular national political party. Although this means that over a hundred parties are represented in the Parliament, fragmentation is avoided because many of these parties have formed political groups. As in most EU Member States, two main political groups – the centre-left and the centre-right – account for two-thirds of the seats and tend to dominate the Parliament's activity. The centre-left grouping in the EP is called the Party of European Socialists, the centre-right group is called the European People's Party.

National delegations of MEPs do not sit together. As in most parliaments, the European Parliament's physical, left-to-right seating arrangement reflects the left-to-right ideology of the MEPs. In the 2009–14 Parliament, the left flank is occupied by the radical left (communist, former communist, extreme left parties and the Nordic Green Left parties). Continuing left to right, the next is the Progressive Alliance of Socialists and Democrats (which includes the Party of the European Socialists), the Greens and European Free Alliance (e.g. European Green Party and regional parties from Spain), the Liberals and Democrats (e.g. the European Liberal Democrat and Reform Party, and European Democratic Party), and the European People's Party (a coalition of centre-right members and the largest group in the Parliament). On the far right flank are European Conservatives and Reformists, the Europe of Freedom and Democracy party, and 'non inscrits' members.

Details on the size and national composition of the European Parliament can be found on www.europarl.eu.int. These party groups have their own internal structure, including Chairs, secretariats, staffs, and 'whips' who keep track of attendance and voting behaviour. The political groups receive budgets from the Parliament.

Statistical analysis of MEPs' voting patterns shows that they vote more along party lines than they do along country lines. Indeed, cohesion within European political groupings is comparable to that in the US Congress, while cohesion of country delegations is significantly lower and is declining.

Location

The Parliament is not located in Brussels, the centre of EU decision making, but rather in Strasbourg (Fig. 2.9) owing to France's dogged insistence (the Parliament's predecessor in the European Coal and Steel Community, the Common Assembly, was located in Strasbourg since it was near to the heart of the coal and steel sectors). Equally determined insistence by Luxembourg has kept the Parliament's secretariat in Luxembourg. Since Brussels is where most of the political action occurs, and is also the location of most of the institutions that the Parliament is supposed to supervise, the Parliament also has offices in Brussels (this is where the various Parliamentary committees meet).

The staffs of the Parliament's political groups work in Brussels. It is not clear how much this geographic dispersion hinders the Parliament's effectiveness, but the time and money wasted on shipping documents and people among three locations occasionally produces negative media attention.

Democratic control

The Parliament and the Council are supposed to be the primary democratic controls over the EU's activities. The MEPs are directly elected by EU citizens, so European Parliamentary elections are – in principle – a way for Europeans to have their voices heard on European issues. In practice, however, European Parliamentary elections are often dominated by standard left-versus-right issues rather than by EU issues. Indeed, European Parliamentary elections are sometimes influenced by pure national concerns, with the voters using the elections as a way of expressing disapproval or approval of the

Figure 2.9 The European Parliament's building in Strasbourg (it also has buildings in Brussels and Luxembourg)

Source: wikimedia.org

ruling national government's performance. Moreover, in many Member States, voter turnout for European Parliamentary elections is low and declining. The first elections in 1979 saw a participation rate of 62 per cent; only 43 per cent of eligible voters voted in the last elections (in 2009). This is quite low compared to the turnout for national government elections.

2.4.5 Court of Justice of the European Union

In the EU, as in every other organization in the world, laws and decisions are open to interpretation and this frequently leads to disputes that cannot be settled by negotiation. The role of the European Court of Justice (ECJ, or sometimes known as the 'EU Court' or EC Court) is to settle these disputes, especially disputes between Member States, between the EU and Member States, between EU institutions, and between individuals and the EU. As discussed above, the EU Court is the highest authority on the application of EU law.

As a result of this power, the Court has had a major impact on European integration. For example, its ruling in the 1970s on non-tariff barriers triggered a sequence of events that eventually led to the Single European Act (see Chapter 4 for details). The Court has also been important in defining the relations between the Member States and the EU, and in the legal protection of individuals (EU citizens can take cases directly to the EU Court without going through their governments).

The European Court of Justice, which is located in Luxembourg (Fig. 2.10), consists of one judge from each Member State. Judges are appointed by common accord of the Member States' governments and serve for six years. The Court also has eight 'advocates-general' whose job is to help the judges by constructing 'reasoned submissions' that suggest what conclusions the judges might make. The Court reaches its decisions by majority voting. The Court of First Instance was set up in the late 1980s to help the EU Court with its ever-growing workload.

Figure 2.10 Headquarters of the European Court of Justice in Luxembourg

Source: European Commission

The Lisbon Treaty extended the Court's authority over many issues in the old third pillar. It also tidied up the organization of the EU's judiciary. The lower court that was set up to help with the workload – the Court of First Instance – is now called the General Court. A new umbrella organization – the Court of Justice of the European Union – now has as its sub-courts the European Court of Justice (now to be called the 'Court of Justice'), the General Court and the Civil Service Tribunal.

2.5 Legislative processes

The European Commission has a near-monopoly on initiating the EU decision-making process. That is to say, it is in charge of writing proposed legislation, although it naturally consults widely when doing so. More importantly, this right of initiative allows the Commission a good deal of power over which new legislation gets considered. For example, if France and Germany want a particular EU law to be passed, they have to first convince the Commission that it would be a good idea.

Once developed, the Commission's proposal is sent to the Council for approval. Most EU legislation also requires the European Parliament's approval, although the exact procedure depends upon the issue concerned. (The Treaties specify which procedure must be used in which areas.) The main procedure, called the codecision procedure before the Lisbon Treaty and now called the 'ordinary legislative procedure', gives the Parliament and the Council equal power in terms of approval/rejection and amendment. Before Lisbon, the Council had more power as there were several important areas where Parliament was only 'consulted', or was ignored altogether. The areas where Parliament gained power include immigration, criminal judicial cooperation, police cooperation, and trade and agricultural policy. These are added to the areas where Parliament already had an equal voice, namely, most areas of economic integration such as free movement of workers, creation of the single market, research and technological development, the environment, consumer protection, education, culture and public health.

The ordinary legislative procedure is highly complex but, simplifying for clarity's sake, it starts with a proposal from the Commission and then goes through two readings by the Council and the Parliament. Passing the act requires a 'yes' vote from the Council and Parliament. The Council decides by qualified majority, while the Parliament decides by a simple majority. If the Council and Parliament disagree after the second reading, a conciliation procedure is started. If this does not produce agreement, the act is dropped. For details, see Box 2.9.

Box 2.9   The ordinary legislative procedure in detail

The procedure starts with a Commission proposal. The Parliament then gives its 'opinion', i.e. evaluates the proposal and suggests desired amendments, by simple majority. After seeing the Parliament's opinion, the Council adopts a 'common position' by a qualified majority, except in the fields of culture, freedom of movement, social security and coordination of the rules for carrying on a profession, which are subject to a unanimous vote. The Parliament then receives the Council's common position and has three months in which to take a decision. If the Parliament expressly approves it, or takes no action by the deadline, the Act is adopted immediately. If an absolute majority of Parliament's Members rejects the common position, the process stops, and the Act is not adopted. If a majority of MEPs adopts amendments to the common position, these are first put to the Commission for its opinion and then returned to the Council. The Council votes by a qualified majority on Parliament's amendments, although it takes a unanimous vote to accept amendments that have been given a negative opinion by the Commission. The Act is adopted if the Council approves all Parliament's amendments no later than three months after receiving them. Otherwise the Conciliation Committee is convened within six weeks.

The Conciliation Committee consists of an equal number of Council and Parliament representatives, assisted by the Commission. It considers the common position on the basis of Parliament's amendments and has six weeks to draft a joint text. The procedure stops and the Act is not adopted unless the Committee approves the joint text by the deadline. If it does so, the joint text goes back to the Council and Parliament for approval. The Council and Parliament have six weeks to approve it. The Council acts by a qualified majority and the Parliament by an absolute majority of the votes cast. The Act is adopted if Council and Parliament approve the joint text. If either of the institutions has not approved it by the deadline, the procedure stops and the Act is not adopted.

The other legislative procedures are called special legislative procedures in the Lisbon Treaty; basically they are re-labelling of existing procedures. In areas that are especially sensitive (mostly on grounds of national sovereignty), the role of the Parliament is reduced to discussion or consent. These are:

- *Consultation procedure*. Here the Council can adopt legislation based on a proposal by the European Commission after merely consulting the European Parliament. Consultation is still used for legislation concerning internal market exemptions, and competition law.

- *Consent procedure*. This procedure (which used to be called the assent procedure) allows the Council to adopt legislation (proposed by the Commission) after obtaining the consent of Parliament. In this way, Parliament can reject the law, but it cannot formally propose amendments. The procedure applies to things like the admission or withdrawal of members.

National parliaments

Member states' parliaments are not part of the EU institutional superstructure, but the Lisbon Treaty gives them a heightened role in guarding against competence creep, i.e. the EU overstepping its authority and legislating in areas where it should not. For example, if a sufficient number of national parliaments is convinced that a legislative initiative should better be taken at a local, regional or national level, the Commission either has to withdraw it or give a clear justification why it does not believe that the initiative is in breach with the principle of subsidiarity.

While national parliaments are mentioned in several places, the clearest examples are in the creation of what are known as 'yellow and orange cards'. These give national parliaments the right to express concerns on subsidiarity directly to the institution which initiated the proposed legislation. Under the 'yellow card' procedure, any parliament can, within two months of the release of a draft law, submit an opinion that the law violates the principle of subsidiarity. This triggers a voting system among national parliaments. If at least one-third approve the opinion, the Commission has to reconsider the law. The Commission can persevere but it must justify its actions.

The 'orange card', which applies to the ordinary legislative procedure, is tougher. If a majority of available parliaments votes against a proposed law, the Commission must review the law as before, but in addition to the Commission providing justification, the European Parliament and Council must also consider the national parliaments' objections. Plainly these measures give no direct power to the national parliaments, but any law that attracted a yellow or orange card would surely be subjected to brutal media scrutiny. The idea is that this would deter the Commission from proposing such laws in the first place, or encourage it to modify them to meet the concerns.

2.5.1 Enhanced cooperation

The tension between the 'vanguard' members, who wish to broaden the scope of EU activities, and the 'doubters', who do not, led to the introduction of a new type of integration process called 'closer cooperation' in the Amsterdam Treaty and renamed 'enhanced cooperation' in the Nice Treaty. This allows subgroups of EU members to cooperate on specific areas while still keeping the cooperation under the general framework of the EU.

Subgroups of Member States have long engaged in closer intergovernmental cooperation. What the Amsterdam Treaty did by creating 'closer cooperation' was to allow such subgroups to proceed while at the same time keeping them under some form of EU discipline and coordination.

However, the conditions for starting new closer cooperations were so strict that no new closer cooperation was established under the Amsterdam rules. The Nice Treaty made it easier to start such subgroups and re-labelled them as 'enhanced cooperation' arrangements (ECAs). Although this form of integration has not yet been used, the increased diversity of members and difficulty of decision making that came with the 2004 and 2007 enlargements may make it more important in coming years. The point is that the diversity of members' preferences for integration will become even more diverse, so subsets of members may well find that starting an ECA is the only way to get things done. See Baldwin et al. (2001) for an analysis of this possibility. The first 'enhanced cooperation' may concern divorce law (Box 2.10).

There are potentially serious risks involved in integration led by such clubs-within-the-club schemes. For instance, we may see calls for an ECA with respect to tighter police and intelligence cooperation, especially with respect to terrorism and organized crime. Given the uneven quality of governments in the new Member States, the ECA may seek to exclude nations whose intelligence services are not up to standard. This, of course, would be divisive. By allowing a separation of members into groups, it risks fragmenting the EU politically. Moreover, ECAs could result in an erosion of existing integration, and in so far as ECAs create diversity in integration, they might erode the consistency of European economic and social integration.

Another example can be found in the meeting of finance ministers of the Eurozone nations. Just before the standard Council of Ministers meeting for finance ministers (ECOFIN), the Eurozone nations gather to discuss issues. Since these 12 constitute a substantial majority in terms of voting power, the non-Eurozone nations can sometimes feel that decisions have been sewn up in advance by the Eurozone-12.

To guard against these twin risks, the Nice Treaty gives the Commission a central role in the decision to create and enlarge any enhanced cooperation. Specifically, the Commission can veto ECAs covering deeper economic integration (i.e. first-pillar areas) and it controls subsequent membership enlargements of these. In other areas, the Commission has a strong voice in the process of setting up and expanding ECAs, but less so in the Security and Foreign Policy area (second pillar) than in Justice and Home Affairs areas (third pillar). It can also be the administrator of such groups.

Box 2.10   Divorce and the first enhanced cooperation

Divorce is never an easy thing, but it can get nightmarishly complicated with a mixed nationality couple with children. Even within the EU, divorce laws vary widely – from the no-fault, automatic policy of secular Sweden to devotedly Catholic Malta's lack of recognition of divorce – and it is not always clear which laws should apply.

The EU tried to simplify things and avoid spouses engaging in a trying and costly search for the 'best' set of divorce laws by agreeing a regulation (known as Rome III) that would have specified which laws apply. The absolute refusal of Sweden and Malta to agree to the regulation (which must be agreed unanimously since such legal cooperation is a third-pillar issue) induced a subset of nations to proceed by requesting an enhanced cooperation on the matter. The group included Austria, France, Greece, Hungary, Italy, Luxembourg, Romania, Slovenia and Spain from the beginning; Germany, Belgium, Portugal and Lithuania are considering joining the initiative.

2.6 Some important facts

EU nations are very different, one from another. This simple fact is the source of a large share of the EU's problems, so it is important to understand it in detail. This section covers the facts on populations, incomes and economic size. Students can easily find the most updated figures for this section in the freely downloadable data from the Eurostat website, epp.eurostat.ec.europa.eu.

2.6.1 Populations and incomes

There are about 500 million EU citizens, a figure that is substantially larger than the corresponding US and Japanese figures, but substantially smaller than those of China and India.

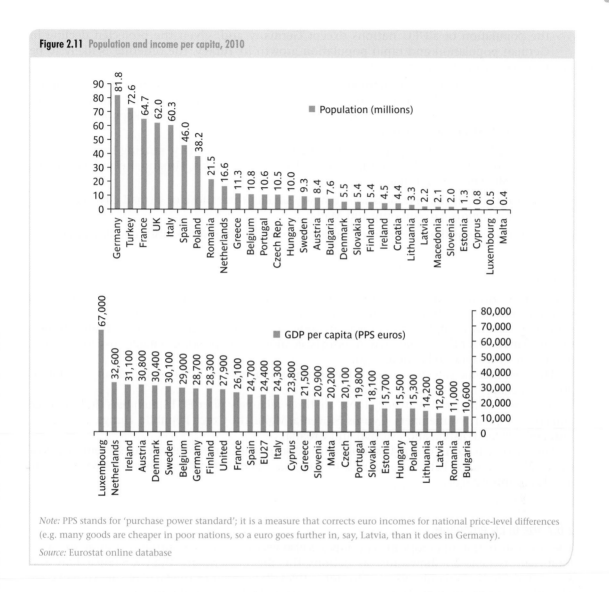

Figure 2.11 Population and income per capita, 2010

Note: PPS stands for 'purchase power standard'; it is a measure that corrects euro incomes for national price-level differences (e.g. many goods are cheaper in poor nations, so a euro goes further in, say, Latvia, than it does in Germany).

Source: Eurostat online database

The EU27 nations and the 'candidate countries' (Croatia, Macedonia and Turkey) vary enormously in terms of populations, as the upper panel of Fig. 2.11 shows. The differences are easier to remember when the nations are grouped into big, medium, small and tiny – where these categories are established by comparison with the population of well-known cities.

■ The 'big' nations are defined here as having 35 million people or more – clearly more people than even the largest city in the world (Mexico City's population is about 20 million). In the EU27 there are six of these – Germany, the UK, France, Italy, Spain and Poland. Germany is substantially larger than the others, more than twice the size of the smallest in the group. The total population of the 'Big-6' accounts for about three-quarters of the 497 million people in the EU27 nations. Turkey, with whom the EU started membership negotiations in October 2005, has over 70 million inhabitants. This exceeds the population of all EU nations except Germany and, given the projected decline in German population and rapid population growth in Turkey, the ordering is likely to be reversed within ten years.

- The 'medium' nations are defined as having populations of between 8 and 11 million, something like that of a really big city, say Paris with its surroundings. There are eight medium nations in the EU27 (Greece, Portugal, Belgium, the Czech Republic, Hungary, Sweden, Austria and Bulgaria).
- The 'small' nations have populations along the lines of a big city, ranging from Barcelona (4 million) to Lyons (1.4 million). These are Denmark, Slovakia, Finland, Ireland, Lithuania, Latvia, Slovenia and Estonia.
- The 'tiny' nations have populations that are smaller than those of a small city like Genoa. The list is Cyprus, Luxembourg and Malta.
- The only nations that fall between these categories are the Netherlands and Romania.

Incomes

The average income level of the people in these nations also varies enormously. Again, it is useful to classify the nations into three categories – high, medium and low. Luxembourg is in a super-rich class by itself; Luxembourgers are more than twice as rich as the French and Swedes. One explanation for this is that Luxembourg is, economically speaking, a medium-sized city and incomes in cities tend to be quite high.

The high-income category – defined as incomes above the EU27 average (about €24,400 in 2010) – includes 12 of the EU27 nations.

In the medium-income category there are three relatively poor EU15 members (Italy, Greece and Portugal), ten new members (Cyprus, Slovenia, Malta, the Czech Republic, Hungary, Slovakia, Lithuania, Poland, Latvia and Estonia) and Croatia.

Low-income nations, defined as those with per-capita incomes of about 50 per cent or less of the EU27 average, are Latvia, Romania and Bulgaria. Candidate nations Turkey and Macedonia are also in this category.

2.6.2 Size of EU economies

The size distribution of European economies is also very uneven, measuring economic size with total GDP. As Table 2.1 shows, just six nations, the 'Big-5' (Germany, the UK, France, Italy and Spain) and the Netherlands, account for more than 80 per cent of the GDP of the whole EU27. The other nations are small, tiny or minuscule, using the following definitions:

- 'Small' is an economy that accounts for between 1 and 3 per cent of the EU27's output.
- 'Tiny' is one that accounts for less than 1 per cent of the total.
- Minuscule is one that accounts for less than one-tenth of 1 per cent.

2.7 The budget

The EU budget is the source of a great deal of both solidarity and tension among EU members, so a full understanding of the EU requires some knowledge of the budget. This section looks at

Table 2.1   Size distribution of EU27 economies

	GDP (billion euros), 2010	Share of EU27 (%)		GDP (billion euros), 2010	Share of EU27 (%)
Germany	2,477	20	Ireland	156	1
France	1,933	16	Czech Rep	149	1
UK	1,700	14	Romania	122	1
Italy	1,549	13	Hungary	97	1
Spain	1,063	9	Slovakia	66	1
Netherlands	588	5	Luxembourg	40	0.3
Belgium	354	3	Bulgaria	36	0.3
Poland	354	3	Slovenia	35	0.3
Sweden	347	3	Lithuania	28	0.2
Austria	286	2	Latvia	18	0.1
Denmark	234	2	Cyprus	17	0.1
Greece	227	2	Estonia	14	0.1
Finland	180	1	Malta	6	0.1
Portugal	173	1			

Note: Data for 2010 not adjusted for national cost of living differences since we are interested in the relative size of economies rather than individual income levels.
Source: Eurostat online database

the following questions in order. What is the money spent on? Where does it come from? Who gets the most on net? How does the budget process work?

2.7.1 Expenditure

Total EU spending is now over €120 billion (€122 billion in 2010). While this sounds like a lot to most people, it is really fairly small – only about 1 per cent of total EU27 GDP – just €250 per EU citizen. The first priority here is to study how this money is spent. We look first at spending by area and then spending by EU member.

Expenditure by area

As with so many things in Europe, understanding EU spending in all its detail would take a lifetime, but understanding the basics takes just a few minutes. Starting at the broadest level, the EU spends its money on farming, poor regions and other things.

Under Commission President Barroso all the names of the main spending categories were changed to make them sound more positive. For example, the EU spends almost half its budget on the payments to farmers despite the sector's meagre contribution to EU growth, income and employment. To make this sound more in line with a forward-looking, dynamic EU, these expenditures were labelled 'Preservation and management of natural resources'. The expenditures by the new-century names are given in Table 2.2.

Table 2.2 EU expenditures in 2010 (formal labels)

	Million euros
1a. Comptetitiveness	11,275
1b. Cohesion	36,372
2. Preservation and management of natural resources	58,136
3a. Freedom, security, justice	736
3b. Citizenship	739
4. The EU as a global player	7,788
5. Administration	7,907
Total	122,956

Source: © European Union, 1995–2012.

The easiest way to remember the facts is to turn to plain English and focus only on the biggest areas. This is shown in Fig. 2.12. Farming takes up about half the budget and poor regions take about one-third. The rest is split among many different uses. Spending on agriculture and poor regions is so important that we have written separate chapters dealing with each, so we do not go into further detail here (see Chapter 9 on agriculture and Chapter 10 on poor regions).

At a slightly finer level of analysis, we break the 'other things' category into three areas:

1 Internal policies (10 per cent of budget). This refers to policies where the money is spent inside the EU but not on agriculture and poor regions. This category is very diverse. The biggest item is research (about 5 per cent) but it also includes spending on trans-European transport networks, energy projects, spending on training and student mobility, the environment, culture, information and communication, etc.

2 External policies (6 per cent of budget). This money is spent mainly on humanitarian aid, food aid and development assistance in non-member countries throughout the world. The big items are pre-accession assistance (payments to candidate nations to help them with the accession process), European Neighbourhood policies (assistance to European neighbouring nations that are not candidates), humanitarian aid, and development cooperation (overseas aid). Spending on EU farmers is about 60 times greater than EU humanitarian aid.

3 Administration (7 per cent of budget). This concerns the cost of running the European Commission, the European Court of Justice and all other European institutions. Taken together, they employ surprisingly few people (about 30,000). The Commission accounts for less than half the amount.

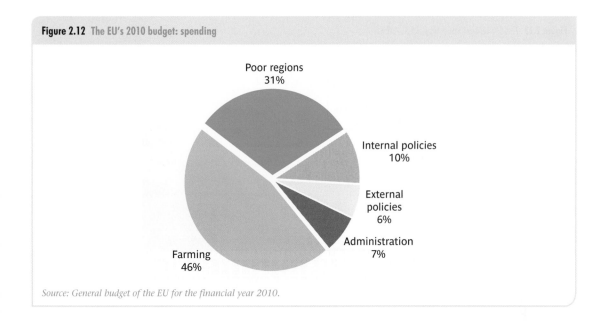

Figure 2.12 The EU's 2010 budget: spending

Poor regions
31%

Internal policies
10%

External
policies
6%

Administration
7%

Farming
46%

Source: General budget of the EU for the financial year 2010.

Historical development of EU spending by area

The EU's spending priorities and the level of spending have changed dramatically since its inception in 1958. This is shown graphically in Fig. 2.13.

As the top panel shows, the budget grew rapidly, but started at a very low level (just 8/100ths of 1 per cent of the EEC6's GDP). EU spending was negligible until the late 1960s, amounting to less than €10 per EU citizen. This changed as the cost of the Common Agricultural Policy (CAP) started to rise rapidly in the 1960s and Cohesion spending started to rise in the 1980s. From the early 1970s to the early 1990s, the budget grew steadily as a fraction of EU GDP, starting from about 8/10ths of 1 per cent and rising to 1.2 per cent in 1993. Since the 1994 enlargement, the budget as a share of GDP has remained quite stable at about 1 per cent.

The bottom panel of the figure depicts the spending by area in shares to illustrate how the EU's budget priorities have changed over the past half century. Until 1965, the budget – tiny as it was – was spent mainly on administration (this was the period when all the European institutions were set up and the customs union was being implemented). CAP spending began in 1965 and soon dominated the budget. For almost a decade, farm spending regularly took 80 per cent or more of total expenditures; at its peak in 1970, it made up 92 per cent of the budget!

From the date of the first enlargement, 1973, Cohesion spending began to grow in importance, pushing down Agriculture's share in the process. Indeed, the sum of the shares of these two big-ticket items has remained remarkably steady, ranging between 80 and 85 per cent of the budget. In a very real sense, we can think of Cohesion spending as steadily crowding out CAP spending over the past three decades.

2.7.2 Expenditure by member

By far the most important benefit from EU membership is economic integration. By comparison, the financial transfers involved in EU spending are minor. Remember that the whole budget is only about 1 per cent of EU GDP and the net contributions (payments to the EU minus payments from the EU) are never greater than one-tenth of 1 per cent. Be this as it may, it is interesting to see which members receive the largest shares of EU spending. Many disputes in the EU are over

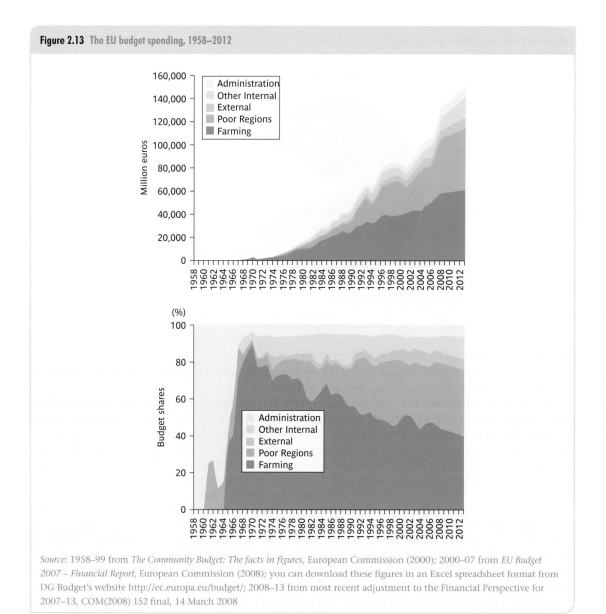

Figure 2.13 The EU budget spending, 1958–2012

Source: 1958–99 from *The Community Budget: The facts in figures*, European Commission (2000); 2000–07 from *EU Budget 2007 – Financial Report*, European Commission (2008); you can download these figures in an Excel spreadsheet format from DG Budget's website http://ec.europa.eu/budget/; 2008–13 from most recent adjustment to the Financial Perspective for 2007–13, COM(2008) 152 final, 14 March 2008

budget allocations, although the basic outlines of spending have been set up to 2013 in the new long-term budget plan that was agreed in 2005.

The amount of EU spending varies quite a lot across members, in terms of both the total amount and its nature, as the top panel of Fig. 2.14 shows. France and Spain are the top recipients, with most of their money coming from EU payments to farmers and poor regions. Not surprising, farm payments matter most for members with relatively big farm sectors like Denmark and Ireland, while spending on poor regions is more important in the poorer Member States. Almost all of Luxembourg's receipts come from administrative spending.

The figures, however, are entirely different when we look at receipts per capita (see bottom panel of the figure). By far the largest receiver per capita is Luxembourg, about €3,000. This

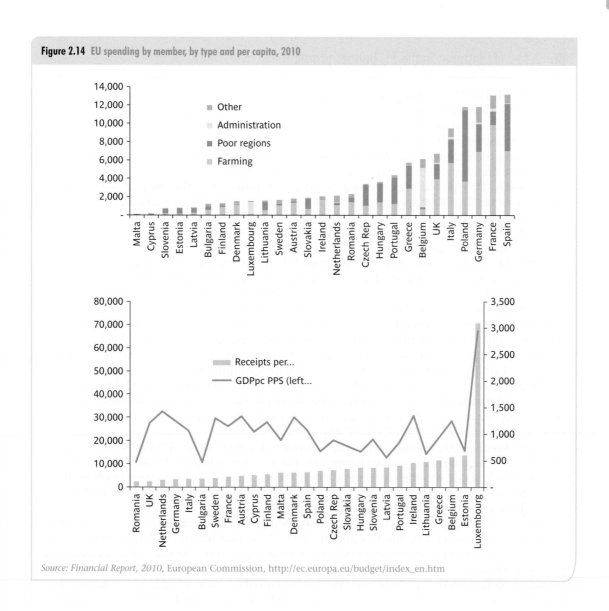

Figure 2.14 EU spending by member, by type and per capita, 2010

Source: Financial Report, 2010, European Commission, http://ec.europa.eu/budget/index_en.htm

sounds like a lot, but since incomes are so high in the Grand Duchy, about twice the EU average at €70,000, this EU spending does not have as large an impact as one might think.

Readers may find the figures in the second panel rather strange. Why should rich nations like Luxembourg, and Belgium, be above-average recipients of EU spending? The answer, which lies in the nature of the EU's decision-making process, is pursued in much greater depth in Chapter 3.

2.7.3 Revenue

The EU's budget must, by law, be balanced every year. All of the spending discussed above must be financed each year by revenues collected from EU members or carried over from previous years.

Up to 1970, the EEC's budget was financed by annual contributions from the members. A pair of Treaties in the 1970s and a handful of landmark decisions by the European Council

---

Box 2.11 Milestones in the EU budget procedure

1958–70. The EU's budget was financed by contributions from its members.

April 1970. The Luxembourg European Council. The 'own resources' system is introduced. These included customs duties, agricultural levies (i.e. variable tariffs) and a share of VAT revenue collected by EU members. The Treaty of July 1975 refined and reinforced the system, establishing the European Court of Auditors to oversee the budget and giving the European Parliament the formal right of rejection over annual budgets.

1975–87. This period was marked by sharp disputes over the budget contributions and ever-expanding CAP spending. The UK's Margaret Thatcher in particular complained repeatedly about the UK's position as the largest net contributor.

1984. The Fontainebleau European Council. The VAT-based revenue source was increased and the UK was awarded its famous 'rebate'.

1988. Delors I package. This reform established the basis of the current revenue and spending system. It introduced a fourth 'own resource' based on members' GNPs, established an overall ceiling on EU revenue as a percentage of the EU's GNP, and started reducing the role of VAT-based revenue. The package, decided at the Brussels European Council in June, also established the EU's multi-year budgeting process whereby a Financial Perspective sets out the evolution of EU spending by broad categories. Substantively, the Financial Perspective adopted provided for a major reorientation of EU spending from the CAP to Cohesion spending; Cohesion spending was doubled and CAP spending growth was capped.

1992. Delors II package. The Edinburgh agreement of December 1992 increased the revenue ceiling slightly to 1.27 per cent, and further reduced the role of VAT-based revenue. It also adopted a new Financial Perspective for 1993–99, which amplified the shift of EU spending priorities away from the CAP and towards Cohesion.

1999. Agenda 2000 package. The Berlin European Council adopted the 2000–06 Financial Perspective. There were no major changes on the revenue side and the only major change on the spending side was the creation of a new broad category, 'Pre-accession' expenditures, meant to finance programmes in central and eastern European nations and provide a reserve to cover the cost of any enlargements in this period.

2005. After a failure to reach agreement at their June 2005 Summit, the issue of setting the seven-year Financial Perspective for the 2007–13 period fell to the UK Presidency. The basic idea was to move spending slowly away from agriculture, to make the spending on poor regions more coherent and concentrated, and increase spending on competitiveness measures such as R&D. The 2004 and 2007 enlargements, however, added 12 new members with below-average incomes and many farmers, so large changes in budget priorities proved politically impossible.

---

established the system we have today in which there are four main sources of revenue. (See Box 2.11 for further details.) According to the EU Treaties, the Union is legally entitled to this revenue, so it is known as 'own resources' in EU jargon.

There are four main types of these own resources and Fig. 2.15 shows how their relative importance has varied over the years. Two of the four have long been used, and indeed in the early days of the Union they were sufficient to finance all payments. These so-called traditional own resources are:

■ Tariff revenue stemming from the Common External Tariff (CET). Although trade within the EU is tariff free, tariffs are imposed on imports from non-member nations. This money accrues to the EU rather than to any particular member.

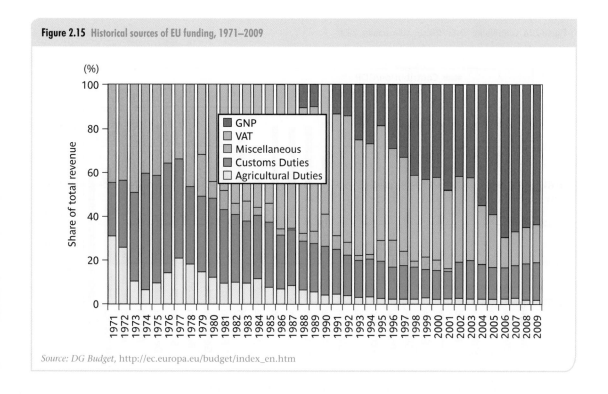

Figure 2.15 Historical sources of EU funding, 1971–2009

Source: DG Budget, http://ec.europa.eu/budget/index_en.htm

- 'Agricultural levies' are tariffs on agricultural goods that are imported from non-members. Conceptually, these are the same as the previous category (they are both taxes on imports from third nations), but are viewed as distinct since the levies are not formally part of the CET. Historically, the level of these tariffs has fluctuated widely according to market conditions (they were part of the CAP's price support mechanism; see Chapter 9).

The importance of these two revenue items has fallen over the years to the point where they are no longer major items (together, they make up only one-seventh of the revenue needs). This reduced importance stems from the way that the level of the CET has been steadily lowered in the course of WTO rounds (e.g. the 1986–94 Uruguay Round). Moreover, EU enlargement and the signing of free trade agreements with non-members means that a very large fraction of EU imports from non-members is duty free. The level of the agricultural levies has also been reduced in the context of CAP reform. The third and fourth types of 'own resources' provide most of the money. They are:

- 'VAT resource'. As is often the case when it comes to tax matters, the reality is quite complex, but it is best thought of as a 1 per cent value added tax. The importance of this resource has declined and is set to decline further.
- GNP based. This revenue is a tax based on the GNP of EU members. It is used to top up any revenue shortfall and thus ensures that the EU never runs a deficit.

The other revenue sources – labelled 'miscellaneous' in the diagram – have been relatively unimportant since 1977. Now, they include items such as taxes paid by employees of European institutions (they do not pay national taxes), fines, and surpluses carried over from previous years. Until the 1970s budget treaties came fully into effect, 'miscellaneous' revenue included direct member contributions, which were a crucial source of funding in the early years.

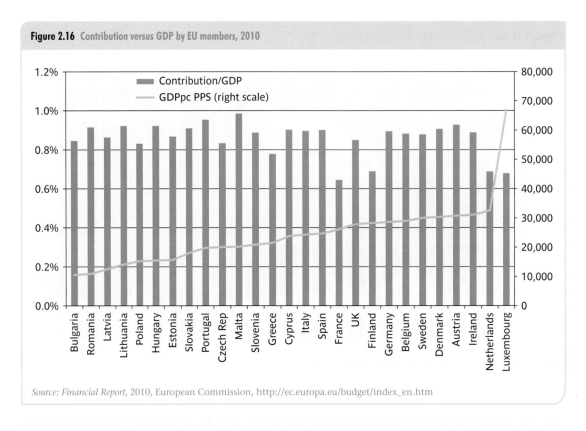

Figure 2.16 Contribution versus GDP by EU members, 2010

Source: Financial Report, 2010, European Commission, http://ec.europa.eu/budget/index_en.htm

Budget contribution by member

On the contribution side, EU funding amounts to basically 1 per cent of each member's GDP. Some observers find this anomalous since taxation in most nations, especially in Europe, is progressive, i.e. the tax rate that an individual pays rises with his or her income level.

The precise figures are shown in Fig. 2.16. Here we see that the contributions as a share of GDP do not vary much. The highest figure in 2010 was about 1 per cent for Malta. The lowest figure was for France. The precise contribution rate varies from year to year by Member State due to the complexities of the system.

For comparison, the nations are ordered by increasing income (the line in the figure shows the national GDP per capita). The figure makes it clear that the EU's 'tax' system is not progressive like that of most of its members. In other words, nations that have higher incomes do not pay a higher proportion of their income. The 'tax rate' is approximately 1 per cent for all members.

2.7.4 Budget process

The EU's annual budget is guided primarily by a medium-term agreement on spending priorities, called 'Financial Perspectives' as mentioned above. The current Financial Perspective sets out broad spending guidelines for the annual budgets from 2007 to 2013 (you can download this from http://ec.europa.eu/budget/index_en.htm). Since the Financial Perspective is adopted by all the institutions involved in budgeting (the Commission, the European Parliament and the Council), its existence reduces dispute over each annual budget.

The procedure for drawing up the annual budget (as laid down in the Treaties) calls for the Commission to prepare a preliminary draft budget. The Commission's draft is presented to the Council for amendments and adoption. Once it has passed the Council, the budget goes to the European Parliament which has some power to amend the budget. After two readings in the Council and the Parliament, it is the European Parliament which adopts the final budget, and its President who signs it. This formal procedure has been augmented by inter-institutional arrangements between the Parliament, the Council and the Commission that are meant to improve cooperation. For more information, see http://ec.europa.eu/budget/index_en.htm.

2.8 Summary

This chapter covered seven very different topics.

Economic integration

The economic integration in the EU was designed to create a unified economic area in which firms and consumers located anywhere in the area would have equal opportunities to sell or buy goods throughout the area, and where owners of labour and capital should be free to employ their resources in any economic activity anywhere in the area. This is implemented via the 'four freedoms', the free movements of goods, services, people and capital.

EU organization

The EU is organized into three pillars. The first pillar (supranational decision making and the authority of supranational institutions such as the Commission and EU Court) encompasses economic integration. The other pillars include areas where EU integration proceeds on an intergovernmental basis. The second and third pillars encompass the Common Foreign and Security Policy, and Home and Judicial Affairs, respectively. Formally, the European Union is the 'roof' covering the three pillars and the European Community (EC) is the first pillar.

Law

The EU is unique in that it has a supranational system of law. That is, on matters pertaining to the European Community, EU law and the EU Court take precedence over Member States' laws and courts. The key principles covered were 'direct effect', 'primacy' and 'autonomy'.

Institutions and legislative procedures

While there are many EU institutions, only five really matter for most things. These are the European Council, the Council of Ministers, the Commission, the Parliament and the Court.

These five institutions work in concert to govern the EU and to pursue deeper and wider European economic integration. Under the main legislative procedure, now called the 'ordinary legislative procedure', the Commission proposes draft laws which have to be approved by the Council of Ministers and the European Parliament before taking effect. Most EU legislation has to be turned into national law by each Member State's parliament.

Facts

A dominant feature of the EU members is their diversity in size and income levels.

Budget

The EU budget is rather small, representing only 1 per cent of the EU's GDP. It is spent mainly on a set of agricultural programmes known as the Common Agricultural Policy (roughly half the budget), and on Cohesion, resources destined for poor regions in the EU (roughly a third of the budget). The budget is funded through four complicated mechanisms but the result is that each EU member pays roughly 1 per cent of its GDP to the Commission, regardless of its income level. The distribution of net contributions (receipts minus contributions) by Member State is quite unequal. The biggest net recipients are Luxembourg (the richest member) and the three poorest members (Greece, Portugal and Spain).

Self-assessment questions

1 Draw a diagram that summarizes the connections between the Council of Ministers, the European Commission and the European Parliament when it comes to passing laws. Use the example of the codecision procedure (now called the ordinary legislative procedure).
2 Draw a schematic representation of the steady deepening of EU economic integration.
3 Draw a diagram that shows the main steps (and dates) in the development of the Big-5 EU institutions. (Hint: You may have to turn to the websites referred to in the text to find the dates.)
4 Develop an easy way of remembering the names of all of the EU15 members (e.g. there are four big ones, four small ones, four poor ones and three new ones). Do the same for the twelve newcomers who joined between 2004 and 2007.
5 Explain in 25 words or fewer the difference between EC law and EU law.
6 List the main sources of EU revenue and the main spending priorities. Explain how each of these has developed over time.
7 Explain why it is important that the EU Court's rulings cannot be appealed in Member States' courts.
8 Make a table of the major changes to each of the Big-5 Institutions implied by the Lisbon Treaty.

Essay questions

1 The general term for the way in which the EU institutions interact is the 'Community Method'. Describe what this is and how it has evolved over time.
2 Analyse the reasons why the harmonization of corporate income taxes has not been part of EU integration effects.

3 Describe the historical origins of the European Council and how its role has evolved over time. Be sure to cover the way it is addressed in the Lisbon Treaty.

4 The European Parliament has progressively gained strength since the EU's inception. Describe this process and explain the forces driving it forward.

5 Compare the powers of the European Parliament to those of the parliament in your nation.

6 If the EU Court decides on a matter, is there any way that EU leaders can overrule that decision?

7 Find where the key elements of EU law discussed in this chapter are transcribed into the Lisbon Treaty. Do you think it is a good idea to have these principles in the Treaty?

8 Download the publication *The Community Budget: The Facts in Figures*, European Commission, and illustrate the evolution of receipts and payments of your favourite EU member in recent years.

9 Ireland is the only EU member that is a large recipient of both CAP spending and Cohesion spending. Did Ireland gain or lose from the shift in EU spending priorities that has, since 1986, reduced the CAP's budget share at the expense of Cohesion's share?

10 Compare and contrast the reasons behind the French and Dutch 'no' votes on the Constitutional Treaty.

11 Is the Lisbon Treaty a 'treaty' or a 'constitution'?

12 Did the EU have a constitution before the Lisbon Treaty in the same sense that Britain has a constitution?

13 Write an essay on the main institutional reforms undertaken to prepare the EU for eastern enlargement.

Further reading: the aficionado's corner

For more economic statistics on Europe, see the most recent issue of the *Eurostat Yearbook*. This is well organized and provides directly comparable figures for all EU members. Eurostat, which used to charge for data, now allows free downloads of most data series. Much of the same information can be found in the Statistical Appendix of the Commission publication called *European Economy*; see http://europa.eu.int/. The OECD also provides an excellent statistical overview in its 'OECD in figures'. You can download the latest issue for free from www.oecd.org.

On EU law, an excellent source is *The ABC of Community Law* by **Borchandt** (2010); this webbook can be freely downloaded from http://europa.eu.int/eur-lex/en/about/abc/. It is still the best freely downloadable text. The basic principles of European law have not changed since its publication.

Comprehensive information on EU institutions and legislative processes is provided by:

Hix, S. (1999) *The Political System of the European Union*, Palgrave, London.
Peterson, J. and M. Shackleton (2002) *The Institutions of the European Union*, Oxford University Press, Oxford.

A good source for further information on the budget is:

Peet, J. and K. Ussher (1999) *The EU Budget: An Agenda for Reform?*, CER Working Paper, February.

See also the Commission publication 'The budget of the EU: How is your money spent?', downloadable from http://europa.eu.int/budget/.

Information on the Lisbon Treaty is provided by:

Norman, P. (2005) 'The accidental constitution', EuroComment, Brussels.
Open Europe (2008a) 'A guide to the constitutional treaty', Second edition February 2008 (Open Europe considers the Lisbon Treaty to be equivalent to the abandoned Constitution). Download from www.openeurope.org.uk/research/guide.pdf.

Useful websites

The European Parliament's factsheets provide excellent, authoritative and succinct coverage of EU law, institutions, decision-making procedures and the budget process. These pages are especially useful in that they provide brief accounts of the historical development of various institutional aspects of the EU. See www.europarl.eu.int/factsheets/default_en.htm.

The most exhaustive source for information on EU law is the Commission's excellent website: http://europa.eu.int/scadplus/.

References

Baldwin, R., et al. (2001) *Nice Try: Should the Treaty of Nice be Ratified?*, CEPR, London.

Borchandt, K.-D. (2010) *The ABC of European Union Law*. Download from http://eur-lex.europa.eu/en/editorial/abc_toc_r1.htm.

House of Lords (2008) 'European Union Committee: 10th Report of Session 2007–08, The Treaty of Lisbon: an impact assessment'. Download from www.publications.parliament.uk/pa/ld200708/ldselect/ldeucom/62/62.pdf.

Milward, A. (1992) *The European Rescue of the Nation-state*, Cambridge University Press, Cambridge.

Mongelli, F.P., E. Dorrucci and I. Agur (2007) 'What does European institutional integration tell us about trade integration?', *Integration and Trade (IADB)*, 11(26).

Noury, A. and G. Roland (2002) *European Parliament: Should it have more power?*, Economic Policy.

Open Europe (2008b) 'Open Europe parliamentary briefing #5: Foreign policy and defence'. Download from www.openeurope.org.uk/research/cfspbriefing.pdf.

Chapter 3

Decision making

Nothing is more difficult, and therefore more precious, than to be able to decide.

Napoleon Bonaparte

Chapter Contents

Introduction

Chapter 2 described how EU institutions work and how they make their decisions. This chapter presents a framework for thinking about EU decision making at a more abstract and more analytical level. The discussion is organized around two major questions:

1 Who should be in charge of what? That is, which decisions should be taken at the EU level and which should be taken at the national or sub-national levels?

2 Is the EU-level decision-making procedure efficient and legitimate?

In answering these questions we shall examine the EU's actual practice and develop a number of specific analytic tools. Moreover, we shall look at proposed reforms of the system since recent and future enlargements challenge the EU's decision-making structure.

3.1 Task allocation and subsidiarity: EU practice and principles

Governments set policies in many areas – speed limits on roads, school curriculums, monetary policy, taxation, import taxes on Chinese t-shirts, development of nuclear weapons, deployment of troops abroad, etc. Plainly, not all of these policies are made by the same level of government. Most European nations have at least three levels of government (local, provincial and national) and EU members have a fourth level of government, the EU.

Although European nations differ in the general attitude towards centralization (e.g. France tends to centralize many more issues than Spain), there is usually a fairly clear allocation of tasks to the four levels of government in each nation. Typically, local speed limits are set by the local government, but motorway speed limits are determined at the national level. Anything to do with military matters is dealt with at the national level, but local nature reserves are likely to be addressed at the provincial level. But what is the logic behind this allocation of tasks? This is the main question addressed by the first two sections of this chapter.

We begin by covering the existing EU principles guiding the allocation of policies between the EU and Member States. The section briefly covers the actual allocation of tasks in the EU. The next section presents an analytic framework for organizing thinking about the appropriate allocation of tasks among the various levels of government.

3.1.1 Introduction to 'competences'

Some tasks and decisions are assigned to the EU level, some are shared between the EU and Member States, and others are set exclusively by national governments. In EU jargon, this task allocation is called the question of 'competences'. Areas where the EU alone decides are known as 'exclusive competences' or 'Union competences'. Those areas where responsibility is shared between the EU and Member States are called 'shared competences'. There are two types of shared competence: those where members cannot pass legislation in areas where the EU already has, and those where the existence of EU legislation does not hinder members' rights to make policy in the same area (see Table 3.1 for examples). The third type is 'supporting, coordinating or complementary competence' where the EU can pass laws that support action by members. The most common names are 'supporting competence' and 'supporting action'. Finally, tasks where national or sub-national governments alone decide are called 'national competences'.

There are some clear examples of national competences, such as the secondary school curriculum; and there are clear examples of exclusive competences, such as competition policy where the EU has the final say on, for example, mergers that affect the European market. However, as is true of so many things in the EU, the exact dividing lines are unclear – even though the Lisbon Treaty substantially improved clarity on this point.

The basic source of ambiguity is that areas of exclusive Union competence are defined partly by reference to specific fields (e.g. the customs union), but partly by reference to functional descriptions. For example, the Union has exclusive competence when it comes to international agreements when it is 'necessary to enable the Union to exercise its internal competence, or insofar as its conclusion may affect common rules or alter their scope'. Plainly the meaning of 'necessary' would be open to interpretation in many cases. As Chapter 2 pointed out, the Treaties' objectives are enormously ambitious, so this proviso puts a great many tasks in the grey area between Community competence and national competence. Often, the dividing line has been established by the EU Court.

Task allocation is further blurred by the so-called flexibility clause which allows the EU to obtain additional competences when necessary; however, this requires an elaborate procedure (see flexibility clause below).

3.1.2 Principle governing the allocation of competences

The touchstone principle is that the EU has no powers intrinsically. Article 1 of the Treaty on European Union says that it is the members that confer competences on the EU in order to attain objectives they have in common. This is the 'principle of conferral'. Competences not granted to the EU remain with the members (Article 4 TEU).

While the limits of EU competences are governed by the principle of conferral, the use of these is governed by the principles of 'subsidiarity' and 'proportionality'. Both words have distinct meaning in the EU.

Subsidiarity and proportionality

The principle of subsidiarity pursues two contrasting goals: (i) to allow the EU to act if a problem cannot be adequately addressed by national policies alone, and (ii) to guard national sovereignty in those areas that cannot be dealt with more effectively at the EU level. The overarching goal is thus to is keep decisions as close to the citizen as possible without jeopardizing win–win cooperation at the EU level. As Borchandt (2010) puts it: 'when it is not necessary for the EU to take action, it is necessary that it should take none'.

The principle of proportionality comes to play when EU action is necessary, i.e. when the objectives of the Treaties can be better achieved at the EU level, or in an area where the EU has exclusive competence. In such situations, the proportionality principle says that the EU should undertake only the minimum necessary actions.

Here is an example of how the subsidiarity and proportionality principles work. The uncoordinated setting of VAT rates would hinder the smooth functioning of the internal market by, for example, leading to massive cross-border shopping driven by VAT differences. The principle of subsidiarity thus suggests that coordinating action at the EU level would be better than uncoordinated action at the national level. In short, the EU should do something to harmonize VAT rates. The principle of proportionality, however, suggests that all that is needed is *some* harmonization, *not complete* harmonization. In keeping with the principle of proportionality, the EU agreed to minimum and maximum VAT rates but let members decide their own rates within the band.

Practically, these principles mean that the 'burden of proof' lies on the instigators of EU legislation. They must make the case that there is a real need for common rules and common action in the area and that the proposed rules or actions are the least restrictive of national sovereignty.

National parliaments are what might be called 'subsidiarity watchdogs' in the sense that they have the right and obligation to check that new EU laws respect the principles of conferral, subsidiarity and proportionality. They are the natural 'watchdogs' since violations of these principles take away their power. (See the discussion of 'yellow card' and 'orange card' in Chapter 2.)

Flexibility clause

The conferral principle says that the EU can act only in areas where Member States have conferred power to it in the Treaties; however, there are situations when a new challenge – one not foreseen in the Treaties – arises that requires action at the EU level. One way to deal with this would be to require a Treaty modification each time such things arose. As Chapter 1 showed plainly, changing treaties can be a long and tricky process.

3.1.3 Competences in practice

The Treaties as amended by the Lisbon Treaty spell out the EU's competences more clearly and more explicitly than was the case before. Indeed this is one of its major accomplishments.

Table 3.1 Allocation of competences to the EU

Exclusive	Shared		Support, coordinate or supplement
Customs union	Exclusive if EU has policy	Non-exclusive	Certain human health policies
Competition policy	Internal market	R&D policies	Industry
Eurozone monetary policy	Certain social policy	Outer space policies	Culture
Conservation of marine resources	Cohesion policy	Development cooperation	Tourism
Common commercial policy	Agriculture and fisheries	Humanitarian aid	Education and training
	Environment		Civil protection and disaster prevention
	Consumer protection		Administrative cooperation
	Transport		Coordination of economic, employment and social policies
	Energy		Common foreign, security and defence policies
	Old third pillar 'Area of freedom, security and justice'		
	Certain public health polices		

Source: The main provisions are in TEU Articles 1, 4, 5, 6, Protocol No. 2

Table 3.1 lists the areas where the EU has competences. All other areas are exclusive competences of the members since any power not explicitly conferred upon the EU remains with the members. Importantly, TEU Article 6 explicitly states that inclusion of the Charter of Fundamental Rights does not extend the EU's competences in any way.

The biggest switch is, as noted in Chapter 2, the switch of Home and Justice Affairs from intergovernmental treatment (i.e. where the EU had no competences at all) to shared competence. This is a natural follow-on from decades of tight economic integration. Europeans are just more tied up with each other, and so many face cross-border legal issues that rarely arose in the last century – things like marriage contracts, retirement plans and house buying.

The third category, support, coordinate or supplement, is new and very useful as the Commission has increasingly turned to this sort of 'soft law' approach in the face of resistance to more direct policies. For example, when it comes to competitiveness, it provides frameworks and benchmarking structures that help member coordination without actually requiring them to do anything specifically. By putting this category of action into the Treaties, the legal status of such actions was clarified.

3.2 Understanding the task allocation: theory of fiscal federalism

The last section considered EU principles and practices, but it did not explain the logic underpinning them. This section uses economic reasoning to help students understand the allocation of tasks in a systematic way. Of course, practice and theory differ – as Albert Einstein is alleged to have said: 'The difference between theory and practice is greater in practice than it is in theory' – but most students find it easier to remember the practice if they understand the underpinning logic.

This section presents a framework for thinking about which is the most appropriate level of government for each type of task. A complete consideration of this question, however, would take us into subjects (political science, sociology, national identity, etc.) that are too far afield for this book. The main line of thinking presented here is called the theory of 'fiscal federalism'. Even though this provides only an incomplete approach to the question, it proves to be a very useful framework for organizing one's thinking about the basic trade-offs.

3.2.1 The basic trade-offs

We focus on five important considerations when thinking about the appropriate allocation of policy-making tasks to the various levels of government. In the real world, the five blend together in complex ways. To clarify our thinking, however, we consider each in isolation. The first concerns local diversity.

Diversity and local informational advantages

When people have very different preferences, centralized decision making creates inefficiencies. There is an obvious aspect and a subtle aspect to this point.

The obvious aspect is that a single, centrally chosen policy will typically be a compromise. By definition, a compromise will not be the right policy for everybody. Take the example of road speed limits. Suppose the German federal government could choose only one speed limit for the whole country. The result would be a limit that was too slow for the autobahn but too fast for residential neighbourhoods. (Of course, for some policies, choosing one policy for the whole nation might reduce costs but we put that aside for clarity's sake and deal with it below under 'scale economies'.)

The subtle aspect concerns local information about diverse situations and preferences. The speed limit example seemed strained since the federal government could set different speed limits for different roads. The subtle point is that, if many different limits are to be set, local governments are probably better at determining which limit to apply to which roads in their localities. This is basically an issue of the cost of acquiring the information necessary to adapt policies to local conditions and preferences. As a general principle (to which there are many exceptions), local governments can acquire such information more cheaply and so the decision-making task should be allocated to the local level.

The general idea is more concretely illustrated in Box 3.1.

Scale economies

The advantage of localized decision making in terms of information efficiency is really quite a robust result. Yet in many situations there are offsetting cost savings from a one-size-fits-all policy that arise from scale economies, i.e. the notion that the per-person cost of a service falls as more people use the service.

For example, in the case of bus services, it seems reasonable to believe that the cost per kilometre of bus service tends to fall as the number of buses gets larger. A large bus company can more easily ensure that the right number of drivers is available, the fixed cost of a maintenance centre can be spread over more buses, and the per-bus cost of administration may fall – at least up to a point – when the bus company is larger. Imagine an extreme situation where every bus in, say, Paris was

---

Box 3.1   Economic inefficiency of a one-size-fits-all policy

To illustrate this general idea more concretely, we turn to Fig. 3.1. (The figure employs supply and demand analysis and the notion of consumer surplus; see Chapter 4 if you are unfamiliar with this type of reasoning.)

Figure 3.1 Diversity of preferences and decentralization

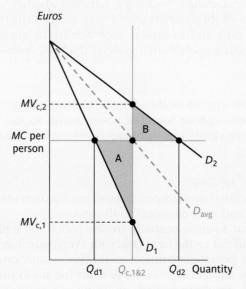

Note: The diagram assumes that individuals in each region are identical and the governments are 'benevolent'.
Technical note: The MC per person = MV criterion is identical to Samuelson's famous sum of MV condition since $MC/N = MV$ implies $MC = N * MV$, where N is the number of people in the region.

The figure shows demand curves for a particular public service. One is for an individual located in region 1 (marked as D_1) and the other for a person in region 2 (marked as D_2). We assume that, for some reason, people in the two regions have different preferences for public services. For example, if we are talking about the density of public bus service, people in region 2 might live in a city where commuting by car is difficult, so they prize bus service more highly than the people in region 1. These relative preferences can be seen from the fact that D_1 is below D_2; from the consumer surplus analysis in Chapter 4, this means that the marginal value of a slight increase in the density of bus service is lower for individuals in region 1 than it is for individuals in region 2.

To start the analysis, we work out the level of bus service that would be provided if the levels were chosen separately by the region 1 and region 2 governments.

The region 1 government would best serve its citizens by choosing the level where a typical region 1 person's marginal value of a denser bus service (i.e. more buses per day and/or more routes) was just equal to the per-person cost of providing the extra service. In the panel, this optimal level is Q_{d1} for region 1 (the 'd' stands for decentralized and '1' for region 1). Region 2's government would choose a higher level, namely Q_{d2}. (This assumes, for simplicity, that the marginal cost is constant at all levels of service and identical across regions.)

Contrast this with the situation where the policy decision is centralized so that the same level is chosen for both regions. In this case, the central government would look at the average preference for bus services as reflected by the average demand curve marked as D_{avg}. Using the same reasoning as with local governments, the optimal average provision is shown by $Q_{c, 1\&2}$.

How do these two situations compare in terms of people's welfare? Taking the decentralized choice as the initial situation, the figure shows that people in both regions are made worse off by centralizing the decision. The people in region 1 are forced to pay (via their taxes) for a level of bus service that is too high for their preferences. The loss to a typical region 1 person is given by the triangle 'A' since this measures – for each extra increase in Q – the gap between the marginal value of the denser service and the marginal cost. The marginal value is given by the demand curve D_1 and the marginal cost is given by the *MC per person* line. Region 2 residents also lose, but for them the loss stems from the fact that they would like a denser service than is provided when decision making is centralized. In particular, area B shows their losses since it measures, for each unit reduction of Q, the gap between their marginal value (given by D_2) and the marginal cost (given by *MC per person*).

Choosing a one-size-fits-all policy leads to an inferior outcome when people have diverse preferences.

If the Q_s are chosen separately for the two regions, there is no reason to centralize the decision. It will typically be cheaper for local authorities to determine what is optimal for their region. More specifically, suppose it costs X euros more for the central authorities to get the information than it would cost local authorities. Since the decision would be the same in both cases (Q_{d1} and Q_{d2} are chosen), the centralized decision making is worse since taxpayers will have to pay the extra information-gathering cost, X.

owned and operated by separate companies versus the situation where all the buses were owned by a single company. Surely the latter would be more efficient in terms of costs.

To sum up, economies arising from joint decision making tend to favour centralization, while diversity of preferences and local information advantages favour decentralization. We turn next to another key issue that arises when the decisions made in one region affect people in other regions. In economics jargon, these are called 'spillovers'.

To understand the economics of the scale versus diversity trade-off, see Box 3.2.

Spillovers

The next major consideration guiding task allocation is 'spillovers', i.e. an economic side-effect, known in economics jargon as an 'externality'.

Many public policy choices involve multi-region effects. National defence is one extreme. The presence of an army almost anywhere in the country deters foreign invasion for the country as a whole, so all the nation's citizens benefit from the army. It would be silly in this case to have taxpayers in each city decide separately on the army's size since, in making their decision, each set of taxpayers is likely to undervalue the nationwide benefit of a slightly bigger army. This is why the size of the army is a decision that is made at the national level in almost every nation. This is an example of what are called 'positive spillovers', i.e. where a slightly higher level of a particular policy or public service in one region benefits citizens in other regions.

A similar line of reasoning works when there are negative spillovers, i.e. when one region's policy has a negative effect on other regions. A good example of this is found in taxation. The value added tax (VAT) rate is set at the national level in all EU nations, so consider why this is so. If the VAT were chosen by each region, regions might be tempted to lower their VAT rate in an attempt to lure shoppers. For example, if the VAT in the centre of Frankfurt were 25 per cent, one of its suburbs might set its VAT at, say, 15 per cent in order to draw shoppers to its shops.

Box 3.2   Economic gains from scale vs. losses from one-size-fits-all

The widespread presence of scale economies in the provision of public services – transport services, medical services, etc. – tends to favour centralization. To see this point, we refer to Fig. 3.2. The diagram focuses only on the impact of centralization on the typical region 1 individual. In the decentralized situation the marginal cost per person of a denser bus service is shown by the line marked *MC p.p. (decentralized)*. In the case of centralized service, the marginal cost is lower, namely *MC p.p. (centralized)* due to scale economies.

Figure 3.2 Scale economies and centralization

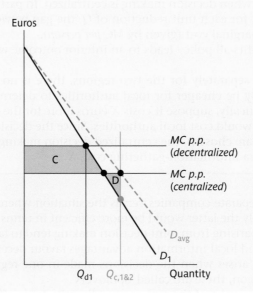

The figure shows that there is a trade-off between having the level of service precisely adjusted to local preferences and having a lower service cost due to scale economies. When the decision is local, the optimal provision is – as in Fig. 3.1 – Q_{d1}. When it is centralized, the marginal cost is lower so the intersection of marginal value of the average citizen (D_{avg}) and marginal cost is at $Q_{c,1\&2}$. As before, the level that is optimal for the average citizen is not right for region 1 people, so there is inefficiency; again, this is measured by a triangle, marked D in Fig. 3.2. This inefficiency, however, is offset by the gain from scale economies. That is, the region 1 person faces a lower marginal cost; the benefit of this is shown by the four-sided area, C. (The gain is just like a price reduction in standard consumer surplus analysis; see Chapter 4 for details.)

It appears, from the figure, that the gain from scale economies outweighs the loss from one-size-fits-all decision making. But, of course, if the scale economies were less important (i.e. the *MC* fell by less), or preferences were more diverse (i.e. the D_{avg} curve was further from the D_1 curve), then decentralization would be the superior outcome. The analysis for region 2 is quite similar and so it is omitted for the sake of brevity.

In fact, if this tax undercutting were effective enough, the suburb would actually see its tax collection rise. (If the rate reduction was more than matched by an increase in local sales, the total VAT collected by the suburb would increase.) Of course, if the suburb's tax cutting worked, Frankfurt would probably have to respond by lowering its rate to 15 per cent. In the end, both Frankfurt and the suburb would charge VAT rates below what they would like, but neither would gain shoppers by doing so. This negative spillover is so famous that it has a name: 'race to the bottom'. Again, the solution that is adopted by most nations is to set the VAT rate at the national level, but this time it is done to avoid negative spillovers.

As it turns out, cross-border shopping is not much of a problem in most parts of the EU, so there is little incentive to completely harmonize VAT rates at the EU level. The EU does, however, require VAT rates to fall within a wide band so that the maximum difference between VAT rates cannot be massive.

In summary, the existence of important negative or positive spillovers suggests that decisions made locally may be suboptimal for the nation (or EU) as a whole. The very existence of spillovers, however, does not force centralization. First, it may be possible to take account of the spillovers via cooperation among lower-level governments. This does not work for all policies, however, since cooperation is very difficult to sustain when the policies are difficult to observe directly and the spillovers are difficult to quantify. Moreover, even if decentralized cooperation does not work well, one may still resist centralization when there are big differences in preferences. A very interesting case study in this sort of fiscal federalism trade-off concerns the EU's different treatment of general VAT and extra sales taxes, or excise taxes on alcohol and tobacco. National preferences within the EU vary enormously when it comes to alcohol and tobacco, so although there is at least as much an argument for partly harmonizing these taxes as there is for harmonizing general VAT rates, the EU has never been able to do so. See Box 3.3 for details.

Box 3.3   Beer, cigarettes and VAT harmonization

Since 1 January 1993, EU travellers have been allowed to buy unlimited quantities of alcohol and tobacco (for their own use) in any Member State, and, as long as they pay taxes due in the Member State where they bought the goods, no additional taxes are due when they return home. This has posed some problems for British fiscal authorities since Britain has some of the highest 'sin' taxes in Europe.

While there has been some progress towards the harmonization of excise duties across the EU (incorporated into EC directives adopted on 19 October 1992), this effort consists of establishing specific minimum rates that are quite low. As Commons (2002) notes: 'The sheer variation in duty rates between countries made any closer form of harmonization politically infeasible.' For example, in the UK beer duty is 34p per pint (5p in France, 3p in Germany and 7p in the Netherlands), duty on a 70 cl bottle of spirits is £5.48 (£2.51 in France and £1.19 in Spain), duty on a 75 cl bottle of wine is £1.16 in the UK (2p in France and 0p in Spain), and the total excise duty on a packet of 20 cigarettes is £2.80 in the UK (£1.22 in France, £1.00 in the Netherlands and 99p in Belgium).

Such differences could, of course, lead to massive tax fraud, if, for example, all British publicans stocked up in France, claiming that their truck load of beer was for personal use. To prevent this, Britain sets indicative levels for how much alcohol and tobacco constitutes 'for personal use'. These levels are rather generous: 10 litres of spirits, 20 litres of fortified wines, 90 litres of wine, 110 litres of beer, 200 cigars, 400 cigarillos, 800 cigarettes and 1 kg of smoking tobacco. The problem has become so severe that the UK has begun to seize the vehicles used in this sort of fiscal smuggling – taking over 10,000 vehicles in 2000–01.

> The Commission felt this was too harsh and referred Britain to the EU Court. As Frits Bolkestein, European Commissioner for taxation and customs union at the time, said: 'I understand any member state's need to fight fraud but the Commission simply cannot accept penalties that are so disproportionate that they interfere with the rights given to EU consumers by the EU single market to go shopping in other Member States.' In 2006, the dispute was settled out of court. The UK modified its seizure policy and clarified its laws. For example, first-time offenders can choose between forfeiting the goods and paying a penalty.
>
> *Source:* This box is based on Commons (2002) and www.cec.org.uk

Democracy as a control mechanism

The analysis up to this point has assumed that governments are interested only in the well-being of their citizens. The next major consideration in task assignment takes a more cynical view of governments' motives.

There are perfect public servants in this world, but not all government officials and politicians are totally selfless. For example, it is quite common for politicians to systematically favour politically powerful special-interest groups – e.g. granting them tax breaks, subsidies and favourable laws – even when this is bad for the average citizen.

Because of this divergence of interests between voters and decision makers, all European nations have adopted arrangements that check the power of politicians and force governments to stay close to the interest of the people. Democracy is the most powerful of these mechanisms.

Since politicians must win approval of the citizens on a regular basis, they are reluctant to misuse their decision-making power. From this perspective, democracy can be thought of as a control mechanism. The importance of this observation is that it helps to inform the allocation of policy making among levels of government. To understand this, however, we need to think more carefully about how elections discipline politicians.

Although democratic procedures vary across European nations, the following is a stylized version that fits many instances. When a politician runs in an election, the politician or his or her party presents a package of promises to the voters. The voters choose between packages and hope that the winner will actually do what he or she promised (deviations without good reason can be punished in the next election). The fact that issues are packaged together and that voters face a limited range of packages gives politicians some leeway. That is to say, their package does not have to fully represent the best interest of the voters; it only has to be good enough to get elected. This means that parties and politicians have room to slip in policies that favour small but influential special-interest groups. Because special-interest groups tend to provide money and other support in election campaigns, skewing the package in favour of these groups tends to increase the likelihood of winning an election.

Given this logic, voters' control over their elected decision makers depends upon the breadth of the package of promises. If democracy consists only of electing national officials once every four or five years, the package of promises must include a vast range of things. This gives politicians and parties a great deal of room to undertake policies that are not in the interest of the general public. By contrast, if the election is for a town mayor, the package will be quite specific and this tends to reduce the room for special-interest politics.

This logic is important. It underpins the basic presumption that decisions should be made at the lowest practical level of government. Or, to put it differently, decisions should be made as close to the voters as possible. As mentioned in the previous chapter, the EU's 'subsidiarity principle' does just this.

Jurisdictional competition

The final element to consider also favours decentralized decision making. It is called 'jurisdictional competition'. Voters can influence the sort of government they live under in two main ways, 'voice' and 'exit'. Voice is what we just discussed – the ability to control politicians and parties by speaking up, in particular by voicing one's opinion at the ballot box. The other way is to leave the jurisdiction that imposed the policy. This is exit.

While exit is not an option for most voters at the national level, it usually is at the subnational level. For example, if someone strongly objects to a lack of, say, parks and green areas in a particular town, they could move to a different town. This is called jurisdictional competition since the fact that people can move forces decision makers to pay closer attention to the wishes of the people. By contrast, if all decisions are centralized, voters do not have the exit option. This reduces the pressure on local governments to be efficient in the provision of public services. To put this differently, even if voters rarely move, the fact that they could move if things got bad enough goes some way to ensuring that politicians keep things from going terribly wrong.

To recap, decentralization tends to improve government since it allows (or forces) regions to compete with each other in providing the best value for money in local services. In the marketplace, competition usually improves quality and reduces prices; in local government, competition provides the same sort of benefits.

3.2.2 From theory to practice

The five points discussed above provide principles rather than precise guidelines. The situation with respect to particular policies can be extremely complex, making it difficult or impossible to determine the 'correct' level of government for each task. Such debate inevitably turns on personal judgements and so takes us into an area where economists have no particular advantage. Be that as it may, it is interesting to speculate briefly on how our framework helps us to think about the EU's actual allocation of tasks between the EU level and national level.

The one thing that is clear is that subsidiarity is probably a good idea. When in doubt, allocate the task to the lowest practicable level since higher-level decisions are less subject to democratic control via voice and exit. Going further is trickier.

In the EU, the main area of centralization has been economic policies (the old first pillar), especially policies affecting the Single Market. As the discussion of the Treaty of Rome in Chapter 2 showed, virtually every policy that directly affects the competitiveness of particular industries is subject to control at the EU level. For example, import taxes, government subsidies (called state aid in EU jargon), exceptional tax benefits, and anticompetitive behaviour by firms are subject to EU-wide rules that are enforceable in the EU Court. The thinking here is that such policies are marked by important and systematic negative spillovers. When one EU nation subsidizes its firms in a particular industry, firms in other EU nations suffer from the artificially intensified competition. As in the tax example above, a likely outcome is a Prisoners' Dilemma – all EU nations end up providing subsidies, but the subsidies cancel each other out. Likewise, each nation might be tempted to introduce idiosyncratic product regulation in an attempt to favour local firms, but the end result would be a highly fragmented European market with too many small firms (see Chapter 6 for an analysis of the economics of this).

The exceptions to centralization in economic policy can also be understood in the light of our five principles. The EU does not attempt to harmonize most social policies or general labour market policies. Nor does it centralize decision making on general taxes, such as income taxes and corporate taxes. As explained in Chapter 1, general policies like these do not necessarily affect the competitiveness of particular firms and so are subject to a much lower level of negative spillovers. Moreover, national preferences for such policies are very diverse. In Spain, for example, the primary form of labour market protection for workers is employment protection legislation, i.e. laws that make it difficult to fire workers. Germany relies much more on unemployment benefits. Given this divergence of nation preferences, the losses from a one-size-fits-all policy would be likely to outweigh any gains in efficiency or avoidance of negative spillovers. Of course, one can argue with this and it is impossible to settle the argument scientifically. For example, German labour unions insisted that nationalized, one-size-fits-all wage bargaining should also apply to the Eastern Länder despite the great diversity of economic conditions, and they insisted on the same homogeneity of labour market laws.

Most non-economic policies are decided at the national level. For example, most foreign policy, defence policy, internal security and social policies are made at the national level. Of course, various nations cooperate on some of these policies – a good example is the agreement between France, Germany, Spain and the UK to produce a common military transport plane – but the decision making is allocated to the national level and cooperation is voluntary.

Roughly speaking, the old first-pillar policies (i.e. economic integration) are where there are important spillovers, where national preferences are not too great and common policies tend to benefit from scale economies. The theory of fiscal federalism thus helps us to organize our thinking about why such policies are centralized.

The old second-pillar policies – Common Foreign and Security Policies – are marked by enormous scale economies. For example, unifying all of Europe's armies would result in a truly impressive force and allow Europe to develop world-class weapon systems. However, second-pillar policies are also marked by vast differences in national preferences. Some EU members – France and the UK, for example – have a long history of sending their young men to die in foreign lands for various causes. Other EU members – such as Sweden and Ireland – shun almost any sort of armed conflict outside their own borders. Given this diversity of preferences, the gains from scale economies would be more than offset by adopting a one-size-fits-all policy. Because of this, the only common EU policies in these areas are those arrived at by common consent, i.e. by cooperation rather than centralization.

The old third-pillar policies lie somewhere between first- and second-pillar policies, both in terms of the gains from scale economies and in terms of the diversity of preferences. As discussed above, many Europeans find themselves, or their pensions, or their marriages, or their land purchases subject to multiple legal jurisdictions. Thus the uncoordinated nature of such national laws is increasingly creating negative spillovers. Moreover, as Europeans' incomes converge upwards, there is a strong tendency for the differences in their legal preferences to converge. Both reasons – narrower preference differences and more people affected by negative spillovers – can be taken as the deep reason that the Lisbon Treaty essentially merged the old first and third pillars. As explained in Chapter 2 in detail, it did this by formally removing the pillars, but it maintained a sharp distinction between supranational and intergovernmental areas of cooperation by specifically the nature of the cooperation that applies article-by-article in the Treaties.

3.3 Economical view of decision making

The previous sections looked at factors affecting the allocation of tasks between the EU and its Member States. This abstracted from the actual process by which EU-level decisions are made. In other words, we simplified away the question of how decisions were made at the EU level in order to study the issue of which decisions should be made at the EU level.

In this and subsequent sections we reverse this simplification, focusing on the question of how the EU makes decisions. In particular, we shall concentrate on how the decision-making mechanisms affect the EU's ability to act how they affect the distribution of power among EU nations and how they affect democratic 'legitimacy'.

Efficiency, power and legitimacy are inherently vague concepts. To make progress, we adopt the tactic of progressive complexity. That is, we start by taking what may seem to be a very shallow view of political actors and their motives. These simplifying assumptions allow us to develop some very precise measures of efficiency, legitimacy and national power in EU decision making. The benefit is that these precise measures permit us to comment on how efficiency and legitimacy have evolved in the EU and how they evolved with the 2004 and 2007 enlargements and how they will evolve when the Lisbon Treaty rules come into effect.

Before turning to the measures, however, we consider the decision-making rules in detail.

3.3.1 Qualified majority voting (QMV)

The EU has several different decision-making procedures; however, about 80 per cent of EU legislation is passed under what was called the 'Codecision Procedure' and is now called the 'ordinary legislative procedure' since the Lisbon Treaty came into force in 2009. This requires the Council of Ministers (as it was traditionally known – the Lisbon Treaty re-labels it as simply 'the Council') to adopt the legislation by a 'qualified majority voting' (QMV) and the European Parliament to adopt it by a simple majority. As the Parliament's voting is straightforward – the usual 50 per cent majority threshold with one vote per Member of Parliament, we focus on the Council's voting rules.

The current rules: Nice Treaty QMV

The rules governing Council of Minister voting since 2004 are those adopted by the Nice Treaty. The Lisbon Treaty will simplify these rules (more on this below), but not before 2014. Moreover, a last-minute political compromise means that an EU member can invoke the Nice Treaty rules up to 2017.

Under current QMV rules, each Member State's minister casts a certain number of votes in the Council. More populous members have more votes, but fewer than population proportionality would suggest. For example, Sweden has 10 votes and 9 million citizens while France has six times more citizens but only 29 votes; Cyprus has about 10 per cent of the Swedish population but 40 per cent as many votes (4 versus 10). See Fig. 3.3. If a proposal is to pass the Council, it must receive yes votes for members that have at least 255 of the 345 total votes, i.e. about 74 per cent. But that is not all. There are two additional thresholds – one concerning the number of yes-voters and the other concerning the share of EU population that they represent. The number-of-members threshold is 50 per cent and the population threshold is 62 per cent.

3.3.2 EU ability to act: decision-making efficiency

EU leaders have been trying to reform EU institutions in preparation for eastern enlargement since the mid-1990s. The process is now complete, but the new Lisbon-Treaty rules will not take effect until 2014 at the earliest. The goal of this long series of reform attempts has been to keep the EU's decision-making procedures 'efficient' and democratically legitimate. We deal first with decision-making efficiency.

In economics, 'efficiency' usually means an absence of waste. In the EU decision-making context, the word has come to mean 'ability to act'. While 'ability to act' is more specific than efficiency, it is still a long way from operational. For instance, on some issues the EU finds it very easy to make decisions, yet on other issues it finds it impossible to find a coalition of countries that would support a particular law. The perfect measure of efficiency would somehow predict all possible issues, decide how the members would line up into 'yes' and 'no' coalitions, and use this to develop an average measure of how easy it is to get things done in the EU. Such predictions, of course, are impossible given the uncertain and ever-changing nature of the challenges facing the EU.

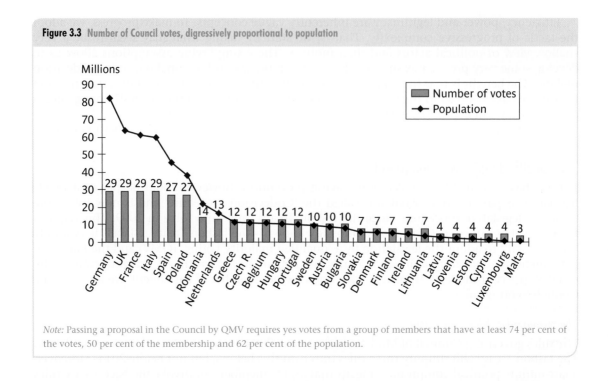

Figure 3.3 Number of Council votes, digressively proportional to population

Note: Passing a proposal in the Council by QMV requires yes votes from a group of members that have at least 74 per cent of the votes, 50 per cent of the membership and 62 per cent of the population.

An alternative approach, which we shall study here, sounds strange at first, but is really the best way of thinking systematically about the issue. Rather than trying to predict details of decision making on particular topics, we adopt a 'veil of ignorance'. That is, we focus on a randomly selected issue – random in the sense that no EU member would know whether it would be for or against the proposition.

A quantitative measure of efficiency: passage probability

The specific measure we focus on is called the 'passage probability'. The passage probability measures how easy it is to find a majority under a given voting scheme. Specifically, it is the number of all possible winning coalitions divided by the number of all possible coalitions. The idea is that if each conceivable coalition of voters is equally likely, then the measure tells us the likelihood of approving a randomly selected issue; that is why it is called the passage probability. The idea behind assuming all coalitions are equally likely is that, on a randomly selected issue, each voter is as likely to say 'yes' as he or she is to say 'no'.

To explain this concept, consider a simple example. Suppose there are only three voters, whom we call A, B and C. The first step is to see what all the possible coalitions are, i.e. all possible arrays of yes and no votes. With three voters, there are eight possible coalitions. All eight are listed in the first three columns of Table 3.2. To keep things really simple, suppose that the three nations all have ten votes. The fourth column shows the number of yes votes for each of the eight coalitions. The fifth column checks whether each coalition would win, assuming it takes 50 per cent (i.e. at least 15 votes) to pass the proposal.

The passage probability is calculated in the second to last row. With the simple equal vote allocation #1, half of all possible coalitions pass the proposal, so the passage probability is 50 per cent.

To illustrate the usefulness of the passage probability concept, consider what would happen to this organization's ability to act if the allocation of votes became more concentrated, but

Table 3.2   Passage probability in a simple example

A	B	C	Vote allocation #1		Vote allocation #2	
			10 votes each	Qualified majority? (50%)	20 votes to A 5 to B and C	Qualified majority? (50%)
Yes	Yes	Yes	30	yes	30	yes
No	Yes	Yes	20	yes	10	no
Yes	No	Yes	20	yes	25	yes
Yes	Yes	No	20	yes	25	yes
No	No	Yes	10	no	5	no
Yes	No	No	10	no	20	no
No	Yes	No	10	no	5	no
No	No	No	0	no	0	no
Passage probability (50% majority threshold)				50.0%		37.5%
Passage probability (70% majority threshold)				12.5%		37.5%

there was no change in the majority threshold. For example, say that nation A now has 20 votes and nations B and C only 5 each. Just thinking intuitively, one would be hard put to form a judgement on whether the shift from 10 votes each to the 20, 5, 5 allocation would make it harder or easier to pass a random proposal. With the passage probability, however, we see that the second allocation of votes leads to fewer ways of forming a winning coalition and so the change in vote allocation reduces the decision-making efficiency.

The second thing that affects the passage probability is the majority threshold. It is intuitively obvious that raising the threshold makes it harder to find a coalition. Comparing the last two rows confirms this intuition. For vote allocation #1, raising the threshold from 50 per cent (i.e. 15 votes) to 70 per cent (21 votes) lowers the passage probability from 50 to 12.5 per cent. However, the details matter. Note that under allocation #2, the higher threshold does not make it any harder to find winning coalitions. The point is that there are no coalitions with a number of votes that lies between the old threshold (15 votes) and the new higher threshold (21 votes).

When looking at the real EU Council, the principle is the same, but the calculations are much, much more tedious. The main point is that the number of possible yes/no coalitions among 27 votes is 2 raised to the power of 27 – which is a very big number, over 134 million. To find the passage probability, one needs a computer and the right software.

The level of the passage probability is affected by the number of members, the distribution of votes and, above all, the majority threshold. It is important to note, however, that the exact level of the passage probability is not very important. As Chapter 2 explained, most EU legislation is proposed by the European Commission, and the Commission often refrains from introducing legislation that is unlikely to pass.

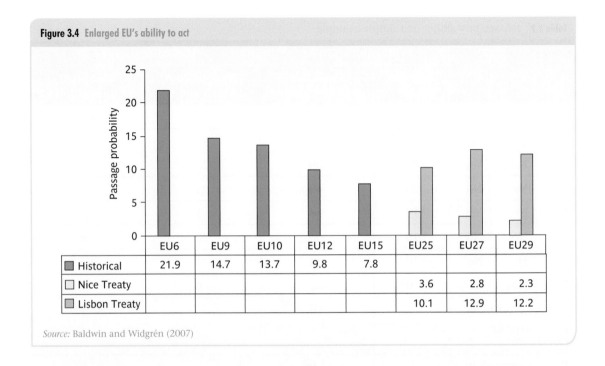

Figure 3.4 Enlarged EU's ability to act

	EU6	EU9	EU10	EU12	EU15	EU25	EU27	EU29
■ Historical	21.9	14.7	13.7	9.8	7.8			
☐ Nice Treaty						3.6	2.8	2.3
☐ Lisbon Treaty						10.1	12.9	12.2

Source: Baldwin and Widgrén (2007)

Historical efficiency and Treaty of Nice reforms

It is interesting to see how the EU's efficiency has changed over time. Above all, it is interesting to see how enlargement affects the EU's decision-making efficiency.

The five leftmost bars in Fig. 3.4 show the passage probability for qualified majority voting (QMV) in the historical EUs with 6, 9, 10, 12 and 15 members. These indicate that, although efficiency has been declining, past enlargements have only moderately hindered decision-making efficiency. The 1994 enlargement lowered the probability only slightly, from 10 to 8 per cent, and the Iberian expansion lowered it from 14 to 10 per cent. The figures also hide the fact that the Single European Act, which took effect in 1987, greatly boosted efficiency by shifting many more decisions from unanimity to qualified majority voting.

Notice that the 2004 enlargement greatly reduces the passage probability. This is true even with the Nice Treaty voting reforms (which were supposed to maintain the enlarged EU's ability to act). In fact, the Nice Treaty's complex rules made matters slightly worse than they would have been with no reform at all. The results show that accepting 12 newcomers without reform would dramatically reduce efficiency, cutting the current passage probability by something like a third, from 7.8 to 3.6 per cent.

This point, which became widely accepted after 2001, was why EU leaders asked the European Convention to reconsider the EU's decision-making rules – the request that eventually led to the Lisbon Treaty's new double majority rule for the Council. Note that the decision-making rules in the Parliament and Commission were not viewed as problematic and thus were not reformed in the Constitution or the Lisbon Treaty.

The role of the Commission and Parliament

In the mainstay legislative process, the ordinary legislative procedure (i.e. the old codecision procedure), both the Commission and the Parliament play critical roles. But they do not really affect the decision-making efficiency.

The Commission proposes legislation and drafts the first version. This gives it a good deal of power, as will be discussed in more depth below. But it has always had this power, so the increasing difficulty of passing EU legislation is not related to the Commission's role. A more plausible link would be with the enlargement of the European Parliament. After all, if enlarging the Council makes it harder to pass laws, doesn't enlarging the Parliament do the same thing?

To address this, it is necessary to realize a special feature of the 50 per cent majority rule that the Parliament uses. When the winning coalition needs only half the votes, the passage probability is unrelated to the number of voters. Upon reflection, this is obvious. There is an almost unfathomable number of possible yes/no coalitions in the Parliament with its 785 members (2 raised to the power of 785 is something like 2 with 236 zeros after it), but when you only need half to win, it is clear that half of all coalitions will be winners. Thus the passage probability is always 50 per cent regardless of the number of voters.[1] This is why we can ignore the Parliament when considering the passage probability.

Of course, in the real world things are much more complex than the passage probability, but this concept provides a good point of departure for judging how various things like enlargement and voting reform can affect the EU's capacity to act.

3.4 The distribution of power among EU members

The next aspect of EU decision making that we address is the distribution of power among EU members. As with efficiency, there is no perfect measure of power. The tactic we adopt relies on the Law of Large Numbers. That is, we look to see how likely it is that each member's vote is crucial on a randomly drawn issue. Before turning to the calculations, however, we lay out our specific definition of power.

For our purposes, power means influence, or, more precisely, the ability to influence EU decisions by being in a position to make or break a winning coalition in the Council. Of course, no one has absolute power in the EU, so we focus on the likelihood that a Member State will be influential. On some things Germany's vote will be crucial, on others it will be irrelevant, and the same goes for all other members. What determines how likely it is that a particular nation will be influential?

The most direct and intuitive measure of political power is national voting shares in the Council. Under current EU rules, each Member State has a fixed number of votes in the Council. Up to the 2004 enlargement, 87 Council-of-Minister votes were divided among the 15 EU nations, with large nations receiving more votes than small ones (see Chapter 2 for details). It seems intuitively plausible that nations with more votes are more likely to be influential on average, so the first power measure to try is a nation's share of Council votes. But how can we tell if this power measure captures anything real? See Box 3.4.

3.4.1 Empirical evidence on power measures' relevance

One cannot measure a nation's power in EU decision making directly, but the exercise of power does leave some 'footprints' in the data. Budget allocations are one manifestation of power that is both observable and quantifiable. To check whether our power measure is useful, we see if it can help to explain the budget allocation puzzles we discussed in Chapter 2.

To understand why our power measure should be related to outward signs of power such as the budgetary spending allocation, we need to briefly review the budget process explained in detail in Chapter 2 and then discuss 'back scratching' and 'horse trading'.

---

[1] This is not exactly true with an odd number of voters but the difference is negligible.

Box 3.4   Why Parliament reform does not affect national power distributions

Most EU legislation these days must be approved by both the Council and the Parliament. As it turns out, the allocation of seats in the European Parliament does not affect national power, per se. The reason rests on three facts: (i) the national distribution of Council votes and MEP seats is quite similar, as Fig. 3.5 shows; (ii) to pass the Council, a proposal must garner at least 71 per cent of votes; and (iii) to pass the Parliament, a proposal needs to win only half the MEP votes.

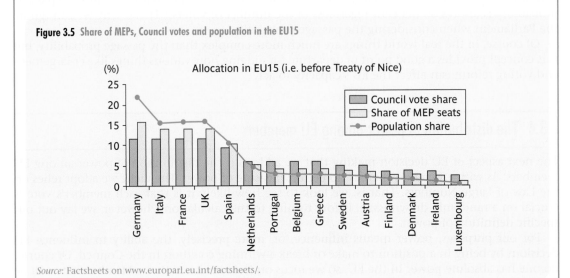

Figure 3.5 Share of MEPs, Council votes and population in the EU15

Source: Factsheets on www.europarl.eu.int/factsheets/.

To illustrate how these three facts affect the Parliament's power from a purely national perspective, we must cover a few preliminaries. First, we start with a simple assumption – that MEPs act as national representatives and indeed that their votes are controlled directly by national governments (obviously this is false, but going to this extreme helps to build intuition for more realistic cases). Second, recall that we define power as the ability to break a winning coalition, so the question is: 'Can a nation use the votes of its MEPs to block a coalition that it cannot otherwise block?' If the answer is 'no', then the votes of MEPs do not affect a nation's power, even under the extreme assumption that MEP votes are controlled by governments. And, of course, if national power is not affected by MEP votes when they are directly controlled, national power is certainly not affected when the MEPs vote by their own conscience. Finally, we assume that each nation's share of Council votes is identical to its share of MEP votes (rather than just similar). Under these assumptions, we can think of the actual procedure as a double majority system. To pass, a proposal needs to attract the votes of Member States that have at least 50 per cent of MEP votes, and 71 per cent of Council votes.

Now here is the main point. The first criterion is redundant since the Council vote threshold is higher than the MEP threshold. That is, since the distributions of Council and MEP votes are assumed to be identical, any coalition that has 71 per cent of Council votes will automatically have 71 per cent of MEP votes, which is plainly more than the 50 per cent necessary. Some careful thought and a little mental gymnastics reveal the implications of this for national power; there are no instances when a nation's MEP votes increase its power to block. In every instance where it can block on the basis of MEP votes, it can also block on the basis of Council votes.

Even under a more realistic view of the process, the same conclusion holds. The fact that the distribution of MEP votes is similar to the distribution of Council votes, teamed with the fact that the Council threshold is much higher than the Parliament's threshold, means that MEPs' votes could never increase a nation's ability to block, even if the MEPs voted on strictly national lines.

Interestingly, this suggests one indirect reason why the Parliament has tended to form cross-national coalitions. If they acted on purely national lines, MEPs would, on typical issues (i.e. where the national government accurately represents the national view), act as rubber-stampers. If they form cross-national coalitions, they may bring something new to the process.

An important caveat to all this is the fact that EU nations are made up of diverse groups. Since some groups are less well represented in their nation's government than they are in the European Parliament (e.g. labour unions when a conservative government is in power), having more seats means that these special-interest groups will have a larger say in EU decision making.

For a more detailed analysis, see Bindseil and Hantke (1997).

The annual budget must be passed by both the Council and the European Parliament (EP). These annual budgets, however, are constrained by medium-term budget plans called 'Financial Perspectives' (the current one covers 2007–13). The Financial Perspectives require unanimity in the Council, but the annual budgets are passed on the basis of a qualified majority. For both the Financial Perspectives and the annual budgets, EP decision making is on the basis of a simple majority. As it turns out, the EP does not matter from a national power perspective. This notion is explained in detail in Box 3.4. For this reason, we focus solely on vote shares in the Council.

As already pointed out, about 80 per cent of Council decisions are made on the basis of qualified majority voting. Since the Council decides many issues each year, and members do not care dearly about all of them, countries tend to trade their votes on issues that they view as minor in exchange for support on an issue that they view as major, even if the two issues are totally unrelated. This sort of natural activity is referred to by the colourful names of 'back scratching' and 'horse trading'.

Now that we have discussed the background, we can turn to the main reasoning. Citizens in EU nations, or at least some citizens, benefit when EU money is spent in their district. Successful politicians, responding to the desires of their citizens, use their political clout to direct money homewards. For example, suppose that countries ask for a little 'gift' each time they find themselves in a position that is critical to a winning coalition. In the data, the 'gift' ends up as EU spending, but the actual mechanism could be subtle, say a more favourable treatment in the allocation of EU subsidies to hillside farmers, a more generous allocation of milk quotas or inclusion of reindeer meat in the CAP's price support mechanism. In this light, it seems natural that a country's power measure would equal its expected fraction of all special gifts handed out. If one goes to the cynical extreme and views the whole EU budget as nothing more than a pile of 'gifts', then our power measures should meet the EU's budget allocation perfectly. If high-minded principles such as helping out disadvantaged regions also matter, then the power measure should only partially explain the spending pattern.

As it turns out, voting power goes a long way towards solving the 'puzzle' of EU budget allocation discussed in Chapter 2. Statistical evidence by Kauppi and Widgrén (2004) shows that, although standard elements do matter – such as a member's dependency on farming and its relative poverty – voting power always turns out to be an influential determinant of budget allocations.

3.4.2 Vote shares as a power measure: the shortcomings

While voting shares are a natural measure of power, they have problems. To illustrate the potential pitfalls of vote weights as a power measure, consider a 'toy model' of the Council. Suppose there are only three countries in this toy model – imaginatively called A, B and C – and they have 40, 40 and 20 votes, respectively. Decisions are based on a simple majority rule (+50 per cent to win). If we used voting weights as a measure of power, we would say that countries A and B, each with their 40 votes, were twice as powerful as C with its 20 votes. This is wrong.

With a bit of reflection you can convince yourself that all three nations are equally powerful in this toy Council. The point is that any winning coalition requires two nations, but any two nations will do. Likewise, any pair of nations can block anything. As a consequence, all three nations are equally powerful in the sense that they are equally likely to make or break a winning coalition.

The level of the majority threshold can also be important for power. For example, continuing with our toy model, raising the majority rule from 50 to 75 per cent would strip nation C of all power. The only winning coalition that C would belong to is the grand coalition A&B&C, but here C would not be able to turn it into a losing one by leaving the coalition. Therefore C's vote can have no influence on the outcome. Again, vote shares in this example would give a very incorrect view of power.

More generally, power – i.e. the ability to make or break a winning coalition – depends upon a complex interaction of the majority threshold and exact distribution of votes. Indeed, the useless vote-situation in which nation C found itself in our second example actually occurred in the early days of the EU. See Box 3.5 for details.

Box 3.5 Luxembourg's useless vote, 1958–73

The 1957 Treaty of Rome laid down the rules for qualified majority voting in the EEC6. The big three – Germany, France and Italy – got 4 votes each, Belgium and the Netherlands got 2 each, and Luxembourg got 1. The minimum threshold for a qualified majority was set at 12 of the 17 total votes.

A little bit of thought shows that the Treaty writers did not think hard enough about this. As you can easily confirm, Luxembourg's 1 vote never matters. Any coalition (group of 'yes' voters) that has enough votes to win can always win with or without Luxembourg. According to formal power measures, this means that Luxembourg had little power over issues decided on a QMV basis. As Felsenthal and Machover (2001) write: 'This didn't matter all that much, because the Treaty of Rome stipulated that QMV would not be used until 1966; and even in 1966–72 it was only used on rare occasions. Still, it seems a bit of a blunder.' All changed from 1973 on when the weights were altered to allow for the accession of Britain, Denmark and Ireland. Indeed, since then Luxembourg's votes have turned out to be crucial in a surprisingly large number of coalitions. Maybe that is why Luxembourg has the highest receipt per capita in the EU despite being the richest nation by far.

Source: This box is based on the excellent webbook, Felsenthal and Machover (2001), which provides a much better in-depth look at voting theory.

Simple counterexamples such as these led to the development of several more sophisticated power indices. We shall focus on the 'Normalized Banzhaf Index'.

3.4.3 Power to break a winning coalition: the Normalized Banzhaf Index

In plain English, the Normalized Banzhaf Index (NBI) gauges how likely it is that a nation finds itself in a position to 'break' a winning coalition on a randomly selected issue. By way of criticism, note that the set-up behind the NBI provides only a shallow depiction of a real-world voting process. For instance, the questions of who sets the voting agenda, how coalitions are formed and how intensively each country holds its various positions are not considered. In a sense, the equal probability of each coalition occurring and each country switching its vote is meant to deal with this shallowness. The idea is that all of these things would average out over a large number of votes on a broad range of issues. Thus, this measure of power is really a very long-term concept. Another way of looking at it is as a measure of power in the abstract. It tells us how powerful a country is likely to be on a randomly chosen issue. Of course, on particular issues, various countries may be much more or much less powerful.

The easiest way to understand this concept more deeply is to calculate it for our simple example in Table 3.2. To make it interesting, we take the uneven vote allocation case (#2) and assume a 70 per cent majority threshold, so winning takes 21 votes. As before, we line up all eight possible coalitions and decide which are the winning ones (Table 3.3). These are the first three. Then we ask who the critical players are in these winning coalitions – critical in the sense that they would turn the winning coalition into a losing coalition if they changed their vote. In the first coalition, only A is critical since the defection of either B or C would not change the outcome; nation A and the remaining other nation would have enough votes to win. In the second and third coalitions, where the majority is narrower, both nations are critical, namely A and C in the second and A and B in the third.

Thus there are five situations where a nation would find itself critical. Nation A finds itself in this situation three of the five times, while B and C are critical in only one of the five times. Thus, in this sense, A is more powerful than B and C. The NBI for A is three-fifths, while it is one-fifth for B and C.

The calculation of NBI for all EU members is a topic that may fascinate some readers, but it is not essential to our study of EU decision making, so we relegate its discussion to Box 3.6.

Table 3.3 Critical players with 70% majority threshold

A	B	C	Yes votes	70% majority?	Critical player(s)
Yes	Yes	Yes	30	yes	A
Yes	No	Yes	25	yes	A, C
Yes	Yes	No	25	yes	A, B
Yes	No	No	20	no	
No	Yes	Yes	10	no	
No	No	Yes	5	no	
No	Yes	No	5	no	
No	No	No	0	no	

Box 3.6   Calculating the Normalized Banzhaf Index (NBI)

The mechanical calculation of the NBI is easy to describe and requires nothing more than some patience and a PC with lots of horsepower. To work it out, one asks a computer to look at all possible coalitions (i.e. all conceivable line-ups of yes and no votes) and identify the winning coalitions. Note that listing all possible coalitions is easy to do by hand for low numbers of voters; in a group of 2 voters there are only 4, in a group of 3 there are 8. However, the general formula for the number of all possible coalitions for a group of n voters is 2^n, so determining which coalitions are winners by hand quickly becomes impractical; in the EU15, 32,768 coalitions have to be checked. In the EU27, the number is over 134 million. The computer's next task is to work out all the ways that each winning coalition could be turned into a loser by the defection of a single nation. Finally, the computer calculates the number of times each nation could be a 'deal breaker' as a fraction of the number of times that any country could be a deal breaker. The theory behind this is that the Council decides on a vast array of issues, so the NBI tells us how likely it is that a particular nation will be critical on a randomly selected issue.

For the EU15, it turns out that the theoretically superior power measure (NBI) is not very different from the rough-and-ready national vote-share measure. The measures are also quite similar for EU27. Readers who distrust sophisticated concepts should find their confidence in the Banzhaf measure bolstered by this similarity – and the same applies to readers who distrust rough-and-ready measures.

3.4.4 Power shifts in 2014 (or 2017)

The fate of the Lisbon Treaty was finally settled in 2009; however, the new voting rules will not come into effect until 2014. Moreover, at the insistence of Poland the new voting rules can be suspended at the wish of a single member up to 2017 (TFEU Protocol No. 35); if this suspension is requested, the old Nice rules apply.

The NBI is a useful tool for understanding Poland's problems with the Lisbon rules and for understanding many of the struggles among Member States over EU institutional reforms – past, present and future. A good example can be found in the switch between the Nice Treaty rules (which are in effect today) and the Lisbon Treaty voting rules.

As pointed out in Chapter 1, the Nice, Constitutional and Lisbon Treaties all had a very hard time getting accepted by EU leaders. Much of the difficulty turned on the voting rules in the Council. Specifically, the voting rule proposed by Giscard d'Estaing was included in the Italian President's draft presented to the European Council in December 2003. This was rejected for many reasons, but the main sticking point was the power changes implied, especially for Spain and Poland. Council voting rules were also one of the hardest issues in the 2004 discussions that finalized the Constitutional Treaty. Finally, after the Constitution had been abandoned, the deal on its replacement (Lisbon Treaty) was hung up on the Council voting issue right until the end.

Switching from the current rules in place (those in the Nice Treaty) to the Lisbon Treaty rules changes the power distribution between large and small nations. The Lisbon Treaty would grant some additional power to the smallest states, but it would provide a huge boost to Germany's power. Since power is measured by shares and shares must add to 100 per cent, the German and tiny-nation power gains must be paid for by the other members. As Fig. 3.6 shows, Spain and Poland will be the big losers, but the middle-sized EU Member States will also suffer from the Lisbon rules.

Figure 3.6 Winners and losers under the Nice rules and Lisbon voting rules

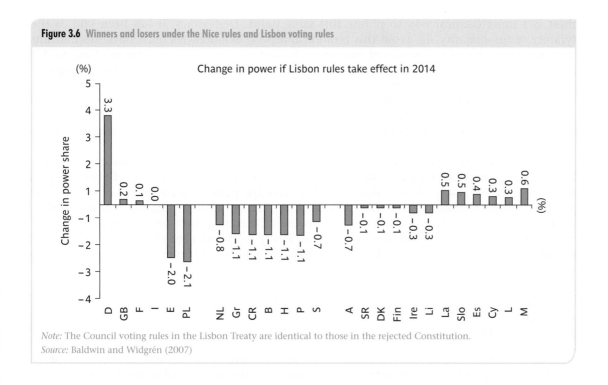

Note: The Council voting rules in the Lisbon Treaty are identical to those in the rejected Constitution.
Source: Baldwin and Widgrén (2007)

3.5 Legitimacy in EU decision making

The EU is a truly unique organization. Nowhere else in the world has so much national sovereignty been transferred to a supranational body. As Chapter 1 pointed out, the massive death and destruction of two world wars is what led the EU's founders to contemplate this transfer, but the continual willingness of the current generation of Europeans to accept it depends upon much more practical considerations. One consideration is the EU's ability to deliver results, but another important consideration is the democratic legitimacy of the EU's decision-making process.

3.5.1 Thinking about democratic legitimacy

What makes a decision-making system legitimate? This is a difficult question so it helps to start with an extreme and obviously illegitimate voting scheme and to think about why it seems illegitimate. Almost every European would view as illegitimate a system that allowed only landowning males the right to vote. Why? Because those without votes would find it unjust. And if the landowning men were forward looking, they would also find it illegitimate since they or their male offspring might one day lose their land. In short, a good way to think about legitimacy is to apply the 'in the other person's shoes' rule. A system is legitimate if all individuals would be happy with any other individual's allocation of voting power, which, if you think about it, requires equality. Equal power per citizen is thus a very natural legitimacy principle.

But what constitutes a citizen? In the EU there are two answers: nations and people. The EU is a union of states, so each state is a citizen and should thus have equal voting power. The EU is also a union of people, so people are citizens and so each person should have equal voting power. This makes it impossible to apply the equality principle in a simple manner. Note that there is a more classical way to phrase this same point. Democracy, it has been said, is the tyranny of the majority. To avoid this tyrannical aspect, democracies must have mechanisms that protect the rights and wishes of minorities. Indeed, many nations provide mechanisms for giving disadvantaged groups larger than proportional shares of power, but the starting point for such departures is one vote per person. In the EU, the over-weighting of small nations' votes was one such mechanism. For example, equality of power per person would grant Germany 2000 per cent more power than Ireland; equality per member would grant Luxembourgers 160 times more power per person than Germans. Given the dual-union nature of the EU, neither extreme is legitimate.

Using the NBI described above, we have a very precise (albeit crude) measure of 'power per person' and 'power per nation'. The 'fair' power distribution for the Union-of-States view is trivial; in the EU27, each member should get 1/27th of the power. For the Union-of-People view power should be distributed such that each EU citizen has equal power regardless of nationality. As it turns out, the Nice Treaty voting rules favoured the equal-power-per-person view (since it shifted power to big nations). The Constitutional Treaty rules had a less clear-cut impact since it greatly boosted Germany's power, but also boosted the power of EU members with populations below that of a medium-large city.

3.6 Summary

Just to continue to operate, the EU must make a steady stream of decisions to adjust to the ever-changing economic and political landscape. This chapter looked at the EU decision-making process from two perspectives. First, it considered the EU current allotment of 'competences' between the EU level and national governments of its members. In terms of actual practices and principles, the key points were:

* Policy making is categorized into areas where the EU has 'exclusive competence', i.e. where the decision is made only at the EU level; areas where competence is shared; areas where the EU can undertake supporting, coordinating or complementary actions; and areas where the EU has no competence, i.e. where decisions are made only at the national or sub-national level.

* The allocation of policy areas to these categories is determined by the Treaties and, when necessary, by decision of the EU Court. This allocation, however, is blurred since the Treaties do not always refer to specific fields. Sometimes they refer only to areas by functional description, e.g. the internal market, which themselves are only vaguely defined (or at least vague from a legalistic perspective). To clarify the allocation, the EU operates on the principle of subsidiarity and proportionality, which says that unless there is a good reason for allocating a task to the EU level, all tasks should be allocated to national or sub-national governments, and even then the EU should take only the minimum necessary action. The old three-pillar structure of the EU helped to clarify the allocation, namely first-pillar (Community pillar) issues were under EU competence while second- and third-pillar issues were not. The Lisbon Treaty removed the pillars, but essentially merged the old third and first pillar into one supranational area while keeping the old second pillar (foreign and defence policy) as intergovernmental.

The chapter also presented a framework for thinking about how tasks should be allocated between various levels of government (theory of fiscal federalism). This framework stresses four trade-offs that suggest whether a particular decision should be centralized or not:

* Diversity and information costs favour decentralized decision making.
* Scale economies favour centralization.
* Democracy-as-a-control-device favours decentralization.
* Jurisdictional competition favours decentralization.

The second part of the chapter considered the EU decision-making process in more detail, focusing on efficiency (i.e. the EU's ability to act), national power shares and democratic legitimacy. These three concepts are inherently vague, but the chapter assumes a series of simplifications that enable us to present precise measures of all three. Of course, the necessary simplifications mean that the resulting measures provide only shallow measures of efficiency, power and legitimacy, but at least the measures permit a concrete departure point for further discussion. These measures were:

* *Efficiency*. We measured efficiency by the 'passage probability', i.e. the likelihood that a randomly selected issue would win a 'yes' vote in the Council. We showed that enlargement has continually lowered the EU's passage probability, but that the 2004 enlargement lowered it by a large and unprecedented amount. We also saw that the voting reforms in the Treaty of Nice will make matters worse, even though they were intended to maintain decision-making efficiency.

* *National power distributions*. We showed that the vote shares of small nations far exceed their population shares. Interpreting vote shares as a measure of power, this says that power in the EU is biased towards small nations. We also showed that this allocation of power goes a long way to explain why actual EU spending patterns may seem strange, i.e. that several rich nations receive above-average receipts per capita. This section also presents a more sophisticated measure of power called the Normalized Banzhaf Index; it measures the probability that a given nation will find itself in a position where it can break a winning coalition.

* *Legitimacy*. This is by far the vaguest of the three concepts. The approach we adopt is to check whether the allocation of votes in the EU's Council lines up against two notions of legitimacy. If the EU is viewed as a Union-of-People, a natural yardstick is equal power per citizen. If the EU is viewed as a Union-of-States, the natural metric is equal power per Member State. Under the principle of equal power per EU citizen, the mathematics of voting tells us that this requires that the Council's votes per country rise with the square root of the country's population. The benchmark of equal power per EU Member State requires an equal number of votes per nation.

Self-assessment questions

1 List the main trade-offs stressed by the theory of fiscal federalism. Discuss how the tension between negative spillovers and diversity can explain the fact that the EU has adopted only very limited harmonization of social policies. (Hint: See Annex A of Chapter 1.)

2 In many European nations, the trend for the past couple of decades has been to decentralize decision making from the national level to the provincial or regional level. How could you explain this trend in terms of the theory of fiscal federalism?

3 Using the actual Council votes that came into force after the 2004 enlargement, list five blocking coalitions that you might think of as 'likely'. Do this using the Nice Treaty definition of a qualified majority. Do the same using the qualified majority definition proposed in the draft Constitutional Treaty.

4 The formal power measure discussed in the chapter assumes that each voter has an equal probability of saying 'yes' or 'no' on a random issue, and that the votes of the various voters are uncorrelated. That is, the likelihood that voter A says 'yes' on a particular issue is unrelated to whether voter B says 'yes'. However, in many situations, the votes of a group of voters will be correlated. For example, poor EU members are all likely to have similar views on issues concerning spending in poor regions. Work out how this correlation changes the distribution of power (defined as likelihood that a particular voter can break a winning coalition). To be concrete, assume that there are five voters (A, B, C, D and E), that each has 20 votes, that the majority rule is 51 per cent, and that A and B always vote the same way.

5 Using the definition of legitimacy proposed in the text (equal power per person), try to determine whether the US Congress is 'legitimate'. Note that the US Congress has two houses: the Senate and the House of Representatives. In the Senate, each of the 50 states has two Senators, while the number of Representatives per state is proportional to the state's population.

Essay questions

1 Obtain a copy of the Constitutional Treaty produced and use the theory of fiscal federalism to discuss the appropriateness of the allocation of competences between the EU and Member States.

2 Using the QMV voting weights in the EEC6 (see Box 3.5), calculate all possible coalitions, i.e. combinations of 'yes' and 'no' votes among the Six. (Hint: There are 26 = 64 of them.) Identify the winning coalitions and find the passage probability.

3 The 2004 enlargement greatly increased the diversity of preferences inside the EU. Use the theory of fiscal federalism to discuss how this change might suggest a different allocation of competences between the EU and the Member States.

4 Discuss how 'enhanced cooperation' agreements (see Chapter 2 for details) fit into the theory of fiscal federalism. Do you think the increase in the diversity of preferences in the EU stemming from the 2004 enlargement will make these agreements more or less attractive to Member States?

5 The Constitutional Treaty produced by the European Convention was first released in draft form in May 2003. Download this draft and compare the Council of Minister's voting scheme to the scheme in the final version in terms of efficiency and legitimacy.

6 Comparing the Nice Treaty's Declaration on the Future of Europe and the Laeken Declaration's list of questions on the allocation of competences to the Constitutional Treaty's Title III Part I, write an essay on how well the European Convention accomplished its task on the competence issue.

Further reading: the aficionado's corner

More wide-ranging introductions to fiscal federalism applied to the European Union can be found in:

Dewatripont, M. et al. (1995) *Flexible Integration: Towards a More Effective and Democratic Europe*, CEPR Monitoring European Integration 6, CEPR, London.

Berglof, E. et al. (2003) *Built to Last: A Political Architecture for Europe*, CEPR Monitoring European Integration 12, CEPR, London.

The latter includes a general discussion that applies the theory to the Constitutional Treaty.

For an opinionated view of what decisions should be allocated to the EU, see:

Alesina, A. and Wacziarg, R. (1999), *Is Europe Going too Far?*, Carnegie-Rochester Conference on Public Policy. Although this contains several factual errors concerning EU law and policies, it contains a highly cogent application of the theory of fiscal federalism to decision making in the EU.

To learn more about formal measures of power and legitimacy, see:

Felsenthal, D. and M. Machover (2001) *Enlargement of the EU and Weighted Voting in the Council*, LSE webbook on www.lse.ac.uk.

For historical power distributions, see:

Laruelle, A. and M. Widgrén (1998) 'Is the allocation of voting power among EU Member States fair?', *Public Choice*, 94: 317–39.

See also:

Baldwin, R. (1994) *Towards an Integrated Europe*, CEPR, London.

Baldwin, R., E. Berglof, F. Giavazzi and M. Widgrén (2001) *Nice Try: Should the Treaty of Nice be Ratified?*, CEPR Monitoring European Integration 11, CEPR, London.

Begg, D. et al. (1993) *Making Sense of Subsidiarity: How Much Centralization for Europe?*, CEPR Monitoring European Integration 4, CEPR, London.

Peet, J. and K. Ussher (1999) *The EU Budget: An Agenda for Reform?*, CER Working Paper, February.

Useful websites

Extensive explanation and use of formal voting measures can be found on http://powerslave.val.utu.fi.

References

Baldwin, R. and M. Widgrén (2007). 'Pandora's (Ballot) Box', CEPR Policy Insight No.4, www.cepr.org/pubs/policyinsights.

Bindseil, U. and C. Hantke (1997) 'The power distribution in decision making among EU Member States', *European Journal of Political Economy*, 13: 171–85.

Borchandt, K.-D. (2010) *The ABC of European Union Law*. Download from http://eur-lex.europa.eu/en/editorial/abc_toc_r1.htm

Commons (2002) 'Crossborder shopping and smuggling', House of Commons Library, Research Paper 02/40, London.

Felsenthal, D. and M. Machover (2001) *Enlargement of the EU and Weighted Voting in the Council*, LSE webbook on www.lse.ac.uk.

Kauppi, H. and M. Widgrén (2004) 'What determines EU decision making? Needs, power or both?', *Economic Policy*, 19(39): 221–6.

Part II

The Microeconomics of Economic Integration

Part II

The Microeconomics of
Economic Integration

Chapter 4

Essential microeconomic tools

> *Everything should be made as simple as possible, but not simpler.*
>
> Albert Einstein

Chapter Contents

Introduction

This chapter presents the tools that we shall need when we begin our study of European economic integration in the next chapter. The tools are simple because we make a series of assumptions that greatly reduce the complexity of economic interactions.

The primary simplification in this chapter concerns the behaviour of firms. In particular, all firms are assumed to be 'perfectly competitive', i.e. we assume that firms take as given the prices they observe in the market. Firms, in other words, believe that they have no impact on prices and that they could sell as much as they want at the market price. A good way of thinking about this assumption is to view each firm as so small that it believes that its choice of output has no impact on market prices. This is obviously a very rough approximation since even medium-sized firms – the Danish producer of Lego toys or the Dutch brewer of Heineken, for example – realize that the amount they can sell is related to the price they charge.

The second key simplification concerns technology, in particular scale economies. Scale economies refer to the way that per unit cost (average cost) falls as a firm produces more units. Almost every industry is subject to some sort of falling average cost, so considering them (in Chapter 6) will be important, but a great deal of simplification can be gained by ignoring them. This simplification, in turn, allows us to master the essentials before adding in more complexity in subsequent chapters.

4.1 Preliminaries I: supply and demand diagrams

Assessing many economic aspects of European integration is made clearer with the help of a simple yet flexible diagram with which to determine the price and volume of imports, as well as the level of domestic consumption and production. The diagram we use – the 'import supply and import demand diagram' – is based on straightforward supply and demand analysis. But to begin from the beginning, we quickly review where demand and supply curves come from. Note that this section assumes that readers have had some exposure to supply and demand analysis; our treatment is intended as a review rather than an introduction. Readers who find it too brief should consult an introductory economics textbook such as Mankiw (2011).

Well-prepared readers may want to skip this section, moving straight on to Section 4.2.

4.1.1 Demand curves and marginal utility

A demand curve shows how much consumers would buy of a particular good at any particular price. Generally speaking, consumers strive to spend their money in a way that maximizes their material well-being. Their demand curve is thus based on some sort of optimization exercise. To see this, the left-hand panel of Fig. 4.1 plots the 'marginal utility' curve for a typical consumer, i.e. the 'happiness' (measured in euros) that consumers would get from consuming an extra unit of the good given that they are already consuming a certain number of units. For example, if we are considering the demand for cups of coffee, the marginal utility curve shows how much extra joy a consumer gets from having one more cup starting from any given number of cups already consumed. Typically the extra joy from an extra cup falls with the number of cups bought per day. For example, if the consumer buys very few cups of coffee per day, say c' in the diagram, the gain from buying an extra one is likely to be pretty high, for example mu' in the diagram. If, however, the consumer buys lots of cups already, then the gain from one more is likely to be much lower. This is shown by the pair, c'' and mu''.

This marginal utility curve allows us to work out how much the consumer would buy at any given price. Suppose the consumer could buy as many cups as she likes at the price p^*. How many would she buy? If the consumer is wise, and we assume she is, she will buy cups of coffee up to the point where the last one bought is just barely worth the price. In the diagram, this level of purchase is given by c^* since the marginal benefit (utility) from buying an extra cup exceeds the cost of doing so (the price) for all levels of purchase up to c^*. At this point, the consumer finds that additional cups would not be worth the price. For example, the marginal utility from buying c^* plus one cups of coffee would be below p^*. As usual, one gets the market demand for cups of coffee by adding all consumers' individual marginal utility curves horizontally (e.g. if the price is p^* and there are 100 identical consumers, market demand will be 100 times c^*).

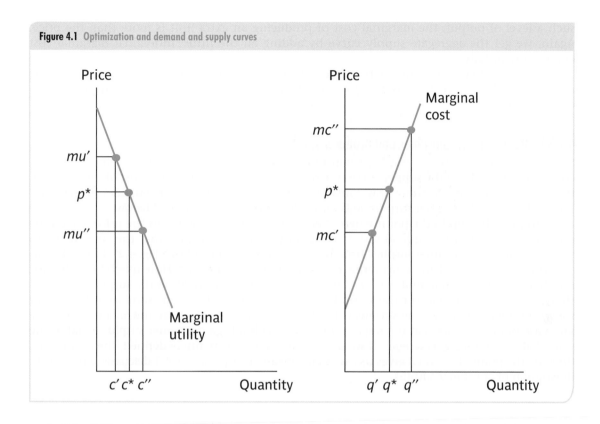

Figure 4.1 Optimization and demand and supply curves

A key point to retain from this is that the price that consumers face reflects the marginal utility of consuming a little more.

4.1.2 Supply curves and marginal costs

Derivation of the supply curve follows a similar logic, but here the optimization is done by firms. The right-hand panel of Fig. 4.1 shows the 'marginal cost' curve facing a typical firm (assume they are all identical for the sake of simplicity), i.e. the extra cost involved in making one more unit of the good. While the marginal cost of production in the real world often declines with the scale of production, allowing for this involves consideration of scale economies and these, in turn, introduce a whole range of complicating factors that would merely clutter the analysis at this stage. To keep it simple, we assume that firms are operating at a point where the marginal cost is upward sloped, i.e. that the cost of producing an extra unit rises as the total number of units produced rises. The curve in the diagram shows, for example, that it costs mc' to produce one more unit when the production level (e.g. the number of cups of coffee per day) is q'. This is less than the cost, mc'', of producing an extra unit when the firm is producing q'' units per year.

Using this curve we can determine the firm's supply behaviour. Presuming that the firm wants to maximize profit, the firm will supply goods up to the point where the marginal cost just equals the price. For example, if the price is p^*, the firm will want to supply q^* units. Why? If the firm offered one less than q^* units, it would be missing out on some profit. After all, at that level of output, the price the firm would receive for the good, p^*, exceeds the marginal cost of producing it. Likewise, the firm would not want to supply any more than q^* since, for such a level of output, the marginal cost of producing an extra unit is more than the price. Again, we get the aggregate supply curve by adding all the firms' individual marginal cost curves horizontally.

A key point here is that under perfect competition, the price facing producers reflects the marginal production cost, i.e. the cost of producing one more unit than the firm produces in equilibrium.

4.1.3 Welfare analysis: consumer and producer surplus

Since the demand curve is based on consumers' evaluation of the happiness they get from consuming a good and the supply curve is based on firms' evaluation of the cost of producing it, the curves can be used to show how consumers and firms are affected by changes in the price. The tools we use, 'consumer surplus' and 'producer surplus', are described below.

Consumers buy up to the point where their marginal utility just equals the price. For all the other units bought, the marginal utility exceeds the price. This means that the consumer gets what is known as 'consumer surplus' from buying c^* units at price p^* (see Fig. 4.2). In words, this says that consumers get more (in terms of utility) than they pay for. How much? For the first unit bought, the marginal unit was mu' but the price paid was only p^*, so the surplus is the area shown by the rectangle a. For the second unit, the marginal utility was somewhat lower (not shown in the diagram), so the surplus is lower, specifically it is given by the area b. Doing the same for all units shows that buying c^* units at p^* yields a total consumer surplus equal to the sum of all the resulting rectangles. If we take the units to be very finely defined, the triangle defined by the points 1, 2 and 3 gives us the total consumer surplus. Box 4.1 discusses a real-world illustration of consumer surplus.

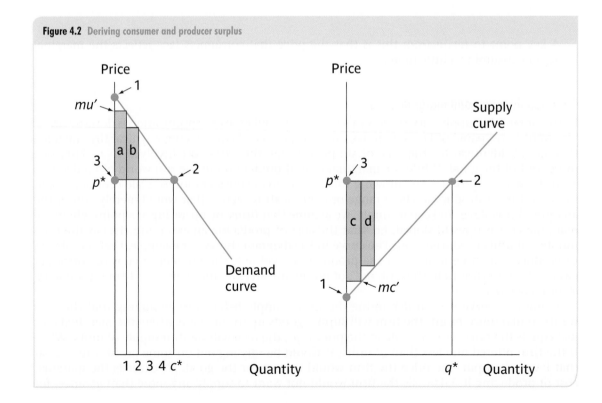

Figure 4.2 Deriving consumer and producer surplus

Box 4.1   Consumer surplus and Swiss Rail's Half Fare Card

Switzerland's wonderful rail system can be expensive, so many tourists buy the Half Fare Card; in 2011, it cost 85 GBP for a one-month pass. The fact that people pay to get unlimited access to a lower price is an example of consumer surplus in action. To see this, ask yourself what would be the maximum you would pay for being able to buy half-price tickets. For example, suppose you were planning a two-week trip that involved 20 individual train trips. Suppose the average price was 10 GBP, so you would spend 200 GBP without the card. With the card you spend only 100 GBP, so you would be willing to pay up to 100 pounds for a Half Fare card. In fact, you would probably be willing to pay a bit more than 100 GBP since at the lower per-trip price (i.e. 5 GBP versus 10), you would probably take a few trips more than you found optimal at the full price.

An analogous line of reasoning shows us that the triangle formed by the points 1, 2 and 3 in the right-hand panel gives us a measure of the gain firms get from being able to sell q^* units at a price of p^*. Consider the first unit sold. The marginal cost of producing this unit was mc' but this was sold for p^* so the firm earns a surplus, what we call the 'producer surplus', equal to the rectangle c in the right-hand panel. Doing the same exercise for each unit sold shows that the total producer surplus is equal to the triangle defined by the points 1, 2 and 3.

By drawing similar diagrams on your own, you should be able to convince yourself that a price rise increases producer surplus and decreases consumer surplus. A price drop does the opposite.

4.2 Preliminaries II: introduction to open-economy supply and demand analysis

This section introduces the 'workhorse' diagram – the open-economy supply and demand diagram – that is essential to our study of European economic integration. Well-prepared readers may consider skipping, moving straight on to the tariff analysis in Section 4.3. The diagram, however, is used throughout this chapter and the next, so even advanced students may wish to briefly review the diagram's foundations; if nothing else, such a review will help with the terminology.

4.2.1 The import demand curve

We first look at where the import demand curve comes from; Fig. 4.3 facilitates the analysis.

The left-hand panel of the diagram depicts a nation's supply and demand curves for a particular good. As usual, the domestic price is on the vertical axis; quantity is on the horizontal axis. If imports of the good were banned for some reason, the nation would only be able to consume as much as it produced. The result would a market price of P^* since this is the price where the amount that consumers want to buy just matches the amount that firms want to produce. Plainly, import demand is zero at P^* (for simplicity, we assume that imported and domestic goods are perfect substitutes). This zero-import point is marked in the right-hand panel as point 1; this diagram has the same price on the vertical axis, but plots imports on the horizontal axis.

How much would the nation import if the price were lower, say P'? The first thing to note is that the import price will fix the domestic price. Imports are always available at P', so no consumer

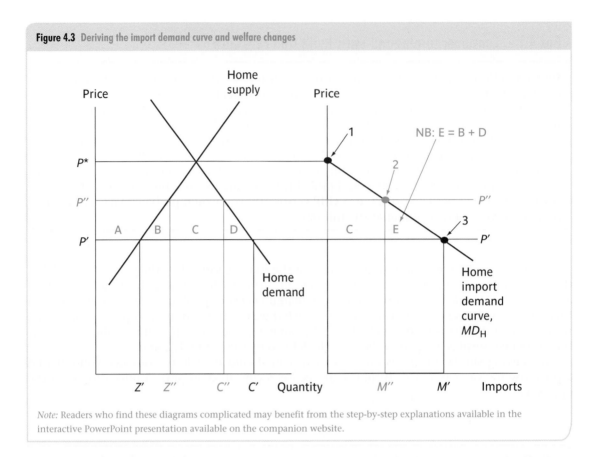

Figure 4.3 Deriving the import demand curve and welfare changes

Note: Readers who find these diagrams complicated may benefit from the step-by-step explanations available in the interactive PowerPoint presentation available on the companion website.

would pay more than P'. Of course, domestic producers must match the import competition, so P' becomes the domestic price.

The second thing to note is the impact of P' on consumption, production and imports. Consumption demand would be C' and domestic production would be Z'. As C' exceeds Z', consumers buy more than domestic firms are willing to produce at P'. The 'excess' demand is met by imports. That is to say, imports are the difference between C' and Z' (in symbols, $M' = C' - Z'$).

What this tells us is that import demand at P' is M'. This point is marked in the right-hand panel of the diagram as point 3. Performing the same exercise for P'' yields point 2, and doing the same for every possible import price yields the import demand curve, i.e. the amount of imports that the nation wants at any given domestic price. The resulting curve is shown as MD_H in the right-hand panel. (For convenience, we often call the nation under study 'Home' to distinguish it from its trade partner which we call 'Foreign'.)

Welfare analysis: MD curves as the marginal benefit of imports

When studying European economic integration, a critical question that arises time and again is the extent to which a policy raises or lowers nations' welfare. In answering such questions, it is useful to know how to do welfare analysis with the import demand curve.

Consider a rise in the import price from P' to P''. As argued above, the higher import price means the domestic price rises by the same amount. The corresponding equilibrium level of imports drops to M'', since consumption drops to C'' and production rises to Z''. We can see the welfare analysis in the left-hand panel using the standard notions of consumer and producer surpluses (see Section 4.1). Specifically, the price rise lowers consumer surplus by A + B + C + D. The same price rise increases producer surplus by A. The right-hand panel shows how this appears in the import demand diagram. From the left-hand panel, the import price rise means a net loss to the country of B + C + D, since the area A cancels out (area A is a gain to Home producers and loss to Home consumers). In the right-hand panel, these changes are shown as areas C and E; as it turns out area E equals area B + D.

A powerful perspective: trade volume effects and border price effects

It proves insightful to realize that the MD_H curve shows the marginal benefit of imports to Home. Before explaining why this is true, we show that it is a useful insight. As we saw above, Home loses areas C and E when the price of imports rises from P' to P''. Area C is easy to understand. After the price rise, Home pays more for the units it imported at the old price. Area C is the size of this loss. (Say the price rise was €1.2 per unit and M'' was 100; the loss would be €1.2 times 100; geometrically, this is the area C since a rectangle's area is its height times its base.) Understanding area E is where the insight comes in handy. Home reduces its imports at the new price and area E measures how much it loses from the drop in imports. The marginal value of the first lost unit is the height of the MD_H curve at M''. But since Home had to pay P' for this unit, the net loss is the gap between P' and the MD_H curve. If we add up the gaps for all the extra units imported, we get the area E. The jargon terms for these areas are the 'border price effect' (area C) and the 'import volume effect' (area E).

To understand why MD_H is the marginal benefit of imports we use three facts and one bit of logic: (i) the MD_H curve is the difference between the domestic demand curve and the domestic supply curve; (ii) the domestic supply curve is the domestic marginal cost curve, and the domestic demand curve is the domestic marginal utility curve (see Section 4.1 if these points are unfamiliar); and (iii) the difference between domestic marginal utility of consumption and domestic marginal cost of production is the net gain to the nation of producing and consuming one more unit. The logical point is that an extra unit of imports leads to some combination of higher consumption and lower domestic production, and this leads to some combination of higher utility and lower costs; the height of the MD_H curve tells us what that combination is. Or, to put it differently, the nation imports up to the point where the marginal gain from doing so equals the marginal cost. Since the border price is the marginal cost, the border price is also an indication of the marginal benefit of imports.

To see these points in more detail, see the interactive PowerPoint presentations available for free on http://hei.unige.ch/~baldwin/PapersBooks/BW/BW.html.

4.2.2 The export supply curve

Figure 4.4 uses an analogous line of reasoning to derive the import supply schedule. The first thing to keep in mind is that the supply of imports to Home is the supply of exports from foreigners. For simplicity's sake, suppose that there is only one foreign country (simply called 'Foreign' hereafter) and its supply and demand curves look like the left-hand panel of the figure. (Note that the areas in Fig. 4.4 are unrelated to the areas in Fig. 4.3.)

As with the import demand curve, we start by asking how much Foreign would export for a particular price. For example, how much would it export, if the price of its exports was P'? At price P', Foreign firms would produce Z' and Foreign consumers would buy C'. The excess production (equal to $X' = Z' - C'$) would be exported. (Note that as in the case of import demand, the export price sets the price in Foreign; Foreign firms have no reason to sell for less since they can always export, and competition among Foreign suppliers would prevent any of them from charging Foreign consumers a higher price.) The fact that Foreign would like to export X' when the export price is P' is shown in the right-hand panel at point 2.

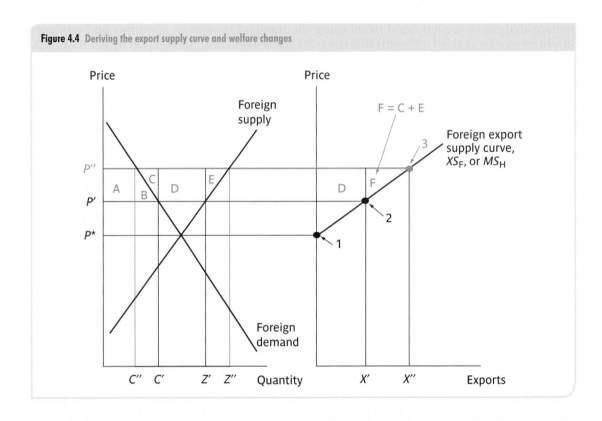

Figure 4.4 Deriving the export supply curve and welfare changes

As the price for Foreign exports (i.e. the Home's import price) rose, Foreign would be willing to supply a higher level of exports for two reasons. The higher price would induce Foreign firms to produce more and Foreign consumers to buy less. For example, the price P'' would bring forth an import supply equal to X'' (this equals $Z'' - C''$); this is shown as point 3 in the right-hand panel. At price $P*$, exports are zero. Plotting all such combinations in the right-hand panel produces the export supply curve XS_F. We stress again the simple but critical point that the Foreign export supply is the Home import supply, thus we also label XS_F as MS_H.

Welfare

The left-hand panel also shows how price changes translate into Foreign welfare changes. If the export price rises from P' to P'', consumers in Foreign lose by A + B (these letters are not related to those in the previous figure), but the Foreign firms gain producer surplus equal to A + B + C + D + E. The net gain is therefore C + D + E. Using the export supply curve XS_F, we can show the same net welfare change in the right-hand panel as the area D + F. Note that the insight from the MD_H curve extends to the XS_F curve, i.e. the XS_F curve gives the marginal benefit to Foreign of exporting.

This review of import supply and demand was very rapid – probably too rapid for students who have never used such diagrams and probably too slow for students who have. For those who find themselves in the first category, there are interactive PowerPoint presentations that go over the diagram in great detail available on http://hei.unige.ch/~baldwin/PapersBooks/BW/BW.html.

4.2.3 The workhorse diagram: *MD–MS*

The big payoff from having an import supply curve and an import demand curve is that it permits us to find the equilibrium price and quantity of imports. The equilibrium price is found

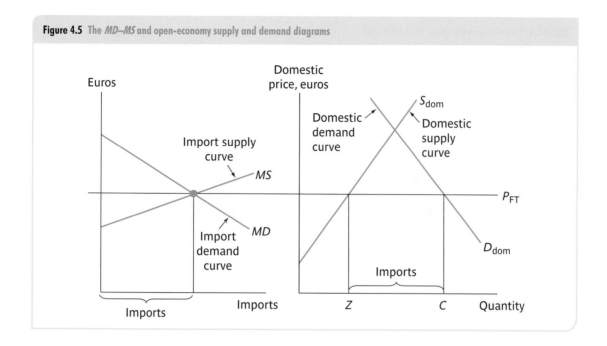

Figure 4.5 The *MD–MS* and open-economy supply and demand diagrams

by putting together import demand and supply as shown in the left-hand panel of Fig. 4.5; we drop the 'H' and 'F' subscripts for convenience.

Assuming imports and domestic production are perfect substitutes, the domestic price is set at the point where the demand and supply of imports meet, namely P_{FT} (FT stands for free trade). While the import supply and demand diagram, or *MD–MS* diagram for short, is handy for determining the price and volume of imports, it does not permit us to see the impact of price changes on domestic consumers and firms separately. This is where the right-hand panel becomes useful. In particular, we know that the market clears only when the price is P_{FT}, so we know that Home production equals Z and Home consumption equals C. The equilibrium level of imports may be read off either panel. In the left-hand panel, it is shown directly; in the right-hand one, it is the difference between domestic consumption and production.

Having explained these basic microeconomic tools, we turn now to using them to study a simple but common real-world problem – the effects of a tax on imports from all nations. Such taxes are called tariffs.

4.3 MFN tariff analysis

To build from simple to complex, we preface the analysis of preferential trade liberalization in Europe with a simpler example, but one that nevertheless is useful for understanding the world. That is, we introduce the basic method of analysis and gain experience in using the diagrams by first studying the impact of removing the simplest type of trade barrier – a tariff that is applied to imports from all trade partners. We call this a non-discriminatory liberalization.

Although this is not what happened when Europe integrated economically, we first look at the non-discriminatory case since it is less complex. An extra benefit of taking this detour is that it helps us understand the effects of the EU lowering its common external tariff – as it does in the

Figure 4.6 Price and quantity effects of an MFN tariff

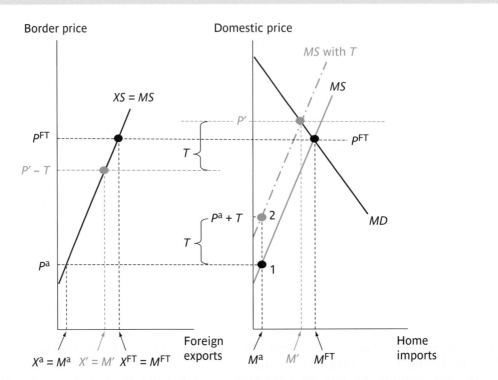

Note: Observe the distinction between the domestic and border prices. The domestic price is the price that domestic consumers pay for the good. The border price is the price foreign producers receive when they sell the good to Home. They can differ because of the tariff (a tariff is nothing more than a tax on imports). When you buy a coffee at a café for, say, 1 euro, the café owner does not get the full euro because the owner has to pay a tax, called the VAT, on your purchase. As a result, the price that the café owner receives is only 80 cents (the VAT is 20 per cent in this example) even though you pay 100 cents. In exactly the same way, foreigners receive a price (the border price) that equals the domestic price minus the tariff.

context of world trade talks (see Chapter 12). For historical reasons, a non-discriminatory tariff is called a 'most favoured nation' tariff, which provides the handy abbreviation, MFN.

4.3.1 Price and quantity effects of a tariff

The first step is to determine how a tariff changes prices and quantities. To be concrete, suppose that the tariff imposed equals T euros per unit.

The first step in finding the post-tariff price is to work out how the tariff changes the *MD–MS* diagram; here Fig. 4.6 facilitates the analysis. (See Section 4.2 if you are unfamiliar with the *MD–MS* diagram.) The right panel of Fig. 4.6 shows the pre-tariff import demand and import supply curves as *MD* and *MS*, respectively. The left-hand panel shows the foreign export supply curve as *XS*. Note that the vertical axis in this right-hand panel shows the domestic price, while the vertical axis in the left-hand panel shows the border price – the difference between the two is simple, but critical (see the note to Fig. 4.6).

A tariff shifts up the MS curve

Imposition of a tariff has no effect on the *MD* curve in the right-hand panel since the *MD* curve tells us how much Home would like to import at any given *domestic* price. By contrast, imposing a tariff on imports shifts up the *MS* curve by *T*. The reason is simple. After the tariff is imposed, the domestic price must be higher by *T* to get Foreign to offer the same quantity as it offered before the tariff. Consider an example. How much would Foreign supply before the tariff, if the Home domestic price before the tariff were P^a? The answer, which is given by point 1 on the *MS* curve, is M^a. After the tariff, we get a different answer. To get Foreign to offer M^a after the tariff, the domestic price must be $P^a + T$ so that Foreign sees a border price of P^a.

Having shown that the tariff shifts up the *MS* curve, consider next the tariff's impact on equilibrium prices and quantities.

The new equilibrium prices and quantities

Even without a diagram, readers will surely realize that a tariff raises the domestic price and lowers imports. After all, a tariff is a tax on imports and it is intuitively obvious that putting a tax on imports will raise prices somewhat and lower imports somewhat. Why do we need a diagram?

The diagram helps us be more specific about this intuition; this specificity allows us to work out how much the nations gain or lose from the tariff. Returning to our analysis, note that after the tariff, the old import supply curve is no longer valid. The new import supply curve, labelled *MS with T*, is what matters and the equilibrium price is set at the point where the new import supply curve and the import demand curve cross. As intuition would have it, the new price – marked P' in the diagram – is higher than the pre-tariff price P^{FT} (as already noted, FT stands for free trade). Because of the higher domestic price, Home imports are reduced to M' from M^{FT}. To summarize, there are five price and quantity effects of the tariff:

1 The price facing Home firms and consumers (domestic price) rises to P'.
2 The border price (i.e. the price Home pays for imports) falls to $P' - T$; this also means that the price received by Foreigners falls to $P' - T$.
3 The Home import volume falls to M'.

The other two effects cannot be seen in Fig. 4.6, but are obvious to readers who worked through Fig. 4.3. The higher domestic price stimulates production and discourages consumption. Specifically:

4 Home production rises.
5 Home consumption falls.

There are also production and consumption effects of the tariff inside the exporting nation. Since the border price falls, Foreign production drops and Foreign consumption rises. We could see this explicitly if we put a diagram like the left-hand panel of Fig. 4.4 to the left of the diagram in Fig. 4.6. You may want to do this as an exercise to test your familiarity with the diagrams.

4.3.2 Welfare effects of a tariff

Having worked out the price and quantity effects, it is simple to calculate the welfare effects of the tariffs, that is to say, who wins, who loses and by how much. The analysis is really just a combination of what we did in Figs 4.3 and 4.4; this is done in Fig. 4.7. The left panel shows Home's supply and demand, the middle panel shows the world market for imports and the right panel shows the Foreign supply and demand. We start with Home.

As shown in Fig. 4.7, the MFN tariff raises the Home price of the good (to P') while lowering the border price (to P' – T). Home consumers lose A + B + C + D, Home producers gain A and

Figure 4.7 Welfare effects of an MFN tariff

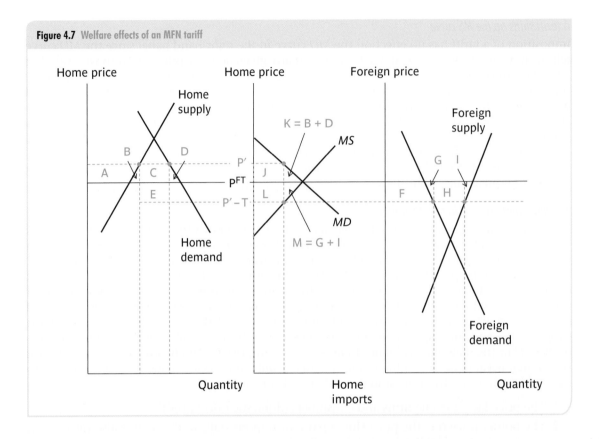

Home government gains tariff revenue C + E. The net Home welfare effect is +E − B − D. This can be positive or negative depending upon the size of the tariff (you can show that it will be negative for very large tariffs, but positive for sufficiently small tariffs).

Turning to Foreign, we see that Home's tariff has lowered the border price facing Foreign exporters and this in turn brings down the price faced by Foreign producers and consumers. Foreign consumers gain F while Foreign firms lose F + G + H + I. There is no change in tariff revenue (the tariff is paid to the Home government), so the net impact on Foreign is −G − H − I. This is plainly negative regardless of the tariff's size.

A useful condensation

The first time one works through these welfare calculations, it is useful to consider the full distributional effects as we did in Fig. 4.7. (i.e. the impact on consumers, producers and government revenue). Yet, once one is familiar with the diagrams, it is convenient to condense the analysis into a single diagram, like the centre panel in Fig. 4.7. This lets us show the overall welfare effects of Home tariff on both nations. Using the area labels in the centre panel, Home's welfare changes by +J − K, Foreign's welfare changes by −L − M, so world welfare falls by −K − M.

To summarize, we find:

- The tariff reduces Foreign welfare since it means they sell less and receive a lower price.
- The tariff creates private-sector winners and losers (Home firms gain, Home consumers lose), but the losers (consumers) lose more than gainers (firms) gain.
- Home collects tariff revenue equal.

- The overall Home welfare change is +L – K; this net effect may be positive or negative; the relative sizes of L and K depend upon the slopes of the *MD* and *MS* curves and on the size of *T*.
- The global impact of the tariff, adding Home and Foreign welfare changes together, is definitely negative.

4.3.3 Tariffs as a way of taxing foreigners

The result that a tariff might make the Home country better or worse off is worth looking at from a different angle. The two parts of Home's net welfare impact, namely +L – K, represent very different kinds of changes.

- The area L is the 'border price effect', i.e. the gain from paying less for imports.

We can also think of it as the amount of the new tariff revenue that is borne by foreigners. This statement requires some explaining. In the real world, the importing firm pays the whole tariff, so one might think that the importing firm bears the full burden of the import tax. This would be wrong. Part of the burden is passed on to Home residents via higher prices. How much? Well pre-tariff, the domestic price was P^{FT} and post-tariff it is P', so the difference shows how much of the tariff is passed on to Home residents. Since this price hike applies to a level of imports equal to M', we can say that the share of the tariff revenue borne by Home residents is area J. Using the same logic, we see that some of the tariff burden is also passed back to Foreign suppliers. The before-versus-after border price gap is P^{FT} minus $(P' - T)$ and this applies to M' units of imports. So area L is a measure of how much of the tariff revenue is borne by foreigners.

- Area K is the 'trade volume effect', i.e. the impact of lowering imports.

Here is the argument. The *MD* curve shows the marginal benefit to Home of importing each unit (see Section 4.2 if this reasoning is unfamiliar to you). Given this, the gap between the *MD* curve and P^{FT} gives us a measure of how much Home loses for each unit it ceases to import. The area of the triangle C is just all the gaps summed giving the change in imports.

- To put it differently, area L represents Home's gain from taxing foreigners while area K represents an efficiency loss from the tariff.

Given all this, we can say that if *T* raises Home welfare, then it does so only because the tariff allows the Home government to indirectly tax foreigners enough to offset the tariff's inefficiency effects on the Home economy. That is, *T* causes economic inefficiency at Home but *T* is also a way of exploiting foreigners. Since the exploitation gains may outweigh the inefficiency effects, Home may gain from imposing a tariff.

4.3.4 Global welfare effects and retaliation

The global welfare impact is simply a matter of summing up effects; as we saw, it is negative and equal to –K – M.

Put in this way, the possibility that Home might gain from a tariff is clearly suspect. For example, if Home and Foreign were symmetric and both imposed tariffs, both would lose the efficiency triangle K and the gain to Home of L on imports would be lost to Home on its exports to Foreign. Home would also lose the deadweight triangle M on exports, so the net loss to each of the symmetric nations would be –K – M.

In short, protection by all nations is worse than a zero-sum game. It is exactly this point that underpins the economics of WTO tariff-cutting negotiations. If only one nation liberalizes, it might lose. If, however, the nation's liberalization is coordinated with its trading partners' liberalization, the zero-sum aspect tends to disappear.

4.4 Types of protection: an economic classification

Tariffs are only one of many types of import barriers that European integration has removed. The first phase of EU integration, 1958–68, focused on tariff removal, but the Single Market Programme that was started in 1986 focused on a much wider range of non-tariff barriers.

While there are several methods of categorizing such barriers, it proves useful to focus on how the barriers affect so-called trade rents. A tariff, for instance, drives a wedge between the Home price and the border price (i.e. the price paid to foreigners). This allows someone (in the tariff case it will be the Home government) to indirectly collect the 'profit' from selling at the high domestic price while buying at the low border price. For historical reasons, economists refer to such profits (area A + B in Fig. 4.8) as 'rents'. When it comes to welfare analysis, we must watch the trade rents closely. For some import barriers, Home residents get the rents, but for others no rents are created, or foreigners get the rents. This distinction is highlighted by distinguishing three categories of trade barriers: domestically captured rent (DCR) barriers; foreign captured rent (FCR) barriers; and 'frictional' barriers. We consider them in turn.

4.4.1 DCR barriers

Tariffs are the classic DCR barrier. Here, the Home government gets the trade rents. From a Home nationwide welfare perspective, however, it does not really matter whether the government, Home firms or Home consumers earn these rents, as long as the rents are captured domestically. What sorts of barriers other than tariffs would lead to domestically captured rents? Some forms of quotas are DCR barriers. A quota is a quantitative limit on the number of goods that can be

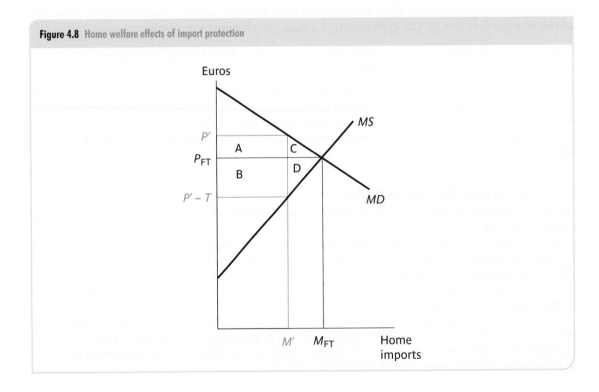

Figure 4.8 Home welfare effects of import protection

imported per year. To control the number of foreign goods entering the country, the government hands out a fixed number of import licences and 'collects' one licence per unit imported. The price and quantity effects of a quota that restricts imports to M' in Fig. 4.8 are identical to the effects of a tariff equal to T. The point is that, if imports are limited to M', then the gap between domestic consumption and production can be no more than M', implying that the domestic price must be driven up to P'. Another way to say this is that T is the 'tariff equivalent' of the quota. Now consider the trade rents. With a quota, whoever has the licence can buy the goods at the border price $P' - T$ and resell them in the Home market for P'. This earns the licence holders $A + B$. If the government gives the licences to Home residents, then the quota is a DCR barrier. If it gives them to foreigners, the quota is an FCR barrier.

4.4.2 FCR barriers

A prime example of an FCR barrier is a 'price undertaking' in the context of an anti-dumping tariff. Under EU law, the Commission can impose a tariff on an non-member nation if that nation's firms are selling goods below cost in the EU market (so-called dumping). In some cases, an anti-dumping tariff is imposed but in other cases no tariff is imposed but rather the exporting firm promises to raise its price instead. These promises are called 'price undertakings'.

For example, if the agreed level were P' from Fig. 4.8, the price undertaking would have the same price and quantity effects as a tariff T. Importantly, however, the undertaking allows foreign producers, rather than the Home government, to garner the rents $A + B$. Throughout the industrialized world, and in the EU in particular, it is very common for trade barriers to be arranged so that foreigners earn the rents. One reason is that trade rents are used as a kind of gift to soothe foreign companies and governments that are likely to be angered by the imposition of a trade barrier.

Finally, note that an FCR barrier harms EU welfare more than a DCR barrier. Specifically, the welfare cost of an FCR is always negative, i.e. $-A - C$, instead of being ambiguous, i.e. $B - C$. Moreover, the foreign welfare impact is now $A - D$, so an FCR may end up helping foreigners!

4.4.3 Frictional barriers

An important type of trade barrier that still remains inside the EU consists of what are sometimes called 'technical barriers to trade' (TBTs). Western European countries often restrict imports by subjecting them to a whole range of policies that increase the real cost of buying foreign goods. Some examples are excessive bureaucratic 'red-tape' restrictions and industrial standards that discriminate against foreign goods. One of the most famous examples is discussed in Box 4.2.

Since frictional barriers are bad for a nation, one may ask why they are so prevalent. Box 4.3 provides one explanation.

Box 4.2   Cassis de Dijon: a history-making technical barrier to trade

One very common type of frictional barrier concerns health and safety regulations that have the side effect of hindering trade. Perhaps the most famous of these was a German regulation that forbade the importation of certain low-alcohol spirits, including the sweet French liqueur, Cassis – used in making the famous white wine drink, Kir. This regulation was challenged before the EU's Court of Justice as a barrier to trade. When challenged on this regulation, the German government argued that the prohibition was necessary to protect public health (since weak spirits more easily promote alcohol tolerance) and to protect consumers (since consumers might buy weak spirits, thinking they were strong). In 1979, the Court ruled that the measure was not necessary since widespread availability of low-alcohol drinks (e.g. beer) in Germany made the prohibition ineffective in furthering public health. It also found that putting the alcohol content on the label was sufficient to protect consumers, so the import ban was not necessary for the protection of consumers. This Court ruling resulted in the frictional barrier being removed. More importantly, it established the basic principle known as 'mutual recognition' whereby goods that are lawfully sold in one EU nation shall be presumed to be safe for sale in all EU nations. Exceptions to this principle require explicit motivation. By the way, the formal name for this Court case is 'Rewe-Zentral AG v. Bundesmonopolverwaltung für Branntwein'; no wonder it is called Cassis de Dijon.

Box 4.3   Why do frictional barriers arise so often?

Government agencies charged with formulating and enforcing standards are often 'captured' by special-interest groups from the regulated industries. Moreover, the Home firms that are to be subjected to the standards often play an important role in setting the standards. For example, when regulating a highly technical field such as elevators, the government (which probably does not employ many full-time elevator experts) naturally asks the opinions of domestic firms that produce elevators. With an eye to their foreign competitors, they quite naturally push for standards that raise the cost of imported goods more than the cost of locally produced goods.

An example can be found in the paper industry. Sweden and Finland produce paper mainly from new trees, while French and German paper producers use a lot of recycled paper and rags. In the early 1990s, the EU was considering a regulation that would require all paper sold in the EU to contain a certain fraction of recycled paper. This sounds like a 'public interest' regulation. However, it also would have had the effect of eliminating the resource-based advantage of Swedish and Finnish firms, much to the joy of French and German firms. In other words, it would have raised the real cost of imports (since the Nordic producers would have had to switch to less efficient techniques). As it turns out, it is not clear which production method is 'greener'. Recycling paper requires lots of chemicals that may be released into the environment, while setting up more tree farms is, well, green – a point that was not raised by French and German paper producers.

Since Finland and Sweden joined the EU, the regulation was not adopted, but this shows the subtle mixing of public interest and protectionism that inevitably arises when nations adopt regulations and standards. Of course, nations do need health, safety, environmental and industrial standards, so we cannot eliminate frictional barriers by just abolishing all regulation. This is one of the things tackled by the EU's 1992 programme.

One important class of frictional – i.e. cost-creating – barriers involves industrial and health standards that are chosen at least in part to restrict imports. For example, some countries refuse to accept safety tests that are performed in foreign countries, even in highly industrialized nations. This forces importers to retest their products in the local country. Beyond raising the real cost of imported goods, this sort of barrier delays the introduction of new products. While this clearly harms consumers, Home producers may benefit since it may give them time to introduce competing varieties. Another example involves imposing industrial, health, safety or environmental standards that differ from internationally recognized norms. It is often difficult to know objectively whether an unusual regulation or standard represents a valid 'public interest' concern or whether it is just a protectionist device. In fact, both motives are usually behind the adoption of such measures.

Regardless of why such policies are adopted, they have the effect of protecting Home producers or service providers. Home firms design their products with these standards in mind, while foreign firms, for whom the Home market may be relatively unimportant, are unlikely to do so. Bringing imported products into conformity raises the real cost of imports.

For example, all cars sold in Sweden must have wipers for the headlights. While this policy may have some merit as a safety regulation (in the old days Sweden had lots of dusty rural roads), it also has the effect of raising the price of imported cars more than it raises the price of Swedish cars. From the drawing board onwards, all models of Volvos and Saabs – and their production facilities – are designed with these headlight wipers in mind. For other car makers, take Renault as an example, the Swedish market is far too small to really matter. The design of Renaults and Renault's mass production facilities are not optimized for the installation of headlight wipers. Consequently, while it is expensive to put headlight wipers on both Swedish and French cars, it is much more so for French cars. This gives the Swedish car makers an edge in Sweden. Similar sorts of barriers give the French an edge in their domestic market.

4.5 Summary

This chapter presented the essential microeconomic tools for trade policy analysis in the simplified world where we assume there is no imperfect competition and no scale economies. The two most important diagrams are the open-economy supply and demand diagram (right-hand panel of Fig. 4.5), and the MD–MS diagram (left-hand panel of Fig. 4.5). The MD–MS diagram provides a compact way of working out the impact of import protection on prices, quantities and overall Home and Foreign welfare. The open-economy supply and demand diagram allowed us to consider the distributional impact of import protection, i.e. to separate the overall effect into its component effects on Home consumers, Home producers and Home revenue.

The chapter also discussed types of trade barriers in Europe and classified them according to what happens to the trade 'rents'. Under the first type, DCR barriers, the rents go to domestic residents. For FCR barriers, the rents go to foreigners, and with frictional barriers the rents disappear. European integration consisted primarily of removing DCR barriers up until the mid-1970s. Subsequent goods-market liberalization has focused on frictional barriers.

Self-assessment questions

1 Using a diagram like Fig. 4.8, show the full Foreign welfare effects of imposing a Home tariff equal to T, i.e. show the impact on Foreign producers and Foreign consumers separately.

2 In August 2005, EU clothing retailers such as Sweden's H&M complained about the new EU restrictions on imports from China that were imposed after complaints from EU clothing producers based in Italy, France, Spain, Portugal and Greece. Use a diagram like Fig. 4.8 to explain the positions of the various EU interest groups.

3 One way to think about the slope of the MS curve is in terms of the 'size' of the home nation. The idea is that the demand from a very small nation has a very small impact on the world price. For example, Switzerland could probably increase its oil imports by 10 per cent without having any impact on the world oil price. Using a diagram like Fig. 4.7, show that the welfare costs of imposing an MFN tariff are larger for smaller nations, interpreting this in terms of the MS curve's slope. Show that when the MS curve is perfectly flat, the welfare effects are unambiguously negative.

4 Using a diagram like Fig. 4.7, show that a country facing an upward-sloped MS curve can gain – starting from free trade – from imposing a sufficiently small tariff. (Hint: Starting from a small tariff, the rectangle gains and triangle losses both increase in size as the tariff gets bigger, but the rectangle gets bigger faster.) Show that any level of a frictional or FCR barrier lowers Home welfare.

5 Using the results from the previous exercise, consider the impact of Home imposing a tariff on Foreign exports and Foreign retaliating with a tariff on Home's exports. Assume that the MS and MD curves for both goods (Home exports to Foreign and Foreign exports to Home) are identical. Starting from a situation where Home and Foreign both impose a tariff of T, show that both unambiguously gain if both remove their tariffs, but one nation might lose if it removed its tariff unilaterally. By the way, this exercise illustrates why nations that are willing to lower their tariffs in the context of a WTO multilateral trade negotiation are often not willing to remove their tariffs unilaterally.

6 Using a diagram like Fig. 4.5, show that an import tariff equal to T has exactly the same impact on prices, quantities and welfare as a domestic consumption tax equal to T and a domestic production subsidy equal to T. (Hint: A production subsidy lowers the effective marginal cost of domestic firms and so lowers the domestic supply curve by T.)

7 Using a diagram like Fig. 4.7, show the impact on quantities, prices and welfare when Home has no tariff, but Foreign charges an export tax equal to T.

8 Using a diagram like Fig. 4.5, show the impact on quantities, prices and welfare when Home has no tariff, but Foreign imposes an export quota with a tariff-equivalent of T.

9 Using a diagram like Fig. 4.7, show that the welfare effects of a quota that restricts imports to M' are exactly the same as a tariff equal to T; assume that each quota licence (i.e. the right to import one unit) is sold by the government to the highest bidder.

Essay questions

1 The concepts of consumer surplus, producer surplus and tariff revenue are meant to capture the key welfare effects of trade policy. Discuss two or three aspects of socio-economic well-being that are not captured by these concepts.

2 The welfare analysis in this chapter assumes that governments weight one euro of consumer surplus and producer surplus equally. Find an account in a newspaper of a real-world trade policy change and summarize the analysis in the article (the basic facts, the points of view reported, etc.). Does the newspaper article make it seem as if the government cares equally about consumers and producers?

3 Go on to the European Commission's website and find an example of a frictional barrier that the Commission is trying to remove. Explain what the barrier is, how it is justified by Member States and why it was not removed during the 1992 Single Market Programme. One URL to try is: europa.eu.int/comm/internal_market/en/index.htm.

4 Write an essay describing the events that led up to the EU's and USA's imposition of new protection against Chinese clothing exports. Be sure to mention the role of the Uruguay Round agreement on the elimination of the Multifibre Agreement, the surge of exports, the Chinese export tax and reactions of buyers and makers of clothing in the EU and the USA. Use the diagrams developed in this chapter to explain the positions taken by the US, EU and Chinese governments as well as the positions of EU and US buyers and makers of clothing.

Further reading: the aficionado's corner

Every undergraduate textbook on international economics has a chapter on tariff analysis that covers the same material as this chapter. One particularly accessible treatment can be found in:

Krugman, P. and M. Obstfeld (2005) *International Economics*, 7th edition (or earlier), HarperCollins, New York.

For much more on the economics of trade protection see:

Vousden, N. (1990) *The Economics of Trade Protection*, Cambridge University Press, Cambridge.

Useful websites

The World Bank's website provides extensive research on trade policy analysis. This includes many papers on non-discriminatory trade policy but also a very large section on preferential trade arrangements under the heading of 'regionalism'. See www.worldbank.org.

The Commission's website on trade issues can be found at http://ec.europa.eu/trade/. It has lots of information on the latest EU trade policy changes.

References

Mankiw, G. (2011) *Principles of Economics*, 6th edition (or earlier), South Western Publishing, New York.

Chapter 5

The essential economics of preferential liberalization

> . . . the ideas of economists and political philosophers, both when they are right and when they are wrong, are more powerful than is commonly understood. Indeed the world is ruled by little else. Practical men, who believe themselves to be exempt from any intellectual influences, are usually the slaves of some defunct economist.
>
> John Maynard Keynes, 1935

Chapter Contents

Introduction

This chapter begins our study of the microeconomics of European integration, focusing on the preferential (i.e. discriminatory) aspects. This is critical since discrimination (the nicer word is preferential) is the heart and soul of European economic integration. Over the past six decades, Europe has liberalized trade and factor markets – but not with everyone. By 1968, EU members charged zero tariffs on all imports from each, while imposing significant tariffs on imports from the USA, Canada and Japan. Likewise, the Single Market Programme instituted the principle of mutual recognition of product standards on a discriminatory basis. In principle, goods made and sold in one EU nation could be sold in all EU nations, but this privilege did not extend to goods made in third nations. Discriminatory effects also played a central role in the political economy of European integration – especially the domino effects discussed in Chapter 1.

The main goal of this chapter is to provide a framework for analysing the essential economics of preferential liberalization. As usual, we start simple and add complexity as we go. For simplicity's sake, we continue with the last chapter's simplifying assumptions of no imperfect competition and no increasing returns (NICNIR). While these assumptions are both monumentally unrealistic, they are pedagogically convenient. They allow us to study the main economic logic of discriminatory liberalization without having to invest a lot of time in learning new tools (that is postponed until the next chapter).

5.1 Analysis of unilateral discriminatory liberalization

The simplest form of preferential liberalization is a unilateral preferential liberalization, so we turn to this first. Specifically, this section looks at what happens when a nation removes its tariff on imports from only one of its trading partners. We postpone consideration of changes in partner tariffs until the next section. This two-step approach is useful for two distinct reasons:

■ While European economic integration almost always involves two-way integration (e.g. France and Germany lowered their tariffs against each other's exports at the same time during the 1960s), the analysis of a two-way (i.e. reciprocal) liberalization is basically an easy extension of the analysis of a one-way (i.e. unilateral) liberalization.

■ The EU extends unilateral preferences to almost every developing nation in the world; the analysis in this section is directly applicable to EU programmes such as 'Everything but Arms' (which removes tariffs and quotas on imports from the world's poorest nations), and the Generalised System of Preferences. (More on these in Chapter 12.)

The basic logic in words: Vinerian insights

Before turning to diagrams, which may strike some readers as complex, it is worth presenting the basic economic logic in words. This helps boost intuition for the diagrams. It may also be sufficient for readers in a hurry.

There are only three elemental effects we really need to understand when it comes to the ABCs for preferential liberalization.

■ The first general point, namely 'Smith's certitude', was made by Adam Smith.

When a nation 'exempt[s] the good of one country from duties to which it subjects those of all other … the merchants and manufacturers of the country whose commerce is so favoured must necessarily derive great advantage' (Adam Smith as quoted in Pomfret, 1997).

The economic logic behind Smith's certitude is straightforward and easily illustrated with an example of a world where firms from two nations – call them Partner and Rest-of-World (RoW) – are competing in a third nation – call it Home. Without preferences, Home charges the same tariff on imports from Partner and RoW. Now suppose Home unilaterally removes tariffs on imports from Partner but not from RoW. The fruits of this reduced import tax will – as usual with tax removals – be shared between consumers and producers. Home consumers will see lower prices and Partner exporters will see higher prices. The higher border price for Partner firms induces them to sell more to Home. Plainly this is good for Partner – its firms sell more and obtain a higher price. In short, Smith's certitude stems from the fact that Partner firms enjoy a rise in both prices and sales to Home.

■ The second elemental effect was identified when Gottfried Haberler (1937) asserted that third nations – those excluded from the preferences – must lose; this is 'Haberler's spillover'.

Haberler's spillover can be illustrated with the same simple case. To remain competitive in the Home market while still paying the tariff, RoW firms must accept a lower pre-tariff price for their exports since their post-tariff price must match the competition's price. This pushes them down their export supply curve so RoW exports fall. Thus Haberler's spillover shows up as RoW exports suffer a drop in both prices and sales to Home. Or to put it differently, what is preference to Partner (Smith's certitude) is discrimination to RoW (Haberler's spillover).

As we shall see in the next sections, Smith's certitude and especially Haberler's spillover are the linchpins of the political economy of the traditional view of regionalism.

■ The third elemental effect is called Viner's ambiguity.

Jacob Viner (1950) demonstrated that preferential liberalization might harm the preference-giving nation; this is 'Viner's ambiguity'. Viner, who was blissfully ignorant of post-war mathematical economics, couched his argument in the enduring but imprecise concepts of 'trade diversion' and 'trade creation'. The basic economics nevertheless is clear from his terms. Discriminatory liberalization is both 'liberalization' – which removes some price wedges and thus tends to improve economic efficiency and Home welfare – and 'discrimination' – which introduces new price wedges and thus tends to harm efficiency and welfare. Viner associated the liberalization part with 'trade creation' and the discriminatory part with 'trade diversion'. It is not possible to say a priori whether the sum of these effects is positive or negative, i.e. its sign is ambiguous.

5.1.1 The PTA diagram

To get a deeper and clearer understanding of the economics of preferential liberalization, it is necessary to turn to diagrams. The diagrams, unfortunately, are more complex than those in the previous chapter for one simple reason – we need a minimum of three nations in the analysis (Home, Partner and RoW). Our first task is to extend the workhorse *MD–MS* diagram from Chapter 4 to allow for two sources of imports. Figure 5.1 shows how.

Before starting, we note that the theory of preferential liberalization is often taught using an additional simplifying factor called the 'small economy' assumption. While this simplifies the analysis of Viner's ambiguity from the perspective of the Home country, it also assumes away the critical impact that preferential liberalization has on other nations (Smith's certitude and Haberler's spillover). Interested readers can find this case in Annex A at the end of the chapter.

Free trade equilibrium

We open our study of the PTA diagram by working out the free trade equilibrium. That is to say, we want to identify the equilibrium price and quantities when no tariff is imposed by Home.

Box 5.1   Smith, Haberler and Viner

The three men responsible for the elemental effects were all interesting characters. Adam Smith, who died in 1790, is the father of economics since his 1776 book, *The Wealth of Nations*, defined the basic approach to markets that is at the heart of modern economic thinking. Not content with launching economics, he was also a social philosopher and a leading figure in the Scottish Enlightenment – a collaborator of David Hume.

Gottfried Haberler was born 1900 in Austria where he earned degrees in political science and law before moving to Harvard University in the 1930s. His most famous work reformulated the case for free trade based on the concept of opportunity cost. As part of this, he invented the production possibility frontier. He was the thesis adviser of the father of one of this textbook's authors (Richard Baldwin).

Jacob Viner, born in 1892, grew up in Montreal, earning his first degree at McGill and then a PhD at Harvard. He taught at the Universities of Chicago, Stanford, Yale and Princeton, and twice at the Graduate Institute of International and Development Studies in Geneva (where both the authors of this textbook teach today). Apart from his elemental contribution to the analysis of preferential trade liberalization, he introduced the long-run and short-run cost curves used in every economics textbook today. At Chicago and Princeton, many students were frightened by the thought of studying under him. His most famous student was Milton Friedman.

To find the free trade price, we need to find the intersection between the *MD* curve and the *MS* curve, as in Chapter 4. But what is the *MS* curve with two trade partners?

The two leftmost panels of Fig. 5.1 show the export supply curves for two individual countries, which we call Partner and RoW. (To minimize complications, we assume that Partner and RoW are identical, so their *XS* curves are identical.) Because there are two suppliers of imports, we must aggregate them in the standard microeconomics way, namely by forming the horizontal sum of the two export supply curves. This summed curve is shown as *MS* in the right-hand panel. Note that the *MS* curve is flatter than XS_P or XS_R since a given price increase will raise supply from both Partner and RoW.

With the *MS* curve in hand, we see that the free trade equilibrium price is P_{FT} (as before, FT stands for 'free trade'), i.e. the point where *MS* and *MD* intersect. The corresponding level of imports is *M* as shown. As we shall be interested in changes to the imports coming from Partner and RoW, we identify the initial free imports. We do this by using each supplier's *XS* curve to

Figure 5.1 The PTA (preferential trade arrangement) diagram

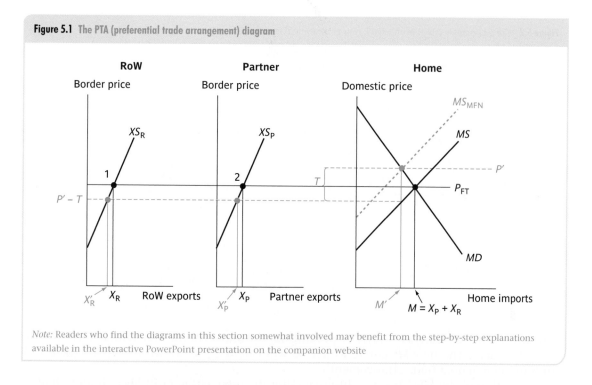

Note: Readers who find the diagrams in this section somewhat involved may benefit from the step-by-step explanations available in the interactive PowerPoint presentation on the companion website

see how much would be offered at the price P_{FT}. The answers are given by the points 1 and 2 in the diagram, namely X_R and X_P (the subscripts R and P stand for RoW and Partner respectively).

MFN tariff with two import suppliers

Working out the free trade equilibrium was just the first step. Next we have to see what would happen to prices and quantities if Home put on a non-discriminatory tariff (i.e. an MFN tariff as in Chapter 4). The reason we do this is to be able to have a baseline for comparison when we study – in the third step – what happens when Home removes the tariff but only on imports coming from Partner.

What happens when Home imposes a tariff equal to T on imports coming from both nations? As always, the first task is to find how the tariff affects the MS curve. As we saw in Chapter 4, an MFN tariff shifts the MS curve up by T since the domestic price would have to be T higher to elicit the same quantity of imports after the tariff is imposed. The new MS curve is shown in the diagram as the curve marked MS_{MFN}. As usual, imposing a tariff does nothing to the MD curve (see Chapter 4 if this point is not obvious).

The intersection of MS_{MFN} and MD tells us that the post-tariff equilibrium domestic price for imports is P' and the new import level is M'; with P' as the new domestic price, the new border price is $P' - T$. At this border price, both import suppliers are willing to supply less, namely X_R and X_P, as shown in the diagram. See Chapter 4 if the concept of 'border price' is not familiar to you.

Finally, we are ready for the third step – an analysis of a discriminatory unilateral liberalization by Home.

5.1.2 Price and quantity effects of discriminatory liberalization

What happens when Home removes T but only for imports from Partner, i.e. when Home unilaterally liberalizes on a preferential basis?

Figure 5.2 Price and quantity effects of unilateral, discriminatory tariff liberalization

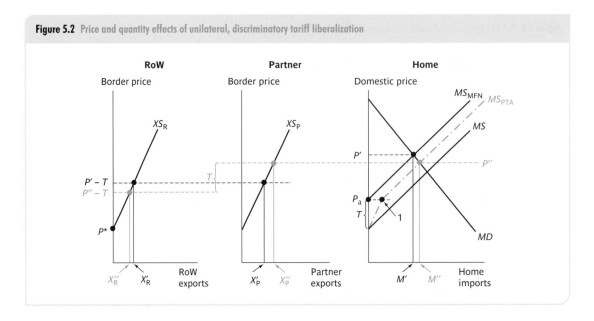

To answer this, we start, as always, by working out the impact of the preferential liberalization on the *MS* curve. The new *MS* curve, which we will call MS_{PTA}, is shown in Fig. 5.2 (here PTA stands for 'preferential trade arrangement').

The position of the MS_{PTA} is quite intuitive. After the preferential tariff liberalization, half of Home's import suppliers get duty-free access; the other half pays T. It seems natural therefore that MS_{PTA} lies halfway between the free-trade MS_{FT} and the MFN tariff MS_{MFN}. One small qualification, however, is necessary; considering this helps us see how MS_{PTA} is constructed.

The tariff prevents RoW firms from exporting until the domestic price in Home rises above the price marked Pa in Fig. 5.2. When Home's domestic price is below P_a, we have that the border price faced by RoW exports is below their zero-supply price (marked as P^* in the diagram). Partner-based firms, by contrast, would export when Home's domestic price is slightly below P_a since they face Home's domestic price (not the Home price minus the tariff). As a consequence, Partner firms – but only Partner firms – will supply imports at the domestic price P_a and this corresponds to the point marked 1 in the diagram. Thus the MS_{PTA} curve is Partner's *XS* curve up to point 1. After that, both foreigners supply imports, so the MS_{PTA} resumes its normal slope.

The domestic price change and conflicting border price changes

Having worked out the new *MS* curve, namely MS_{PTA} , we are ready to find the new equilibrium price. This is, as always, given by the intersection of the *MD* curve and the MS_{PTA} curve, namely P''. This is the new, post-PTA domestic price. As you might have expected even without going through the analysis, the new domestic price is lower than the old MFN tariff price. After all, imports from Partner can now enter duty free.

The impact on the border price is twofold because only RoW continues to pay the tariff. For Partner-based firms, the liberalization means that they now face Home's domestic price, P'', so for them the border price is P''. For RoW-based firms, which still have to pay T, the border price is $P'' - T$. This means that RoW sees its border price fall (this is the price-part of Haberler's spillover). Partner firms sees the border rise (this is the price-part of Smith's certitude). The source of this conflicting border price change is the fact that RoW must cut its border price to stay competitive with Partner firms' exports which benefited from T's removal.

Next we consider the quantity effects.

Supply switching

Given that Partner firms see a price rise, they increase exports from X'_P, X''_P (this is the quantity-part of Smith's certitude). RoW exports fall from X'_R to X''_R because their border price has fallen (this is the quantity-part of Haberler's spillover). This combination of higher Partner sales and lower RoW sales is known as 'supply switching', or 'trade diversion'. Defining it directly, supply switching occurs when a discriminatory liberalization induces the Home nation to switch some of its purchases to import suppliers who benefit from the PTA and away from suppliers based in nations that did not benefit from the PTA.

Did this sort of supply switching actually occur in Europe? When the EEC eliminated tariffs on a discriminatory basis during the formation of its customs union between 1958 and 1968, Box 5.2 shows that supply switching did occur. We discuss more recent econometric evidence for other preferential trade agreements in Section 5.5.

Summary: Price and quantity effects

To summarize, the price and quantity effects are:

- Home's domestic price falls from P' to P''.
- The border price falls from $P' - T$ to $P'' - T$ for RoW imports.
- The border price rises from $P' - T$ to P'' for Partner imports.
- The RoW exports fall.
- The Partner exports rise.
- Total Home imports rise from M' to M''.

These price and quantity effects may seem strange at first – especially the fact that Home buys more imports from the supplier whose border price has risen. This strangeness is simple to understand. The discriminatory liberalization distorts price signals so that Home consumers are not aware of the fact that Partner goods cost the nation more than RoW goods. To the Home consumer, imports from the two sources cost the same, namely P'. Supply switching is coming from the behaviour of firms: Partner firms see a higher border price and thus sell more; RoW firms see a lower border price and thus sell less.

Interested readers may want to add a fourth panel to the diagram by drawing a standard open-economy supply and demand figure for Home to the right of the MD–MS panel. Doing so allows you to see that Home production falls and Home consumption rises due to the domestic price drop.

5.1.3 Welfare effects

Having worked out the price and quantity effects, we are ready to study the welfare consequences for Home, Partner and RoW. As it turns out, showing the welfare implications in the same figure as the price and quantity effects would complicate the diagram too much. Thus Fig. 5.4 reproduces the previous figure but omits unnecessary lines to reduce the 'clutter factor'. As we saw in Chapter 4, all welfare effects stem from price and quantity changes, so these are all that we really need to keep track of.

The welfare effects on foreigners are straightforward. Partner gains D since it gets a higher price and sells more. In other words, Partner experiences a positive border price effect and a positive trade volume effect (see Chapter 4 if you are not familiar with these terms). RoW's losses are E for the reverse reasons; it gets a lower price and sells less (a negative border price effect and a negative trade volume effect).

Home's welfare effects are slightly more complex due to the conflicting border price changes. The direct way of gauging Home's net welfare effect is to use the concepts of 'trade volume effects' and 'border price effects' that were introduced in Chapter 4. This direct approach is also

Box 5.2 The supply-switching effects of the formation of the EEC customs union

Figure 5.3 shows the trade volume effects that occurred when the EEC6 removed their internal tariffs between 1958 and 1968. In the left-hand panel, the columns show the import shares broken down into intra-EEC6 imports, imports from six other European nations (the ones who joined in the EU's first three enlargements), and the rest of the world.

Note that as the EEC6 share of exports to itself rose from about 30 per cent in 1958 to about 45 per cent in 1968, the share of EEC imports from other nations had to fall. Part of the displacement occurred with respect to imports from other non-EEC European nations. As the dark bars show, the import share from six other western European nations (UK, Ireland, Portugal, Spain, Denmark and Greece) fell during this period by a small amount, from 8–9 per cent to 7 per cent. The main displacement came from the rest of the world, mainly imports from the USA. The right-hand panel, however, shows that imports from all sources were in fact growing rapidly. Thus we have to interpret the 'supply switching' as a relative thing. That is, if the customs union had not been formed, imports from non-EEC6 members would have risen even faster.

Figure 5.3 Supply switching and formation of the Common Market, 1958–70

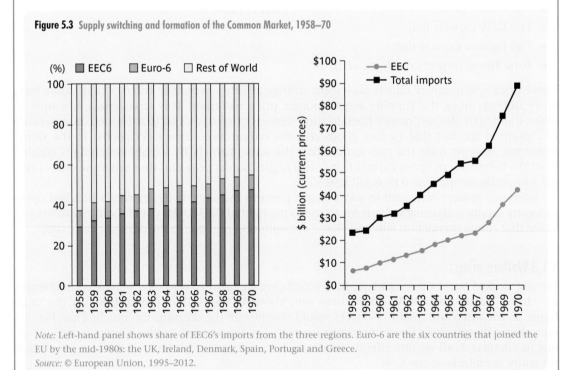

Note: Left-hand panel shows share of EEC6's imports from the three regions. Euro-6 are the six countries that joined the EU by the mid-1980s: the UK, Ireland, Denmark, Spain, Portugal and Greece.
Source: © European Union, 1995–2012.

the easiest way to remember the Home welfare effects and it is the easiest way to understand them, so this is what we do in Fig. 5.4. Some readers, however, may benefit from working through the welfare impact using the indirect method of adding up the separate impact on consumer surplus, producer surplus and tariff revenue (see Box 5.3). The two methods lead to the same answer.

Figure 5.4 Welfare effects of unilateral discriminatory liberalization

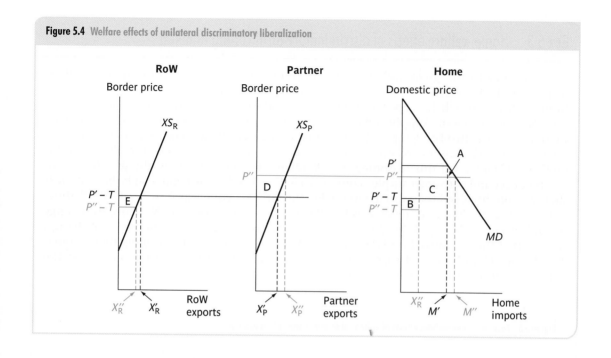

Following the direct analysis, we note that the preferential tariff liberalization has increased imports. By the usual reasoning (see Chapter 4), the increase in imports raises Home welfare, with the exact measure being the gap between the MD curve and P'' summed over all the extra units imported. This equals the area marked as A in Fig. 5.4.

Consider next the conflicting border price effects using these key facts: (i) Home imports amounted to M' before the PTA; (ii) after the PTA, an amount equal to X_R'' comes from RoW; and (iii) the rest of M', namely $M' - X_R''$, comes from Partner. Next we line up these quantities with the relevant price changes.

- The goods coming from RoW have fallen in price, so Home gains on these. The exact size of the gain is just the amount of imports affected times the price drop; in the figure this gain equals the area B.

- The goods coming from Partner have risen in price, so Home experiences a loss. The size of the loss is again the amount of imports affected (namely, $M' - X_R''$) times the price rise, namely the difference between $P' - T$ and P''. Graphically, this is the area C.

What about the border price effect on the extra imports, $M'' - M'$? The border price effect does not apply to these units; since Home did not import them to begin with, it does not make sense to talk about how much more or less they cost post-liberalization. The welfare impact of the extra imports shows up in the trade volume effect, i.e. area A.

Putting together the trade volume effect and the border price effects, Home's overall welfare change is equal to the areas A plus B minus the area C. A key point to remember is that this welfare effect may be positive or negative (this is Viner's ambiguity).

Summary: Welfare effects

To sum up:

- Partner gains area D (Smith's certitude);

Box 5.3   Home welfare effects of discriminatory tariff cutting in detail

Here, we consider the 'gross' welfare implications of the price and quantity changes derived in Fig. 5.4. To see consumer and producer surplus separately, we put the rightmost panel from Fig. 5.4 in the left-hand panel of Fig. 5.5 and add to it a right-hand panel consisting of a standard open-economy supply and demand diagram. (As we are focusing on Home welfare, we shall drop the two Foreign panels.) Turn first to the right panel. The drop in the domestic price from P' to P'' raises consumer surplus by $D + A_2 + A_1 + A_3$, but lowers producer surplus by D (see Chapter 4 if this reasoning is unfamiliar). The net change in the private surplus (i.e. producer and consumer surplus combined) is $A_2 + A_1 + A_3$. The change in tariff revenue is slightly more involved than usual. Originally, the tariff revenue was $A_1 + B_1 + C$ (i.e. T times M'). After the PTA, the tariff revenue is $B_1 + B$ since T is charged only on X''_R. Thus, the change in tariff-revenue is $B - A_1 - C$. Adding the private surplus change and the net revenue change, we find that the net impact on Home is: $A_2 + A_1 + A_3 + B - A_1 - C$. Cancelling, this becomes $A_2 + A_3 + B - C$. In Chapter 4 we showed that $A_2 + A_3$ equals A in the left-hand panel, so the net effect is just $A + B - C$, as in Fig. 5.4.

Figure 5.5 Focus on Home welfare effects of unilateral discriminatory liberalization

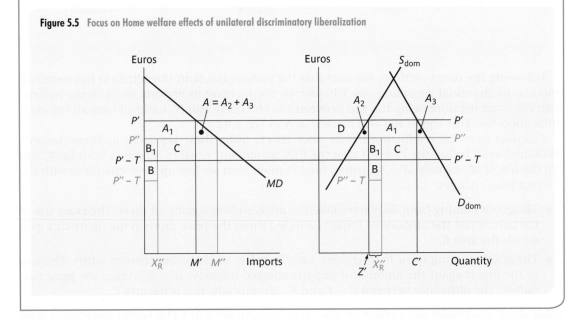

- RoW loses area E (Haberler's spillover); and
- Home's welfare changes by A + B − C, which may be positive or negative (Viner's ambiguity).

As Fig. 5.4 is drawn, the net welfare impact looks negative. Interested readers should be able to show that discriminatory liberalization will lead to a welfare gain if T is large enough. Moreover, as usual with tax analysis, the slopes of the supply and demand curves also affect the size of the welfare effects.

Box 5.4   Terminology in detail: trade creation, trade diversion

If one were to sneak into the bedroom of almost any famous international economist, shake that famous economist awake and shout loudly 'Free trade area – good or bad?', the first words out of the economist's mouth would surely include 'trade creation and trade diversion'. Indeed, these terms are so influential that one really must know them despite their shortcomings.

It should be clear to readers who have worked through the PTA diagram that this terminology fails to capture all welfare effects of discriminatory tariff liberalization, and, as we shall see in Section 5.2.3, it is completely useless when it comes to the type of barriers European integration has addressed since the mid-1970s, i.e. non-tariff barriers. One economist who has studied the history of 'customs union theory' suggests that the terms persist since they are 'highly effective tools of focusing policy makers' attention on the ambiguous welfare effects of PTAs' (Panagariya, 1999).

Economists have dealt with the incompleteness of Viner's terms in two ways. Some stretch the original meaning of his terms to cover the full effects in the simplest case where the *MS* curves are flat (see Annex A at the end of this chapter). Others have introduced new jargon – adding terms like 'internal versus external trade creation' and 'trade expansion'. All this variance in literary interpretation is possible because Viner did not use diagrams in his book and certainly no maths, so there is some debate over exactly what he meant. The most convincing translation of Viner's words into modern economics was undertaken by Nobel Laureate James Meade in his famous 1955 book, *The Theory of Customs Unions*. That book employed a general approach based on the powerful toolkit developed by, among others, Paul Samuelson, Kenneth Arrow, James Mirrles, and Meade himself. Namely, he breaks down net welfare effects into what we have called trade volume effects and border price effects.

5.2 Analysis of a customs union

Until now we have considered only unilateral tariff cuts. European integration, however, involves reciprocal, i.e. two-way, preferential liberalizations, so it is important to think through the case of two-way preferential liberalization. In our simple model, that means Home and Partner both set their tariffs to zero on each other's exports.

As it turns out, the study of a customs union is an easy stretch of the unilateral PTA analysis. The main extra insight we get from studying a customs union (a free trade agreement with a common external tariff) arises from the fact that a customs union (CU) is systematically more favourable for participating countries than unilateral liberalization schemes since Home exporters gain from Partner tariff cuts.

To keep things simple, we shall look at the formation of a CU between Home and Partner, assuming that all three countries (Home, Partner and RoW) are symmetric initially in all aspects, including the MFN tariff they initially impose on all imports. To do this carefully, we must address the question of the three-nation trade pattern. Again to streamline the analysis, we adopt the simplest combination that permits us to study the issues. This leads us to assume that three goods are traded (goods 1, 2 and 3). Each country produces all three goods, but cost structures are such that each nation exports two of the three goods while importing the remaining one. The trade pattern, shown schematically in Fig. 5.6, entails Home importing good 1 from Partner and RoW, and Partner importing good 2 from Home and RoW.

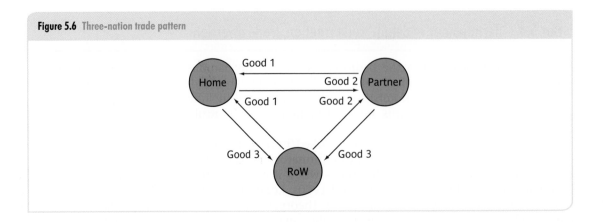

Figure 5.6 Three-nation trade pattern

5.2.1 Price and quantity effects

A CU is formed between Home and Partner when Home eliminates T on imports of good 1 from Partner, and Partner eliminates T on imports of good 2 from Home. The tariffs facing RoW exports are not changed, and since Home's and Partner's MFN tariffs were identical to start with, there is no need to harmonize their tariffs towards RoW; T becomes the common external tariff.

We first address the price and quantity effects. Plainly, the impact of Home's discriminatory liberalization is exactly the same as the impact shown in Fig. 5.2, so there is no need to repeat it here. The impact of Partner's discriminatory liberalization of imports of good 2 from Home can also be seen using the same diagram. Here is the key point.

A moment's reflection reveals that, given the assumed symmetry of nations, what happens to Home's exports when Partner lowers its barriers is exactly what happened to Partner's exports when Home lowered its barriers. We can, therefore, rely on analysis with which we are already familiar. More specifically, the price of good 2 in Partner falls from P' to P'' (see Fig. 5.2) but the border price facing Home exporters when they sell good 2 to Partner rises; it rises from $P' - T$ to P''. Nothing happens to domestic prices in RoW (since they did not liberalize), but RoW exporters face a lower border price for their exports to Partner. The trade volume effects are similarly simple. Partner imports rise from M' to M'' and Home exports to Partner rise; using the terminology from Fig. 5.2, Home exports to Partner rise from X'_p to X''_p. RoW's exports to Partner fall, as in Fig. 5.2.

5.2.2 Welfare effects

The welfare effects are also just a matter of adding up effects illustrated above. On Home's import side (i.e. in the market for good 1), Home gains the usual A + B − C in the right-hand panel of Fig. 5.7. On Home's export market (good 2), Home's situation is shown in the left-hand panel, so it gains area D. The welfare effects on Partner are identical to this, due to the assumed symmetry of goods and nations.

It is useful to study the welfare effects a bit more closely, using Fig. 5.8. This diagram shows only the two liberalizing nations, Home and Partner. To be concrete, suppose this is the market for good 1, which Home imports and Partner exports. The diagram is based on the two rightmost panels of Fig. 5.7 but we have added further detail to the areas. In particular, the trade price loss associated with area C is here split into two parts, C_1 and C_2, for a good reason.

Recall that Home loses $C_1 + C_2$ because the tariff cut raised the price it paid for imports from Partner (from $P' - T$ to P''). The first area, C_1, identifies how much it pays for the units it

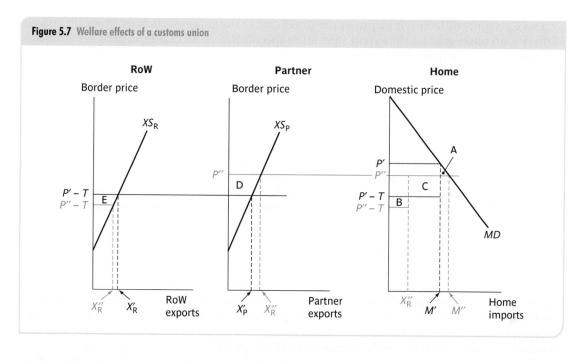

Figure 5.7 Welfare effects of a customs union

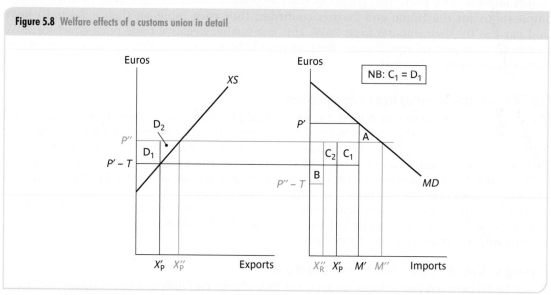

Figure 5.8 Welfare effects of a customs union in detail

continues to import from Partner ($M' - X'_p$). Home's loss of C_1, however, is exactly matched by a gain to Partner of the same size; the higher price for the X'_p units transfers C_1 from Home to Partner. The key point is that, because C_1 is just a transfer between CU members, Home's loss of C_1 on its imports of good 1 will be offset by a gain of $D_1 = C_1$ on its exports of good 2 to Partner. After all, Partner also lowers its tariff against Home exports, so we know that Home will gain an area exactly equal to C_1 in its exports of good 2. In addition, Home will gain D_2 in its export market.

Area C_2 is quite different. It identifies the direct cost of the supply switching (trade diversion), so there is no offset gain on the export side. More specifically, recall that from pre-CU symmetry, we know that RoW exports to Home pre-CU were equal to X'_p. After the CU, RoW exports are $X''_{R'}$, so the difference, $X'_p - X''_{R'}$, measures the amount of supply switching. This quantity is multiplied by the price change ($P' - T$ to P'') to get the welfare cost of the supply switching.

In summary, using the fact that $D_1 = C_1$, the net gain to Home is $+A + B + D_2 - C_2$. This net welfare effect may still be negative, but it is clear that the welfare change from a CU is more positive (or less negative) than the welfare change from a unilateral discriminatory liberalization with Partner.

The losses to RoW from the CU are twice the size of their losses shown in Fig. 5.7, since they lose E both on the exports of good 1 to Home and on their exports of good 2 to Partner. Readers who find this reasoning a bit complex may benefit from the step-by-step explanations in the interactive PowerPoint presentations that can be freely downloaded from http://heiwww.unige/ch/~baldwin/BW/BW.htm.

General equilibrium effects: second-order terms of trade changes

Lastly, we must consider the indirect or second-round implications of the CU.

RoW experiences a reduction in the value of its exports, yet has not reduced the value of its imports from Home and Partner. While this sort of trade deficit may be sustainable in the short run, eventually RoW must turn the situation around. In the real world, this is usually accomplished by a real depreciation of its currency (or a terms of trade worsening if it is in a monetary union). This makes all RoW exports to Home and Partner cheaper and simultaneously makes imports from those two countries more expensive. Both changes have positive welfare implications for the Home and Partner countries; they earn more on their exports to RoW and pay less for their imports from RoW. This is a further negative trade price effect for RoW stemming from general equilibrium effects of the CU between its trading Partners. Such effects, however, are likely to be small.

5.2.3 Customs unions versus free trade agreements

The 1957 Treaty of Rome committed the six original EU members to eliminating all tariffs and quotas on trade among themselves but it also committed them to completely harmonizing their tariffs on imports from non-member nations. In reaction to this customs union, other western European nations formed another trade bloc – known as the European Free Trade Association (EFTA) – in 1960. This was not a customs union, only a free trade area since EFTA members did not adopt a common external tariff. (See Chapter 1 for details.)

What are the key differences between a customs union and a free trade area? Why did the EEC go for a customs union while EFTA went for an FTA? We address these questions in order, starting with the main economic differences.

Stopping tariff cheats: 'trade deflection' and 'rules of origin'

When tariffs between two nations are zero, yet they charge two different tariffs on imports from third nations, firms have an incentive to cheat on tariffs. Take our three-nation example. If all Home–Partner trade is duty free, yet Home charges a 10 per cent tariff on imports from RoW while Partner charges only a 5 per cent tariff on goods coming from RoW, Home-based buyers of RoW goods would be tempted to import the goods first into Partner (thus paying only a 5 per cent tariff) and then to import them duty free from Partner to Home. To thwart this practice – known as trade deflection – Home and Partner have two choices. They can eliminate the temptation by harmonizing their external tariffs (thus turning their FTA into a customs union), or they can stay with the FTA but restrict duty-free treatment to goods that are actually *made* in Home or Foreign. The set of rules that enforce the latter option are called 'rules of origin'.

One problem with rules of origin, and thus with FTAs, is that it can be difficult to know where a product is made in today's highly globalized markets. Personal computers made in, say, Switzerland will contain components from all over the world. The Swiss company may be doing little more than customized assembly of parts from the USA and Asia. In the extreme, it may be doing nothing more than opening the box of a US-made computer and putting in an instruction manual translated into, say, Norwegian. Should the full value of this computer be given duty-free treatment when it is exported to Norway? (Switzerland and Norway are both EFTA members.)

The costs of rules of origin

For manufactured goods, the EU's basic rule of origin is that some fixed percentage of the product's value-added – say 50 per cent – must be done in the exporting nation. For example, if Switzerland exports a specialized type of computer set-up to Germany but imports the monitors and computers from Asia, then the Swiss export will only qualify for zero-tariff treatment if the final price of the good is more than 50 per cent higher than the value of the imported components. For many products, the rules can be much more complex.

Because they can be very expensive to comply with, rules of origin can act as trade barriers, or as barriers that de facto nullify the benefits of a de jure trade agreement. A good example of this can be seen in the EU's unilateral preference schemes for developing nations. Brenton and Manchin (2003) show that only one-third of EU imports from developing countries which were – in principle – eligible for preferences actually entered the EU market with reduced duties. The reason is that the EU's rules of origin in developing nations' exports (e.g. textiles and clothing) are very difficult and expensive to comply with, so the developing nation exporters prefer to pay the EU's high common external tariff rather than comply with the rules of origin and pay zero tariff.

An additional problem with rules of origin is that they can end up as hidden protection. Since rules of origin are specified at the product level, they can be difficult for non-experts to evaluate – just as is the case with technical barriers to trade. As a consequence, rules of origin are usually written in consultation with domestic firms who have an incentive to shape the rules into protectionist devices.

One great advantage of a customs union like the EU is that firms do not have to demonstrate the origin of a product before it is allowed to cross an intra-EU border duty free. Any good that is physically in Germany was either made in Germany or paid the CET when it entered. In either case, the good deserves duty-free passage into France, or any other EU member, without any documentation at all.

5.2.4 Political integration and customs unions

Most preferential trade arrangements in the world are free trade agreements rather than customs unions, like the EU. The reason is simple – political integration. Getting a group of nations to agree on a common external tariff at the launch of a customs union is difficult, but the real problems begin as time passes. For instance, if one member nation believes its industry is being undercut by some non-member nation which is exporting its goods at a price that is below cost (so-called dumping), it may want to impose tariffs to offset the dumping. In a customs union, all nations must agree on every dumping duty since external tariffs must always remain constant. Likewise, nations typically reduce their tariffs in the context of GATT/WTO negotiations. For a customs union, this requires all members to agree on a common negotiating position on every single product.

In practice, keeping the Common External Tariff (CET) common requires some integration of decision making. In the EU, the Commission formally has the power to set tariffs on third-nation goods (even though it naturally consults with Member States before doing so), but very few groups of countries are willing to transfer that amount of national sovereignty. As a result, most trade blocs, including EFTA and the North American Free Trade Agreement, are free trade areas rather than customs unions.

Another way to 'solve' the decision-making problem is for the members to let one nation decide everything. This is the case in all the successful customs unions in the world apart from the EU. For example, South Africa is the dominant nation in the Southern African Customs Union and Switzerland is the dominant nation in the Swiss–Liechtenstein customs union.

5.3 Frictional barriers: the 1992 Programme

Hereto we have dealt with tariff liberalization. This was an important part of early European economic integration, but after the free trade agreements between the EU and EFTA nations were signed in 1973, tariff liberalization was a minor part of intra-European economic integration (see Chapter 1 for details).

Since the mid-1970s – and especially since the 1986 Single European Act – most of the economic integration in Europe has involved the removal of 'frictional' barriers to trade. As Chapter 4 explained, this type of barrier hinders trade without raising revenue. Frictional barriers often involve intricate differences between national regulations, so a critical frictional-barrier-liberalizing element of the 1986–92 Single Market Programme was the mutual recognition principle which made it difficult for EU members to use health, safety and environmental regulations as subtle forms of trade barriers.

This section extends the basic Fig. 5.4 reasoning in a way that allows us to study the impact of preferential frictional barriers liberalization. At a basic level, this is easy to do since frictional barriers can be conceptualized as tariffs where the tariff revenue is thrown away. As we shall see, for such barriers Smith's certitude and Haberler's spillover still hold, but Viner's ambiguity disappears.

5.3.1 Price and quantity effects

To keep things simple, we continue to work with the simplified reality of three nations, and we assume that they all initially impose a frictional barrier whose tariff equivalent is T. Note that the 'tariff equivalent' is a useful way of measuring the importance of a frictional barrier since it identifies the size of the tariff, T, that would drive an equivalent wedge between the border price and the Home price.

To be specific, we assume that Home and Partner fully remove the frictional barrier on each other with no change in the frictional barrier applied to RoW–Home or Partner–RoW trade. In this sense it is a preferential frictional barrier liberalization.

Not surprisingly, the price and quantity effects of the preferential liberalization are very similar to those discussed in Fig. 5.2. After all, a frictional barrier can be thought of as a tariff where the tariff revenue is thrown away. The only change concerns the border price.

As discussed in Chapter 4, the importer's and exporter's border prices differ with a frictional barrier. In particular, the importer's border price (i.e. what the importing nation actually pays for the imports) is higher than that of the exporter's border price (i.e. what the exporter actually gets paid for the export). Specially, the different is T and it reflects the real costs involved in overcoming the frictional barrier. Given this, frictional barriers liberalization lowers Home's border price while at the same time raising the border price faced by Partner's exporters.

Using the Fig. 5.7 terms, the reciprocal, preferential frictional barrier liberalization:

- lowers Home's domestic price from P' to P'';
- lowers Home's border price from P' to P'';

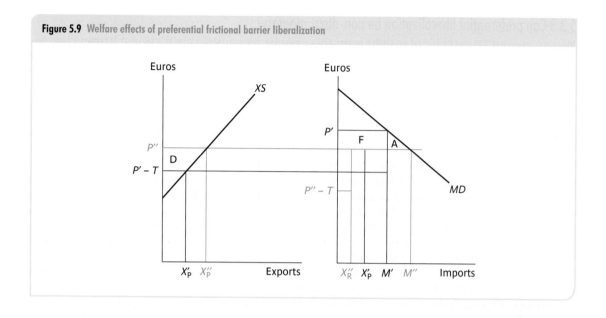

Figure 5.9 Welfare effects of preferential frictional barrier liberalization

- raises the price received by Partner exporters from $P'' - T$ to P''; and
- lowers the price received by RoW exporters from $P' - T$ to $P'' - T$.

The quantity effects follow from the price changes. Namely:

- Home imports rise from M' to M''.
- Partner exports rise from X'_P to X''_P.
- RoW exports fall from X'_R to X''_R.

Combining the last two, we see that supply switching still occurs.

5.3.2 Welfare effects

The welfare effects on Home are simple. As with tariffs, the change in Home private surplus equals areas F + A in Fig. 5.9. This is not offset by a loss in tariff revenues, as was the case in Fig. 5.4; this is why Viner's ambiguity fails in the frictional barrier case. Removing frictional barriers – even on a preferential basis – always lowers the price that the nation pays for its imports. Although both Partner and RoW exporters see changes in the prices they receive for exports to Home, and this leads to supply switching, this 'trade diversion' has no welfare consequences for Home.

Since we are looking at a reciprocal liberalization like the Single European Act, we have to also consider the changes that affect Home's and RoW's exporters to Partner (i.e. in the good-2 market using the Fig. 5.6 labels). In this market, Home is an exporter to Partner, and the welfare effect is also positive. Home exporters get a higher price and sell more, so they gain the area D.

Thus the overall welfare effect of the reciprocal, preferential frictional barrier liberalization FTA is +D + F + A for Home, and the same for Foreign by symmetry. RoW loses the equivalent of area E from Fig. 5.4 twice (once on its exports to Home and once on its exports to Partner). A key point is that Viner's ambiguity has disappeared. With frictional barriers, any kind of liberalization will lead to positive border price effects and positive trade volume effects since the border price equals the domestic price with frictional barriers.

5.3.3 Can preferential liberalization be non-discriminatory?

We can eke out an extra bit of insight from this exercise by considering frictional barrier changes that do not come with 'rules of origin'. That is, some aspects of European economic integration have made it easier for firms from all nations to do business in the EU – not just EU firms.

For example, consider the trade effects of introducing the euro. Clearly a common currency lowered the cost of, say, French firms doing business in Germany. But the euro also made it easier for, say, Japanese firms or British firms to do business with Eurozone members. Before the euro, a Japanese firm that wanted to sell, say, specialized GPS sports watches in Germany would have had to set up a bank account in Germany and set up internal arrangements to deal with the Deutschmarks it got from sales. For a market the size of Germany this might be worthwhile, but for a market the size of Austria, the Japanese firm might not find it worthwhile setting up all the arrangements that would be necessary to deal with sales in Austrian schillings. The euro's introduction, however, removed the extra cost. The arrangements that make it possible to sell in euros now give access to all Eurozone markets at no extra cost. In this way, we can think of the euro – which otherwise might be thought of as a preferential economic integration – as a non-discriminatory removal of frictional barriers.

In fact this is exactly what happened when the euro was introduced. Baldwin (2006) estimates that the euro boosted trade among Eurozone nations by about 9 per cent and it was accompanied by no supply switching. Indeed Eurozone imports from non-Eurozone EU members rose by 7 per cent.

We covered the analysis of MFN liberalization of frictional barriers in Chapter 4 (Section 4.4.2). The key point is that the price and quantity effects would be just those of the removal of an MFN tariff. Specifically, the MFN frictional barrier liberalization would lower Home's price and raise the border price of both Partner and RoW along with both of their exports to Home. Thus there would be no supply switching and no 'trade diversion'.

5.4 WTO rules

The world trading system is governed by a set of rules overseen by the World Trade Organization (WTO). The most important guiding principle of the WTO/GATT is non-discrimination in trade policy, i.e. the so-called most favoured nation principle, or MFN for short. This says that nations should, in principle, impose tariffs on a non-discriminatory basis. Of course, all of the preferential liberalization discussed above contradicts this principle, so why is it allowed? As it turns out, the GATT created an explicit loophole for FTAs and customs unions. Allowing this loophole was important for some of the early GATT members since they wished to maintain existing preferential arrangements (especially Britain's Commonwealth Preferences).

The loophole, formally known as Article 24, specifically allows preferential liberalization, subject to a few restrictions, the most important of which are:

- Free trade agreements and customs unions must completely eliminate tariffs on 'substantially all the trade' among members.
- The phase-out of tariffs must take place within a reasonable period.

Although there are no hard definitions, 'substantially all trade' is usually taken to mean at least 80 per cent of all goods and a 'reasonable period' is taken to be ten years or less.

For a customs union, there is the additional requirement that the common external tariff (CET) 'shall not on the whole be higher or more restrictive' than before the customs union. That is, when forming the customs union, the members cannot harmonize the CET to the highest level of any member. In the case of the EEC's customs union formation, external tariff harmonization generally involved a reduction in French and Italian tariffs, a rise in Benelux tariffs and little change in German tariffs.

5.5 Empirical studies of supply switching

A large number of recent studies in the economics literature have examined the trade-creating and trade-diverting effects of preferential agreements. A recent review of the evidence (Freund and Ornelas, 2010) notes that most studies find evidence of trade creation and little or no evidence of trade diversion for most PTAs. However, the EU may be an exception. Magee (2008) uses data from the late twentieth century to estimate the creation/diversion effects of 15 separate PTAs including NAFTA, the 1986 enlargement of the EU, and 1992 bilateral PTAs between the EU and several central European nations. Of the eight PTAs that were found to have positive trade creation effects, only 2 were found to be trade diverting. Those two were the 1986 EU enlargement, and the EU Association agreements with central and eastern European Countries in the early 1990s.

A more recent study using twenty-first century data measures trade creation and diversion for many PTAs around the world (Archarya et al., 2010). Their estimates show that most PTAs – including the EU and EFTA – had positive trade creation effects and reverse trade diversion effects, i.e. the PTAs raised the partners' imports from each other and from nations outside the agreement. This is not consistent with our study of the economic effects of a preferential tariff liberalization; however, it is consistent with the idea that many of today's PTAs – especially the EU and EFTA – are really pursuing frictional barrier liberalization that tends not to be discriminatory for the reasons discussed in Section 5.3.3.

5.6 Summary

This chapter introduced the verbal logic and graphical methods necessary to study preferential trade liberalization in a NICNIR setting. After going over the preliminaries, we studied the price and quantity and welfare effects of the formation of a customs union. The main technical points are:

* Formation of a preferential trade arrangement such as the EEC's customs union, or EFTA's free trade area, tends to lower domestic prices and raise imports overall, but the discriminatory aspects of these liberalizations also produce supply switching, that is to say, a switch from non-member suppliers to member-based suppliers.

* The welfare effects of any trade liberalization, including PTA liberalization, can be captured by standard public-finance concepts, which we here call trade volume effects and border price (or trade price) effects.

* The welfare impact of preferential tariff liberalization is ambiguous for the liberalizing nations; this is called Viner's ambiguity. The deep fundamental reason is that PTAs are discriminatory liberalizations; the liberalization part – what Viner called trade creation – tends to boost economic efficiency, while the discrimination part – what Viner called trade diversion – tends to lower it. The impact on excluded nations is always negative.

* Estimates of the welfare impact of trade liberalization in the NICNIR setting are inevitably very small. This suggests to most observers that one has to look to more

complicated frameworks if one is to understand why trade liberalization in general, and European integration in particular, matter.

The bigger lessons from the chapter concern the way in which the economic analysis helps us to understand the big-think trends in European integration.

∗ The NICNIR framework helped us to study the impact of discriminatory liberalization on outsiders in an intellectually uncluttered setting. This helps us to understand why outsiders always reacted to the deepening and widening of EU integration. As we showed, preferential liberalization definitely harms excluded nations since it leads them to face lower prices for their exports to the customs union and lower export sales. It seems natural, therefore, that the outsiders would react either by forming their own preferential arrangements (as happened in the 1960s with EFTA), or by deepening the integration between the outsiders and the EU (as outsiders did in the 1970s and again in the 1990s), or by joining the EU (as nine formerly outsider western European nations had done by 1994).

Self-assessment questions

The NICNIR was the backbone of 'customs union theory' for years, so quite a number of extensions and provisos were put forth in the NICNIR setting. Some of them are still insightful and the following exercises illustrate the basic points.

1 (Kemp–Wan theorem.) Starting from a situation like that shown in Fig. 5.1, where the three nations are symmetric in everything, including the initial MFN tariff T, suppose that Home and Partner form a customs union *and* lower their common tariff against RoW to the point where the new, post-liberalization border price facing RoW exporters is the same as it was before the liberalization, i.e. $P' - T$. Show that this 'Kemp–Wan' adjustment ensures that Home and Partner gain while RoW does not lose from this CU-with-CET-reduction scheme.

2 (Cooper–Massell extended.) We can think of a preferential unilateral liberalization in the following roundabout manner. Home lowers its tariffs to zero on an MFN basis, but then raises it back to T on imports only from RoW. Now suppose that Home faces a flat MS curve for imports from both Partner and RoW (this is the 'small country' case). Moreover, suppose that Partner's *MS* is somewhat above that of RoW's.

First work out the welfare effects on Home. (Hint: This is covered in Annex A.)

Second, show that Home would gain more from a unilateral MFN liberalization than it would from a unilateral preferential liberalization. (Historical note: Taking their NICNIR analysis as definitive, this result led Cooper and Massell to suggest that small countries must join customs unions for political reasons only. You can see that this is only a partial analysis by realizing that a customs union also lowers tariffs facing Home-based exporters.) Try to figure out how Home gains from Partner's tariff removal on Home-to-Partner exports. After doing this, see if you can say definitely whether Home gains more from unilateral free trade, or from joining the customs union. You should also be able to show that the optimal policy for a small nation is to have unilateral free trade *and* join every FTA that it can.

3 (Large Partner rule of thumb.) Redo the FTA formation exercise from the text, assuming that RoW is initially a much smaller trading partner of Home and Partner in the sense that most of Home's imports are from Partner and most of Partner's imports are from Home when all three nations impose the initial MFN tariff, T. Show that the 'net border price effect' (area $B - C_1 - C_2$ in Fig. 5.8) is smaller when RoW is initially a less important trade partner of Home and Partner nations. (Hint: Focus on the Home country and start with a diagram like Fig. 5.1. Keep the vertical intersections of XS_P and XS_R at the same height, but make the XS_R steeper and the XS_P flatter in a way that does not change P''; our thanks to Jonathan Gage for help with this problem.)

4 (Growth effects and RoW impact.) Suppose that signing an FTA between Home and Partner produces a growth effect that raises their income level and thus shifts their MD curves upwards. Use a diagram like Fig. 5.4 to show how big the upward shift would have to be to ensure that RoW did not lose from the Home–Partner FTA. (In the 1970s, this was the informal explanation for why the EEC6 formation did not lead to trade diversion.) Can you show the welfare impact of this growth on Home?

5 (Hub-and-spoke bilateralism.) Using PTA diagrams, show what the price, quantity and welfare effects would be of a hub-and-spoke arrangement among three nations. (Hub-and-spoke means that country 1 signs FTAs with countries 2 and 3, but 2 and 3 do not liberalize trade between them.) Assume that there are *only* frictional barriers in this world, that initially all import barriers have a tariff equivalent of T, and that the FTAs concern only frictional barrier liberalization. Be sure to look at the price, quantity and welfare impact on (i) a typical spoke economy (2 or 3) and (ii) the hub economy.

6 (Sapir, 1992.) Consider a situation where Home and Partner have formed a customs union but have not eliminated frictional barriers between them. Specifically, assume that all trade flows among Home, Partner and RoW are subject to frictional trade barriers equal to T' and additionally the tariff on trade between the CU and RoW is equal to T''. Show that eliminating frictional barriers inside the CU might harm welfare since it leads to a reduction in the amount of tariff revenue collected on imports from RoW.

7 Suppose Home has no trade barriers, except anti-dumping measures. These anti-dumping measures take the form of price undertakings, i.e. instead of Home imposing a tariff on RoW and Partner imports, Home requires Partner and RoW firms to charge a high price for their sales to Home. Show the price, quantity and welfare effects of imposing this import price floor (look at all three nations). Next, show the price, quantity and welfare effects of removing the price undertaking (i.e. allowing free trade) only for imports from Partner. Be sure to illustrate the impact on all three nations. (Hint: The price undertaking is a price floor, so it does not act just like a tariff; be very careful in constructing the MS_{PTA} for this situation.)

Essay questions

1 Using the analysis of a customs union in this chapter, explain how the domino theory of integration could explain the fact that virtually all nations in and around western Europe now have or want to have preferential trade arrangements with the European Union.

2 Using the economic analysis in this chapter, together with the political economy logic of special-interest groups (well-organized groups often have political weight that is far in excess of their economic weight), explain why the WTO restrictions on customs unions and free trade areas might be a good idea.

3 Using the economic analysis in this chapter and political economy logic, explain why most trade liberalizations are reciprocal rather than unilateral.

4 Some international trade experts believe that formation of the EU's customs union led to pressures from the USA and Japan for a multilateral tariff-cutting round called the Kennedy Round. Use the economic analysis in this chapter, together with the political economy logic of special-interest groups, to explain why this view might make sense. (Hint: US and Japanese exporters are a very powerful special-interest group.)

5 When Bismarck led the drive to unify the many small regions and nation-states of Germany, he used a customs union (*Zollverein*) as both a carrot and a stick to encourage unification. Use the economic analysis in this chapter (especially the impact on RoW) to make sense of this strategy.

Further reading: the aficionado's corner

The modern study of European economic integration began life under the name of 'customs union theory' with **Viner** (1950). Viner's seminal text triggered a flood of work. At the time, tariffs were the key trade barriers and theorists had few tools for dealing with imperfect competition, so the early literature focused on tariff removals in the NICNIR setting. For a highly readable survey of this literature, see:

Pomfret, R. (1986) 'The theory of preferential trading arrangements', *Weltwirtschaftliches Archiv*, 122: 439–64.

A review of pre-Vinerian literature is provided by:

O'Brien, D.P. (1975) 'Classical monetary theory', in *The Classical Economists*, Clarendon Press, Oxford, pp. 140–69.

Following Viner's theory, which associated welfare effects with changes in trade flows, early empirical studies focused on trade creation and diversion. Surveys of this literature include:

Mayes, D. (1978) 'The effects of economic integration on trade', *Journal of Common Market Studies*, XVII: 1–25.

Srinivasan, T.N., J. Whalley and I. Wooton (1993) 'Measuring the effects of regionalism on trade and welfare', pp. 52–79 in K. Anderson and R. Blackhurst (eds) *Regional Integration and the Global Trading System*, Harvester Wheatsheaf for the GATT Secretariat, London.

Winters, L.A. (1987) 'Britain in Europe: a survey of quantitative trade studies', *Journal of Common Market Studies*, 25: 315–35.

A more extensively graphic presentation of pre- and post-1958 trade flows in Europe can be found in:

Neal, L. and D. Berbezat (1998) *The Economics of the European Union and the Economics of Europe*, Oxford University Press, London.

See also:

Baldwin, R.E. and A. Venables (1995) 'Regional economic integration', in G. Grossman and K. Rogoff (eds) *Handbook of International Economics* Volume III, North-Holland, Amsterdam.

Mankiw, G. (2000) *Principles of Economics*, Thomson Learning, New York.

Useful websites

While the EU's customs union has been completed for over three decades, some policy issues occasionally arise. See the Commission's website http://europa.eu.int/comm/taxationcustoms/.

The history of EFTA's free trade area can be found on www.efta.int/.

Further information on WTO rules concerning preferential trade arrangements can be found on www.wto.org.

References

Acharya, R., J.-C. Crawford, M. Maliszewski and C. Renard (2011) 'Landscape', chapter 2 in J.-P. Chauffour and J.-C. Maur (eds) *Preferential Trade Agreement Policies for Development: A Handbook*, World Bank Publications, Washington, DC.

Baldwin, R. (2006) *In or Out: Does it Matter? An Evidence-based Analysis of the Trade Effects of the Euro*, Centre for Economic Policy Research, London.

Brenton, P. and M. Manchin (2003) 'Making EU trade agreements work: the role of rules of origin', *The World Economy*, 26(5): 755–69.

Cooper, C. and D. Massell (1965) 'Towards a general theory of customs unions in developing countries', *Journal of Political Economy*, 73: 256–83.

Freund, C. and E. Ornelas (2010) *Regional Trade Agreements*, Policy Research Working Paper Series 5314, The World Bank.

Haberler, G. (1937) *The Theory of International Trade with its Applications to Commercial Policy*, Macmillan, New York.

Kemp, M. and H. Wan (1976) 'An elementary proposition concerning the formation of customs unions', *Economic Journal*, 6: 95–7.

Magee, C.S.P. (2008) 'New measures of trade creation and trade diversion', *Journal of International Economics*, 75(2): 340–62.

Meade, J. (1955) *The Theory of Customs Unions*, Oxford University Press, London.

Panagariya, A. (1999) 'Preferential trade liberalisation: the traditional theory and new developments', University of Maryland mimeo (download from www.bsos.umd.edu/econ/panagariya/song/surveypt.pdf).

Pomfret, R. (1997) *The Economics of Regional Trading Arrangements*, Clarendon Press, London.

Sapir, A. (1992) 'Regional integration in Europe', *Economic Journal*, 102(415): 1491–506.

Viner, J. (1950) *The Customs Union Issue*, Carnegie Endowment for International Peace, New York.

Annex A Discriminatory liberalization: small country case

This background appendix presents the classic analysis of unilateral preferential tariff liberalization for the 'small country' case. The so-called small country case means that we make the simplifying assumption that the volume of a nation's imports is unrelated to the price of those imports. In this case, we do not need the import supply and demand diagram discussed above. Rather, we can work directly with a simpler open-economy supply and demand diagram.

Figure A5.1, which allows for two potential sources of imports (countries A and B), helps to organize the reasoning. To set the stage, suppose that Home initially imposes a tariff of T on imports from A and B. (Goods produced in the countries A, B and Home are perfect substitutes.) The Home nation is assumed to face a flat import supply curve from both countries. The idea behind this simplification is that Home is so small that it can buy as much or as little as it wants without affecting the price. Specifically, the import supply curves from A and B are the flat curves at the levels P_A and P_B. We can see that country A producers are more efficient since they can offer the goods at a lower price. That is, importing from A costs Home consumers $P_A + T$, while importing from B costs $P_B + T$. Plainly, all imports initially come from the cheaper supplier, namely A.

Adding together the three sources of supply (Home, A and B), we find the pre-liberalization total supply curve to be TS_1. Because it is the horizontal sum of the Home supply curve and the two import supply curves, it follows the Home supply curve up to $P_A + T$ and, beyond that, it follows A's import supply curve. The equilibrium Home price (i.e. the price facing Home consumers and producers) is $P_A + T$, since this is where total supply meets demand. The border price, namely the price that Home as a country pays for imports, is P_A.

Next, we ask what would happen if the tariff were removed on a discriminatory basis. That is to say, if it were removed on imports from only A or only B. Both cases must be considered. We turn now to the price, quantity and welfare effects of the two cases.

Figure A5.1 Price and quantity effects of discriminatory liberalization (small nation)

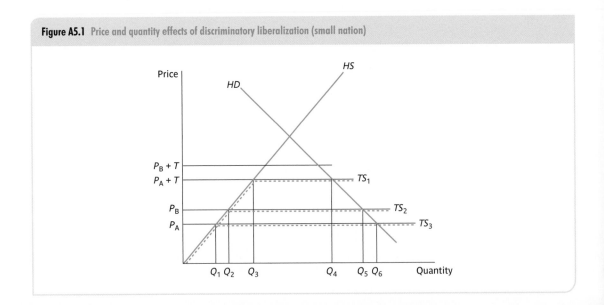

A5.1 Price and quantity analysis, liberalization with low-cost country

In the first case, the liberalization is applied to Home's current trading partner, namely A. The total supply curve becomes TS_3, so the Home price falls to P_A. Home consumption rises, Home production falls, imports rise and nothing happens to the border price of imports. To summarize:

- The price in the Home market of both imports and Home import-competing goods falls to P_A.
- Home production falls from Q_3 to Q_1.

  Home consumption rises from Q_4 to Q_6.

- The import volume rises from the difference between Q_3 and Q_4 to the difference between Q_1 and Q_6.
- The border price (i.e. the price of imported goods before the imposition of the tax) remains unchanged at P_A.

With some thought, it is clear that discriminatory liberalization with the low-cost country has the same impact as an MFN liberalization. After all, both types of liberalization remove the tariff on all imports (the preferential tariff cut leaves the tariff on goods from B, but no imports come from B before or after the liberalization).

A5.2 Welfare analysis: liberalization with low-cost country

As with the price and quantity analysis, in this case the welfare analysis is identical to that of non-discriminatory liberalization. Home consumer surplus rises and Home producer surplus falls because of the liberalization. Since more units are consumed than produced domestically, the sum of consumer and producer surpluses rises. Part of this gain is offset by a loss in tariff revenue. Using Fig. A5.2 to be more precise:

- Consumer surplus rises by the sum of all the areas A through J.
- Producer surplus falls by the area A + E.

Figure A5.2 Small country welfare analysis

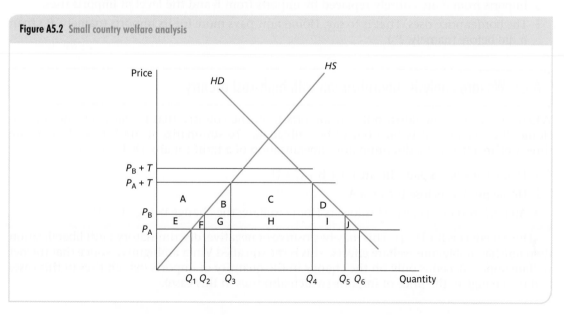

- Government revenue falls by C + H.
- The net effect is unambiguously positive and equal to (B + F + G) and (D + I + J).

A5.3 Liberalization with high-cost country: supply switching

The analysis is only slightly trickier when the preferential trade arrangement is signed with the high-cost country.

Graphically, as shown in Fig. A5.1, this results in a total supply curve of TS_2 and a Home price of P_B. Recall that since country B is the high-cost supplier (i.e. P_B is above P_A) nothing was imported from B initially. Granting duty-free access to goods from B artificially changes the relative competitiveness of goods from A and B – at least in the eyes of Home consumers. Goods from B cost P_B while goods from A cost P_A + T. Quite naturally, Home importers of goods will divert all their import demand from A towards B. We call this the 'supply-switching' effect of discriminatory liberalization; it is the first of two elements that arise with discriminatory liberalization but do not arise with non-discriminatory liberalization. Note, however, that discriminatory liberalization does not always lead to supply switching. It can only do so when it is done with the high-cost country. The second novel aspect of discriminatory liberalization is the border price impact. That is, as consumers switch from the low-cost source to the high-cost source (country B), the Home border price rises. We call this the 'border price' effect, or the import-price-rising effect. The importance of this price change should be clear – such liberalization will raise the cost of imports to the country as a whole.

To summarize, there are six price and quantity effects:

1 The preferential liberalization increases competition from imports and thereby forces down the Home price of locally made and imported goods to P_B.
2 Consumption rises to Q_5.
3 Some high-cost Home production is replaced by lower-cost imports. This amount is equal to $Q_3 - Q_2$.
4 The new Home production level is Q_2.
5 Imports from A are entirely replaced by imports from B and the level of imports rises.
6 The border price rises. That is to say, Home now pays more for its imports (namely, P_B) than it did before (namely, P_A).

A5.4 Welfare analysis: liberalization with high-cost country

When the tariffs come down only on imports from the country that initially sells nothing to Home, the welfare effects turn out to be ambiguous. To summarize using Fig. A5.2, there are three welfare effects of a discriminatory liberalization of a tariff (or any DCR barrier):

1 Home consumers gain the area A + B + C + D.
2 Home producers lose the area A.
3 All tariff revenue is lost. This lowers Home welfare; the change being −C − H.

The net effect is B + D − H. This may be positive or negative; discriminatory tariff liberalization therefore has ambiguous welfare effects. This is the so-called Viner ambiguity. Notice that the net welfare impact depends only on the change in the quantity of imports (which rises in this case) and the change in the price of imports (which also rises in this case).

Chapter 6

Market size and scale effects

The countries of Europe are too small to give their peoples the prosperity that is now attainable and therefore necessary. They need wider markets.

Jean Monnet, 1943

By its size – the biggest in the world – the single market without frontiers is an invaluable asset to revitalize our businesses and make them more competitive. It is one of the main engines of the European Union.

Jacques Delors, July 1987

Chapter Contents

Introduction

Market size matters. From its very inception in the 1950s, an important premise behind European economic integration was the belief that unification of European economies would – by allowing European firms access to a bigger market – make European firms more efficient and this, in turn, would allow them to lower prices, raise quality and gain competitiveness in external markets.

This chapter explores the economic logic of how European integration can lead to fewer, larger firms operating at a more efficient scale and facing more effective competition. The EU policy responses to these changes – notably the enforcement of rules that prohibit unfair subsidization of firms and rules restricting anti-competitive behaviour – are studied in Chapter 14. In the EU, such policies are called, respectively, 'state aids' policy and 'competition policy'.

6.1 Liberalization, defragmentation and industrial restructuring: logic and facts

We start the chapter by verbally explaining the logic that links European integration to industrial restructuring before presenting some facts on mergers and acquisitions (M&As) and the effects on competition.

Europe's national markets are separated by a whole host of barriers. These included tariffs and quotas until the Common Market was completed in 1968 and tariffs between the EEC and EFTA until the EEC–EFTA free trade agreements were signed in 1974. Yet, even though intra-EU trade has been duty free for over three decades, trade among European nations is not as free as it is within any given nation. Many technical, physical and fiscal barriers still make it easier for companies to sell in their local market than in other EU markets. While most of these barriers seem trivial or even silly when considered in isolation, the confluence of thousands of seemingly small barriers serves to substantially restrict intra-EU trade. As a result, EU firms can often be dominant in their home market while being marginal players in other EU markets (think of the European car market). This situation, known as market fragmentation, reduces competition and this, in turn, raises prices and keeps too many firms in business. Keeping firms in business is not, of course, a bad thing in itself. The problem is that this results in an industrial structure marked by too many inefficient small firms that can get away with charging high prices to cover the cost of their inefficiency. Owing to the absence of competition, poor and/or low-quality services and goods may also accompany the high prices (think of the European telephone service before liberalization).

Tearing down these intra-EU barriers defragments the markets and produces extra competition. This 'pro-competitive effect', in turn, puts pressure on profits and the market's response is 'merger mania'. That is, the pro-competitive effect squeezes the least efficient firms, prompting an industrial restructuring where Europe's weaker firms merge or get bought up. In the end, Europe is left with a more efficient industrial structure, with fewer, bigger, more efficient firms competing more effectively with each other. All this means improved material well-being for Europeans as prices fall and output rises. In some industries, restructuring may be accompanied by a sizeable reallocation of employment, as firms cut back on redundant workers and close inefficient plants and offices (a painful process for workers who have to change jobs). In other industries, however, liberalization can unleash a virtuous circle of more competition, lower prices, higher sales and higher employment.

In the remainder of the chapter we work through the logic of what was just presented informally. Schematically, the steps can be summarized as: liberalization → defragmentation → pro-competitive effect → industrial restructuring. The result is fewer, bigger, more efficient firms facing more effective competition from each other.

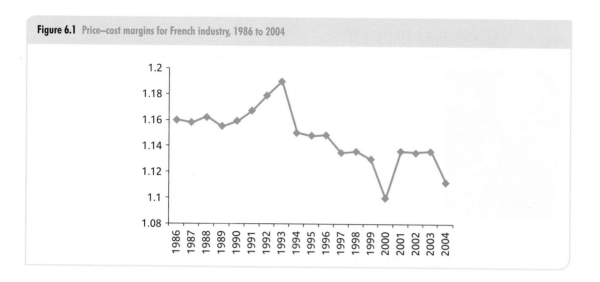

Figure 6.1 Price–cost margins for French industry, 1986 to 2004

6.1.1 Some evidence

As the verbal explanation made clear, the cutting edge of the scale effects turns on the pro-competitive effect and this can be measured by the price–cost ratio. A study of French manufacturing data calculated the the price–cost ratio shown in Fig. 6.1 (Bellone et al., 2008). The authors calculate that implementation of the Single Market Programme and its follow-up in the Economic and Monetary Union treaty (Maastricht Treaty) lowered the margin 4 to 5 percentage points.

Econometric evidence from Allen et al. (1998a, 1999b) suggests that the Single Market Programme reduced price–cost margins by 4 per cent on average, in line with the estimate for France. This impact varied from quite high, e.g. −15 per cent in the office machinery sector, to quite small, e.g. −0.1 per cent in brewing. It is noteworthy that in the auto sector – a sector that was granted a bloc exemption from the Single Market Programme – the price–cost margin actually rose.

Another study, Badinger (2007), used data on ten EU Member States over the period 1981–99 for each of three major industry groups (manufacturing, construction and services) and 18 more detailed industries to test whether the EU's Single Market Programme reduced firms' price–cost mark-ups, i.e. had a pro-competitive effect. He found mark-up reductions for aggregate manufacturing and construction. In contrast, mark-ups have gone up in most service industries since the early 1990s. He suggests that this latter finding confirms the weak state of the Single Market for services and suggests that anti-competitive defence strategies have emerged in EU service industries.

More recently, Chen et al. (2009) find evidence of a pro-competitive effect from economic integration using disaggregated data for EU manufacturing over the period 1989–99. They find that foreign import penetration has a strong competitive effect, with prices and mark-ups falling and productivity rising.

6.2 Theoretical preliminaries: monopoly, duopoly and oligopoly

To study the logic of European integration's impact on scale and competition we need a simple yet flexible framework that allows for imperfect competition. The framework we employ below – the *BE–COMP* diagram – assumes a knowledge of simple imperfect competition models, so by way of preliminaries, we briefly review the simplest forms of imperfect competition – monopoly,

> ### Box 6.1 Joan Robinson (1903–83)
>
>
>
> Joan Robinson, one of the most prominent economists of the twentieth century, made many fundamental contributions to various areas of economics, including what is widely recognized as the seminal contribution on imperfect competition in her 1933 book, *The Economics of Imperfect Competition*. Robinson, who taught at Cambridge University, was a colleage of Keynes and a prominent socialist. She actively spoke out against the social and economic injustices in the developing world. Other works by Robinson include *An Essay on Marxian Economics* (1942) and *The Accumulation of Capital* (1956).
>
> Many economists feel that she should have been awarded the Nobel Prize, but she worked at a time of blatant sex discrimination. For instance, despite her monumental contributions to economic theory in the 1930s and 1940s, she became a full professor only in 1965.

duopoly and oligopoly. Advanced readers may want to skip this section and move directly to the *BE–COMP* diagram in Section 6.3, but since it introduces notation and basic concepts, even advanced readers may find it useful.

As usual, we start with the simplest problem – namely, the decision faced by a firm that has a monopoly. The monopoly case is easy because it avoids strategic interactions. When a firm is the only seller of a product, it can choose how much to sell and what price to charge without considering the reaction of other suppliers. The only restraint a monopolist faces is the demand curve. A downward-sloping demand curve is a constraint because it forces the monopolist to confront a trade-off between price and sales; higher prices mean lower sales. When considering the impact of European integration on imperfectly competitive firms, we need to determine how various policy changes will alter prices and sales. The first step in this direction is to see what determines a monopolist's price and sales in a closed economy. The natural question then is: 'What is the profit-maximizing level of sales for the monopolist?'

An excellent way to proceed is to make a guess at the optimal level, say, Q' in the left-hand panel of Fig. 6.2. Almost surely this initial guess will be wrong, but what we want to know is whether Q' is too low or too high. To this end, we calculate the profit earned when Q' units are sold at the highest obtainable price, namely P'. The answer is A + B, since the total value of sales is price times quantity (area A + B + C) minus cost (area C).

Would profits rise or fall if the firm sold an extra unit? Of course, to sell the extra unit, the firm will have to let its price fall a bit to P''. The change in profit equals the change in revenue minus the change in cost. Consider first the change in revenue. This has two parts. Selling the extra unit brings in extra revenue (represented by areas D + E), but it also depresses the price received for all units sold initially (lowering revenue by an amount equal to area A). The net change in revenue – called 'marginal revenue' for short – is given by the areas D + E minus the area A. The change in cost – called marginal cost for short – is area E. Plainly, profit only increases if the extra revenue (D + E – A) exceeds the extra cost E, i.e. if D – A is positive. As it is drawn, D – A appears to be negative, so marginal revenue is less than marginal cost at $Q' + 1$. This means that raising output from Q' would lower profits, so the initial guess of Q' turned out to be too high.

To find the profit-maximizing level using this trial-and-error method, we would consider a lower guess, say Q' minus 4 units, and repeat the procedure applied above. At the profit-maximizing level, marginal revenue just equals marginal cost. This level must be optimal since any increase or

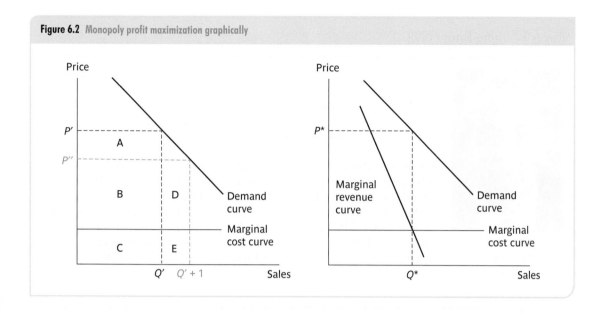

Figure 6.2 Monopoly profit maximization graphically

decrease in sales will lower profit. Increasing sales beyond this point will increase cost more than revenue, while decreasing sales would lower revenue more than cost. Both would reduce profit.

The right-hand panel of Fig. 6.2 shows an easier way to find the point where marginal revenue equals marginal cost. The diagram includes a new curve, called the marginal revenue curve. This shows how the marginal revenue (measured in euros) declines as the level of sales rises. (It declines since area A from the left-hand panel gets very small for low levels of sales.) At the sales level marked Q^*, marginal revenue just equals marginal cost. The firm charges the most it can at this level of sales, and this is P^*. These are the profit-maximizing levels of sales and price.

6.2.1 Lessons

Several deep aspects of imperfect competition come through even in the monopoly case. First, in setting up the problem, we had to assume things about the firm's beliefs concerning the behaviour of other economic agents. In this case, the monopolist is assumed to believe that consumers are price-takers and that the trade-off between prices and sales depends only on the demand curve (rather than, for example, on the reaction of firms in other markets). Second, the critical difference between perfect and imperfect competition comes out clearly. As part of the definition, perfectly competitive firms are assumed to take the price of their output as given (a classic example is a wheat farmer who cannot set his own price; he just sells at the current market price). This means that such firms are assumed to be ignorant of the fact that selling more will depress the market price. In terms of the diagram, perfectly competitive firms ignore the area A, so they maximize profits by selling an amount where price equals marginal cost. Of course, any increase in sales would have some negative impact on price, so it is best to think of perfect competition as a simplifying assumption that is close to true when all firms have market shares that are close to zero. By stepping away from this simplification, imperfect competition allows firms to explicitly consider the price-depressing effect – area A – when deciding how much to sell.

6.2.2 Duopolist as monopolist on residual demand curve

The monopoly case is instructive, but not very realistic – most European firms face some competition. Taking account of this, however, brings us up against the strategic considerations

Box 6.2 John Nash (1928–)

Early work on imperfect competition (see Box 6.1) was hampered by the problem of strategic interactions among firms. The 'Nash equilibrium' was the concept that cleared away confusions and opened the door to thousands of books and articles on imperfect competition.

The brilliant but troubled creator of the Nash equilibrium concept is a mathematician whose career has attracted an unusual amount of public attention. Since Nash's path-breaking publications have been interspersed with periods of paranoid schizophrenia, Hollywood found it easy to cast him in the cherished stereotype of a mad genius, making his life the subject of a big-budget film entitled *A Beautiful Mind* in 2001. The basis of the Nash equilibrium concept was his 1950 article entitled 'Non-cooperative games'. Just 27 pages long, it earned him the Nobel Prize in economics in 1994. An autobiographical account of his life is on www.nobel.se/economics/laureates/1994/index.html.

Source: www.nobel.se

discussed above. The convention we adopt to sort out this interaction is the so-called Cournot–Nash equilibrium that won John Nash a Nobel prize (see Box 6.2). That is, we assume that each firm acts as if the other firms' outputs are fixed. The equilibrium we are interested in is where each firm's expectations of the other firms' outputs turn out to be correct, i.e. no one is fooled. This no-one-fooled notion proves to be somewhat difficult to comprehend in the abstract but, as we shall see below, it is easy in specific applications.

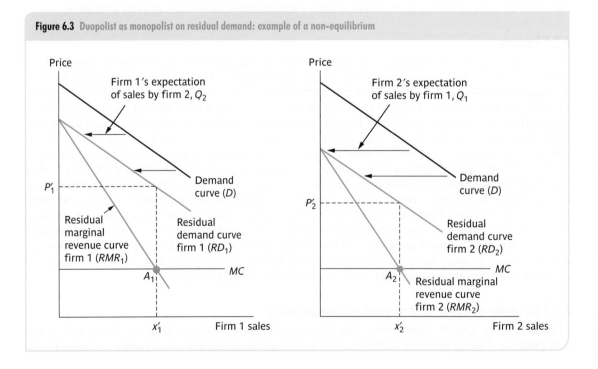

Figure 6.3 Duopolist as monopolist on residual demand: example of a non-equilibrium

The residual demand curve shortcut

Since firms take as given the sales of other firms, the only constraint facing a typical firm is the demand curve shifted to the left by the amount of sales of all other firms. In other words, each firm believes it is a monopolist on the shifted demand curve (we called the shifted demand curve the 'residual demand curve'). This realization is handy since it means that we can directly apply the solution technique from the monopolist's problem; the only change is that we calculate the marginal revenue curve based on the residual demand curve instead of the demand curve.

This trick is shown in Fig. 6.3 for a competition between two firms producing the same good – a situation that economists call 'duopoly'. For simplicity, we assume that the firms have the same marginal cost curves. Taking firm 2's sales as given at Q_2, firm 1 has a monopoly on the residual demand curve labelled RD_1. Firm 1's optimal output in this case is x_1' (since at point A_1, the residual marginal revenue curve, RMR_1, crosses the marginal cost curve MC). The right-hand panel shows the same sort of analysis for firm 2. Taking firm 1's output as fixed at Q_1, firm 2's optimal output is x_2'.

Note that the situation in Fig. 6.3 is not an equilibrium. To highlight the importance of the difference between expected and actual outcomes, the diagram shows the solutions of the two firms when their expectations about the other firm's output do not match the reality. The consistent-expectations outcome, i.e. the Nash equilibrium, is shown in Fig. 6.4, but we first consider why Fig. 6.3 is not an equilibrium.

As drawn, x_1' and x_2' are not a Cournot–Nash equilibrium since the firms' actual output levels do not match expectations; firm 1 produces x_1', which is greater than what firm 2 expected (namely, Q_1), and likewise, firm 2 produces x_2', which is greater than what firm 1 expected (namely, Q_2).

Figure 6.4 Duopoly and oligopoly: expectation-consistent outputs

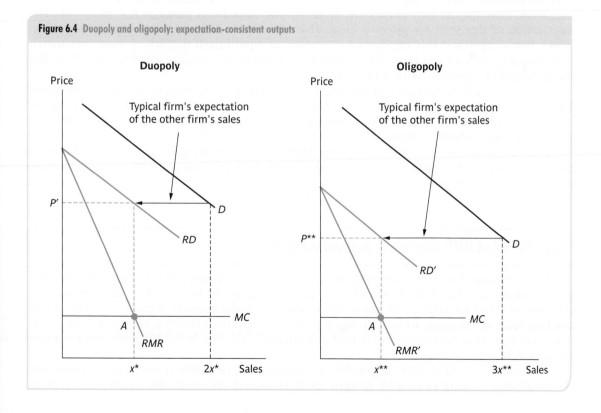

We can also see the problem by observing that the implied prices are not equal. If x'_1 and x'_2 were actually produced by the firms, then firms would not be able to charge the prices they expected to charge. In other words, this is not an equilibrium because the outcome is not consistent with expectations.

Finding the expectations consistent equilibrium

How do we find the expectation-consistent set of outputs? The easiest way is to use the assumed symmetry of firms. In the symmetric equilibrium, each firm will sell the same amount. With this fact in mind, a bit of thought reveals that the residual demand curve facing each firm must be half of the overall demand curve. This situation is shown in the left-hand panel of Fig. 6.4 for a duopoly. Some facts to note are that: (i) the optimal output for a typical firm is x^*, given by the intersection of *RMR* and *MC*; (ii) the total sales to the market are $2x^*$ and at this level of sales the overall market price (given by the demand curve, *D*) is consistent with the price each firm expects to receive given the residual demand curve, *RD*; and (iii) the outputs of the identical firms are equal in equilibrium.

6.2.3 Oligopoly: Cournot–Nash for an arbitrary number of firms

While allowing for two firms was more realistic than just allowing for only one firm, studying the impact of European integration on mergers and acquisitions requires us to allow for an arbitrary number of firms. In economists' jargon, this situation is called an oligopoly. As it turns out, this situation is straightforward to deal with when firms are symmetric. The right-hand panel of Fig. 6.4 shows the argument for the case of three firms.

As more firms are competing in the market (here we consider three instead of two), the residual demand curve facing each one shifts inwards, so the residual marginal revenue curve also shifts inwards; the new curves are shown in the right-hand panel as *RD'* and *RMR'*. The implication of this shift for prices is clear. The new *RMR = MC* point occurs at a lower level of per-firm output and this implies a lower price. In equilibrium (i.e. where outcomes match expectations), each of the three firms produces an identical amount, identified as x^{**} in the diagram, and charges an identical price, p^{**}.

Given that we have worked through the 1, 2 and 3 firm cases, readers should be able to see what would happen as the number of firms continues to rise. Each increase in the number of competitors will shift inwards the RD facing each one of them. This will inevitably lead to lower prices and lower output per firm.

Of course, this analysis is just formalizing what most readers would expect. If one adds more competitors to a market, prices will fall along with the market share of each firm. As is so often the case, the brilliant concepts are simple.

6.3 The *BE–COMP* diagram in a closed economy

To study the impact of European integration on firm size and efficiency, the number of firms, prices, output and the like, it is useful to have a diagram in which all of these things are determined. The presentation of this diagram, which actually consists of three sub-diagrams, is the first order of business. To keep things simple, we begin with the case of a closed economy. The diagram is an extensive elaboration of one originally used by Nobel Laureate Paul Krugman (see Box 6.3).

The heart of the *BE–COMP* diagram is the sub-diagram in which the number of firms and the profit-maximizing price–cost margin are determined. As usual, the equilibrium will be

the intersection of two curves, the *BE* curve and the *COMP* curve. We start by presenting the *COMP* curve.

6.3.1 The COMP curve

It is easy to understand that imperfectly competitive firms charge a price that exceeds their marginal cost; they do so in order to maximize profit. But how wide is the gap between price and marginal cost, and how does it vary with the number of competitors? These questions are answered by the *COMP* curve.

If there is only one firm, the price–cost gap – what we call the 'mark-up' of price over marginal cost – will equal the mark-up that a monopolist would charge. If there are more firms competing in the market, competition will force each firm to charge a lower markup. We summarize this 'competition-side' relationship between the mark-up and the number of firms as the '*COMP* curve' shown in Fig. 6.5. It is downward sloped since competition drives the mark-up down as the number of competitors rises, as explained above. We denote the mark-up with the Greek letter μ, pronounced mu, since 'mu' is an abbreviation for mark-up. We call it the *COMP* curve since the size of the mark-up is an indicator of how competitive the market is.

While this intuitive connection between price and marginal cost may suffice for some readers, extra insight is gained by considering the derivation of the *COMP* curve in more detail. This is done in Annex A.

6.3.2 The break-even (BE) curve

The mark-up and number of firms are related in another way, summarized by the *BE* curve.

When a sector is marked by increasing returns to scale, there is only room for a certain number of firms in a market of a given size. Intuitively, more firms will be able to survive if the price is far above marginal cost, i.e. if the mark-up is high. The curve that captures this

Figure 6.5 The *COMP* and *BE* curves

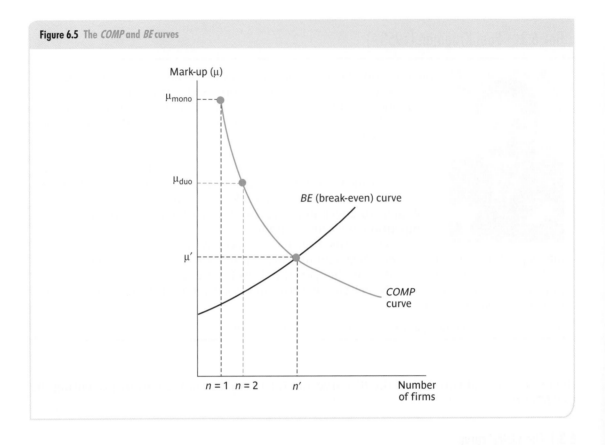

relationship is called the 'break-even curve', or zero-profit curve (*BE* curve, for short) in Fig. 6.5. It has a positive slope since more firms can break even when the mark-up is high. That is to say, taking the mark-up as given, the *BE* curve shows the number of firms that can earn enough to cover their fixed cost, say, the cost of setting up a factory.

Again, this intuitive presentation of the *BE* curve will suffice for many readers, but might well raise questions in the minds of more advanced readers. These questions are addressed in Annex A.

6.3.3 Equilibrium prices, output and firm size

It is important to note that firms are not always on the *BE* curve since they can earn above-normal or below-normal profits for a while. In the long run, however, firms can enter or exit the market, so the number of firms rises or falls until the typical firm earns just enough to cover its fixed cost. By contrast, firms are always on the *COMP* curve since firms can change prices quickly in response to any change in the number of firms.

With this in mind, we are ready to work out the equilibrium mark-up, number of firms, price and firm-size in a closed economy using Fig. 6.6. The right-hand panel combines the *BE* curve with the *COMP* curve. The intersection of the two defines the equilibrium mark-up and long-run number of firms. More specifically, the *COMP* curve tells us that firms would charge a mark-up of μ' when there are n' firms in the market, and the BE curve tells us that n' firms could break even when the mark-up is μ'. The equilibrium price is – by definition of the mark-up – just the equilibrium mark-up plus the marginal cost, *MC*. Using the *MC* curve from the left-hand panel, we see that the equilibrium price is p' (this equals μ' plus *MC*). The middle panel shows

Figure 6.6 Prices, output and equilibrium firm size in a closed economy

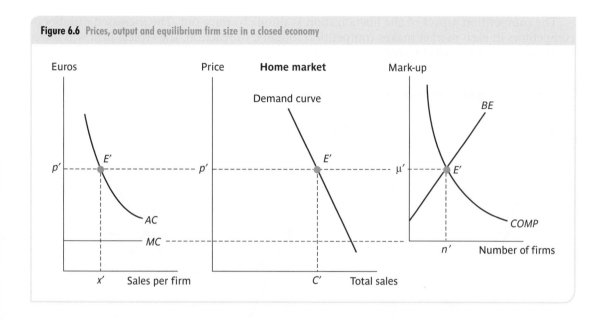

the demand curve and this allows us to see that the total level of consumption implied by the equilibrium price is C'.

The left-hand panel helps us to find the equilibrium firm size, i.e. sales per firm, which we denote as x'. This sub-diagram shows the average and marginal cost curves of a typical firm. As a little bit of reflection reveals, a typical firm's total profit is zero when price equals average cost (when price equals average cost, total revenue equals total cost). Since we know that total profits are zero at the equilibrium and we know the price is p', it must be that the equilibrium firm size is x' since this is where the firm's size implies an average cost equal to p'.

In summary, Fig. 6.6 lets us determine the equilibrium number of firms, mark-up, price, total consumption and firm size all in one diagram. With this in hand, we are now ready to study how European integration has sparked a wave of industrial restructuring.

6.4 The impact of European liberalization

European integration has involved a gradual reduction of trade barriers. The basic economic effects of this gradual reduction can, however, be illustrated more simply by considering a much more drastic liberalization – taking a completely closed economy and making it a completely open economy. To keep things simple, we suppose that there are only two nations, Home and Foreign, and that these nations are identical. Since they are identical, we could trace through the effects looking at either market, but we focus on Home's market for convenience.

6.4.1 No-trade-to-free-trade liberalization
The immediate impact of the no-trade-to-free-trade liberalization is to provide each firm with a second market of the same size and to double the number of competitors in each market. How does this change the outcome?

The competition aspect of the liberalization is simple to trace out. The increased number of competitors in each market makes competition tougher. In reaction, the typical firm will lower its mark-up in each market to point A in Fig. 6.7.

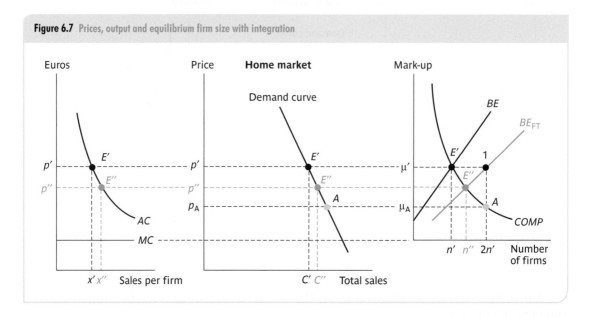

Figure 6.7 Prices, output and equilibrium firm size with integration

The doubling of the market size facing each firm also has an important effect. The liberalization adds a new market for each firm, so it makes sense that more firms will be able to survive. To see how many more firms can survive, we work out the impact of the liberalization on the *BE* curve. As it turns out, the liberalization shifts the *BE* curve to the right, specifically to BE_{FT}, as shown in the diagram. Why? Shifting *BE* to the right means that at any given mark-up more firms can break even. This is true since as the market size increases the sales per firm increases, thus providing a higher operating profit per firm at any given level of mark-up.

The size of the rightward shift is determined without difficulty. If there were no changes in the mark-up (there will be in the new equilibrium, but ignore this for the moment), then double the number of firms could break even since each firm would be selling the same number of units. In other words, the new *BE* curve must pass through the point marked '1' in the diagram; at point 1, the mark-up is μ', the number of firms is $2n'$, and logic tells us that this combination of μ and n would result in all firms breaking even. Point 1, however, is merely an intellectual landmark used to determine how far out the *BE* curve shifts. It is not where the economy would be right after liberalization since the mark-up would immediately be pushed down to μ_A.

Because the increase in competition would immediately push down the mark-up to μ_A, the two newly integrated markets will initially be at a point that is below the *BE* curve. We know that all firms will be losing money at point *A* since the actual mark-up (μ_A) is less than what would be needed to have all $2n'$ firms break even. Now, this loss of profit is not a problem in the short run since firms only need to break even in the long run. Indeed, the profit losses are what would trigger the process of industrial restructuring that will eventually reduce the number of firms.

The corresponding effect on prices is shown in the middle diagram as the move from *E'* to *A* and then to *E''*. Before explaining this, observe that the middle panel shows the demand curve for Home only, so the no-trade-to-free-trade liberalization does not shift the demand curve. The Foreign market has an identical demand, but since exactly the same thing goes on in Foreign, we omit the Foreign demand curve to reduce the diagram's complexity.

As mentioned above, the initial impact of the extra competition ($2n'$ firms selling to the Home market instead of n') pushes the equilibrium mark-up down to $\mu_{A'}$, so the price falls to p_A. Thus during this industrial restructuring phase, the price would rise to p'' (from p_A), but this rise does not take the price all the way back to its pre-liberalization level of p'.

The impact of this combination of extra competition and industrial restructuring on a typical firm is shown in the left-hand panel. As prices are falling, firms that remain in the market increase their efficiency – i.e. lower their average costs – by spreading their fixed cost over a larger number of sales. Indeed, since price equalled average cost before the liberalization and in the long run after liberalization, we know that the price drop is exactly equal to the efficiency gain. In the left-hand panel, this is shown as a move from E' to E''. Increasing returns to scale are the root of this efficiency gain. As the equilibrium scale of a typical firm rises from x' to x'', average costs fall.

To summarize, the no-trade-to-free-trade liberalization results in fewer, larger firms. The resulting scale economies lower average cost and thus make these firms more efficient. The extra competition ensures that these savings are passed on to lower prices. It is useful to think of the integration as leading to two steps.

Step 1. Short term: defragmentation and the pro-competitive effect (from E′ to A)

We start with the short-term impact, that is to say, the impact before the number of firms can adjust. Before the liberalization, each market was extremely fragmented in the sense that firms in each nation had a local market share of $1/n'$ and a zero share in the other market. After the liberalization, the market share of each firm is the same in each market, namely $n'/2$. This elimination of market fragmentation has a pro-competitive effect, which is defined as a decrease in the price–cost mark-up. This is shown in the right-hand panel of Fig. 6.7 as a move from E' to A. The short-term impact on prices and sales can be seen in the middle panel as a drop from p' to p_A.

Step 2. Long term: industrial restructuring and scale effects (from A to E″)

Point A is not a long-term equilibrium since the operating profit earned by a typical firm is insufficient to cover the fixed cost. We see this by noting that point A is below the BE curve and this tells us that the mark-up is too low to allow $2n'$ firms to break even. To restore a normal level of profitability, the overall number of firms has to fall from $2n'$ to n''. In Europe, this process typically occurs via mergers and buy-outs, but in some cases the number of firms is reduced by bankruptcies. As this industrial consolidation occurs, the economy moves from point A to point E''. During this process, firms enlarge their market shares, the mark-up rises somewhat and profitability is restored.

Welfare effects

The welfare effects of this liberalization are quite straightforward. The four-sided area marked by p', p'', E' and E'' in the middle panel of Fig. 6.8 corresponds to the gain in Home consumer surplus. As usual, this gain can be broken down into the gain to consumers of paying a lower price for the units they bought prior to the liberalization, and the gains from buying more (C'' versus C'). Note that the exact same gain occurs in the Foreign market (not shown in the diagram).

As it turns out, this four-sided region labelled **A** in Fig. 6.8 is Home's long-term welfare gain because there is no offsetting loss to producers and there was no tariff revenue to begin with. Firms made zero profits before liberalization and they earn zero profits after liberalization. Note, however, that this long-term calculation ignores the medium-term adjustment costs. These costs, which stem from the industrial restructuring, can be politically very important. Indeed, many governments attempt to thwart the restructuring by adopting a variety of policies such

Figure 6.8 Welfare effects

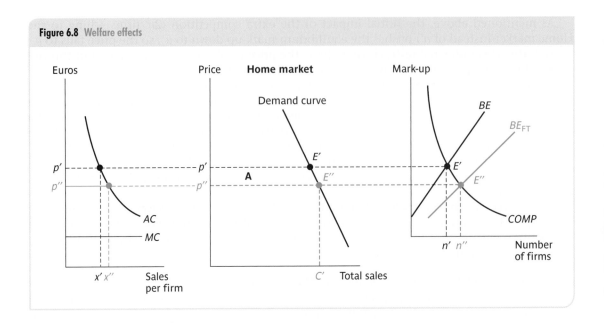

as industrial subsidies and various anti-merger and anti-acquisition policies (discussed further in Chapter 14). We should also note that the welfare gains shown can be rather substantial. Roughly speaking, the percentage gain in real GDP equals the share of the economy affected (industry in the EU, for instance, accounts for about 30 per cent of output) times the percentage drop in price.

6.4.2 Slow and fast adjustments

The discussion above has shown that the integration initially leads to big price reductions and large profit losses. These profit losses are eliminated as the number of firms falls and profits are restored to normal levels. During this industrial restructuring process, prices rise slightly. This sequence of steps – sometimes called industry 'consolidation' or an industry 'shake-out' – is relevant to some industries, for example air travel. Here, Europe's liberalization has resulted in large profit losses for many European airlines and big price reductions for consumers. At first, airlines were reluctant to merge – largely because most airlines were government-owned and their governments were willing to use taxpayer euros to cover the losses. More recently, however, European airlines are rationalizing their costs by forming cooperative alliances. While the actual number of firms has not yet fallen, the number of planes flying a particular route is reduced. For example, before the two firms went bankrupt, cooperation between Swiss Air and Sabena meant that instead of having two planes flying the Geneva–Brussels route (one Swiss Air and one Sabena), only one plane flew. Nevertheless, Swiss Air called it a Swiss Air flight and Sabena called it a Sabena flight. Such 'code-sharing' arrangements are a way of achieving scale economies without actually eliminating a national carrier. Interestingly, both airlines eventually went bankrupt but the Swiss and Belgian governments stepped in to create replacement airlines, Swiss and SN Brussels Airlines.

In other industries, firms anticipate the increased competition and undertake the mergers and acquisitions quickly enough to avoid big losses. European banking is an example. The introduction of the euro and continuing liberalization of the banking sector mean that European banks will have to become fewer and bigger in order to break even. However, instead of waiting for profit losses to become intolerable, banks have launched a record-breaking series of mergers and acquisitions. In terms of Fig. 6.8, this would look like a move from E' directly to E''.

6.4.3 Empirical evidence

There is ample empirical evidence that European industry is marked by fewer, bigger, more efficient firms since the Single Market Programme. For example, the 1996 Single Market Review by the European Commission presents several studies illustrating these trends (see Commission, 1996, for a brief review of this multi-volume study). Unfortunately, there is little direct evidence in Europe that industry consolidation was caused by market integration, although this is what most economists believe is the obvious explanation. More direct evidence linking market size with efficiency and competition can be found in Campbell and Hopenhayn (2002). The authors study the impact of market size on the size distribution of firms in retail-trade industries across 225 US cities. In every industry examined, establishments were larger in larger cities. The authors conclude that their results support the notion that competition is tougher in larger markets and this accounts for the link between firm size and market size.

6.5 Summary

Three main points have been made in this chapter:

* One very obvious impact of European integration has been to face individual European firms with a bigger 'home' market. This produces a chain reaction that leads to fewer, bigger, more efficient firms that face more effective competition from each other. Understanding the economic logic driving this chain reaction is the main goal of this chapter. This logic can be summarized as follows. Integration defragments Europe's markets in the sense that it removes the privileged position of national firms in their national markets. As a result, all firms face more competition from other firms in their national market, but at the same time they have better access to the other EU markets. This general increase in competition puts downward pressure on price–cost mark-ups, prices and profits. The profit-squeeze results in industrial restructuring, a process by which the total number of firms in Europe falls. The lower prices and lower number of firms mean that the average firm gets larger and this, in turn, allows firms to better exploit economies of scale. This efficiency increase, in turn, permits the firms to break even despite the lower prices.

* The industrial restructuring is often politically painful since it often results in layoffs and the closure of inefficient plants. Governments very often attempt to offset this political pain by providing 'state aid' to their national firms. Such state aid can be viewed as unfair and the perception of unfairness threatens to undermine EU members' interest in integration. To avoid these problems, the founders of the EU established rules that prohibited state aid that distorts competition. The Commission is charged with enforcing these rules. These rules are covered in Chapter 14.

* Industrial restructuring raises another problem that led the EU's founders to set out another set of rules. As integration proceeds and the number of firms falls, the temptation for firms to collude may increase. To avoid this, the EU has strict rules on anti-competitive practices. It also screens mergers to ensure that mergers will enhance efficiency. Again, the Commission is charged with enforcing these rules. These rules are covered in Chapter 14.

Self-assessment questions

1 Suppose that liberalization occurs as in Section 6.4 and the result is a pro-competitive effect, but instead of merging or restructuring, all firms are bought by their national governments to allow the firms to continue operating. What will be the impact of this on prices and government revenues? Now that the governments are the owners, will they have an incentive to continue with liberalization? Can you imagine why this might favour firms located in nations with big, rich governments?

2 Use a three-panel diagram, like Fig. 6.6, to show how the number of firms, mark-up and firm size would change in a closed economy if the demand for the particular good rose, i.e. the demand curve shifted out.

3 Using your findings from Question 2, you should be able to consider the impact of a no-trade-to-free-trade integration between a large and a small nation, where size is defined by the position of the demand curve (the demand curve in the large nation will be further out than the demand curve for the small nation). To do this, you will need two of the three-panel diagrams of the Fig. 6.6 type to show the pre-integration situation. Then use a three-panel diagram of the Fig. 6.7 type to show what happens to prices, firm size and the number of firms in the integrated economy. Note that you will want to show both demand curves in the middle panel. As usual, assume that all firms have the same marginal cost. What does this analysis tell you about how integration affects firms in small nations versus large nations?

4 Consider a sequence of EU 'enlargements' where each enlargement involves a no-trade-to-free-trade addition of one more member. Specifically, suppose there are three initially identical economies, each of which looks like the one described in Section 6.3. Initially, all nations are closed to trade. Now, consider a no-trade-to-free-trade integration between two of the nations (just as in Section 6.4). Then consider a no-trade-to-free-trade integration of a third nation. (Hint: The second step will be very much like the integration between unequal-sized economies explored in Question 3.) Calculate how much the third nation gains from joining and compare it to how much the existing two-nation bloc gains from the third nation's membership. Who gains more in proportion to size: the 'incumbents' or the 'entrants'?

Essay questions

1 When the Single Market Programme was launched in the mid-1980s, European leaders asserted that it would improve the competitiveness of European firms vis-à-vis US firms. Explain how one can make sense of this assertion by extending the reasoning in this chapter.

2 Has the strategy of defragmenting Europe's markets worked in the sense of promoting bigger, more efficient firms facing more effective competition? Choose an industry, for example telecoms, chemicals, pharmaceuticals or autos, and compare the evolution of the EU industry with that of the USA or Japan. You can find information on these and many more industries at the Commission website. Search the site http://europa.eu.int/comm/enterprise/index_en.htm with Google to find specific information on specific sectors.

3 Some EU members allow their companies to engage in 'anti-takeover' practices. Discuss how differences in EU members' laws concerning these practices might be viewed as unfair when EU industry is being transformed by a wave of mergers and acquisitions.

4 Write an essay on the historical role that the scale economies argument played in the economic case for deeper European integration. Start with the Spaak Report (see www.ena.lu) and the Cockfield Report, Completing the Internal Market, White Paper, COM(85) 310 final (you can find it in French, 'Livre blanc sur l'achèvement du marché intérieur', on www.ena.lu under the subject 'The Delors White Paper').

Further reading: the aficionado's corner

Consideration of imperfect competition and scale effects was made possible in the 1980s with development of the so-called new trade theory:

Helpman, E. and P. Krugman (1985) *Market Structure and Foreign Trade: Increasing Returns, Imperfect Competition and the International Economy*, MIT Press, Cambridge, MA.

Helpman, E. and P. Krugman (1989) *Trade Policy and Market Structure*, MIT Press, Cambridge, MA.

The new theory was naturally applied to the analysis of the Single Market Programme when it was first discussed in the mid-1980s. Many of the classic studies are contained in:

Winters, L.A. (1992) *Trade Flows and Trade Policies after '1992'*, Cambridge University Press, Cambridge.

A synthetic, graduate-level survey of this literature is provided by:

Baldwin, R. and A. Venables (1995) 'Regional economic integration', in G. Grossman and K. Rogoff (eds) *Handbook of International Economics*, North-Holland, New York.

An alternative presentation of the theory and a thorough empirical evaluation are provided by:

Allen, C., M. Gasiorek and A. Smith (1998a) 'European Single Market: how the programme has fostered competition', *Economic Policy*, 13(24): 441–86.

Other useful works are:

Brander, J. and P. Krugman (1983) 'A "reciprocal dumping" model of international trade', *Journal of International Economics*, 15 (November): 313–21.

Mas-Colell, A., M. Whinston and J.R. Green (1995) *Microeconomic Theory*, Oxford University Press, New York.

Useful websites

A large number of evaluations of the Single Market, most of which employ ICIR frameworks, can be found on http://europa.eu.int/comm/economy_finance/publications/. The document *The Internal Market: 10 Years without Frontiers* is especially useful. This site also posts the annual *State Aids Report*, which provides the latest data on subsidies.

References

Allen, C., M. Gasiorek and A. Smith (1998a) 'European Single Market: how the programme has fostered competition', *Economic Policy*, 13(24): 441–86.

Allen, C., M. Gasiorek and A. Smith (1998b) 'The competition effects of the Single Market in Europe', *Economic Policy*, 13(27): 439–86.

Badinger, H. (2007) 'Has the EU's Single Market programme fostered competition? Testing for a decrease in mark-up ratios in EU industries', *Oxford Bulletin of Economics and Statistics*, 69(4): 497–519.

Bellone, F., P. Musso, S. Antipolis, L. Nesta and F. Warzynski (2008). 'L'effet pro-concurrentiel de l'intégration européenne: une analyse de l'évolution des taux de marge dans les industries manufacturières françaises', OFCE, N° 2008-09, Paris.

Brander, J. and P. Krugman (1983) 'A "reciprocal dumping" model of international trade', *Journal of International Economics*, 15 (November): 313–21.

Campbell, J. and H. Hopenhayn (2002) *Market Size Matters*, NBER Working Paper 9113, Cambridge, MA.

Chen, N., J. Imbs and A. Scott (2009) 'The dynamics of trade and competition,' *Journal of International Economics*, 77(1): 50–62.

Commission (1996) *The 1996 Single Market Review: Background Information for the Report to the Council and European Parliament*, Commission Staff Working Paper, Brussels. Download from http://europa.eu.int/comm/internal_market/en/update/impact/index.htm.

European Economy (2001) Supplement A, No. 12, December. This contains many facts on the M&A wave. Download from http://europa.eu.int/comm/economy_finance/publications/supplement_a_en.htm.

Helpman, E. and P. Krugman (1985) *Market Structure and Foreign Trade: Increasing Returns, Imperfect Competition and the International Economy*, MIT Press, Cambridge, MA.

Annex A Details on the *COMP* and *BE* curves

A6.1 *COMP* curve in detail

Consider how the profit-maximizing mark-up changes when the number of firms increases. To keep the reasoning concrete, consider an increase from 1 firm (the monopoly case) to 2 firms (the duopoly case).

The solid lines in the left-hand panel of Fig. A6.1 show the usual problem for a monopolist, with the demand curve marked as D and the marginal revenue curve marked as MR. (See Section 6.2 if you are not familiar with the monopolist case.) The profit-maximizing output, x_{mono}, is indicated by the point A, i.e. the intersection of marginal cost (marked as MC in the diagram) and marginal revenue (marked as MR in the diagram). The firm charges the most it can for the level of sales xmono, i.e. p'. The price–marginal cost mark-up (called the mark-up for short) equals $p' - MC$, as shown. We can also see the size of operating profit (i.e. profit without considering fixed cost) in the diagram since it is, by definition, just the monopolist mark-up times the monopoly level of sales x_{mono}. In the diagram, this is shown by the area of the box marked by the points p', A', A and MC.

When a second firm competes in this market, we have a duopoly rather than a monopoly. To solve this, we adopt the standard 'Cournot–Nash' approach of assuming that each firm takes

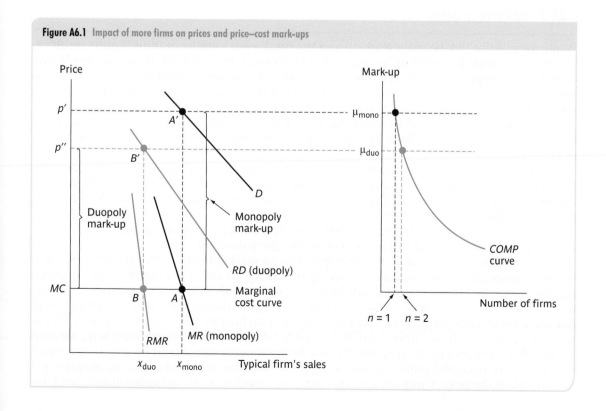

Figure A6.1 Impact of more firms on prices and price–cost mark-ups

as given the output of the other firm(s). Practically speaking, this means that each firm acts as if it were a monopolist on the 'residual demand curve', i.e. the demand curve shifted to the left by the amount of other firms' sales (marked as *RD* in the diagram). The exact equilibrium price and output are found by identifying the intersection of the residual marginal revenue curve (*RMR*) and the marginal cost curve; again, firms charge the highest possible price for this level of sales, namely p''. In drawing the diagram, we have supposed that the two firms have identical marginal cost curves (for simplicity), so the outcome of the competition will be that each firm sells an equal amount. You can verify that p'' is the price that the full demand curve, *D*, says would result if two times x_{duo} were sold.

The net result of adding an additional firm is that the price drops from p' to p'' and thus lowers the equilibrium mark-up. We also note that more competition lowers the level of sales per firm, although the sum of sales of the two competing firms exceeds the sales of a monopolist. Finally, note that adding in more firms lowers each firm's operating profit since it reduces the mark-up and sales per firm. The duopoly operating profit is the duopoly mark-up times x_{duo}; this is shown by the area p'', B', B, *MC* in the diagram.

Here we have looked only at the switch from one to two firms, but it should be clear that continuing to add in more firms would produce a similar result. As the number of firms rose, the residual demand curve facing each firm would shift inwards, resulting in a lower price, lower level of output per firm and, most importantly, a lower price–cost margin, i.e. a lower mark-up. In the extreme, an infinite number of firms would push the price down to marginal cost, eliminating the price–cost margin and all operating profits; each firm would be infinitely small (this is why perfectly competitive firms are sometimes called atomistic).

A6.2 *BE* curve in detail

While the positive link between mark-up and the break-even number of firms is quite intuitive, it is useful to study the relationship more closely. To keep the reasoning as easy as possible we consider the simplest form of increasing returns to scale, namely a situation where the typical firm faces a flat marginal cost curve and a fixed cost of operating. The fixed cost could represent, for example, the cost of building a factory, establishing a brand name, training workers, etc.

This combination of fixed cost and flat marginal cost implies increasing returns since the typical firm's average cost falls as its scale of production rises, as shown in the left-hand panel of Fig. A6.2.

If a firm is to survive in this situation, it must earn enough on its sales to cover its fixed cost. The amount it earns on sales is called its 'operating profit', and this is simply the mark-up times the level of sales. For example, if the mark-up (i.e. price minus marginal cost) is €200 and each firm sells 20,000 units, the operating profit per firm will be €4 million. As we shall see, this simple connection between the mark-up, sales and operating profit makes it quite easy to figure out the number of firms that can break even at any given mark-up.

Since all firms are identical in this example, a given mark-up implies that the price will also be given; specifically, it will equal the mark-up plus marginal cost. For example, if the mark-up is μ_0 as in Fig. A6.2, then the price will be $p_0 = \mu_0 + MC$. At this price, the demand curve tells us that the level of total sales will be C_0. Finally, we again use the symmetry of firms to work out the level of sales per firm; this will be total sales divided by the number of firms, which, in symbols, is C_0/n. To see how many firms can break even when the mark-up is μ_0, we turn to the left-hand panel in the diagram. With a little thought, you should be able to see that a firm will make zero total profit (i.e. operating profit plus the fixed cost) when its average cost exactly equals the price. Using the average cost curve, marked as *AC* in the left-hand panel, we

Figure A6.2 The *BE* curve in detail

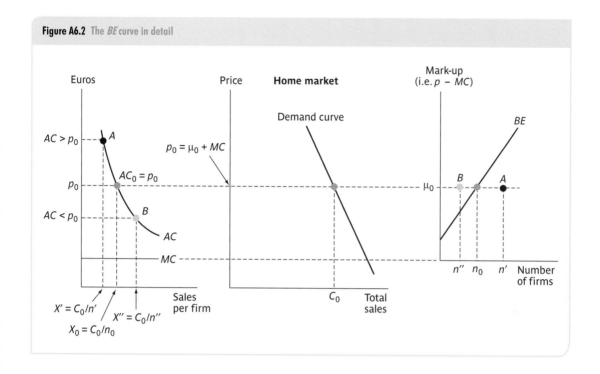

see that the typical firm's average cost equals price when the sales of the typical firm equal x_0. Because we know that sales per firm will be C_0/n, we can work out the number of firms where the sales per firm just equal x_0. In symbols, the break-even number of firms, call this n_0, is where C_0/n_0 equals x_0.

It is instructive to consider what would happen if the mark-up were μ_0, but there were more than n_0 firms, say n' firms, in the market. In this case, the sales per firm would be lower than x_0, namely $x' = C_0/n'$, so the typical firm's average cost would be higher and this means that the average cost of a typical firm would exceed the price. Plainly, such a situation is not sustainable since all the firms would be losing money (earning operating profits that were too low to allow them to cover their fixed cost). This case is shown by point *A* in the left-hand panel of the diagram. The same point *A* can be shown in the right-hand panel as the combination of the mark-up μ_0 and n'; we know that at this point firms are not covering their fixed cost, so there would be a tendency for some firms to exit the industry. In the real world this sort of 'exit' takes the form of mergers or bankruptcies. The opposite case of too few firms is shown in the right-hand and left-hand panels as point *B*; here firms' average cost is below the price and so all are making pure profits (i.e. their operating profit exceeds the fixed cost). Such a situation would encourage more firms to enter the market.

To work out all the points on the *BE* curve, we would go through a similar analysis for every given level of mark-up. The logic presented above, however, makes it clear that the result would be an upward-sloped *BE* curve.

Chapter 7

Growth effects and factor market integration

The Union has today set itself a new strategic goal for the next decade: to become the most competitive and dynamic knowledge-based economy in the world capable of sustainable economic growth with more and better jobs and greater social cohesion.

Presidency Conclusions, Lisbon European Council, March 2000

Chapter Contents

Introduction

The two previous chapters looked at 'allocation effects' of European integration, i.e. the impact on the efficiency with which economic resources within nations are allocated across economic activities. Allocation effects are 'one-off' in the sense that a single policy change leads to a single reallocation of resources. European leaders, however, have long emphasized a different type of economic effect – the growth effect. Growth effects operate in a way that is fundamentally different from allocation effects; they operate by changing the rate at which new factors of production – mainly capital – are accumulated, hence the name 'accumulation effects'.

Factor market integration is another channel by which European integration can change the supply of productive factors within EU members. Under EU rules, citizens of any EU nation may work in any other EU nation. Similar rules guarantee the free movement of capital, so this aspect of European integration can – in principle – alter the amount of productive factors employed in any given EU member. Or, to put it differently, capital and labour movements can look like an allocation-of-resources effect from the EU perspective, but like an accumulation effect from the national perspective. This chapter therefore also studies the economics of factor market integration.

7.1 The logic of growth and the facts

The link between European integration and growth rests on the logic of growth. The logic of growth is simple, but widely misunderstood, so before looking at the facts, we briefly present the logic of growth in words.

7.1.1 The logic of growth: medium-run and long-run effects

Economic growth means producing more and more every year. Per-capita growth means an annual rise in the output per person. In most western European nations, output per capita rises at between 1 and 3 per cent per year in normal times. How does this happen?

If a nation's workers are to produce more goods and services year after year, the economy must provide workers with more 'tools' year after year. Here 'tools' is meant in the broadest possible sense – what economists call capital – and three categories of capital must be distinguished: physical capital (machines, etc.); human capital (skills, training, experience, etc.); and knowledge capital (technology).

Given this necessity, the rate of output growth is hitched straight to the rate of physical, human and knowledge capital accumulation. Most capital accumulation is intentional and is called investment. Accordingly, we can say that European integration affects growth mainly via its effect on investment in human capital, physical capital and knowledge capital. The qualification 'mainly' is necessary since integration may unintentionally affect accumulation, for instance by speeding the international dissemination of technological progress (this is especially important in central European nations).

Growth effects fall naturally into two categories: medium term and long term. An instance of medium-term effects is 'induced physical capital formation'. For all the reasons documented in the previous chapters, European integration improves the efficiency with which productive factors are combined to produce output. As a side effect, this heightened efficiency typically makes Europe a better place to invest, so more investment occurs. The result is that the initial efficiency gains from integration are boosted by induced capital formation. While the above-normal capital formation is occurring, the economies experience a medium-term growth effect. This growth effect is only medium term, since it will eventually peter out; as the amount of capital per worker rises, the gain from investing in each further unit of capital diminishes.

Eventually the gain from investing in an extra unit reaches the cost of doing so and the above-normal capital formation stops. A good example of this is the investment boom that Spain experienced around the time of its accession to the EU.

Long-term growth effects involve a permanent change in the rate of accumulation, and thereby a permanent change in the rate of growth. Since the accumulation of physical capital faces diminishing returns, long-run growth effects typically refer to the rate of accumulation of knowledge capital, i.e. technological progress.

To summarize the logic of growth effects schematically: European integration (or any other policy) → allocation effect → improved efficiency → better investment climate → more investment in machines, skills and/or technology → higher output per person. Under medium-run growth effects, the rise in output per person eventually stops at a new, higher level. Under long-run growth effects, the rate of growth is forever higher.

7.1.2 Post-war European growth: the evidence

Any informed discussion of European integration and economic growth must begin with a fistful of overarching facts. We first cover these facts before setting out a prima facie case that European integration has, broadly speaking, been favourable to growth in the post-war period.

Phases of European growth

By historical standards, continuous economic growth is a relatively recent phenomenon. Before the Industrial Revolution, which started in Great Britain in the late 1700s, European incomes had stagnated for a millennium and a half. It has been estimated that the real earnings of a typical British factory worker in 1850 were no higher than those of a typical free Roman artisan in the first century (Cameron and Neal, 2003). Between the glory years of the Roman Empire and the Industrial Revolution, periods of prosperity were offset by famines, plagues and warfare that brought the average person back to the brink of starvation.

With industrialization, which had spread to most of continental Europe by 1870, incomes began to rise at a respectable rate of something like 2 per cent per year. Growth rates, however, were hardly constant from this date – four growth phases are traditionally defined, as Table 7.1 shows. During the 1890–1913 period (often called the *Belle Époque*) real GDP grew at 2.6 per cent. This is considered to be a very good growth rate, and is enough to double GDP every 27 years. Since population was also growing rapidly in this period, real GDP per person rose at only 1.7 per cent per annum.

Table 7.1 European growth phases, 1890–1992

Period	Real GDP	Real GDP per capita	Real GDP per hour
1890–1913	2.6	1.7	1.6
1913–1950	1.4	1.0	1.9
1950–1973	4.6	3.8	4.7
1973–1992	2.0	1.7	2.7
Whole period 1890–1992	2.5	1.9	2.6

Notes: Figures are annual average percentages for 12 nations (Austria, Belgium, Denmark, Finland, France, Germany, Italy, Netherlands, Norway, Sweden, Switzerland, United Kingdom, all adjusted for boundary changes)

Note that the 1950–73 period is the aberration. Both before and after this period, growth rates were just under 2 per cent per annum (excluding the unusual 1913–50 period). The Golden Age was also the most intensive period of European integration and it was this correlation that first started economists thinking about the growth effects of European integration.
Source: Crafts and Toniolo (1996), p. 2

These rates were approximately halved during the 1913–50 period (i.e. from the First World War until the end of the post-Second World War reconstruction period). Despite this, the GDP per hour worked accelerated slightly to 1.9 per cent since the average hours worked per year fell with the introduction and spread of labour unions and social legislation.

The period from 1950 to 1973 is called the Golden Age of growth; throughout the world, but especially in Europe, growth rates jumped. Real GDP growth rates more than tripled and per-capita GDP growth almost quadrupled. At this pace, per-capita incomes would double every 18.6 years, implying that the material standard of living would quadruple in an average lifetime. Unfortunately, the Golden Age ended after only 23 years for reasons that are still not entirely understood. Since 1973, the date of the first oil shock, per-capita incomes have progressed at only 1.9 per cent per year. However, as the working week has been further shortened during this period, GDP-per-hour-worked continued to progress at a respectable 2.7 per cent per annum.

Growth performance during the 1913–50 period was far from homogeneous. This phase, which Crafts and Toniolo (1996) aptly call the 'second Thirty Years War', contains the two world wars and the Great Depression, each of which was responsible for massive income drops. It also, however, contains the most spectacular growth phase that Europe has ever seen, namely the years of reconstruction, 1945–50. Table 7.2 shows various aspects of this 'reconstruction period' for 12 European nations. The first point (a point we also made in Chapter 1) is that the Second World War caused enormous economic damage. It cost Germany and Italy four decades or more of growth and put Austrian and French GDPs back to nineteenth-century levels. Despite this, recovery was remarkably rapid. By 1951, every European nation was back on the pre-war growth path. This resurgence was due to a short period of truly astonishing growth. All the growth rates were double digit (except Belgium's); France, for instance, grew at almost 20 per cent a year for four consecutive years and the Netherlands grew at almost twice that pace for two years. To a large extent, however, this rapid growth is a bit of an illusion. It consisted of merely setting back up, or repairing, production facilities created in earlier years. This also indicates that much of the Second World War drop in GDP was due to the temporary disorganization of Europe's economy rather than permanent destruction.

Table 7.2 Growth in the post-Second World War reconstruction phase

Period	The setback: pre-war year when GDP equalled that of 1945	Back-on-track year: year GDP attained highest pre-war level	Reconstruction: growth rate during reconstruction years (1945 to column 2 year) (%)
Austria	1886	1951	15.2
Belgium	1924	1948	6.0
Denmark	1936	1946	13.5
Finland	1938	1945	n.a.
France	1891	1949	19.0
Germany	1908	1951	13.5
Italy	1909	1950	11.2
Netherlands	1912	1947	39.8
Norway	1937	1946	9.7
Sweden			
Switzerland	These countries actually grew during the Second World War		
UK			

Source: Crafts and Toniolo (1996), p. 4

7.1.3 Are growth and European integration related?

The prima facie case

The Brothers Grimm's tale of the rooster who believes that his crowing makes the sun rise each day (See, it works every morning!) should alert us to the dangers of confusing correlation and causality. There is, nonetheless, some general evidence – what might be called prima facie evidence in a court of law – that supports the integration-fosters-growth hypothesis.

The first element of the prima facie case concerns a country-by-country analysis of growth during the 1950–73 period. Recall from Chapter 1 that this period saw rapid integration among European nations. From 1950 to 1958, the main liberalization was common to western European nations, but from 1958 to 1968 the EEC6 integrated much faster than did EFTA members (UK, Sweden, Switzerland, Finland, Norway, Austria, Portugal and Iceland). Table 7.3 shows the growth performance of various OEEC members during this period. Focusing, first, on the third column, we note that the EEC6 (data for Luxembourg was not available) rose in the GDP per-capita rankings. Germany jumped five places, Italy jumped two, while the Netherlands and Belgium slipped slightly. By contrast, the EFTAns lost ground, with the UK and Norway dropping five and four places, respectively, with Sweden and Denmark gaining one and Austria gaining two.

The non-EEC, non-EFTA nations also lost, especially Ireland, which was tightly linked to EFTA by a bilateral free trade agreement with the UK. Note also that the average growth performance of the EEC members was almost 50 per cent better than that of the EFTAns, although much of this may be explained by a 'catching-up' phenomenon (EEC nations were poorer than EFTAns in 1950 and poorer nations tend to grow more quickly than rich nations).

What is particularly striking is the performance of the 'big four' nations: France, Germany, Italy and the UK. The first three were members of the EEC and grew between 1.7 and 2.1 times faster than the UK. Again catch-up played some role in this, but by 1973 both France and Germany were richer than the UK, so the catch-up roles were reversed by the end of the period. This suggests a correlation between integration and growth since the economic integration in the EEC was much tighter than that of EFTA during this period.

Of course, not much should be read into such simple correlation, but at the time the UK's laggard growth performance in the face of the Continental growth booms played an important role in shaping British attitudes towards EEC membership. Or, to put it more bluntly, regardless of whether EEC integration was responsible for the Six's superior growth performance, political leaders at the time believed there was a connection.

Another line of indicative evidence comes from comparing the before and after growth rates of nations that have joined the EU. The facts are shown in Table 7.4. We have data for four enlargements (the 2004 enlargement is too recent). Growth picked up in half the cases (the third and fourth), but slowed in the other half. However, many things affect growth apart from EU membership. The world experienced serious growth slowdowns during the first oil shock (1973–75) and when OECD central banks decided to fight inflation with restrictive monetary policies (1981–83). One way to partially control for this is to compare the growth rate of the entrants to the average western European growth rate over the same period. We see that all the enlargements have been pro-growth by this rough measure, except Greece's.

The combined GDP of the first entrants (Britain, Denmark and Ireland) was growth much slower than the European average during the five years before accession in 1973, but only slightly less fast in the five years following membership (i.e. 18.5 versus 12.5 per cent compared with 5.8 versus 4.8 per cent). For the third and fourth enlargements, the five-year growth rates for the entrants were behind the pan-European average before but ahead of it after they joined. The one exception is that of Greece – a theme that comes out clearly in a closer examination of the data below.

Table 7.3   GDP per capita and rankings, 1950 and 1973 (1990 international dollars)

	1950 GDP (1990 $)	European rank 1950	Change in rank 1950–1973	GDP growth rate 1950–1973
EEC average	4825	8.0	+1.2	4.2
Netherlands	5850	5	−1	3.4
Belgium	5346	6	−2	3.5
France	5221	7	+2	4.0
Germany	4281	9	+5	5.0
Italy	3425	13	+2	4.9
EFTA average	6835	3.6	−1.4	3.0
Switzerland	8939	1	0	3.1
UK	6847	2	−5	2.4
Sweden	6738	3	+1	3.1
Denmark	6683	4	+1	3.1
Norway	4969	8	−4	3.2
Finland	4131	10	0	4.2
Austria	3731	11	+2	4.9
Others average	2401	14.3	−0.3	5.2
Ireland	3518	12	−3	3.1
Spain	2397	14	+1	5.8
Portugal	2132	15	+1	5.6
Greece	1558	16	0	6.2
For comparison				
USA	9573			2.4
Japan	1873			8.0

Source: Crafts and Toniolo (1996), p. 3

Formal statistical evidence

There are better ways to isolate the impact of integration and growth than simply comparing to the western European growth average. These techniques involve statistical methods – regression analysis – that are standard in the scientific literature on trade and growth. The consensus in this literature is that economic integration is good for income growth, although the exact relationship is not fully understood. The literature on European integration per se is much less developed. A recent pair of papers by Harald Badinger suggest that, although there is no long-run

Table 7.4 Growth rates five years before and five years after accession

	West Europe (%)	Britain + Denmark + Ireland (%)	Greece (%)	Spain + Portugal (%)	Finland + Austria + Sweden (%)
Pre-1968–72	18.5	12.5			
Post-1973–77	5.8	4.8			
Pre-1976–80	10.2		9.0		
Post-1981–85	7.4		0.1		
Pre-1981–85	7.4			2.7	
Post-1986–90	16.2			23.0	
Pre-1989–93	3.7				–5.0
Post-1994–98	12.7				12.4

Notes: Real GDP in constant prices; 5-year average, not annualized. West Europe is all the nations that eventually ended up in the EU or EFTA, i.e. the EU15 plus Iceland, Norway and Switzerland.
Source: Penn World, Table 6.1 (RGDPL)

(i.e. permanent) boost to growth, tighter European integration does produce a sizeable medium-run growth effect (Badinger, 2005, 2008).[1]

The point is illustrated in Fig. 7.1. In reality, European integration did occur and this produced the income growth we can observe in the data. To work out the fraction of this income that was

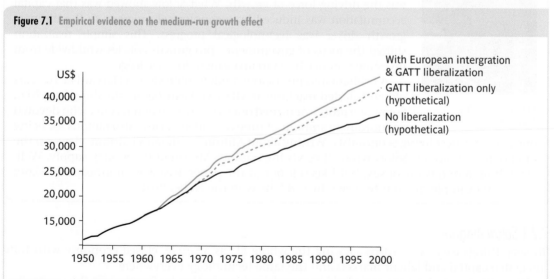

Figure 7.1 Empirical evidence on the medium-run growth effect

Note: The top line shows EU income growth. The middle and lower lines show a simulation of how much lower EU income per worker would have been under two hypothetical situations, without European integration (middle) and without any integration (lower). The difference between the middle and top line is Badinger's estimate of the medium-run growth effect.
Source: Badinger (2005), working paper version, with permission from the author

---

[1] Also see Henrekson et al. (1997), Coe and Moghadam (1993) and Italianer (1994).

due to an integration-induced growth effect, one needs to simulate what income would have been *without* European integration. The difference is the medium-run growth effect.

We turn now to a more careful consideration of *how* integration might affect growth. Establishing such an analytical framework is useful to understanding the growth–integration link, but more importantly, it allows us to make more pointed predictions that can be confronted with the data.

7.2 Medium-term growth effects: induced capital formation with Solow's analysis

Spain's accession to the EU in the mid-1980s and Estonia's accession in 2004 were accompanied by an investment boom that raised their GDP growth by several percentage points for a few years. In this section, we consider ways of understanding how EU membership could yield such a medium-term growth bonus.

The key to the medium-term growth bonus is 'induced capital formation'. That is to say, integration induces firms to raise the level of capital per worker employed. For the moment, we focus exclusively on the machine per worker (i.e. physical-capital to labour) ratio, so the first step is to identify a means of determining the equilibrium capital/labour ratio. The approach we adopt was discovered by Nobel Laureate Robert Solow in the 1950s (see Box 7.1). It assumes that people save and then invest a fixed share of their income.

Box 7.1   Robert Solow (1924–)

Photo: © Adephs,
2003–2005

Robert Solow's most famous contributions to economics, published in the late 1950s, revolutionized thinking about the causes of growth. Before Solow, the dominant thinking was that capital accumulation by itself was the driving force of growth. What Solow showed was that capital accumulation was induced by technological progress, so the ultimate growth driver was technological progress. This simple realization shifted the focus of governments' pro-growth policies worldwide from investment in machines to investment in knowledge.

A brilliant and precocious student (enrolled in Harvard at 16 years old and started teaching at MIT two years before finishing his PhD), Solow as a professor turned out to be an excellent teacher who devoted an inordinate amount of time to students. He is also famous for being one of the wittiest living economists. Writing about Milton Friedman's hardline views on the importance of money, Solow wrote, 'Everything reminds Milton of the money supply. Well, everything reminds me of sex, but I keep it out of the paper' (see www.minneapolisfed.org for recent examples in an interview). In 1987, he won the Nobel Prize.

7.2.1 Solow diagram

To keep things easy, we start by viewing the whole EU as a single, closed economy with fully integrated capital and labour markets and the same technology everywhere.

We begin our study of the logic linking growth and integration by focusing on the connection between GDP-per-worker and capital-per-worker. When a firm provides its workers with more and better equipment, output per worker rises. However, output per worker does not increase in proportion with equipment per worker. To see this, consider the example of the efficiency of your studying and your personal capital/labour ratio. The most primitive method of studying would be just to go to lectures and listen. Buying some paper and pencils would allow you to take notes and this would enormously boost your productivity in terms of both time and quality. Going further, you could buy the book and again this would boost your productivity (i.e. the effectiveness per hour of studying) but not as much as the pencils and paper. It would also be nice to have a calculator, a laptop, high-speed connection to the internet at home, and a laser printer of your own.

Each subsequent increase in your 'capital' would boost your effectiveness, but each euro of capital investment would provide progressively lower increases in productivity. As it turns out, this sort of 'diminishing returns' to investment also marks the economy as a whole. Raising the capital/labour ratio in the economy increases output per hour worked, but the rate of increase diminishes as the level of the capital/labour ratio rises.

This sort of less-than-proportional increase in efficiency is portrayed by the GDP/L curve. This shows that raising the capital/labour ratio (K/L, which is plotted on the horizontal axis) increases output per worker, but a 10 per cent hike in K/L raises GDP/L by less than 10 per cent. This is why the curve is bowed downwards in Fig. 7.2. (Alternatively, think of the curve as rising less rapidly than a straight line.)

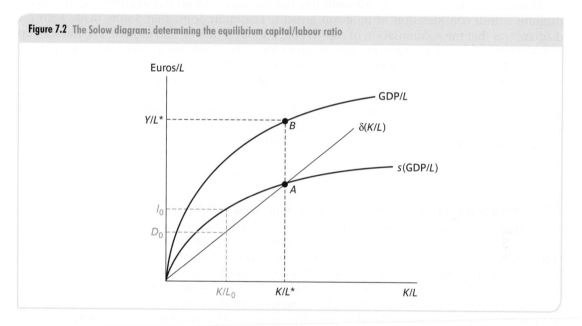

Figure 7.2 The Solow diagram: determining the equilibrium capital/labour ratio

The GDP/L curve shows us what output per worker would be for any given K/L; but what will the K/L be? The equilibrium K/L ratio depends upon the inflow and outflow of new capital per worker. The inflow is investment – firms building new factories, buying new trucks, installing new machines, etc. The outflow is depreciation – factories, trucks and machinery break down with use and must be repaired or replaced. The equilibrium K/L is where the inflow of new investment just balances depreciation of capital. The reason is simple. If the flow of savings exceeds the depreciation of capital, then K/L rises. If depreciation outstrips investment, K/L falls. The next step is to find the inflow and outflow of capital.

Solow simply assumed that people save and invest a constant fraction of their income each year, so the inflow of capital is just a fraction of GDP/L; in the diagram, this constant savings and investment fraction is denoted as s, so the inflow-of-capital curve is marked as s(GDP/L). (In European nations, s is somewhere between 20 and 35 per cent.) The investment-per-worker curve has a shape that is similar to that of the GDP/L curve but it is rotated clockwise since the savings are a fraction of GDP/L. As for depreciation, Solow made an equally simple assumption. He assumed that a constant fraction of capital stock depreciates each year. In the figure, the constant fraction of the capital stock that depreciates each year is denoted with the Greek letter 'delta', δ. (In Europe, something like 12 per cent of the capital stock depreciates each year.) The depreciation per worker line is shown as $\delta(K/L)$. It is a straight line since the amount of depreciation per worker increases in proportion to the amount of capital per worker.

The important point in the figure is point A, the crossing of the $s(GDP/L)$ curve and the $\delta(K/L)$ line. This occurs at K/L^*. At this capital/labour ratio, the inflow of new investment just balances the outflow. For a ratio below K/L^*, the capital/labour ratio would rise since investment outstrips depreciation. For example, if K/L were K/L_0, then the inflow would be I_0 and the outflow would be D_0. Since I_0 is higher than D_0, the amount of new capital per worker installed would be greater than the amount of capital per worker lost to depreciation. Naturally, the capital/labour ratio would rise. With more capital being installed for a ratio higher than this, depreciation surpasses investment, so K/L would fall. The last thing to work out is the output per worker implied by the equilibrium K/L. The answer, which is given by the GDP/L curve at point B, tells us that output per worker in this equilibrium will be Y/L^*.

Although it is not essential to our main line of analysis, we finish our discussion of the Solow diagram with a consideration of long-run growth. The main point that Solow made with his diagram was that the accumulation of capital is not a source of long-run growth. Capital rises up to the point where the K/L ratio reaches its equilibrium value and then stops, unless something changes. To explain the year-after-year growth we see in the modern world – about 2 per cent per year on average – Solow relied on technological progress. He assumed that technological advances would rotate the GDP/L curve upwards year after year, pulling the $s(GDP/L)$ curve up with it. As can be easily verified in the Solow diagram, such progress will lead to an ever-rising output per worker and an ever-rising capital/labour ratio. When we look at the growth effects of European integration, we shall be referring to growth that is higher than the growth that would have otherwise occurred due to technological progress.

We next use the Solow diagram to study how European integration might boost growth.

7.2.2 Liberalization, allocation effects and the medium-run growth bonus

The verbal logic of growth effects is straightforward. Integration improves the efficiency of the European economy by encouraging a more efficient allocation of European resources. Not surprisingly, this improved efficiency also makes Europe a better place to invest and thus boosts investment beyond what it otherwise would have been. The extra investment means more tools per worker, and this raises the output per worker. As workers get more tools than they would have without integration, output per worker rises faster than it would have done otherwise. To put this differently, integration produces extra growth as the capital/labour ratio approaches its new equilibrium output. This is the medium-run growth bonus introduced by Baldwin (1989). It is medium term since the higher growth disappears once the new equilibrium capital/labour ratio is reached.

Medium-run growth bonus in detail

Figure 7.3 allows us to portray the logic in more detail. The first step is to realize how 'allocation effects' of European integration alter the diagram. For all the reasons presented in Chapters 4 to 6, European integration has improved the effectiveness with which capital, labour and technology are combined to produce output. To take one concrete example, we saw that integration can lead to fewer, more efficient firms. From the firm-level perspective, this improved efficiency means lower average cost. From the economy-wide perspective, the improved efficiency means that the same amount of capital and labour can produce more output. How can we show this in the Solow diagram?

The positive allocation effect shifts the GDP/L curve to the dashed line marked GDP/L'. The new GDP/L curve is the old one rotated up counter-clockwise since the improved efficiency means that the economy is able to produce more output, say, 2 per cent more, for any given capital/labour ratio. This is the first step. The impact of the higher efficiency on output is shown

Figure 7.3 Medium-run growth bonus from European integration

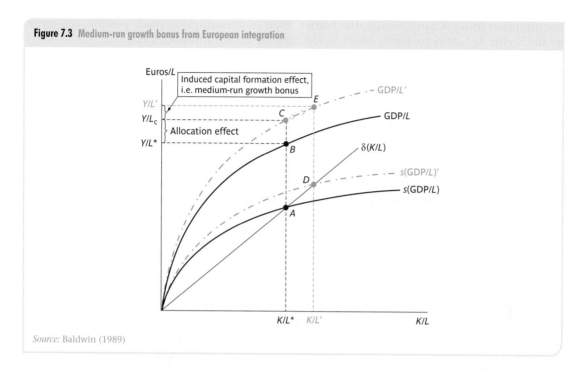

Source: Baldwin (1989)

by point C. That is, holding the capital/labour ratio constant at K/L^*, output would rise from Y/L^* to Y/L_c. This is not the end of the story, however, since K/L^* is no longer the equilibrium capital/labour ratio. This brings us to the second step.

The shift up in the GDP/L curve to GDP/L' also shifts up the investment curve to $s(\text{GDP}/L)'$. After all, the fixed investment rate now applies to higher output and so generates a higher inflow of investment for any given capital/labour ratio. This is shown in the diagram by the dashed curve $s(\text{GDP}/L)'$. Since the inflow has risen, K/L^* is no longer the equilibrium. At K/L^*, the inflow exceeds the outflow, so the economy's capital/labour ratio begins to rise. The new equilibrium is at the new intersection of the inflow and outflow curves, namely point D, so the new equilibrium capital/labour ratio is K/L'. The rise from K/L^* to K/L' is called 'induced capital formation' and reflects the fact that improved efficiency will tend to stimulate investment.

What are the growth implications? As the capital/labour ratio rises from K/L^* to K/L', output per worker rises from Y/L_c to Y/L'. This is shown in the diagram as the movement from point C to point E. Since the capital stock builds up only slowly, the movement between C and E can take years. The key to the second step is to realize that the rise in output per worker between C and E would show up as faster than normal growth until the economy reaches point E. At that time, the growth rate would return to normal.

Summary in words

In words, the integration-causes-growth mechanism is: integration → improved efficiency → higher GDP/L → higher investment-per-worker → economy's capital/labour ratio starts to rise towards new, higher equilibrium value → faster growth of output per worker during the transition from the old to the new capital/labour ratio. This is the so-called medium-term growth bonus from European integration.

When it comes to welfare, however, it is important to note that higher output is not a pure welfare gain. In order to invest more, citizens must save more and this means forgoing consumption today. Consequently, the higher levels of consumption made possible tomorrow by the higher K/L ratio are partly offset by the forgone consumption of today.

7.2.3 Other medium-run growth effects: changes in the investment rate

The Solow diagram relied on an extremely convenient simplifying assumption – a constant investment rate. Unfortunately, taking the investment rate as given severely limits the range of growth effects that we can study. As the introduction pointed out, the basic logic of growth rests on the decision to invest in new physical capital (machines), new human capital (skills) and/or new knowledge capital (innovations). Many growth effects operate by altering the costs and/or benefits of investing and thus by altering the investment *rate*, what we called s in the diagram. For instance, many people claim that the euro makes it easier, cheaper and safer to invest in Europe. If this turns out to be true, the extra investment would boost growth at least in the medium term, but how would we get this into the Solow framework?

If European integration raises the investment rate from, say, s to s', the inflow of capital curve, namely $s(GDP/L)$, will rotate upwards, as shown in Fig. 7.4. This change would in turn alter the equilibrium capital/labour ratio. Following the logic we considered above, the inflow of capital at the old capital/labour ratio K/L^* would exceed the outflow, so the capital stock per worker would rise to the new equilibrium shown by point C in the diagram. As before, the rising K/L would raise output per worker from Y/L^* to Y/L' (these Y/L^* and Y/L' are unrelated to those in previous figures). During this process, growth would be somewhat higher than it would have otherwise been.

This shows that it is straightforward to illustrate this second type of growth effect in the Solow diagram. We postpone our discussion of how various aspects of European integration might raise the investment rate to Section 7.3, where we consider EU capital market integration.

7.2.4 Evidence from EU accessions

Western Europe grew rapidly in the post-war period and experienced rapid integration. The problem, however, is that it is very difficult to separate the effects of European integration from

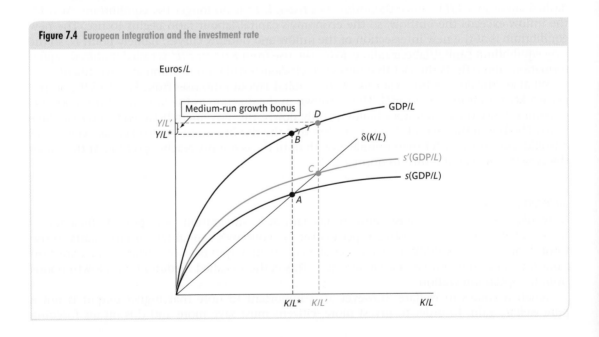

Figure 7.4 European integration and the investment rate

the many other factors affecting growth. One natural experiment is to look at what happened to nations that joined the EU. These nations experienced a rather sudden and well-defined increase in economic integration when they joined. In particular, we shall look at the impact of EU membership on Portugal and Spain (which joined in 1986), Latvia, Lithuania and Estonia (which joined in 2004), and Greece (which joined in 1981).

The logic sketched out above explains how integration may raise a nation's steady-state capital stock. What sort of 'footprints' would this leave in the data? First, heightened efficiency makes investment more worthwhile, i.e. it tends to raise the real return to capital. Moreover, this will normally be associated with an increase in the profitability of existing capital and this, in turn, should show up in the average behaviour of the stock market (as long as the stock market reflects a broad sample of firms). An important caveat comes from the fact that liberalization usually harms some firms and sectors even when it is beneficial for the nation as a whole. If the stock market is dominated by, say, state-controlled 'white elephants' that will face increased pressure in a more liberal economy, a drop in the stock market index may accompany the enlargement. Second, the Solow diagram is too simple to distinguish between domestic and foreign investors, but we presume that an improvement in the national investment climate should attract more investment from both sources. These two effects are likely to leave three kinds of 'footprints' in the data:

1 Stock market prices should increase.
2 The aggregate investment to GDP ratio should rise.
3 The net direct investment figures should improve.

Portugal and Spain

The case that EU membership induced investment-led growth is the strongest for the Iberians. Following restoration of democracy in the mid-1970s, Portugal and Spain applied to the EU in 1977, with membership talks beginning in 1978. The talks proved difficult, so accession occurred only in 1986. Growth in Portugal picked up rapidly and stayed high both during the negotiations and after accession; and between 1977 and 1992, Portugal expanded 13 per cent more than France (the country we have chosen as a 'control'). In Spain, however, growth was worse than that of France until accession. From 1986, it picked up significantly and between 1986 and 1992 Spain's cumulative growth edge over France amounted to 7.5 per cent, about the same as Portugal's.

As the lower panel of Fig. 7.5 shows, much of this rapid growth was due to a higher rate of physical capital formation. Portugal's investment rate responded strongly and quickly to the combination of democracy and the prospect of EU membership. The importance of membership probably stems from some mixture of reduced uncertainty concerning the nation's stability and the prospect of improved market access. Note, however, that as a member of EFTA, Portugal already had duty-free access to the EU market for industrial goods. The pattern of the Spanish investment rate, in contrast, did not differ significantly from that of our 'control' country until accession actually occurred. At that point, however, the Spanish investment-rate pattern does follow the predictions of integration-induced investment-led growth.

The top-left panel of the figure shows the same pattern for the stock market price indices. Spain's index tracked that of France until accession but thereafter showed signs of a significant improvement in the investment climate. Portuguese data are available only from 1987, but clearly show a better-than-average performance in subsequent years. The top-right panel displays the evidence for net foreign direct investment. Here the prospect of membership and domestic market-oriented reforms boosted the attractiveness of Spain and Portugal as industrial locations. Note that the boom in Portuguese foreign direct investment came only after accession.

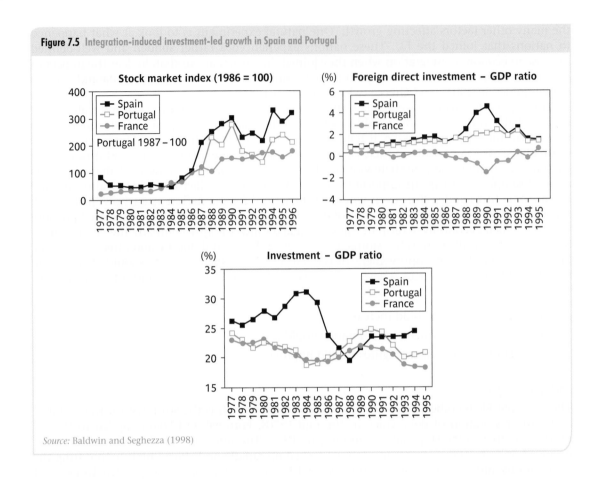

Figure 7.5 Integration-induced investment-led growth in Spain and Portugal

Source: Baldwin and Seghezza (1998)

The Baltic States

Latvia, Lithuania and Estonia were republics of the USSR up until 1991. Upon independence they approached the EU for closer ties. From the mid-1990s it was clear that they would eventually become EU members and would certainly be part of the first enlargement wave. As history would have it, that wave came in 2004.

Since these nations were under strict communism up till 1991 – and thus their economies were subject to central planning – data for the 1990s is a confusion of factors. These nations were making the difficult transition from planning and socialism to European-style social market economies. At the same time, they were preparing for EU member and signing a series of trade agreements with the EU, EFTA, each other, Finland, Sweden, etc. From 2000, however, we see the clear signs of investment-led growth in Fig.7.6. The investment to GDP ratio was far above that of France (again included as a control) and rising. There is no jump when enlargement came since the 2004 enlargement was widely anticipated more than a year in advance. The drop in investment from 2007 is a consequence of the global economic crisis that started with the subprime crisis in the USA.

The facts for FDI are not as convincing as they were for Spain when it comes to Latvia and Lithuania. The case of Estonia – which shares close lingual, historical and geographic ties with high-tech and high-wage Finland – is quite clear. Once it was clear that property rights in Estonia would be enforced to EU standards, Estonia experienced a big inward surge of FDI, especially from Finland and Sweden. The evidence from stock markets is quite clear. As EU membership

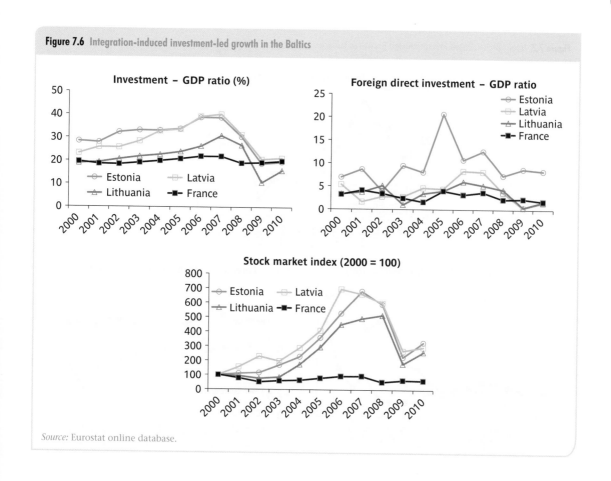

Figure 7.6 Integration-induced investment-led growth in the Baltics

Source: Eurostat online database.

approached, investors bid up the price of Baltic companies – a sign that EU accession was improving the investment climate in the Baltics.

Greece

As in the case of Portugal and Spain, the Greek accession (1981) came just after a period of undemocratic governments. However, unlike the Iberians, Greece continued its pervasive state controls of the economy. These controls prevented the Greek economy from reacting flexibly to any shock, and EU membership turned out to be one such example. Moreover, the poor macroeconomic management of the Greek economy further harmed the investment climate. The high and unstable inflation rate provides an example. While most European nations brought inflation down during the 1981–91 period, the Greek inflation rate hardly moved (from 25 per cent in 1981 to 20 per cent in 1991). Moreover, during this period inflation fluctuated greatly, jumping up or down by more than 3 percentage points in a single year in five out of the ten years.

Given this background, it is not surprising that we find no evidence of investment-led growth in Greece. Figure 7.7 shows the Greek numbers for the five years prior to, and ten years subsequent to, accession. None of the figures suggests that EU membership had any impact on our three indicators.

The sharp contrast between the Greek case and the others provides an important lesson. While integration may improve the investment climate in a nation, this can certainly be offset by other factors.

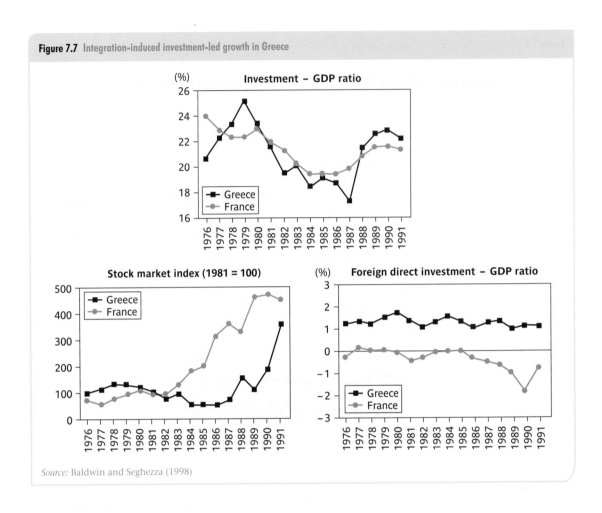

Figure 7.7 Integration-induced investment-led growth in Greece

Source: Baldwin and Seghezza (1998)

7.3 Long-term growth effects: faster knowledge creation and absorption

Up to this point we have focused on physical capital. Here, we focus on knowledge capital, i.e. technology. Although both technology and machines are capital in the sense that they provide a flow of productive services over time, there is an enormous difference between the two. The most important, for our purposes, concerns diminishing returns. It is easy to see that raising the physical capital is subject to diminishing returns. Is knowledge capital subject to the same effects? The answer is clearly no.

The stock of knowledge per worker has risen steadily at least since the Enlightenment in the seventeenth century. Moreover, even as the knowledge stock rises, there seems to be no tendency for the usefulness of more knowledge to diminish. In the late nineteenth century, at the end of a particularly impressive burst of innovation called, by some, the second industrial revolution, the chief of the US Patent Office made the famously incorrect statement that Congress should close the Patent Office since everything had already been invented. This myopic viewpoint seems humorous exactly because knowledge, by its very nature, does not seem to be subject to the same sort of limits as physical capital.

As we pointed out in Section 7.2.1, technological progress shifts the GDP/*L* curve up in the Solow diagram and this raises output per worker in exactly the same way as we saw in the Fig. 7.3

analysis. In short, we can think of technological progress as an allocative efficiency gain that comes every year, but instead of the gain being driven by European integration, it is driven by technology.

From this perspective, it is clear that the rate of technological progress is the key to understanding the long-term growth rate. The key point from our perspective is that, in principle, European integration can alter the rate of technological progress.

7.3.1 Solow-like diagram with long-term growth

To study this possibility in closer detail, we draw a Solow-like diagram where we focus on knowledge capital accumulation, rather than physical capital accumulation. The key difference is that knowledge capital does not face diminishing returns, so the GDP/L curve rises in a straight-line fashion with respect to the knowledge-per-worker ratio, referred to as K/L in Fig. 7.8 (note that the K/L here is not the same as K/L in the previous figures; here, it is knowledge capital per worker instead of physical capital per worker).

To keep things simple, we continue to assume that each nation invests a constant fraction of its national income in the accumulation of knowledge capital – this rate (referred to as s in the diagram) could be measured by the fraction of a nation's income invested in R&D, i.e. typically something like 3 to 5 per cent in European nations. To see how the total investment in new knowledge changes with the knowledge/labour ratio (K/L), we plot $s(GDP/L)$ as before. However, now it is a straight line since the GDP/L curve is a straight line.

We also continue to assume that depreciation is constant in the sense that a given fraction of the national knowledge capital stock 'depreciates' each year. When it comes to knowledge, we usually say the knowledge capital has become obsolete rather than saying it has depreciated, but the wording does not change the logic. In both cases, a certain fraction of the capital becomes worthless every year.

As drawn in Fig. 7.8, the investment rate exceeds the depreciation rate at all levels of K/L. For example, at a moment in time when the K/L ratio equals K/L^*, the amount of new knowledge capital per worker that is created is given by point A, while the amount of knowledge per worker that becomes obsolete is B. Since the inflow of new knowledge exceeds the outflow, the

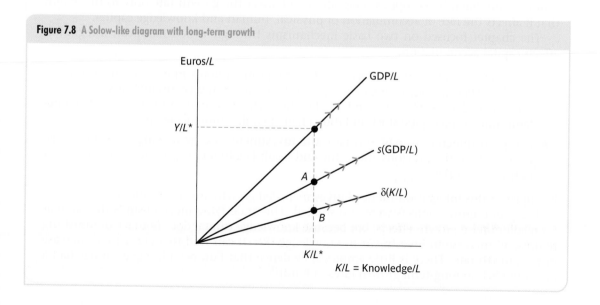

Figure 7.8 A Solow-like diagram with long-term growth

knowledge capital stock rises. This is shown by the arrow on the horizontal axis that suggests that K/L will continually rise.

As K/L rises for ever, the output per worker will rise for ever, along with the amount of new knowledge created and the amount of new knowledge that depreciates. These points are shown by the arrows on the GDP/L line, the s(GDP/L) line and the $\delta(K/L)$ line.

The diagram does not let us directly see how fast output per worker is rising, but it is easy to work this out. The further s(GDP/L) is above $\delta(K/L)$, the larger is the annual net addition to K/L. Thus as s rises, the nation will accumulate knowledge capital faster, and thus its income will rise faster.

Does European integration affect the long-term growth rate?

The evidence on long-term growth effects of European integration is much harder to find. The overarching fact is that long-term growth rates around the world, including those in Europe, returned to their pre-Golden Age levels. Since the level of European integration was rising more or less steadily during the whole post-war period, one would have to tell a complicated story to explain how the long-run growth rate returned to its pre-integration average, if integration strongly boosted long-run growth. Badinger (2005) confirms this with statistical evidence (also see Deardorff and Stern, 2002). For this reason, it is probably best to focus on medium-term growth effects, i.e. investment booms that are associated with European integration.

The experience of the new Member States will provide an important opportunity for testing the growth effects of EU membership, but as yet we do not have enough data to undertake serious statistical analysis.

7.4 Summary

The logic of accumulation effects of European integration is based on the fundamental logic of economic growth. A nation's per-capita income can rise on a sustained basis only if its workers are provided with a steadily rising stock of physical, human and/or knowledge capital. Consequently, European integration will affect the growth rate only to the extent that it affects the rate of accumulation of physical, human and knowledge capital.

The chapter focused on two basic mechanisms through which European integration affects capital accumulation:

  ✳ In so far as European integration makes the European economy more efficient, i.e. leads to a positive allocation effect, it raises output and this – assuming a constant investment rate – leads to more investment. The end result of this higher level of investment is a higher long-term equilibrium capital stock and thus a higher equilibrium income per person.

  ✳ European integration may also raise the investment rate by making investment less risky. As with the previous effect, the end result is a higher capital stock and a higher output per worker.

Examples of this integration-induced investment-led growth are fairly common.

Long-term growth effects were also studied. The underlying mechanism is the same as for medium-term growth effects, but because knowledge capital does not face diminishing returns, an increase in investment in knowledge (R&D) can lead to a permanent increase in the growth rate. There is little empirical evidence that European integration has had a major impact on long-term growth rates in Europe.

Self-assessment questions

1. When the German reunification took place, Germany's labour force rose much more than its capital stock (since much of East Germany's capital stock was useless in the market economy). Use a diagram to analyse what the medium-term growth effects should have been. Go on the internet to find out what actually happened to German growth after reunification.

2. It is often said that the prospect of EU membership made central European nations a better, safer place to invest. Using the Solow diagram, show how this would affect medium-term growth in these nations. What sort of 'footprints' would this leave in the data?

3. Use a diagram to analyse the medium-term growth effects of the following situation. Assume: (1) Serbia's K/L was pushed below its long-term equilibrium by war damage to its capital stock, and (2) the EU signs a free trade agreement with Serbia that has two effects: (2a) it increases the efficiency of the Serbian economy (allocation effect), and (2b) it raises the Serbian investment rate (s) but only temporarily, for, say, ten years. (i) Show what (1), (2a) and (2b) would look like; (ii) show where the Serbian economy would end up in the long run (i.e. after s returned to its normal rate); and (iii) show how the integration would affect Serbia's growth path.

4. Just after the Second World War, the economies of the Six experienced massive destruction of physical capital. Although many workers also died, the war tended to do more damage to the capital stocks than it did to the labour force. Use a diagram to illustrate how this may help explain the 'miraculous growth' in the late 1940s and 1950s.

Essay questions

1. In most analyses, growth in per-capita GDP is taken to be a good thing. Write an essay that critiques GDP as a measure of economic welfare. Be sure to consider issues of income distribution and leisure time.

2. Write an essay that puts the attitude towards capital market integration of the founders of the EU into historical perspective. Focus on the period after 1914.

3. Write an essay that discusses and analyses the post-1989 growth experience of one central European nation. Be sure to use the concepts introduced in this chapter.

Further reading: the aficionado's corner

An extensive description and analysis of growth in Europe can be found in:
Crafts, N. and G. Toniolo (1996) *Economic Growth in Europe since 1945*, Cambridge University Press, Cambridge.

An alternative presentation of the Solow model, one that allows for several extensions such as population growth and continuous technological progress, can be found in:
Mankiw, G. (2000) *Principles of Economics*, Thomson Learning, New York.

An advanced treatment of neoclassical and endogenous growth can be found in:
Barro, R. and X. Sala-I-Martin (1995) *Economic Growth*, McGraw-Hill, New York.

Other useful works are:

Baldwin, R. and R. Forslid (2001) 'Trade liberalization and endogenous growth: a q-theory approach', *Journal of International Economics*, 50: 497–517.

Commission (1996) *The 1996 Single Market Review: Background Information for the Report to the Council and European Parliament*, Commission of the European Communities, SEC (96) 2378, Brussels. Download from http://europa.eu.int/comm/internal_market/en/update/impact/bgrounen.pdf.

Useful websites

For the latest data on European growth and forecasts, see the website of DG Economy and Finance: http://europa.eu.int/comm/economy_finance/.

References

Badinger, H. (2005) 'Growth effects of economic integration: evidence from the EU member states', *Weltwirtschaftliches Archiv*, 141(1): 50–78.

Badinger, H. (2008) 'Technology- and investment-led growth effects of economic integration: a panel cointegration analysis for the EU-15 (1960–2000)', *Applied Economics Letters*, 15(7): 557–61.

Baldwin, R. (1989) 'The growth effects of 1992', *Economic Policy*, 9: 247–82.

Baldwin, R. and E. Seghezza (1998) 'Regional integration and growth in developing nations', *Journal of Economic Integration*, 13(3): 367–99.

Cameron, R. and L. Neal (2003) *A Concise Economic History of the World*, Oxford University Press, Oxford.

Coe, D. and R. Moghadam (1993) 'Capital and trade as engines of growth in France', *IMF Staff Papers*, 40: 542–66.

Deardorff, A. and R. Stern (2002) *EU Expansion and EU Growth*, Ford School of Public Policy, Working Paper 487.

Henrekson, M., J. Torstensson and R. Torstensson (1997) 'Growth effects of European integration', *European Economic Review*, 41(8): 1537–57.

Italianer, A. (1994) 'Whither the gains from European economic integration?', *Revue Economique*, 3: 689–702.

Chapter 8

Economic integration, labour markets and migration

As the extent of economic integration approaches that of the United States, labour market institutions and labour market outcomes may also begin to resemble their American counterparts. [. . .] Full and irreversible economic integration may call for harmonization of social and labour-market institutions within the European Union.

Giuseppe Bertola (2000)

Chapter Contents

Introduction

For most people, a good job is an essential element of a good life. This is why employment is a critical political and economic issue throughout Europe. Rightly or wrongly, European citizens expect Europe to improve their lot. The failure to deliver full employment throughout Europe, therefore, is a major failure. Even though labour market policies remain a national prerogative, this failure challenges the whole integration process. The rejection of the Constitution is a symptom of a widespread discontent that does not spare Europe and its institutions. The job difficulties faced by millions of people throughout the continent are due to poor national policies and institutions, but can European integration make the situation better, or worse? This chapter explores the linkages between jobs and European integration. It covers two main topics: unemployment, and how it is related to trade integration, and migration, one of Europe's four freedoms.

The chapter starts by describing the situation of the European labour markets. It shows that in many countries unemployment is high and employment is low. We next present a simple analytical framework that explains the unemployment phenomenon. This framework shows that socially desirable features of the labour market have serious economic costs. Put differently, social protection results in labour market rigidities. With these basics in place, we next examine the impact of European integration on Europe's labour markets. We show that economic and labour market integration encourages labour market flexibility. The last section looks at migration. Migration is another form of integration. From an economic point of view, it allows for a more efficient allocation of resources. But it also helps build up a better understanding of people. In contrast to widespread fears of huge migratory movements, the evidence is that Europeans move little.

8.1 European labour markets: a brief characterization

In contrast to goods markets, each national labour market in Europe is on its own. There are two main reasons for that. First, there is not much 'trade' in labour, because migration within the EU is very limited. Second, each country has its own social customs, a historical heritage that leads to very different legislations and practices. As a result, we cannot talk of a 'European labour market' but of as many markets as there are countries. Still, on average, the EU is generally

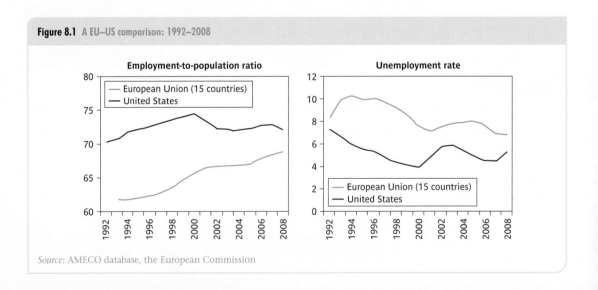

Figure 8.1 A EU–US comparison: 1992–2008

Source: AMECO database, the European Commission

not doing well. Figure 8.1 shows two measures of labour market performance (see Box 8.1 for an explanation of these and other definitions). The employment-to-population ratio is the percentage of the working-age population (conventionally set at 15 to 64 years) that has a job. The average employment-to-population ratio in the EU27 countries is growing, but remains significantly below the US rate. In 2008, the EU27 employment-to-population ratio stood at 69 per cent. This means that 31 per cent of the working-age population does not have a proper job. Some of these people may be disabled. The others are not working for two main reasons: some cannot find a job; others are not interested in looking for work, in some cases because they are taking care of the household. The right-hand chart shows the unemployment rate, the percentage of people who want to work but do not find a job. It is higher in Europe than in the USA. It is also the case that more Europeans are apparently not keen to work. Labour is a

Box 8.1   Labour market concepts

Categories

A country's total population can be broken down into several categories (Table 8.1). The first distinction is between the total population and the working-age population, conventionally defined as all valid people from 15 to 64 years old. Thus the working-age population excludes the young, the retired and the invalid.

Table 8.1   Decomposition of the population of the EU27 countries (millions), 2008

Employed (1)	Unemployed (2)	Labour force (3) = (1) + (2)	Out of the labour force (4)	Employment-age population (5) = (3) + (4)	Population (6)
226	16	242	93	334	497

Source: AMECO database, the European Commission

The working-age population (N) can be decomposed into three groups: 1, those who are employed (E); 2, those who are unemployed (U); and 3, those who are out of the labour force (O):

$$N = E + U + O$$

The labour force includes the employed and the unemployed:

$$L = E + U$$

and the working-age population is the sum of the labour force and the others:

$$N = L + O$$

People out of the labour force are those who do not want to work and those who are too discouraged even to seek a job and thus qualify as unemployed.

Ratios

The unemployment rate (u) is the ratio of the number (U) of people who declare themselves unemployed (they have no job and are actively looking for one) to the labour force (L):

$$u = \frac{U}{L}$$

The employment rate (e) is the remaining proportion of the labour force, composed of those who hold jobs:

$$e = \frac{E}{L} = 1 - u$$

The participation rate (p) is the ratio of the labour force to the working-age population:

$$p = \frac{L}{N} = 1 - \frac{0}{N}$$

The employment-to-population ratio, which is shown in Figs 8.1 and 8.2, is the proportion of people of working age who hold a job:

$$eR = \frac{E}{N} = \frac{E}{L}\frac{L}{N} = ep$$

How are people counted?

This is not an innocuous question. Each country carries out census polls and other formal population-counting procedures. The employed, E, are identified from firms reporting taxes and various welfare contributions, and from surveys. The unemployed, U, are identified either through polls or because they are officially registered as such (the difference matters as each country has its own procedure; the International Labour Office produces harmonized data based on surveys). This leaves those out of the labour force, O, as a residual ($O = N - E - U$). Precision is not the name of the game as the black market can include 10 or 20 per cent of the working-age population.

An important distinction is between voluntary and involuntary unemployment. In principle, people who do not want to work are classified as out of the labour force (O). In practice, however, things are less clear cut: some people counted in U are really voluntarily unemployed or actually employed, whereas others counted in O are involuntarily unemployed. Three main reasons explain this discrepancy. First, some unemployed people are really working in the black market (they are counted in U whereas they should be in E). Second, being unemployed opens the door to a range of welfare payments, mainly unemployment insurance benefits. It is believed that these benefits enable workers to be choosier and to reject some job offers or to search less than would otherwise be the case; yet, they must identify themselves as involuntarily unemployed either by registering or when polled. Finally, some people who have searched for a job for a long time become discouraged and simply drop out of the labour force (i.e. they are counted in O whereas they really are in U).

Note: These concepts are further defined and explained in International Labour Organization (ILO) publications. See www.ilo.org.

country's most precious input, because it is its people and their talents and because each country spends considerable resources to educate its population. A non-employment rate of 31 per cent thus represents a massive waste of talent and a huge loss in income. Just as bad is that those who do not have a job feel estranged from society.

While, on average, European labour markets underperform, the situation varies considerably from one country to another. This is illustrated in Fig. 8.2, which displays the average employment-to-population ratios and the unemployment rates over 2005–08 for each EU country as well as

Figure 8.2 Employment-to-population ratios and unemployment rates in 2005–08: EU27 and comparable non-EU countries

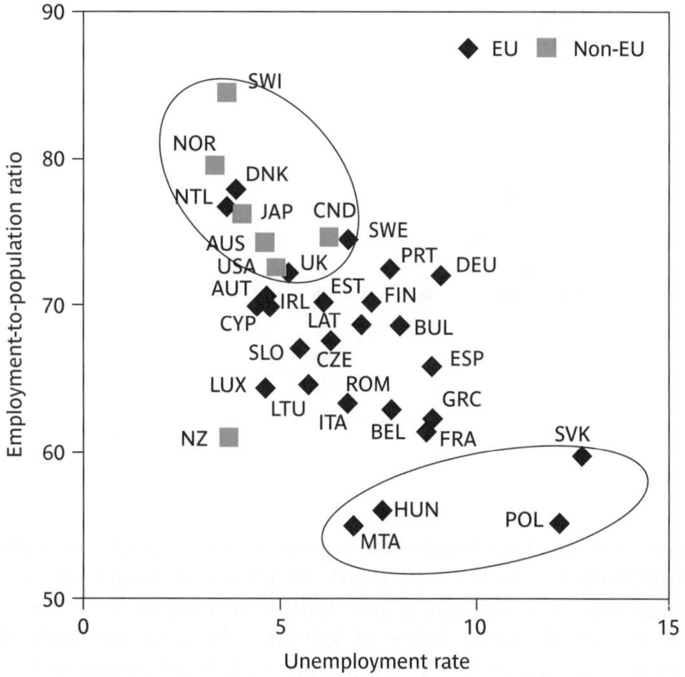

Note: The non-EU27 countries are Australia, Canada, Japan, New Zealand, Norway, Switzerland and the USA.
Source: AMECO database, the European Commission

for similar non-EU countries. The countries with the best-performing labour markets are closer to the top-left corner, while poorly performing countries appear in the bottom-right corner. With one exception (New Zealand), the non-EU countries have better-performing labour markets than the EU countries. Only two EU countries (Denmark and the Netherlands) clearly join the top league and two others (Sweden and the UK) come close. The four worst performers are among the new EU members (from left to right: Malta, Hungary, Poland and Slovakia).

8.2 Labour markets: the principles

We start with the essential tools that will guide us throughout this chapter. We look at the demand for labour by firms, at the supply of hours of work by individuals, and ask why unemployment is a general feature. This question leads us to realize that the labour market is a very special market, similar to none other.

8.2.1 Demand

Jobs exist because firms employ people. When deciding whether to hire an additional worker, a firm looks at the cost and the benefit. The cost is the wage, to which must be added the

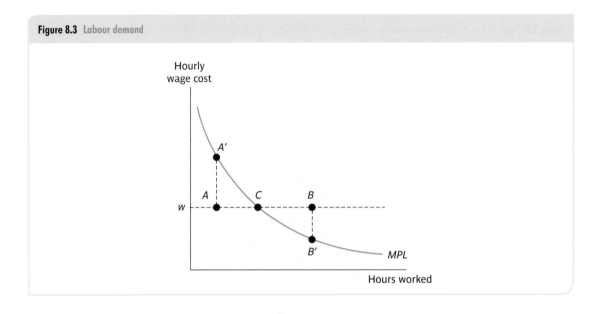

Figure 8.3 Labour demand

various contributions that most governments impose (contributions to health, unemployment and retirement programmes). As we will think in terms of hours of work, let us call this total the hourly wage cost. The benefit is the additional output that the worker will deliver, which is called the marginal productivity of labour – because we look at the margin, the output from one more hour of work. A key feature of labour productivity is that it declines as more hours are being performed. One reason is that, at any point of time, the equipment available in the firm is given, so that more workers will have to share it. Another reason is that longer hours mean that workers get tired and equipment is used up faster and breaks down more often. The principle of declining labour marginal productivity is captured in Fig. 8.3 by the downward-sloping curve labelled *MPL*.

Now imagine a firm facing an hourly labour cost *w*. If it chooses to buy the number of hours corresponding to point *A* in Fig. 8.3, its cost is lower than its benefit, which corresponds to point *A'*. Hiring one more hour is therefore highly profitable, and there is no reason for the firm not to do so and move rightward from point *A*. How far? Imagine that the firm goes all the way to point *B*, where the hourly labour cost is now higher than the marginal productivity of labour, as point *B'* indicates. Hiring more hours would entail losses. Reducing one hour would mean saving on the wage bill by *w* and giving up output by *MPL*, hence a saving for the firm. This means that the firm does well by moving leftward from point *B*. Clearly, the best position is at point *C*, on the *MPL* curve. If *w* rises, the point corresponding to point *C* will move up the *MPL* curve. This shows that the firm will always hire the number of hours that corresponds to the marginal productivity of labour. Put differently, the *MPL* curve represents the firm's demand for labour.[1]

8.2.2 Supply

Labour is supplied by people. As we all know too well, work is tiring and less pleasurable than leisure. This is why we ask for remuneration. How much we ask will depend on our skills and

---

[1] Note that the marginal productivity is measured in units of output. To be comparable, we also need to measure wage costs in the same units, e.g. one hour of work gets you three beers or one-thousandth of a car, more generally a portion of GDP. In the terminology of Chapter 9, we consider here the real wage, which is represented as the ratio of the nominal wage W to the price level P, $w = W/P$.

Figure 8.4 Demand and supply

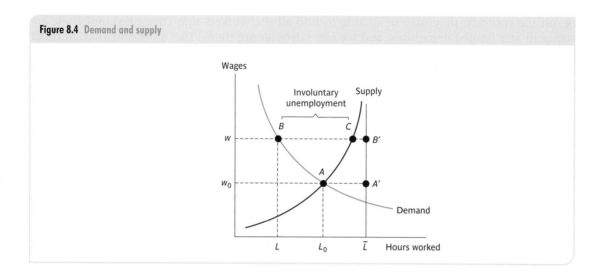

personal characteristics, including our inclination to stay at home. We consider the 'average' worker, so we ignore these personal characteristics. Instead, we ask what has to happen to the wage to convince the average worker to work one more hour. If the worker is unemployed, ignoring for the time being any welfare income such as unemployment benefits, almost any salary is better than nothing. If the worker already works quite a lot, one more hour is not that attractive and it will take a fairly good salary to convince her to stay longer on the job. This reasoning suggests that the supply of labour can be represented by an upward-sloping curve, as shown in Fig. 8.4. The curve is steeper the choosier the worker is.

8.2.3 Equilibrium and more realism

Equipped with the demand and supply apparatus, we are tempted to conclude that the outcome occurs at point A in Fig. 8.4 where demand and supply meet.[2] Note that, in this situation, both firms and workers are perfectly satisfied with the situation. In particular, the total amount of work L_0 corresponds precisely to what workers are willing to supply at the going wage w_0. That does not mean that every worker has a job or that every employed person works full time. Such a case of full employment corresponds to L. The distance AA' represents unused labour or unemployment. This is a special form of unemployment, however, for these hours are voluntarily not worked. Given the wage rate, some people do not wish to work at all or to work long hours – this is the meaning of the supply curve.

If, as Fig. 8.4 presumes, the labour markets operated like other markets, there would be no involuntary unemployment. This is why equilibrium at point A is unrealistic. Since in every country a number of people are involuntarily unemployed, we have to admit that this is not a good description of real-life labour markets. Indeed, labour markets are very special, and for a good reason. The goods that are bought and sold on this market are people's time, talent and effort. Quite obviously, these are not standard goods.

Looking at Fig. 8.4, we see that involuntary unemployment can only occur if workers are not on their supply curve. More precisely, they must be kept involuntarily somewhere to the left of the supply curve. On the other hand, firms are usually on, or close to, their demand curve. True, firms can have more workers than they want because they are forbidden to dismiss workers

---

[2] Here we ignore the various charges that make wage costs different from what workers take home. Section 8.3.3 shows how to deal with this issue.

or, on the contrary, they may be unable to find all the workers that they need. But these are transient and limited departures, and we can safely ignore them. This all means that, in order to explain involuntary unemployment, we have to imagine that the economy lies on the labour demand curve somewhere up above point A, for example at point B. In this case, employment is L, and the distance BC measures involuntary unemployment while CB' captures voluntary unemployment.

How can point B be a lasting equilibrium? The salient feature of point B is that the wage w is above its no-involuntary-unemployment level w_0. The challenge, therefore, is to understand why such an outcome is possible. If the labour market were a market like all others, the wage rate would decline until it reached w_0. This is not what happens. Somehow, wages do not move up and down, and they very rarely move down. A number of characteristics explain this feature:

- Salaries, the price of labour, are not set like the price of oil or corn, through bidding. They are collectively negotiated by representatives of employers and employees.

- Negotiations take place at more or less regular intervals and agreements hold for periods that usually extend to one year or more. Thus labour markets react slowly to changing conditions.

- Wage contracts are often regulated. For example, in many countries minimum wages legislation hampers downward adjustments.

- Conditions under which workers are hired and dismissed are also the object of specific legislation and customs.

- Unemployment benefits, designed to limit the hardship of becoming unemployed, can backfire, as explained below.

8.2.4 The economics of collective negotiations

The most crucial feature, perhaps, is the collective nature of labour negotiations. We now amend the demand–supply diagram to illustrate their economic effects. Workers resort to a collective representation – let's call it a trade union for the sake of simplicity – because it allows them to achieve better wages. If the arrangement works – if it did not, it would not have survived – the trade union's action delivers a higher wage than individual workers would achieve on their own. In Fig. 8.5 we distinguish between the individual supply curve S^{ind}, which describes how individuals trade off income from work against leisure time, and a collective supply curve S^{coll}, which lies above the previous one.

Figure 8.5 The role of collective negotiations

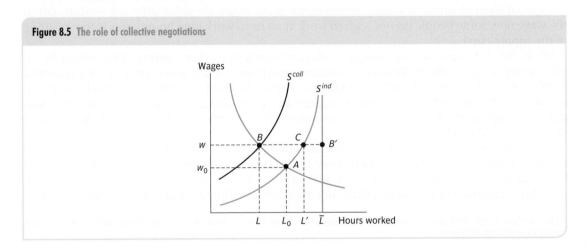

Point *A* shows the outcome of the free interplay of individual demand and supply in the labour market in the absence of any rigidity: employment is L_0, the real wage is w_0 and there is no involuntary unemployment. With collective negotiations, the outcome of the negotiation is now represented by point *B*. As collective negotiations raise the real wage to *w*, firms respond by aiming at production processes that are less labour intensive and employment declines to *L*. Note that, at the new, higher wage level *w*, the amount of labour that workers wish to supply increases to *L'*, corresponding to point *C*. The result is involuntary unemployment represented by the distance *BC*. This unemployment is collectively voluntary, however.

Why is this feature of labour markets so widespread? The workers who negotiate wages are, by definition, those who hold a job. They are the insiders. Reducing their own wages would allow some of those currently unemployed, the outsiders, to find jobs. But outsiders have no voice in the negotiations and the insiders have no interest in accepting wage cuts. This is why point *B* is stable in the sense that there is no mechanism that would change the situation. From a social and political viewpoint, this is understandable. Politically, the overwhelming majority of workers are employed since the highest unemployment rates rarely exceed 10–15 per cent, at least in the developed countries. Democratically, therefore, they support an institution that delivers higher wages, even at the cost of unemployment. Socially, the insiders ask for assistance for the unemployed. Unemployment benefits are usually financed, partly at least, through taxes paid by the employed, who then feel that the outcome is beneficial to them and fair to the unemployed. Yet, from a strict economic point of view, these arrangements can be analysed as rigidities that prevent the labour markets from being flexible enough to avoid involuntary employment, sometimes on a very large scale, as Table 8.1 shows.

Collective negotiations provide a first explanation of the involuntary unemployment phenomenon, but many other common features conspire to make things worse. This is the case of high and, especially, long-lasting, unemployment benefits. These benefits have an obvious justification. Losing a job is already a traumatic experience; at least those who face this hardship, and their families, should live decently until they find a new job. But experience shows that a by-product of these benefits is that unemployed people feel less pressure to take up new jobs, and therefore remain unemployed for longer periods of time, which further lessens the pressure on insiders to allow for more wage flexibility. Figure 8.6 shows that, in many EU countries, a large number of people remain unemployed for more than one year. This is an important example of the fact that many European countries have long attached more weight to social protection than to economic efficiency. They tend to run socially generous but economically inefficient unemployment programmes. Some countries have found a way of combining both concerns. This is the case in the Scandinavian countries, which provide generous unemployment benefits coupled with the obligation to take up job offers.

8.2.5 The cyclical impact of wage rigidity

An important implication of wage rigidity can be seen by considering the case of a cyclical downturn when the wage is fixed at *w*. We start in Fig. 8.7 from a situation where employment takes place at point *B*, with involuntary unemployment measured by *BC*. Now imagine that the economy slows down, for reasons explained in Chapter 17. Firms cannot sell all their products. Given that their equipments are in place anyway – their stock of capital cannot be reduced – the marginal product of labour declines and the demand for labour shifts down from *D* to *D'*. If the wages were perfectly flexible, we would have started at point *A* and moved to point *A'*. Employment and wages would have declined, voluntary unemployment would have risen but there would still be no involuntary unemployment. With wages rigidly maintained at w, we move to *B'*, employment declines from *L* to *L'* and involuntary unemployment rises to *B'C*. It is easy to imagine the opposite case of an economic expansion, which would result in higher employment and lower involuntary unemployment. We see that wage rigidity explains the fact that cyclical fluctuations are accompanied by variations in involuntary unemployment.

Figure 8.6 Long-term unemployment, 2010

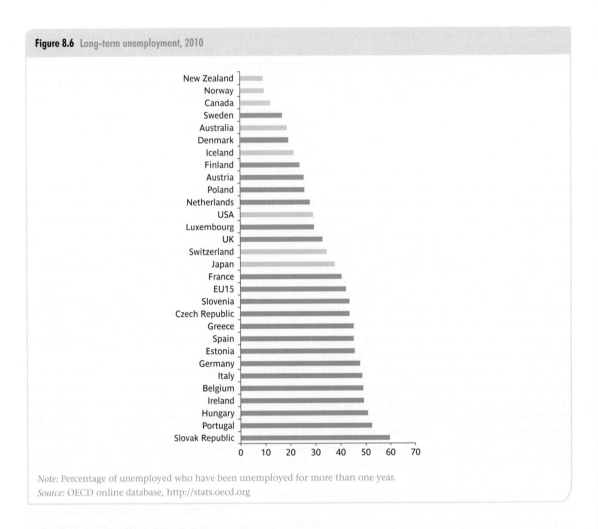

Note: Percentage of unemployed who have been unemployed for more than one year.

Source: OECD online database, http://stats.oecd.org

Figure 8.7 A cyclical downturn

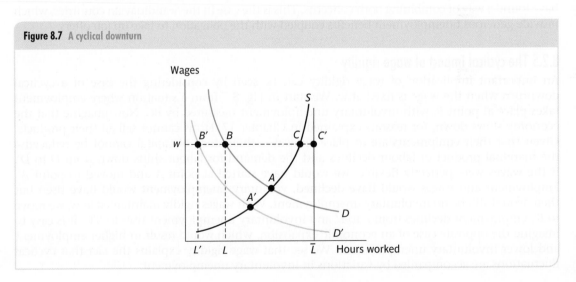

8.3 Effects of trade integration

The previous chapters have focused on the effects of the Single Market on the goods and services markets and on overall economic growth. This section looks at the effects on the labour markets. In order to compete in the goods and services markets, producers must fight on all fronts; first and foremost, their production costs. Production costs include three main components: labour costs, the price of equipment and the price of materials.

Both equipment and material costs are largely determined internationally (since domestically produced goods must compete with imports) and therefore are not a source of comparative advantage. Labour costs, which typically amount to over 50 per cent of total production costs, on the other hand, are a key source of competitiveness. Competition in the goods market, in turn, has deep implications for the labour markets. Through goods markets, national labour markets indirectly compete against each other. This section examines some implications of this observation.

8.3.1 Economic effects of trade integration

Chapter 4 shows the distortionary effects of barriers to trade. When these barriers are eliminated, Chapter 5 shows that protected import-competing industries shrink while the export industries expand. In terms of the analysis above, this can be seen as shifts in the labour demand curve that take place at the sectoral level.

If the labour markets are fully flexible, wages should rise in the industries that expand and they should decline in the industries that shrink. This, in turn, should trigger workers to move from the shrinking to the expanding industries, until wages are the same in both sectors. Wages could rise or decline, depending on the relative importance of the various adjustments, but there would still be no involuntary unemployment.[3]

A more realistic description must recognize the labour market rigidities presented in Section 8.2. As an illustration, we can either assume that wages are downward-rigid, as in Section 8.2.3, or think of the distinction between individual and collective labour supply, as in Section 8.2.4. We do both in Fig. 8.8, where we imagine that trade opening separates out the economy into two broad sectors, an expanding one and a contracting one. Additionally, we take the extreme case where workers are specialized and cannot move from one sector to the other, at least not until they have undergone retraining.

The initial situation is represented by point A in both charts. With collective labour bargaining, involuntary unemployment is measured by AB in each sector. The left-hand chart describes the expanding industry, where the demand for labour increases and the curve shifts from D to D'. The opposite happens in the contracting sector, shown in the left-hand chart. The new situation is represented by points A' in both charts and involuntary unemployment is measured by $A'B'$. It is not clear whether involuntary unemployment increases or decreases, both in each sector and in total. If the S^{coll} and the individual labour supply S^{ind} curves are parallel, there is no unemployment effect. There is a priori no reason to expect trade integration to raise or lower unemployment. This lines up with the facts. As previously noted, the tighter integration of European markets has been accompanied by steady or rising unemployment rates in some EU members such as France and Germany, but falling unemployment rates in members such as the UK, Sweden and Spain.

The only clear effect is that wages rise in the first sector and they decline in the second one. This may be seen as a source of growing inequality if wages were previously higher in the

---

[3] The Hecksher–Ohlin theory predicts that wages will increase if the country is capital-intensive relative to its trading partners and that wages will decrease if labour is relatively more abundant. This reasoning ignores the subsequent impact on capital accumulation.

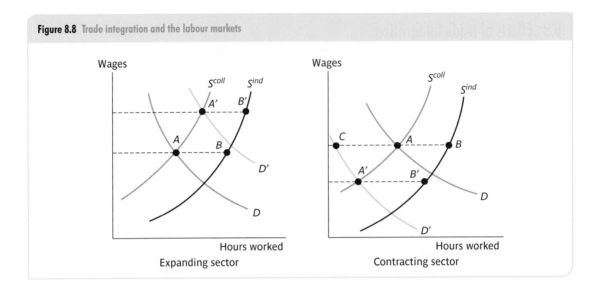

Figure 8.8 Trade integration and the labour markets

now-expanding sector, but inequality could be declining in the opposite case. At least, workers in the contracting sector may see the impact of trade integration as unfair.

We can briefly also consider what happens if, in addition, wages are downward-rigid, meaning that they can rise but not decline, because of legislative arrangements, social customs or the prevalence of minimum wage legislation. This does not matter for the expanding sector, since wages there increase. In the contracting sector, however, downward wage rigidity implies that the outcome is found at point C and involuntary unemployment, measured by CB, unambiguously increases.

In the end, trade integration does affect unemployment, unless the rigidities are severe. In that case, unemployment and inequalities are likely to rise. Yet trade is being blamed for creating unemployment. In fact, trade is only the messenger, which reveals the adverse effects of underlying distortions. This message, however, is very difficult to convey – the analysis presented here is far from trivial – and protectionism is never far below the surface. This is one reason why Europe's ability to dismantle *all* trade barriers is rather exceptional.

8.3.2 Institutional effects of trade integration

Labour market distortions are almost always related to institutional arrangements that reflect a country's political and social history. These institutions imply various degrees and forms of rigidity, with various effects on productive efficiency and unemployment. Such a deep change as European integration is unlikely to leave the institutions untouched. This section shows that labour market institutions and economic integration interact, with influences running in both directions:

■ Economic integration affects the nature of labour market institutions. These institutions arise from a compromise between economic and social imperatives, reached under conditions that prevail at some point in time. When faced with deep economic integration, labour market institutions become a strategic characteristic in the quest for competitiveness, i.e. economic effectiveness. The ability of firms to compete across borders on the Single Market depends on the ability of employers and employees to react adequately to adverse shocks. In addition, if the labour markets are too inflexible, integration may result in job losses with no job gains and possibly even no general economic gain either. This changes the incentives that justified the initial institutional arrangements and, quite likely, opens the way to labour market reforms that raise the effectiveness of labour markets. Figure 8.1 shows that, indeed, some progress has been achieved in the EU.

- Labour market institutions affect integration. Economic integration almost always creates winners and losers, but typically the winners win more than the losers lose. Europeans' willingness to elect leaders who push ever-deeper integration hinges critically on their belief that labour market institutions along with social safety nets will spread the net benefits of integration and dampen the pain felt by the losers. In the absence of some degree of fairness, broad political support for ever-closer economic integration is unlikely to be maintained in EU nations.

One important question is how national labour market institutions stand to be affected by the process of EU integration. In principle, since trade competition becomes competition among national social arrangements, survival of the fittest should guarantee that, eventually, all European states will gravitate towards the most efficient arrangements. This principle, however, must face the fact that European integration can be challenged, and even possibly reversed, if it is perceived as unfair.

8.3.3 Economics of 'social dumping'

A good example of this situation is the widely held view that European integration undermines valuable social protection, a view summarized as 'social dumping'. Indeed, workers in many of the older Member States (EU15) are convinced that competition from the 12 new Member States (EU12) will force a reduction of the level of social protection that they enjoy today. By the time they joined, wages were much lower in the EU12 countries (see Table 8.2) and in some of them the level of social protection was also considerably lower than in the EU15. There is nothing new here; it is an old, old concern. It was, for example, the crux of a major debate over the shape of

Table 8.2 Median weekly private sector earnings, February 2005–2010

	Feb. 2005	Feb. 2008	Feb. 2010
Bulgaria	5	6	7
Croatia	22	26	30
Czech Republic	19	26	29
Estonia	13	19	21
Hungary	20	19	17
Latvia	7	12	18
Lithuania	10	14	14
Poland	16	25	21
Romania	7	11	16
Slovakia	15	15	34
Slovenia	33	30	46

Source: Federation of European Employers (www.fedee.com)

the Treaty of Rome in the 1950s. In the early 1950s, French workers worried that lax social policy in Italy and Germany would undermine French social policy. Half a century later, in 2005, French workers voted against the European Constitution, partly because they feared competition from the famed 'Polish plumber'. As history would have it, since the 1950s social protection of workers rose spectacularly throughout western Europe despite (or maybe because of) the deep integration between nations that initially had very different wage and social protection levels. Much the same is happening now in the EU12 countries. Table 8.2 shows that the wage gap is often narrowing.

Such fears lead to calls for social harmonization. The leaders of the six founding nations of the European Union already worried about 'social dumping'. Yet, they decided that harmonization of most social policies was not a necessary component of European integration. The economic logic behind this judgement continues to affect EU policy, so it is worth considering in some detail.

To get a handle on the basic issues, we start by making strong assumptions to radically simplify the range of issues at hand. We will add back in some important aspects of reality after having established the basic points. Taking the example of France, we start by supposing that, as in Section 8.2.3, labour markets operate like other markets, so the wage adjusts to make sure that there is no involuntary unemployment. Moreover, to keep things simple, suppose France starts without any social policies and initially is closed to trade. The equilibrium, shown in the left-hand panel of Fig. 8.9, is where the real wage is w and the employment level is L.

Now suppose the French government adopted a whole series of social policies, e.g. limits on working hours, obligatory retirement benefits, maternity leave, sick leave, six weeks of annual holidays, etc. These policies would undoubtedly be good for most workers. Indeed, most Europeans view these as necessities, not luxuries. Yet, however good these policies are for workers and society at large, such policies are expensive for firms. To be specific, suppose that they raise the cost of employing workers by T euros per hour. What happens to wages and employment? The demand schedule shifts vertically down by T, since labour cost has increased by that amount. The new equilibrium wage paid to workers – this is called the 'take-home' pay – with the general policy will be w'.[4] It is useful to think of the social policy 'tax' being paid partly by consumers (in the form of higher prices) and partly by workers (in the form of lower take-home wages). The firms we consider here are competitive and so cannot bear any part of T (they earn zero profits both before and after T is imposed).

Figure 8.9 Social policy and distortions

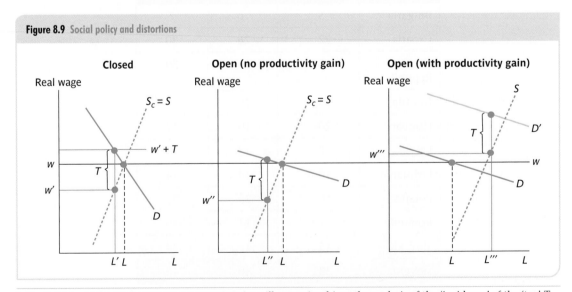

---

[4] Readers who had a good course in microeconomics will recognize this as the analysis of the 'incidence' of the 'tax' T.

Why does the take-home wage fall when social policies are imposed? Firms hire workers up to the point where marginal labour productivity is equal to the wage cost, as explained in Section 8.2.1. This cost includes wage and non-wage costs, such as the cost of social policies. Firms cannot pay higher labour costs if they want to avoid losing money. Given this iron law of the labour market – firms hire workers up to the point where all included employment costs equal the workers' value to the firm – everything that raises non-wage labour costs must force down the take-home pay of workers. In essence, the social policies are a way of 'forcing' workers to take part of their remuneration in the form of non-wage 'payment', e.g. four weeks of paid holiday or generous sick leave, instead of in the direct form of take-home pay.

Next, consider the impact of freeing trade in goods between France and other nations. As far as the labour market is concerned, freer trade has two main impacts:

1 As discussed at length in Chapters 4, 5, 6 and 7, trade tends to boost the productivity of an economy. It does this by allowing a nation's capital and labour to be allocated more efficiently. For example, Chapter 6 showed how freer trade produced fewer, larger, more efficient firms that faced more effective competition from each other.

2 Trade also tends to flatten the demand curve since it heightens the competition between national firms and foreign firms. For example, if real wage costs rise by €100 per week, firms will have to raise prices. The negative impact of higher prices on output, and therefore employment, is greater in the presence of foreign competition. Or, to put it more directly, greater integration of goods markets means that workers in different nations compete more directly with each other.

We begin with the second concern since this is closest to the everyday concerns of many workers in Europe. The middle panel in Fig. 8.9 shows the impact of the flatter demand curve on French labour. The way the diagram is drawn, openness per se would have no impact if there were no social policy. Without the tax T, wage and employment levels would be as in the closed economy case (i.e. w and L). The non-wage costs, i.e. T, however, change things. Since labour demand is now more responsive to total labour costs, the take-home wage of French workers will fall more, to w'' rather than w' when T is imposed. The reason is simple. Greater openness gives consumers a wider range of options; when T is imposed more of it gets paid by workers than by consumers. In other words, the greater price sensitivity forces workers to bear more of the burden of the social-policy 'tax'.

The result that greater openness reduces wages flies in the face of Europe's experience. The incomes of European workers have been growing steadily as European markets have become more tightly integrated. Moreover, as discussed in Chapter 7, some of the fastest income growth occurred in the 1960s when European trade integration was proceeding at its fastest pace. How can we explain this? The efficiency-enhancing effects of trade integration are the answer.

The third panel in Fig. 8.9 shows the labour market implications of trade-induced efficiency gains. As productivity rises, the value of workers to firms rises and this shows up as a shift up the demand curve to D'. Now we see that, even if trade integration makes the demand curve flatter, the shift up in the labour demand curve more than offsets flattening. In the figure, the take-home wage has risen to w'' and employment has increased to L''.

So far we have put the issue of unemployment to the side by assuming that the labour market clears. To consider unemployment, we allow the 'collective' labour supply curve (S^{coll}) and the individual labour supply curve (S^{ind}) to differ, as in Section 8.2.4. This is done in Fig. 8.10, which corresponds to the second panel of Fig. 8.9. The initial position is characterized by unemployment U, with employment L and supply L_s. The social policy distortion reduces employment to L' and supply to L_s'. The effect on unemployment is not clear, however, and this is also the case of the trade-opening effect, as we have already seen in Section 8.3.1. Here again, trade integration has no direct impact on unemployment, only on employment.

Figure 8.10 Social policy distortions with involuntary unemployment

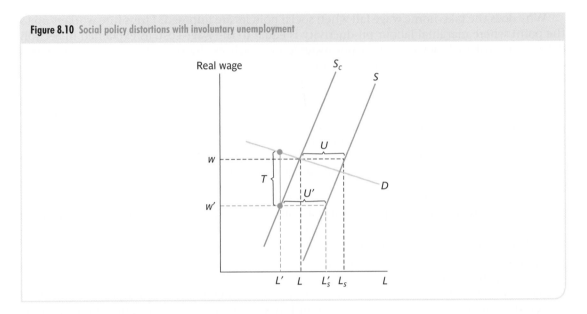

What has all this got to do with social dumping? What we have shown is that the total cost of employing workers – wage and non-wage costs – is tied to the productivity of workers. If governments raise social policy standards, the economy will adjust by lowering employment and reducing the wages (of course, wages rarely fall; what would happen is that wages would rise more slowly than productivity for a number of years, as happened in France when the 35-hour week was introduced). When an economy is more open, the wage and employment adjustments tend to be greater, other things equal. Or, to put it more colloquially, the anti-employment effects of social policies are magnified by greater openness.

This does not necessarily put pressure on social policies. The key point is that the same mechanism is at work in France's trade partners. If the other nations have lower social policy standards, their workers will have higher take-home pay than otherwise, since the foreign firms hire workers up to the point where their total labour cost matches their workers' productivity. Social harmonization would result in lower wages in these countries but would have little impact on the competitive pressures facing French employers. Turning this around, the same logic tells us that lowering French social policy standards would not boost French competitiveness in anything but the short run.

The upshot of all this should be clear. The logic of competition ties the sum of wage and non-wage costs to workers' productivity. The founders of the EU therefore believed that the division between wage and non-wage costs could be left to the choice of each Member State exactly because this division has only a moderate impact on external competitiveness.

8.4 Migration

Along with the other freedoms of movement (goods, services, capital), the free movement of workers is the cornerstone of EU integration and has been so since its inception in the 1950s. The goal is both economic and political. Allowing workers to move freely within the Union should enhance economic efficiency by allowing workers to find the jobs that best suit their skills and experience, while simultaneously allowing firms to hire the most appropriate workers. On a political level, the architects of the EU hoped that mobility would foster mutual understanding among the peoples of Europe. As many readers will know from first-hand experience, the fact that many young Europeans spend some time living, studying or working in other EU nations has had a big impact on the way Europeans view each other. This section considers European migration. We start with some facts.

8.4.1 Some facts

We start with global migration patterns. Figure 8.11 presents the net migration record – the excess of immigrants over emigrants, so that negative numbers indicate an outflow of workers while positive numbers mean an inflow – of continents since the 1950s, with forecasts for the period 2005–10. The figure confirms that people move from 'the South' to 'the North' and increasingly so. It also shows that Europe has switched from net emigration to net immigration. This is explained by Europe's spectacular growth during the late 1950s and the 1960s, which brought about conditions of full employment and led governments and firms to seek out foreign labour. The turnaround of Europe's economic fortunes, starting with the 1973 recession, temporarily stopped the evolution, but the trend has been resumed. This pattern reflects the two basic reasons why people leave their countries: (1) they flee poverty and (2) they flee political instability and related violence. In general, political instability breeds poverty.

Global numbers should not conceal important differences within Europe. For decades, southern Europe (Italy, Spain, Portugal and Greece) and south-eastern Europe (mainly Turkey) were prime sending nations, while the northern European nations (the EEC6 less Italy plus the Nordic and Alpine countries) were big receiving nations. Since the early 1980s, with growth picking up, the southern European nations have become net importers as well. Some of this migration involves the return of Spanish, Italian and Portuguese workers who had previously emigrated, but it also

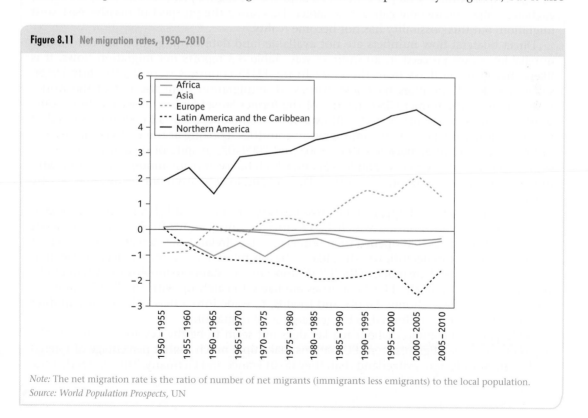

Figure 8.11 Net migration rates, 1950–2010

Note: The net migration rate is the ratio of number of net migrants (immigrants less emigrants) to the local population.
Source: World Population Prospects, UN

reflects an increasing inflow of non-European workers from places such as Africa or Latin America. Within Europe, Turkey has been joined in its role as a provider of migrants by central and eastern European nations that dropped, by the end of the 1980s, general restrictions on emigration imposed by their previous regimes.

Migration within the EU is, in principle, free. Yet, when the EU was expanded in 2004, special provisions were temporarily imposed on the ten new members to limit migration from these countries to the incumbent 15 members. Similar restrictions were imposed on Bulgaria and Romania upon accession in 2007. We return to this issue in Section 8.4.4. Box 8.2 explains why fears of massive immigration from central and eastern Europe have been unjustified. In fact, seven out of ten foreign workers in EU Member States are from non-EU countries. The policies that govern labour flows from non-member nations are entirely national – the EU does not try to impose what might be called a common external migration policy. To put it differently, being part of the EU's common labour market does not seem to matter very much for migration.

Box 8.2   The flood that was not to be

The 2004 and 2007 enlargements brought 12 countries and about 100 million new citizens into the European Union. Table 8.2 shows that most workers in the EU12 countries are paid substantially less in their home nations than they would get if they held similar jobs in the EU15. According to the principles laid out in Section 8.2.1, this difference is primarily due to higher labour productivity in the EU15. The income gap between the east and the west in Europe is approximately 50 per cent when adjusted for higher prices in the west; at current exchange rates, the income gap is even larger. This raised the prospect of massive east–west migration, but this possibility has not become reality.

Direct bilateral flow numbers are not available (and data on migration are notoriously unreliable), so we proceed in an indirect way. Table 8.3 reports net migration flows. It is likely that gross outflows from the EU12 to the EU15 countries were significantly larger, since most EU12 countries have also witnessed immigration from the rest of the world, including from the former CIS countries of the former Soviet Union, as well as from some southern European countries. Net outflows have declined in all EU12 countries, several of which have actually become net immigration countries. Looking at the EU15 countries, net inflows mostly declined between 1997–2003 and 2004–07, in spite of sustained flows from the rest of the world. A good example is Spain, which has seen rising immigration from Latin America. The main exceptions are Austria, Finland and Ireland, each one being a special case of its own.

Why didn't the flood happen? One possible reason is that most EU15 nations negotiated long transition periods during which EU12 citizens cannot move freely into their labour markets. But countries that opened their borders, such as Ireland, Sweden and the UK, report no or little increase in net inflows. Most likely, the low migration numbers reflect the fact that the 'New Europeans' share much of the 'Old Europeans'' resistance to moving (see Chapter 11). With the prospect that the EU12 countries are likely to catch up with the EU15 countries, the incentives to leave home, family and friends, to wade into a new culture with another language, have been too limited to trigger large-scale migration.

Being part of a common labour market does not seem to be the key to determining the origin of migrants. Migrants from EU nations make up a much higher percentage of foreign workers in Norway and Switzerland than they do in France and Germany. This shows that the

⊃

discriminatory liberalization implied by the free mobility of workers within the EU (i.e. workers from one EU nation are free to work in any other EU nation, but they need special permission to work in non-EU nations such as Norway) is not a dominant factor in determining migration patterns. This contrasts sharply with discriminatory liberalization of goods. As Chapter 7 shows, the composition of imports is strongly influenced by implementation of the customs union.

Table 8.3 Net immigration before and after enlargements (thousands of people)

	Belgium	Denmark	Germany	Ireland	Greece	Spain	France	Italy
1997–2003	164	71	1146	193	302	2596	853	1197
2004–2007	202	42	237	245	162	2558	358	1753

	Luxembourg	Netherlands	Austria	Portugal	Finland	Sweden	UK	Total EU15
1997–2003	27	266	164	344	32	143	924	6522
2004–2007	12	−60	179	131	40	157	842	5557

	Bulgaria	Czech Rep.	Estonia	Cyprus	Latvia	Lithuania	Hungary	
1997–2003	−213	32	−14	41	−33	−96	97	
2004–2007	−1	174	1	52	−5	−28	71	

	Malta	Poland	Romania	Slovenia	Slovakia			
1997–2003	17	−497	−592	18	−14			−186
2004–2007	7	−79	−23	29	17			262

Note: A positive number indicates net immigration, a negative number signals net emigration.
Source: Eurostat online database

There is nothing really new here. We already mentioned that, in the 1950s and 1960s, nations across north-western Europe were experiencing such rapid growth that industry found itself short of workers. Individual nations responded by facilitating inward migration from many different nations. Not surprisingly, nations that wanted to 'import' workers found it easiest to induce migration from nations with low wages and relatively high unemployment. The fact that Spain, Portugal and Greece were not at the time members of the EU did little to hinder the flow of their workers into EU members such as Germany. Indeed, German immigration policy in the 1960s was at least as welcoming to Turks and Spaniards as it was to southern Italians. Moreover, nations such as Sweden and the UK, whose industries also experienced labour shortages, managed to attract migrants – including some migrants from EU nations such as Italy – even without being part of the Common Market. In short, the western European policies that fostered the big migration flows in the 1960s were basically unrelated to the policies of the Common Market.

8.4.2 Economics of labour market integration

Labour migration is probably the most contentious aspect of economic integration in Europe. In most western European nations, popular opinion holds immigrants responsible for high unemployment, abuse of social welfare programmes, street crime and deterioration of neighbourhoods. As a result, a number of explicitly anti-immigration political parties have fared well in elections. How does immigration affect the sending and receiving nations, and who gains and loses from it?

Simplest framework

We start with the simplest analytical framework that allows us to organize our thinking about the economic consequences of labour migration. We start with the case where migration is not allowed between two nations (Home and Foreign) which initially have different wages. Figure 8.12 shows a situation where workers initially earn better wages in Home than in Foreign. The length of the horizontal schedule represents total labour available in both countries, L in Home and L^* in Foreign. For the time being, we will assume full employment, $L + L^*$ in total for both countries. The marginal productivity of labour in Home is measured on the left vertical axis. The corresponding MPL curve is downward sloping as employment in Home is measured along the horizontal axis from left to right. The foreign marginal productivity of labour is measured on the right vertical axis. The corresponding MPL^* curve seems upward sloping, but it is not, since employment in Foreign is measured in the opposite of the usual direction, from right to left.

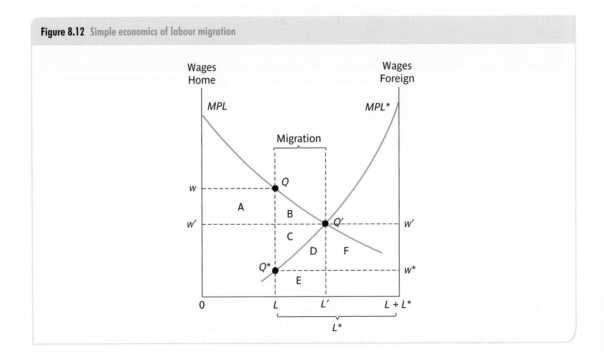

Figure 8.12 Simple economics of labour migration

Initially, the situation in Home is represented by point Q, with wage w and employment L. Point Q^* describes the initial situation in Foreign, with wage w^* and employment L^*.

Now allow migration. Given the wage difference, labour will flow from Foreign to Home. This will push down wages in Home and thus harm the Home workers – while benefiting Home capital owners. The opposite happens in Foreign. As some Foreign labour moves to Home, Foreign wages tend to rise, making the remaining Foreign workers better off – and Foreign capital owners worse off. If there is no impediment – legal, personal reticence or other – migration will go on until wages are equalized. This is represented by point Q', with wages w' in both countries.

We find that, in each country, some lose and some gain from migration, but what about each country? Start with Home country. We need to understand the impact of migration on the earnings of workers and capital-owners. To that effect we look at Fig. 8.13, which enlarges the Home country situation around point Q. The area under the MPL curve represents total Home output. The reason follows directly from the definition of the marginal product of capital. The first unit of labour employed produces output equal to the height of the MPL curve at the point where $L = 1$. The amount produced by the second unit of capital is given by the level of MPL at the point where $L = 2$, and so on. Adding up all the heights of the MPL curve at each point yields the area under the curve.

The total earnings of Home labour is just the wage rate w times the amount of labour L, which is measured in Fig. 8.13 by the rectangle below and to the left of point Q. Since we are assuming that capital and labour are the only two factors of production in this simple world, capital receives all the output that is not paid to labour. Graphically this means that capital's income corresponds to the triangle between the MPL curve and w line.

With this in hand, we turn now to the welfare effects of capital flows. We saw that the 'native' Home workers lose. As they move from Q to Q', their wages decline by $w - w'$. Their loss is represented by the rectangle marked A in Fig. 8.12. Home capital-owners increase their earnings by area A plus the triangle B. Thus the total economic impact on Home citizens is positive and equal to the triangle B. Another way of seeing that Home gains from migration is to note that the immigrant workers raise total output in Home by the areas B + C + D + E, but some of it, equal to areas C + D + E (i.e. w' times the labour flow $L^* - L'$), does not benefit 'native' workers since it is paid out to the immigrants.

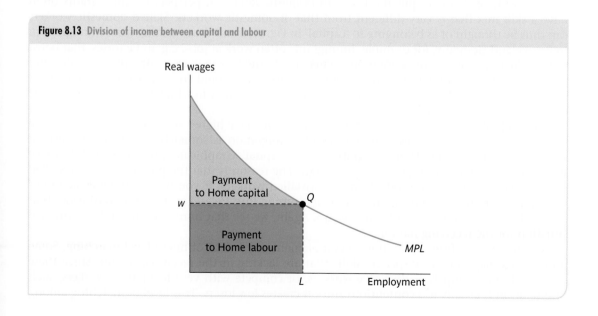

Figure 8.13 Division of income between capital and labour

The Foreign workers who remain in their country see their wages rise from to w^* to w'. The size of this gain is shown by rectangle F. With production falling, Foreign capital-owners lose by D + F. Combining all these losses and gains, the factors of production that remain in Foreign lose overall by an amount measured by triangle D. However, if we count the welfare of the emigrant workers as part of Foreign's welfare, the conclusion is reversed. Foreign workers abroad used to earn E, now they receive C + D + E, so they gain C + D. Altogether, Foreign gains by an amount equal to the triangle C.

In short, while migration creates winners and losers in both nations, collectively both nations gain. The deep reason for this has to do with efficiency. Without labour mobility, the allocation of productive factors was inefficient. For example, on the margin, Foreign workers were less productive. Migration improves the overall efficiency of the EU economy and the gains from this are split between Home and Foreign. Foreign gets area C; Home gets area B. This all assumes that there is no unemployment to start with and therefore seems unrealistic; we return to this issue in Section 8.4.3 below.

Broader interpretation: complementarity vs. substitutability

The analysis above classifies all productive factors into two categories: capital and labour. It is important to note, however, that for most EU nations we should interpret 'capital' as including 'human capital', i.e. highly educated workers. The reason has to do with the economic notion of 'complementarity' versus 'substitutability'.

Consider the example of how productive factors combine to produce hotel services. Apart from material inputs such as food and bed linen, hotels require unskilled workers (cleaners, etc.), skilled workers (managers, marketing people, etc.) and capital (the building, furniture, etc.). In a country such as Norway, unskilled labour is very costly so hotels are very expensive; consequently there are relatively few hotels. If Norway allowed hotels to hire foreign workers at lower wages, some factors would be hurt – the unskilled workers who earned high wages before the immigration – but other factors would be helped. Skilled workers and capital would find that their rewards rise. As the price of hotel rooms fell, the hotel industry would expand, raising the demand for highly skilled workers and capital. In this situation, we say that unskilled workers are complements to skilled workers and capital: demand for skilled workers and capital rises as the supply of unskilled workers increases and their price falls.

The point of this is to put the losses to domestic labour in perspective. Immigrants often have a skill mix that is very different from that of domestic workers. Skilled domestic workers can thus be thought of as belonging to 'capital' in Fig. 8.12 and thus winning from immigration. In France and Germany, for example, immigrants often work at jobs, e.g. in factories, that boost the productivity of native workers in related fields such as management, finance, sales and marketing. Indeed, immigrants often fill jobs that no native would take, such as kitchen workers, street sweepers, etc.; this is an extreme form of complementarity in which there are no economic losers in the receiving nation.

We can look at the opposite case, when immigrants have higher skill levels than the average native worker. In these cases, the analysis of immigration is somewhat different. Instead of shifting L from Foreign to Home, migration shifts 'capital'. Graphically this raises the *MPL* curve in Fig. 8.12 for Home and lowers it for Foreign. The reason is that the presence of more skilled workers tends to raise the productivity of unskilled workers. If you want a mental picture of this process, think of American entrepreneurs coming into Ireland and starting businesses that hire Irish workers away from the farm sector. Again, we see that immigration can be a win–win situation for the receiving nation.

Another insight from the notion of complementarity is that of micro-level matching. Some immigrants may have very specific skills that are lacking in the receiving nation. Since these workers do not compete with native workers, or compete with very few native workers, such immigration is usually less contentious since it creates few losers. This level of matching among countries can proceed to an even lower level. For example, even within a single company, the experiences of workers vary, and free mobility of labour may make it easier to move workers into jobs that best fit their experience. Again, it is entirely possible that everyone gains from such matching. More generally, immigrants who have skills that are complementary to the skill mix in the receiving nation are typically less likely to create losers in the receiving nation.

Empirical evidence

So much for the theory. What does the evidence tell us? Given the importance of immigration in the various national debates in Europe, economists have done a great deal of work estimating the impact of migration on the wages of domestic workers. Generally, these studies find that a 1 per cent rise in the supply of workers via migration changes the wages of native workers by between 1 per cent and −1 per cent, with most studies putting the figure in the even narrower range of ±0.3 per cent. There are two key points to take away from these findings. First, it is not obvious that immigration always lowers wages. Since nations tend to let in workers who have skills that are complementary to those of domestic workers, the impact is often positive. Second, whether it is slightly positive or slightly negative, the impact is quite small. Again, this outcome is due in part to the fact that countries tend to restrict the types of labour inflow that would have large negative effects on wages.

Table 8.4 provides some information regarding the complementarity/substitutability issue. It shows the education levels of workers employed in the EU15 countries, according to where they come from, in percentage of all employed workers. Immigrants from the other EU15 countries are generally better educated and occupy higher-skill jobs than the natives. This suggests micro-level matching and explains why this type of immigration is not controversial. Immigrants from outside the EU are complementary in the opposite direction: they are often less educated and fill in elementary tasks/jobs. Immigrants from the EU10 – the ten countries that acceded in 2004 – are in-between as far as education is concerned and they tend to accept less skilled jobs.

Table 8.4 Education level and skills of recent immigrant workers in the EU15 countries in 2005 (percentage of total)

	Overall EU employed	Immigrant workers from:		
		EU15	EU10	Outside EU
Education				
Low	27	15	15	36
Medium	47	41	63	40
High	26	44	22	23
Occupation				
High-skilled white collar	40	55	16	20
Low-skilled white collar	26	24	28	25
Skilled manuals	25	12	27	21
Elementary tasks	10	9	30	35

Source: Survey of the European Union, OECD, Sept 2007

8.4.3 Unemployment

Framework

One common belief is that immigrants cause unemployment. The framework presented in the previous section cannot help us assess this view since it explicitly assumes that all workers get jobs. Instead, we use the framework presented in Section 8.2.4 and apply it to the employment of native workers. In Fig. 8.14, in the absence of immigration, the labour market is at point A and involuntary unemployment is AB.

Now suppose that some immigrants enter the country. We have to imagine how the immigrants will operate in the labour market. One extreme assumption is that the immigrants are willing and able to perform the same jobs as natives but at a wage that is below the union-set wage w. Being cheaper, they displace the native workers. The demand curve for native workers shifts to the left from D to D'. The idea here is that firms first hire cheap immigrants and then turn to the native market to fulfil any remaining demands. The distance AC measures the share of employment taken over by immigrant workers. The result is that the market moves to point A'. The union-set wage and native employment fall to w' and L', respectively. Two points are worth stressing. First, even in this extreme case – where firms are able to hire immigrants at below market wages – the drop in native employment $(L - L')$ is less than the number of immigrants (AC). As a consequence, total employment, counting both natives and immigrants, rises. This dampening is due to the drop in native wages, which allows firms to produce more output and therefore expand jobs.

Second, there may be no change in unemployment. Because unemployment is a result of the labour market's structure, immigration will affect unemployment only to the extent that it affects the structure of the labour market. In the particular example shown in the diagram, where the two labour supply curves S^{ind} and S^{coll} are drawn as parallel, there is no change in the number of unemployed natives. In that case, the drop in wages from w to w' decreases the number of native workers who want to work at the going wage by as much as the drop in native employment. If we had not drawn the two supply curves as parallel, we would have got a different answer.[5] The

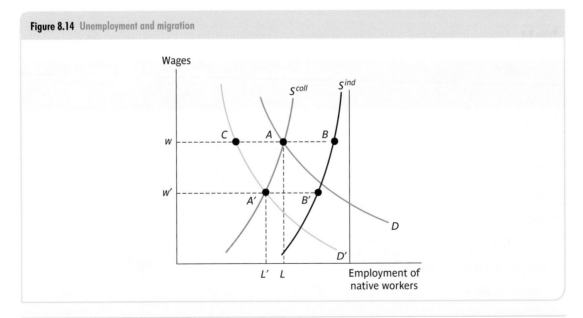

Figure 8.14 Unemployment and migration

---

[5] How are the curves in reality? Truth is that we don't know. The proof of the pudding is in the eating, namely in the empirical evidence discussed below.

main point, however, is that if immigration is to affect unemployment, it must do so by altering labour market structure.

Another possible assumption is the opposite one, that immigrants participate in the labour market in exactly the same way as native workers do. In this case (not shown in the diagram), both curves S_{ind} and S_{coll} shift to the right. The results would be qualitatively identical to those shown in Fig. 8.14. There would be some drop in the wage and some increase in employment. Since the true impact of immigrants on national labour markets is probably somewhere between these two extremes, it seems reasonable to believe that the standard impact of immigration will be some increase in employment, some decrease in wages and an ambiguous effect on unemployment.

Empirical evidence

The empirical evidence on the effect of immigration on unemployment is mixed. A visual inspection of Fig. 8.15 does not suggest any link. Some studies have found that immigrants increase the chance of unemployment for some groups of workers, but have the opposite effect on other groups of workers. This is clearly linked to the complements and substitutes analysis. Other authors find little or no effect of immigration on the risk of being unemployed. In summary, the empirical evidence we have to date does not support the notion that immigration has large, negative effects on European labour markets. As usual, this lack of convincing evidence is due in part to the fact that countries tend to pick and choose their immigrants, presumably with a view to avoiding large negative effects on employment and/or unemployment.

Figure 8.15 Foreign population and unemployment, 2007

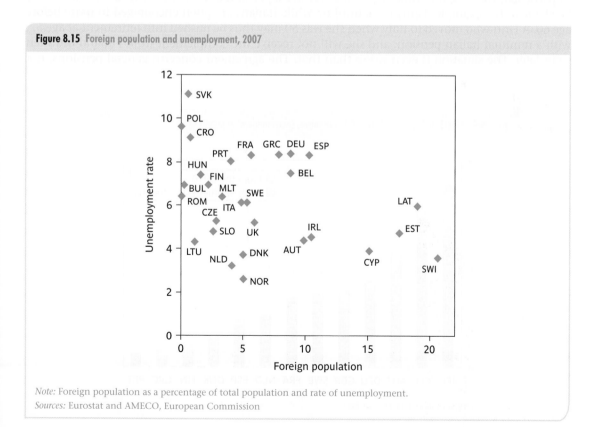

Note: Foreign population as a percentage of total population and rate of unemployment.
Sources: Eurostat and AMECO, European Commission

8.4.4 Barriers to mobility

Two key results emerge: (1) immigration is likely to raise employment and national income; and (2) immigration is unlikely to affect unemployment in either direction. These results provide a strong endorsement for the fundamental principle of freedom of movement of workers within the EU. Figure 8.16 indicates that few people take advantage of this opportunity. One reason is that EU citizens do not regard freedom of establishment as an attractive option. Another is that, in spite of the stated policy, there remain a large number of barriers, some explicit, most implicit.

The first barrier is the explicit temporary arrangement concerning the new EU members, except Cyprus and Malta. Starting in 2004, all countries may apply restrictive measures for up to seven years following accession. Except Ireland, the UK and Sweden, all EU15 countries and Hungary chose to implement this clause. In 2006, obviously reassured that migration was moderate, a number of countries allowed unrestricted entry from the 2004 acceding countries.

Other implicit barriers concern social protection. Health insurance does not raise serious difficulties since any EU worker is allowed to enter the local system upon settlement, paying local dues and receiving equal treatment. In order to simplify the transition process, a European Health Card was introduced in 2004.

The situation is more complicated as far as pension rights are concerned. The principle is simple: workers collect pension rights wherever they go; upon retirement, they apply to their country of residence to establish their pension rights on the basis of work performed anywhere in the EU. However, the rights acquired in each country of previous residence are assessed on the basis of that country's system. This 'detail' means that pension rights act as a strong barrier to mobility. The reason is that rules to accumulate rights differ widely from one country to the next. This concerns, in particular, the length of time required to receive a pension and the age at which pensions can be claimed. For example, Finns work until 67 while Italians are often encouraged to retire before age 60. A Finn who moved to Italy when she was 50 may thus be pushed into retirement at age 57, with a minimal Italian pension, and she will not receive the complement from Finland until ten years later. The situation is even worse than that. The agreement concerns general pensions, not

Figure 8.16 Proportion of EU15 and EU10 workers in EU15 countries (percentage of population)

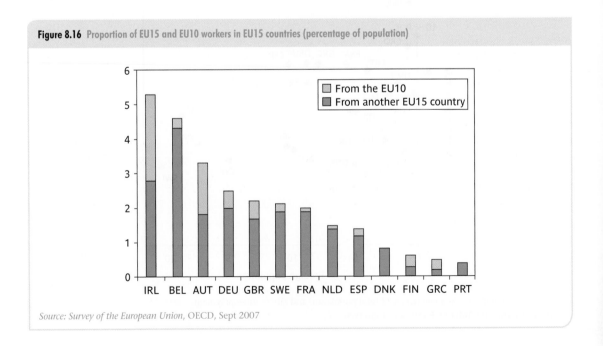

Source: Survey of the European Union, OECD, Sept 2007

those tied to a company or a profession. In several countries, such occupational pensions represent the larger share of retirement income.

Similarly, unemployment benefits discourage mobility. Existing agreements allow an unemployed worker who moves elsewhere within the EU to keep receiving the benefits for up to three months. Imagine the case of a worker who moves from a high to a low unemployment country after having lost his job. If he does not find a job within three months of arrival, he loses his unemployment benefit and is without income. This is a powerful deterrent to migration. The rule might seem strange, but it is designed to discourage 'welfare tourism', the possibility that people move not to seek jobs but to gain access to generous welfare payments.

A last barrier worth mentioning concerns the regulated professions. Obviously, not everyone can set himself up as a medical doctor. In principle, the EU countries recognize each other's qualifications, so doctors, architects, nurses or lawyers can practise anywhere they wish. But the rule does not apply to all regulated professions. For instance, in order to open a hairdressing salon in France, one has to satisfy surprisingly exacting conditions, which rule out all other European hairdressers.

These are examples of the many barriers that limit labour mobility within Europe. Add languages and customs, distance from home, frequent housing shortages, and you start understanding why the freedom of establishment is not delivering. The European Commission is regularly advancing proposals to beat back all regulatory barriers, but many initiatives fail because myriads of local private interests – such as French hairdressers – are opposed to the free entry of competitors.

8.5 Summary

This chapter has dealt with two related topics: the link between trade integration and labour markets and migration, and the view that the EU may be moving to a single integrated labour market. Both issues are politically sensitive but there is surprisingly little substance behind widely held fears that workers systematically get the wrong end of the stick.

Relative to comparable advanced economies, many European countries exhibit low rates of employment and high rates of unemployment. This represents a waste of our most precious resources and a source of anxiety. The situation, though, is very uneven, reflecting the diversity of labour market arrangements inherited from each country's history. Labour market regulations are needed to protect workers but many of them introduce rigidities that prevent the achievement of full employment.

European integration affects the labour markets in two main ways:

* Trade integration indirectly leads to competition between labour markets. It affects the labour markets in two ways. It creates winners and losers and it shifts production patterns, which require labour market flexibility to avoid job losses. In general, countries with more flexible labour markets have a comparative advantage in goods markets. This has led countries with more rigid markets to complain about social dumping, as they resist economic pressure to reform their labour markets. The principle remains that labour markets and social policies are a national prerogative. Theory and evidence support this principle.

* The EU treaty guarantees the freedom of movement of workers. Here again, many citizens fear that competition from foreign workers will lower wages and create more unemployment. The fear is commonplace in the EU15 countries where wages are much higher than in the EU12 countries. Theory and evidence suggest that these fears are largely misplaced. In fact, for a number of cultural and institutional reasons, there is too little mobility of workers in Europe, in spite of the general principle of freedom of movement.

Self-assessment questions

1 Explain what happens to a firm's profits as it moves in Fig. 8.3 from point *A* to point *B*.

2 Using the diagram of Fig. 8.4, explain what happens to voluntary and involuntary unemployment as workers individually ask for higher wages for the same amount of work. Answer the same question using Fig. 8.5, assuming that there is no change in the collective supply of labour.

3 Figure 8.17 depicts the evolution of the unemployment rate in France and in the UK, distinguishing between a trend and deviations from the trend. In the UK, the rate tends to deviate more from its trend than in France. Can you explain this pattern?

Figure 8.17 Unemployment rates in France and the UK (% of labour force)

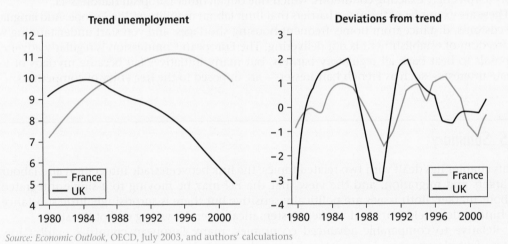

Source: *Economic Outlook*, OECD, July 2003, and authors' calculations

4 Figure 8.8 shows the effect of trade integration in the presence of collective bargaining. What would things look like in the absence of collective bargaining but when wages are downward-rigid?

5 Same question as (4) but looking at the effects of migration in Fig. 8.14.

6 Explain why the immigration of low-skilled workers can hurt native low-skilled workers and benefit high-skilled workers.

7 Capital accumulation and technological innovations raise the marginal productivity of capital. Graphically, in Fig. 8.13 the *MPL* curve shifts up. Starting from point *Q*, consider two cases: (a) wages rise but employment remains unchanged at *L*; (b) employment increases but wages rise. Compare the changes to the income shares of capital and labour and interpret your results.

8 Looking at Fig. 8.2, there seems to be a weak inverse relationship between the unemployment rate and the employment-to-population ratio. Why? And why is this relationship not tighter?

Essay questions

1 'Compared to Americans, Europeans care more about equity than efficiency.' Comment.

2 It is argued – and it is the case in some countries – that the minimum wage should be set at different levels for the young, for the older, for the unskilled or for particular industries. Evaluate this argument.

3 The distinction between voluntary and involuntary unemployment is not as clear-cut as presented in this chapter. Explain why, providing examples.

4 'Hard line' trade unions push for higher wages while 'cooperating' trade unions push for more jobs. What do these differences imply for the working of the labour market and for output? (Hint: Capture the distinction in terms of the shape of the S^{coll} curve.)

5 'Social magnets' are countries that offer generous unemployment and other welfare benefits. This is one key reason why unemployment benefits are not served to migrants for more than three months. Explain why, otherwise, this could be a serious problem in Europe in view of the freedom of movement of workers.

6 'The poorer EU countries should reduce their welfare programmes to better take advantage of accession.' Evaluate this advice.

7 Use the distinction between complementarity and substitutability to evaluate the effects of immigration in your country from neighbouring countries.

Further reading: the aficionado's corner

For general overviews, see:

Bean, C., S. Bentolila, G. Bertola and J. Dolado (1998) *Social Europe: One for All?*, CEPR Monitoring European Integration 8, Centre for Economic Policy Research, London.

Blanchard, O. (2006) 'European unemployment: the evolution of facts and ideas', *Economic Policy*, 45: 5–60.

Boeri, T., M. Burda and F. Kramarz (2008) *Working Hours and Job Sharing in the EU and USA*, Oxford University Press, Oxford.

Freeman, R.B. (2004) 'The European labour markets: are European labour markets as awful as all that?', *CESifo Forum*, 5(1): 34–9.

Nickell, S. (2002) *Unemployment in Europe: Reasons and Remedies*. Download from www.cesifo.de.

Portugal, P. and J.T. Addison (2004) 'The European labour markets: disincentive effects of unemployment benefits on the paths out of unemployment', *CESifo Forum*, 5(1): 24–30.

The articles collected in: **Bertola, G., T. Boeri and G. Nicoletti (eds)** (2001) *Welfare and Employment in a United Europe*, MIT Press, Cambridge, MA.

On the trade-off between economic efficiency and social concerns, see:

Atkinson, A. (1999) *The Economic Consequences on Rolling Back the Welfare State*, MIT Press, Cambridge, MA.

On trade unions, see:

Calmfors, L., A. Booth, M. Burda, D. Checchi, R. Naylor and J. Visser (2001) 'What do unions do in Europe? Prospects and challenges for union presence and union influence', in T. Boeri, A. Brugiavini and L. Calmfors (eds) *The Role of Unions in the Twenty-first Century*, Oxford University Press, Oxford.

Checci, D. and C. Lucifora (2002) 'Unions and labour market institutions in Europe', *Economic Policy*, 35: 361–408.

On migration, see:

Boeri, T. and H. Brücker (2005) 'Why are Europeans so tough on migrants?', *Economic Policy*, 44: 629–704.

Diez Guardia, N. and K. Pichelmann (2006) *Labour Migration Patterns in Europe: Recent Trends, Future Challenges*, Economic Papers No. 256, European Commission. Download from http://ec.europa.eu/economy_finance/publications/publication644_en.pdf.

European Commission, *Job Mobility Action Plan*. Download from http://ec.europa.eu/social/main.jsp?catId=540&langId=en.

Hatton, T. (2007) 'Should we have a WTO for international migration?', *Economic Policy*, 50: 339–84.

Nickell, S. (2007) *Immigration: Trends and Macroeconomic Implications*, Nuffield College, Oxford. Download from www.nuffield.ox.ac.uk/users/nickell/papers/Immigration-Trends&MacroeconomicImplicationsDec07.pdf.

OECD (2007) *Survey of Europe*, September.

To find a job in the EU:

The European Commission's job mobility portal EURES: www.europa.eu.int/eures/home.jsp?lang=en.

Useful websites

The website of the Rodolfo de Benedetti Foundation, dedicated to European labour market issues: www.frdb.org.

References

Bertola, G. (2000) 'Labour markets in the European Union', *Ifo-Studies*, 46(1): 99–122.

Part III

EU Micro Policies

Chapter 9

The Common Agricultural Policy

There is a common misconception that the CAP is about helping small struggling farmers and looking after the European rural environment. But in reality the bulk of these funds end up in the pockets of the wealthiest farmers and processors while also doing enormous harm to developing countries.

Luis Morago, Head of Oxfam International in Brussels

In Europe the CAP has been so successful in achieving food security that consumers have come to take it for granted. But the EU has now dismantled almost every instrument that created this stability.

Pekka Pesonen, Secretary General of COPA-COGECA (EU farm lobby)

Chapter Contents

Introduction

The Common Agricultural Policy (CAP) is a set of policies aimed at raising farm incomes in the EU. The CAP is problematic. It accounts for almost half the EU budget but farmers continue to leave the land. It accounts for many of the quarrels among EU members and between the EU and third nations, yet it is extremely difficult to reform. Given all these problems and its dominant role in the budget, a good understanding of the CAP is essential to the study of European integration. This chapter presents the essential elements and economics of the CAP.

Today's CAP is a massively complex matrix of policies, but it was not always that way. The CAP started life in 1962 as a straightforward policy of keeping agricultural prices high and stable. This simple policy had unintended consequences that created huge problems and triggered a reform process that has been going on since the early 1980s. The need and general direction of this reform has been obvious from the beginning, but because farming is so politically sensitive in so many members, reform has been piecemeal and very, very slow. That is why the CAP is so complex. What we see today is not a well-designed policy aimed at achieving well-thought-out objectives. It is a snapshot of an ongoing adjustment process.

The radical transformation of European agriculture goes a long way to explaining why this process is so politically painful and slow. Figure 9.1 shows a three-horse ploughing team in St Justin, near Montreuil. Such a world required a great deal more farm workers than today's world of tractors and high-tech production methods. This technological progress – combined with the fact that Europeans do not really eat much more food than they used to – means that numbers in the farm sector have been falling steadily for decades.

Figure 9.1 French farming in the 1950s

Source: Fox Photos/Getty

Table 9.1 Importance of agriculture, 1955 vs. 2009

	Agriculture's share of GDP (%)		Agriculture's share of employment (%)	
	1955	2009	1955	2009
Belgium	7.9	0.6	9.3	1.5
Luxembourg	9.3	0.2	19.4	1.4
Netherlands	11.4	1.3	13.2	2.8
Germany	8.0	0.5	18.5	1.7
France	11.4	1.2	26.9	2.9
Italy	20.7	1.5	40.0	3.7
EEC6	11.5		21.2	
UK	4.8	0.5	4.6	1.1
Denmark	18.4	0.7	24.9	2.5

Source: European Commission (2011) and Zobbe (2001)

Table 9.1 shows how important agriculture was in western Europe in the mid-1950s and how unimportant it is now in terms of employment and GDP. In 1955, agriculture accounted for double-digit shares of employment in all the original Six members. In France the share was more than a quarter and in Italy it was a shocking 40 per cent. The shares in GDP were much lower, reflecting the low level of productivity in the sector. In the twenty-first century, agriculture has shrunk to a minor share of employment in all west European nations. The special situation in Britain is also shown in the table. Owing to its long history of free trade, the British agricultural sector had already completed a great deal of its downsizing by the 1950s. Comparing the numbers for 1955 and 2009 for Britain versus the other nations, it is clear that the downsizing of farming has been a much bigger headache on the Continent. This goes a long way to explaining why Britain has always had a problem with the EU's agricultural policy, which was basically designed for nations in very different situations.

To a large extent the CAP has been a programme aimed at buffering the worst pain of this inevitable downsizing. As the agricultural sector changes, so too must the CAP.

The CAP is a policy that is in the politically painful process of moving from one simple economic logic to another simple economic logic. This suggests that the best way to understand the CAP is to study the CAP's original simple economic logic before discussing the unintended problems that are driving EU leaders to reform the CAP towards its new simple economic logic.

Once we have these analytic organizing frameworks in place, we consider the details of the CAP's policy instruments and commodity regimes.

9.1 The old simple logic: price supports

The simple economic logic of the early CAP was to establish a price floor. This was enforced by a tariff, and when necessary, direct purchases. The EU set price floors for many major farm products, including grains, dairy products, beef, veal and sugar. For most of the CAP's existence, these prices were between 50 and 100 per cent higher than world prices, and even higher than this for dairy products and sugar.

These price floors were enforced by guaranteed, unlimited purchase by CAP authorities at the price floor, but such purchases were only the last resort. In the early days of the CAP, the EU was a net importer of most farm products, so it could ensure that supply and demand matched at high prices by manipulating the amount of foreign food that entered the EU market. The manipulation was done with import tariffs, so the best way to understand the early CAP is with a standard open-economy supply and demand diagram of the type we considered in Chapter 4.

9.1.1 Basic price-floor diagram for a net importer

The economics of the tariffs used to raise EU food prices above the price floor are quite similar to the standard tariff analysis presented in Chapter 4. For convenience, we briefly repeat the analysis here – pointing out the minor differences as we go (the presentation in Chapter 4 provides much more detail and explanation).

The goal of these CAP tariffs – called 'variable levies' in CAP jargon since they changed daily according to world market conditions – was to ensure that imports never pushed EU prices below the price floor.

The left-hand panel of Fig. 9.2 helps us to analyse the impact of such a price floor in cases where it is set above the world price (P_w) but below the level where the EU would import no food (in agricultural economics, this level is called the point of 'self-sufficiency', so we mark the level as p_{ss} in the diagram). As we saw in Chapter 4, the domestic price ends up as the world price plus the tariff. No one in the EU would pay more than $P_w + T$, and the inability of domestic producers

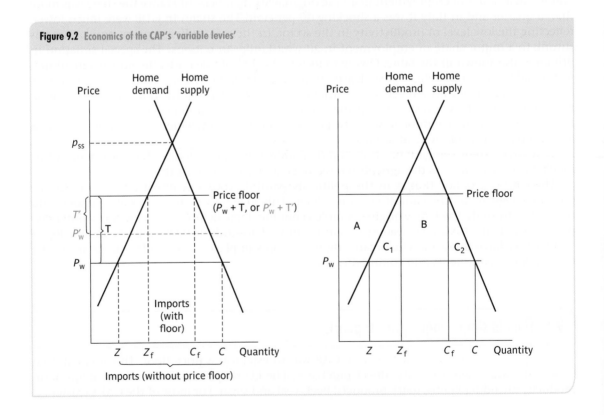

Figure 9.2 Economics of the CAP's 'variable levies'

to make enough food to satisfy the demand at $P_w + T$ means that EU farmers would never have to accept a price lower than $P_w + T$, so the EU price becomes $P_w + T$. At this price, all domestic production (equal to Z_f) is sold at the price floor. Domestic consumption is C_f and the difference between consumption and production equals the level of imports. The subscript 'f' indicates 'floor'.

What is the economic impact of having a price floor above the world price?

- The higher price induces EU farmers to produce more (Z_f instead of Z).
- The higher price is to discourage food consumption (C_f instead of C).
- The EU consumption reduction and production increase move the EU towards self-sufficiency in food.
- Since the price floor is enforced by a variable tariff, the EU receives tariff revenue equal to the area B in the right-hand panel.

The food tax and subsidy interpretation

To get at the economic fundamentals of the CAP's impact and to help understand the politics of CAP reform, it is useful to recast the economics of the tariff. As it turns out, any tariff can be thought of as an all-in-one package consisting of (i) free trade in the presence of (ii) a consumption tax equal to T and (iii) a production subsidy equal to T. This way of thinking about the tariff is less direct, but the extra work is compensated by a good deal of insight.

Consider the impact of the free trade with tax and production subsidy. The consumption tax means that consumers pay the world price plus the consumption tax T (this is exactly equal to the price floor in the left-hand panel of the diagram). EU producers sell at the world price but they also receive the production subsidy T (i.e. they sell all output at the world price but they also get a payment from the government equal to T for each unit of output they sell); thus the price they actually receive is $P_w + T$, which is just equal to the price floor. So far, so good. The tax-and-subsidy means that consumers and producers see the same price as with the tariff and so consume and produce exactly the same amounts (C_f and Z_f); as imports are just the difference between EU consumption and production, the level of imports is also exactly the same with the tax-and-subsidies package. What about the revenue implications?

The revenue from the consumption tax is the level of consumption C_f times the tax T; the cost of the production subsidy payment to farmers is production Z_f times T. What this means is that the government's receipt net of its payments is equal to $(C_f - Z_f) \times T$. This is exactly equal to revenue collected under the CAP tariff (area B).

This way of looking at the price floor is insightful since it makes it quite plain that consumers are the ones who pay for a price floor enforced with a variable levy. Part of what they pay goes to domestic farmers (area A), part of it goes to the EU budget (area B) and part is wasted (areas C_1 and C_2). This interpretation is important when we think about the distributional impact of price floors in more detail.

Aggregate welfare effects

The overall welfare effects of the tariff are familiar from Chapter 4. The right-hand panel of Fig. 9.2 recaps the analysis. The higher price ($P_w + T$ instead of P_w) means that consumer surplus falls by $A + C_1 + B + C_2$. The first part of this, $A + C_1 + B$, reflects the higher cost that consumers pay for the food they continue to consume. The second part, C_2, is what they lose from the tariff-induced drop in consumption. For producers, the gain in producer surplus is equal to area A. We can think of this impact on producers as consisting of the impact of getting a higher price for the amount they would have produced without the tariff plus the gain in producer surplus from the higher sales.

The diagram leaves out one effect that is important in the real world. Since the EU would be a large importer of food under free trade, the tariffs tend to lower the world price. This effect, not shown in the diagram for the sake of simplicity, counts as a welfare improvement for the EU. (The *MD–MS* diagram in Chapter 4 can be used to show the impact of a tariff on the world price.)

The variable levy (i.e. tariff)

Price instability is a key feature of food markets, so we also need to consider what happens when the world price changes to, say, P'_w. In this case, maintaining its price floor requires the EU to apply a lower tariff. Specifically, the tariff must be lowered to T' so that the new world price (P'_w) plus the new tariff (T') equals the old price floor. The levels of EU production, consumption and imports are held constant. The only thing that varies in this simple example is the tariff.

9.1.2 Farm size, efficiency and distribution of farmer benefits

The overall welfare analysis that lumps all EU farms together is useful for some things, but it hides a very important effect of price floors – the distribution of benefits among farms. This fact is at the heart of one of the problems that continues to plague today's CAP, so it is worth studying its basic economic logic in a simple setting.

Anyone who has done much travelling in Europe realizes that a 'farm' means very different things in different places. A wheat farm in the Paris Basin and a farm on a small Greek island, for example, are very dissimilar. On the Parisian plain, farms tend to be very large and very, very high tech. They use expensive, high-yield, disease-resistant seeds to boost their 'yield' (food produced per hectare), they apply large quantities of pesticides to control bugs, large quantities of chemical fertilizers to maintain the soil's fertility, and they use massive, labour-saving machines to plant, tend and harvest. In the Greek islands, farms are smaller and less efficient. As we shall see, these differences have important implications for the distribution of gains from price floors.

The basic facts are shown in Fig. 9.3. The chart shows five classes of farm size, from small (less than 5 hectares) to very large (more than 50 hectares). The top bars show the distribution of the EU27's farmland among the size groups. The fact that jumps out is that most of the land, 62.6 per cent, is in the form of large farms. However, the bottom bars show that most farms,

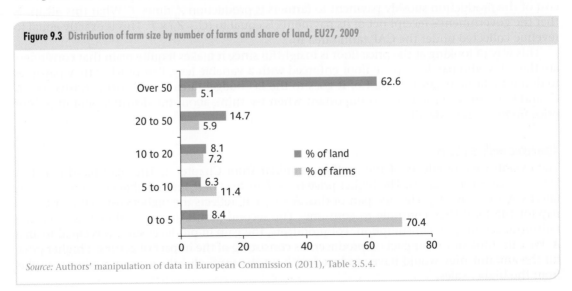

Figure 9.3 Distribution of farm size by number of farms and share of land, EU27, 2009

Source: Authors' manipulation of data in European Commission (2011), Table 3.5.4.

70.4 per cent, are of the small type. In other words, almost two-thirds of the farmland are held by about 5 per cent of the 'farmers'. Here we must put farmer in quotes since many of these land holdings are owned by absentee landowners.

The logic is best illustrated with the help of Fig. 9.4. To keep things simple, suppose there are only two farms in the EU, one large and one small. The small-farm supply curve is shown in the left-hand panel, that of the large farm in the middle panel, and the total supply curve in the right-hand panel. Note that the small farm's supply curve is above the large farm's supply curve, reflecting the large farm's greater efficiency. (Remember from Chapter 4 that the supply curve shows marginal cost, so a higher supply curve means that the small farm has higher marginal cost at any level of output.)

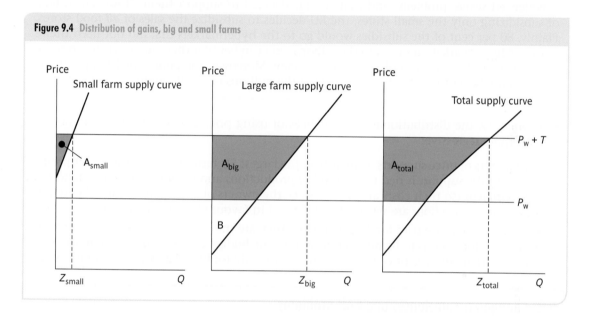

Figure 9.4 Distribution of gains, big and small farms

The world price is marked as P_w. Note that at this price only the large farm would produce anything. The small farm would stop farming with free trade since the price would be below its marginal cost of producing even a small amount. With the price floor at $P_w + T$, however, both farms produce. Specifically, the small farm produces Z_{small} and the large farm produces Z_{big}. Total output is just the sum of the two.

From Fig. 9.4 we see that the producer surplus generated by the price floor is quite unevenly distributed. The small, low-technology, high-cost family farm earns only A_{small}, while the large, modern industrial farm earns A_{big}. This should be intuitively obvious. Since a price floor helps producers in proportion to their production, big producers will benefit more from the policy.

How is this connected with income levels? The benefit from owning a farm is the producer surplus it yields, so the income generated by the small farm is A_{small} and the income for owners of the large farm is $A_{big} + B$, since B measures the producer surplus that the large farm would have without the price floor. Plainly, the owners of big farms tend to be richer than the owners of small farms. This is the main point. Price floors help all farmers but most of the gains go to large farmers who tend to be richer; after all, they own larger farms.

This uneven-distribution point is critical – the key to many of the CAP's paradoxes – so it is worth presenting it from another angle. Few readers will be familiar with modern farming, but everyone has been to a food store. Box 9.1 presents an analogy by considering what would happen if CAP-like policies were used to support the owners of European food stores.

> ### Box 9.1   An analogy with hypothetical support for food stores
>
> In most European nations, there are many, many food stores, but food sales are dominated by huge supermarket chains. Simplifying to make the point, we can think of there being two types of store: small, family-run stores and hypermarkets. The small stores are much more numerous, but since many people do their main food shopping at hypermarkets, the total sales of the many small stores is only a fraction of the hypermarkets' sales. To be concrete, suppose that the hypermarkets account for only 20 per cent of the total number of stores, but account for 80 per cent of the sales. Now suppose that small, family-owned stores experienced severe problems and that the EU decided to support them. However, instead of subsidizing only the small stores, the EU decides to subsidize the sales of *all* food stores. Plainly, 80 per cent of the subsidies would go to the hypermarkets that did not need them. Once the hypermarkets got used to the billions, you can bet that they would engage in some pretty fierce politicking to hold on to the money. Moreover, the public might support the policy in the belief that the funds are helping the millions of small, family-owned stores.

In summary, the distributional consequences of using price floors to support the EU farm sector are quite regressive:

■ The benefits of price supports go mainly to the largest EU farms because large farms produce a lot (and the support is tied to the level of production) and because large farms tend to be more efficient (so their costs are lower). Since the owners of large farms tend to be rich, the benefits of a price floor are systematically biased in favour of large, rich farmers.

■ Since price floors are paid for by consumers (they are the ones that have to pay the higher price), and food tends to be more important in the budget of poor families than it is in the budget of rich families, price floors are in essence paid for by a regressive consumption tax.

9.2 Changed circumstances and CAP problems

In its first few years of life, the CAP was a politician's dream. The price floors provided higher and stable prices to farmers, so they were happy. They also substantially raised food production and this, at the time, was viewed as a good thing, reducing EU dependence on imported food. Higher farm incomes suited the EU's goal of fostering 'social cohesion' between rural and urban Europe. The variable tariffs even generated revenue for the EU budget. The only ones who might have objected were European consumers, since they paid for the policy via higher prices. As it turned out, consumers were also happy about the CAP:

■ Average incomes in the 1950s and 1960s rose rapidly – much faster than food prices – so the share of people's income spent on food actually fell, although not as fast as it would have done without the CAP.

■ During the Second World War and its aftermath, food was in short supply and rationed in most European nations. The memory of this – and the hunger that came with it – was still fresh in people's minds in the early 1960s. More food and lower dependence on food imports seemed like good ideas to most Europeans.

■ Consumers had a great deal of empathy with farmers. As is still the case today, most Europeans viewed agriculture as a form of economic activity unlike others.

The CAP's 'honeymoon', however, was soon to end.

9.2.1 The 'green' revolution

The post-war period saw revolutionary advances in the application of science to agriculture. Crops and farm animals were selectively bred to boost yields. A whole agrochemical industry sprang up, producing pesticides to control insects, herbicides to control weeds and chemical fertilizers to boost soil fertility. Huge planting and harvesting machines were developed to save labour. Strange as it may seem today, this chemical-, energy- and machine-intensive technology was known as the 'green revolution'.

Since the CAP rewarded output, EU farmers – especially those with large farms – switched to these new, more intensive farming methods. The result was impressive. EU farm production rose rapidly – so much so that the EU swung from a net importer to a net exporter in most farm products.

In most sectors, this sort of rapid productivity growth would be a cause for celebration. In European agriculture, it was called the 'supply problem'. Other European sectors that have experienced rapid technological progress – e.g. telecoms – saw rapid price falls as the efficiency gains were passed on to consumers. The political power of the EU farm lobby, however, was strong enough to prevent this. EU food prices continued to be fixed far above the world price.

Cascade of unintended consequences

This combination of high, fixed prices and rapid technological progress created a whole cascade of unintended consequences. To understand these, we study the impact of a price floor in the presence of a positive supply shock. Figure 9.5 shows the situation. Technological improvements shifted the supply curve down (recall that the supply curve is marginal cost, so cost-lowering technology shifts the whole curve downwards; see Chapter 4).

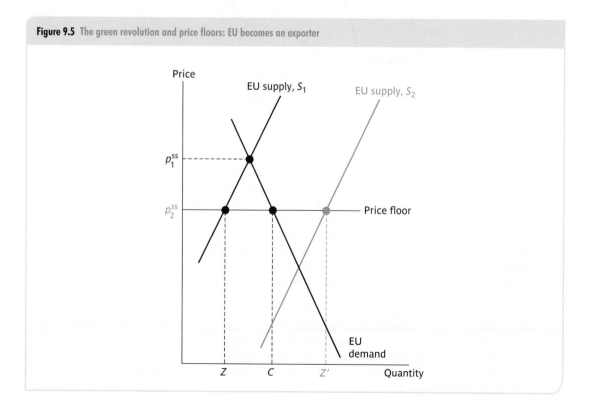

Figure 9.5 The green revolution and price floors: EU becomes an exporter

Before the supply shift, the EU was a food importer and the price floor worked as in Fig. 9.2. After the shift, the EU supply curve is S_2 with the price floor in place, so the EU has surplus food production; production level Z' exceeds the consumption level, C. Since the EU is no longer a food importer, the price floor cannot be maintained with a tariff. The EU actually has to purchase the surplus food (i.e. Z' minus C). In fact, this is exactly what the CAP was doing in the late 1970s and 1980s. This supply problem set off a cascade of problems.

The budget problem

The immediate difficulty was budgetary. Instead of earning money by imposing tariffs, the EU had to dole out large sums from its budget to buy the 'excess' food. The CAP came into operation in 1962 and did not incur a positive expenditure until 1965. After this, however, its cost and share of the budget started to grow exponentially, rising from 8 per cent in 1965 to 80 per cent in 1969 (Fig. 9.6). Fights over how to pay for these hindered EU cooperation through the 1970s and early 1980s.

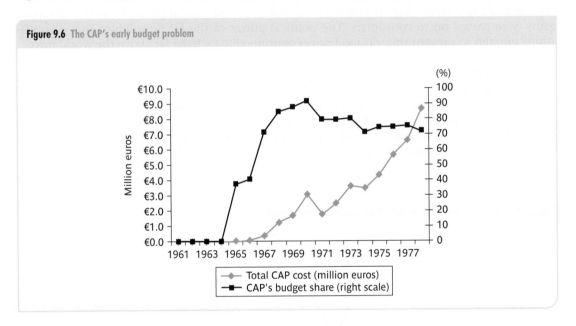

Figure 9.6 The CAP's early budget problem

The disposal problem: wheat, beef and butter mountains

Apart from the cost of buying all this food, the EU faced the problem of what to do with it. When the food 'surpluses' first appeared, the EU viewed them as temporary. The main solution was to store the food, hoping that market prices would rise above the price floor. This was not to be. High and stable prices teamed with steady technological progress made investment in agriculture very attractive. The supply curve continued to shift out, so the EU had to continue buying food. The EU found itself the owner of what the media called 'wheat, beef and butter mountains'. In 1985, the EU had 18.5 million tonnes of cereals stored, about 70 kilos for each of its citizens. Much of this rotted, causing a major public relations problem (it looks bad to pay high prices for food and then allow it to rot).

To reduce the budget and disposal problems, the EU sold the food at subsidized prices. Some was sold to non-standard consumers within the EU. For example, a sixth of the wheat crop in 1969 was rendered unfit for human consumption and sold as animal feed at a subsidized price. The major destinations for the subsidized sales were foreign markets. This practice of buying high domestically and selling cheap abroad is called 'dumping', although the EU jargon for it is 'export restitution' or 'export subsidies'.

Dumping and international objections

Disposing of EU 'surplus' food abroad created the next problem – a foreign trade problem. Under WTO rules for manufactured goods, dumping is normally not permitted, especially when the practice is driven by government export subsidies. However, before the 1994 Uruguay Round agreement, the WTO placed no restrictions on the dumping of agricultural goods.

The EU's food dumping drove down world food prices. As we saw in Chapters 4 and 5, a drop in the world price is a gain for net importers but a loss for net exporters. While the world's net food importers did not complain, EU dumping infuriated the world's large food exporters: Argentina, Australia, Bolivia, Brazil, Chile, Colombia, Costa Rica, Guatemala, New Zealand, Paraguay, the Philippines, South Africa, Thailand, Uruguay, Canada and – most importantly – the USA. (See Box 9.2 for details.)

Box 9.2 Economics of the CAP's impact on world food markets

Even in the early days, the CAP's price floor policy harmed other nations. By shutting off EU markets to the exports of non-members, the CAP reduced the world price of food as well as reduced the volume of non-members' exports. As the EU's food surplus grew, and the EU started to subsidize its exports, non-members were further harmed.

The economics of this can be seen in Fig. 9.7. The solid lines marked *MD (no CAP)* and *MS (no dumping)* show the world import demand (i.e. *MD*) and import supply (i.e. *MS*) without the CAP's tariffs and without the CAP's dumping. The price would be $pw0$. In the first stage, the tariff imposed by the EU, one of the largest importers of food in the world, shifted the world import demand inwards to *MD (CAP)*. This resulted in lower export prices for non-EU members (to P'_w). When the EU started subsidizing exports, the world *MS* curve shifted to *MS (with dumping)*.

Many countries impose some form of import protection on food, so while the CAP's tariffs were harmful to the world market, they were not viewed as particularly out of line with the rest of the world's practice. The subsidized export of food, however, was more unusual. Additionally, the USA and the EU were, at the time, the only major subsidizers and often engaged in subsidy wars.

Figure 9.7 Impact of CAP protection and dumping on world markets

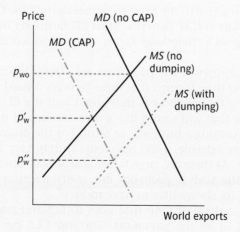

The farm income problem

Despite its massive budgetary cost and high implicit tax on European food consumers, the CAP failed to bring the reward to farming in line with the incomes of average EU citizens. In 1990, the average income from farming per worker in agriculture averaged less than 40 per cent of the income per worker in the EU12 economy as a whole (European Commission, 1994). While most farm family income was augmented by some non-farm earnings, farming was not a very attractive activity.

Farmers showed their discontent with the CAP by 'voting with their feet', i.e. quitting the sector. The number of farms and farmers has declined steadily since the CAP's inception (Fig. 9.8). This is the truest indication that the average EU farmer found that, even with CAP support, farm incomes were not keeping up with those in the rest of the economy.

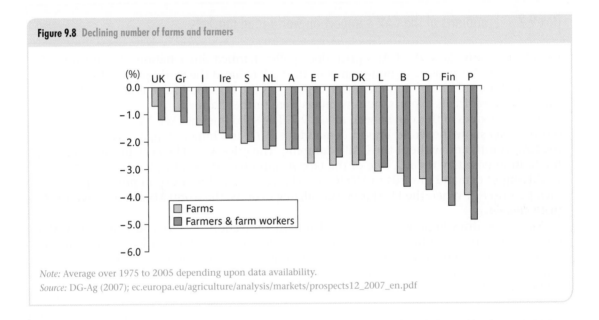

Figure 9.8 Declining number of farms and farmers

Note: Average over 1975 to 2005 depending upon data availability.

Source: DG-Ag (2007); ec.europa.eu/agriculture/analysis/markets/prospects12_2007_en.pdf

The CAP paradox

How could farming be unattractive to the average farmer despite the CAP's billions? The solution lies in the uneven distribution of CAP benefits. Most EU farms get little from the CAP since the lion's share of the support goes to help large farms, most of which are owned by rich people or corporations.

Table 9.2 shows just how uneven the payments are. The categories of payment size are on the left; they range from less than 0 euros (i.e. these farmers owned the CAP money!) to over a half million euros. What the figures show is that about half the EU farmers (48.1 per cent) get less than 3900 euros. While that will sound like a nice amount of money to most readers, it is peanuts when it comes to running a business, or farm. For the disfavoured half, the CAP is not really helping. On the other extreme, 1300 recipients (surely very large, rich landowners) get almost a million euros each. As these are large farms and almost surely run as modern industrial agricultural corporations, the CAP is probably not really necessary – although as Benjamin Franklin said, 'rich or poor, its always nice to have money'.

The table also shows the share of CAP that goes to big and small recipients. The bottom half split just 2.1 per cent of all the payments. The top 17.6 per cent of the recipients get 85.3 per cent of the money.

Table 9.2 Extremely uneven distribution of CAP payments, EU27, 2008

Size of payment	1000s recipients	Average payment (euros)	Cumulative share of recipients	Cumulative share of payments
< 0 EUR	6.3	–	0.1%	0.0%
> 0 and < 500 EUR	3,910.2	205	48.1%	2.1%
> 500 and < 1,250 EUR	1,383.0	800	65.2%	5.1%
> 1,250 and < 2,000 EUR	544.2	1,585	71.9%	7.4%
> 2,000 and < 5,000 EUR	855.9	3,215	82.4%	14.7%
> 5,000 and < 10,000 EUR	541.2	7,109	89.1%	24.9%
> 10,000 and < 20,000 EUR	419.4	14,221	94.2%	40.8%
> 20,000 and < 50,000 EUR	345.7	30,676	98.5%	69.0%
> 50,000 and < 100,000 EUR	88.6	67,066	99.6%	84.7%
> 100,000 and < 200,000 EUR	21.0	132,311	99.8%	92.1%
> 200,000 and < 300,000 EUR	3.7	241,864	99.9%	94.5%
> 300,000 and < 500,000 EUR	2.1	377,176	99.9%	96.7%
> 500,000 EUR	1.3	965,044	99.9%	100.0%

Source: @ European Union, 1995–2012

To put it starkly, more than half the CAP payments go to big, rich farms, while for the vast majority of EU farmers, the CAP payments are just enough to keep them on the edge of bankruptcy. For example, Queen Elizabeth of the United Kingdom receives over a million euros a year in CAP support (more on this below).

This situation has not changed since 2006, but the Commission has stopped releasing detailed information like this.

Industrialization of farming: pollution and animal welfare

The 'industrialization of farming' had a negative environmental impact. As the public's environmental concerns reawakened in the 1980s and 1990s, these harmful effects of the CAP eroded public support for the CAP.

According to a 2002 report to the British agricultural ministry (JNCC, 2002), the CAP harmed the environment in many ways:

- Encouraged by the CAP, many farmers have sought to raise yields through increased use of fertilizers and pesticides and higher stocking densities. The associated changes in the way land is managed have led to a decline in the area of semi-natural habitats, populations of associated wildlife species and the diversity of landscape features. The amount of available land has been increased through the removal of hedges, walls, farm ponds, etc. These changes have allowed easier access for larger machinery, which in turn has reduced farm labour requirements and led to damaging effects on soil structure and functionality.

- The CAP has encouraged specialization of particular crops (e.g. cereals, oilseeds and peas, beans) and livestock enterprises (e.g. dairy). Such changes have encouraged monocultures with the loss of mixed farming enterprises, and have had impacts on land use, landscape character and biodiversity in these areas.

- Deteriorating water quality due to the application of chemical fertilizers is a problem. Chemical fertilizers, which are necessary to restore the soil's fertility when it is intensively farmed, are a main culprit in the nitrate and phosphate pollution of EU water supplies. Nitrates and phosphates tend to soak through the soil into the groundwater or get into streams and rivers via runoff from fertilized farmland. High levels of these chemicals tend to 'kill' lakes by over-stimulating water plants, which in turn reduces aquatic biodiversity. In extreme cases, nitrogen can be a threat to human health. In some areas where pork and beef production are particularly intensive (Holland, for example), animal manure is even more of a problem than agrochemicals. Pesticides also pose a threat; high levels of pesticides reduce the biodiversity of ecosystems.

Animal welfare and 'factory farming'

Just as science improved the yields of crops, science has also been applied to boost the efficiency with which animal products – meat, eggs, milk, etc. – are produced. Efficiency in this sense typically means producing the most meat at the least cost. Doing so has involved studying the most efficient density of animals, the use of antibiotics to control disease and promote growth, the scientific design of animal feed and the breeding of higher-yielding, disease-resistant animals. While raising farm productivity, these practices have moved modern farming a very long way from the pastoral scenes still in the minds of many Europeans. As the non-governmental organization Compassion in World Farming puts it:

> CAP has encouraged the industrialization of agriculture, giving rise to factory farming practices and widespread animal suffering. Through the CAP, animals have been taken off the land and put into overcrowded buildings, straw-based housing has been replaced with bare concrete or slatted floors and live animals have been transported over much greater distances. The CAP also pays very generous subsidies to dealers who export live cattle from Europe to the Middle East. The long journeys often inflict tremendous suffering on the animals and end in slaughter in far away abattoirs where all too often the conditions can only be described as appalling.

(www.ciwf.co.uk)

Some aspects of industrial farming became known to the wider public as the result of two animal diseases:

1 BSE –'mad cow' disease, which was spread by the practice of processing the carcasses of dead cows (some of which had the disease) into feed that was then given to healthy cows; and

2 'foot and mouth' disease in which large numbers of animals were destroyed to mitigate the economic consequences; the disease does not kill the animals but renders them uneconomical; the alternative to 'culling' (killing massive numbers of animals) was vaccination, but this would have made the export of healthy animals very difficult.

Some Europeans reacted strongly against this 'factory farming' as inhumane treatment of animals. While there are some extremists, the concern has become quite mainstream. For instance, a million EU citizens signed a 1991 petition to the European Parliament calling for animals to be given a new status in the Treaty of Rome as sentient beings. The petition worked. The Maastricht Treaty now includes a 'Declaration on the Protection of Animals' and the Lisbon Treaty goes further.

Concern for developing nations

The last problem facing the CAP was the growing realization that the dumping of food on the world market was harming the prospects of developing nations. The dumping of sugar and protection of cotton were particularly harmful to some of the world's poorest nations. As EU citizens started to realize this, attitudes started to change.

See Box 9.3 for a discussion of the EU sugar policy's impact on Mozambique.

Box 9.3   EU sugar policy and Mozambique

The CAP's sugar policy is one of the oldest and most complex EU policies. EU sugar prices are maintained at about three times the world price, but not for all production. At the high price, many EU farmers would find it profitable to switch to growing sugar beet. EU leaders recognized this impending 'supply problem' from the beginning, so the amount of sugar for which farmers receive the high price is capped. Since the EU produces more sugar than it consumes at the high prices, the EU has to subsidize the export of the excess, but again, not for all production. The EU sets a quota for the maximum amount of exports it will subsidize; anything beyond this must be sold at world prices. One strange thing about EU sugar policy is that it actually taxes EU farmers in order to raise the money for the export subsidies. High EU tariffs shut off almost all imports, but again with an exception. The EU allows entry for some imported sugar from its former colonies, the so-called ACP nations (ACP stands for African, Caribbean and Pacific), but the EU must re-export this, with subsidies, since it already produces more sugar than it consumes. Note that more than half the EU's sugar is grown in Germany and France.

All this manipulation has made the EU the world's largest exporter of white sugar (it accounts for about two-fifths of world white-sugar exports). EU subsidies depress the world price and its tariffs deny other nations the opportunity to sell in the EU market. Taken together, the CAP's sugar policy has a powerfully negative impact on poor countries, especially on poor nation farmers – a group that tends to be the poorest people in poor countries.

By way of illustration, the non-governmental organization Oxfam has highlighted the impact of EU sugar policies on Mozambique (Oxfam, 2002, www.oxfam.org.uk). This points out that per-capita income in Mozambique is under €250 per year and two-thirds of the population live below the poverty line. The 80 per cent of the population that live in rural areas rely mainly on agriculture for their living, with sugar production being the single largest source of jobs in the country. Oxfam estimates that Mozambique is one of the lowest-cost producers of sugar in the world, with a production cost under €300 per tonne. Removal of EU sugar tariffs would help Mozambique directly, but even a cessation of export subsidies would be welcome. For example, the EU exports almost a million tonnes of sugar to Algeria and Nigeria, nations that would otherwise be natural markets for Mozambique's sugar.

Since 2006, the system has been getting less distortionary, with support prices coming down about 40 per cent. The reform increased EU imports to the benefit of developing country sugar exporters. However, the developing nation exporters that get limited preferential access to the EU market are harmed by this (the ACP nations, see Chapter 12 for details). These exporters face the same price reduction.

9.3 The new economic logic of the CAP

The solution to these problems is obvious now, and has been since the supply problem first appeared in the 1970s. The heart of the problem is the overproduction and over-intensification of agriculture, which in turn is caused by the EU price floor being above the world price. Eliminating the price floor would eliminate the problem. This, however, was not politically feasible.

Although there are few EU farmers – less than 5 per cent of the population even back in the 1970s (around 4 per cent now in the EU15; 6 per cent for the EU27 overall) – their political power was, and still is, enormous. Large commercial farmers have become used to the extra millions that the high prices brought them.[1] Just think about the numbers involved. The EU 2007–13 budget package, which was agreed by EU leaders in a stormy December 2005 summit, spends €330 billion on payments to farmers and on keeping farm prices high. There are only 12.6 million people working in the farm sector. If the money were divided evenly, that would be about €26 000 per person – certainly something worth fighting for. The money, however, is not distributed evenly. Most of the money goes to farm owners, with most of it going to the largest farm owners. For example, in 2006, the EU25 paid €33.1 billion to 7.3 million farmland owners, with about 70 per cent of the money going to just 10 per cent of these (the ones with the largest landholdings). For these large landowners, the CAP is a gold mine. Just as real gold-mine owners hire armed guards to protect their investment, large farmland owners are willing to spend millions on politicking that guards their virtual gold mine – the CAP.[2]

Moreover, farmers had invested heavily in restructuring their farms to focus on the goods most heavily supported by the CAP. Small farmers earned much less from the CAP but, without the higher prices, many would be driven out of farming altogether. In a nutshell, the CAP meant loads of cash for the happy few (large farms) but it was a matter of survival for the 80 per cent of EU farmers with small operations. In addition to the cold-hearted political logic of cash, part of the farmers' disproportionate power stems from the warm-hearted feeling that the average European has towards the sector; opinion polls show that most EU citizens approve of CAP spending in general.

The farm sector's political strength meant that it was impossible to just eliminate the price floor. EU leaders had to 'bribe' the farmers into allowing them to undertake CAP reform that was good for the EU as a whole. This was done by linking the lowering or elimination of price floors to compensation payments paid directly to farmland owners. The direct payment amounts per farm were more or less linked to the amount of money each farm got under the old price-support system. To break the link between the payments and overproduction, the payments were 'decoupled', i.e. the size of the payment was not related to the amount currently produced – it was set according to historical production levels. (Note to non-native English readers: decouple is the verb one uses when a railroad car is disconnected from the train engine.)

9.3.1 Price floor liberalization and decoupled payments: the economics

This is the new simple economic logic that the CAP is heading for – market-determined prices with direct payments to farmers that are not related to production levels. Before turning to the actual reform, we study the basic economics driving the direction of the reform, namely the economics of switching from a price-support system to market-determined prices with direct payments to compensate farmers for the price reduction.

Figure 9.9 considers a product, such as wheat, where the EU is a net exporter even without the CAP price floor. To keep things simple, we assume that in the pre-reform situation all the surplus food was dumped on the world market. The cost of this is the difference between the price floor (the price paid by the EU when it buys excess food) and the world price (the price

---

[1] It is important to note that the EU's special treatment of farmers was not unusual. In the early 1990s, the EU's generosity was only in the middle of the OECD pack. OECD (2004) reports that the subsidy equivalent per EU farmer was $13, 000, less than half the amount for EFTA members (Sweden, Switzerland, Norway, Finland and Austria) and about equal with that of the USA and Japan.

[2] See http://ec.europa.eu/agriculture/fin/directaid/2006/annex1_en.pdf for details.

the EU gets when it sells on the world market) times the surplus, namely the area b + c + d.[3] Observe that the EU still needs high tariffs to make the price floor work. Although no imports come into the EU with the tariff shown, they would if the tariff were removed. Every farmer in the world would like to sell at the EU's price floor instead of the world price; to reserve the higher price only for EU producers, the world price plus the EU tariff must exceed the price floor.

The decoupling reform lowers the price faced by EU farmers and consumers from the price floor to the world price. EU production falls from Z to Z' and consumption rises.

EU consumers gain from the lower prices by the area a + b (this is the consumer surplus gain; see Chapter 4 if you are unfamiliar with this concept). EU farmers lose the producer surplus equal to area a + b + c, and the EU budget saves b + c + d. Overall, the reform is welfare improving since the net gain is area d + b, i.e. (a + b) plus (b + c + d) minus (a + b + c).

If the farmers are to be fully compensated, the direct payments must equal a + b + c. Since this may well be larger than the cost of dumping the surplus, this policy reform is unlikely to reduce the cost of the CAP.

Notice that this reform solves most of the CAP's problems: the disposal problem, the dumping problem and the over-intensification of farming problem. The surplus disappears, so there is no disposal problem and thus no need to dump food on world markets. Overproduction is no longer being stimulated by the CAP, so, although the industrialization of EU farming may persist, it cannot be blamed on EU farm policy. Moreover, the EU's actual decoupling policy has linked the payments to greater respect for the environment and animal welfare, so the switch improves the environmental impact of EU farming.

The only problems not fixed by decouple-with-compensation reform are the budget problems and the farm income problem.

Having laid out the basic economics of this new system, we turn to a brief discussion of the decades of reform that have moved the CAP gradually from the pure price-support system of Fig. 9.2 to the decouple-with-compensation system of Fig. 9.9.

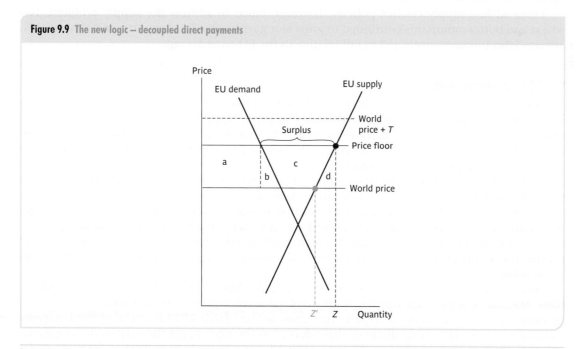

Figure 9.9 The new logic – decoupled direct payments

---

[3] In practice, it is not the EU that does this; the EU pays private companies – mostly multinational agro-commodity firms – to buy high in the EU and sell low on the world market. For example, the sugar multinational Tate & Lyle receives hundreds of millions of euros a year to dump EU sugar abroad.

9.4 CAP reform

Up to the mid-1980s, the primary way of dealing with higher CAP costs was to increase the contribution from the members. This changed when Spain and Portugal joined in 1986 and the politics in the Council of Ministers shifted importantly.

The CAP did little to help Spanish and Portuguese farmers since their climates prevented them from producing the goods that the CAP supported the most, i.e. dairy, sugar, wheat, rice and beef. The newcomers, who were reluctant to see their national contributions to the budget rise year after year in order to subsidize the production of rich northern European farmers, teamed up with the two incumbent poor nations (Ireland and Greece) to shift EU spending priorities towards 'structural spending' in poor nations (see Chapter 3 for further details). One option would have been to expand the EU budget to pay for the extra structural spending, but the EU net contributors (especially Germany, Denmark and the UK) opposed this.

9.4.1 Ad hoc supply control attempts

This situation posed a reform dilemma; lowering farm prices faced a political roadblock, but buying all the excess food was too expensive. The EU's first reaction was to try to work around the problem, dealing with the surplus situation without fundamentally changing the price-floor system. As European Commission (1994) puts it, the 1983 to 1991 period was 'years of experimentation' with supply controls.

The CAP during this period became fantastically complex. Fortunately, most of these experiments have been dropped, so most students of European integration have no need to study their details. What is important is the outcome of these new policies. The CAP's share of the budget began to fall to meet the new political imperative of spending more of the EU budget on poor members and regions.

These ad hoc supply control policies, however, failed to address the supply problem. The wheat and butter mountains continued to grow along with subsidized exports, and, despite this, average farm incomes continued to fall relative to the EU-wide average.

9.4.2 The MacSharry reforms

The first really big reform was driven by pressure from the EU's trade partners who were fed up with seeing the market for their exports ruined by export subsidies (the USA also subsidized its exports). The issue came into sharp relief when the global trade talks, known as the Uruguay Round, failed in December 1991 when the EU refused to commit to phasing out its export subsidies and open its agriculture markets.

Since these global trade talks were viewed as vital to European exporters of goods, services and intellectual property, Europe's highest-powered exporters started to push for CAP reform. The political power of poor regions who wanted to use the money and European exporters who wanted the Uruguay Round to succeed was sufficient to get a major reform accepted by the Council of Ministers. The resulting reform package (the MacSharry reforms) put the CAP on the road to the economic logic of Fig. 9.9. All subsequent reforms to date have followed its main outlines.

There have been three major CAP reforms since the MacSharry package, which pushed the basic MacSharry logic even further. Both involved further price cuts that were compensated by direct payments to landowners. The first came at the March 1999 meeting of the European Council in Berlin. The prime driver of this reform was the need to get the CAP ready for eastern enlargement and to prepare the CAP for a falling budget share in the 2000 to 2006 Financial Perspective. The second came in 2003.

The 2003 CAP reform

The driving force was the current WTO trade talks (the so-called Doha Development Agenda). Developing countries were reluctant to start new WTO talks and were only convinced when the EU members and other rich nations promised in November 2001 to liberalize agricultural markets as part of the Doha Round. With the crucial mid-term meeting of ministers scheduled for September 2003 in Cancun, Mexico, the EU had to come up with a reform of the CAP that would allow it to fulfil its liberalization pledge. The Cancun meeting ended in failure. Although there is plenty of blame to go round, many observers believe that the meagre liberalization contained in the CAP reform was at least one major reason for the failure. The 2003 reform has been followed up by a series of sector-specific reforms in recent years.

Health Check 2008

This agreement pushed the market orientation of the CAP even further and took a big step towards liberalizing one of the most resistant sectors – dairy. The reform abolished arable set-aside (i.e. paying farmers to not grow food). It is also relaxing the restrictiveness of milk quotas gradually, with the goal of eliminating them in 2015. Moreover, the unfairness of the direct payments was mitigated under the name of 'modulation'. This means that some direct payments to farmers are reduced and the money transferred to the Rural Development Fund. Lastly, the direct payments are no longer linked to the production of a specific product.

9.5 Today's CAP

Today's CAP has two pillars. The first concerns direct payments and the cost of the remaining price supports. The second is called 'Rural Development'. We address the first pillar first.

9.5.1 CAP's first pillar

With the 2003 reform of the CAP – a reform process that is being phased in slowly (delayed up to 2014 in some sectors) – the CAP continues to approach the simple economic logic of Fig. 9.9. The backbone of the system is the 'Single Payment Scheme', or SPS as it is known in EU literature (sometimes SFP for Single Farm Payment). To explain how it works, consider an example provided by this extract from the 22 September 2003 article by Peter Hetherington in *The Guardian* (a leading British newspaper):

> *The harvest has been good for Oliver Walston and many other farmers. . . . With 2000 acres (800 hectares) of prime arable land at Thriplow, near Cambridge, Mr Walston runs a medium-sized undertaking . . . Mr Walston volunteers that he gets around £165,000 annually in subsidies . . .*

Since the 2003 reforms were phased in from 2005 to 2007, Farmer Walston is talking about the old system set up by the MacSharry reforms.

Under the old system, Farmer Walston's payment was linked to his historical production of particular products, say wheat. To get the £165,000 (about €230,000), he had to continue growing wheat. In this sense, payments were only partially decoupled; payment was linked to growing wheat, but the size of this year's payment was not related to the amount of wheat grown this year.

Under the new system, the Single Payments Scheme, he would get the £165,000 regardless of what he grows – he need not continue to grow wheat to get the cash. This completes the decoupling of CAP payments and production. There are exceptions, as always with the CAP, many of which sound a bit fanciful to non-specialists. (For example, farmers receiving the new Single Farm Payment can produce any commodity on their land except fruit and vegetables and table potatoes.)

The size of the single payment is based on historical payments in the old EU15. There are two methods of determining the historical payment: either it is the average amount the particular farm received in the period 2000 to 2002 (historical model) or it is based on the number of hectares farmed during the first year of the scheme and the average payment for the region (regional model). Member States choose which to apply. Since the new Member States (central and eastern European nations) entered the CAP only upon accession in 2004, they hand out money per hectare, with the amount limited by national ceilings that were agreed in their Accession Treaties.

Cross-compliance

To get the single payment, farmers are supposed to comply with the EU and national rules governing the CAP's environmental impact, European food safety and animal welfare. Importantly, these requirements were already in place. The idea is that tying the cash to compliance makes it more likely that farmers will obey the existing laws.

The rules to comply with are complex and vary somewhat from nation to nation. There are two basic categories:

1 'Good agricultural and environmental conditions'. For the UK, the first category includes things such as: soil protection, post-harvest land management, waterlogged soil, crop residue burning, overgrazing and unsuitable supplementary feeding, heather and grass burning, stone walls, protection of hedgerows and watercourses, etc.

2 'Statutory management requirements'. These include rules on: wild birds, groundwater, sewage sludge, nitrate-vulnerable zones, pig identification and registration, restrictions on the use of plant protection products, restrictions on the use of substances having 'hormonal or thyrostatic action and beta-agonist' in farm animals, control of foot-and-mouth disease, certain animal diseases and bluetongue, welfare of calves, etc.

Exceptions

The political resistance to the 2003 reform was vicious (see Box 9.4). Some Member States insisted on maintaining the link between the payment and the crop produced for some crops. Moreover, the most powerful lobby, sugar, escaped reform altogether. Political pressure also dampened reform in many sectors, such as wine, durum wheat, protein crops, rice, nuts, energy crops, starch potatoes, milk and milk products, seeds, cotton, tobacco, fruit and vegetables, and olive groves. Since 2003, most of these sectors have had to adopt reforms leading to decoupling. For example, the EU lost a WTO case against its sugar policy and was forced to reform that sector or face retaliation. That led to a reform in 2006, which goes some way towards reducing the CAP-induced waste and a long way to reducing the EU's need to dump sugar on the world market. Reform of the fruit and vegetables sector came in 2007, and for the wine sector in 2008.

9.5.2 CAP's second pillar: rural development

One interesting aspect of the 2003 reform is that it shifts money from direct payments to rural development, which is now called the 'second pillar' of the CAP (the first pillar being price and

Box 9.4   Name-calling and national positions

Since the CAP pays millions of euros to Europe's large, rich farmers and these farmers are extremely well organized politically, any change in the CAP is politically difficult. In particular, former French President Jacques Chirac has always counted on the political support of French farmers. He could not help but view CAP reform as a threat to his personal political base.

When the reform was first broached at an October 2002 European Council meeting in Brussels, UK Prime Minister Tony Blair and French President Jacques Chirac got into a heated conversation over the Frenchman's attempt to sideline the reforms. The headline in the British newspaper *The Daily Telegraph* was: 'Chirac and Blair trade insults over farm reform' (29 October 2002). The article, by Toby Helm and Philip Delves, states: 'The argument flared in front of other EU leaders in the middle of the Brussels meeting after Mr Blair accused M Chirac of trying to renege on a commitment to reform farm policy in 2004. M Chirac . . . reportedly told Mr Blair: "You have been very rude and I have never been spoken to like this before." ' The problem was that 'Mr Blair discovered on arrival at the Brussels meeting that M Chirac and Gerhard Schröder, the German chancellor, had already struck a deal to keep CAP spending at around its present levels until 2013. The Prime Minister was furious not only because he was excluded by Europe's two biggest power brokers, but by what they had decided behind his back. Mr Blair had called for a root and branch reform of CAP and viewed the deal as a ploy by the French to dodge a 1999 commitment by EU leaders for a revamp in 2004.'

At the June 2003 European Council meeting in Athens, Chirac again tried to prevent the reforms. *The Daily Telegraph* covered this under the headline, 'Chirac snubbed in farm dispute'. The story states:

> "*M Chirac astounded fellow leaders by threatening to veto reform of the Common Agricultural Policy unless France got its way. Losing his patience as two weeks of marathon talks by farm ministers in Luxembourg began to turn against France, he switched tack on Thursday night and insisted for the first time that the matter should be dealt with directly by European Union prime ministers. But Costa Simitis, the Greek prime minister and summit host, rejected the proposal, saying it should be left to farm ministers properly briefed on the subject. M Chirac's veto threat could cause a major crisis. France does not have a legally binding veto on farm policy since decisions are taken by majority voting. In theory, Paris could invoke 'vital national interests' as a last resort, but this safeguard, known as the Luxembourg Compromise, has fallen into disuse and is not recognised by the European Court. . . . The proposals, which have the loose backing of the northern 'scrap-the-CAP club' of Germany, Britain, Holland, Sweden and Denmark, are intended to cut the link between subsidies and production.*
>
> *Funds would be switched gradually to eco-friendly 'green' agriculture and help for village communities, reducing the excess production that has flooded Third World economies with dumped EU goods. Commission officials said M Chirac, a former farm minister, believed he could outmanoeuvre his colleagues on farm aid, provided he could pin them down at yesterday's summit, without the presence of their key advisers.*"

(21 June 2003, article by Ambrose Evans-Pritchard)

income support). The rural development schemes supported by this money are wide ranging. The 2003 reforms listed several programmes that seem very forward looking and helpful to rural society (as opposed to merely giving money to the biggest, richest farmers!). These include:

- New quality incentives for farmers. The idea is to improve the quality of agricultural products and the production processes and inform consumers of these changes.
- New support to help farmers to meet standards. The idea is to ease the pain farmers face in adjusting to regulations on the environment, public, animal and plant health, animal welfare and occupational safety.
- A new 'Farm Advisory System'. The idea is to help modernize the farm sector and make it easier for farmers to adjust to reforms by providing technical advice.
- Covering animal welfare costs. The idea is to help farmers committed to improving the welfare of farm animals beyond the regulator levels.

In 2005, the second pillar was expanded and strengthened, with the Council of Ministers adopting a rural development policy for 2007–13. The new regulation focuses on three axes:

1 improving agricultural competitiveness;
2 managing the land in an environmentally friendly, sustainable manner; and
3 improving the quality of life in rural areas.

The third axis seems to be the way of the future as EU agriculture moves closer to market principles. One particularly interesting programme is called LEADER. It is supposed to help rural actors consider the long-term potential of their local region and act accordingly. It supports integrated territorial development strategies, supports cooperation between rural territories and fosters networking.

Modulation

The rural-development pillar is paid for in part by a small reduction in single payments (up to 5 per cent). The smallest farms are not affected as the first €5000 are not subject to this 'modulation'.

Funding allocation

The second pillar is mainly under the control of Member States and they have a good deal of leeway in how much and how they spend on the second pillar. As Fig. 9.10 shows, the new Member States plan to spend a larger fraction on rural development than the EU27's average of about 20 per cent.

9.6 Remaining problems

Today's CAP shares some of the problems discussed above. For example, not all of the payments are fully decoupled, so the production distortions persist in some sectors. Moreover, with or without the CAP, the most productive farming is industrial farming and this almost inevitably involves chemical and energy usage that harms the environment.

9.6.1 Social inequality and CAP payments

The complete decoupling of the single payments is good economics, as we saw in Fig. 9.9, but it poses what might be called a public relations problem for the CAP as a whole. Full decoupling turns the single payment into a subsidy to farmland ownership. Since many of the EU's landowners are not the ones who farm it, the CAP is increasingly looking like an excuse for paying very large sums of money to rich landowners. Paying millions of euros to wealthy landowners is not what most Europeans think of as a good idea. For a long time, the allocation of the payments was

Figure 9.10 Planned spending on first and second pillars, 2007–13, by member

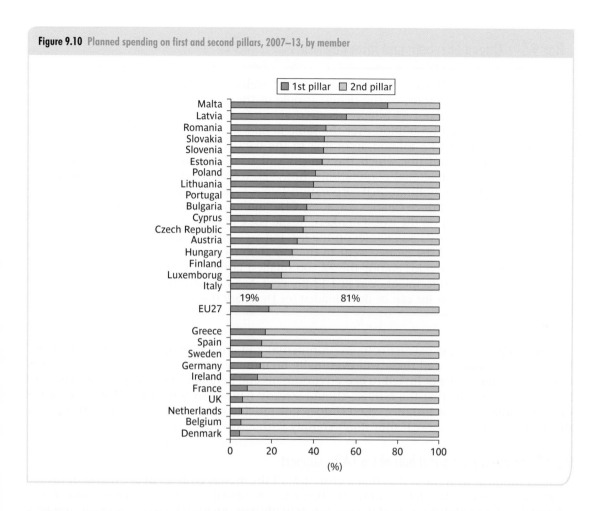

kept secret, but journalists using new 'freedom of information' laws forced some governments to reveal who was getting the cash. This includes Queen Elizabeth II and other royalty (Box 9.5).

The Commission is quite set against this iniquitous allocation of CAP money and has tried many times to trim payments to the largest landowners. As part of its campaign, it has begun to publish annual data on the size distribution of payments in each Member State. Moreover, as part of the EU's new transparency goals, the Commission adopted a rule in March 2008 that requires the full name, municipality and postal code of every recipient. The first full list came in April 2009. A good deal of information is already available on the Commission's web page on the CAP (ec.europa.eu/agriculture/funding/index_en.htm).

This sort of transparency puts a political bomb under the massive payments to rich landowners. Local media is likely to highlight the anomalies. For example, we have already seen that some of the ministers in charge of reforming the CAP are in fact receiving CAP payments (Box 9.6). Increasingly, CAP spending will be seen as welfare for the rich and support for first-pillar payments is likely to erode.

This makes it easier to understand why governments have opposed the release of detailed information on who is getting the taxpayers' money. As more EU nations reveal the names of CAP recipients, the pressure to reform the welfare-for-rich-landowners aspects of the CAP is likely to grow. One proposal put forth several times by the European Commission (and rejected by the Council) would put an upper bound on the payment per farm.

> ## Box 9.5   Queen Elizabeth and farm payments
>
> The list of English CAP recipients (the Scottish and Welsh governments refuse to release the information) includes some of the richest people in the realm. The Duke of Westminster, whose net worth is about €7 billion, received about €1 million over two years, the Duke of Marlborough got €1.5 million over the same period, and the Queen and Prince Charles received more than €1.5 million according to the data. The royal family is also a major landowner in Scotland (for which the data is still secret), so this is probably a serious underestimate. Multinational corporations, however, received even more. At the head of the subsidy list is the multinational corporation Tate & Lyle. It received more than ten times what the Queen and Prince Charles got, some €180 million (most of this went to paying for the dumping of sugar on the world market). Nestlé got €30 million.
>
> Overall, there were 24,525 names on the list, but an eighth of the payments went to the top 20 names; half of the money went to the top 2000 recipients. Or, to put it differently, half the money was divided among the 22,500 smallest farms. The share of payments going to the bottom 10,000 recipients was just 13 per cent. See *The Guardian* newspaper's website for a full list. A similar list can be downloaded for Denmark from www.dicar.dk.

The linking of these payments to environmental and animal welfare concerns is popular, but the details matter and these will eventually be more widely publicized. The key point is that the payments are not linked to *new* environment and animal welfare regulations, they are linked to regulations that the farmers should already have been following. This is not done in other industries. For instance, the EU does not provide millions to the auto industry and threaten to take them away if they don't comply with environmental regulations.

9.6.2 Farmers only get about half of the CAP's support

Another problem with the CAP is that a great deal of the money ends up in the hands of people other than farmers. An OECD study in 2003 that examined the actual beneficiaries of the reformed CAP found that much of the support actually ends up in the pockets of input suppliers such as non-farming landowners and agrochemical firms.

When it comes to direct payments based on hectares, one euro of payment ends up having a minimal impact on the earning of farm household labour. Since the payments are tied to the land, it is the land price that soaks up most of the subsidy. This is not a problem for farmers who owned their land before the area payments were instituted, but about 40 per cent of EU farmland is not owned by the people who farm it.

The OECD calculates that about 45 cents of every euro of direct payment benefits non-farming landowners instead of farmers. The other major CAP policy – market price support – does even worse. Farmers get only 48 cents in the euro, with 38 cents going to real resource costs and input supplies.

9.6.3 Future reform

The Commission is in the process of reviewing the CAP once again. The reason is that the five-year budget plan (the Financial Perspective 2009–13) is about to come to an end. Since the CAP represents such a large chunk of the budget, it is impossible for the EU to plan for other areas until it decides what to do with agriculture. This provides an enormous opportunity for reform, but it also creates an enormous opportunity for special-interest groups to get (or keep) their hands on CAP monies.

Box 9.6   Government ministers receiving CAP payments

In the Dutch and Danish cases, some scandal has been caused by the fact that the politicians charged with overseeing the CAP are actually getting some of the money personally. For example, four of the 18 Danish ministers or their spouses, including the Farm Minister, received CAP money. The biggest scandal to date, however, involved the Dutch Farm Minister Cees Veerman. He receives about €190,000 annually in CAP subsidies for the farms he owns.

The scandal was revealed when British Premier Tony Blair suggested a reform of the CAP in the summer of 2005. The Dutch Prime Minister Jan Peter Balkenende at first supported Blair, but Veerman threatened to resign in protest if Balkenende backed Blair. According to an *International Herald Tribune* article (19 August 2005), a spokesman for the Dutch Ministry of Agriculture claimed that there was no connection between Veerman's cash receipts and his opposition to CAP reform. One can question this, since Veerman referred to his farms as 'my pension' according to a report in *The Guardian* newspaper.

The Commission's proposal was released just days before this chapter went to press, so the full implications are still unclear. Moreover, as the Parliament now has a great deal more to say about CAP spending – and the Parliament is less interested in farming matters than most Member States – it is possible that the final post-2013 CAP will look very different from the Commission's proposal. Be that as it may, here are the basic elements of the Commission plan:

- An almost complete shift away from price support (market intervention). As Fig. 9.11 shows, the Commission proposes to keep the total spending on CAP approximately unchanged, but the amount spent on distorting prices will be greatly reduced. Note that the gradual expansion of the second pillar – a trend that has been en route since the 1990s – is halted. The emphasis of the new CAP will be on giving money to farmers.

- A fairer distribution of direct payments. The disparity between the high levels of support for the rich, large landowners and the poor small farmers is to be addressed in three ways. First, the basic income support (directly payments) will cover only active farmers. Second, it will be reduced from €150,000 per holding (i.e. per farm) and capped at €300,000. It will also be distributed more equitably between members, with the eastern and central European famers seeing a big increase in their receipts in order to reduce the current discrepancies between new and old members.

- A 'Green' payment for preserving long-term productivity and ecosystems. To bolster environmental sustainability, the proposal allots 30 per cent of direct payments specifically to those that engage in improving the use of natural resources – measures such as crop diversification, maintenance of permanent pasture, the preservation of environmental reservoirs and landscapes.

- A simpler CAP. Administrative burdens will be reduced by a set of reforms, especially concerning small farms for which a flat rate of €500 to €1000 per farm per year will be created.

There are already many objections to the proposal as it fails to seize the opportunity for substantially downsizing the share of the EU budget that goes to this small sector. While political realities demanded that farmers be compensated for price cuts in the 1990s, much of this argument has faded. It seems odd to 'compensate' farmers for ever for the removal of a massive subsidy when every other sector of the economy is undergoing austerity on an historic scale. Moreover, as the farmers in the eastern and central European nations never experienced the high prices, it is hard to see why they should be compensated.

Figure 9.11 Proposed shift of CAP money towards direct payments

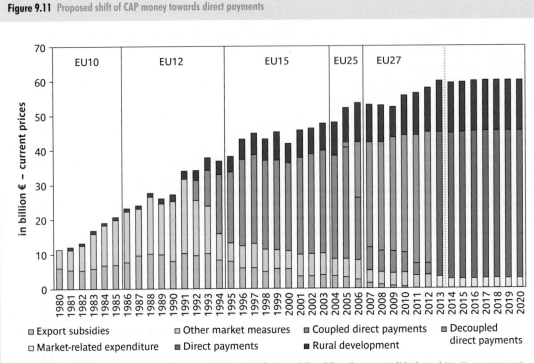

Source: 'The CAP towards 2020, Legal proposals', DG Agriculture and Rural Development, slideshow, http://ec.europa.eu/agriculture/cap-post-2013/legal-proposals/slide-show_en.pdf

At first glance, the Commission's reform looks like a coterie of technocrats and special-interest groups getting together to divide up a pie that they have come to view as theirs by right. One hopes that the Parliament will see through this and decide that this small sector of the EU economy can get by with a greatly reduced share of the EU budget. There are, after all, important things to be done to boost EU competitiveness in the big-employment sectors like services and industry.

One direction could be to nationalize the CAP. For example, most of the CAP spending could be done by turning over the CAP payments to Member States. In this way, the French taxpayers would be free to continue handing millions to large landowners and multinationals without asking poor Poles to pay for it. In the terminology of Chapter 3, the CAP is a classic situation where local information and a lack of scale economies make national decision making the superior choice. This is especially true as the reversion to market-based pricing has removed most of the negative spillovers that used to plague European agriculture.

9.7 Summary

The CAP started in the 1960s as a way of guaranteeing EU farmers high and stable prices. Because agricultural technology advanced rapidly, and because the high prices encouraged farm investment, EU food production rose rapidly, much faster than EU food demand. As a consequence, the EU switched from being an importer of food to being an exporter of food. This change meant that supporting prices required much more than keeping cheaper foreign food out with high tariffs. The EU began to purchase massive amounts of food – an operation that became very expensive, consuming over 80 per cent of the EU's budget in the 1970s. Since the EU had no use for the food it bought, it disposed of the surplus by storing it or dumping it on the world market. The former was expensive and wasteful; the latter had serious international repercussions since it tended to ruin world markets for farmers outside the EU.

A combination of budget constraints and pressure from EU trade partners forced a major reform of the CAP in the 1990s, the so-called MacSharry reform. This reform lowered the guaranteed prices, and thus reduced the amount of food the EU had to buy, but it compensated farmers for the price-cut by providing them with direct payments. This type of price-cut-and-compensate reform was carried further by the so-called Agenda 2000 reforms and the June 2003 reforms.

The economic impact of the CAP is quite unusual at first glance. Despite high prices and massive subsidies, the EU farming population continues to decline because CAP support is distributed in an extraordinarily unequal way. The largest farms, which are typically owned by rich citizens or corporations, receive most of the money, while the small farms get very little. In short, CAP payments to most EU farms are too small to prevent many farmers from quitting. Yet, despite the small size of most payments, the total cost of the CAP is huge because payments to big farms are big. The MacSharry and Agenda 2000 reforms did little to change this because the direct payments are related to farm size.

The CAP was seriously reformed in 2003, with a trail of related reforms in 2005 and 2008. These moved the CAP a long way from a price-support system to an income-support system with market-determined prices. This has solved many of the trade conflicts that arose from the EU's dumping and it has eliminated the food mountains.

The CAP, however, still has problems as most of the money still goes to rich landowners. Future reforms seem quite likely, but nothing important will be done before the end of the current Financial Perspective in 2013.

Self-assessment questions

1 In 2003, the world wheat price is above the CAP's target price so the price floor has become a price ceiling. (i) Using a diagram like Fig. 9.2, show how the EU could implement the price ceiling with an export tax. (ii) What are the effects of this in the EU and in the rest of the world (prices, quantities and welfare)?

2 Some developing nations accuse the EU of using technical standards for food (pesticide content, etc.) as a barrier to trade. Suppose they are correct. Use diagrams to show how you would analyse the impact of such protection on EU and RoW welfare. (Hint: See Chapter 4's analysis of 'frictional' barriers.)

3 Before the UK adopted the CAP, it supported its farmers with a system of 'deficiency payments', which is the agro-jargon for production subsidies. Using a diagram like Fig. 9.2, analyse this policy assuming that the import of food was duty free, but the government directly paid farmers the difference between the market price and a target price for each unit of food they produced. Be sure to consider the implications for world prices, UK production and UK imports as well as the welfare implications for UK farmers, consumers and taxpayers.

4 Suppose that the EU allowed free trade in food and subsidized production on small farms only. Analyse the price, quantity and welfare implications of this policy using a diagram.

5 The text mentions that since direct payments are tied to the land, it is the land price that soaks up most of the subsidy. Use a classic supply and demand diagram to demonstrate this result. (Hint: This is a standard exercise in what is known as the 'incidence of a tax' since a subsidy is just a negative tax.)

6 The European Commission has proposed putting an upper limit on the total direct payment per farm of approximately €300,000. What would be the impact of this on prices, output and the distribution of farm incomes?

Essay questions

1 Compare the EU's agricultural policy to that of the USA. The EU's policy is based on price support plus direct payments. Does the USA have the same system? Which policy provides a higher level of support to farmers? (Hint: The US Department of Agriculture has an excellent website, and the OECD annually publishes a comparison of farm policies.)

2 What sort of CAP reforms are proposed by environmental groups in Europe? Choose one group's policy recommendations and discuss its implications for the overall level of support to the farm sector, its distribution among farmers and its implications for world food markets.

3 Select a particular European nation and investigate the political influence of its farmers. In particular, identify the main farm lobby group(s) and show how they put pressure on politicians to continue the high level of support.

4 What is the overall impact of the EU's CAP on farmers in developing nations? (Hint: The IMF published a study on this issue in its September 2002 *World Economic Outlook*.)

5 Using the theory of fiscal federalism presented in Chapter 2, can you argue that agricultural policy should be set at the EU level?

Further reading: the aficionado's corner

A wide-ranging and accessible consideration of the CAP can be found in:

Hathaway, K. and D. Hathaway (eds), *Searching for Common Ground. European Union Enlargement and Agricultural Policy*, FAO, Rome.

Other useful works are those listed below:

ERS (1999) *The EU's CAP: Pressures for Change*, US Department of Agriculture Economic Research Service, International Agriculture and Trade Reports, WRS-99 – 2. Download from www.ers.usda.gov/publications/wrs992/wrs992.pdf.

EU Court of Auditors (2000) *Greening the CAP*, Special Report No. 14/2000.

European Commission (1994) *EC Agricultural Policy for the 21st Century*, European Economy, Reports and Studies, No. 4.

European Commission (1999) *Agriculture, Environment, Rural Development: Facts and Figures – A Challenge for Agriculture*, DG Agriculture. Download from http://europa.int/comm/agriculture/envir/report/en/.

Farmer, M. (2007) *The Possible Impacts of Cross Compliance on Farm Costs and Competitiveness*, Institute for European Environmental Policy, 21, January.

Halverson, D. (1987) *Factory Farming: The Experiment That Failed*, Animal Welfare Institute, London.

Milward, A. (1992) *The European Rescue of the Nation-state*, University of California Press, Berkeley.

Moehler, R. (1997) 'The role of agriculture in the economy and society', in K. Hathaway and D. Hathaway (eds) *Searching for Common Ground: European Union Enlargement and Agricultural Policy*, FAO, Rome, www.fao.org/docrep/W7440E/w7440e00.htm.

Molle, W. (1997) *The Economics of European Integration*, Ashgate, London.

Nevin, E. (1990) *The Economics of Europe*, Macmillan, London.

Swinnen, J. (2002) *Towards a Sustainable European Agricultural Policy for the 21st Century*, CEPS Task Force Report No. 42, Brussels.

Useful websites

For a non-institutional view of the CAP, and a series of readable and informative essays, see http://members.tripod.com/~WynGrant/WynGrantCAPpage.html.

The Commission's website http://europa.eu.int/comm/agriculture/ provides a wealth of data and analysis, although much of it is politically constrained to be fairly pro-CAP. The US government's Agricultural Department provides even more analysis and tends to be more openly critical of the CAP; the pages of the Economic Research Service are especially informative. See www.ers.usda.gov/briefing/EuropeanUnion/PolicyCommon.htm.

Every year, the OECD publishes an excellent report on the agricultural policy of all OECD members (this includes the CAP). For the latest figures and exhaustive analysis, see www.oecd.org.

References

DG-Ag (2007) 'Situation and prospects for EU agriculture and rural areas', Note to file. Download from http://ec.europa.eu/agriculture/analysis/markets/prospects12_2007_en.pdf.

European Commission (1994) *EC Agricultural Policy for the 21st Century*, European Economy, Reports and Studies, No. 4.

European Commission (2011). 'Agriculture in the EU, Statistical and Economic, Information Report 2010', DG-Ag, http://ec.europa.eu/agriculture/agrista/2010/table_en/2010enfinal.pdf.

IMF (2002) *World Economic Outlook*, September. Download from www.imf.org.

JNCC (2002) *Environmental Effects of the Common Agricultural Policy and Possible Mitigation Measures*, Report prepared for the Department for Environment, Food and Rural Affairs by the Joint Nature Conservation Committee. Download from www.jncc.gov.uk.

OECD (2003) *Farm Household Income: Issues and Policy Responses*, Paris.

OECD (2004) *Analysis of the 2003 CAP Reform*, Paris.

Oxfam (2002) 'Stop the dumping', Oxfam Briefing Paper 31. Download from www.oxfam.org.uk/resources/policy/trade/downloads/bp31_dumping.pdf.

Zobbe, H. (2001) *The Economic and Historical Foundation of the Common Agricultural Policy in Europe*, Working paper, Royal Veterinary and Agricultural University, Copenhagen. Download from www.flec.kvl.dk/kok/ore-seminar/zobbe.pdf.

Chapter 10

Location effects, economic geography and regional policy

. . . the Community shall aim at reducing disparities between the levels of development of the various regions and the backwardness of the least favoured regions or islands, including rural areas.

Treaty establishing the European Community, 1957

Chapter Contents

Introduction

When deeper European economic integration took off in the 1950s, rural Europe was really poor. Electricity and telephones were far from standard in rural households and many were without indoor plumbing. Europe as a whole was booming, but cities and a few industrial regions were leaving rural Europe behind. The EU's founders made a concern for rural Europe one of the key goals of European integration. As the 2004 and 2007 enlargements added large swaths of poor rural areas to the EU, helping Europe's rural communities remains a touchstone of today's EU.

This chapter looks at the facts, theory and policy connecting European integration to the location of economic activity in Europe.

10.1 Europe's economic geography: the facts

Regional incomes in the EU follow a clear pattern. Rich regions are located close to one another and form the 'core' of the EU economy. Poor regions tend to be geographically peripheral. (See Combes and Overman, 2004, for more detail.) These points are clear in Fig. 10.1. This shows a map of Europe's night-time light pollution. Since light pollution lines up very closely with economic activity at this scale, we can think of this as showing the spatial distribution of economic activity. The 'heart of Europe' is clearly made up of western Germany, the Benelux nations, north-eastern France and south-eastern England. This region contains only one-seventh of the EU's land but a third of its population and half its economic activity. It is the economic

Figure 10.1 Europe at night – light 'pollution'

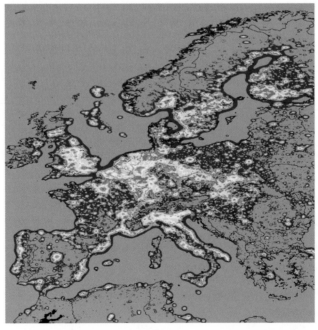

Source: P. Cinzano, F. Falchi (University of Padova), C.D. Elvidge (NOAA National Geophysical Data Center, Boulder, CO). Copyright Royal Astronomical Society. Reproduced from the Monthly Notices of the RAS by permission of Blackwell Science (www.lightpollution.it/dmsp/)

centre of Europe. Roughly speaking, the concentration of economic activity drops as one moves away from the core, although the map shows that there is also a massive concentration of economic activity in northern Italy and various hot spots in Iberian and Nordic regions.

The map also serves to make an important point about nations and regions. The focus of our analysis in the earlier chapters has been on nations' economies and the integration of nations. Looking at Fig. 10.1, it is not hard to see that national borders are not really the best way to think about economic activity in Europe. In short, regions matter.

Although distance is continuous, when we discuss the economics below we frequently refer to the 'core' and the 'periphery'. The core is the regions with the brightest lights in Fig.10.1, the rest is the periphery. Plainly it is very blunt to put regions into just two categories, but it proves analytically convenient.

10.1.1 Why does peripherality matter?

Why should anyone care about the location of economic activity? There are, after all, very few people in northern Finland. Why is it a problem that there is also very little economic activity there? For reasons we discuss below, incomes tend to be lower for people living in the periphery regions – although, as always, there are exceptions, especially around key but remote cities such as Rome, Madrid, Dublin, Edinburgh, Stockholm and Helsinki (see Fig. 10.2). Note that:

Figure 10.2 Income disparity in the EU, 2007 (regional GDP per capita adjusted for prices PPS)

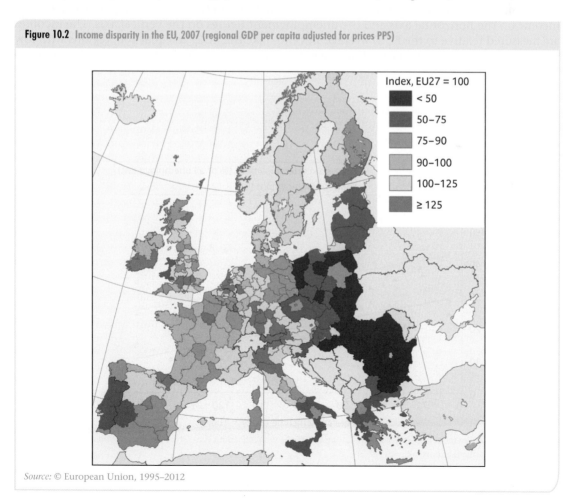

Index, EU27 = 100
- < 50
- 50–75
- 75–90
- 90–100
- 100–125
- ≥ 125

Source: © European Union, 1995–2012

■ Most regions in the 12 new members have incomes that are below those of the EU15 nations. The differences are stark. The poorest region in the EU27 is Romania's Severozapaden region, which has a per-capita income that is 28 per cent of the EU27 average. The richest region, Inner London, had an average income that is 343 per cent higher than the EU27 average.

■ Apart from the western-most and southern-most parts of the Continent, none of the EU15 regions have incomes below 75 per cent of the EU27 average. Although it is not shown on the map, the northern extremes of the Continent would also have very low incomes if it were not for the colossal income transfers and special programmes undertaken by Sweden and Finland. One of the most striking things about the map is how regional incomes seem to fall with the region's distance from the 'heart of Europe' (again apart from the Nordic cases).

The wide disparity in income levels is a problem from a social point of view, but it is also a problem from the political perspective. Large income gaps between regions foster bitter political disputes that can hinder cooperation on things such as European integration. Giving the poorer regions hope that they will catch up is an important role for the EU's regional policies.

The disadvantages of the poor regions range much further than low incomes. Many standard indicators of social misfortune suggest that many of Europe's poor regions have many problems. For instance, the poor regions also often have higher levels of youth unemployment, long-term unemployment and lower levels of investment and education.

This point is illustrated for the regions of Italy and Spain in Fig. 10.3, which plots each region's income on the horizontal axis and the unemployment figures on the vertical axis. The incomes are measured relative to the EU27 average since we take the EU27 to equal 100; regions with low numbers are poor relative to the EU average. What the figure shows is that poor regions tend to

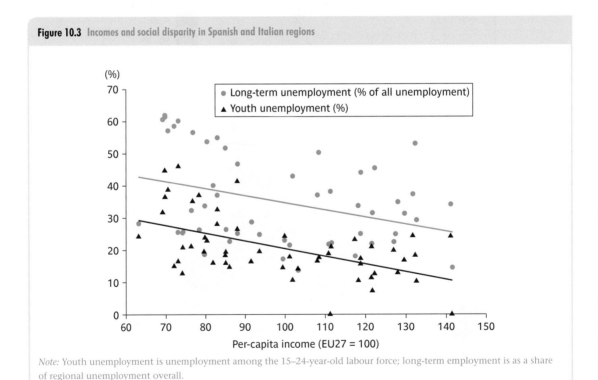

Figure 10.3 Incomes and social disparity in Spanish and Italian regions

Note: Youth unemployment is unemployment among the 15–24-year-old labour force; long-term employment is as a share of regional unemployment overall.

Source: © European Union, 1995–2012.

have more problems with long-term unemployment and youth unemployment. Although the connection is far from perfect, it helps illustrate that the problems of Europe's remote regions concern more than money.

Note that the regions in the new members are different in many ways from those in the old EU15. The new member regions are almost universally dynamic, with fast-rising incomes, employment and productivity. Much of this is simply a quick catch-up to the investment and technology standards of western Europe. The poor/remote regions of the old members tend to be areas that have suffered prolonged decline in output, investment and populations as people and industry headed for the cities.

Much more detail on the state of the EU's economic and social cohesion can be found in the Cohesion reports and annual updates (http://europa.eu.int/comm/regional_policy/). This includes downloadable data at the regional level and statistical mapping software.

10.1.2 Evolution over time: narrower national differences, wider regional differences

While the dispersion of income levels across nations is still very high, the gaps among EU members have been steadily narrowing, as Fig. 10.4 shows. The EU15 members have on average seen a significant convergence of their incomes to the EU15 average (shown in each year as EU15 = 100). Note that Sweden, Finland and Austria only joined in 1995, but had participated in much of the economic integration with the EU even before they joined (see Chapter 1). The real success stories are Spain, Portugal, Greece and, above all, Ireland, which went from one of the poorest to the second richest Member State. The obvious exception to the convergence story is Luxembourg, which started above average and continued to diverge. The fact that it is a net recipient of EU funds (see Chapter 3) has little to do with this performance; most of it is due to the Grand Duchy's development of a highly lucrative financial service sector based in part on its low taxes and banking secrecy.

The convergence of the new Member States is also clear in the chart, although the process has been gradual and their membership in 2004 did not lead to any visible jump.

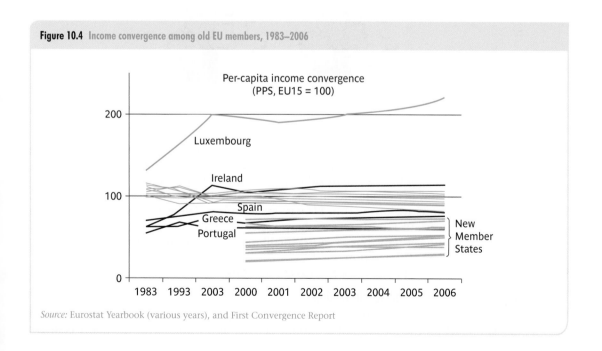

Figure 10.4 Income convergence among old EU members, 1983–2006

Per-capita income convergence
(PPS, EU15 = 100)

Luxembourg

Ireland

Spain

Greece

Portugal

New Member States

1983 1993 2003 2000 2001 2002 2003 2004 2005 2006

Source: Eurostat Yearbook (various years), and First Convergence Report

Divergence within nations

The convergence across nations, however, hides an important trend. Income inequality across regions within each EU nation has been rising steadily. We can see this clearly by taking the example of the UK. The left-hand map in Fig. 10.5 shows the distribution of per-capita income in 1995, region by region. The right-hand map shows the same for 2005. To ease comparison between 1995 and 2005, we look at each region's per-capita income compared to the UK average. Thus a region with a per-capita income equal to 100 is just at the UK average, while those with figures below 100 have below-average incomes. In 1995, Greater London was the only region with more than 140 (i.e. more than 40 per cent above the UK average). Two other regions – Scotland and the region below London – had above-average incomes. All the rest had below-average incomes. In 2005, London retains its first place but Scotland is no longer above average. Additionally, two of the regions in the west see their incomes drop below 90 per cent of the average. Overall, there is a clear increase in regional inequality between 1995 and 2005.

Figure 10.5 GDP per capita in British regions, 1995 vs. 2005

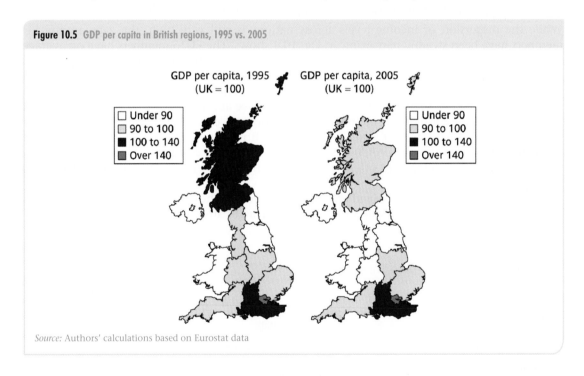

Source: Authors' calculations based on Eurostat data

A similar pattern holds generally across the EU. For example, Poland has been growing rapidly during this time and in fact all regions saw their incomes rise. However, some regions – such as Warsaw – grew much faster than others, so their share of Polish GDP rose. Roughly speaking, regions with low per-capita incomes have lost out in the race for national GDP shares. In short, inequality among regions within EU nations has risen. There are many exceptions, as always. For instance, western French regions have seen their GDP shares rise, as have some of the poorer parts of southern Italy, but even in equalitarian Sweden, the northern regions have shrunk relative to the rest of the nation.

10.1.3 Integration and production specialization

The evidence presented up to this point suggests that European economic integration has had only a modest impact on the location of economic activity as a whole, with the many changes occurring within nations rather than across nations. Lumping together all economic activity (i.e. measuring activity by total GDP), however, may hide changes in the composition of economic activity within each nation or region. European integration may have encouraged a clustering of manufacturing by sector rather than by region. To explore this possibility, we look at regions' and nations' industrial structures and their evolution. We focus on industry since it is difficult to get comparable data on services.

Figures for European nations

Using a particular measure of specialization – called the Krugman specialization index – we look at how different the industrial structures are in various European nations and how they have evolved. The Krugman index tells us what fraction of manufacturing activity would have to change sector in order to make the particular nation's sector-shares line up with the sector-shares of the average of all other EU15 nations.

The indices for the EU27 are shown in Table 10.1. Since almost all the changes are positive, we conclude that the industrial structures of most nations are diverging from the average EU industrial structure. In other words, taking the EU average as our standard, most European nations experienced an increase in the extent to which they specialized in the various manufacturing sectors. The only major exception is that of Spain, whose industrial structure became substantially more similar to the EU average over this period.

Table 10.1 Specialization by nations, 1980 to 1997

	1980–83 (%)	1988–91 (%)	1994–97 (%)
Ireland	62	66	78
Greece	58	66	70
Finland	51	53	59
Denmark	55	59	59
Portugal	48	59	57
Netherlands	57	55	52
Sweden	39	40	50
Belgium	35	38	45
Italy	35	36	44
Germany	31	35	37
Austria	28	28	35
Spain	29	33	34
UK	19	22	21
France	19	21	20
EU15 average (weighted)	30	33	35

Source: Midelfart-Knarvik and Overman (2002)

How important is this increase in specialization? To take one example, Ireland's index in 1970–73 was 70 per cent, which means that 35 per cent of total production would have to change sector to bring it into line with the rest of the EU. Ireland's index had increased by 8 per cent by 1997, so by 1997, 38 per cent of Ireland's manufacturing would have to change sector to get in line with the EU average. For most EU nations, the change has been fairly mild, on the order of 5 or 10 per cent.

10.1.4 Summary of facts

To summarize, the facts are:

- Europe's economic activity is highly concentrated geographically at the national level as well as within nations.
- People located in the core enjoy higher incomes and lower unemployment rates.
- While the income equality across nations has narrowed steadily with European integration, the geographical distribution of economic activity within Member States has become more concentrated (taking income per capita as a measure of economic activity per capita).
- As far as specialization is concerned, European integration has been accompanied by only modest relocation of industry among nations, at least when one lumps all forms of manufacturing together.
- The little movement that there has been tends to lean in the direction of manufacturing activities having become more geographically dispersed across nations, not less.
- Most European nations have become more specialized on a sector-by-sector basis.
- At the sub-national level, we see that industry has become more concentrated spatially.

10.2 Theory part I: comparative advantage

We now turn to the economic logic that connects European integration and the location of economic activity, focusing on two aspects in particular: specialization at the international level and agglomeration at the international level.

To keep things simple, we consider each effect in isolation, using a separate framework for each. The first framework focuses on natural differences among European nations – what economists call comparative advantage. The second framework – which is presented in the following section – focuses on the tendency of closer integration to encourage the geographic clustering of economic activity.

10.2.1 Comparative advantage and specialization

Opening up trade between nations raises economic efficiency. This is just the 'magic of the market'. When trade is very difficult, each nation has to make the most of what it consumes. Trade allows nations to 'do what they do best and import the rest'. Trade allows a nation to concentrate its productive resources in sectors where it has an edge over other nations. The jargon word for the edge is 'comparative advantage'. This effect of liberalization can have important effects on the location of industry because it encourages a nation-by-nation specialization. The main purpose of this section is to explain how comparative advantage and European economic integration help explain the type of industrial specialization that happened in Europe in the 1980–97 period and is likely to continue into the future.

An example

To see the basic idea more clearly, think about what Europe would look like without any trade. European nations have different supplies of productive factors – and different types of goods use factors in different proportions – so without trade the output of a nation would be largely determined by its supplies of factors. Focusing on labour supplies, consider the current distribution of labour among EU members, dividing labour into three types: those with little education (less than secondary), those with at least secondary education, and highly educated workers (researchers). To make the numbers comparable, we compute each nation's supply of low-education workers relative to its total supply of workers and compare this to the same ratio calculated for the EU as a whole (EU's supply of low-educated labour to overall labour) – and we do the same for the other two labour types.

The numbers are shown in Fig. 10.6. For example, we see that Portugal's supply of low-education workers (divided by Portugal's total supply of workers) is 83 per cent above the EU average. Germany's is 52 per cent below the EU average. Now consider what this means for the price of a good that uses low-education labour intensively, such as clothing. Without any trade, Germany and Portugal would have to make all their own clothes. Since the factor that is used intensively in clothes production is relatively abundant in Portugal and relatively scarce in Germany, we should expect clothing to be more expensive in Germany than in Portugal, if there were no trade.

Now think about what would happen if trade between Germany and Portugal opened up. Since clothes are relatively cheap in Portugal, we would see Portugal exporting clothing to Germany. But what would Germany export to Portugal in exchange? As Fig. 10.6 shows, Germany is

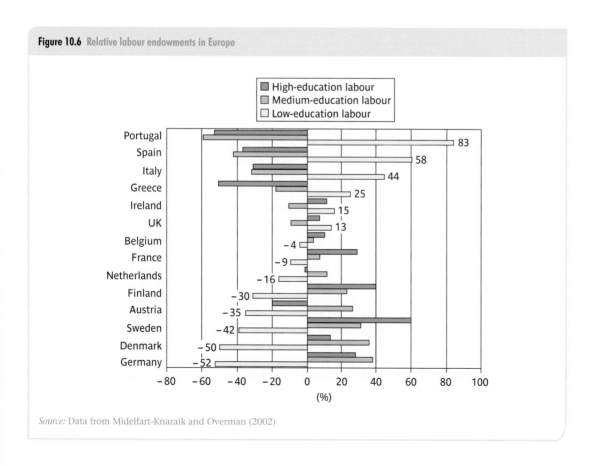

Figure 10.6 Relative labour endowments in Europe

Source: Data from Midelfart-Knaraik and Overman (2002)

relatively abundant in high-education labour. Using the same logic that told us clothing would be relatively cheap in Portugal without trade, we know that goods that are intensive in their use of high-education labour – for example, pharmaceuticals – would be relatively cheap in Germany. In this highly simplified world with trade only between Portugal and Germany, we would see Portugal exporting clothing (and other goods that are intensive in the use of low-education labour) in exchange for pharmaceuticals (and other goods that are intensive in the use of high-education labour) from Germany.

Germans would get their clothes for less and Portuguese would get the pharmaceuticals for less, so this exchange would be good for both nations (although individual workers might be hurt by the implied structural adjustment). The key to this 'gain from trade' is the way in which trade allows for a more efficient allocation of production across countries. Instead of each nation having to make everything it consumes, trade allows production to locate in its 'natural' place. In this case, some production of low-education-intensive goods shifts to the nation that is relatively abundant in this type of labour.

Before turning to the main point – the implication of this trade liberalization for the spatial allocation of manufacturing – it is worth stressing the logical necessity of each nation having a comparative advantage in something. The way we defined our measure of relative factor abundance, each nation's labour supplies must either be exactly in line with the EU average (Belgium's is very close to this), or it must be abundant in some types of labour and scarce in others. Thus, without trade, each nation would have some goods that were relatively expensive and some goods that were relatively cheap. This type of comparative advantage, based on relative factor endowments, is known to economists as 'Heckscher–Ohlin' comparative advantage (it is named after the two Swedish economists who worked out its logic in the 1920s and 1930s).

The spatial implications of Heckscher–Ohlin comparative advantage

How does trade change the geographical pattern of production in this framework? In the example, trade induces an expansion in Portuguese sectors that are intensive in the use of low-education labour. Since the resources needed to expand output in these sectors must come from somewhere, trade also induces a contraction of other Portuguese sectors, in particular the sectors that had relatively high prices without trade, e.g. pharmaceuticals and other goods that are intensive in the use of high-education labour. In the simple example, the mirror-image shift would occur in Germany's industrial structure. If we view this from the international level, the resulting structural changes would look like a shift of clothing production from Germany to Portugal and a shift of the production of pharmaceuticals in the opposite direction. As a result, the industrial structures of both Portugal and Germany would become more specialized.

Of course, European integration is not limited to two nations. Allowing for many nations makes the analysis much more difficult, but it does not change the basic results that freer trade induces nations to specialize in producing products that they are relatively good at and importing products that they are relatively bad at producing. Consequently, trade liberalization of any type – including European economic integration – tends to lead nations to specialize on a nation-by-nation basis. Economic resources get shifted between sectors within each nation and, as a result, it seems as if production is being reallocated sector by sector across nations.

From the point of view of economic geography, this shows up as an increase in national specialization sector by sector. While this is not the only possible explanation for the increased specialization we saw in Table 10.1 (more on this below), it provides a very natural way of understanding why European integration was so systematically associated with an increase in specialization by nation.

We turn now to the logic behind the increased concentration of economic activity within European nations.

10.3 Theory part II: agglomeration and the new economic geography

The deep economic logic of the comparative advantage mechanism just discussed concerns how a nation's productive factors – i.e. its capital, skilled and unskilled labour, etc. – are employed *across sectors within the same nation*. To keep things simple, we implicitly assumed that there was only one region per nation so the issue of the geographic location of economic activity within a nation never arose.

In this section, we switch to the opposite extreme, where the key question is: 'How does European integration affect the location of economic activity *across regions within the same nation?*' To keep things simple, we assume that there is only a single industry in a nation but several regions within the nation.

The basic issues we are trying to understand in this section can be illustrated with a pair of maps – one showing the geographic distribution of economic activity (i.e. GDP) and one showing the population. Economic integration within the UK has, for decades, encouraged the shift of economic activity within Britain towards southern England. The facts for the 1995–2005 period are shown in Fig. 10.7. The left-hand map shows how each region's share of the UK's total economic activity has changed; darker colours indicate bigger increases. The right-hand map shows the same figures for regional population shares.

The dominant fact that comes out clearly from the maps is that the rise in GDP shares is closely matched by the rise in population shares. In other words, what we see here is a movement of productive factors across regions within a nation. Economic activity and population are agglomerating in southern England. Population figures are easy to obtain, but if we could find

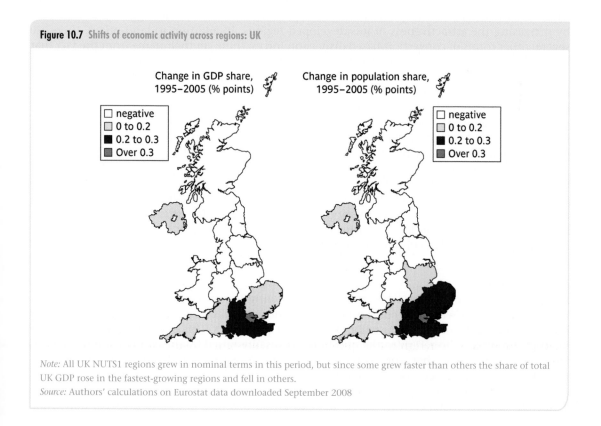

Figure 10.7 Shifts of economic activity across regions: UK

Change in GDP share, 1995–2005 (% points)

- □ negative
- ☐ 0 to 0.2
- ■ 0.2 to 0.3
- ▧ Over 0.3

Change in population share, 1995–2005 (% points)

- □ negative
- ☐ 0 to 0.2
- ■ 0.2 to 0.3
- ▧ Over 0.3

Note: All UK NUTS1 regions grew in nominal terms in this period, but since some grew faster than others the share of total UK GDP rose in the fastest-growing regions and fell in others.

Source: Authors' calculations on Eurostat data downloaded September 2008

regional statistics on capital stocks and other types of productive factors, we would see the same pattern of spatial agglomeration accompanied by a spatial agglomeration of productive factors.

But what causes what? Is economic activity clustering in southern England because this is where the workers are clustering, or is it the other way around? To organize our thinking on this question and related questions, we need to study the basic elements of economic geography. In what follows, the concepts are introduced with verbal logic alone.

10.3.1 Agglomeration and dispersion forces in general

The logic of economic geography rests on two pillars – dispersion forces and agglomeration forces. Agglomeration forces promote the spatial concentration of economic activity while dispersion forces discourage such concentration. The spatial distribution of economic activity at a moment in time depends upon the balance of the pro-concentration (agglomeration) forces and anti-concentration (dispersion) forces. The main question we want to answer is: 'How does European integration affect the equilibrium location of an industry?' To set the stage for the equilibrium analysis, we first consider dispersion and agglomeration forces in isolation.

Dispersion forces

Dispersion forces favour the geographic dispersion of economic activity. Land prices are the classic example. The price of land – and therefore the price of housing, office space, etc. – is usually higher in built-up areas, such as Central London, than it is in rural areas, such as North Wales. What this means is that if everything else were equal, firms and workers would prefer to locate in less built-up areas. Of course, we know other things are not equal, but the forces that make built-up areas more attractive are called agglomeration forces and we put them aside for the moment to focus on dispersion forces. Dispersion forces counteract agglomeration forces by increasing the attractiveness of less-developed regions. In addition to land prices, there are several other forms of congestion-based dispersion forces; these get their name from the fact that living in a congested area has many downsides (light, noise and air pollution, etc.).

While congestion-based dispersion forces are important in the real world, we shall ignore them in our theory. There are two very good reasons for this. First, such dispersion forces are not changed by European economic integration. Thus, when we go to see how European integration affects the geographic dispersion of economic activity, consideration of such forces will not add anything important. Second, including such forces in our theory complicates matters, so for simplicity's sake we put them aside. (See Box 10.2 for what happens when they are put back into the framework.)

The only dispersion force we consider is the so-called local competition force. That is, given trade costs and imperfect competition, firms are naturally attracted to markets where they would face few locally based competitors. For example, an entrepreneur thinking about setting up a new convenience store is likely to choose a location that is far from other competitors. In seeking to avoid local competition, firms spread themselves evenly across markets. In this way, local competition tends to disperse economic activity.

Agglomeration forces

An agglomeration force exists when the spatial concentration of economic activity creates forces that encourage further spatial concentration. This definition is more circular than the straight-line chain of causes and effects usually presented in economics. This circularity, however, is the heart of the subject. To return to the question of causality raised by the comparison of maps in Fig. 10.7, the answer is that workers move because the jobs concentrate *and*, at the same time, the jobs concentrate since workers concentrate.

There are many agglomeration forces, but some of them operate only on a very local scale. These explain, for instance, why banks tend to group together in one part of London while dance clubs cluster in another part of the city. The study of agglomerations at this level – it is called urban economics – is fascinating, but it is not the level of agglomeration that interests us. European policy is concerned with the impact of European integration on agglomeration at the level of regions and nations. At this geographic level, many of the city-level agglomeration forces are unimportant.

The two most important agglomeration forces that operate across great geographical spaces are called demand linkages and cost linkages (also known as backward and forward linkages, respectively).

Demand-linked and cost-linked agglomeration forces

To illustrate the circular-causality logic of demand-linked and cost-linked agglomeration forces as simply as possible, we make a couple of bold assumptions. First, we assume that firms will choose one location (see Box 10.1 for the economics behind this assumption). Second, we assume that there are only two possible locations, a region called 'north' and a region called 'south'. The demand-linked circular causality rests on market-size issues (hence its name). Firms want to locate where they have good access to a large market. Consider the UK example again. In 2005, much but not all UK demand was in southern England. If a firm locates in the north, it has to incur high shipping costs to sell to southern customers, although it has low costs of selling to customers in the north. (It is cheaper to sell to nearby customers.) Since there are more customers in the south, northern firms can reduce their shipping by moving to the south. This is where the circular causality of demand linkages starts. Other things equal, firms want to be in the big market.

Box 10.1   How scale economies force manufacturing firms to choose a location

By definition, a firm that is subject to scale economies is one whose average cost – i.e. the per-unit cost – of producing a good falls as the scale of production rises. This means that firms whose production is subject to scale economies will benefit from concentrating production in a single location – think of it as a single factory, rather than setting up a factory near every market. For example, contrast the production of car engines, which is marked by huge scale economies, with the production of cheese, which is economical even at fairly low levels of output (there are thousands of these around Europe). Owing to scale economies, most European car companies make all engines of a particular type in a single factory located somewhere in Europe. The reason is that the per-engine cost of production is much lower in big factories. When it comes to cheese, however, the cost reduction from having a single massive cheese factory would not lower per-kilo production costs by much. For this reason, companies tend to put cheese factories near the milk production rather than ship massive quantities of milk to a massive cheese factory.

The causality becomes circular because the movement of firms from the small market in the north to the big market in the south makes the big market bigger and the small market smaller. The reason is that, by moving to the south, the firms create jobs in the south and this induces workers to move to the south. This affects market size since workers tend to spend their incomes locally. For example, when a firm leaves Dijon to set up in Paris, it moves jobs to Paris. This makes it somewhat harder to get a job in Dijon and somewhat easier to get a job in Paris, so this move encourages workers to move to Paris. We call this an 'agglomeration force' since spatial concentration (the Dijon-to-Paris move) of economic activity creates forces (the change in market sizes) that encourage further spatial concentration.

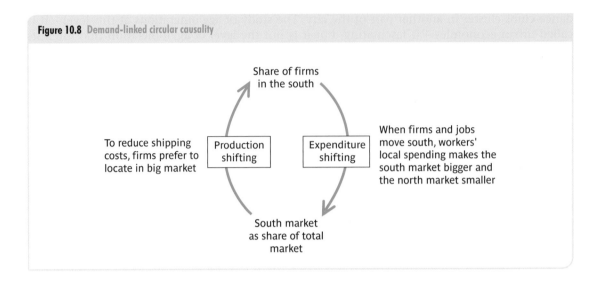

Figure 10.8 Demand-linked circular causality

The basic idea is illustrated in Fig. 10.8. It is useful to separate two things that are closely related: market size (i.e. 'south market as a share of total market', or the spatial distribution of firms), and firm location (i.e. 'share of firms in the south', or the spatial distribution of firms).

Starting from the left arrow, we see that the market size affects the location of firms. The logic rests on firms' desire to minimize shipping costs. The right arrow shows that the location of firms affects relative market size. The logic is simply that firms employ workers and workers tend to spend their incomes locally. If no dispersion forces were in operation, this circular causality would continue until the north was entirely empty of jobs and firms.

This brings us to the second major type of agglomeration force: cost-linked circular causality. This agglomeration force works in a fashion that is similar to demand-linked circular causality, but it involves production costs rather than market size.

It is a fact that, in the modern economy, firms buy plenty of things from other firms. These range from raw materials and machinery to specialized services such as marketing, accounting and IT services. Since it is cheaper to find and buy such input from firms that are nearby, the presence of many firms in a location tends to reduce the cost of doing business in that location. Thinking this through, we can see that a similar circular causality will encourage agglomeration. Figure 10.9 helps explain this.

The figure separates two things that are closely related but worth keeping distinct: firm location (i.e. 'share of firms in the south', or the spatial distribution of firms), and the cost-advantage of producing in the big market (i.e. 'cost of producing in the south', or the spatial distribution of production costs).

Starting from the left arrow, we note that, if many firms are already in the south, then doing business in the south will – all else equal – be cheaper than doing business in the north. This production-cost differential influences the location of firms. The right arrow shows how the relocation of firms from the north to the south tends to improve the business climate in the south and worsen it in the north, at least in terms of the range of available inputs. Again, if there were no dispersion forces (e.g. wages in the north being lower than those in the south), this circular causality would empty out the north entirely.

In other words, cost-linked circular causality describes the way in which firms are attracted by the presence of many suppliers in the big market and how firms moving to the big market widens the range of suppliers and thus makes the big market even more attractive from a cost-of-production point of view.

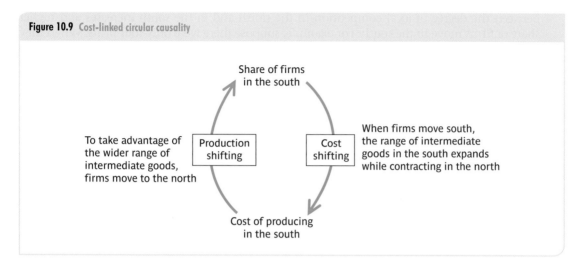

Figure 10.9 Cost-linked circular causality

10.3.2 The locational effects of European integration

European integration affects the balance of agglomeration and dispersion forces in complex ways. Such complexity is important for understanding the real world since – as the facts presented above show – the locational effects of European integration are far from simple. The best way to understand this complex logic, however, is to follow the principle of progressive complexity. We start with a set of simplifying assumptions that allow us to focus on the critical logical relationships. Once we have understood this logic in a simplified setting, we add back in complicating factors.

A very simple analytic framework

To simplify, we start by assuming away all dispersion forces except 'local competition'. We also assume away cost-linked circular causality (by assuming firms buy no intermediate inputs). This leaves us with only one pro-agglomeration consideration and one pro-dispersion consideration:

- The pro-agglomeration force is that firms would, all else equal, prefer to locate in the big market in order to save on trade costs, i.e. to be close to more of their customers than they would be if they were located in the small market.
- The pro-dispersion force is that firms would, all else equal, prefer to be in the market where there are few local competitors and that means locating in the small market.

The final simplifying assumption is that we ignore the circular causality in the demand-linked agglomeration force. One way to think of this is by supposing that workers spend all their income in their native region regardless of where they work. Thus the south market starts out bigger, but firms moving to the south does not make the market bigger.

To study the balance of the agglomeration and dispersion forces, it helps to have a simple diagram. Figure 10.10 serves this purpose. The diagram plots the strength of agglomeration and dispersion forces on the vertical axis. The horizontal axis plots the share of all firms that are located in the big region, i.e. the south.

- The 'agglomeration force' line is flat since we assume away circular causality for simplicity's sake. The market-size difference does not vary with the share of firms in the south, so the strength of the agglomeration force as we move out along the agglomeration force line does not change.
- The 'dispersion force' line is rising since the benefit of staying in the small region rises as more firms move to the southern market. To understand the positive slope, note that the difference

between the degree of local competition in the north and in the south increases as a higher share of firms move to the south. For example, suppose there were only four firms. When they are split 2–2 between the regions, the local competition is even. When they are split 3–1, the local competition is more intense in the region with three firms (the south). Finally, if the split is 4–0, then the difference in local competition is even greater. Connecting these observations, we see that the dispersion force (i.e. the attractiveness of the small market) rises as the share of firms in the south rises. Graphically, this means that the 'dispersion force' curve is upwards sloped.

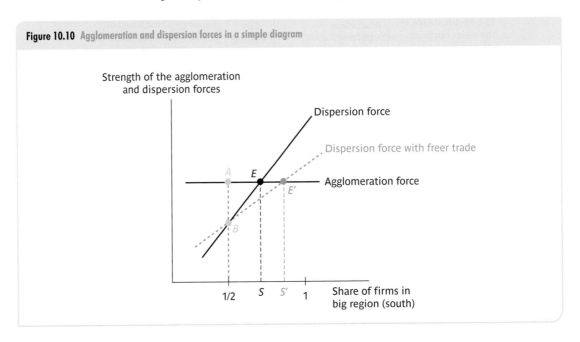

Figure 10.10 Agglomeration and dispersion forces in a simple diagram

The locational equilibrium is shown by point E; this is where the share of firms in the south rises to the point where incentives to agglomerate are just balanced by incentives to disperse. It is instructive to consider why other points are not the equilibrium. For example, consider the point where half the firms are in the north. For this equal distribution of firms, the strength of the agglomeration force is shown by point A; the strength of the dispersion force is shown by point B. Because A is greater than B, we know that the agglomeration force – i.e. the force leading more firms to move to the south – is stronger than the dispersion force – i.e. the force leading firms to move to the north. As a consequence, having only half the firms in the south cannot be an equilibrium. Moreover, since the agglomeration force is stronger than the dispersion force, some firms will move from the small north to the big south.

As firms move southward, the gap between the agglomeration force and the dispersion force narrows. The location equilibrium is where the two forces just offset each other, namely point E, where the share of firms in the south is S. Although it is not shown in the diagram, readers can easily convince themselves that points to the right of point E involve a situation where the dispersion forces are larger than the agglomeration forces so the share of firms in the big region would tend to fall back to point E.

The location effects of tighter European integration

Finally, we come to the main subject of this section: How does tighter economic integration affect the location of industry inside a nation? We think of greater economic integration as lowering shipping costs. Note that here we are speaking of the trade costs among regions within a nation. Such cost reductions come with improvements in technology and improvements in transportation infrastructure and competition. All of these are fostered directly and indirectly by various elements of European integration. This is especially true for EU regional spending on roads, airports, seaports – the sort of thing we discuss below. It is worth noting, however, that such within-nation integration would proceed even without European integration. For the purposes of the diagram, we do not care about the exact reason trade costs are falling, we simply assume they do fall and trace out the impact on the spatial dispersion of firms.

How do we show the trade cost reduction in the diagram? The first point is that the agglomeration force line does not move. The agglomeration force is based on the fact that the northern market is bigger and this fact does not change when trade gets freer. Nothing happens to the 'agglomeration force' line.

Freer trade, however, has a very direct effect on the 'dispersion force' curve. The source of the dispersion force is that trade costs protect firms located in the small market from competition from firms located in the big market. It is clear, then, that something will happen to the dispersion force line. To get a handle on this, consider a very particular point on the line, the point where the share of firms in the big region is ½. At this point, the level of trade costs has no influence on the relative attractiveness of the two regions. Whether trade costs are high or low, the degree of local competition in the two markets will be identical. The thrust of this is that the dispersion force line must always pass through point B in the diagram. Any change will be a rotation of the line around point B.

For points to the right, the dispersion force line must come down. The reason is that, with more firms in the south than the north, the advantage of being in the low-competition north (low competition since there are fewer firms there) is reduced by lower trade costs. In other words, the lower trade costs provide less protection against competition from south-based firms. For this reason, the local competition advantages of being in the north are reduced. Since this is true for all points to the right of ½, this shows up graphically as a clockwise rotation of the 'dispersion force' line around the ½ point.

Given that the dispersion-force curve rotates clockwise and the agglomeration-force curve stays put, the new locational equilibrium is at point E'. Note that this involves a higher share of firms in the big region. In other words, free trade promotes the agglomeration of economic activity in the initially big region. As we saw in Fig. 10.2, this within-nation concentration of economic activity is a widespread phenomenon in Europe.

The simplifying assumptions above made it very easy to study integration's impact on the location of economic activity in Fig. 10.10. While it assumed away many important factors affecting the location of economic activity, it is sufficient for understanding the basic economic logic of how tighter European integration can be expected to favour the location of industry in Europe's core regions. Some readers, however, will want to explore the economics of this in greater depth. Box 10.2 shows how some factors can be included in a modified version of Fig. 10.10.

We can consider other dispersion forces by shifting the dispersion-force curve up or twisting it at the ends. For dispersion forces that are not related to the share of firms in the north, the dispersion-force curve is shifted up vertically. For example, it could be that the one region is intrinsically more pleasant to live in. Since the impact of this on location does not depend upon the share of firms in the south, we allow for such forces by shifting the curve either up or down. Interested readers can easily check that a downward shift will lower the equilibrium share of firms in the south. Other dispersion forces, however, are related to the share of firms. For example, the concentration of firms in southern England drives up the wages of workers in this region. Other things equal, this acts as a dispersion force in that it discourages some firms from moving to the south. We can reflect this in the diagram by rotating the dispersion-force line counter-clockwise around the ½ point.

Box 10.2   Considering additional complicating factors

As it turns out, it is not very difficult to add back in a number of complicating factors that we assumed away to start with.

For example, we can easily allow for circular causality in the agglomeration force. We do this by drawing the agglomeration-force line as upward sloped (Fig. 10.11). If the line slopes upward, it says that the strength of the agglomeration force rises as a larger share of firms move to the big northern region. This addition raises an extra complication concerning the impact of freer trade. Freer trade rotates the dispersion-force line as in the text; however, now it also reduces the agglomeration force for any level of firms in the north. The reason is clear; the agglomeration force stemmed from the fact that locating in the big market helps a firm reduce its shipping costs. Since lower overall shipping costs narrow this difference between the markets, the agglomeration-force line shifts down. The complication is that there is now a graphical possibility that the new E' will be to the left of the old E. A careful study of the logic shows that this cannot occur (see Annex A). Roughly speaking, the free trade reduces the agglomeration forces by less than the dispersion forces so the new location equilibrium involves more spatial concentration.

Figure 10.11 Allowing for circular causality

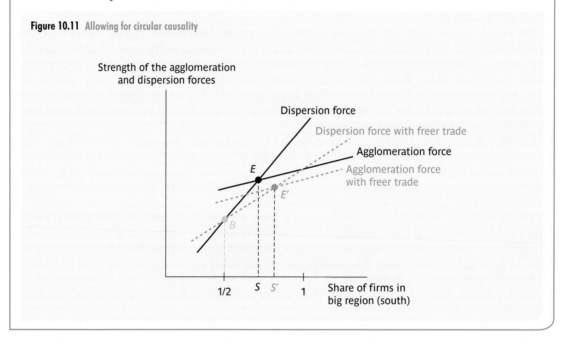

10.4 Theory part III: putting it all together

The facts presented above showed that European integration was accompanied by location effects within nations that are quite different from those between nations. European integration seems to be associated with a more even dispersion of economic activity in the sense that per-capita GDP figures tended to converge nation by nation. Within nations, however, the opposite has happened. In most Member States, regional disparities have grown as European integration has deepened. The theory presented above helps us to understand the difference. The key factor is the mobility of capital and labour.

While there are few remaining restrictions on intra-EU labour flows, workers seldom move across national borders in the EU. Labour mobility between regions within a nation is higher, but still not enormous – as we can see with the huge variation in regional unemployment rates. However, labour mobility has not always been low within nations. The post-war period, for example, saw a massive shift of the population from rural regions to urban regions and this often involved a move across regional boundaries. Moreover, other productive factors are more mobile; for example, capital and skilled workers are quite mobile between regions within the same nation.

Oversimplifying to make the point, think of all factors as perfectly mobile within nations, but perfectly immobile across nations. In this case, removing barriers to trade allows nations to specialize in the sectors in which they have a comparative advantage. The resulting efficiency gain allows all nations to increase their output. Moreover, deeper aspects of integration, such as foreign direct investment and mobility of students, suggest that European integration would also be accompanied by a convergence of national technology frontiers to the best practice in Europe, with the technological laggards catching up with the technological leaders. Both of these factors would promote a convergence of per-capita incomes across European nations. Importantly, the lack of factor mobility across nations means that agglomeration forces are not dominant at the national level. That is to say, the cycles of circular causality that might lead all economic activity to leave a region have no chance of starting. This conclusion must be modified to allow for sector-specific clusters. Even if productive factors do not move across national boundaries, agglomeration forces operating at the sectoral level could result in nations specializing in particular industries. For example, deeper integration could foster greater geographic clustering of, say, the chemicals industry and the car industry, but in the end each nation ends up with some industry.

By contrast, the much greater mobility of factors within nations permits backward and forward linkages to operate. As one region grows, it becomes attractive to firms for demand reasons and cost reasons, so more firms and more factors move to the region, thereby fuelling further growth.

10.4.1 Regional unemployment

The analysis so far has assumed that wages are flexible enough to ensure full employment of all labour. Since regional unemployment is a serious problem in Europe, we turn to the economic logic connecting delocation and unemployment. As usual, we follow the principle of progressive complexity by starting simple.

If wages were adjusted instantaneously across time and space, we would have no unemployment. The wage rate paid for each hour of work would adjust so that the amount of labour that workers would like to supply at that price just matched the amount that firms would like to 'buy' (hire). In this hypothetical world, the wages would instantaneously jump to the market-clearing level, i.e. the level where labour supply matches labour demand. Things are not that simple, however.

For many reasons, most European nations have decided to prevent the wage – the 'price' of labour – from jumping around like the price of crude oil or government bonds. (See Chapter 8 for a more formal treatment of unemployment.) All sorts of labour market institutions, ranging from trade unions and unemployment benefits to minimum wages and employment protection legislation, mean that the price of labour is systematically stabilized at a level that exceeds the market-clearing wage level. The direct logical consequence is that workers systematically want to offer more labour at the going wage than firms are willing to hire; this is the definition of unemployment. As in any market, if the price is fixed too high, the amount offered for sale will exceed the amount that is bought.

In most European nations, there is a strong spatial element to this price-fixing of labour. Take Germany, for example. For many reasons, labour productivity in the eastern Länder is lower than it is in the western Länder. Thus, firms would only be willing to employ all the eastern labour offered if wages were lower in the east. However, German labour unions have methodically prevented eastern wages from falling to their market-clearing level, either in an attempt to avoid downward pressure on their own wages, or, more charitably, in the spirit of solidarity with the eastern workers who actually do get employed. Whatever the source of regional wage inflexibility, its logical consequence is regional unemployment. Moreover, since firms can leave a region much more easily than workers, a continual within-nation clustering of economic activity will tend to be associated with high levels of unemployment in the contracting regions and low levels in the expanding regions.

Finally, it should be clear that this sort of mismatch of migration speeds (firms move faster than workers) – teamed with a lack of regional wage flexibility – has the effect of creating an agglomeration force. A little shift of industry raises unemployment in the contracting region and lowers it in the expanding region. Since unemployment is an important factor in workers' migration decisions, the initial shift makes workers more likely to migrate to the expanding region. Such migration, however, changes the relative market sizes in a way that tends to encourage more firms to leave the contracting region. (For a detailed account of geographical clustering of unemployment in Europe, see Overman and Puga, 2001).

10.4.2 Peripherality and real geography

Our theoretical discussion has intentionally simplified physical geography considerations by working with only two nations, both of which are thought of as points in space. Real-world geography, of course, is much more interesting and this matters for the location of economic activity. We can use the basic logic of demand-linked agglomeration forces to consider how one can put real geography back into the picture.

As discussed above, firms that want to concentrate production in a single location tend, other things being equal, to locate in a place that minimizes transportation costs. With only two markets, this means locating in the bigger market, but when the economic activity is spread out over real geography, the answer can be less obvious. However, the fact that economic activity is highly concentrated in Europe makes the problem easier. As the map in Fig. 10.2 showed, the core of Europe is fairly compact from a geographical point of view, i.e. it is concentrated in the northeast corner of the continent. This is why it is useful to abstract Europe's geography as consisting of two regions, the core and the periphery, what we called the north and the south in the previous section.

There are many complicating factors, however. For example, despite the Alps forming a wall between northern Italy and the big French, German and UK markets, northern Italy has quite good road access thanks to several tunnels and passes through the Alps.

Economists have a way of taking account of the various real-geography features, known as the accessibility index (also called the market potential index); see Fig. 10.12 for a recent example. The accessibility index for each region measures the region's closeness to other regions that have a lot of economic activity. For example, to calculate the accessibility of the region that contains Paris, the Ile de France, one calculates how long it would take to get from the centre of Paris to the main urban centre of every other region in the EU (the calculation varies somewhat according to the form of transport used; the map here works with road transportation). Finally, one weights each of these transport times by the destination region's share of the EU's total economic activity. Adding up these weighted times gives us an idea of how close Paris is to the bulk of EU economic activity. Doing the same for every other region gives us an index of accessibility by region.

Figure 10.12 Real geography and market accessibility

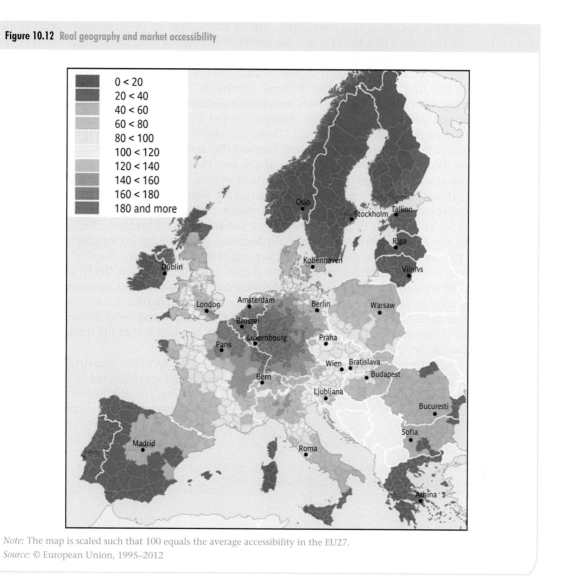

	0 < 20
	20 < 40
	40 < 60
	60 < 80
	80 < 100
	100 < 120
	120 < 140
	140 < 160
	160 < 180
	180 and more

Note: The map is scaled such that 100 equals the average accessibility in the EU27.

Source: © European Union, 1995–2012

10.5 EU regional policy

As mentioned in the introduction, a concern for Europe's disadvantaged regions has always been a headline goal of the European Union. For the first three and a half decades of the EU's existence, however, the task of helping less-favoured regions was left firmly in the hands of national governments. All European nations, both inside and outside the EU, spent huge sums on rural infrastructure during the 1950s, 1960s and 1970s. They extended their electricity and telephone grids to every city, town, village and farmhouse. They built roads, rails and provincial universities in an effort to develop their less-favoured regions. In many cases, modern banking was extended to the rural community via the state-owned PTTs (Post, Telephone and Telegraph).

The EEC, as it was known at the time, did have some programmes for rural regions, but despite real poverty in some members' regions – like Italy's Mezzogiorno – the level of EU funding was negligible. Structural spending was only 3 per cent of the budget in 1970, rising to only 11 per cent by 1980. To the extent that the EEC was not involved in helping rural communities at all, it did so by artificially raising the price of agricultural goods via the Common Agricultural Policy (CAP).

Major EU funding for less-favoured regions would have to wait for a change in Community politics. When the first 'poor' member, Ireland, joined in 1973, a new fund – the European Regional Development Fund (ERDF) – was set up to redistribute money to the poorest regions, but its budget was minor. The situation changed in the 1980s when the EU admitted three new members, Greece, Spain and Portugal. These nations were substantially poorer than the incumbent members, and, importantly, their farmers did not produce the goods that the CAP supported most heavily (mainly wheat, sugar, dairy and beef). If these nations were to benefit financially from the EU's budget, EU spending priorities would have to be changed.

As it turned out, the voting power of Spain and Portugal, teamed with the votes of Ireland and Greece, was sufficient to produce a major realignment of EU spending priorities (see Chapter 3 for an analysis of how power politics shapes the EU budget). During the Iberian accession talks, the EU promised to substantially increase spending on poor regions. The official rationale for the increase was the assertion that economic integration, implied by the 1986 Single European Act, favoured Europe's industrial core (an assertion that fits in perfectly with the economics of agglomeration described in the previous section). As the Commission's website puts it, the policy was 'designed to offset the burden of the single market for southern countries and other less-favoured regions'. Whether it was caused by a new-found concern for less-favoured regions, simple power politics or a combination of the two, the fact is that EU spending on poor regions rose sharply in the mid- to late 1980s, as Fig. 10.13 shows.

When the issue of monetary union was raised in talks leading up to the Maastricht Treaty, the 'poor-4' again managed to obtain a significant increase in regional spending via the creation of a new fund (the Cohesion Fund) that could be spent only in Greece, Ireland, Spain and Portugal. Again, the justification was that tighter economic integration would mostly favour Europe's

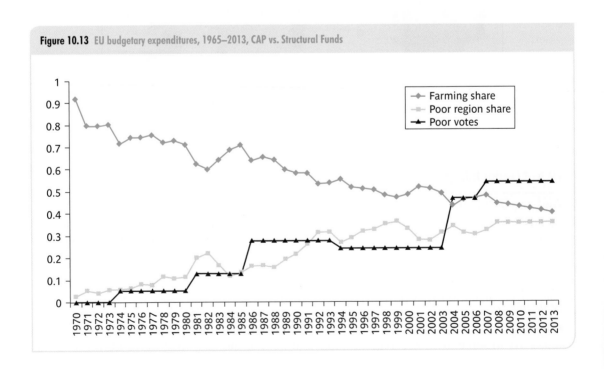

Figure 10.13 EU budgetary expenditures, 1965–2013, CAP vs. Structural Funds

industrial core, so peripheral regions should be compensated by a big increase in EU money for poor regions, what is known as 'structural spending' in EU jargon. The practical outcome was that structural spending doubled its share of the EU budget between 1986 and 1993.

10.5.1 Politics and the allocation of EU regional spending

This link between the political power of poor countries and the budget is clear to see in Fig. 10.13. The share of the EU budget going to poor regions rises in tandem with the share of poor countries' votes in the Council of Ministers. Up to the most recent enlargement, when Austria, Finland and Sweden joined, the correlation was remarkably good. Since 1994, however, the connection between poor nations and structural spending has been greatly diluted. Large parts of Finland and Sweden were designated as eligible, and even some Austrian regions, together with all of the former East Germany, were deemed as poor. The figure also shows the power of 'poor nations' after ten new members joined in 2004 and two more in 2007. The budget plan for 2007–13 shows that the spending share on poor regions will rise, but nowhere near in line with the poor regions' voting share. This may be in part explained by the fact that many of the new members are both poor and highly agrarian, so they may not be as clearly interested in downsizing the CAP as were Spain, Greece and Portugal (who benefited little from the CAP).

10.5.2 Instruments, objectives and guiding principles

The EU spends about a third of its budget on less-favoured regions. How is this money allocated? As mentioned above, politics plays a role, but the EU does have a set of guidelines, objectives and principles that help to channel the spending to where it will do the most good. Here we just touch upon the main points. (Interested readers can find well-written documentation of all the details at http://ec.europa.eu/regional_policy/index_en.htm.)

The EU's regional policy for the period 2007–13 has three main objectives: convergence, regional competitiveness and employment, and territorial cooperation (Table 10.2). The main changes from the previous seven-year period are that the money is more concentrated in the poorest areas and the spending should be linked to the Lisbon goals of making the EU the most competitive economy in the world.

Convergence

Most of the money (€283 billion, or about 80 per cent of total cohesion spending) is spent on the first objective, which is called 'convergence' since it is aimed at reducing income differences

Table 10.2 Share of cohesion budget for convergence, regional competitiveness and employment, and territorial cooperation

	% Cohesion budget	% of EU27 population covered
Convergence	82	Standard convergence regions (34), Phase-out convergence regions (3), Cohesion Fund nations (34)
Regional competitiveness and employment	16	All non-convergence regions (66)
Territorial cooperation	2	100

Source: 'EU Cohesion Policy 1988–2008: Investing in Europe's future', InfoRegio, June 2008

across EU regions. There are three ways to qualify for this money. The main way is to be a NUTS 2 region with GDP per capita that is less than 75 per cent of the average GDP of the EU25 (which is the reference even after the 2007 enlargement). There are 84 of these regions with a total population of 154 million (31 per cent of the EU27 population). The second is to be a so-called phasing-out region, which are regions that got this sort of money before the eastern enlargement, but do not qualify under the new 75 per cent threshold since the newcomers, being much poorer than the EU15, lowered the threshold. This covers only 16 million people (about 3 per cent of the EU27 population), but includes some poor regions in rich nations such as Germany, Austria, Britain and Italy.

Finally, the Cohesion Fund spending (about €70 billion of the €283 billion) is allocated by country rather than by region; all regions in the cohesion countries are eligible regardless of their wealth. This is a holdover from an earlier programme (set up in 1992); the nations that benefited from it, especially Spain, Portugal and Greece, used their political power to maintain the programme. The qualifying threshold is a national income below 90 per cent of the EU25 average. Spain, which is technically too rich as a nation to qualify, used its political power in the Council of Ministers to get itself included on a transitory basis. Since the poorest regions in Spain, Portugal and Greece already qualify under the first criterion, the Cohesion Fund allows convergence money to be spent in the richer regions of Spain, Portugal and Greece.

Regional competitiveness and employment

The second objective is called 'regional competitiveness and employment'. Under this heading, all the non-convergence regions are eligible. The goal is to strengthen the competitiveness and attractiveness of the regions, as well as regional employment. This objective approaches the problem in two ways. First, development programmes are designed to help regions promote economic change through innovation and encouragement of the 'knowledge society' as well as entrepreneurship, protection of the environment, and improvement of the regions' accessibility. It also encourages more and better jobs by helping regions to adapt their workforce.

European territorial cooperation

This objective aims to reinforce cooperation at cross-border, transnational level. It collects under one objective a handful of small programmes that already exist. The sum total budget of all these projects is just €9 billion, or 2 per cent of total cohesion spending. All EU citizens are covered by at least one of the 'transnational cooperation' and about a third live in regions that are considered to be 'cross-border areas'.

The map in Fig. 10.14 shows which regions are eligible for the first- and second-objective spending.

The many structural funds

For historical reasons, most EU regional spending is channelled through three 'funds': two 'Structural Funds' and the 'Cohesion Fund', and the CAP's second pillar which is run separately from the rest of the regional policy. Although there are three funds, they are subsumed in an overall strategy aimed at fighting unemployment and stimulating growth in poor regions. The details of the funds are only important for experts, but for the record, the two structural funds are: the European Regional Development Fund (which funds all three objectives) and the European Social Fund (which funds the first two), plus the Cohesion Fund which helps with the convergence objective. Politically and administratively, the CAP is quite separate from the EU's Regional Policy, so the second pillar of the CAP is only loosely connected with the regional policy.

Figure 10.14 EU first- and second-objective regions

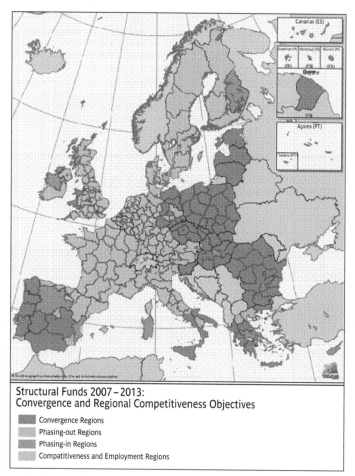

Structural Funds 2007–2013:
Convergence and Regional Competitiveness Objectives

- Convergence Regions
- Phasing-out Regions
- Phasing-in Regions
- Compatitiveness and Employment Regions

Notes: The convergence regions plus the 'phasing-in regions' are eligible for convergence objective spending; the rest are eligible for the competitiveness and employment objective spending. the European territorial cooperation regions are not shown (see http://ec.europa.eu/regional_policy/).

Box 10.3   Relationship with old 2000–06 cohesion objectives

The new objectives are not a substantial reorganization of the basic programmes, although there has been additional concentration on the poorest regions, and much of the cohesion spending has to be explicitly motivated as helping regions meet the Lisbon criteria of boosting growth, jobs and innovation.

Table 10.3 shows what has happened to the old objectives and miscellaneous cohesion projects.

Table 10.3 The old and new objectives compared

2000–06	2007–13
Objective 1: Regions lagging behind in development terms Cohesion Fund (money set aside for Spain, Portugal, Greece and Ireland)	Convergence

Objective 2: Economic and social conversion zones
Objective 3: Training systems and employment policies
 	
    Miscellaneous cohesion programmes
    Interreg III
    URBAN II(*) ERDF
    EQUAL (*) ESF
	Regional competitiveness and employment
	
	European territorial cooperation

Common Agricultural Policy based programmes
 	
    Leader + EAGGF-Guidance
    Rural development and restructuring of the fishing sector beyond Objective 1
	CAP second pillar

Source: Derived from *Cohesion Policy 2007–13: Commentaries and Official Texts*, January 2007, DG Regio, p. 10 (http://ec.europa.eu/regional_policy/sources/docof.c/of.cial/regulation/pdf/2007/publications/guide2007_en.pdf)

Spending priorities

What is this money spent on? Although there are many types of project, a good deal goes to physical infrastructure such as roads, bridges, regional airports, etc. The 2007–13 Regional Policy programme calls for a new generation of programmes that earmark a certain proportion of the resources for projects connected to the EU's so-called Lisbon Agenda (formally, the Strategy for Growth and Jobs). These include research and innovation, infrastructures of European importance, industrial competitiveness, renewable energies, energy efficiency, eco-innovations and human resources.

The proportion devoted to these more forward-looking projects must be at least 60 per cent of the total available funding in convergence regions and 75 per cent in all other regions. According to plans laid in 2007 and 2008, around €200 billion will be allocated to such projects; compared to the previous seven-year budget period, this is a €50 billion increase.

Guiding principles

The Structural Funds are not spent on projects chosen at the European level. The choice of projects and their management are solely the responsibility of the national and regional authorities. The projects, however, are co-financed from both national and Community funds. As a matter of principle, the so-called additionality principle, Community funding should not be used to economize on national funds. This principle is naturally difficult to verify. National budgetary priorities change frequently, so it is hard to know how much the members would have spent if the Community funding were not available.

Besides additionality, the structural spending is characterized by five other basic rules:

1 *Concentration*. The spending should be geographically concentrated.
2 *Coherence*. Spending should be in the context of broad development programmes that are drawn up by EU members and approved by the Commission.
3 *Coordination*. The Commission, the Member State concerned, the regional and local authorities, industry, and labour unions should cooperate in the spending.
4 *Monitoring and evaluation*. The spending should be monitored and evaluated.
6 *Consistency and complementarity*. The spending should be consistent with the provisions of the Treaties and other Community policies such as the Single Market, the CAP and the Common Fisheries Policy.

10.5.3 Political allocation

As part of its responsibilities within the framework of Structural Funds management, the European Commission takes decisions on the concrete implementation of the regulations. This includes allocating the money by objective and by EU member. The outcome of the most recent deal is shown in Table 10.4. Note that this is set in advance for the whole seven-year period.

This allocation was decided as part of the political struggle surrounding the seven-year Financial Perspective for the 2007–13 period (see Chapter 2 for details). While Poland, which is both populous and relatively poor by EU standards, gets by far the most money, well-to-do nations such as Germany, Italy and Spain are also top beneficiaries.

The last two columns show the facts on the per-capita cohesion spending and the per-capita incomes measured in PPS terms (PPS stands for purchasing power standard, i.e. it is a measure that adjusts for the fact that prices tend to be higher in some nations, especially rich nations). Comparing the columns shows that there is a clear distinction between the cohesion countries (i.e. the 12 new members plus Portugal, Greece and Spain) and the other members. The cohesion countries all get substantially more per person than the richer nations. However, among the cohesion countries the allocation does not line up at all well with per-capita income. Chapter 3 discusses issues of power and EU decision making which may help account for these facts.

10.6 Empirical evidence

The chapter has stressed three main determinants of the location of economic activity: regional policy and two purely economic determinants (comparative advantage and agglomeration). We now consider the importance of these three forces.

To evaluate the determinants of industrial location in the EU, researchers try to explain how regional and national shares of various types of manufacturing vary with regional and national characteristics, where it is useful to divide the national characteristics into three broad groups: relative labour supplies, economic geography features, and policies affecting industrial location.

For instance, the theory section explained why we should expect nations that have a relatively high share of the EU's skilled labour also to have a relatively high share of the EU's manufacturing sectors that are relatively intensive in their use of skilled labour. The same link should be expected for relative endowments of other types of labour – low-skilled and medium-skilled workers – and

Table 10.4   Country allocations in the financial perspective, 2007–13 (million euros)

	Convergence objective	Regional competitiveness and employment objective	European territorial cooperation objective	Total	Per-capita cohesion spending (euros)	Per-capita income (2008, PPS)
Poland	66,553		731	67,284	1,765	14,100
Spain	26,180	8,477	559	35,217	778	27,000
Italy	21,641	6,325	846	28,812	2,034	15,100
Czech Rep.	25,883	419	389	26,692	112	31,000
Germany	16,079	9,409	851	26,340	1,821	25,300
Hungary	22,890	2,031	386	25,307	204	36,900
Portugal	20,473	938	99	21,511	2,026	18,900
Greece	19,575	635	210	20,420	2,519	16,200
Romania	6,565		455	19,668	914	10,800
France	3,191	10,257	872	14,319	320	28,900
Slovakia	3,906	449	227	11,588	2,146	18,300
UK	177	6,979	722	10,613	173	29,400
Lithuania	6,775		109	6,885	134	71,000
Bulgaria	6,674		179	6,853	805	23,700
Latvia	4,531		90	4,620	2,045	16,100
Slovenia	4,101		104	4,205	2,076	23,100
Estonia	3,404		52	3,456	324	30,000
Belgium	638	1,425	194	2,258	897	10,100
Netherlands		1,660	247	1,907	116	33,600
Sweden		1,626	265	1,891	206	32,200
Finland		1,596	120	1,716	225	28,100
Austria	177	1,027	257	1,461	212	30,000
Ireland	0	751	151	901	483	25,500
Malta	840	0	15	855	2,082	19,700
Cyprus	213	399	28	640	2,571	21,300
Denmark		510	103	613	2,577	18,600
Luxembourg		50	15	65	175	32,500
Interregional			445	445		

Source: Cohesion Policy 2007–13: Commentaries and Official Texts, January 2007, DG Regio

sectors that use these types of labour intensively as well as regional endowments of agricultural land and industries that use agricultural inputs intensively.

The theory section also explained that the spatial allocation of demand affects the location of industry since sectors where firms tend to concentrate production in a single location (i.e. those marked by important economies of scale) will tend to favour locations that are near large markets. This so-called demand linkage (firms want to be near the demands for their goods) is complemented by so-called supply linkages – that is, firms in sectors that use lots of intermediate inputs will tend to favour locations with concentrations of their suppliers.

Finally, policy can directly encourage the location of particular types of sectors in particular locations and this effect can either amplify or dampen the impact of factor endowments and economic geography factors on the location of industry.

Although the research in this area is limited – mainly owing to a lack of data on the location of manufacturing and regional labour endowments – the results so far suggest that all three factors matter. Interestingly, it seems that labour endowments have become more important in determining location as European economic integration has become tighter. One of the two agglomeration forces – namely, supply linkages – seems to be getting stronger, while the demand linkage is getting weaker. (See Redding et al., 2001, for a survey of empirical results. This can be downloaded from http://econ.lse.ac.uk/staff/ajv/research_material.html.)

Given that EU regional policy has been operating at a significant level only since the mid-1980s, results on the impact of policy are even more tenuous. The best study in this area, Midelfart-Knarvik and Overman (2002), finds that EU policy has significantly affected the geographical location of industries. In particular, these authors find that EU structural spending did affect the location of high-skilled intensive industries. For an integrated survey of the empirical evidence, see Combes and Overman (2004).

10.7 Summary

Europe's economic activity is highly concentrated geographically at the national level as well as within nations. This is a problem for social cohesion since people located in the 'core' enjoy higher incomes and lower unemployment rates. European integration seems to have led to a narrowing of income equality across nations, but an increase in inequality within nations. Nevertheless, European integration has been accompanied by only modest relocation of industry among nations, but the little movement we have seen has been in the direction of manufacturing activities having become more geographically dispersed, not less, while most European nations have become more specialized on a sector-by-sector basis.

The chapter presented two main theories that could account for these facts. The first – the comparative advantage framework – explains why nations have become more specialized while at the same time income differences have narrowed. The second – based on the so-called new economic geography – focuses on agglomeration forces that account for the way in which tighter economic integration can foster the clustering of economic activities within nations.

The chapter also presented the main outlines of the EU's regional policy. The goal of this policy is to help to disperse economic activity to less-favoured regions. Most of the money is spent on so-called convergence regions that typically have per-capita incomes that are less than 75 per cent of the EU average. The EU spends about a third of its budget on these policies.

Self-assessment questions

1 Draw a diagram with the extensions to the agglomeration diagram suggested in Box 10.2.

2 Download the European Commission's proposal for reforming structural spending and compare them to the principles of the system in place up to the end of 2006.

3 The educational level in all EU nations is rising. How would this affect the spatial allocation of production in the Heckscher–Ohlin framework?

Essay questions

1 EU regional policy was reformed in the context of 'Agenda 2000'. What were the major reform themes and how successfully were they implemented?

2 When the ten newcomers joined, some Objective 1 regions became 'statistically' rich. That is, the lowering of the EU average pushed their incomes above the 75 per cent threshold for Objective 1 status. Referring to the two theoretical frameworks discussed in the chapter, do you think it is correct for the EU to remove their Objective 1 status?

3 Many of the ten newcomer members are both very agrarian and very poor. Some of them have agricultural land that is well suited to the production of the products that the CAP supports most. How do you think these nations will vote when the new long-term budget plan is drawn up for the post-enlargement period? (Hint: Think about special-interest group politics and the position of farmers in the political life of the newcomer countries.)

4 Using the theory of fiscal federalism presented in Chapter 2, can you argue that regional policy should be set at the EU level?

Further reading: the aficionado's corner

For a more extensive discussion of the facts concerning changes in the location of economic activity in the EU, see:

Brülhart, M. and R. Traeger (2003) *An Account of Geographic Concentration Patterns in Europe,* Cahiers de Recherches Economiques du Département d'Econométrie et d'Economie Politique (DEEP), Université de Lausanne. Download from www.hec.unil.ch/deep/publications-english/e-cahiers.htm.

Each year, the Commission produces a report on 'cohesion' in the EU. This contains a large number of maps showing things such as unemployment, declining population, share of the economy in agriculture, industry and services. It also presents a large number of indicators of social cohesion, such as youth unemployment and income distribution. See:

European Commission (1996) *European Cohesion Report,* so-called First Cohesion Report; see http://europa.eu.int/comm/regional_policy/sources/docoffic/official/repor_en.htm.

European Commission (2001) Second Report on Economic and Social Cohesion.

European Commission (2003) *Communication from the Commission: Second Progress Report on Economic and Social Cohesion,* COM(2003) 34 final. Download from http://europa.eu.int/scadplus/leg/en/lvb/g24004.htm.

For an advanced treatment of the new economic geography, see part I of:

Baldwin, R., R. Forslid, P. Martin, G. Ottaviano and F. Robert-Nicoud (2003) *Economic Geography and Public Policy,* Princeton University Press, Princeton, NJ. This is freely downloadable from http://heiwww.unige.ch/~baldwin/.

Useful websites

The webpage www.europarl.eu.int factsheets provide a wealth of information on EU regional policy.

The Commission department devoted to regional policy (DG Regio) has an extensive website that provides masses of data and several highly readable explanations of EU policy in the area. There is also a very handy facility to display regional data on maps.

References

Combes, P.-P. and H.G. Overman (2004) 'The spatial distribution of economic activities in the European Union', in J.V. Henderson and J.-F. Thisse (eds) *Handbook of Regional and Urban Economics*, Volume 4: *Cities and Geography*, Elsevier, Oxford.

Midelfart-Knarvik, K.-H. and H.G. Overman (2002) 'Delocation and European integration: Is structural spending justified?', *Economic Policy*, 17 (35): 321–59.

Overman, H. and D. Puga (2001) 'Regional unemployment clusters: nearness matters within and across Europe's national borders', *Economic Policy*, 17(34): 115–47.

Redding, S., H.G. Overman and A. Venables (2001) *The Economic Geography of Trade, Production and Income: A Survey of Empirics*, CEPR Discussion Paper, London.

Chapter 11

EU competition and state aid policy

Competitive markets make our companies more innovative, more productive and more cost effective, and at the same time deliver lower prices, better quality, new products and greater choice for our citizens. Competitive markets require a strong competition policy, rigorously enforced, and the EU's state aid rules are an intrinsic part of this.

Neelie Kroes, 28 October 2008

Chapter Contents

Introduction

Deeper European economic integration – together with more general trends such as WTO trade liberalization and globalization – has put European manufacturing and service sector firms under a great deal of pressure. As discussed in Chapter 6, the long-run outcome of this heightened competitive pressure is typically a reshaped industry marked by fewer, bigger, more efficient firms engaged in more effective competition among themselves. However, in the short and medium run firms may be tempted to collude in order to avoid or postpone industrial restructuring, and Member State governments may be tempted to provide subsidies that delay the necessary but painful restructuring.

The founders of the European Union understood that pressures to collude and subsidize would arise in the course of economic integration. They also understood that anticipation of such unfair practices could reduce political support for economic integration in all nations; an 'I will not liberalize since the others are not playing fair' feeling could halt all deeper integration, especially in the sectors where it is most critical, i.e. those marked by important scale economies and imperfect competition.

To guard against these pressures, they wrote into the Treaty of Rome broad prohibitions on private and public policies that distort competition. Of course, the Treaty of Rome has several provisions that have not been followed seriously, and the founders understood that this is frequently the fate of many provisions in many treaties. Yet, the Treaty writers felt that enforcing fair play in the internal market was so important that EU competition policy required special institutional arrangements – arrangements that would ensure that political expediency would not hinder the maintenance of a level playing field.

To this end, the Treaty grants the European Commission the sole power (exclusive competence in EU jargon; see Chapter 2) to regulate the EU's competition policy. The Commission's decisions can be overturned by the EU Court but they are not subject to approval by the Council (i.e. what was called the Council of Ministers before the Lisbon Treaty) or the European Parliament. Of course, the Commission is not a 'Lone Ranger' in such matters. It continuously consults with Member States, especially via their respective competition authorities, but the Commission has the final word on whether mergers are allowed, whether particular business practices are allowed, and whether aid provided by Member States to firms is allowed. We can say that competition policy is one area where the Member States have truly transferred substantial sovereignty to a supranational level. The Lisbon Treaty confirmed the special position of competition policy and the control of state aids.

This chapter opens by providing an introduction to the economics of anti-competitive practices by private firms and subsidies by governments. It then proceeds to discuss the EU's actual policies.

11.1 The economics of anti-competitive behaviour and state aid

Before turning to how the European Commission regulates competition and state aid, it is important to understand the economics that lead private firms to engage in anti-competitive behaviour and what the effects of this are on the broader economy. This is the task we turn to first. Here, we study basic issues using the framework introduced in Chapter 6. The discussion here assumes readers have mastered the *BE–COMP* diagram, which is explained at length in Chapter 6.

11.1.1 Allowing collusion in the *BE–COMP* framework

As the EU's Single Market gets less fragmented, firms experience greater competition and this forces them to restructure in a way that lowers their costs. Frequently, such adjustments involve waves of mergers and acquisitions. An alternative, however, is for the firms to collude in order to avoid or postpone industrial restructuring. Or, to put it more directly, in many sectors firms face the choice between perishing and engaging in anti-competitive behaviour; some firms choose the latter.

Examples of cartels

In April 2011, the Commission fined Procter & Gamble and Unilever €300 million for operating a cartel together with Henkel in the market for household laundry powder detergents in eight EU countries. Henkel was implicated in the cartel, but got immunity for revealing the cartel to the Commission (this is one of the Commission's most powerful tools in getting 'convictions'). The companies ran the cartel for three years with the goal of 'stabilizing' market positions and coordinating prices.

In December 2010, the Commission fined six LCD panel producers €650 million for operating a cartel. The convicted companies were Samsung Electronics and LG (from Korea), AU Optronics, Chimei InnoLux Corporation, Chunghwa Picture Tubes, and HannStar Display Corporation (from Taiwan). Samsung received full immunity in exchange for information that allowed the Commission to convict the others.

Interested readers can find the latest convictions on the website of DG Competition, http://ec.europa.eu/competition/cartels/cases/cases.html.

Theory

While price-fixing reactions by firms under competitive pressure may be understandable, it is illegal under EU law and economically harmful for Europe as a whole. In a nutshell, allowing collusion among firms can result in too many, too small firms who must charge high prices to compensate for their lack of efficiency. The high prices result in lower demand and production. Thus protecting existing firms can end up reducing the overall level of industrial production.

One very clear real-world example was seen in telecoms services. Before liberalization, each European nation had its own monopoly provider, services were expensive since firms were small and as a result consumers did not spend much on telecoms. Since liberalization, competition has forced a massive industrial restructuring, a massive increase in the size of firms and a massive reduction in the price of services. The result has been a boom in the amount of telecoms services produced and consumed in Europe.

We illustrate this general point with an extended version of the *BE–COMP* framework from Chapter 6.

The BE–COMP diagram

Reviewing it briefly, the *BE–COMP* diagram, shown in Fig. 11.1, has three panels:

1 The middle panel shows the demand curve facing the sector in a typical nation (the diagram assumes that there are two identical nations; the middle panel shows the demand curve for one of them, the Home market). This panel is used for keeping track of consumer surplus and the connection between price and industry-wide production (which must equal consumption). For example, in the closed-economy case, the long-run price is P'. This means that total consumption must equal C'. This in turn means that total production must be C'.

2 The left-hand panel shows the average and marginal cost curves for a typical firm (all firms are identical). The diagram assumes that firms enter or exit until all pure profit is eliminated, i.e. until price equals average cost. This panel is used to keep track of the typical firm's size, x, and its efficiency, as measured by its average cost (lower average cost means higher efficiency). The long-run equilibrium firm size is deduced from the long-run equilibrium price since we know that pure profits are zero in the long run, so the long-run price must equal the average cost of the typical firm. The average cost curve, AC, thus tells us how large the typical firm must be to have an average cost equal to the long-run equilibrium price. For example, if the long-run price is P', the typical firm size must be x' to ensure that price equals average cost.

3 The right-hand panel shows two equilibrium relationships between the mark-up and the number of firms. Recall that the mark-up is price minus marginal cost and that we denote it with the Greek letter 'mu', i.e. μ. The number of firms is denoted n. The $COMP$ curve shows the equilibrium combinations of μ and n assuming normal competition; as expected, more firms corresponds to more competition and thus a lower mark-up. The BE (break-even) curve is upward sloped since, as the number of firms rises, the sales per firm fall and so firms would need a higher mark-up in order to cover their fixed costs.

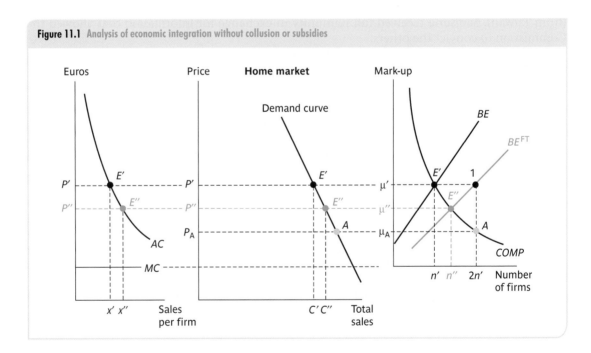

Figure 11.1 Analysis of economic integration without collusion or subsidies

The equilibrium in the three panels identifies the equilibrium number of firms, n, mark-up, μ, price, P, firm size, x, and total output/consumption, C.

As in Chapter 6, we model European integration as a no-trade-to-free-trade liberalization between two identical nations. The equilibrium with no trade is marked by E'; the one with free trade between the two identical nations is marked E''.

There are two immediate and very obvious effects from the no-trade-to-free-trade liberalization:

1 Market size: post-integration, each firm has access to a second market of the same size.

2 Degree of competition: post-integration, each firm faces twice the number of competitors.

The market-size effect shifts the *BE* curve to the right, specifically out to the point marked '1' (see Chapter 6 for a detailed explanation). The competition aspect is the simplest to illustrate in the diagram, Fig. 11.1. Immediately upon opening the markets, i.e. before the industry has had time to adjust, the number of firms is $2n'$. Thus the typical firm will lower its mark-up in each market to point A – assuming, of course, that firms do not collude (recall that the *COMP* curve shows the mark-up under normal competition).

The extra competition forces mark-ups down to point A, and this pushes prices down to P_A. At this combination of sales per firm and mark-up, all firms begin to lose money (i.e. A is below the relevant break-even line, BE^{FT}). This 'profit pressure' forces industrial reorganization (mergers, acquisitions and bankruptcies) that gradually reduces the number of firms to the new long-run equilibrium number, n''. Note that after this long-run 'industry shake-out', firms are bigger and more efficient (the left-hand panel shows that x has increased to x'' and average cost has decreased to P''); they are also facing more effective competition than before the liberalization (the right-hand panel shows that the price–cost margins drop to μ'').

To summarize in words, deeper European integration boosts the degree of competition and this in turn requires the industry to consolidate so as to better exploit scale economies. Naturally, this consolidation involves the exit of some firms. The classic examples are telecoms, airlines, banking and autos where market integration has resulted in a wave of mergers.

The key point as far as competition policy is concerned is that deeper European integration will generally be accompanied by a long-run reduction in the number of firms. This is important for two reasons:

- First, it means that Europe must be even more vigilant to ensure that the fewer bigger firms do not collude.

- Second, it means that firms may be tempted to engage in anti-competitive practices in order to avoid or delay the industrial restructuring.

We turn now to showing what anti-competitive practices look like in the *BE–COMP* diagram. Box 11.1 provides a real example of how four firms conspired to raise the price of beer in the Netherlands.

Box 11.1   Collusion in the Dutch beer market

The Commission convicted four brewers of running a cartel in the Netherlands (the Heineken group, Grolsch, Bavaria, and the InBev group). Beer is big business for the Dutch; yearly consumption is something like 80 litres per inhabitant! The four brewers involved sold a total of around €1 billion annually, and had a combined market share of over 90 per cent. The collusion was quite formally coordinated. According to the Commission's investigation, between 1996 and 1999 the four brewers held numerous unofficial meetings, during which they coordinated prices and price increases of beer. All this was successfully hidden from the authorities; however, a break came when the Commission uncovered a cartel on the Belgian beer market. One of the players in that case – InBev – gave evidence to the Commission in order to reduce its fine. This is a tactic – the so-called leniency policy – that the Commission uses with great effect as it essentially faces the cartel members with a Prisoners' Dilemma. After the tip-off from InBev, the Commission raided ('surprise inspection') brewers in France, Luxembourg, Italy and the Netherlands.

The raids collected handwritten notes taken at unofficial meetings and proof of the dates and places when these meetings, called 'agenda meetings', 'Catherijne meetings' or 'sliding scale meetings' took place. These coordinated prices, and price hikes at pubs as well as store sales. The Commission also found evidence that board members, the managing director and national sales managers actually participated in these meetings. Moreover, evidence was gathered that showed that the companies were well aware that what they were doing was illegal. Indeed, they employed cloak-and-dagger techniques to avoid detection (code names, abbreviations, etc. as well as holding the meetings in various hotels and restaurants). One wonders whether they brought their own beer to avoid the high prices!

In the words of then Competition Commissioner Neelie Kroes (the Commissioner who over saw an historic expansion in the effectiveness of the EU's competition policy): 'It is unacceptable that the major beer suppliers colluded to hike up prices and carve up the market between themselves.' The companies were fined a total of about €270 million. InBev got off without a fine.

Perfect collusion

The *COMP* curve in Fig. 11.1 assumes that firms do not collude. Both before and after the integration, we assumed that firms engaged in 'normal' competition in the sense that each firm decided on how much to sell, taking as given other firms' sales. In other words, each firm decided its output without any coordination among firms.

This assumption of 'normal' competition is quite reasonable for many industries, but it is not the most profitable behaviour for firms. If firms were allowed to collude, they could raise profits by reducing the amount they sell and raising prices. We consider some real-world examples in the policy section below (Section 11.2), but interested readers may wish to go to ec.europa.eu/comm/competition/cartels/cases/cases.cfm for details on the latest cases where the European Commission has caught firms colluding.

There are many, many forms of collusion in the world. The first form of collusion we consider is the simplest form to study. Instead of assuming no collusion on output, we consider the extreme opposite of perfect collusion on output.

If all firms could perfectly coordinate their sales, i.e. if they could act as if they were a single firm, they would limit total sales to the monopoly level. This would allow them to charge the monopoly price and to earn the greatest possible profit from the market. After all, the monopoly price–sales combination is – by definition – the combination that extracts the greatest profit from the market. In the diagram, this is shown by the mark-up, μ^m, that corresponds to one firm ($n = 1$). The resulting price is the monopoly price, shown as P^m.

The hard part of collusion is finding a way to divide up the monopoly level of sales among the colluding firms. The problem is that, because the price is so much higher than marginal cost, each firm would like to sell a little more than its share. To keep things simple, we assume that the firms manage the collusion by allocating an equal share to all firms. This type of behaviour can be illustrated in the *BE–COMP* diagram with the 'perfect collusion' line shown in Fig. 11.2. This line extends horizontally since it assumes that the mark-up always equals the monopoly mark-up, μ^m, regardless of the number of firms.

If all firms did charge the monopoly mark-up, then the maximum number of firms that could break even is shown by the point '2'. This would involve new entry – an outcome that we rarely observed after liberalization. Another possibility is that all $2n''$ firms would stay in business, without any new firms entering; this is shown as the point A'. Note that, at this point, all firms are making pure profits owing to the collusion (since E^m is above the AC curve in the left-hand panel and it is above the BE^{FT} curve in the right-hand panel).

Figure 11.2 Perfect collusion

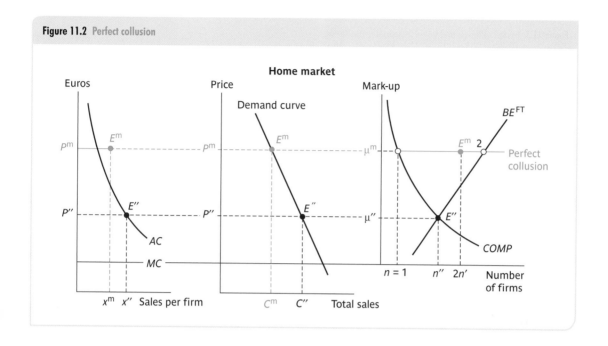

This collusion is good for firms' profits, but it is bad for society as a whole. Comparing the perfect collusion outcome to the long-run outcome without collusion (equilibrium marked with E'), we see that the price is higher, and consumption and production are lower. Moreover, since firms are smaller (since overall production is lower with collusion, the output of each firm must be smaller), average costs are higher, so the industry is less efficient.

Partial collusion

Perfect collusion is difficult to maintain since the gains from 'cheating' on other colluders are quite high. To reduce the incentive to cheat, the actual degree of collusion may be milder than perfect collusion. This sort of partial collusion restricts sales of all firms but not all the way back to the monopoly level, so the mark-up is lower than the monopoly mark-up but higher than the *COMP* mark-up. With the mark-up lower, it is easier to sustain the collusion since the benefits from cheating are not quite as large.

But how much lower would the mark-up be under partial collusion? As it turns out, an understanding of advanced economics is needed to formalize this notion of 'partial collusion', so we do not address it here explicitly (see Mas-Colell et al., 1995, for an advanced treatment). Fortunately, the basic idea can be easily depicted in Fig. 11.3.

The curve labelled 'partial collusion' shows a level of collusion where the mark-up is somewhere between the monopoly mark-up and the no-collusion mark-up shown by the *COMP* curve. We do not specify exactly where it lies between the two as it does not change the qualitative analysis. All we need to assume is that the partial collusion curve lies between the *COMP* curve and the perfect collusion curve as shown in the diagram.

If the $2n'$ firms all engaged in this partial collusion, then the mark-up would be shown by the point A''. This mark-up is higher than the long-run equilibrium mark-up without collusion (μ''), so we see that this partial collusion offsets, to some extent, the increase in competition induced by integration. (Recall from Chapter 6 that the size of the mark-up is an indicator of the degree of competition.)

Figure 11.3 Partial collusion and failed industrial restructuring

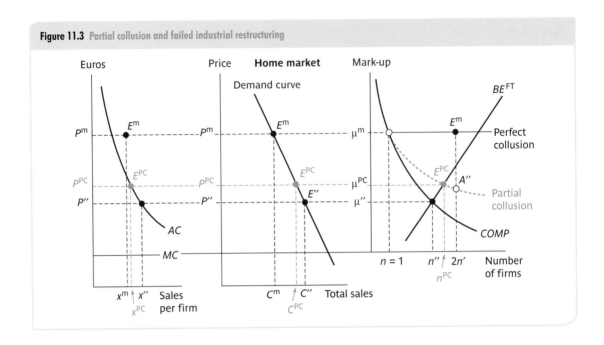

Note, however, that although this mark-up is higher than under normal competition, it is not high enough for all the firms to break even. We can see this from the fact that point A'' is below the break-even curve (BE^{FT}). What this means is that even with partial collusion, some firms will exit the market. In the long run, the number of firms adjusts to restore zero pure profits, and this is where the partial competition curve and the break-even curve intersect, namely point E^{PC}.

Point E^{PC} is the long-run equilibrium since with n^{PC} firms the mark-up would be μ^{PC} and, with this mark-up, n^{PC} firms would all break even. As before, we can read off all the important aspects from the diagram. The level of consumption in the Home market (which is half of total consumption since Foreign is assumed to be identical) is C^{PC}. Since supply equals demand in equilibrium, we know that C^{PC} is also the total production in each nation. As usual, the equilibrium price also tells us the equilibrium efficiency, i.e. the typical firm's average cost. Using the average cost curve, we also know that the size of the typical firm is x^{PC}.

Now we study the economic implications of such collusion, comparing it to the long-run equilibrium with normal competition, i.e. equilibrium E''. To summarize the price and quantity changes, we note that, compared to the normal competition equilibrium, the partial collusion equilibrium involves firms that are smaller, less efficient and more numerous. The mark-up is higher along with the price, so consumption and total production are lower.

Long-run economic costs of collusion

The first point is that collusion will not in the end raise firms' profits to above-normal levels. Even allowing for the way that partial collusion raises prices above P'', the initial number of firms after liberalization, namely $2n'$, is too high for all of them to break even. Industrial consolidation proceeds as usual, but instead of the zero-profit level being reached when the number of firms has dropped to n'', the process halts at n^{PC}. As noted above, this is where pure profits – which started at zero in the pre-integration long-run equilibrium described in Fig. 11.1 – are returned to zero. In other words, the higher prices do not result in higher long-run profits. They merely allow more small, inefficient firms to remain in the market. The welfare cost of the collusion is measured by the four-sided area marked by P^{pc}, P'', E'' and B. This is just the consumer surplus loss, but since there is no change in pure profits (it is zero in the long run with or without collusion), the change in consumer surplus is the full welfare effect.

To summarize, collusion prevents the full benefits of restructuring from occurring. By keeping too many firms in the market, anti-competitive behaviour thwarts part of the industry's adjustment that is the key to the gains from integration.

Having presented a general analysis that suggests why deeper European integration and competition problems tend to go hand in hand, we turn now to considering four types of anti-competitive practices in more detail. We start with cartels.

11.1.2 Anti-competitive behaviour

Firms like to make money. Competition hinders this, so some firms try to limit competition. One age-old way of doing this is to form a cartel with other firms in the industry. For example, one of the best-known cartels, the Organization of the Petroleum Exporting Countries (OPEC), has been controlling the international price of crude oil since the early 1970s.

Horizontal anti-competitive practices: cartels and exclusive territories

The classic example of a cartel in Europe is the vitamins cartel (see Box 11.2). As Fig. 11.4 shows, the economic effects of cartels are rather straightforward (see Chapter 4 if you need a refresher on this sort of economics). The diagram depicts the impact of the price-raising effects of a cartel.

The diagram shows the situation for a particular market, say DRAM, where the price without the cartel would be P. This initial price is shown as being equal to average costs (AC), which indicates zero profits even before the cartel; the analysis follows through even if the initial price

---

Box 11.2   The DRAM cartel

Memory chips are a key component is almost every bit of modern electronics – especially Dynamic Random Access Memory, or DRAM. They are used as the main memory for loading, displaying and manipulating applications and data and as such are critical to personal computers, servers and workstations.

The production of DRAMs is extremely capital intensive (the cost of plants runs into the billions), but the marginal cost of each chip is very low. This combination makes collusion especially tempting and the small number of producers globally makes it feasible.

In May 2010, the Commission decided that ten DRAM producers were running a cartel and fined them over €331 million. All the convicted companies but one are non-European (Infineon is German), but the case was based on their European sales. The convicted companies were Micron, Samsung, Hynix, Infineon, NEC, Hitachi, Mitsubishi, Toshiba, Elpida and Nanya, but Micron paid no fine as it testified against the others.

The companies ran the cartel between 1998 and 2002 via a network of contacts and the sharing of secret information bilaterally. Specifically, they had regular contacts where the companies secretly exchanged information on pricing intentions and general pricing strategy. They also swapped commercially sensitive data to identify specific contract customers. In this way, they shared, verified, and monitored prices charged to major electronics manufacturers. The companies used the secret information to set their own price quotes.

Source: This box is based on information from DG Competition's website http://ec.europa.eu/competition/cartels/cases/cases.html

Figure 11.4 Economic analysis of cartels

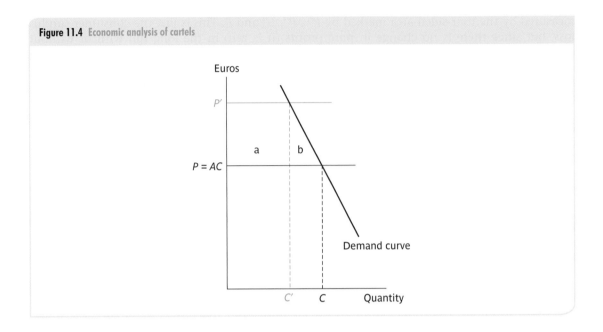

were above *AC*, but this way makes it easier to see the effects. When the cartel raises the price to *P'* by reducing the volume of sales to *C'*, consumer surplus is reduced by the areas 'a' plus 'b'. The cartel's profit rises by the area 'b'.

This analysis illustrates the two main problems with cartels: the rip-off effect and the inefficiency effect.

First, the fact that they allow firms to profit at the expense of customers is considered by most people (and by EU law) to be unfair – a rip-off to put it colloquially. Second, the gain to firms is less than the loss to consumers, so the cartel is inefficient from a purely technical point of view. Specifically, the net economic loss is the area 'b'. While few Europeans know or care about the efficiency loss, almost all would find that the rip-off effect was something their governments should do something about.

Another rather common way of restricting competition is for firms to agree upon so-called exclusive territories. For example, one company would agree to sell only in its local market in exchange for a similar promise by its foreign competitors. One example of this can be found in the market for video games.

Nintendo and seven of its official distributors in Europe teamed up in the 1990s to boost profits by dividing up Europe's markets and charging higher prices where consumers had a higher ability to pay. Under this practice, distributors had to prevent games being shipped from their territory to that of another EU market where prices were higher. Independent customers who allowed such sales among territories were punished by being given smaller shipments next time or by being cut off altogether. In this way, these companies managed to maintain big price differences for play consoles and games in various EU markets (e.g. Britons enjoyed prices that were 65 per cent cheaper than those faced by the Germans and Dutch). The European Commission fined Nintendo and the seven distributors €168 million.

Thinking more broadly, it is clear that such practices offset all the goals of European integration, which is exactly why the Treaty of Rome prohibited such behaviour.

Figure 11.5 shows a situation where a firm would like to charge a different price in the German and UK markets.

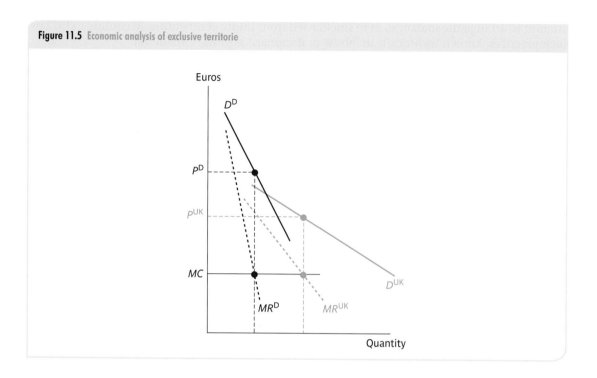

Figure 11.5 Economic analysis of exclusive territorie

The diagram shows the two demand curves; the German demand curve D^D is steeper than the British demand curve D^{UK}. The steepness of a demand curve reflects a 'willingness to pay' since it tells us how much consumption of Nintendo products would drop for a given price increase. The German curve is drawn as steeper to reflect the fact that Germans have fewer options when it comes to consumer electronics and games (owing to the smaller number of people who speak German versus English worldwide, and to widespread restrictions on retail outlets in Germany). In economics jargon, German demand is more inelastic, i.e. more unresponsive to price. In this situation, Nintendo would maximize profits by selling the quantities in Germany and Britain that correspond to the intersections of the marginal revenue curves (MR^D and MR^{UK}) and marginal cost curves (MC); see Chapter 6 if this reasoning is unfamiliar. The quantities are not shown explicitly, but the resulting prices are marked as P^D and P^{UK}.

In an integrated market, independent firms, often called 'traders', could arbitrage the price gap by buying Nintendo goods in the UK and shipping them to Germany. Such shipments – which are known as 'parallel trade' – would lower Nintendo's profits and that of its official distributors. To preserve their profits, Nintendo and its distributors attempted, illegally, to prevent such trade.

Bullies in the market: abuse of dominant position

Business leaders and stock markets often evaluate a company's performance based on the growth of its market share, so many firms aim to conquer the market. Firms that are lucky or possess excellent products can succeed in establishing very strong positions in their market. This is not a problem if the position reflects superior products and/or efficiency – Google's triumph in the market for search engines could be one example. However, once a firm has a dominant position, it may be tempted to use it to extract extra profits from its suppliers or customers, or it may attempt to arrange the market so as to shield itself from future competitors. According to EU law, such practices, known technically as 'abuse of dominant position', are illegal.

The classic example of this is Microsoft. Most computer users are happy that Microsoft has standardized the basics of personal computing around the world – especially those that move between nations or use more than one machine on a regular basis. In other words, computer operating systems are subject to network externalities. That is, computer operating system software becomes more valuable to each user as more people use it.

To understand how and why network externalities work, just think about why the English language has spread so widely and continues to do so; more and more people learn it since so many people speak it. Just as with English, industries characterized by network externalities tend to be marked by a dominant firm, or a handful of firms.

In the case of Microsoft, which has dominated the operating system software market for decades, the question is how it came to dominate applications with products such as Word and Excel. Although it has never been proved in court, many observers believe that the company used frequent updates of its operating system to induce users to drop competing applications (as recently as ten years ago, Microsoft had real competition from rival products such as WordPerfect and Lotus). The details of Windows updates are available to engineers updating Microsoft applications but not to those updating rival applications, so new versions of rival applications often had glitches caused by incompatibilities with the latest version of Windows. Even if a user preferred the other applications, incompatibilities with successive versions of DOS and Windows meant it was easier to switch to Microsoft's applications than it was to deal with the glitches. Moreover, when competing firms came up with innovative programs, Microsoft typically responded with similar programs and gave them away for free. Today, for example, Microsoft charges a high price for Word, where it no longer has any real competitors, but it charges a zero price on software where it has significant rivals, such as media readers and web browsers. See Box 11.3 for details.

Box 11.3   The Microsoft case

The case against Microsoft was triggered by one of its competitors, Sun Microsystems, asserting that Microsoft refused to supply information that it needed to make its products work with Microsoft's PC operating system. Since Microsoft dominated the market, Sun could not really do business without the information, so the denial of information was a possible abuse of Microsoft's dominant position. During its investigation, the Commission found evidence of additional illegal behaviour by Microsoft and it broadened the scope of the investigation to include Microsoft's conduct with regard to its Windows Media Player product. In particular, it seemed that Microsoft was using its dominant position in the operating system market to push out rivals that had developed innovative products for playing various forms of audio and video files.

The investigation dragged on for years and, during this time, Microsoft engaged in additional practices that the Commission suspected. Finally, the Commission concluded its investigation on 24 March 2004 and issued a decision. As Chapter 2 points out, these are EU rulings that have direct effect in all Member States. The decision found that Microsoft had abused its dominant position in the PC operating system market in two ways: (1) by refusing to supply competitors with the information they needed to compete with Microsoft products – the decision ordered Microsoft to make that information available on reasonable terms, and (2) harming competition through the tying of its separate Windows Media Player product to its Windows PC operating system. The decision ordered Microsoft to provide a version of Windows without Windows Media Player. The European Commission also fined Microsoft €497 million at the time.

The problems did not stop there, however. The Commission decided in December 2005 that Microsoft was failing to comply with the ruling by not releasing information in a way and at a price that fostered competition. The Commission decided to fine Microsoft more than a million euros a day until the company complied.

The daily fine was levied in July 2006, at €1.5 million per day (16 December 2005 to 20 June 2006) for a total of €280 million. The Commission also threatened to increase the fine to €3 million a day from July 2006, if Microsoft did not comply by then. EU Competition Commissioner Neelie Kroes said, 'I regret that, more than two years after the decision . . . Microsoft has still not put an end to its illegal conduct.' Predictably, Microsoft appealed. In September 2007, it lost the appeal against the European Commission's case and was forced to pay most of the Commission's court costs.

Despite all this, Microsoft continued in its non-compliance and the Commission imposed an €899 million fine in February 2008. This was for non-compliance between 21 June 2006 and 21 October 2007, the date that the Commission determined Microsoft to be in compliance with its 2004 ruling.

Although the total fine amounted to €1.7 billion since 2004, that is only about two weeks' worth of the company's cash flow. For example, Microsoft posted a record profit of $4.7 billion in the second quarter of 2008. Moreover, Microsoft has a long history of paying antitrust fines, e.g. $750 million to AOL/Time-Warner in 2003, $1.1 billion to California in 2003, $536 million to Novell in 2004, $1.6 billion to Sun in 2004, $775 million to IBM in 2005, $776 million to Real Networks in 2005.

In January 2008 the Commission launched fresh investigations into Microsoft's behaviour in the market for its Office software and its Internet Explorer. Finally in 2010, Microsoft gave in and agreed to remove barriers to consumer choice in browsers. From March 2010, all Windows users are able to choose which web browser they want to use on their computer by means of a browser Choice Screen; the 12 most popular web browsers are included (e.g. Mozilla Firefox, Google Chrome, Apple Safari and Opera).

11.1.3 Merger control

In many European industries, the number of firms is falling as firms merge or buy each other out. This sort of concentration of market power is a natural outcome of European integration, as Fig. 11.1 showed, but it may also produce cartel-like conditions. The basic trade-off can be illustrated with the so-called Williamson diagram in Fig. 11.6.

Consider a merger that allows the merged firms to charge a higher price, but which also allows them to lower average cost by eliminating redundant capacities in marketing, accounting, sales representatives, etc. The price rise is shown in the diagram by the increase in price from P to P' (the diagram assumes that the market was in long-run equilibrium with $P = AC$ to start with). The efficiency gain is shown by the drop in average cost from AC to AC'. The gain to the firm's profitability is strongly positive. Before, $P = AC$ meant there were no profits. After, profits are the areas 'a' plus 'c'. The merger is bad for consumers, since the price hike implies a loss of

Figure 11.6 Basic economics of mergers: market power vs. efficiency gains

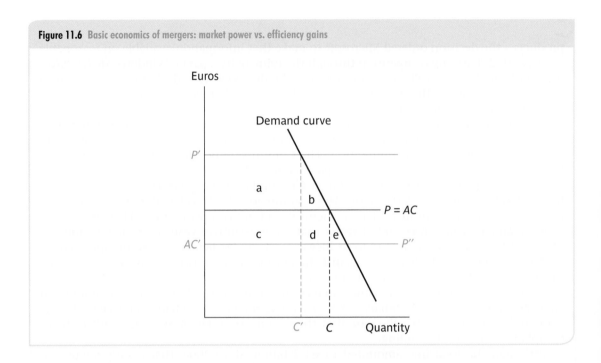

consumer surplus equal to the area a + b. The overall gain to society, taking profits and consumer surplus together, is the area 'c' minus the area 'b' since area 'a' is just a transfer from consumers to firms.

There is a point here that is important for understanding the EU's new rules on mergers. Notice that if entry and exit in the industry are unrestricted, and the remaining firms do not collude, then the long-run outcome of this merger will be to drive the price down to the lower average costs, $P'' = AC'$. This is essentially what happens when the equilibrium shifts from E' to E'' in Fig. 11.1. In this case, the merger-with-efficiency gain is always positive and equal to area c + d + e since the consumer surplus gain from the lower long-run price, P'', is not offset by any loss of producer surplus; profits were zero to start with ($P' = AC'$) and to end with ($P'' = AC'$). Since entry and exit in most EU industries are fairly unrestricted, there is a presumption that mergers will generally be of the type that boosts efficiency and passes on this efficiency to consumers.

Note that our treatment of competition here is highly simplified. The impact of mergers on pricing and costs can be extremely complicated and highly dependent on the nature of the industry. Examples of such reasoning can be found in the Commission's analysis of actual merger cases on their website: europa.int.eu/comp/.

11.1.4 State aid

The Fig. 11.1 logic linking integration and industrial restructuring presumes that profit-losing firms would eventually leave the industry – that they would be bought out by another firm, merged with other firms or, in rare cases, go bankrupt. All three of these exit strategies may involve important job losses in specific locations, or at the very least an important reorganization that may require workers to change jobs. Since job losses and relocations are painful, governments frequently seek to prevent them. For example, if the firm is government owned, trade unions may force the government to continue to shore up the money-losing enterprise. If it is privately owned, the government may provide subsidies through direct grants or through long-term loans that may not be repaid.

What we want to do here is to look at the long-run economics of such subsidies – called 'state aid' in EU jargon – under two distinct scenarios. The first is where all governments provide such support. The second is where only one does.

EU-wide subsidies: thwarting the main source of gains

Start by supposing that both governments provide subsidies that prevent restructuring. To be concrete, we make the additional, more specific assumption that governments make annual payments to all firms exactly equal to their losses. Under this policy, all $2n'$ firms in the Fig. 11.1 analysis will stay in business, but, since firms are not making extraordinary profits, no new firms will enter. The economy, in short, remains at point A owing to the anti-restructuring subsidies.

An insightful way to think about this subsidy policy is as a swap in who pays for the inefficiently small firms. Before integration, prices were high, so consumers paid for the inefficiency. After liberalization, competition drives down the price but this comes at the cost of extra pay-outs from the national treasuries, so now the taxpayers bear the burden of the industry's inefficiency. Moreover, since all the firms stay in business, integration is prevented from curing the main problem, i.e. the too-many-too-small firms problem. Firms continue to be inefficient since they continue to operate at a too small a scale. As a consequence, the subsidies prevent the overall improvement in industry efficiency that was the source of most of the gains discussed in Chapter 6.

Do nations gain from this liberalize-and-subsidize scheme? As it turns out, both nations do gain overall, even counting the cost of the subsidies. We shall show this with a diagram, but before turning to the detailed reasoning, it is instructive to explain the deep reason for this result. Imperfect competition is inefficient since it leads prices to exceed marginal costs. Recalling from Chapter 4 that the consumer price is a measure of marginal utility, the fact that price exceeds marginal cost implies that the gain to consumers from an extra unit would exceed the resource cost of providing the unit. In short, society tends to gain from an expansion of output when price exceeds marginal cost. Because of this, policies that increase output tend to improve welfare. In the jargon of public economics, the subsidy is a 'second-best' policy since it reduces the negative effects of market-power distortion, even if it does not solve the root of the problem.

Note, however, that this reasoning is very partial. This sort of 'reactive' subsidy turns out to be a very bad idea in the long run. The subsidies are paid to prevent firms from adapting to changed circumstances. While the government may occasionally improve things by preventing change, a culture of reactive interventionism typically results in a stagnant economy. Staying competitive requires industries to change – to adapt to new technologies, to new competitors and to new opportunities. When firms get used to the idea that their governments will keep them in business no matter what, the incentive to innovate and adapt is greatly weakened. Firms with this sort of mindset will soon find themselves far behind the international competition.

Welfare effects of the liberalize-and-subsidize policy

To explain the welfare effects of the liberalize-and-subsidize policy, we refer to Fig. 11.7. The policy we consider freezes the economy at point A in the right-hand and middle panels (this point A corresponds exactly to the point A in Fig. 11.1). We know that the price falls from p' to p^A and consumption rises from C' to C^A. Since the number of firms has not changed but total sales in each market (which must equal total consumption in each market) have increased, we know

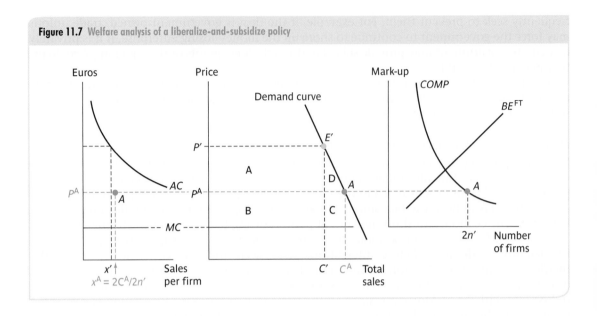

Figure 11.7 Welfare analysis of a liberalize-and-subsidize policy

that the sales of each firm have increased somewhat, as shown in the left-hand panel from x' to x^A. At this point, firms are losing money, but the government offsets this with a subsidy.

How big will the subsidy be? The easiest way to make this comparison is to adopt a roundabout approach. First, consider the total size of operating profit that the whole Home industry needs to cover all fixed cost before the liberalization. The answer is already in the middle panel. Before the liberalization, the industry broke even by selling a total of C' units at the price p'. The operating profit on this was the area A + B in the middle panel of the diagram, i.e. the gap between price and marginal cost times the units sold. After the liberalization, the industry's operating profit is area B + C (the new price–cost gap, $p^A - MC$, times the new sales, C^A). The drop in operating profit is thus area C minus area A. The subsidy we are considering would have to exactly offset the loss, so the subsidy would equal area A – C. With these facts established, we turn to the welfare calculation.

The consumer part of the welfare calculation is simple. Consumers see a lower price so consumer surplus rises by the area +A + D. To see the overall welfare effect, we subtract the subsidy, which equals A – C. The net welfare effect is A + D – (A – C), which equals D + C. We know this is right since this area is the gap between price and marginal cost summed over all the extra units consumed. Notice that this is the classic gain from partially redressing a market power distortion.

Only some subsidize: unfair competition

EU members' governments differ over how much they can or want to subsidize loss-making firms. Yet, when only some governments subsidize their firms, the outcome of the restructuring may be 'unfair' in the sense that it gets forced upon the firms in nations that do not subsidize, or stop subsidizing before the others. The real problem with this is that it may create the impression that European economic integration gives an unfair advantage to some nations' firms.

To examine this problem more closely while keeping the reasoning as tangible and simple as possible, we continue with the Fig. 11.1 example of two nations engaged in an extreme no-trade-to-free-trade integration. The integration moves each identical economy from the point E' to A.

At A, all firms in both nations are losing money. Now suppose that restructuring takes, say, five years in the sense that after that time the number of firms has adjusted from $2n'$ to n''. In our simple example, there is no way of telling which of the surviving firms will be Home firms and which will be Foreign firms. Symmetry suggests that half the remaining firms would be Foreign, but nothing in the example ensures that this is the case. This is where subsidies can make a big difference.

To be concrete, suppose that prior to the liberalization there were ten firms in Home and ten in Foreign, and that after restructuring there will be 12 firms in total. Furthermore, suppose that Home provides a five-year subsidy to all of its ten firms, with the size of the subsidy being large enough to offset the liberalization-induced losses. The Foreign government, by contrast, is assumed to pursue a laissez-faire policy, i.e. it allows the market to decide which firms should survive – either because it believes in the market, or because it cannot afford the subsidies. In this situation, it is clear that eight of the ten Foreign firms will go out of business, while all ten Home firms will survive. At the end of the five-year period, the Home government no longer needs to subsidize its firms since the exit of eight Foreign firms restores the industry to profitability.

From a purely economic perspective, the Foreign nation might have been the winner since having firms in our example brings nothing to national welfare (firms earn zero profit in the best of cases). The Home nation's subsidies were merely a waste of taxpayers' money. Two comments are relevant at this stage. First, this sort of conclusion shows that our simple example is actually too simplistic in many ways. For example, we did not consider the cost of workers having to switch jobs and possibly being unemployed for some time. Second, it shows that economics is only part of the picture.

The politics of state aid disciplines: I'll play only if the rules are fair

From a political perspective, this sort of unfair competition would be intolerable. Indeed, if trade unions and business groups in Foreign anticipated that this would be the outcome, they might very well block the whole integration exercise. To avoid this sort of resistance to liberalization, the EU establishes very strict rules forbidding such unfair competition. In this sense, one of the most important effects of disciplines on state aid is the fact that it allows governments to procede with painful and politically difficult reforms.

11.2 EU competition policy

Having laid out the basic logic of collusion and subsidies, we turn now to considering actual EU policy that constrains such actions by private actors (anti-competitive practices) and governments (subsidies).

11.2.1 Institutions: the European Commission's power

The EU's founders were fully aware that integrating Europe's markets would result in restructuring and that this would produce incentives for private and public actors to resist consolidation. This is very clear, for example, in the 1956 Spaak Report which was the economic blueprint for the Treaty of Rome (*Rapport des chefs de délégation aux ministres des affaires étrangères*, Bruxelles, 21 avril 1956). Moreover, they feared that the perception that some nations might 'cheat' in an effort to shift the burden of consolidation onto others would, in itself, make deeper European integration politically impossible. To ensure that the prevailing attitude was 'I will reform since the rules are fair' instead of 'I cannot reform since other nations will cheat', the Treaty of Rome prohibited any action that prevents, restricts or distorts competition in the common market.

Importantly, the Treaty puts the supranational Commission in charge of enforcing these strictures. Just as European leaders decided to forgo their control over monetary policy (by making central banks independent) since they knew in advance that short-run politics would lead to bad long-run policy, the Treaty of Rome grants a great deal of power on competition policy directly to the European Commission. The idea was that the politicians in the Council of Ministers might not be able to resist the short-run pressure of special-interest groups opposed to the consolidation that is necessary to obtain the long-run gains from European economic integration. In fact, competition policy is probably the area in which the Commission has the greatest unilateral power.

The Commission has considerable powers to investigate suspected abuses of EU competition law, including the right to force companies to hand over documents. Most famously, the Commission has the right to make on-site inspections without prior warning, which the media often call 'dawn raids'. With a court order, the Commission can even inspect the homes of company personnel.

The Commission has the power to prohibit anti-competitive activities. It does this by issuing injunctions against firms. To back up these demands, the Commission has the right to impose fines on firms found guilty of anti-competitive conduct. The fines vary according to the severity of the anti-competitive practices, with a maximum of 10 per cent of the offending firm's worldwide turnover. When it comes to subsidies, the Commission has the power to force firms to repay subsidies it deems to be illicit.

Unlike most other areas where the Commission acts, the Commission's decisions are not subject to approval by the Council of Ministers or the European Parliament. The only recourse is through the European Court. This is an area where Member States truly did pool their sovereignty to ensure a better outcome for all.

11.2.2 EU law on anti-competitive behaviour

EU law on anti-competitive practices was first laid out in the Treaty of Rome (formally, the Treaty establishing the European Community, or TEC for short). These have not been changed since the Treaty of Rome apart from occasional renumbering of the articles (most recently in the Lisbon Treaty). Here we review the main provisions, but it is important to note that this gives only a hint as to actual policy. EU competition policy has been subject to many decisions of the EU Court and one must master the details of these cases in order to fully understand which practices are prohibited and why. Moreover, the Commission publishes its own administrative guidelines so that firms can more easily determine whether a particular agreement they are contemplating will be permitted by the Commission.

Article 101 of the Treaty on the Functioning of the EU, TFEU (as the Treaty of Rome was re-labelled by the Lisbon Treaty) outright forbids practices that prevent, restrict or distort competition, unless the Commission grants an exemption. This article is clearly written and worth reading in its entirety (Box 11.4).

Typically, the restrictions in Article 101 are classified as preventing horizontal or vertical anti-competitive agreements. Horizontal agreements are arrangements, like cartels and exclusive territories, upon competitors selling similar goods. Vertical agreements are arrangements between a firm and its suppliers or distributors (e.g. agreements by retailers to charge not less than a certain price, and tie-in arrangements whereby goods are only supplied if the vendor agrees to purchase other products).

The first part of Article 101 is so categorical that it rules out an enormous range of normal business practices, which can in fact be good for the European economy. The final part therefore allows the Commission to grant exemptions to agreements where the benefits outweigh the anti-competitive effects. The Commission does this for individual agreements notified to the Commission for exemption, but it also has established the policy of 'block exemptions' that grant permission to broad types of agreements. These exist for technology transfer and for R&D

Box 11.4   Article 101 (Article 81 pre-Lisbon; Article 85 in the original TEC)

1 The following shall be prohibited as incompatible with the common market: all agreements between undertakings, decisions by associations of undertakings and concerted practices which may affect trade between Member States and which have as their object or effect the prevention, restriction or distortion of competition within the common market, and in particular those which:

(a) directly or indirectly fix purchase or selling prices or any other trading conditions;

(b) limit or control production, markets, technical development, or investment;

(c) share markets or sources of supply;

(d) apply dissimilar conditions to equivalent transactions with other trading parties, thereby placing them at a competitive disadvantage;

(e) make the conclusion of contracts subject to acceptance by the other parties of supplementary obligations which, by their nature or according to commercial usage, have no connection with the subject of such contracts.

2 Any agreements or decisions prohibited pursuant to this Article shall be automatically void.

3 The provisions of paragraph 1 may, however, be declared inapplicable in the case of:

■ any agreement or category of agreements between undertakings;

■ any decision or category of decisions by associations of undertakings;

■ any concerted practice or category of concerted practices, which contributes to improving the production or distribution of goods or to promoting technical or economic progress, while allowing consumers a fair share of the resulting benefit, and which does not:

(a) impose on the undertakings concerned restrictions which are not indispensable to the attainment of these objectives;

(b) afford such undertakings the possibility of eliminating competition in respect of a substantial part of the products in question.

---

agreements. Political pressure has also forced the Commission to grant a block exemption to the anti-competitive practices in the distribution of motor vehicles.

The second major set of policies – restrictions on the abuse of a dominant position – are found in Article 102 of the TFEU (see Box 11.5). A dominant position usually depends upon a firm's market share. Abuse is a general term but it includes refusal to supply, unfair prices and conditions, predatory pricing, loyalty rebates, exclusive dealing requirements, and abuse of intellectual property rights.

11.2.3 Control of mergers

The EC Treaty does not contain specific provisions on mergers, but since mergers can affect competition the Treaty requires the Commission to oversee merger activity. The Commission realized that the 1992 programme for the completion of the internal market would produce a

---

Box 11.5　Article 102 (formerly Article 82 pre-Lisbon; 86 in original TEC)

Any abuse by one or more undertakings of a dominant position within the common market or in a substantial part of it shall be prohibited as incompatible with the common market insofar as it may affect trade between Member States.

　　Such abuse may, in particular, consist in:

(a) directly or indirectly imposing unfair purchase or selling prices or other unfair trading conditions;

(b) limiting production, markets or technical development to the prejudice of consumers;

(c) applying dissimilar conditions to equivalent transactions with other trading parties, thereby placing them at a competitive disadvantage;

(d) making the conclusion of contracts subject to acceptance by the other parties of supplementary obligations which, by their nature or according to commercial usage, have no connection with the subject of such contracts.

---

flurry of merger activity. To promote transparency and allow firms to better understand whether a particular merger will be allowed, the EU set out explicit rules in Council and Commission Regulations starting in the late 1980s.

　　The current set of regulations are called simply 'Merger Regulation'. This regulation, which reformed a string of earlier regulations to include new thinking and various EU Court decisions, was introduced in January 2004 and entered into force with the Union's enlargement. The Regulation does not stand by itself but rather is one pillar in a merger control edifice that also includes guidelines on the assessment of horizontal mergers and on best practice in merger investigations, and reforms within the Commission. For details see the Commission (2010).

　　The Merger Regulation defines anti-competitive behaviour as: 'A concentration which would significantly impede effective competition, in the common market or in a substantial part of it, in particular by the creation or strengthening of a dominant position, shall be declared incompatible with the common market.' Under the new rules, mergers that meet the relevant criteria do not have to be notified to the Commission since they are presumed to be compatible with competition.

　　The new rules also give a prominent role to national competition authorities and courts, under the so-called European Competition Network which facilitates coordination among EU and national competition authorities and courts. See Box 11.6 for some merger decision examples.

11.2.4 EU policies on state aid

The EU's founders realized that the entire European project would be endangered if EU members felt that other members were taking unfair advantage of the economic integration (see Box 11.7 for an example of unfair competition in the EU energy market). To prevent this, the 1957 Treaty of Rome bans state aid that provides firms with an unfair advantage and thus distorts competition. Importantly, the EU founders considered this prohibition to be so important that they actually empowered the supranational European Commission to be in charge of enforcing the prohibition. Indeed, the Commission has the power to force the repayment of illegal state aid, even though the Commission normally has no say over members' individual tax and spending policies.

> ## Box 11.6   Some merger decision examples
>
> The European pharmaceutical sector has experienced a wave of consolidation and, as part of this, two mega-mergers were brought to the attention of the European Commission, the Sanofi and Synthélabo link-up and the Pfizer and Pharmacia fusion. The Commission determined that both would lessen competition in certain market segments by limiting the choice of some drugs. The Commission, however, recognized the need for efficiency gains and believed that the mergers could be useful. The outcome was that the Commission allowed the mergers subject to conditions. The firms were required to transfer some of their products to their competitors so as to redress potential anti-competitive effects. For example, Sanofi/Synthélabo sold off certain antibiotics, hypnotics and sedatives.
>
> Another case involved a mainly domestic merger between TotalFina and Elf Aquitaine, which were the main players in the French petroleum sector. The Commission determined that their merger would have allowed them to push up costs for independent petrol station operators (e.g. supermarkets) and the combined company would have operated around 60 per cent of the service stations on French motorways. The combined firms would also have been the leading supplier of liquid petroleum gas. The European Commission believed that this level of market power would be anti-competitive and agreed to the merger only on the condition that TotalFina/Elf sell off a large proportion of these operations to competitors. For example, it sold 70 motorway service stations in France to competitors.

The EC Treaty prohibits state aid that distorts competition in the EU. The Treaty defines state aid in very broad terms. It can, for instance, take the form of grants, interest relief, tax relief, state guarantee or holding, or the provision by the state of goods and services on preferential terms.

Some state aid, however, is allowed according to the Treaty since subsidies, when used correctly, are an essential instrument in the toolkit of good governance. The permitted exceptions include

> ## Box 11.7   Subsidies and unfair competition in the energy market
>
> The market for electricity was one of the few markets left largely untouched by the sweeping liberalization of the EU's Single Market Programme between 1986 and 1992. Until the 1990s, the sector was dominated by government-owned or -controlled firms, but as part of the general trend towards market-oriented policies, many EU members privatized their state-owned energy monopolies and opened their markets to foreign competition. These moves, however, were not part of a coordinated EU strategy. The resulting difficulties provide an excellent illustration of how important the EU's anti-state-aid policy is to keeping European economic integration on track.
>
> As with much of European industry, the energy sector was and still is marked by too many firms which are too small to be truly competitive. As in many other sectors, a process of consolidation and industrial restructuring has begun. Unlike other EU sectors, however, liberalization varies greatly across Member States. France is one of the most closed markets

in two senses. It is difficult for foreign firms to supply French customers and the French energy monopoly Electricité de France (EdF) is tightly controlled by the government so that it cannot be bought. Moreover, EdF receives various subsidies that give it an advantage in the market.

Other EU members feared that France had embarked on a cynical campaign of ensuring that EdF would be one of the survivors of the industrial restructuring that would inevitably come when energy was eventually liberalized. For example, France consistently opposed full liberalization of energy markets, and when the EU adopted a partial opening measure in which members were bound to open up their energy markets to third-party competition, France delayed passing the necessary laws. The real trouble began when EdF launched an aggressive campaign of expanding rapidly into the power markets of neighbouring Member States (Britain, Germany, Italy and Spain) while remaining a state-owned monopoly in its home market.

Such expansion would be unremarkable in other sectors, but the perception that EdF's moves were 'unfair' led other EU members to postpone or restrict their own liberalization efforts. For example, in 2001, German Economy Minister Werner Mueller threatened to prevent the French state-owned power giant EdF from importing electricity into Germany as long as France did not open up its power market to foreign companies. Italy had a similar reaction after EdF began to take over the Italian company Montedison. As Italy's Treasury Minister Vincenzo Visco explained, it was 'unacceptable to let a player with a rigged hand of cards join the game'. The Italian government quickly introduced measures designed to block further takeovers.

To prevent this action–reaction chain from ruining prospects for liberalization, the Commission launched an investigation in 2002 into EdF's state aid. Following the formal investigation procedure initiated by the Commission on 2 April 2003, the French government agreed to end EdF's unlimited state guarantee by 2005. Mario Monti, the Competition Commissioner at the time, said: 'I welcome the favourable outcome reached in this highly sensitive case. . . . A competitive situation has for the first time been created for EdF, without distortions due to state aid. The introduction of conditions of fair competition and the correction of past distortions is all the more important in sectors such as energy which are in the process of being liberalized and will enable all the positive effects to be reaped from that liberalization.'

Source: This box is based mainly on BBC news stories dated 12 June 2001 and 16 October 2002 (see www.bbc.co.uk)

social policy aid, natural disaster aid and economic development aid to underdeveloped areas. More generally, state aid that is in the general interest of the EU is permitted. For example, the Commission has also adopted a number of bloc-exemption rules that explain which sorts of state aid are indisputable. These include aid to small and medium-sized enterprises, aid for training and aid for employment. More information can be found in DG Competition's highly accessible document *Competition Policy and Consumers*, downloadable from europa.eu.int (use Google to find the exact link since the Commission occasionally reshuffles its websites).

A contentious example: airlines in trouble

The Commission is frequently in the headlines over its state aid decisions since these often produce loud protests from firms and/or workers who benefited from any state aid that the DG Competition judges to be illegal. An excellent example concerns the airline industry – an industry where there are clearly too many firms in existence and the tendency to subsidize is strong. Many European airlines are the national 'flag carrier' and as such are often considered a symbol of nation pride.

Consolidation of the European airline industry has been on the cards for years, but the problem was exacerbated by the terrorist attacks of 11 September 2001. The ensuing reduction in air travel caused great damage to airlines all around the world and led to calls for massive state aid. To prevent these subsidies from being used as an excuse to put off restructuring, the Commission restricted subsidies to cover only the 'exceptional losses' incurred when transatlantic routes were shut down immediately after 11 September. To date, the Commission has managed to resist the desire of several Member State governments to support their national airlines to the same extent that the US government has supported US airlines.

It is easy to see the logic of the Commission's stance. Low-cost airlines, such as Ryanair and easyJet, have done well without subsidies. Moreover, artificial support for inefficient national carriers hinders the expansion of low-cost airlines. As Bannerman (2002) puts it:

> *No-one will benefit from a return to spiralling subsidies, which damage the industry by encouraging inefficiency. Both consumers and taxpayers would suffer as a result. As for the national carriers, they would probably benefit from some market consolidation, creating fewer, leaner, pan-European airlines – although this process would need monitoring for its competitive effects on key routes. If the airline industry can use the crisis to create more efficient carriers, it will probably be the better for it. But this long-term view cuts little ice with workers who stand to lose their jobs, or with some politicians, for whom a flag carrier is a symbol of national pride. Unfortunately, the benefits of controlling state-aids occur mainly in lower fares and taxes, and are therefore widely diffused among the population. The costs, on the other hand, take the form of job losses, which hurt a small but vocal constituency.*

11.3 Summary

Three main points have been made in this chapter:

* One very obvious impact of European integration has been to face individual European firms with a bigger 'home' market. This produces a chain reaction that leads to fewer, bigger, more efficient firms that face more effective competition from each other. The attendant industrial restructuring is often politically painful since it often results in layoffs and the closure of inefficient plants. Governments very often attempt to offset this political pain by providing 'state aid' to their national firms. Such state aid can be viewed as unfair and the perception of unfairness threatens to undermine EU members' interest in integration. To avoid these problems, the founders of the EU established rules that prohibited state aid that distorts competition. The Commission is charged with enforcing these rules.

* Private firms may also seek to avoid restructuring by engaging in anti-competitive practices and EU rules prohibit this. Moreover, as integration proceeds and the number of firms falls, the temptation for firms to collude may increase.

* To avoid this, the EU has strict rules on anti-competitive practices. It also screens mergers to ensure that mergers will enhance efficiency. Again, the Commission is charged with enforcing these rules.

Self-assessment questions

1 Suppose that liberalization occurs as in Fig. 11.1 and the result is a pro-competitive effect, but instead of merging or restructuring, all firms are bought by their national governments to allow the firms to continue operating. What will be the impact of this on prices and government revenues? Now that the governments are the owners, will they have an incentive to continue with liberalization? Can you imagine why this might favour firms located in nations with big, rich governments?.

2 Look up a recent state aid case on the Commission's website (europa.int.eu) and explain the economic and legal reasoning behind the Commission's decision using the diagrams in this chapter.

3 Look up a recent abuse of dominant position case (Article 82) on the Commission's website (europa.int.eu) and explain the economic and legal reasoning behind the Commission's decision using the diagrams in this chapter.

4 Look up a recent antitrust case (Article 81) on the Commission's website (europa.int.eu) and explain the economic and legal reasoning behind the Commission's decision using the diagrams in this chapter.

5 Using a diagram similar to Fig. 11.2, show what the welfare effects would be following a switch from normal competition to perfect collusion. Be sure to address the change in consumer surplus and pure profits.

Essay questions

1 When the Single Market Programme was launched in the mid-1980s, European leaders asserted that it would improve the competitiveness of European firms vis-à-vis US firms. Explain how one can make sense of this assertion by extending the reasoning in this chapter, and explain why this makes EU competition policy an important part of Europe's external competitiveness.

2 While the case for strengthening European-wide competition policy in tandem with the Single Market Programme is clear, is it obvious that this task should be allocated to the EU level instead of being left in the hands of Member States?

3 Some EU members allow their companies to engage in 'anti-takeover' practices. Discuss how differences in EU members' laws concerning these practices might be viewed as unfair when an EU industry is being transformed by a wave of mergers and acquisitions.

4 Read about the EU's 'Lisbon Strategy' and use the reasoning and logic in this chapter to explain the role that EU leaders expected competition policy to play in making the EU the most competitive economy by 2010.

5 In 2008, the EU began a review of its merger regulations. Read about the various considerations posted on the Commission's website and write an essay on how you think the merger regulations should be changed.

Further reading: the aficionado's corner

For a very accessible introduction to EU competition policy, see:
Neven, D., P. Seabright and M. Nutall (1996) *Fishing for Minnows*, CEPR, London.

Every interested reader should at least skim through the most recent version of the Commission's document, *Competition Policy and the Consumer*. This presents a succinct and authoritative account of EU competition policy. It also presents a large number of examples of EU competition policy in action (most of the examples in this chapter are based on these).

Useful websites

The website of DG Competition has several highly accessible accounts of EU competition policy and information on recent cases; see http://europa.eu.int/comm/competition/.

References

Bannerman, E. (2002) *The Future of EU Competition Policy*, Centre for European Reform. Download from www.cer.org.uk/pdf/p297_competition_policy.pdf.

Commission (2010) 'EU Competition law: Rules applicable to Merger Control, Situation as at 1 April 2010', DG Competition, ec.europa.eu/competition/mergers/legislation/legislation.html.

Mas-Colell, A., M. Whinston and J.R. Green (1995) *Microeconomic Theory*, Oxford University Press, New York.

Chapter 12

EU trade policy

Chapter Contents

Introduction

The European Union is the world's biggest trader. Counting EU exports both within the EU and to non-EU nations, the Union accounts for almost 40 per cent of world trade – about 4 times more than China or the USA. Its dominance of trade in services is even greater. Three of the EU27 members are individually in the top ten trading nations in the world (Germany, Britain and France). The EU is also a leader in the world trade system, both as a key player in the World Trade Organization (WTO) and as a massive signer of bilateral trade agreements and extender of unilateral trade concessions to the world's poorest nations.

While the EU has been one of the staunchest supporters of the WTO's trade rules, many observers traditionally viewed EU trade policy – especially its policy on agricultural goods – as a major roadblock to greater liberalization worldwide. This, however, is changing. The

EU's reform of its massive Common Agriculture Policy (CAP, see Chapter 9 for details) has greatly reduced the extent to which EU farm policy distorts world markets. For example, as this edition was going to press, the EU was committed to eliminating all export subsidies by 2013.

This chapter covers EU trade policy by presenting the basic facts on EU trade, covering the EU's institutional arrangements as they concern trade policy, and finally summarizing the EU's policies towards its various trade partners. It is important to note that EU trade policy – like so much about the Union – is mind-numbingly complex. There is a whole army of specialists who do nothing but follow EU trade issues, and most of these have to specialize in one particular area in order to master all the detail. Plainly, then, this chapter cannot come even close to surveying all EU trade policy. Its goal is rather to present the broad outlines and key issues. Readers who are interested in greater detail on a particular trade partner, sector or policy should start with the European Commission's website: http://europa.eu.int/comm/trade/.

12.1 Pattern of trade and tariffs: facts

The EU trades mainly with Europe, as Fig. 12.1 shows. The right bar shows the share of EU exports that goes to the EU's various partners. The figures include EU sales to non-EU nations as well as exports from one EU nation to another. This gives perspective on the relative importance of intra-EU trade and external trade. The main points are:

- Two-thirds of EU27 exports are to other EU27 nations. More than 90 per cent of this is actually among the EU15, since the ten new Member States are fairly small economically (see Chapter 2 for details).
- If we add in other European nations – EFTA (Switzerland, Norway, Iceland and Liechtenstein) and Turkey – the figure rises to three-quarters. In short, three out of four export euros earned by the EU27 are from sales within Europe, broadly defined.
- After Europe, North America and Asia are the EU27's main markets, but each account for a little less than one-tenth of EU exports.
- Africa, Latin America and the Middle East are not very important as EU export destinations; their shares are each less than 3 per cent.

Rounding off to make the numbers easy to remember, we can say that three-quarters of EU exports go to Europe. The remaining quarter is split more or less evenly among three groups of nations: North America, Asia and all other nations.

The pattern on the import side is very similar (left bar in Fig. 12.1). The biggest difference lies with Asia since the EU imports more from Asia than it exports to Asia. The opposite is true of North America. The EU's trade with the rest of the world is approximately in balance. Again rounding off to make the numbers easy to remember, we can say that three-quarters of EU imports are from Europe, with the fourth quarter split into two more or less even groups of nations – Asia, and all other nations.

It can be useful to take an even closer look by separating out individual nations, as in Table 12.1. Just ten nations account for about two-thirds of EU27 *external* trade, but the list is slightly different on the import and export sides. The US is the number one buyer of EU exports by a very large margin, and China is the biggest exporter to the EU. After China and the USA, the next most important market for EU exports is Switzerland, but the Swiss

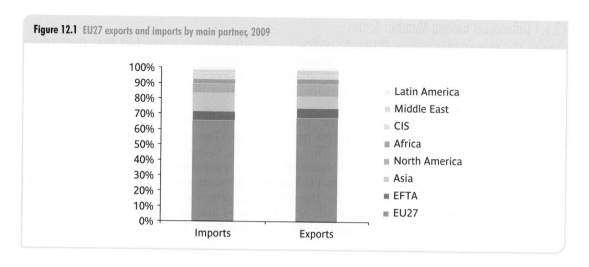

Figure 12.1 EU27 exports and imports by main partner, 2009

buy only 40 per cent as much as Americans (still, this is a big number given that there are 8 million Swiss and 300 million Americans). Russia, Turkey and Japan round out the top five partners – leaving aside imports from Norway (most oil and gas). This role of the so-called emerging economies in EU trade is quite clear from these numbers. Taking the BRICs (Brazil, Russia, India and China) together, they account for 18 per cent of imports and 27 per cent of exports.

Table 12.1   EU's top ten import and export partners, 2010 (€ billions)

Partner	Exports	Share	Partner	Imports	Share
USA	242	18%	China	157	10%
China	113	8%	USA	105	7%
Switzerland	105	8%	Russia	72	5%
Russia	87	6%	Switzerland	68	5%
Turkey	61	5%	Norway	59	4%
Japan	44	3%	Japan	51	3%
Norway	42	3%	Turkey	26	2%
India	35	3%	Korea	26	2%
Brazil	31	2%	India	22	1%
Korea	28	2%	Brazil	19	1%
UAE	28	2%	Libya	16	1%
Hong Kong	27	2%	Taiwan	16	1%

Source: Eurostat © European Union, 1995–2012

12.1.1 Differences among Member States

One of the things that makes EU trade policy a contentious issue is the fact that the various Member States have quite different trade patterns. Some members are landlocked and surrounded by other EU members, while others are geographically and/or culturally close to Africa, North America or Latin America. It is not surprising, therefore, that the importance of various trade partners varies quite a lot across the EU27.

Figure 12.2 illustrates this divergence. The reliance of Member States on imports from the various regions is shown by the 100 per cent bars. The leftmost segment shows the share of imports from non-EU Europe. This ranges from about 5 per cent for Luxembourg to almost 80 per cent for Lithuania. Geography matters a great deal when it comes to trade partners, so it is not surprising that non-EU Europe countries – which include Ukraine and Russia – play a big role in the imports for the central European members such as Poland and the Baltic States. The importance of North America varies almost as much. North America's share in Irish external imports is about 40 per cent, while for the Baltic States it is 10 per cent or less.

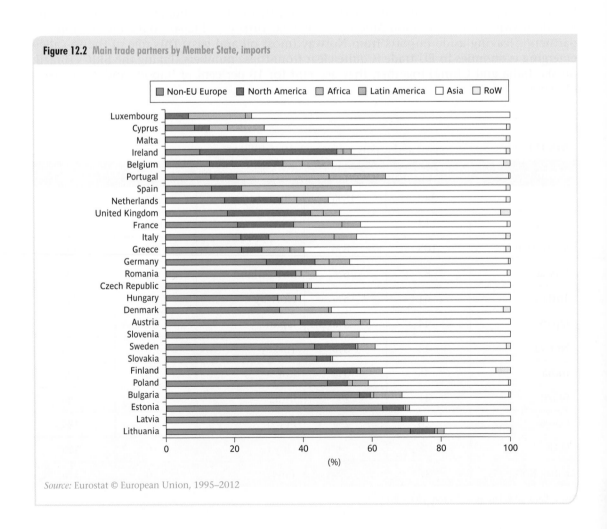

Figure 12.2 Main trade partners by Member State, imports

Source: Eurostat © European Union, 1995–2012

The figure also shows some fairly natural linkages. The Iberians import a large share of their external trade from Latin America and Africa. Africa's share is also over 15 per cent for Italy and France.

Asia's role is more constant, although it tends to be larger for members with easy access to the sea, such as Britain, Denmark and Poland.

12.1.2 Composition of the EU's external trade

What sorts of goods does the EU27 export and import to and from the rest of the world? As Fig. 12.3 shows, the answer is 'mainly manufactured goods'. The main points from the diagram are:

- Manufactured goods account for almost 90 per cent of EU exports, with about half of all exports being machinery and transport equipment.
- On the import side, about two out of every three euros spent on imports go to buy manufactured goods.
- Being energy poor, the EU27 is a big importer of fuel; about one in every five euros spent on imports goes to pay for fuel.
- Other types of goods play a relatively minor part in the EU's trade.

About 7 per cent of EU27 exports to the rest of the world consist of food (more precisely, food, drinks and tobacco). The EU's imports of such goods account also for 7 per cent of all its imports. As the chapter on the CAP (Chapter 9) showed, Europe's trade in agricultural goods is massively distorted by subsidies to EU farmers, subsidies to EU exports and high barriers against imports. If the CAP were fully liberalized in the direction the Commission is pushing for (see Chapter 9 for details), all trade distortions would be removed and the EU would surely become a net importer of food.

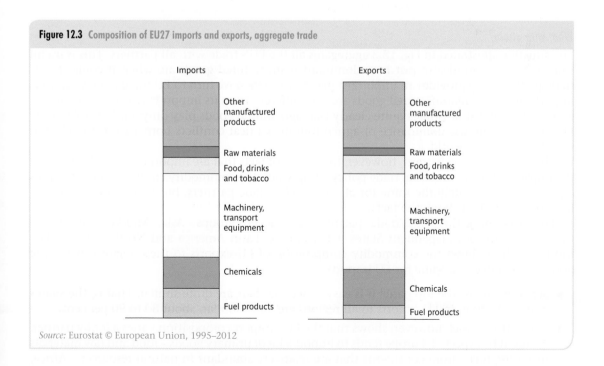

Figure 12.3 Composition of EU27 imports and exports, aggregate trade

Source: Eurostat © European Union, 1995–2012

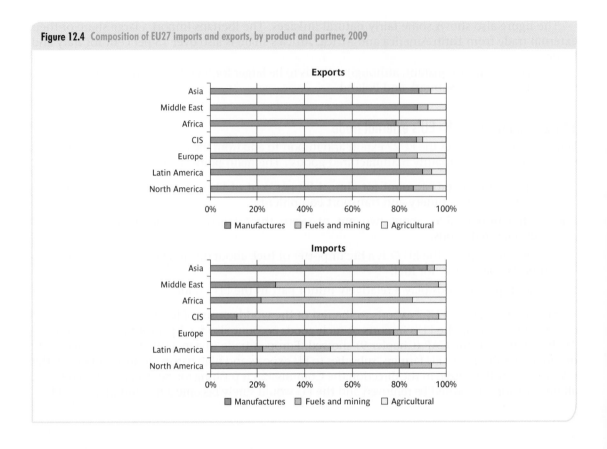

Figure 12.4 Composition of EU27 imports and exports, by product and partner, 2009

What with whom?

The situation illustrated in Fig. 12.3 aggregates all the EU's trade with all partners. This is useful since it gives us an idea of just how dominant manufactured goods are when it comes to EU trade policy. It also provides an important perspective when we turn to EU trade policy, since EU import barriers for manufactured goods are very different from its import barriers on agricultural goods. Moreover, it illustrates quite clearly that agricultural goods play only a minor role in the EU's trade despite the dominance of agriculture in political conflicts both within the EU and with the rest of the world.

The aggregate trade pattern, however, hides a set of facts that are important to understanding the impact of the EU's external trade policy. Simply put, the commodity composition of the EU's *exports* is approximately the same for all of the EU's trade partners, but this is not true for its imports. Figure 12.4 shows the facts.

The diagram gathers EU trade partners into seven groups: Asia, Middle East, Africa, Commonwealth of Independent States (CIS), Europe, Latin America and North America. The top panel show shows the commodity composition of EU exports to these regions, while the bottom panel does the same for EU imports.

- Scanning across the top panel it is easy to see that bars are quite similar. That is, the shares of manufactures in EU exports to all regions are fairly similar, about 80 to 90 per cent.
- The bottom panel, however, shows that the EU's import composition varies a lot by partner. As might be expected, Europe tends to import a lot of primary goods – food and raw materials including fuel – from continents that are relatively abundant in natural resources – Africa,

CIS, Middle East and Latin America. With North America and Asia, the imports consist mostly of manufactures.

■ Food is never a dominant import for any of the partners, but it amounts to almost half of the EU's imports from Latin America (and this figure can be much higher for particular nations, especially small, poor nations).

12.1.3 The EU's Common External Tariff (CET)

The EU has been an active participant in the 60-year-long sequence of global tariff-cutting talks known as GATT Rounds, or since 1995 WTO Rounds. As a result, the EU's tariffs are quite low for most goods that were bargained over in these Rounds. Since agricultural tariffs were not included in these Rounds until the end of the twentieth century, EU tariffs on such goods remain much higher.

As the EU defines individual tariff rates for about 10,000 products, we must generalize to get a handle on the numbers. The average CET rate is about 6 per cent, but this hides a wide variation. About a quarter of the rates on all products are set at zero (mostly industrial goods including electronics) and the average for industrial goods is about 4 per cent. The average on agricultural imports is four times this, namely 16 per cent. The facts for various product categories are shown in Table 12.2.

The table's three columns list the average tariff in the relevant product category, the maximum tariff in the category and the share of such imports that come in duty-free. The first column thus gives an idea of the overall protectionist tendency in the category. For example, the average tariff on animal products (meat, etc.) is 23 per cent, which is fairly high, but only half as high as the protection of dairy products (49 per cent). The maximum tariff in both categories is astronomical – over 160 per cent, as the second column shows. The third column shows the share of the EU's external imports that come in duty-free because of reciprocal or unilateral preference agreements. For example, 10 per cent of EU imports of animal products come in at zero tariffs, but no dairy does. Below we discuss in more detail the various programmes that allow duty-free imports.

Now, looking down the rows we see that imports of primary goods are – with the exception of cotton – taxed at a much higher rate than manufactured goods. The maximum tariffs are also much lower. The share of imports that come in duty-free varies a lot by product. The maximum rates on some manufactured goods are still high, but the average rate on manufactures is always below 5 per cent, except for textiles and clothing where the averages are 7 and 12 per cent respectively.

12.2 EU institutions for trade policy

Formation of a customs union – which means the elimination of tariffs on intra-EU trade and adoption of a common external tariff – was the EU's first big step towards economic integration. A customs union requires political coordination since trade policy towards third nations is an ever-evolving issue. To facilitate this coordination, the Treaty of Rome granted supranational powers to the EU's institutions as far as external trade policy is concerned – what is known in EU jargon as 'exclusive competence' (see Chapter 3 for details). This delegation of sovereignty has never changed and indeed over the decades the various Treaties have granted the EU more power in the area of trade. The 2009 Lisbon Treaty in particular greatly increased the extent to which EU members have delegated power on trade issues to the EU. This section reviews the institutions and practices governing this coordination.

Table 12.2   EU's Common External Tariff (CET), 2010

	Average (%)	Max (%)	Share of extra-EU imports duty free
Animal products	23	162	10
Dairy products	49	163	0
Fruit, vegetables, plants	11	161	12
Coffee, tea	7	55	78
Cereals & preparations	18	111	2
Oilseeds, fats & oils	6	94	70
Sugars and confectionery	28	118	0
Beverages & tobacco	19	166	15
Cotton	0	0	100
Other agricultural products	5	117	68
Fish & fish products	12	26	5
Minerals & metals	2	12	56
Petroleum	3	5	84
Chemicals	5	13	43
Wood, paper, etc.	1	10	85
Textiles	7	12	2
Clothing	12	12	0
Leather, footwear, etc.	4	17	17
Non-electrical machinery	2	10	53
Electrical machinery	3	14	55
Transport equipment	4	22	17
Manufactures, n.e.s	3	14	55

Source: WTO online database, 'World Tariff Profiles', www.wto.org.

12.2.1 EU competences on trade

Trade policy is an EU 'exclusive competence' (see Chapter 3 for details). That is, the EU has the exclusive power to set trade policy with third nations – the so-called Common Commercial Policy. Individual Member States cannot legislate on trade matters or conclude international trade agreements. The logic of a customs union having one trade policy is extremely strong. After all, if each member did bilateral deals on its own, the single market might be undermined by third nations exploiting differences across EU members' external trade policies.

In the twentieth century, the EU's power on trade policy was basically limited to tariffs. This was not an important limitation; back then, tariffs were by far the most important aspect of trade policy. As EU tariffs came down during the course of multilateral trade negotiations, and the nature of international commerce grew more complex, the range of important trade barriers broadened.

As the logic of a unified external trade policy was as strong as ever, this trend created a need to expand the competence of the EU beyond tariffs. This was done in a series of small and practical steps in the Maastricht and Nice Treaties. It took a big step forward with the December 2009 Lisbon Treaty, which extended the Common Commercial Policy to explicitly include trade in services, foreign direct investment and some aspects of intellectual property rights (copyrights, patents, etc.).

Protection and enforcement of intellectual property

A key element in Europe's competitiveness lies in its intellectual property (the general name for things like patents, trademarks, designs, copyrights and geographical indications, like Parma Ham or Champagne). To protect these, the EU and its members have signed many agreements that establish international disciplines that protect this intellectual property. These disciplines are meant to deter piracy, counterfeiting and the like.

A key role of EU trade policy is to see that such standards are respected by third countries. The Commission takes the lead here and pursues the objective in the WTO and bilaterally with third nations. Most recently, the EU participated actively in the negotiation of the Anti-Counterfeiting Trade Agreement (ACTA) which was signed in the autumn of 2011.

Investment

In many industries, investment has become an integral part of trade. For example, BMW and Airbus set up production facilities in China as part of their effort to sell goods to Chinese customers. Likewise, the internationalization of supply chains often involves EU companies investing in factories in third nations. Indeed the EU is the largest generator of foreign direct investment (FDI) in the global economy (FDI is where a company from one nation directly controls an investment in another, say a factory, rather than merely owning some shares in the foreign company).

Such investment is facilitated by clear rules that establish legal rights for investors abroad and for foreign investors in the EU. Establishing, improving and enforcing such rules is the main thrust of EU investment policy. Here the Commission works with the WTO and third nations in the context of bilateral trade agreements (e.g. the EU–Korea FTA that came into effect in 2011).

Currently, the focus is on the negotiation of investment rules in the context of preferential trade agreements that the EU negotiates with third countries. The EU–Korea Free Trade Agreement is the most recent example of an agreement that reflects EU investment policy negotiations.

Prior to the Lisbon Treaty, investment was not part of the EU's responsibility, so Member States signed a large number of bilateral arrangements (called Bilateral Investment Treaties, BITs). It is not yet clear how the EU will deal with this tangle of agreements. For example, Turkey has a BIT with 11 separate EU members. These will presumably be eventually merged into one, but such pre-existing BITs are likely to remain in force for some time.

12.2.2 Allocation of responsibilities

Trade policy in today's globalized world touches on a vast array of issues. Correspondingly, EU trade policy is extremely complex since it has to deal with issues ranging from quotas on men's underwear from China to internet banking to sugar imports. To keep EU policy coherent in the face of this complexity, the Treaties assign to the European Commission the task of negotiating trade matters with third nations on behalf of the Member States (Article 207 of the Treaty on the Functioning of the European Union). In practice, this means that the EU Trade Commissioner (currently Karl de Gucht) is responsible for conducting trade negotiations. These negotiations are conducted in accordance with specific mandates defined by the Council and the Parliament (called 'Directives for Negotiation'). The European Commission also takes the lead in trade policy in the sense that it has the right of initiative on, for example, trade agreements, and it is in charge of enforcement and surveillance of compliance with existing agreements and WTO rules.

The basic frameworks guiding the Commission are jointly decided by the European Parliament and the Council (i.e. what was called the Council of Ministers before the Lisbon Treaty). These decisions are taken on the basis of the 'ordinary legislative procedure' (see Chapter 2), which involves majority voting in the Council and the Parliament. The Council must adopt any agreements negotiated by the Commission after the Parliament has given its consent (i.e. the Parliament can say 'yes' or 'no' but cannot amend the agreements). For agreements that deal with areas under the exclusive competences of the EU, members' national parliaments no longer have to ratify the decision of the Council and Parliament.

The big change in the Lisbon Treaty on trade policy concerns the European Parliament. Specifically, it is now co-legislator with the Council on all basic EU trade legislation, such as anti-dumping tariffs and trade preferences for developing nations. Moreover, the Commission is required to inform the Parliament regularly about ongoing negotiations.

Trade policy and foreign policy

Trade policy has long been one of the EU's most effective foreign policy tools. After Lisbon, the lines between foreign policy and trade policy became even more blurred. The Lisbon Treaty institutes a hierarchy of principles that should be applied to trade policy (as well as other aspects of foreign policy). For example, Article 3 of the Treaty on European Union states: 'In its relations with the wider world, the Union shall uphold and promote its values and interests and contribute to the protection of its citizens. It shall contribute to peace, security, the sustainable development of the Earth, solidarity and mutual respect among peoples, free and fair trade, eradication of poverty and the protection of human rights, in particular the rights of the child, as well as to the strict observance and development of international law, including respect for the principles of the United Nations Charters.'

It is not yet clear how much practical importance this will have, but it certainly means that the EU's general pro-business view of trade agreements will be tempered with more input from players – such as Members of the European Parliament – who are less concerned with exporting and more concerned with human rights, the environment, etc.

Box 12.1   Lisbon Treaty changes on trade in a nutshell

As far as trade policy goes, the Lisbon Treaty involves three big changes:

1 Big increase in European Parliament power on trade policy.

   Before Lisbon, the Parliament's power on EU trade policy was minor. Now its power is very nearly equal to that of the Council (i.e. the old Council of Ministers). Specifically:

   ■ All EU trade laws (e.g. imposition of anti-dumping tariffs, granting of trade preferences, etc.) must be adopted by the 'ordinary legislative procedure' (the old codecision procedure). Under this procedure, the Parliament and Council have equal power.

- All trade agreements must now be approved by Parliament, but Parliament does not have the formal right to suggest amendments. However as the discussion of the EU-Korea free trade agreement showed, Parliament can use its right of refusal to influence the content of agreements.

2 Increased powers for the EU as opposed to EU members.

- Foreign direct investment (FDI) becomes clearly under EU authority, so only the EU can conclude international agreements, and adopt laws on FDI.

- The Lisbon Treaty clearly grants power to the EU on issues such as trade in services and commercial aspects of intellectual property, along with trade in cultural, audiovisual, educational and social and health services (in certain sensitive cases, like culture, the EU power is subject to specific voting rules that grant EU members veto power).

3 Qualified majority voting for most trade issues.

Qualified majority voting (see Chapter 3 for details) is now the general rule in the Council for actions related to trade policy areas (including the new areas such as investment and services). However, members still retain a veto (i.e. unanimity is required in the Council) in certain cases. For example, when commitments in trade agreements might undermine the EU's cultural and linguistic diversity, or seriously disturb members' national organization of social, educational or health services.

Unanimity is also required if the EU law or trade agreement covers issues that would be subject to unanimity for internal laws (e.g. tax harmonization).

Source: This box draws on European Commission (2011)

12.2.3 Anti-dumping and anti-subsidy measures

Under WTO rules, tariff liberalization is a one-way street. Once a nation has lowered its tariff in WTO talks (such talks are often called 'Rounds', e.g. the ongoing one is called the Doha Round), it is not allowed to put the tariff back up. This principle of 'binding' tariffs applies to the EU's external tariffs. The principle, however, is subject to some loopholes, the most important of which are anti-dumping and anti-subsidy tariffs.

Dumping is defined as the selling of exports below some normal price. According to WTO rules, a nation, or more broadly speaking, a customs area (i.e. the EU), can impose tariffs on imports if dumping 'causes or threatens material injury to an established industry'. The EU, together with the USA, is one of the world's leading users of such measures, especially in iron and steel, consumer electronics and chemicals.

The European Commission is in charge of investigating dumping complaints. If the Commission finds that: (i) dumping has occurred (this involves intricate and somewhat arbitrary calculations), and (ii) that material injury to EU producers has or might happen, it can impose a provisional duty (that lasts between six and nine months). The Council of Ministers must confirm the Commission's decision before the tariffs become definitive (these stay in place for five years). Sometimes the Commission avoids imposing tariffs by negotiating 'price undertakings' with the exporting nation; these are promises by the exporters to charge a high price for their goods in exchange for suspension or termination of the Commission's anti-dumping investigation. In terms of EU welfare, price undertakings are worse than tariffs since the EU collects no tariff revenue. Nevertheless, price undertakings are often more expedient politically since they are a way of 'bribing' the exporting nation into not complaining too loudly about the EU's new protection. (See Chapter 4 for the economic analysis.)

Since dumping duties, like all tariffs, help producers but harm consumers and firms that buy the goods (see Chapter 4), the Commission often faces a tricky balancing act among Member States. Frequently, the EU producers are concentrated in one or a few Member States while there are consumers in every Member State. Typically the former want the Commission to impose dumping duties while the latter oppose them. For this reason, the Commission implements anti-dumping measures only when it believes that they are in the broader interest of the EU. For historical and institutional reasons, the EU rarely imposes anti-subsidy duties, preferring to deal with such behaviour as 'below normal' pricing.

Many observers believe that both the EU and the USA employ a cynical manipulation of dumping rules – especially the calculation that determines whether imports have been dumped – in order to provide WTO-consistent protection for sectors whose producers are usually powerful politically. The iron and steel industry and the chemical industry are leading examples.

12.3 EU trade policy: broad goals and means

For most of its life, EU external trade policy meant negotiating:

- reciprocal tariff cuts in FTAs with other Europeans (e.g. the EU–EFTA bilaterals for 1973);
- reciprocal tariff cuts with non-European rich nations in the GATT/WTO (e.g. the 1967 Kennedy Round, or 1994 Uruguay Round); and
- unilateral tariff preferences for developing nations.

This started to change with a 2006 landmark communication from the Commission known as Global Europe. It set out a more global strategy for EU external trade policy as a complement to the renewed 'Lisbon Strategy'. (The Lisbon Strategy was a set of loosely knit initiatives that EU members were supposed to undertake domestically to improve their growth prospects.) Specifically, Global Europe identified ASEAN, Korea, India and Mercosur as priority partners for new FTAs.

The logic behind these choices is still rock solid and demonstrated in Fig. 12.5. Up until about the end of the twenty century, about 60 per cent of world growth came from rich-nation

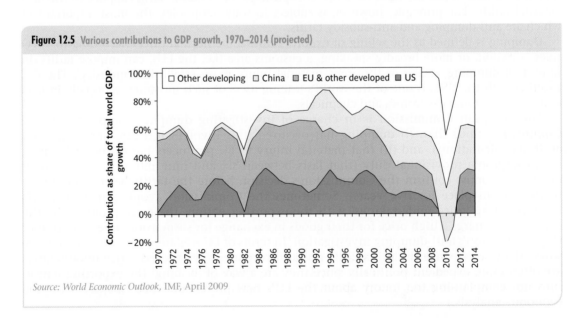

Figure 12.5 Various contributions to GDP growth, 1970–2014 (projected)

Source: *World Economic Outlook*, IMF, April 2009

markets – the USA, EU, Japan, Canada, etc. That share declined rapidly in the new century even before the global economic crisis. According to IMF forecasts, after recovery from the crisis, China and other developing nations will account for more than three-quarters of global growth.

There was also a shift away from 'shallow' FTAs, i.e. agreements that focused on many tariffs, towards deeper agreements that covered issues such as investment, public procurement, competition, IPR enforcement and regulatory convergence issues (i.e. what would be known as approximation of laws inside the EU). Such matters had to be dealt with in FTAs since the ongoing WTO Round – the Doha Round launched in 2001 – was based on an agenda that included few of these subjects.

Europe 2020 and EU trade policy

In March 2010, the European Commission launched a new 10-year strategy (similar to the Lisbon Strategy) aimed at promoting 'smart, sustainable, inclusive growth' (see http://ec.europa.eu/europe2020/index_en.htm for details). This, of course, included a trade and investment policy component laid out in a 2010 Commission communication titled 'Trade, Growth and World Affairs'. The communication notes that world trade has undergone profound changes, especially with respect to the internationalization of supply chains. For example, two-thirds of EU imports involve intermediate inputs which boost the EU's productive capacity. Keeping ahead of the competition in manufacturing and export services requires EU firms to source parts and services from the most competitive locations.

Owing to these changes, the EU trade policy is to continue the tendency, started by Global Europe, of focusing on deeper integration; cutting tariffs is still important, but the big challenge is more complex. The goal is to tackle market access for services and investment, opening public procurement, enforcement of protection of IPR, unrestricted supply of raw materials and energy, and overcoming regulatory barriers. Readers can follow a public debate on this new strategy on the policy portal www.VoxEU.org (just click on the Debate tab and then on 'The Future of EU Trade Policy').

Given this renewed emphasis on 'beyond the borders' barriers to trade – and the continued inability of WTO members to conclude the Doha Round – the EU's emphasis shifts even more towards bilateral FTA. The Doha Round remains the EU's top trade priority; however, getting more than 150 nations to agree on that complex deal is beyond the EU's power.

12.4 EU trade policy: existing arrangements

The EU's external trade policy is extremely complex. A brief summary of its bilateral trade policy is given in Table 12.3. As the figures show, about half of the EU's external trade is with nations with which it has or is planning to have an FTA. In addition to these reciprocal preferential trade policies, the EU extends unilateral preferences to nations under a variety of schemes. The rest of this section considers the more important arrangements.

The best way to gain a broad understanding of EU external trade policy is by grouping the arrangements into categories. We start with the bouquet of trade arrangements that link the EU with its immediate neighbours. Readers who are interested in one or more of these agreements can find all the details on the European Commission's website; at the end of 2011 the URL was http://ec.europa.eu/trade/.

12.4.1 The European Mediterranean trade area

The EU27 encompasses almost all of western Europe and most of central and eastern Europe. The remaining western European nations participate in the Single Market via the European Economic Area agreement (Norway, Iceland and Liechtenstein) or the EU–Swiss Bilateral Accords. Although

Table 12.3   EU FTAs and share of EU external trade, 2010

		Share of EU imports (%)	Share of EU exports (%)
Operational FTAs	Note	**22.3**	**27.7**
Chile, Mexico, South Africa	Developing country FTAs	2.5	3.4
Andorra, San Marino, Turkey, Iceland, Liechtenstein, Norway, Switzerland	Single Market-like access, or customs union	14.6	15.9
Caribbean ACP	EPAs	0.3	0.3
Algeria, Egypt, Israel, Jordan, Lebanon, Morocco, Occupied Palestinian Territory, Tunisia	Euro-Med Association Agreements	4.0	5.9
Albania, Bosnia and Herzegovina, Croatia, Former Yugoslav Republic of Macedonia, Montenegro, Serbia	Stabilisation and Association Agreements	0.9	2.2
Korea	Deep FTA	2.6	2.1
Under negotiation or awaiting ratification		**21.8**	**25.6**
Bolivia, Ecuador, Peru, Colombia	Developing country FTAs	0.4	0.6
Brunei Darussalam, Indonesia, Malaysia, Philippines, Singapore, Thailand, Vietnam	Developing country FTAs	5.4	4.6
Costa Rica, El Salvador, Guatemala, Honduras, Nicaragua, Panama	Developing country FTAs	0.2	0.4
Bahrain, Kuwait, Oman, Qatar, Saudi Arabia, United Arab Emirates	Gulf Cooperation Council	2.0	5.3
Argentina, Brazil, Paraguay, Uruguay	Mercosur	1.5	2.5
Armenia, Azerbaijan, Georgia, Libya, Moldova, Syria, Ukraine, India, Canada	Developing country FTAs	10.0	9.0
ACPs less Caribbean	EPAs	2.3	3.2
Partners with no FTA in progress		**55.8**	**46.7**
Australia, China, Japan, New Zealand, Russia, USA		50.3	38.6
Rest of the world (~ 70 countries)		5.5	8.1

Source: © European Union, 1995–2012

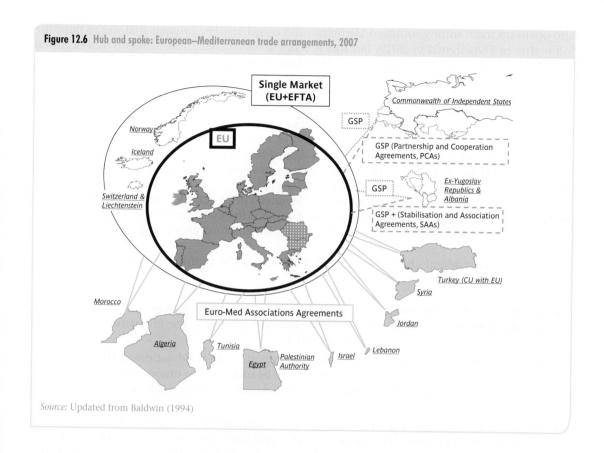

Figure 12.6 Hub and spoke: European–Mediterranean trade arrangements, 2007

Source: Updated from Baldwin (1994)

there are a multitude of exceptions that matter to specialists, understanding is greatly boosted by thinking of European trade arrangements as being characterized by two concentric circles, the EU and the Single Market (see Fig. 12.6). That is to say, every nation in the Single Market circle enjoys the 'four freedoms' with respect to every other nation in the circle. (Trade in food products is generally excluded.) The nations in the EU share even deeper integration in the political, agricultural and several non-economic spheres such as foreign and defence policy.

Euro-Meds

Trade arrangements in Europe go far beyond this inner core of partners. The next most important group of trade links are the so-called Euro-Med Association Agreements that the EU has with ten Mediterranean nations – Algeria, Egypt, Israel, Jordon, Lebanon, Morocco, the Palestinian Authority, Syria, Tunisia and Turkey (although Turkey also has a separate and deeper arrangement with the EU) – the Med-10 for short.

These Euro-Mediterranean Association Agreements are free trade agreements in that they promise bilateral duty-free trade in industrial goods. They are asymmetric, however, in that the EU had to cut its tariffs to zero faster than did its partners. The EU has already phased out its tariffs on industrial goods and is in the process of gradually lowering trade barriers on most food products. The Med-10 promised to eliminate their tariffs on EU industrial goods by 2010, but the Arab Spring disruptions put trade policy reform on a back burner. These EU bilaterals are at the heart of a more ambitious scheme called the Euro-Mediterranean partnership. Launched in 1995 ('Barcelona Process'), it was redesigned in 2008 with the addition of the 'Union for the Mediterranean'. The ultimate goal is a comprehensive Euro-Mediterranean free trade area that also opens up trade among southern Mediterranean countries. The original goal was to have the full matrix of FTAs signed by 2010, but this was not achieved. The trade collapse that occurred in 2008 and 2009 hindered progress and the recent Arab Spring turmoil has brought progress to a full halt. However, there is hope that the radical changes in the region will – as happened in central Europe – open the door to a more integrated trade policy in the region, with the EU helping the process along.

These free trade agreements for goods are being complemented with a number of additional negotiations to open up agricultural trade, services trade, and investment. A plan called the Euro-Mediterranean Trade Roadmap has been agreed beyond 2010. The goals are to complete the table of FTAs in the region, foster closer business ties and ultimately meld these agreements into a comprehensive Euro-Mediterranean free trade area.

The least progress has been made among the Mediterranean nations themselves. The progress to date includes the Agadir Agreement among Tunisia, Morocco, Jordan and Egypt (2007), an Israel–Jordan FTA, and Turkey's bilaterals with Egypt, Israel, Morocco, the Palestinian Territories, Syria and Tunisia.

When thinking about this collection of trade deals, the points worth keeping in mind include:

- The EU market can be thought of as the 'hub' in a regional hub-and-spoke system of trade deals. Exporters in each of these nations depend heavily on the EU market, while each individual nation is negligible for EU exporters.
- Turkey unilaterally sets its tariffs on industrial imports from third nations at the level of the EU's Common External Tariff, so it can be said to be in a customs union with the EU. Turkey, however, has no voice in the setting of EU external trade policy and this customs union does not apply to trade in agricultural goods.
- The EFTA nations have signed similar free trade agreements with all the Med-10 in order to ensure that their exporters compete on an equal basis with firms located in the EU (i.e. so EFTA firms face the same tariffs as EU firms do). Indeed, this is true throughout the world; whenever the EU signs an FTA with a new partner, the EFTA nations sign a similar agreement. This creates what might be called a 'virtual FTA union' between the EU and EFTA nations. Or, to put it in terms of the hub-and-spoke metaphor, EFTA's practice of shadowing the EU's FTA policy has the effect of making EFTA part of the EU's hub, at least as far as preferential tariffs are concerned. EFTA has pursued this strategy for decades; Turkey has recently followed suit, since its customs union with the EU forces it to have the same external trade policy as the EU does.
- The Euro-Med arrangements are more than FTAs since they contain provisions for financial and technical assistance from the EU and they address additional issues such as trade in services and foreign direct investment.

The Balkans

The nations in the Western Balkans region are Albania, Bosnia and Herzegovina, Croatia, Macedonia, Montenegro, Serbia and Kosovo. The EU is engaged with them via an ad hoc collection of initiatives aimed at stabilizing the countries and encouraging their swift transition to a market economy, promoting regional cooperation, and leading to eventual membership of the EU.

Where trade is concerned, they focus on liberalizing trade in goods, aligning rules on EU practice (approximation of laws) and protecting intellectual property. The agreements aim to progressively establish a free trade area between the EU and the Western Balkan countries, with EU membership as the ultimate goal. Since 2000, the EU has granted all these nations unilateral trade preferences that cover nearly all goods; so far the preferences are unilateral rather than reciprocal. To date, there are four such 'Stabilisation and Association Agreements' in force (Macedonia 2004, Croatia 2005, Albania 2009 and Montenegro 2010). The trade aspects of such agreements have been in effect for Bosnia and Herzegovina since 2007, and for Serbia since 2010. So far, only Croatia, Montenegro and Macedonia are formally candidate countries for membership.

From 2007, the EU has encouraged these nations to join the Central European Free Trade Agreement (CEFTA), which was originally set up in the 1990s by Poland, Czechoslovakia and Hungary while they were waiting for membership. CEFTA operates as a single FTA that connects the Balkans and Moldova by replacing a mess of more than 30 bilateral FTAs among them.

12.4.2 Preferential arrangements with former colonies

Europeans were big colonizers in the nineteenth and twentieth centuries and they still had many colonies right up to the 1960s and 1970s – Britain, France and Belgium in particular. Colonial ties almost always involved important trade relations; usually the 'mother' country's market was the main export destination for the colony's traded goods. When this aberrant system came to an end with the independence movements of the 1960s and 1970s, the former colonists typically wanted to maintain preferential treatment for goods coming from their former colonies. Since the EU is a customs union (i.e. all members must have the same tariffs on imports from third nations), these pressures came to bear on the EU's external trade policy. In particular, to avoid putting the Common External Tariff (CET) on imports that had long been duty free, the Six signed agreements with many of their former colonies while they were establishing the EU's customs union in the 1960s. These trade deals were asymmetric in the sense that the EU tariffs were set to zero but the poor nations did not remove theirs.

When the UK joined in 1974, these old agreements (Yaoundé Convention and Arusha Agreement) were rolled into a comprehensive policy that was extended to the poor members of the UK's Commonwealth (this way, Britain avoided imposing the CET on these nations' exports). The combined group was labelled the ACP nations since they are located in Africa, the Caribbean and the Pacific; the new agreement was known as the Lomé Convention. This granted duty-free status to all industrial exports and most agricultural exports of ACP nations (with quotas on sensitive items such as sugar and bananas) without requiring that the ACP nations lower their barriers to EU exports.

The Lomé Convention was based on the now discredited belief that such unilateral preferences would help the former colonies industrialize. Experience has shown that the preferences did not encourage industrialization or growth. Most ACP nations fell further behind, while many Asian and Latin American countries enjoyed rapid industrialization, booming exports to the EU and income growth without preferences. When the Lomé Convention came up for renewal in 2000, the EU and the ACP nations agreed to modernize the deal. Additional impetus came from a WTO ruling that Lomé was inconsistent with the WTO as it distinguished among developing nations on the basis of colonial ties.

The result was the ACP–EU Partnership Agreement, sometimes called the Cotonou Agreement. This is not a hard-nosed trade agreement to win EU exporters better market access. As with the Euro-Med partners, the EU is a major market for the ACP nations, but the ACP markets are marginal markets for EU exporters. The best way to understand the Cotonou Agreement is to view it as an economic and trade cooperation aimed at fostering development in the ACP nations.

The big change from Lomé was that Cotonou commits the ACP nations to eventually removing their tariffs against EU exports. The idea is that gradually phasing in two-way free trade with the EU is a good way of integrating these developing nations into the world economy and that this is a necessary step towards development in the modern, globalized world. For example, although

ACP exporters have enjoyed preferential access to EU markets for three decades, the quantity of exports has fallen.

The EPAs thus seek to go beyond mere tariff preferences by providing a gamut of policies aimed at helping the ACP nations trade more with EU and each other. Thus EPAs include technical assistance, and policies to foster knowledge transfer and strengthen governance, particularly public services.

While the Cotonou Agreement lays out principles, the actual trade bargains are struck in bilateral deals known as Economic Partnership Agreements (EPAs). Interim agreements have been signed with many of the ACP nations, but EU trade policy with respect to these nations has shifted with the change of Trade Commissioners (Peter Mandelson, Catherine Ashton and Karl de Gucht). As is true with much in the world of trade, the global economic crisis that started in September 2008 put EPA negotiations on the back burner as governments focused on more immediate challenges.

12.4.3 Preferences for poor nations: GSP

As mentioned above, many scholars and policy makers in the 1960s and 1970s believed that rich countries could help poor countries develop by granting unilateral preferential tariff treatment for poor nation industrial exports. This notion was formally brought into world trade rules – i.e. the WTO, or GATT as it was known at the time – in 1971 under the name 'Generalized System of tariff Preferences', GSP for short. The EU was the first to implement a GSP scheme, in 1971, and it now grants GSP preferences to almost every developing nation in the world.

As is true of all aspects of its trade policy, the EU's GSP policy is extremely complex. It helps to categorize the various EU GSP policies into two general groups:

- General GSP, which is available to all developing nations at the EU's discretion, and
- Super GSP, which involves extra 'generous' EU unilateral preferences for nations that the EU wishes to encourage for some reason or another.

Currently, 'super GSP' is granted to nations that comply with the EU's idea of labour rights, the EU's idea of environmental protection, the EU's idea of combating illegal drugs, and very poor nations.

Everything But Arms

The latter group, which is more politely called 'least developed nations', gets the most generous form of GSP preferences – a programme called 'Everything But Arms', or EBA as it is known in EU trade jargon. On paper, EBA grants zero-tariff access to the EU's market – without quotas limiting the exports eligible for preferences – for all products from these nations, except arms and munitions. There are, however, some exceptions that are still being phased out (e.g. sugar).

Currently, 49 nations qualify for EBA in principle. The list is: Afghanistan, Angola, Bangladesh, Benin, Bhutan, Burkina Faso, Burundi, Cambodia, Cape Verde, Central African Republic, Chad, Comoros, Congo (Democratic Republic), Djibouti, Equatorial Guinea, Eritrea, Ethiopia, Gambia, Guinea, Guinea Bissau, Haiti, Kiribati, Lao PDR, Lesotho, Liberia, Madagascar, Malawi, Maldives, Mali, Mauritania, Mozambique, Myanmar, Nepal, Niger, Rwanda, Samoa, São Tomé e Principe, Senegal, Sierra Leone, Solomon Islands, Somalia, Sudan, Tanzania, Togo, Tuvalu, Uganda, Vanuatu, Yemen and Zambia.

Note that the EU imposes restrictions on nations it deems to be insufficiently democratic, in violation of international law, or otherwise undesirable. In 2011 this included Burma/Myanmar and Cape Verde.

12.4.4 Non-regional FTAs

In recent years, a number of non-European nations have sought out FTAs with the EU. The EU is almost always open to FTAs (as long as they exclude agriculture) and so it has signed a number of these deals. In late 2011 when this edition went to print, the list included Mexico, Chile, Mercosur (Brazil, Argentina, Uruguay and Paraguay), the Gulf Cooperation Council (Bahrain, Kuwait, Oman, Qatar, Saudi Arabia and United Arab Emirates), India, the ASEAN nations (Indonesia, Malaysia, Philippines, Thailand, Singapore, Vietnam, Cambodia, Burma/Myanmar and Laos) and South Africa. Also, negotiations for an FTA between the EU and Colombia, Peru and Ecuador have started. The first round was in February 2009.

12.5 Summary

This chapter provided a broad introduction to the immensely complex topic of EU trade policy. It started by presenting facts on the EU's trade pattern. The main points there were:

* The EU trades mainly with Europe, with itself in particular.

* The EU is primarily an exporter of manufactured goods.

* Most EU imports are manufactured goods, although imports of primary goods are important for Africa, the Middle East and Latin America.

The next topic was EU decision making on trade. In a nutshell, the European Commission is in charge of negotiating the EU's external trade policy, but its efforts are directed by mandates from the Council of Ministers and all deals are subject to Council approval. Before the Lisbon Treaty, the Parliament had a negligible role, but now it is a co-legislator with the Council on issues like anti-dumping duties, and it must give its consent on new trade agreements.

The last section in the chapter addressed the content of the EU's trade policy. The main points were:

* Trade arrangements in Europe can be characterized as hub-and-spoke bilateralism. The hub is formed by two concentric circles (the EU, which has the deepest level of integration, and EFTA, which participates in the Single Market apart from agriculture). These circles form a 'hub' around which a network of bilateral agreements are arranged with almost every nation in Europe (broadly defined) and the Mediterranean. These bilateral deals fall into three groups: the Euro-Med agreements, the Stabilisation and Association Agreements with Western Balkan nations, and the Partnership and Cooperation Agreements with former Soviet republics in the Commonwealth of Independent States.

* The EU has preferential trade agreements with its former colonies – the so-called ACP nations – that are currently asymmetric (the EU charges zero tariffs but the ACP nations do not), but they are aiming at establishing full-blown two-way FTAs in the coming years.

* The EU grants unilateral preferences of various types to almost all developing nations.

Self-assessment questions

1 What is the role of the Member States and the Commission when it comes to external trade policy? Be sure to distinguish between trade in goods and more 'modern' trade issues such as trade in services, trade in intellectual property rights and foreign direct investment.
2 What does the EU buy from and sell to the five continents Europe, Africa, North America, South America and Asia?
3 What is the most protected good in the EU and which is the least protected good?
4 Why did the EU extend unilateral tariff preferences to former French and Belgium colonies, and why did it extend these to former British colonies in the mid-1970s?
5 Explain the term 'hub-and-spoke bilateralism' as applied to the EU's neighbours in Europe and around the Mediterranean.

Essay questions

1 'In some sense, the trade policy has been the EU's most effective form of "foreign policy", and indeed up until the Maastricht Treaty it could be considered the EU's only foreign policy.' Write an essay evaluating this statement.
2 'Some non-governmental organizations (NGOs) claim that the EU only provides developing nations with tariff preferences that are not worth much, either because the developing nations are not competitive in these goods or because the EU's CET is low on these goods so duty-free treatment is not much different from non-preferential treatment.' Write an essay evaluating this statement.
3 Select a particular European trade partner and investigate all the trade agreements the EU has with it and the EU's imports and exports to this nation. You can find trade data on http://europa.eu.int/comm/trade/, and information on trade agreements on the same site (but also check the more general site, http://europa.eu.int/comm/world/).
4 Write an essay describing the EU's trade policy in a particular sector, such as steel or textiles.
5 Write an account of the EU's recent troubles with Chinese textile exports. Be sure to explain how this illustrates the allocation of competences and the difficult politics within the EU on trade matters.
6 Do you think it would be a good idea for the EU to sign more trade agreements? If so, with which countries and why?
7 Why do you think European nations trade more with their former colonies?

Further reading: the aficionado's corner

A very lengthy and complete treatment of the EU's trade policy can be downloaded from the WTO's website, www.wto.org (follow links to the Trade Policy Reviews, or use Google with the words EU, Trade Policy Review and WTO). This is an independent review of EU trade policy which includes detailed presentation of its preferential, multilateral and sector policies. This also provides references to many academic studies of the impact of EU policies.

A very sceptical presentation of EU trade policy that includes explicit economic evaluation is:

Messerlin, P. (2001) *Measuring the Costs of Protection in Europe: European Commercial Policy in the 2000s*, Institute for International Economics, Washington, DC.

For general information on the WTO, see:

Hoekman, B. and M. Kostecki (2001) *The Political Economy of the World Trading System: The WTO and Beyond*, Oxford University Press, Oxford.
Or the **WTO**'s website, www.wto.org.

For more on the EU trade policy with poor nations, see:

Hinkle, L. and M. Schiff (2004) 'Economic Partnership Agreements between Sub-Saharan Africa and the EU: a development perspective', *World Economy*, 27(9): 1321–34.
Panagariya, A. (2002) 'EU preferential trade policies and developing countries', *World Economy*, 10(25): 1415–32.

For more on GSP in general, see:

GAO (1994) *Assessment of the Generalized System of Preferences Program*, US General Accounting Office, Washington, DC. Download from www.gao.gov.

Useful websites

The best general site is the European Commission DG-Trade site, http://europa.eu.int/comm/trade/.

For information on preferential trade agreements worldwide, see www.bilaterals.org.

References

Baldwin, R. (1994) *Towards an Integrated Europe*, CEPR, London.
European Commission (2011) 'What did the Lisbon Treaty change?' Factsheet, 14 June 2011, Brussels. http://trade.ec.europa.eu/doclib/html/147977.htm
GAO (1994) *Assessment of the Generalized System of Preferences Program*, US General Accounting Office, Washington, DC. Download from www.gao.gov.

Part IV

The Macroeconomics of Monetary Integration

Chapter 13

Essential macroeconomic tools

The point is that you can't have it all: A country must pick two out of three.

Paul Krugman (1999)

Chapter Contents

Introduction

This chapter lays the groundwork for the monetary integration part of the book. From a theoretical viewpoint, it extends the standard closed-economy framework by allowing for trade in goods and services and for international capital flows. It also offers a realistic reinterpretation of monetary policy to modify the classic short-run *IS–LM* framework. From a practical viewpoint, it introduces three principles: interest rate parity, purchasing power parity and the impossible trinity, which describes a fundamental choice that every government faces when deciding on the exchange rate regime.

13.1 Interest parity

13.1.1 The interest rate parity condition

Imagine that you are a trader working for a large bank. You are in charge of a vast amount of money and your job is to find the best return. The world is your playground. As shown in Fig. 13.1, you are perfectly informed about all investment opportunities anywhere. Now suppose that the domestic interest rate is low relative to interest rates elsewhere in the world. Shouldn't you invest your money abroad rather than at home? Consider the two options. Investing at home for, say, one year gets you the principal and interest in the domestic currency after the year has elapsed. In order to invest the same amount abroad, you must first buy the foreign currency at the current interest rate; then, after one year, you receive the principal and higher interest but in foreign currency. To compare with the first option, you will need to convert all that into domestic currency at the then prevailing exchange rate.

If the exchange rate will not change, maybe because it is fixed, then the interest rates fully capture the difference between the two options and, indeed, you will want to invest abroad. If the foreign currency will appreciate, you will get more domestic currency when you sell the foreign currency in one year's time; investing abroad you get both a higher interest rate and a capital gain (the additional domestic currency value of your holdings in the foreign currency). Now, imagine that the foreign currency depreciates over the year. Then you will get less domestic currency, and the loss that you suffer may be even larger than what you gained by investing abroad at a higher interest rate. The conclusion is that you need to compare not just the domestic and foreign interest rates, but you must also make a bet on the likely evolution of the exchange rate. Box 13. 1 provides a formal derivation.

The story becomes even more interesting when you realize that you are not the only trader in the world. Hundreds of colleagues look at the same screens and compare their views about what may happen in the future. If the consensus is that the exchange rate will not change much, they all conclude that investing abroad is the better deal. No one brings money from abroad and all the money available at home leaves the country. Given the huge resources available to international investors, the resulting flows out the domestic currency lead to a depreciation of the current exchange rate. In one year's time, the foreign investments will be sold and demand for the domestic currency will swell, so the exchange rate will appreciate. The combination of a weaker exchange rate today and a stronger exchange rate in one year means that the domestic currency is expected to appreciate or, equivalently, that the foreign exchange rate will depreciate. This undermines the attractiveness of investing abroad. In fact, if the expected foreign currency depreciation exactly undermines the higher foreign interest rate, traders become indifferent between the two options. This is when capital flows between the two countries will come to a halt.

International financial markets are in equilibrium when capital flows of this kind are unnecessary because the returns on domestic and foreign assets are equalized, taking into account likely capital gains or losses. This property of international financial markets is called the interest rate parity condition. It can be stated as:

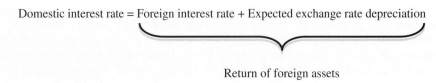

Domestic interest rate = Foreign interest rate + Expected exchange rate depreciation

Return of foreign assets

Figure 13.1 A trader ponders his next move

If it is not right there on one of the screens, any information can be obtained on the phone.
Source: Norges Bank

Written this way, it makes it clear that when our exchange rate depreciates, foreign assets become more valuable when measured in our currency. Conversely, an exchange rate appreciation – a negative depreciation – has the opposite effect and reduces the domestic value of foreign currency investments. For example, if the domestic interest rate is 5 per cent and the foreign rate is 2 per cent, the interest rate parity condition requires that the exchange rate be expected to depreciate by 3 per cent.

Among countries whose financial markets are deeply integrated, this means that the smallest deviation from the interest parity condition instantly triggers huge capital flows. These flows promptly affect domestic and foreign interest rates as well as current and expected future exchange rates and the interest rate parity is instantly re-established. In fact, deviations from the parity condition are fleeting, which is why traders try to spot and act upon them, for they offer profit opportunities to the early birds.

13.1.2 Does the interest rate parity condition work?

The parity condition cannot be directly observed because we cannot measure the expected exchange rate. Anyway, whose expectation are we talking about? There are thousands of traders, each of whom may have her own view. They all play the game of shifting money around all the time. What the condition does is to reveal the 'market sentiment', the average of what traders believe will be the exchange rate in the future. In other words, we interpret the interest parity condition as revealing the 'market expectation':

Expected exchange depreciation = Domestic interest rate – Foreign interest rate

This is not a proof that the parity condition works, simply an interpretation, and a warning that we cannot really observe expectations. But there is some indirect evidence, which leads

---

Box 13.1 The interest parity condition: a formal derivation

A trader wants to invest €1000 for one year and considers the choice between euros where the interest rate is i, say 5 per cent, and dollars where the interest rate is i^*, say 2 per cent. After one year, the euro investment will have become €1000$(1 + i)$, i.e. €1050. The investment in dollars requires selling the euros to acquire dollars. The current exchange rate is E_t, defining how many dollars are obtained by selling one euro, for example 1.3. Selling €1000 gives $1000.$E_t$ – $1300 in our example – which will become $1000.$E_t$.(1 + i^*)$ in one year's time, $1326 when $i^* = 2\%$. Then, the exchange rate is expected to be E_{t+1}, so that selling these dollars will yield €1000.E_t(1 + i^*)/E_{t+1}$, or €1326/$E_{t+1}$.

The interest parity condition is achieved when both strategies yield the same revenue:

$$1000(1 + i) = 1000\,E_t(1 + i^*)\frac{1}{E_{t+1}}$$

This will be verified if the expected exchange rate one year ahead is 1.2629. Note that the initial investment, €1000, appears on both sides of the equation and can therefore be eliminated, which simply means that the interest rate parity condition is independent of the amount involved:

$$(1 + i) = (1 + i^*)\frac{E_t}{E_{t+1}}$$

An approximation yields the condition presented in the text. It involves taking logs on both sides and noting that $ln(1 + i) \approx i$, $ln(1 + i^*) \approx i^*$, and $ln(E_t/E_{t+1}) \approx -(E_{t+1} - E_t)/E_t$:

$$i = i^* - \frac{E_{t+1} - E_t}{E_t}$$

This approximation says that if the euro interest rate is 5 per cent, the dollar interest rate is 2 per cent, the difference in favour of the euro (3 per cent) must be compensated by an expectation of euro depreciation of (about, because this is an approximation) 3 per cent.

---

to refinements. Figure 13.2 shows the interest rate on Greek and German public debts. Greece joined the euro area in January 2001. Before that, the Greek drachma was a weak currency that was perennially depreciating vis-à-vis the German mark. As the interest parity condition predicts, Greek interest rates were above German rates. Once Greece became a euro area member, the exchange rate between the drachma and Germany's new currency was irredeemably fixed. The interest parity condition predicts that the interest rates should become equalized, which they dutifully did, with the Greek rate gradually converging to the German rate until D-day.

13.1.3 The role of risk

This is not the end of the story, though, as Greek rates have again risen since the economic crisis started in 2008. This does not mean that the interest parity condition has failed, but it requires going deeper into the issue.

Figure 13.2 Government bond interest rates

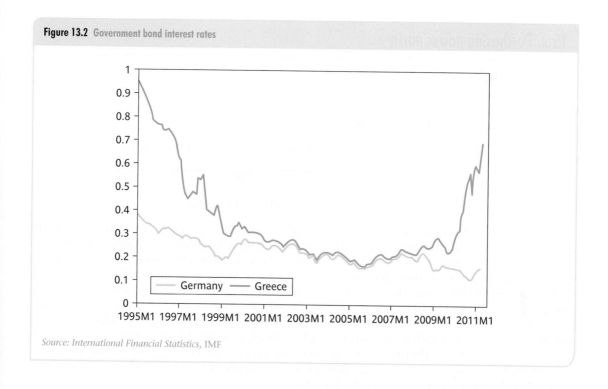

Source: *International Financial Statistics*, IMF

Once a country joins the monetary union, the situation is similar to what we find inside any country: the exchange rate disappears, so there can be no expected change in the exchange rate. Yet, within a country, there is not just one interest rate, but a whole range of rates. Top quality borrowers – rated AAA by rating agencies – pay much lower interest rates than risky borrowers. This can be summarized as follows:

Interest rate of risky asset = Interest rate of safe asset + Risk premium

Up until the crisis, developed country governments were seen as safe borrowers. In 2005, even though the Greek government was more indebted than the German government, its public debt was rated AA, just a notch below the AAA enjoyed by the German government. The risk premium was very small, hardly visible in Fig. 13.2. The crisis changed that, mainly for already highly indebted governments that went on running large deficits. As a result, the Greek debt came to be seen as increasingly risky and, quite naturally, commanded rising risk premia.

This is an example of a general rule. Within a country – or a monetary union – if interest rates are equal for assets that are similarly risky, we say that they belong to the same risk class. Across countries, the interest rate parity condition applies to assets that belong to the same risk class. Across risk classes, risk premia apply on top of the expected change in the exchange rate. From 2008 onwards, the Greek interest rate reflects the perceived increasing riskiness that the government will not be able to honour its debt. It may also reflect the possibility that Greece could leave the euro area, so that the expected exchange rate depreciation is no longer zero.

13.2 Purchasing power parity

13.2.1 The principle

The purchasing power parity (PPP) principle asserts that the rate of change of the nominal exchange rate between two countries is equal to the difference between the inflation rates in these two countries, called the inflation differential:

Exchange rate appreciation = Foreign inflation rate – Domestic inflation rate

Inflation differential

It means that if inflation at home is durably lower than abroad, our currency should appreciate. Conversely, a country with higher inflation sees its exchange rate depreciate vis-à-vis the currency of a country with a lower inflation rate. This principle only holds in the long run... when it holds; the next section gives an important reason why it sometimes fails to hold.[1]

An example of PPP is provided in Table 13.1, which compares Italy and Germany over a very long period, from 1960 to 1998, the year before the adoption of the euro by these two countries. Inflation in Italy had been high, on average 8.0 per cent per year, exceeding the German average rate of 3.2 per cent. The PPP prediction is that the Italian lira should have depreciated vis-à-vis the German mark by the difference, 4.8 per cent on average. In fact, the lira depreciated a bit more, at an average rate of 5.3 per cent. This is a good example of how PPP works: it tells us about the right story, not always very precisely, but close.

Table 13.1 PPP: Italy and Germany, 1960–98

Average annual inflation rate in Italy	8.0%
Average annual inflation rate in Germany	3.2%
Average annual depreciation of the lira	5.3%

Source: IMF

What is the logic behind the PPP principle? The explanation involves the distinction between the nominal and the real exchange rate. The nominal exchange rate is the one that is widely discussed and reported in newspapers. We will define it as the price in foreign currency of one unit of the domestic currency, for instance 1.3 dollars for 1 euro or 2 dollars for 1 pound. One function of the exchange rate is to translate the price of goods from one currency to another. When it changes, it affects the country's international competitiveness. The real exchange rate is designed to provide a measure of competitiveness. It is defined as the ratio of domestic to foreign good prices, expressed in the same currency. Consider the real exchange rate of the euro in terms of dollars. The real exchange rate compares the dollar price of a basket of goods made in Europe to the dollar price, P^*, of a basket of goods made in the USA. To that effect, we need to convert into dollars the basket price of domestic goods in euros, P (e.g. €100):

Price of a basket of European goods in euros: P (e.g. €100)

Exchange rate (dollars per euro): E (e.g. 1.3 \$/€)

Price of the same basket of European goods in dollars: EP (e.g. \$130)

---

[1] It is an implication of the neutrality of money and therefore applies in the same long run, over the duration of a business cycle, e.g. 5 years or more.

Thus we can compare EP with P^*, since both are measured in dollars. The real exchange rate is the ratio EP/P^*. We could instead measure the price of the US basket in euros as P^*/E and compare it to the domestic price in euros as well. When we divide P by P^*/E, we obtain EP/P^* as before. Reassuringly, it does not matter which currency we use. Like price levels, the real exchange rate is an index number, computed to take a simple value (e.g. 1 or 100) in a specified period.

When the real exchange rate increases – we say that it appreciates – it means that domestic goods become more expensive relative to foreign goods: our competitiveness declines. The real exchange rate appreciates when:

- the nominal exchange rate E appreciates;
- domestic prices P rise faster than foreign prices P^*, so that P/P^* increases.

Conversely, a real exchange rate depreciation – a decline in EP/P^* – signals a gain in competitiveness.

The exchange rate E and prices are both nominal variables. The money neutrality principle asserts that neutral variables do not affect real variables in the long run. This implies that changes in the nominal exchange rate and to price levels at home and abroad leave the real exchange rate unaffected in the long run. In fact, PPP implies that the real exchange rate is constant.[2] The mechanism at work is presented in the next section, but we first look at how PPP fares in practice. Figure 13.3 displays the nominal and real exchange rates between sterling and the Deutschmark (the euro after 1998). Year-to-year movements in the nominal exchange rate are mirrored in similar but subdued movements in the real exchange rate; clearly PPP is not a

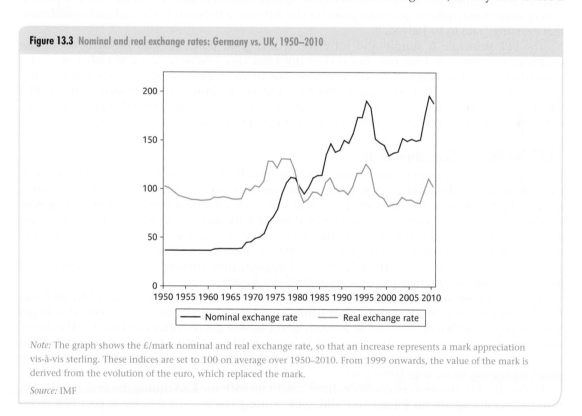

Figure 13.3 Nominal and real exchange rates: Germany vs. UK, 1950–2010

Note: The graph shows the £/mark nominal and real exchange rate, so that an increase represents a mark appreciation vis-à-vis sterling. These indices are set to 100 on average over 1950–2010. From 1999 onwards, the value of the mark is derived from the evolution of the euro, which replaced the mark.

Source: IMF

---

[2] This assertion is mathematically proved as follows. Since the rate of change (e.g. in per cent) of the real exchange rate is $\Delta(EP/P^*)/(EP/P^*) = \Delta E/E + \Delta P/P - \Delta P^*/P^*$, we have $\Delta(EP/P^*)/(EP/P^*) = 0$ when $\Delta E/E = \Delta P^*/P^* - \Delta P/P$.

short-run phenomenon. While it is not constant from year to year, the real exchange moves around a reasonably stable level. Indeed, the fivefold nominal depreciation of the pound since 1950 fails to leave a lasting impression on the real exchange rate.

13.2.2 The equilibrium real exchange rate

The long-run stability of the real exchange rate cannot be a fluke. When its real exchange rate appreciates, a country becomes less competitive. Its current account deteriorates as exports decline – domestic goods are more expensive on foreign markets – and imports rise – foreign goods are cheaper at home. The resulting external deficit cannot go on for ever. Eventually, either the nominal exchange rate must depreciate or prices have to move to re-establish competitiveness. Either way, the real exchange rate must return to its 'normal' level, which is called the equilibrium rate: it is the rate at which trade is balanced. When the real exchange rate is above equilibrium, it is said to be overvalued, and it is undervalued in the opposite case. Over- and under-valuations are instances of misalignments.

This explains why PPP is a long-run concept. External imbalances are possible, indeed they occur all the time, but they must eventually be corrected. It may take a long time for that to happen. In Fig. 13.3, the real exchange rate index is constructed so that, on average, it is equal to 100 over the whole period 1950–2010. If the real exchange rate fluctuates around its equilibrium level, such a long-run average is a pretty good approximation of the equilibrium real rate. Indeed, the £/mark real exchange rate started out at 102.7 in 1950 and was at 103.7 in 2010. How long does it take for misalignments to be corrected? Recent studies tend to conclude that the process is very slow: it may take two to four years for the difference between the actual and equilibrium real exchange rate to be halved.

The PPP principle is simple and intuitive. It is a good point to start thinking about the exchange rate over the long run, but it does not hold very precisely, as we already noted, nor everywhere and at all times. Not only is it very slow to assert itself but it also suffers from many important exceptions. If it works well among countries at similar stages of development, like the developed countries, it can fail badly in other cases, for well-understood reasons. One key reason, which affects the newer members of the EU, is presented in the next section.

13.2.3 The Balassa–Samuelson effect

Italy and Germany compete with each other on broadly similar goods and services, such as cars, insurance or chemicals. These products are very similar, so that competition is mostly a matter of costs, mostly labour costs. India and China also manufacture cars, which they start exporting. Their labour costs are a fraction of those of Italy and Germany, and indeed their cars are considerably cheaper. Yet, Indians and Chinese find it hard to enter the European market because these cars are low-tech, and this is indeed why they must be very cheap, and their labour costs very low. Over the years, though, they will upgrade their products, which will allow them to raise their prices and their wages, as explained in Chapter 7.

This is the Balassa–Samuelson effect.[3] Currently, labour costs in China are about €1 an hour. Fast forward: in 50 years, it is likely that China could have caught up with Europe and wages will not be that different from those in Germany. Chinese goods, priced in euro (in the above notations, EP) are now cheap but they will be comparable to German goods and fetch similar prices (P^*). Seen from China's perspective, this means that the real exchange rate EP/P^* will be on an increasing trend over these years.

Within the EU, the western countries have caught up with the USA during the period 1950–80. Standards of living are no longer very different. Among these countries, we expect PPP to do

---

[3] It is named after Hungarian-born US economist Bela Balassa, who taught at Johns Hopkins University, and Paul Samuelson, Nobel Prize laureate, who taught at MIT; they discovered this effect independently.

well. The central and eastern European countries have been transiting from planned to market economies since the mid-1990s. Starting from a low income level and poor production capacities, they have been catching up on their western neighbours. As they build up their production potential and adopt the best technologies, they climb up the product quality ladder and produce increasingly more sophisticated products that they can sell at higher prices, which allows their workers to earn higher wages. For instance, in 1997, the average hourly labour cost in Hungary was 10 per cent of that in Germany; by 2009, it has increased to 19 per cent. This process is bound to continue over the coming decades, and Hungary's real exchange rate relative to Germany will keep on appreciating, year in, year out.

Real appreciation – an increase in EP/P^* – can occur as the result of an appreciation of the nominal exchange rate – a rise in E – or as a result of faster domestic inflation (P/P^* increases), or any combination of changes in these variables. Table 13.2 shows how this has played out for the central and eastern European countries. For each country, it displays in the first row the inflation differential, the difference between domestic and euro area inflation rates, and the nominal exchange rate appreciation vis-à-vis the euro.[4] In all these countries, inflation has been higher than in the Eurozone. For the real exchange rate to remain constant, they would have had to undergo a nominal depreciation of the same magnitude; in fact, their currencies depreciated by less, even appreciating in the case of the Czech Republic, Lithuania and Slovakia.

Table 13.2 The Balassa–Samuelson effect: average annual changes (%), 1996–2008

	Bulgaria	Czech Republic	Estonia	Latvia	Lithuania
Inflation differential	29.0	1.6	3.2	3.7	1.4
Nominal appreciation	−19.7	2.6	−0.2	0.0	3.2
Real appreciation	9.3	4.2	3.0	3.7	4.6
	Hungary	Poland	Romania	Slovenia	Slovakia
Inflation differential	6.2	3.3	28.3	3.8	4.1
Nominal appreciation	−2.4	−0.2	−20.6	−2.8	1.5
Real appreciation	3.8	3.1	7.7	1.0	5.6

Source: AMECO, European Commission

13.3 The impossible trinity

13.3.1 Monetary policy: a refresher[5]

As already indicated, the long run is the realm of money neutrality: monetary policy effects are limited to nominal variables (price inflation, the nominal exchange rate).[6] In the short run, however, monetary policy can have effects on the real economy (growth, employment,

---

[4] Following the reasoning in footnote 2, we present $\Delta P/P - \Delta P^*/P^*$ in the first row, $\Delta E/E$ in the second row and the real exchange rate is calculated in the last row as $\Delta(EP/P^*)/(EP/P^*) = \Delta E/E + \Delta P/P - \Delta P^*/P^*$, i.e. the sum of the first two rows.

[5] This section starts with a brief review the standard macroeconomic model for an open economy, which can be skipped by students familiar with this framework.

[6] In diagrams that display real output – or the output gap – on the horizontal axis and inflation – or the price level – on the vertical axis, this dichotomy is usually captured by the transition from the short-run aggregate supply curve to the long-run vertical curve.

spending, etc.). These effects are usually explained using the *IS–LM* framework. Here we revisit this framework to introduce two modifications: we examine the implications of economic and financial openness and we capture the fact that nowadays central banks set the interest rate.

The *IS* curve represents the conditions under which the market for goods and services is in equilibrium. It incorporates the Keynesian assumption under which, in the short run, prices are sticky – they move much more slowly that other macroeconomic variables – so that firms produce whatever the market wants to buy. The question is which levels of output, measured by the GDP, are such that total demand adds up exactly to the total production income that supports demand. More precisely, aggregate demand *Y* is decomposed into 4 components: private consumption *C*, private investment spending by firms *I*, public spending *G* and foreign demand for our goods and services, i.e. exports, *X*:

$$Y = C + I + G + X - Z$$

where we subtract imports *Z* from private and public spending $(C + I + G)$, because these are goods and services bought abroad and therefore not produced locally. The difference $(X - Z)$ between exports and imports represents the current account. This is the first extension to the open economy case.

The *IS* curve recognizes that private spending is affected by domestic income, i.e. the GDP *Y*, and by the interest rate *i*. A higher GDP tends to raise consumption and investment spending while a higher interest rate works in the opposite direction because it raises borrowing costs. Thus, if for some reason total GDP rises, it means that more goods and services are available (the left-hand side of the equation above increases). Will they be bought? More production means more income, so consumption and investment (in the right-hand side) will increase, but will that be enough? Experience tells us that the answer is no, in part because some of the additional income will be saved, therefore not spent, and in part because some of the additional spending falls on imported goods and services. It follows that the additional production is not entirely demanded. In order to restore equilibrium between supply and demand, the interest must decline, to generate additional private spending. The *IS* curve captures this equilibrium requirement, as shown in Fig. 13.4. The curve will shift when exogenous events that concern demand for domestic production occur: changes in exports and imports unrelated to domestic income, for example real exchange rate movements, or changes in public spending, or taxes, as they affect resources available to the private sector.

The second change to the *IS–LM* framework is . . . to get rid of the *LM* curve. This curve assumes that the central bank controls the money supply to affect the interest rate. Nowadays, central banks do the opposite. They control the interest rate directly – they put in whatever amount of money is needed to achieve their interest rate target. Graphically, given its objectives, the central bank simply picks a point on the *IS* curve, e.g. point *A* in Fig. 13.4. The *LM* curve is not helpful any more and can be ignored.[7]

The last change concerns financial openness. We know from Section 13.1.1 that capital mobility leads to the interest rate parity condition. This condition says that the domestic interest rate is determined by two factors: the foreign interest rate and the expected change in the nominal exchange rate. There is nothing that we can do about the foreign interest rate, so we must take it as given.[8] Imagine, for the time being, that the expected exchange rate change is also given, then the interest rate parity condition simply imposes upon us our own interest rate. This is represented in Fig. 13.4 by the *IRP* line. In general this line has no reason to pass

---

[7] Formally, the *LM* curve still exists, but it only tells us what the central bank must be doing with the money supply to set the interest rate.

[8] There is one exception: the USA. As the world's largest financial centre, the USA can influence other countries' interest rates. Thus the interest rate parity condition applies to all countries but one, the USA. When the Federal Reserve, the US central bank, decides on its interest rate, this is the *i** that appears in other countries' interest rate parity conditions.

Figure 13.4 The short-run macroeconomic framework

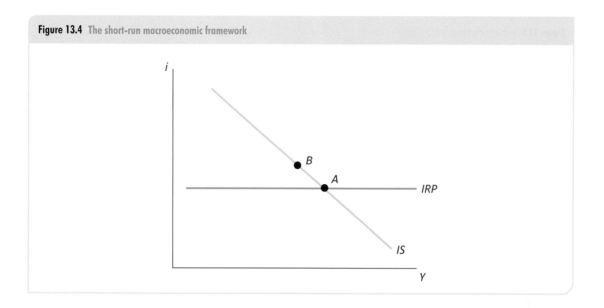

through point *A*, which identifies the interest rate chosen by the central bank. This means that the central bank must either accept being at point *B* or 'do something' about the exchange rate so that the *IRP* line goes through point *A*. The implications of this conclusion are far-reaching. They are examined in the next section.

13.3.2 The impossible trinity principle

The impossible trinity principle is stated as follows:
   Only two of the three following features are compatible with each other:

- full capital mobility
- fixed exchange rates
- autonomous monetary policy.

The incompatibility of these three features can be seen using Fig. 13.4. The first feature, full capital mobility, means that the domestic interest rate is determined by the interest parity condition, so we must be on the *IRP* line. But where exactly is this line? That the exchange rate is fixed implies that the exchange rate should not be expected to change: the domestic interest rate is equal to the foreign interest rate and the *IRP* line is positioned at $i = i^*$. Given the situation on the goods market as represented by the *IS* schedule, full capital mobility and a fixed exchange rate regime therefore require that the economy be at point *A*. Monetary policy autonomy occurs when the central bank is free to choose the interest rate, for instance picking point *B*. Obviously, it cannot do so. The conclusion is that the central bank has no policy autonomy under a fixed exchange rate regime.

The impossible trinity principle is represented in Fig. 13.5 by a triangle. Each angle corresponds to one of the three features and each side represents a feasible combination. The triangle's left side corresponds to the case just described, a fixed exchange rate and capital mobility, but no monetary policy autonomy. Consider now the right side of the triangle, when capital controls

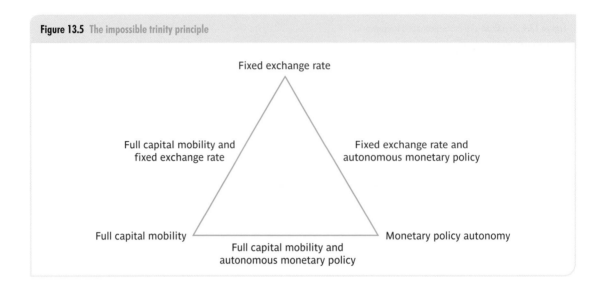

Figure 13.5 The impossible trinity principle

prevent capital mobility – more on controls below. Traders cannot (legally) move their monies freely and the interest parity no longer applies. The *IRP* line does not exist, leaving the central bank free to choose the interest rate that best fits its objectives, irrespective of whether the exchange rate is fixed or not.

The bottom side of the triangle represents the case when the exchange rate floats freely. The impossible trinity is a little bit trickier to understand in this case. Full capital mobility imposes the interest rate parity condition, which involves exchange rate changes, now possible under the prevailing exchange rate regime. Suppose that the central bank chooses point *A* in Fig. 13.4. The question is: Where does the *IRP* line lie? Can it go through point *A*? The answer is yes, if the exchange floats freely. To see why and how, imagine that, initially, the situation is such that the *IRP* line is as drawn, below point *A*. The domestic interest rate is too high for the parity condition to be met. It exceeds the foreign rate *plus* the currently expected exchange rate appreciation or depreciation. The result is that capital flows in and the current exchange rate appreciates. Whatever happens to the *future expected* exchange rate, the *current* exchange rate will keep on appreciating until it is high enough above the future rate to achieve the expected exchange rate change that the interest rate parity requires. An example may help grasp this reasoning.

Imagine that we start from the situation described in the first row of Table 13.3. Although the exchange rate is freely floating, markets do not expect it to change from its current value of 10, and we assume that markets will stick to this forecast.[9] With an interest rate of 5 per cent at home and 2 per cent abroad, the parity condition is not satisfied and traders rush capital into the domestic financial markets, because they are seen as more lucrative. This leads to an exchange appreciation. The exchange rate goes up and up, until it reaches the value of 10.3. Then the rate of expected depreciation becomes 3 per cent and the interest rate parity condition is re-established.[10] Capital flows stop, equilibrium is restored and the central bank has it its own way.

The impossible trinity principle is central to the European integration process. It implies that, for a country that maintains full financial integration, the exchange rate policy, i.e. the choice of an exchange rate regime, is simply the same thing as adopting a monetary policy strategy. Fixing

---

[9] An exercise takes up the case when the future expected exchange rate changes.

[10] This is only approximately true. With the exchange rate expected to be 10, a 3 per cent depreciation occurs when the current exchange rate is 10.3093.

Table 13.3 Restoring the interest parity condition

Domestic interest rate (i)	Foreign interest rate (i^*)	Expected change in the exchange rate $(E_{t+1} - E_t)/E_t$	Current exchange rate (E_t)	Future expected exchange rate (E_{t+1})	Parity condition met? Consequence?
5%	2%	0%	10	10	No. Capital flows in.
5%	2%	− 3%	10.3	10	Yes. Capital flows stop.

the exchange rate means adopting the foreign interest rate; conversely, maintaining the ability to choose the domestic interest rate requires allowing the exchange rate to float freely. Ever since the EU adopted in 1992 the principle of open capital markets as part of the Single Market (see Chapter 1), the choice has been circumscribed to the left or bottom sides of the triangle in Fig. 13.5.

One way of escaping the choice between exchange rate stability and monetary policy autonomy is to restrict capital movements. This is one reason why many European countries operated extensive capital controls until the early 1990s when full capital mobility was made compulsory. Likewise, many of the new EU members only abandoned capital controls upon accession.

13.3.3 Who does what?

Each side of the impossibility triangle has its real-life supporters, a more or less conscious choice. This section gives some examples, with the aim of signalling that there is no optimal choice: as circumstances vary, it may be desirable to adopt a new combination of two of the three features. Governments often want to have all three features at the same time; in Section 13.4 we show that invariably the result is a crisis. Box 13.2 describes a particular episode, the European debt crisis.

Full capital mobility and autonomous monetary policy, flexible exchange rate

In this case, monetary policy is effective but the central bank must give up any pretence at steering the exchange rate. The Eurozone as a whole, the USA, Japan, the UK, Switzerland and Sweden follow this approach. These countries, which gave up capital controls long ago and are committed to full financial openness, have decided to retain full control on monetary policy.

While retaining monetary autonomy sounds like a good idea, it has drawbacks as well. The downside is that the exchange rate can be quite volatile, which affects external competitiveness. For example, the UK has very explicitly decided to retain monetary policy autonomy and negotiated an exemption from the EU obligation to eventually join the monetary union. Figure 13.6 describes the experience since 1999, when the euro was launched. The left-hand chart displays the nominal exchange rate of sterling relative to the euro, along with the corresponding real exchange rate. The nominal rate fluctuates quite widely around the real rate. As periods of overvaluation follow periods of undervaluation, trade is being disrupted. Within the European Single Market, such fluctuations may become a source of irritation.

On the other hand, Britain has retained full control of its monetary policy. Like other central banks, the Bank of England endeavours to carry out short-run stabilization policy without jeopardizing long-run price stability.[11] How helpful is monetary policy autonomy? Quite a

---

[11] This is an implication of the long-run money neutrality principle: monetary policy can affect the real economy in the short but not in the long run. In the long run, monetary policy determines the inflation rate.

Figure 13.6 Flexible exchange rates: the British experience

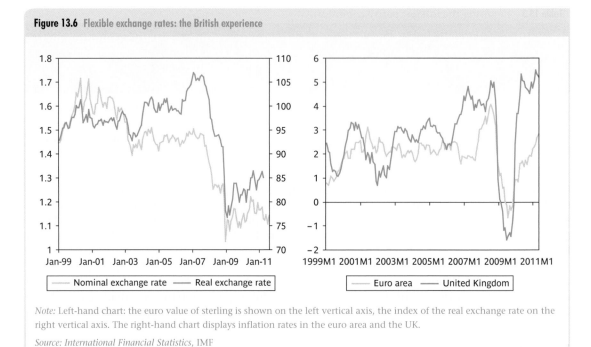

Note: Left-hand chart: the euro value of sterling is shown on the left vertical axis, the index of the real exchange rate on the right vertical axis. The right-hand chart displays inflation rates in the euro area and the UK.

Source: International Financial Statistics, IMF

lot, actually. For instance, facing the recession that followed the economic financial crisis that started in mid-2007, the UK has benefited from a large depreciation (some 50 per cent) of its currency, which boosted its external competitiveness at a time when domestic demand crashed in the wake of bank failures. Yet, the right-hand chart in Fig. 13.6 shows that inflation has risen much more in the UK than in the euro area. More generally, inflation in the UK has been more volatile and on average higher. This shows that monetary policy autonomy carries benefits but also costs.

Full capital mobility and fixed exchange rate

In this case, the central bank must dedicate itself to upholding the fixed exchange rate commitment. This strategy has been adopted in Europe by the current Exchange Rate Mechanism (ERM, presented in Chapter 14) members. Figure 13.7 shows the case of Denmark, which like the UK has been given an exemption and did not join the euro area. In contrast to the UK, which has no intention of adopting the euro, Denmark operates as a shadow euro area member and, to that effect, it is committed to keeping its exchange rate fixed to the euro.[12] The figure shows that the Danish central bank has essentially adopted all decisions taken by the European Central Bank. The distinction between such a policy and euro area membership is tenuous. Euro area member countries have formally given up monetary policy autonomy by transferring the responsibility for monetary policy to the European Central Bank, and Denmark has done the same informally. Of course, Denmark is not involved in ECB decisions.

---

[12] In 1992, the Danish people rejected the Maastricht Treaty, against the wishes of the government, because they wanted to keep their currency. Since European treaties are valid only when ratified by all member countries, Denmark was offered an exemption from euro area membership and a second referendum in 1993 was successful. Yet, the Danish authorities still believe that exchange rate stability is crucial and decided to fix the kroner to the euro.

Figure 13.7 Central bank interest rates: Denmark and the euro area (1999–2011)

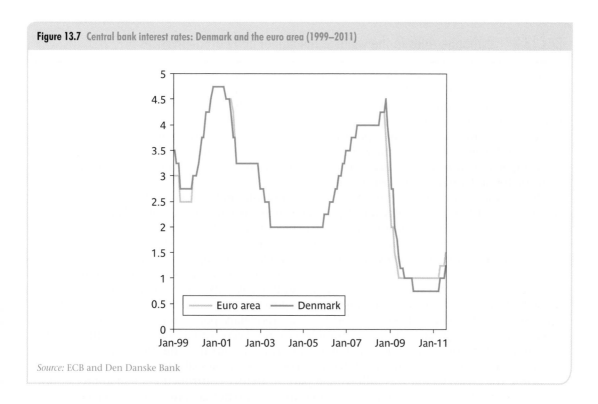

Source: ECB and Den Danske Bank

Fixed exchange rate and monetary policy autonomy, with capital controls

Capital controls make the interest rate parity principle inoperative. There exist a wide variety of capital controls. Some simply forbid the transfer of funds between a country and the rest of the world, or subject these transfers to limits, sometimes to administration authorization. The result is that traders can no longer take advantage of higher returns abroad, or of lower borrowing costs. Being restricted, capital flows cannot establish the parity condition. Many developing and some emerging market countries, for instance China, use this type of control. Another form of capital control imposes taxes on international financial transactions. The result is that traders must factor in these taxes when they compare domestic and foreign interest rates. If the tax rate is high enough, it will discourage a significant portion of capital flows. In recent years, Brazil has adopted this mechanism.

There is no miracle, however. Capital controls allow for monetary autonomy but there are costs. To start with, people try to evade the restrictions and the taxes. This means that one has to build an administration to monitor and enforce the controls, and then to punish those who evade them. The more sophisticated the financial sector, the more expensive and eventually self-defeating the enforcement of capital controls. In addition, while capital flows are occasionally disruptive, they serve a useful purpose. They allow savers to achieve the best returns that the world has on offer, much as they allow borrowers to find the best available loans. Financial autarky prevents these arrangements, which eventually harm investment and economic growth.

The combination of capital controls and fixed exchange rates was widespread under the Bretton Woods system – although some countries such as Germany and Switzerland almost never enforced capital controls. It also characterized Europe's early monetary integration efforts which led to the European Monetary System (see Chapter 14). The removal of capital controls made this option non-viable, which eventually led to the adoption of the euro by most EU countries, and to a free floating of the exchange rate in Sweden and the UK.

Box 13.2 Exchange rates in the wake of the global and European crises

Following the subprime and Wall Street crises in 2007–08, the dollar had to weaken. Then, starting in late 2009, the financial markets have started to question the ability of some euro area member countries to service their soaring public debts (that story is the subject of Chapter 19), which weakened the euro as well. For an exchange rate to depreciate, however, some other currency(ies) must appreciate. We look at three countries: Brazil, China and Switzerland. The evolution of their exchange rates relative to the dollar is shown in Fig. 13.8. For comparison purposes, the exchange rates have been converted into indices that take the value of 100 in January 2007, before the crisis.

Brazil started out with a floating exchange rate and full capital mobility (the lower side of the triangle in Fig. 13.5). Its exchange rate depreciated rapidly when the crisis hit and initial concerns about the impact on its economy led to a deep depreciation, as the real lost about half its value in the second half of 2008. But then it zoomed up and promptly recovered its earlier losses. Afraid that this appreciation could abort the recovery, Guido Mantega, the Finance Minister, talked about a 'currency war' and imposed capital control. This episode illustrates three points. First, floating exchange rates can be highly volatile and this volatility can be highly uncomfortable. Second, when faced with a challenging situation, governments can change the position on the impossible trinity triangle. Brazil decided to retain monetary policy autonomy but wanted to stabilize the exchange rate. Third, the controls have not been entirely successful – although no one knows what would have happened otherwise. This suggests that the effectiveness of capital controls is doubtful in countries that have a well-developed financial sector.

Before the crisis, China was following a path of tightly controlled gradual appreciation, largely to meet international pressure, because its exchange rate was perceived to be undervalued and the cause of large external surpluses. When the crisis started, China again pegged its currency to the dollar. Once fast growth came back, the exchange rate was again allowed to appreciate. This is a fixed exchange rate regime, with the proviso that the exchange rate is guided to rise in value as desired by the authorities. Quite clearly, the government also wants to preserve the autonomy of its monetary policy. Logically, China operates an array of exchange controls. In fact, its currency is not even freely convertible. Sales and purchases of the renminbi[1] require prior authorization, as does every transfer of funds. Figure 13.8 shows that China went through the crisis without any exchange rate instability. On the other hand, the Chinese financial markets are relatively rudimentary. The allocation of resources is under the direct control of the authorities. It is generally believed that China's vast savings are not efficiently channelled to their best uses, resulting in significant waste.

As a financial centre, Switzerland has long been committed to full capital mobility. Its excellent record of prudent monetary policy, delivering low inflation and, via PPP, a strong currency, has also contributed to the attractiveness of its financial industry. This explains the adoption of a flexible exchange rate regime. During the crisis, the Swiss franc has been quite volatile. As the situation deteriorated in Europe in 2010, once again investors saw Switzerland as a safe haven. Although the Swiss interest rate has been kept close to 0 per cent, capital inflows have been heavy, generating a continuing appreciation and thus validating the interest parity condition. The franc has appreciated by 35 per cent, putting the country's competitiveness under heavy stress. The central bank tried several ways of stemming this evolution, until it fixed a limit to appreciation, an arrangement called a one-sided peg.

---

[1] Renminbi is the Chinese pronunciation for RMB, which means People's currency.

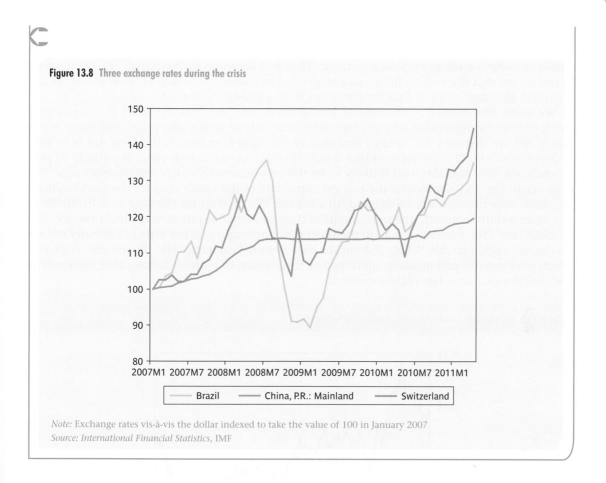

Figure 13.8 Three exchange rates during the crisis

Note: Exchange rates vis-à-vis the dollar indexed to take the value of 100 in January 2007
Source: International Financial Statistics, IMF

13.3.4 Can the impossible trinity principle be ignored?

Policymakers naturally do not like the impossible trinity principle, because it restricts their room for manoeuvre. It is often tempting to ignore it and keep the exchange rate fixed while using monetary policy actively and freeing capital movements.

What happens when one tries to violate the impossible trinity? The answer is simple: a currency crisis. Sooner or later a speculative attack wipes out the fixed exchange rate arrangement. We will show in Chapter 14 that this is precisely what happened in Europe in 1993. Some more recent and prominent examples include Russia and Southeast Asia in 1997 and, in some way, Argentina in 2001. In all these cases, financial liberalization was undertaken as part of the financial globalization process but the authorities did not want to give up either the fixed exchange rate system or monetary autonomy. Eventually, they had to make this choice but in the midst of traumatic crises.

13.4 In practice: exchange rate regimes

13.4.1 When does the exchange rate regime matter?

Trivial as it may sound, the choice of an exchange rate regime only matters if the nominal exchange rate has real effects. If monetary policy were fully neutral, even in the short run, it would have no effect other than determining the rate of inflation. PPP would always hold, the real exchange rate would remain constant and the behaviour of the nominal exchange rate would be irrelevant for any practical purpose. Thus we care about the exchange rate regime only to the extent that the real exchange rate is affected by monetary policy, i.e. that money is not neutral in the short run and that the short run is long enough to matter.

We know that money is not neutral in the short run, and that the short run is not that short; in fact, it extends over several years. Non-neutrality arises because prices and wages move slowly; we say that they are 'sticky'. One way of checking how long is the long run is to look at deviations from PPP among countries where the Balassa–Samuelson effect is unlikely to play a significant role. Arguably, this is likely to be the case between Sweden and the euro area. The evidence in Fig. 13.9 shows that the real exchange rate of the krona vis-à-vis the euro has been trendless since the euro was introduced, this is what PPP predicts for the long run. In the short run, from month to month, the movements of the real exchange rate closely mirror those of the nominal rate. This is evidence that, in the short run, prices move far too little to have any impact on the real exchange rate.[13] This also means that nominal exchange rate movements have real effects over months and quarters, up to two or three years, or more. It follows that, over such a horizon, the exchange rate regime matters.

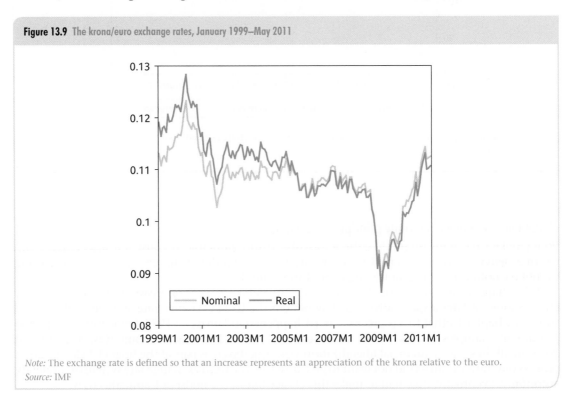

Figure 13.9 The krona/euro exchange rates, January 1999–May 2011

Note: The exchange rate is defined so that an increase represents an appreciation of the krona relative to the euro.
Source: IMF

13.4.2 What's on the menu?

So far we have mentioned just two exchange rate regimes: fixed and flexible. In practice, exchange rate regimes come in all sorts of shapes and forms. Except when the exchange rate is freely floating, all other regimes require choosing a foreign currency to peg to. The main anchors have

---

[13] Formally, if E and EP/P^* move closely together, it must be that P and P^* do not change much, at least relative to each other.

traditionally been the US dollar and the Deutschmark, now replaced by the euro. This section reviews the various possible arrangements, going from full flexibility to full rigidity.

Free floating

The simplest regime is when the monetary authorities decline any responsibility for the exchange rate. The rate is then freely determined by the markets and can fluctuate by any amount at any moment. We already noted (Section 13.3.3) that most developed countries let their exchange rate float freely because they want to conduct autonomous monetary policies and to put their central bank in charge of inflation.

Managed floating

In small and open economies, the authorities are often concerned that a free float results in excessive exchange rate volatility, a pattern sometimes called 'fear of floating'. At the same time, for reasons that will become clear below, they may not want to commit themselves to a particular exchange rate; this is 'fear of fixing'. What they wish is to intervene on the exchange markets from time to time, as they see fit. They operate a managed float, sometimes called a dirty float, which is a halfway house between a free float and a peg. Central banks buy their own currency when they consider it too weak, and sell it when they see it as too strong, but they refrain from pursuing any particular exchange rate target. They are not making any explicit commitment but they are occasionally present on foreign exchange markets with the aim of smoothing short-term movements. This strategy cannot always be distinguished from a free float. European countries that manage their exchange rates to some degree include the Czech Republic, Hungary, Poland and Romania.

Fixed exchange rates or target zones

In a fixed exchange rate regime, the authorities declare an official parity vis-à-vis another currency, chiefly the US dollar or the euro, sometimes vis-à-vis a basket of several currencies. The arrangement normally specifies margins of fluctuations around the central parity, hence the qualification as a target zone. The wider is the band of fluctuation, the closer is the regime to a free float or to a managed float. Practically, the central bank must intervene – and lose policy independence – when the exchange rate moves towards the edges of the target zone, but it can also intervene at any time it wishes, even if the exchange rate is well within its band of fluctuation. The main advantage is that the knowledge that the central bank will intervene for sure as the exchange rate moves towards the margins leads traders to become prudent when this is the case, which has a stabilizing effect – unless they believe that the central bank will not be willing to intervene strongly enough, in which case we may face a speculative attack.

It is understood that the central parity may be infrequently changed, a procedure called realignment. The realignment option is useful to face serious disturbances. It is also needed when domestic inflation durably exceeds that of the anchor currency, which erodes external competitiveness.[14] The realignment option provides some monetary policy autonomy, mainly the ability for the inflation rate to differ from that in the anchor currency country.

From 1945 to 1973, under the Bretton Woods agreement, fixed and adjustable exchange rates were the rule worldwide. The margins were initially set at ±1 per cent until 1971, and then widened to ±2.25 per cent. This widening reflected a desire to maintain monetary policy autonomy as capital movements, strictly limited since the end of the Second World War, were

---

[14] If inflation is higher than abroad, P rises faster than P^* and P/P^* increases. When the nominal exchange rate E is fixed, the real exchange rate EP/P^* appreciates. In order to restore competitiveness and lower the real exchange rate, the country must depreciate the nominal rate, i.e. reduce E.

gradually liberalized. Fundamentally, it reflected attempts to avoid the implication of the impossible trinity and the Bretton Woods system collapsed in the midst of currency crisis.

Between 1979 and 1993, Europe's Exchange Rate Mechanism (ERM) also operated as a system of fixed and adjustable exchange rates, which is studied in the next chapter. Here we just note that attempts to retain monetary policy autonomy led to a serious crisis in 1993 and to the end of the ERM as originally designed.

Crawling pegs

In a crawling peg regime the authorities declare a central parity and band of fluctuation around it. The characteristic of this regime is that the central parity and the associated maximum and lower levels are allowed to slide regularly: they crawl. The rate of crawl is sometimes pre-announced, sometimes not. The difference between a crawling peg and a target zone is not clear cut, since both involve an acceptable range – margins considered narrow enough to qualify as a pegged arrangement are typically less than ±5 per cent around the official parity. Many Latin American countries operated crawling pegs in the 1980s, as did Poland and Russia in the mid-1990s. These arrangements did not last for very long, however, because they really are attempts to escape the logic of the impossible trinity. Figure 13.10 shows the case of Poland; note that the rate of crawl was gradually reduced while the width of the band was progressively widened until the currency was allowed to float freely.

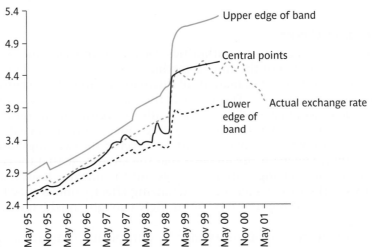

Figure 13.10 Poland's crawling band, May 1995–March 2000

Notes: The exchange rate is an index computed by the National Bank, which rises when the currency depreciates. The crawling band was introduced in March 1995 and lasted until April 2000 when the zloty was allowed to float, and soon appreciated. The anchor was a basket index whose composition was occasionally changed (in 1999 it included the euro, with a 55 per cent weight, and the US dollar, with a 45 per cent weight). The vertical scale (zloty per euro) is inverted so that an upward movement represents a nominal appreciation.

Source: National Bank of Poland

Currency boards

Currency boards are a tight version of fixed exchange rate regimes. Under a pegged regime, monetary policy has to be wholly dedicated to the exchange rate target but, as we saw, the possibility to devalue or revalue and the existence of margins of fluctuation introduce some degree of flexibility. Currency boards are designed to remove this flexibility. In order to ensure that monetary policy is entirely dedicated to support the declared parity, with no margin of fluctuation, the central bank may only issue domestic money when it acquires foreign exchange reserves. If it spends its foreign exchange reserves, the central bank must retire its own currency from circulation and the money supply shrinks.[15]

Currency boards used to exist in the British Empire, and disappeared with it. They were revived by a number of Caribbean islands as they became independent and by Hong Kong in 1983. They became more widespread in the 1990s when countries with weak political institutions, such as Argentina, Bosnia-Herzegovina and Bulgaria, chose this rigorous arrangement to put an end to monetary indiscipline and its corollary, raging inflation. Freshly independent from the Soviet Union, with no history of central banking, Estonia and Lithuania also adopted a currency board. Argentina's system collapsed in 2002, illustrating the dangers of an inflexible arrangement.

Dollarization/euroization and currency unions

A yet stricter regime is to fix the exchange rate irrevocably, which means adopting a foreign currency, hence the term '*dollarization*' (as in Ecuador, El Salvador, Panama, Liberia) or '*euroization*' (as in Kosovo and Montenegro). Without a domestic currency, there obviously can be no monetary policy whatsoever. This regime is typically adopted by small countries with very weak political institutions as they simply rely on a foreign central bank to carry out what is de facto their own monetary policy.

A monetary union is very similar since countries that decide to share the same currency give up national monetary policy. The difference between a currency board and a monetary union is that in the former monetary policy is carried out by a foreign central bank, which only cares about its own country, while the common central bank of the latter cares about all member countries. In addition to Europe, francophone Africa and some Caribbean islands have formed monetary unions, as described in Box 13.3.

Box 13.3 Existing monetary unions

In Africa, the CFA zone was created when the former French colonies reached independence in the 1960s.[1] It includes two unions: the West African Economic and Monetary Union (Benin, Burkina Faso, Côte d'Ivoire, Guinea Bissau, Mali, Niger, Senegal, Togo) and the Central African Economic and Monetary Union (Cameroon, Central African Republic, Chad, Democratic Republic of Congo, Equatorial Guinea, Gabon). These countries never created their own currencies (Mali and Equatorial Guinea did, until they joined the CFA zone in 1985). The two monetary unions are formally independent from each other and each has its own central bank, yet both peg their currency to the French franc at the same rate, and both devalued just once by 50 per cent in 1994. They have been pegged to the euro since 1999. The arrangement is special, a legacy of colonial times and based on a guarantee by France, but it is a true, modern monetary union. Belgium and Luxembourg formed a monetary union until they joined the euro area.

The East Caribbean Common Market (Antigua and Barbuda, Dominica, Grenada, St Kitts and Nevis, St Lucia, and St Vincent and the Grenadines) forms a monetary union. These are small islands that can hardly be compared to the European monetary union.

---

[15] The study of the gold standard in Section 14.1.1 provides the logic of this rule.

Brunei and Singapore also form a currency union.

Other countries have unilaterally adopted a foreign currency and therefore do not actively participate in the running of the central bank. This is the case of Kiribati, Nauru and Tuvalu, which use the Australian dollar; Lesotho, Namibia and Swaziland, which use the South African rand; and Bahamas, Liberia, Marshall Islands, Micronesia, Palau and Panama, which have adopted the US dollar. More recently, Ecuador and San Salvador have also adopted the US dollar since 2001. In Europe, Monaco uses the French franc (now the euro), Liechtenstein the Swiss franc, and San Marino the Italian lira (now the euro). These are not true monetary unions, since the centre country is not committed to take into account the interests and viewpoints of its 'satellites', and actually never does.

[1] The term CFA comes from the old colonial French designation 'Comptoir Français d'Afrique'. The Western Africa's CFA means *Communauté financière d'Afrique* (Financial Community of Africa), while the Central Africa version means *Coopération financière en Afrique centrale* (Financial Cooperation in Central Africa).

13.4.3 The two corners

The 1990s was a decade of violent currency crises. Europe's ERM was hit in 1992–93, Latin America followed in 1995–99, then it was Southeast Asia's turn in 1997–98 and Russia in 1998. These countries were operating one or another form of a peg, but countries like Hong Kong and Argentina, both with a currency board, escaped the apparently contagious wave. This has made popular the 'two-corner' view according to which the only safe regimes are the extremes ones, free floating or 'hard pegs' such as currency boards, monetary unions or dollarization. Hard pegs were seen as impregnable because the central banks have no opportunity to give in to market pressure, even if they – or their governments – wish to do so. Freely floating rates too are presumed to be immune from speculative attacks simply because there is no peg to attack; like soft pillows, they absorb any blow.

The two-corner view is directly related to the impossible trinity principle when capital is freely mobile. In a globalized world of full capital mobility, either monetary policy is completely free or it is entirely committed to uphold the chosen peg. The intermediate regimes, called 'soft pegs', may be seen as a reasonable compromise between fear of floating and fear of fixing, but they run against the impossible trinity principle. As the world went through a wave of capital liberalization over the 1990s, the two-corner view predicted that the middle ground of soft pegs would hollow out.

Figure 13.11 shows the percentage of countries that have adopted the corners and the 'soft middle ground'. This classification is based on actual observed behaviour, not on official announcements (since many countries do not necessarily practise what they claim). The big changes came in the early 1970s when the Bretton Woods system collapsed – the number of fixed exchange rate regimes declined – and in 1999 when the euro was adopted in Europe. It may be surprising that nearly 40 per cent of countries operate de facto a hard peg. Many of them, in fact, share the same currency as part of a monetary union, see Box 13.3, and have done so for quite a long time. On the other hand, freely floating rates, in particular, have made limited headway.

Figure 13.11 Actual exchange rate regimes (per cent of total), 1970–2007

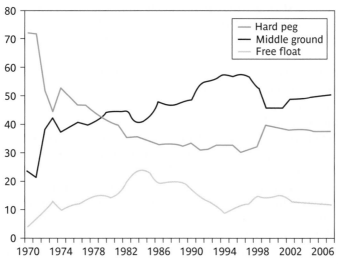

Source: Ilzetzki et al. (2008)

13.5 Summary

This chapter has presented three extensions of the traditional closed economy macroeconomic framework: the role of trade and financial openness, the implication of capital mobility and the long-run link between inflation and the exchange rate. This has left us with three essential tools: the interest rate parity principle, the purchasing power principle and the impossible parity principles.

The first one is a feature of capital mobility and is met permanently. The interest rate parity recognizes that international investors are constantly on the watch for the best possible returns. As they shift capital around, they equalize returns across countries and currencies. The interest parity establishes a tight link between the domestic interest rate and the exchange rate.

The second tool, purchasing power parity, is a long-run consequence of money neutrality. It establishes a link between domestic inflation and the exchange rate. We have not made use of this principle in the present chapter, but it will be useful later on.

The last tool draws the implications for the crucial decision on monetary and exchange rate policy strategies. It asserts that governments must make coherent choices regarding the exchange rate regime, the use of monetary policy and the capital mobility regime. An important implication is that, when capital is free to move, a central bank cannot control simultaneously the interest and the exchange rates.

In practice, really fixed exchange rates and complete free floating are just the two corners of a wide range of intermediate arrangements. These 'soft peg' arrangements either set limits to exchange rate fluctuations – betraying a fear of floating – or seek to introduce some degree of flexibility in fixed rate regimes – revealing a fear of fixing. Attempts to avoid the rigour of fixing and the volatility that comes with floating often amount to violating the impossible trinity principle. In general, the result is a crisis.

Self-assessment questions

1 A currency is called strong when it is usually appreciating. How can a central bank achieve strong currency status? Which currencies are strong?

2 If the nominal exchange rate appreciates by less than the excess of foreign over domestic inflation, is the real exchange rate appreciating or depreciating?

3 Why are fixed exchange rates believed to impose discipline on monetary policy?

4 Why would the exchange rate regime be irrelevant if money were also neutral in the short run? What would make money neutral in the short run?

5 Go back to Table 13.2 and compute for each country what would have been the rate of change of the exchange rate that we would have observed if PPP were to be satisfied.

6 Consider the case where $i > i* + (E_{t+1} - E_t)/E_t$. Explain the capital flows triggered by this intuition and in which direction they are likely to push i, $i*$, E_t and E_{t+1}.

7 Go back to Table 13.3. Assume now that the capital inflows predicated by the first row lead the markets to believe that the future exchange rate will depreciate to 0.97. What is the value of the current exchange rate that re-establishes the interest rate parity. Why would the markets form such a belief?

8 Same question as above, but assume now the markets believe that the future exchange rate will appreciate to 10.3.

9 A standard speculation consists in borrowing in the home country, investing abroad and selling the proceeds from the foreign investment to pay back the original loan. Determine when this strategy is profitable. Explain why it helps re-establish the interest rate parity condition.

Essay questions

1 The real, not the nominal, exchange rate is what matters for the real side of the economy. Why don't central banks attempt to control the real rather the nominal exchange rate?

2 It is often believed that a peg encourages residents (households, firms, banks) to borrow in a foreign currency. Then, if the exchange rate is devalued, many residents face the risk of bankruptcy. Explain and comment.

3 Monetary policy determines the inflation rate in the long run. What can lead some central banks to let prices rise quickly?

4 Central bankers are often described as 'conservatives', meaning that they are concerned more with inflation than with growth. What could explain this feature?

5 Fixed exchange rate regimes usually allow for occasional changes of the central parity. Use the interest parity condition to explain why the reputation of the central bank – its ability to stick by its words – matters for the well-being of the economy.

6 Argue why it may be preferable to adopt a fixed exchange rate regime. Now make the argument in defence of a floating exchange rate.

Further reading: the aficionado's corner

Purchasing power parity is one of the oldest regularity detected by economists, traced back to the sixteenth century and much studied ever since. A classic review of its various incarnations (absolute PPP, relative PPP) and of the evidence is:

Rogoff, K. (1996) 'The purchasing power parity puzzle', *Journal of Economic Literature,* 34(2): 647–68.

The interest rate parity condition too has a long history. While its logic is strong, 'proving' this condition is much more difficult because it deals with expectations and everyone is entitled to her own views. There is no such thing as the 'expectation of the markets'. A large empirical literature has been and still is grappling with the issue. It has become increasingly technical. A good update is:

Lothian, J.R. and L. Wu (2011) 'Uncovered interest-rate parity over the past two centuries', *Journal of International Money and Finance,* 30(3), 448–73.

The impossible trinity comes under a variety of names such as the unholy trinity, the policy trilemma or the triangle of impossibility. It was made clear by Robert Mundell in his classic development of what has come to be called the Mundell–Fleming model. This link is described in detail in:

Burda, M. and C. Wyplosz (2012) *Macroeconomics, A European Text,* 6th edition, Oxford University Press, Oxford.

The Bank for International Settlements surveys the size and functioning of foreign exchange markets every three years. The latest survey is described in:

BIS, *Triennial Survey,* December 2010, available at www.bis.org.

A description of existing capital controls and an evaluation of their effectiveness can be found in:

Ostry, J.D., A.R. Ghosh, K. Habermeier, L. Laeven, M. Chamon, M. S. Qureshi and A. Kokenyne, 'Managing Capital Inflows: What Tools to Use?', IMF Staff Discussion Note, April 5, 2011, available at imf.org.

Useful websites

The IMF presents up-to-date evaluations of exchange rate policies: www.imf.org.

To find out about the exchange rate regime of a particular country, visit its central bank's website.

References

Ilzetzki, E.O., C. Reinhart and K.S. Rogoff (2008) 'Exchange rate arrangements entering the 21st century: Which anchor will hold?', unpublished paper, University of Maryland. Download from www.wam.umd.edu/~creinhar/Papers.html.

Krugman, P. (1999) 'O Canada', *The Dismal Science,* Slate, http://www.slate.com/.articles/business/the_dismal_science/1999/10/o_canada.html.

Chapter 14

Essential facts of monetary integration

It was the 1992 EMS crisis that provided the immediate impetus for monetary unification.

Barry Eichengreen (2002)

Chapter Contents

Introduction

This chapter presents the main steps of the history of monetary integration in Europe. The aim is to reveal the deep logic that has led to the creation of the euro. As we know all too well, the monetary union is far from perfect – more on that in subsequent chapters – and political considerations have been paramount all along, yet there is also an economic logic behind it. Indeed, the concepts developed in the previous chapter provide a powerful interpretation of the main events.

The chapter starts far back in the nineteenth century with a brief review of the gold standard and a long analysis of the Hume mechanism. Interest in both history and an old principle is justified by the fact that, in many respects, a monetary union works like the gold standard. In both cases sovereign countries share the same currency – gold back then, the euro now – and cannot use the exchange rate any more to correct for imbalances. The Hume mechanism explains how correction is achieved, an issue highly relevant in the wake of the current crisis.

The chapter next looks at the inter-war period, which includes the Great Depression, currency crises and the dislocation of international trade as the gold standard crumbled. These were years when policy mistakes were accumulated, offering a large number of important lessons. These lessons, in fact, have played a crucial role in shaping policy makers' thinking, and they still do. For one thing, the Bretton Woods system was shaped to avoid these past mistakes. From a European viewpoint, this system offered exchange rate stability. Its demise left Europe in need of a replacement. The chapter recounts the history of the Snake and its much-improved successor, the European Monetary System (EMS).

The EMS worked well as long as capital controls were pervasive. When these controls were removed, as predicted by the impossible trinity principle developed in Chapter 13, the EMS was no longer the solution to the quest for intra-European exchange stability. The logical response was a common currency.

We will see that the rise of capital mobility within Europe has forced a choice between monetary policy autonomy and intra-European exchange stability. There is no obviously better alternative; both have their advantages and disadvantages. With some notable exceptions (Sweden and the UK, so far), and some countries still undecided (the Czech Republic, Hungary and Poland), the other countries have opted for exchange rate stability. Over several decades, this choice, largely driven by past experience, has triggered a series of moves that made the adoption of a common currency a natural step.

14.1 Prehistory: before paper money

Europe's path to complete monetary integration is spectacular but, in many ways, it is just a return to the situation that prevailed before the introduction of paper money. This section reviews the historical record, partly for its own sake, and partly because some important lessons have been learnt and shape the current thinking of policy makers.

14.1.1 The world as a monetary union

From time immemorial until the end of the nineteenth century, money was metallic (mainly gold and silver) and a bewildering variety of currencies were circulating side by side. Each currency was defined by its content of precious metal and each local lord endeavoured to control the minting of currency in his fiefdom, chiefly because seigniorage was a key source of revenue. When public finances were under pressure and the lord badly needed cash, money was debased through 'shaving': the metallic content was reduced by rubbing off scraps of metal or by re-minting coins to reduce the content of precious metal in the alloy. Exchange rates existed but they merely corresponded to the different contents of precious metal in different coins. With so many coins circulating in every political jurisdiction, life was not easy for shoppers:

> *The multiplicity and diversity of 'sous' and 'deniers' is such that it would be nearly impossible to assess their precise values, and to sort out these various coins. It would lead to deep confusion which would increase work, trouble and other inconveniences of daily traffic.*

> (Nicolaus Copernicus, *Monetae Cudendae Ratio*; written in 1556, first published in 1816; our translation from French)

This is why goods were priced in gold weight and the currencies were used in the reverse order of what we are now accustomed to. If a horse was worth 100 grams of pure gold, the buyer and seller would agree on which coins would be used. If they chose ecus, which included, say, 0.5 gram of pure gold each, the transaction would involve 200 ecus. If they rather settled in thaler, each coin of which contained, say, 0.1 gram of pure gold, the buyer would pay 1000 thaler coins. In effect, gold was *the* currency and monies were merely the materialization of gold. The 'world' was just one monetary union.[1]

It was only during the nineteenth century that people started to identify money and country, a part of the process of building up nation-states.[2] It was also at that stage that efforts were developed to put some order into what we would now call the international monetary system. This led to the gold standard. As Box 14.1 explains, some countries even decided to share the same currency.

Box 14.1 Early European monetary unions

By the early nineteenth century, gold and silver coins circulated side by side. The exchange rate between gold and silver fluctuated depending on discoveries. Britain was the first large country to drop silver and adopt the gold standard. On the Continent, bimetallism survived much longer, even though some countries (Germany, the Netherlands, the Scandinavian countries) favoured silver, until gold discoveries in the 1850s resulted in the disappearance of silver money on much of the Continent.

To preserve bimetallism, Belgium, France, Italy and Switzerland formed the **Latin European Monetary Union** in 1865 – a distant ancestor of today's monetary union. Greece joined in 1868. That effort foundered following the Franco-German war of 1870–71, when the newly established German empire shifted from silver to gold and weakened French finances by imposing war reparations to be paid in gold. When silver discoveries in Nevada depressed the price of silver, the Latin European Monetary Union was abandoned in 1878 and gold became the monetary standard.

The **Scandinavian Monetary Union** was created in 1873 by Denmark, Norway and Sweden, as part of the 'Scandinavianism' movement in support of the symbol of a common krona. These countries' currencies circulated widely in each other's territories. At the outbreak

---

[1] A couple of qualifications are in order. The 'world' here refers to Europe and its colonies. In addition, as mentioned, silver was used alongside gold, so in fact there were two monies and the gold–silver price was the meaningful exchange rate.

[2] Germany and Italy achieved political unification late in that century, and many different currencies still circulated there well into the 1850s. It took Italy two decades after its political unification in 1861 to achieve monetary unification. Similarly, even after the creation of the German Reich in 1871, different monetary standards survived until the Bank of Prussia unified German monies.

of the First World War, the Scandinavian Monetary Union ceased to exist, and was officially pronounced dead in 1924.

These precedents are merely of historical interest and bear little resemblance to modern monetary unions now that the currency is no longer metallic and that central banks create money. These old monetary unions amounted to nothing more than harmonized coinage. They were not associated with any trade agreement and, more importantly, there was no common central bank and very little coordination among the national monetary authorities. When external conditions became difficult (the fall of the price of silver in the case of the Latin European Monetary Union, and the dislocations of war in the case of the Scandinavian Monetary Union), each country reacted in its own way to protect its own interests.

The gold standard remains a fundamental reference because it had a very nice property: it automatically restored a country's external balance. This property, which got lost when we adopted paper money, is known as Hume's price–specie mechanism (see Box 14.2 for a note on Hume). The mechanism is well worth a modern visit because it applies to the internal working of a monetary union. It is presented at some length in the Annex. Briefly stated, the mechanism works as follows. A country whose prices are too high is uncompetitive and runs a trade deficit. This means that importers spend more gold money, which is shipped abroad, than importers receive from abroad in payment for their sales. Overall, therefore, the stock of money declines. Long-run monetary neutrality means that eventually prices will decline and the process will automatically go on until competitiveness is restored. The opposite occurs when prices are too low and the current account is in surplus: inflows of gold eventually lead to higher prices and a correction of the surplus. Thus, even though there is no exchange rate, imbalances cannot last for ever. They are self-correcting.

The automatic return to external balance is the key result of Hume's mechanism. Crucially, it means that the gold standard was inherently stable. Note also that there is no monetary policy autonomy since the stock of gold money is entirely determined by the balance of payments, and there is no paper money.

By the late nineteenth century, paper money started to exist. Gradually, we moved to the gold exchange standard where paper money could circulate internationally, but each banknote was very explicitly defined as representing some amount of gold. The continuing automaticity of the gold exchange standard relied on adherence to three principles, known as the 'rules of the game'. This is the way contemporaries shrewdly sought to implement the impossible trinity principle described in Chapter 13:

1 Full gold convertibility at fixed price of banknotes issued by central banks, so that paper money is merely a convenient surrogate for gold. In other words, the exchange rate is fixed.[3]

2 Full backing. The central bank holds at least as much gold as it has issued banknotes. In the presence of gold inflows, the central bank prints money; with gold outflows it retires previously created paper money. In effect, it means no monetary policy autonomy.

---

[3]   This mimics a currency board arrangement, as described in Chapter 13.

> ## Box 14.2   David Hume (1711–1776)
>
>
>
> Born in 1711 to a well-to-do family in Berwickshire, Scotland, Hume mostly wrote on philosophy, including the *Principles of Morals* (1751), which founded, among other things, the theory of utility. His works were highly influential even though they were denounced at the time as sceptical and atheistic. His economic thinking, mainly contained in *Political Discourses* (1752), had a large impact on Adam Smith and Thomas Malthus.
>
> *Source: National Galleries of Scotland*

3 Complete freedom in trade and capital movements, so as not to interfere with the adjustment mechanism. This means full capital mobility.

The operation of the European monetary union bears more than a passing resemblance to the gold standard. The euro replaces gold since national central banks are no longer allowed to issue national currencies and there is no national exchange rate. Within the Eurozone, when one country runs a balance of payments surplus, it receives an inflow of euros, and conversely, in the case of a deficit, its money supply automatically shrinks. Thus, the Hume mechanism is at work inside the Eurozone. In particular, a deficit country can no longer use the exchange rate to re-establish its competitiveness. This will have to operate through prices (and wages), which will have to increase more slowly than in the rest of the Eurozone, possibly even to decline. The comparison also means that the same 'rules of the game' must be strictly adhered to if national imbalances are to be automatically corrected. Put differently, tinkering with the rules would destabilize the whole monetary union and the rules are therefore part and parcel of Eurozone membership. We will see in Chapter 16 that some rules have been violated in 2010, which precipitated the debt crisis.

14.1.2 The unhappy inter-war period

The gold exchange standard was suspended in 1914 when hostilities disrupted gold shipping. The subsequent inter-war period left a bitter taste in Europe that still haunts the Continent. Belligerent countries had emerged exhausted from the First World War, facing huge debts, and over the next 30 years they would never quite fully recover. In many ways, the post-war European economic and political integration represents an effort to rule out any repeat of the inter-war disaster.

Wars are expensive and strain budgets, especially as governments are loath to raise taxes. The two alternatives are either to issue debt or to run the printing press. Both were used during the First World War. During the war, prices were kept artificially stable through rationing schemes; when war was ended and prices were freed, the accumulated inflationary pressure burst into the open. Some of the most famous hyperinflations erupted during this period, with Germany, Hungary and Greece facing *monthly* inflation rates of 1000 per cent or more in the early 1920s.

Lacking the vision of how a world of paper money could work – many even doubted that it could exist – post-war policy makers committed to return to the gold exchange standard as soon as practical, but at which exchange rate? Different European countries adopted different strategies, which ended up tearing them apart, economically and politically. We look at three prominent cases: the UK, France and Germany.

The UK

Hoping to retain its traditional leadership in international monetary matters in the face of a mounting US challenge, the UK decided to return a much-depreciated sterling to its pre-war gold parity, 'to look the dollar in the face'. This forced appreciation of the pound is shown in Fig. 14.1.[4] This decision has become a landmark policy mistake. Since 1914, prices had increased much more in the UK than in the USA, the newly emerging economic powerhouse. Returning sterling to its pre-war value resulted in overvaluation. Restoring competitiveness required bringing prices back down through deflation, a lengthy and painful process. As the impossible trinity principle suggests, monetary policy autonomy was lost. The result was poor growth, a weak current account and the erosion of trust in sterling, once considered 'as good as gold'. The City of London lost ground to New York's Wall Street.

The economy was already weak when the Great Depression followed the crash on Wall Street in 1929. The UK was in no position to deal with yet more hardship. The exchange markets sensed the vulnerability and repeatedly launched speculative attacks on sterling. When, at long last, the Bank of England withdrew from the gold standard in 1931, sterling promptly lost 30 per cent of its value with respect to gold and the dollar. An ambition was gone, and the price was high: a decade of miserable growth.

France

France, too, initially intended to return to its pre-war gold parity, but it soon lost control of inflation for several years. During the war the French debt had grown much more than the UK's. The government allowed it to rise further after the war on the premise that Germany's huge war reparations would eventually pick up the bill. When, by 1924, it became clear that Germany would not pay and plug the hole, inflation soared to an annual rate of close to 50 per cent. The franc was attacked and sunk. When inflation was finally stopped in 1926, the franc was stabilized at one-fifth of its pre-war parity.

France officially returned to the gold standard in 1928 but, in contrast to the pound, its exchange rate was now undervalued. Over the next few years, the undervaluation allowed France to run surpluses in its balance of payments and the Banque de France accumulated large foreign exchange reserves. When the Great Depression hit, France escaped relatively unscathed because it was highly competitive. Trouble started when many countries followed Britain's 1931 decision to devalue. Their renewed competitiveness came at the expense of France's. The last blow came when the USA too abandoned the gold standard in 1933 and devalued the dollar by 40 per cent. Fighting the inevitable, France and some other countries (Belgium, Luxembourg, Italy, the Netherlands, Poland and Switzerland) formed the Gold Bloc, in an attempt to jointly protect their now overvalued currencies. Overvaluation is the channel though which France was finally hit by the Great Depression. Facing speculative attacks, exactly as the UK had ten years earlier, France finally devalued its currency by a whopping 42 per cent.

---

[4] Note that the exchange rate is expressed as the number of pounds needed to buy one US dollar. A decrease means an appreciation, since fewer pounds are needed to buy one dollar. The same definition is used in the other charts collected in Fig. 14.1.

Figure 14.1 Prices and exchange rates: France, Germany and the UK, 1910–39

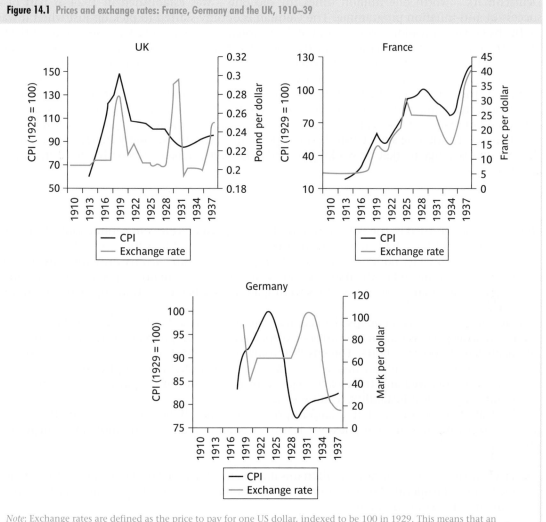

Note: Exchange rates are defined as the price to pay for one US dollar, indexed to be 100 in 1929. This means that an increase represents a depreciation as foreign currency becomes more expensive. We choose this presentation because it makes the PPP link between the exchange rate and the price level clearer: a higher price means a depreciation, hence a higher exchange rate as defined here.
Source: Mitchell (1998)

Germany

In contrast to France and the UK, Germany never considered returning to its pre-war level. Its domestic public debt was huge and massive war reparations imposed in 1919 by the Treaty of Versailles magnified it. As in France, Germany's post-war inflation was high, but in 1922 it slipped out of control.[5] The result was one of history's most violent hyperinflations. A new

---

[5]   This is why pre-hyperinflation prices and exchange rates are not shown in Fig. 14.1.

Deutschmark – worth one million times the old one – was established in 1924 as part of a successful anti-inflation programme. The German economy started to pick up just when it was hit by the Great Depression. Preservation of the restored value of the mark was seen as essential to dispel the ghosts of hyperinflation. Like the franc, the mark became overvalued when more and more countries devalued their own currencies. Germany first suspended its debt and then started to move away from a free trade system. Exchange controls were established. As the depression deepened, the Nazis combined public spending with wage and price increases. This further dented external competitiveness and deepened the trade deficit. The response was to stop the conversion of marks into gold and foreign currencies – an extreme form of capital controls – and to impose ever-widening state controls on imports and exports. Germany bypassed completely the foreign exchange market by working out bilateral barter agreements with one country after another.

Lessons

Once they had returned to the gold standard's hard peg, which rules out capital controls, France and the UK would have had to give up monetary autonomy. When the Great Depression hit, the urge to use monetary policy became too strong. The impossible trinity principle was violated and the result was the end of the fixed exchange rate system. Germany respected the impossible trinity principle, in an extreme way, by severing all market-based relationships with the rest of the world.

Once the gold standard collapsed, exchange rates were left to float, a fairly novel experience. Faced with a deep recession, each country – except Germany – sought relief by letting its exchange rate depreciate to boost exports. The ensuing round of tit-for-tat depreciations, which came to be called beggar-thy-neighbour policies, led nowhere but started to disrupt trade. Protectionist measures soon followed and trade exchanges went into a tailspin, aggravating the depression. The result was political instability, leading to war.

This traumatic period has left a deep imprint in Europe, shaping post-war thinking among policy makers. Among the many lessons learnt, two are relevant for the monetary integration process:

- Freely floating exchange rates result in misalignments that breed trade barriers and eventually undermine prosperity. Most European countries have developed a fear of floating, which remains a key concern today.
- The management of exchange rate parities cannot be left to each country's discretion. We need an international order that deals with the fact that one country's depreciation is another country's appreciation. In other words, we need a 'system'.

14.2 Bretton Woods as an antidote to the inter-war debacle

Even before the end of the Second World War, the USA and the UK started to plan the Bretton Woods conference. The aim was to establish an international monetary system based on paper currencies. Gold remained the ultimate source of value, but the dollar became the anchor of the system, and the US government guaranteed its value in terms of gold. All the other currencies were defined in terms of the dollar. Exchange rates were 'fixed but adjustable' to avoid both unreasonable adherence to an outdated parity (over- or undervaluation) and an inter-war-type free-for-all. The system was a collective undertaking with the International

Monetary Fund (IMF) both supervising compliance and providing emergency assistance. By providing the system's central currency and hosting the IMF in Washington, the USA was the ultimate economic and political guarantor of the system. Capital controls were not outlawed and most countries made abundant use of them. This was compatible with the impossible trinity.

The system unravelled when capital controls started to be lifted in the 1960s. The impossible trinity principle required that exchange rates be freed – including the link between the dollar and gold – or that the authorities give up monetary policy autonomy. Most governments – Canada being a rare exception – refused to make such a choice.

By the late 1960s, reflecting an active use of monetary policy, not always wise, inflation started to rise in a number of countries, including in the USA. The anchor of the system, the US dollar, gradually became overvalued. The Bretton Woods system came under strain when the USA could no longer guarantee the dollar's gold value. The demise of the system came in two steps. First, in 1971, the USA 'suspended' the dollar's convertibility into gold. Then, in 1973, the 'fixed but adjustable' principle was officially abandoned; each country would now be free to choose its exchange rate regime. This effectively ended the Bretton Woods era.

14.3 After Bretton Woods: Europe's snake in the tunnel

For Europe, the Bretton Woods system had provided a ready-made solution to the exchange rate question. Most countries wanted fairly fixed exchange rates and reassurances that competitive devaluations would be held in check. IMF membership provided all of that. Once the Bretton Woods system fell apart, Europe found itself without a solution. Its early reaction charted the way that would lead to a monetary union three decades later. Following up on devaluations in the late 1960s in France and the UK, two high-inflation currencies, speculation soon started to tear European countries apart from each other, as Fig. 14.2 shows. Concerned with the inter-war spectre of over- and undervaluations, the continental countries of Europe promptly resolved to limit exchange rate movements among themselves.

The first response was the 'European Snake', a regional stepped-down version of the Bretton Woods system designed to limit intra-European exchange rate fluctuations. But the Snake was a very loose arrangement, as explained in Box 14.3. It did not deal with the impossible trinity principle: capital controls were often in place but they were not tight and were increasingly evaded, and there was no restriction on national monetary policies. When inflation rose abruptly in the wake of the first oil shock of 1973–74, central banks reacted differently. Some (Germany, the Netherlands and Belgium) succeeded at keeping inflation in check, whereas others (e.g. Italy and the UK) did not. Maintaining exchange rate fixity with very divergent monetary policies was hopeless and, indeed, several countries had to leave the Snake arrangement.

In spite of its eventual failure, the Snake brought about two innovations that shaped subsequent integration efforts. First, it embodied the determination to keep intra-European rates fixed, irrespective of what happened elsewhere in the world. Second, the gold standard and the Bretton Woods system were gone, and with them references to gold and the dollar for European currencies. From there on, European currencies would have to be defined vis-à-vis each other. The Snake was meant to be 'an island of stability in an ocean of instability'. The natural next move was to respond to the Snake's weaknesses. The answer was the creation of the European Monetary System (EMS).

Figure 14.2 Dollar exchange rates, January 1967–December 1977

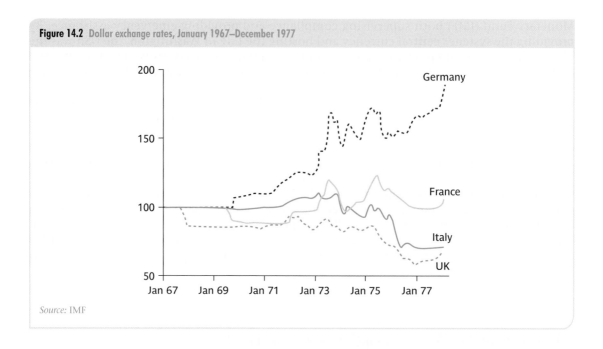

Source: IMF

14.4 The European Monetary System

The decision to create the system was taken in 1978 by German Chancellor Helmut Schmidt and French President Valéry Giscard d'Estaing. They were alarmed by the monetary disorders that had followed the end of the Bretton Woods system and by the inability to sustain the Snake arrangement. They saw large exchange rate movements as a direct threat to the Common Market. They wanted a stronger, more resilient arrangement.

The heart of the EMS is the Exchange Rate Mechanism (ERM), a system of jointly managed fixed and adjustable exchange rates backed by mutual support. Open to all EU countries, the ERM has seen its membership grow and then decline (see Table 14.1) as euro area member countries gave up their national currencies. Several more recent EU member countries have joined the ERM and some left it when they adopted the euro.

Political sensitivities were important in shaping the design of the ERM. Germany would never take the risk of weakening its star currency, the Deutschmark, while France could not be seen to be playing second fiddle to Germany. Additionally, the smaller countries had to be brought along, while the UK was staunchly opposed to a fixed exchange rate regime. The solution came close to squaring the circle. The chosen arrangement was explicitly symmetric, without any currency at its centre, and it established a subtle distinction between the European Monetary System, of which all European Community countries were de facto members, and the Exchange Rate Mechanism, an optional but operational scheme.

14.4.1 Fixed and flexible exchange rates

The ERM rested on four main elements: a grid of agreed-upon bilateral exchange rates, mutual support, possibility of realignments but subject to unanimity agreement and the European Currency Unit (ECU).

All ERM currencies were fixed to each other, with a band of fluctuation of ±2.25 per cent around the central parity (Italy was initially allowed a margin of fluctuation of ±6 per cent, in

Box 14.3 The snake in the tunnel

In 1971, in a last-ditch effort to save the Bretton Woods system, it was decided to widen the margins of fluctuations vis-à-vis the dollar from ±1 per cent to ±2.25 per cent. Non-dollar currencies, like the DM and the franc, would now fluctuate by as much as 9 per cent vis-à-vis each other, as is shown in the upper part of Fig. 14.3. Under the Bretton Woods system, the exchange rates of the French franc and the DM were determined in terms of dollars. Consider the case, represented by both points A, where both currencies are at their opposite extremes vis-à-vis the dollar, the DM is 2.25 per cent above the dollar and the franc 2.25 per cent below it. As a result, the DM is 4.5 per cent above the franc. At the opposite extremes (points B), the DM is 4.5 per cent below the franc, with a total amplitude of 9 per cent. A number of European countries (the EC members as well as Denmark, Ireland, Norway, the UK and Sweden) felt that this was too wide a margin and decided to maintain their bilateral rates within a common ±2.25 per cent band of fluctuation. This was called the 'snake in the tunnel' – a colourful representation of their joint movements vis-à-vis the dollar, as shown in the lower part of the figure. Once the Bretton Woods system ended, the tunnel was gone but the EC countries resolved to keep the Snake, i.e. to limit the range of variation of their bilateral exchange rates to a maximum of 4.5 per cent. The Snake crawled out of the vanishing tunnel and this led directly to the EMS.

Figure 14.3 The European Snake (all currencies relative to the US dollar)

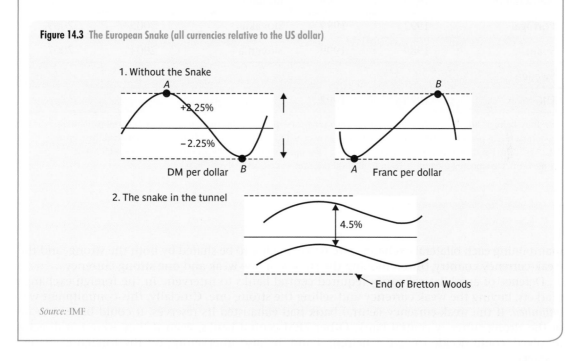

Source: IMF

recognition of its higher rate of inflation and internal political difficulties). The arrangement carried a number of interesting features. First, the system was entirely European, with no reference to the dollar or to gold. Never before had European countries built an exchange rate system standing on its own. Second, the system was fully symmetric: no currency played any special role, in contrast to the dollar in the Bretton Woods system. Third, the responsibility for

Table 14.1 ERM membership

Older EU members	Joined	Left	Recent EU members	Joined	Left
Austria	1995	1999	Bulgaria		
Belgium-Luxembourg	1979	1999	Cyprus	2005	2008
Denmark	1979	1999	Czech Rep.		
Finland	1996	1999	Estonia	2004	2011
France	1979	1999	Hungary		
Germany	1979	1999	Latvia	2005	
Greece	1998	2001	Lithuania	2004	
Ireland	1979	1999	Malta	2005	2008
Italy	1979, 1996	1992, 1999	Poland		
Netherlands	1979	1999	Romania		
Portugal	1992	1999	Slovakia	2005	2009
Spain	1989	1999	Slovenia	2004	2007
Sweden					
UK	1990	1992			

Note: Italy, Portugal and Spain initially operated a wider (±6 per cent) band of fluctuation around the central parity than the normal (±2.25 per cent) band. In 1993, the band was widened to ±15 per cent, but Denmark has retained the narrow (±2.25 per cent) band. All other current members of the ERM operate the wide (±15 per cent) band, except for Latvia (±1 per cent). Luxembourg used the Belgian franc until the euro was created.

maintaining each bilateral exchange rate was explicitly to be shared by both the strong- and the weak-currency country, thus removing the stigma of one weak and one strong currency.

Defence of any bilateral parity required central banks to intervene in the foreign exchange markets, buying the weak currency and selling the strong one. Crucially, this commitment was *unlimited*. If the weak-currency central bank had exhausted its reserves, it could borrow those of the strong-currency central bank. Other ERM central banks, even if they were not directly involved, could decide to give a helping hand, by also intervening on the foreign exchange markets.

How long should interventions be pursued? Clearly, if markets remained unimpressed by the artillery lined up against them, there remained the possibility of depreciating the weak currency, appreciating the strong currency, or both. Realignments, as these actions were called, had to be agreed by all ERM members, which were all involved because all parities were defined bilaterally. The consensus rule implied that, in effect, each country gave up exclusive control of its own exchange rate. The history of realignments is shown in Table 14.2.

Table 14.2   ERM realignments

Dates	24.9.79	30.11.79	22.3.81	5.10.81	22.2.82	14.6.82
No. of currencies involved	2	1	1	2	2	4
Dates	21.3.83	18.5.83	22.7.85	7.4.86	4.8.86	12.1.87
No. of currencies involved	7[a]	7[a]	7[a]	5	1	3
Dates	8.1.90	14.9.92	23.11.92	1.2.93	14.5.93	6.3.95
No. of currencies involved	1	3[b]	2	1	2	2

[a] All ERM currencies realigned.
[b] In addition, two currencies (sterling and lira) leave the ERM.

14.4.2 From divergence to convergence and blow-up

This shows that the ERM's ride has not been smooth. Between 1979 and 1987, realignment occurred no fewer than 12 times, once every eight months on average. Most of these parity adjustments occurred in the midst of serious market turmoil. The reason is that, in violation of the impossible trinity principle, most countries sought to retain monetary policy autonomy. Until the mid-1980s, capital controls were in place in the devaluation-prone countries, so policy autonomy was possible and used to live with different inflation rates. Figure 14.4 readily confirms that inflation rates diverged widely in the 1970s and 1980s, following two large oil-price shocks in 1973 and 1981. As a result, realignments were frequently needed to re-establish competitiveness, an implication of the PPP principle presented in Chapter 13.

Gradually, however, capital controls were lifted, making realignments increasingly destabilizing. This pushed high-inflation and depreciation-prone countries to seek to bring down inflation and therefore to converge to the lowest rate. Germany, the perennial low-inflation country, became the standard to emulate. In effect, Germany's monetary policy became the ERM standard and other countries de facto surrendered monetary policy independence.

With all central banks emulating the Bundesbank, inflation rates started to converge. Realignments were resisted to convey the seriousness of the commitment to achieve low German-style inflation. For nearly six years, from early 1987 to September 1992, there was no realignment.[6] The link became tighter as, in anticipation of the Single European Act 1986, capital controls were formally banned as of July 1990. The impossible trinity principle meant that, with the Deutschmark serving as anchor, monetary policy autonomy was lost for all countries except Germany. A system designed to be symmetric has become perfectly asymmetric.

This unplanned evolution carried two momentous implications. First, the other countries resented the Bundesbank leadership. The next step in the reasoning was: if we give up national monetary policy autonomy, we should share it collectively, not delegate to one national central

---

[6] The 1990 realignment (Table 14.2) was not really a realignment. It was merely a technical adjustment prompted by Italy's decision to switch to the narrow ±2.25 per cent band of fluctuation, a consequence of the 'strong lira' policy. Parity was brought closer (from 6 per cent to 2.25 per cent) to its weak margin.

Figure 14.4 Inflation during the ERM years

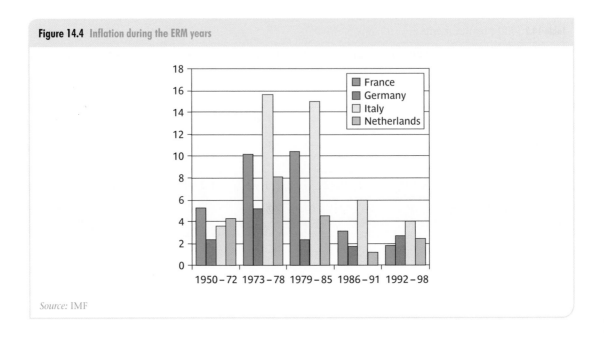

Source: IMF

bank. Of course, Germany was unwilling to relinquish its lock on ERM monetary policies but, in the end, accepted a political deal in 1991: the monetary union in exchange for its own reunification with the former East Germany. This is when the second event occurred and nearly destroyed the ERM in 1992–93.

14.4.3 The crisis of 1992–93

The absence of any realignment for about six years looked good, but inflation rates never fully converged (see Fig. 14.4). While countries such as Denmark and France indeed moved towards the German inflation rate, others, such as Italy, Portugal and Spain, failed to get close enough. For these countries, the fixed exchange rate strategy resulted in a dangerous loss of competitiveness. Any spark could trigger speculative attacks.

German unification was costly and became inflationary once East German wages were brought up to levels that were inconsistent with the low productivity of East German firms. Predictably, the Bundesbank responded by sharply raising its interest rate. Facing a global economic slowdown, the other central banks decided not to follow up and to recover some autonomy. The result of this violation of the impossible trinity principle was bound to trigger speculative attacks on the countries that had lost competitiveness.

Paradoxically, the monetary union project – a huge show of political bravery – provided the final spark. The Maastricht Treaty had been signed in December 1991 and was to be ratified by each member country during 1992. The first country to initiate the ratification process was Denmark, where law mandates that international treaties be submitted to referenda. For a variety of reasons, the Danes voted down the Treaty by a few thousand votes. The Treaty included one provision that stated that it would be void unless ratified by all EU countries. Thus, before the other countries even had a chance to ratify it, the Treaty was technically dead by mid-1992. France then organized its own ratification referendum. Negative polls alarmed the exchange markets. Speculative attacks started immediately, initially targeting Italy (the lira was seriously overvalued by then) and the UK, which had finally joined the ERM a year earlier but at an overvalued exchange rate.[7]

In response to the speculative attacks, as mandated by the ERM agreements, the strong currency central banks initially intervened in support of the embattled Banca d'Italia and Bank of England. By mid-September 1992, the attacks had become so massive that a frightened Bundesbank decided that truly unlimited interventions were not reasonable and stopped its support. Left to themselves, the lira and the pound withdrew from the ERM. The markets concluded that the ERM was considerably more fragile than hitherto admitted. Speculation shifted to the currencies of Ireland, Portugal and Spain. Each of them had to be devalued, twice. Contagion then spread to Belgium, Denmark and France, even though inflation in these countries had converged to below the German level and their currencies were not overvalued. By the summer of 1993, huge amounts of reserves had been thrown into the foreign exchange markets and speculation was still going strong. In order to uphold the principle of the ERM, and save face at the same time, the monetary authorities adopted new ultra-large (±15 per cent) bands of fluctuation.[8] Figure 14.5 shows the ERM history of the DM/French franc parity. The tight ERM was dead.

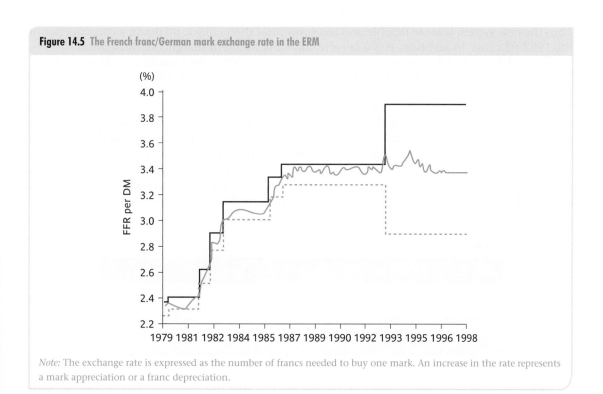

Figure 14.5 The French franc/German mark exchange rate in the ERM

Note: The exchange rate is expressed as the number of francs needed to buy one mark. An increase in the rate represents a mark appreciation or a franc depreciation.

---

[7] The UK had joined the ERM a few months before, soon after John Major had replaced Margaret Thatcher as Prime Minister, largely because her opposition to ERM membership appeared anachronistic in the midst of a wave of Euro-optimism.

[8] Germany and the Netherlands independently agreed to keep their bilateral parity within the old ±2.25 per cent margins. Belgium decided on its own to follow the same rule. In effect, these countries had given up monetary policy autonomy.

14.4.4   The EMS re-engineered

The post-crisis ERM agreed upon in 1993 differed little from a floating exchange rate regime. Bilateral parities could move by 30 per cent, a very wide margin. Unsurprisingly, therefore, the (non)system worked well. For example, Fig. 14.5 shows that the DM/FRF fluctuated slightly outside of its earlier narrow ±2.25 per cent range for a few years and then gently converged to its ultimate EMU conversion rate.

One precondition set by the Maastricht Treaty for joining the monetary union is at least two years of ERM membership (the other conditions are presented in Chapter 16). This means that the ERM is still in use as a temporary gateway but it has been re-engineered. EMS-2, as the new arrangement is called, incorporates most of the features of its predecessor, yet differs in some key aspects:

- While EMS-1 was a symmetric system based on a grid of bilateral parities, in EMS-2, parities are defined vis-à-vis the euro, which is clearly the anchor currency. There is no grid, just a table. The margin of fluctuation is less precisely defined. De facto, the 'standard' band is 15 per cent as in the latter version of EMS-1, but a narrower band is also possible.

- Interventions are still automatic and unlimited, but there is a clear understanding that the European Central Bank (ECB) may decide to suspend this obligation.

Thus the new system is more flexible and less committal than EMS-1, no doubt a consequence of the 1992–93 crisis. In addition, it is à la carte, allowing different margins of fluctuation.

Table 14.3 shows ERM membership as of September 2011. Two countries joined in when EMS-2 came into force in January 1999: Greece, with the standard ±15 per cent band, until it joined the monetary union in January 2001, and Denmark, which has adopted the narrow ±2.25 per cent that prevailed in EMS-1. Sweden and the UK have decided to stay out 'for the time being'. The countries that accessed to the EU since then are all formally committed to adopt the euro and therefore to pass through the ERM beforehand. Four of them promptly joined the ERM (Slovenia in 2004; Cyprus and Malta in 2005; Slovakia in 2006) and then left it when they adopted the euro. Estonia followed suit. In addition to Denmark, the ERM currently includes Latvia and Lithuania. Latvia operates a non-official ±1 per cent band; in fact, it has adopted a currency board arrangement (see Chapter 13 for a presentation of currency boards).

Table 14.3   ERM membership as of September 2011

Country	Date of ERM membership	Band of fluctuation (%)
Denmark	1 January 1999	± 2.25
Lithuania	27 June 2004	± 15
Latvia	2 May 2005	± 15

Unsurprisingly, the new Member States behave just like the previous ones. Many of them value exchange rate stability and want to adopt the euro. They are typically small and very open. The others are lukewarm, especially the larger and less open ones.

14.4.5   Assessment and lessons

The EMS has been a key step in European monetary integration. For the first time, European currencies defined their interrelationship without reference to an external store of value, like gold or the US dollar. It involved deep and comprehensive agreements among sovereign states that remain unmatched elsewhere in the world, with the exception of existing monetary unions. Its difficulties eventually made the monetary union a natural next step.

These difficulties have underlined the importance of the impossible trinity principle. Policy makers have sometimes ignored the principle, because they see it as a constraint on their freedom of action. Each time, the consequence has been a currency crisis. As long as the weaker-currency countries imposed restrictions on capital movements, speculative attacks often accompanied exchange rate realignments, but they were manageable. Once full capital mobility was achieved, central banks soon realized that even large stocks of foreign exchange reserves are too small to repel speculative attacks, and that unlimited interventions are practically impossible. In other words, the conclusion was that monetary integration with separate currencies is a very risky endeavour, possibly a hopeless quest. Monetary union was one response.

14.5 The Maastricht Treaty

Maastricht – unpronounceable by non-Dutch natives – is a picturesque Dutch town. In December 1991, the 12 heads of states and governments of the EU gathered there to sign a treaty that replaced the European Community (EC) with the European Union (EU). The change of name was symbolic. It was meant to signal that the Treaty was not just about economics but also included political considerations. Two new pillars – foreign and defence policies, justice and internal security – were added to the first, economic pillar. Yet, the Maastricht Treaty will remain mostly known for having established the monetary union.

Achieving a monetary union had been in the back of the minds of the signatories of the 1957 Treaty of Rome, which established the European Community and the Common Market. Chapter 1 describes the first attempt that failed, the Werner Report. The second one, the 1989 Delors Report, was successful. The report, commissioned by the European Council, was formally adopted in July 1989. Two intergovernmental conferences followed and their conclusions were presented to the Council meeting held in Maastricht at the end of 1991. Even though the debt crisis that started in 2010 casts a shadow on this achievement – and could lead to the demise of the euro as we know it – the Treaty marks the end of a long road: three decades of attempts to achieve a monetary union, summarized in Table 14.4. Maybe as a bad omen, the Treaty ratification process turned out to be eventful, as recalled in Box 14.4.

The Treaty described in great detail how the system would work, including the statutes of the European Central Bank (ECB) and the conditions under which monetary union would start. Chapter 16 presents the Treaty. Here we only note that it specified entry conditions, also described in Chapter 16. These conditions were established mostly at German request. Germany, which considered the strong Deutschmark as an essential achievement and a key economic success factor, was not willing to swap it against a weaker currency. Against much of his public opinion, Chancellor Helmut Kohl was convinced of the paramount importance of European integration and was ready to abandon the mark, but he requested tough entry conditions. Germany would rather start the monetary union with a small number of like-minded countries than bring on board more countries several of which, in its eyes, had not adopted its culture of price stability. Greece, Italy, Spain and Portugal were not on the list of welcomed members. France neither, but Chancellor Kohl decided that politically France could not be kept out. It is striking that all these countries ended up being caught in the public debt crisis that started in 2009.

The convergence criteria were designed with this objective in mind. Fulfilment of these criteria was to be evaluated by late 1997, a full year before the euro would replace the national currencies. In the end, partly through window-dressing measurements and creative accounting, all the countries that wanted to adopt the euro qualified, with the exception of Greece, which had to wait for another two years.

Table 14.4 Steps of monetary integration

Towards Maastricht		Between Maastricht and the single currency		After Maastricht	
1970	Werner Plan	1994	European Monetary Institute (precursor of ECB)	1999	Monetary union starts
1979	European Monetary System starts	1997	Stability and Growth Pact	2001	Greece joins
1989	Delors Committee	1998	Decision on membership	2002	Euro coins and notes introduced
1991	Maastricht Treaty signed	1998	Conversion rates set	2007	Slovenia joins
1993	Maastricht Treaty ratified	1998	Creation of ECB	2008	Cyprus and Malta join
				2009	Slovakia joins
				2011	Estonia joins

On 4 January 1999, the exchange rates of 11 countries[9] were 'irrevocably' frozen. The old currencies formally became (odd) fractions of the euro, and the power to conduct monetary policy was transferred from each member country to the European System of Central Banks (ESCB), under the aegis of the European Central Bank (ECB) headquartered in Frankfurt. Ordinary citizens had to wait another three years, until January 2002, to see and touch euro banknotes and coins. Since then, six more countries[10] have joined the Eurozone, which includes 17 members as of September 2011.

14.6 The crisis

Starting in 2010, a severe crisis has started to affect public debts, in Greece first, then Ireland and Portugal. At the time of writing, in the summer of 2011, the crisis is threatening Italy and Spain, with early signs of concern about France and Belgium. The policy response to the crisis has already changed the nature of the monetary union. At the same time, there is a serious risk that the union could break up, with incalculable consequences. Chapter 19 is dedicated to the study of these momentous events.

---

[9] Austria, Belgium, Finland, France, Germany, Ireland, Italy, Luxembourg, the Netherlands, Portugal and Spain.
[10] Greece in 2001, Slovenia in 2007, Cyprus and Malta in 2008, Slovakia in 2009 and Estonia in 2011.

Box 14.4 The bumpy ratification of the Maastricht Treaty

Any international treaty must be ratified by the signatories. The ratification procedure varies from one country to another: some countries require a referendum, others must obtain parliament's approval, yet others can decide between these two alternatives. The first country to undertake ratification of the Maastricht Treaty was Denmark, and it had to be by referendum. The Danish people chose to reject the Treaty by a small margin. Since European treaties are all-or-nothing, the Treaty looked dead before the other countries even had a chance to consider it. Yet, hoping that a legal solution would be found, it was decided to continue with the ratification process.

France offered to be the second country to consider ratification. President Mitterrand chose the referendum procedure – he could have asked for approval by the parliament. As the campaign went on, support gradually eroded. When some polls reported a majority against the Treaty, leading to fears of a collapse of the whole project, the exchange markets became jittery and speculation gained momentum. In the event, Italy and the UK were ejected from the ERM and several currencies had to be devalued, some of them many times, as described above. Meanwhile, the French approved the Treaty by a narrow margin.

The Danes were asked to return to the polls, after the Danish government was given the right, included in a special protocol, not to adopt the single currency. This time, the Danes approved the Treaty. Just when the road seemed clear, the German Constitutional Court was asked for an opinion on whether the Treaty was compatible with Germany's constitution. The Court took several months to deliver its opinion, keeping the process hanging. The Court finally decided that the Treaty did not contradict the German Constitution. This allowed Germany to ratify the Treaty in late 1993, the last country to do so.

14.7 Summary

Europe's long process of monetary integration started with an implicit single currency under the gold standard, went through painful dislocation in the inter-war period, followed by various attempts to fix intra-European exchange rates without always paying due respect to the principle. The current solution, the single currency shared by an increasing number of countries and free floating elsewhere, has been shaken by the sovereign debt crisis in 2009.

Hume's price–specie mechanism allows for the automatic elimination of imbalances within the gold standard. For instance, countries with balance of payment surpluses see their money supply increase, which eliminates the surplus through lower interest rates and capital outflows first, and rising prices that undermine external competitiveness next. The same mechanism is also at work in the monetary union.

The EMS was adopted in 1979 in an effort to preserve exchange rate stability within Europe following the end of the Bretton Woods system. Initially created to shield Europe from international monetary disturbances, its success made the monetary union look almost like the natural next step. A new arrangement has been set up following the adoption of the euro. All EU members are members of the EMS but the active part of the system, the ERM, is optional in the sense that some countries (Denmark and the UK) have a derogation while Sweden and some new EU members are postponing membership.

The ERM was based on a grid specifying all bilateral parities and the corresponding margins of fluctuation, normally ±2.25 per cent. ERM members were committed to jointly defend their bilateral parities, if necessary through unlimited interventions and loans. Realignments were possible, but required the consent of all members. This amounted to a tight and elaborate arrangement.

The EMS went through several phases. During the first period, inflation differed quite widely from one country to another and realignments were frequent. Then, all countries decided to adopt the Bundesbank's low-inflation strategy, in effect adopting the Deutschmark as an anchor and avoiding further realignments. Finally, the 1992–93 crisis – which saw two currencies, the Italian lira and the British pound, exit – ended with the adoption of wide margins of ±15 per cent, allowing the ERM to nominally survive until the launch of the euro.

The 1992–93 crisis provides an example of the impossible trinity. The liberalization of financial markets and the fixity of exchange rates were incompatible with divergent monetary policies. For a while, during the late 1980s, most countries did follow the Bundesbank and achieved low inflation. But when Germany went through its unification shock, the Bundesbank adopted a tight policy stance that was incompatible with the low-growth situation in the other ERM member countries.

With the adoption of a single currency, a new EMS was established. EMS-2 differs from EMS-1 mainly in that the euro is now the reference currency and the unlimited intervention obligation no longer exists. As a result, the ERM is asymmetric and its members must rely on their own resources to maintain the declared parities within the standard ±15 per cent band. EMS-2 remains a prerequisite for joining the Eurozone. Nowadays, the ERM is one of the requirements to join the Eurozone. Of the 12 countries that joined the EU in 2004, five joined the ERM until they adopted the euro, two are currently part of the mechanism alongside Denmark, and five have delayed ERM membership.

The Maastricht Treaty, signed in 1991 and ratified over the following two years, established the monetary union, to start on 1 January 1999. It included entry conditions designed to keep out those countries that were not wed to price stability. In the end, all but one candidate countries were found to satisfy these conditions. Greece was admitted two years later. Slovenia. Slovakia, Cyprus, Malta and Estonia joined subsequently. The euro is now – at the time of writing – the currency of 17 countries.

Self-assessment questions

1 During the inter-war era, misalignments led to competitive devaluations, which then prompted a tariff war. Explain the links from one step to the next.
2 What is the difference between the EMS and the ERM?
3 How does EMS-2 differ from EMS-1?
4 What are the margins of fluctuation? What role do they play?
5 Explain the principle of mutual support within the ERM.
6 What do we mean by saying that the EMS-1 had become a 'Deutschmark area'? How did that happen and could it have been foreseen?

7 Some non-Eurozone EU member countries currently allow their exchange rates to float (relatively) freely, others operate hard pegs or soft pegs. Which countries abide by the impossible trinity principle?

8 The Danish people have rejected by referendum joining the Eurozone. So Denmark has been a member of the ERM-2 since it was created in 1999, and the krone has almost never moved by more than 1 per cent vis-à-vis the euro. What difference would Eurozone membership make?

Essay questions

1 In retrospect it is claimed that the 1992–93 crisis of the EMS could have been anticipated. Why and why not? Once the crisis started, could Italy and the UK have stayed in the system, and if so under what conditions?

2 Would the Bretton Woods system have survived had it been patterned after the ERM?

3 'The EMS turned out to be a successful transition to the establishment of the monetary union.' Comment.

4 The inter-war decline of Britain is sometimes imputed to the 1924 return to the gold standard at the overvalued pre-war parity. Explain how and why lasting overvaluations hurt.

5 Proposals to return the world to the gold standard are regularly put forward. Evaluate the pros and the cons of this idea.

6 'The creation of the European Snake was a sign of US decline in monetary matters.' Comment.

7 Why did the ERM succeed while the Snake failed?

8 Britain and Sweden have decided not to adopt the euro. Discuss the economic implications.

9 Some countries are attached to intra-Europe exchange rate stability, others not. Comment.

Further reading: the aficionado's corner

On the gold standard:

Bordo, M. (1999) *The Gold Standard and Related Regimes*, Cambridge University Press, Cambridge. This book offers a comprehensive and modern analysis of the gold standard and its relevance to today's discussions.

On early efforts at monetary unification:

Bergman, M., S. Gerlach and L. Jonung (1993) 'The rise and fall of the Scandinavian currency union 1873–1920', *European Economic Review*, 37: 507–17.

Bordo, M. and L. Jonung (2000) *Lessons for EMU from the History of Monetary Unions*, Institute of Economic Affairs, London.

Holtfrerich, C.L. (1993) 'Did monetary unification precede or follow political unification of Germany in the 19th century?', *European Economic Review*, 37: 518–24.

On the evolution of Europe to the monetary union:

Eichengreen, B. (2007) 'Sui Generis Euro'. Download from www.econ.berkeley.edu/~eichengr/sui_generis_EMU. pdf.

Kenen, P.B. (1995) *Economic and Monetary Union in Europe*, Cambridge University Press, Cambridge.

Padoa-Schioppa, T. (2000) *The Road to Monetary Union in Europe: The Emperor, the Kings, and the Genies*, Oxford University Press, Oxford.

On exchange rate regime choices:
Bordo, M. (2003) *Exchange Rate Regime Choice in Historical Perspective*, Working paper no. 03/160, IMF.
Frankel, J. (1999) 'No single currency regime is right for all currencies or at all times', *Essays in International Finance*, International Finance Section, Princeton University.

Two studies show the difference between the officially declared regime and what countries actually do:
Levy-Yeyati, E. and F. Sturzenegger (2005) 'Classifying exchange rate regimes: deeds vs. words', *European Economic Review* 49(6): 1603–35.
Reinhart, C. and K. Rogoff (2002) 'The modern history of exchange rate arrangements: a reinterpretation', *Quarterly Journal of Economics*, 119(1): 1– 48.

A very useful description of the EMS is given in Chapter 1 of:
Kenen, P. (1995) *Economic and Monetary Union in Europe*, Cambridge University Press, New York.

On the first ten years of the euro:

- A view from the centre: Tenth Anniversary of the ECB, *Monthly Bulletin*, 2008: http://www.ecb.int/pub/pdf/other/10thanniversaryoftheecbmb200806en.pdf
- A view from outside: SNS economic policy group report, *EMU at Ten, Should Denmark, Sweden and the UK join?*, SNS, Stockholm, 2008.

Useful websites

For a concise summary of the EMS, access the European Parliament's factsheet at www.europarl.eu.int/factsheets/5_2_0_en.htm.

The European Commission publishes annual Convergence Reports that evaluate each country's position relative to the EU: http://ec.europa.eu/economy_finance/publications/specpub_list9259.htm.

The Exchange Rate Mechanism is described on the European Commission's site at http://ec.europa.eu/economy_finance/euro/adoption/erm2/index_en.htm.

The European Parliament's factsheet on monetary integration: www.europarl.eu.int/factsheets/5_1_0_en.htm.

General resources on monetary history: www.ex.ac.uk/~RDavies/arian/other.html; www.micheloud.com/FXM/MH/Glossary.htm.

References

Eichengreen, B. (2002) *Lessons of the Euro for the Rest of the World*, December. Download from http://repositories.cdlib.org/cgi/viewcontent.cgi?article=1005&context=ies.
Mitchell, B.R. (1998) *International Historical Statistics: Europe 1750–1993*, Macmillan, London.

Annex A Hume's mechanism

Hume's mechanism is based on several results from Chapter 13: the long-run neutrality of money and PPP, and the short-run effect of money on interest rates. The neutrality principle is represented in panel (a) of Fig. 14.6 by the upward-sloping schedule, which describes the proportionality between the money stock M and the price level P. In the same panel, we add a horizontal line meant to capture long-run PPP. When all prices are defined in terms of gold, the exchange rate is fixed and simply equal to unity ($E = 1$, as one gram of gold is one gram of gold everywhere!). Imagine that the price of domestic goods P rises while the price $P*$ of foreign goods remains unchanged. The domestic economy becomes less competitive and must eventually run a current account deficit.[11] The horizontal line corresponds to the price level P at which exports equal imports and the current account is in equilibrium. Above this line, the current account is in deficit, and it is in surplus below the line. Point E represents the external equilibrium where the money stock M is consistent with price level P.[12]

Where is the gold money stock coming from? Some of it may be dug out from the ground, the rest is imported. Ignoring for the time being financial flows, it is earned through exports and spent on imports. Thus a current account surplus results in an inflow of gold money, the modern-day equivalent of the accumulation of foreign exchange reserves, the counterpart to a balance of payments surplus. Conversely, gold flows out in presence of a deficit. Now consider point A, where the stock of gold money has been large, resulting in a relatively high price level and, therefore, a current account deficit. The country sends more gold abroad to pay for its imports than it receives for its exports. The stock of gold money declines. This mechanism is represented by the downward-sloping schedule in panel (b) of Fig. 14.6. It says that the balance of payment deteriorates as the stock of money increases (because the price level rises, as shown in the top left-hand panel). Point A in both panels describes a situation of external deficit, which corresponds to money stock M'. The deficit means that gold is flowing out and the money stock contracts, which takes us to point A' in both panels. Over time, the price level declines and the deficit is reduced.[13] At A' the deficit is not yet fully eliminated, gold is still flowing out and the money stock keeps contracting, so we continue moving in the same direction. The process will not stop until point E is reached. At point E, the price level is just 'right', the balance of payments is in equilibrium and the money stock is stabilized. Obviously, a surplus such as point B will trigger an inflow of money (specie) and an increase in prices, bringing the economy gradually to point E. This link between money and external balance is Hume's price–specie mechanism.

The mechanism that takes us from a situation of excessively high money and price level (point A) to equilibrium (point E) involves two steps: (1) the link from the balance of payments to the money stock in the right-hand panel, which is instantaneous; and (2) the link from money to the price level in the top left-hand panel, which takes time when prices are sticky. This is a long-run mechanism, as predicted by PPP and monetary neutrality. In the shorter run, most of the action takes place in the financial sector, which has been overlooked so far. To remedy this, we now look at panel (c) in Fig. 14.6, which describes the financial market. The downward-sloping schedule describes the fact that an increase in the stock of money results in a lower interest rate. Since the exchange rate is fixed (remember, money is gold, everywhere), the interest rate parity principle presented in Chapter 13 implies that when the domestic interest rate i is below

---

[11] It is the trade balance that changes. It is assumed that the other components of the current account remain unaffected.

[12] If we normalize the foreign price index to be $P* = 1$, with $E = 1$ the real exchange rate is $EP/P* = P$. Thus the price level P is also the real exchange rate and the horizontal line corresponds to the equilibrium exchange rate.

[13] This is PPP, a long-run proposition. The detailed mechanism involves declining demand because money contracts and interest rates rise. Then, the Phillips curve mechanism predicts declining inflation.

Figure 14.6 Hume's price–specie mechanism

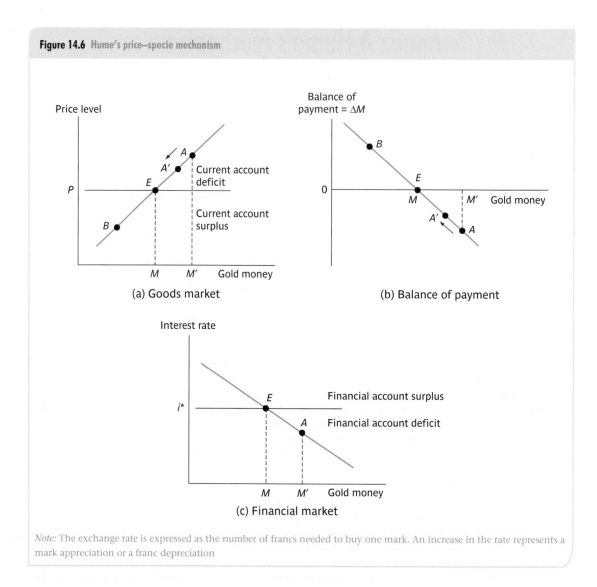

(a) Goods market

(b) Balance of payment

(c) Financial market

Note: The exchange rate is expressed as the number of francs needed to buy one mark. An increase in the rate represents a mark appreciation or a franc depreciation

the rate i^* prevailing abroad, it pays to borrow gold at home where interest is low and to ship it abroad for lending at the higher interest rate. The horizontal line represents the interest rate parity condition. Along this line, the domestic interest rate is the same as abroad ($i = i^*$) and the financial account is in equilibrium. Above this line, the financial account is in surplus; below it, it is in deficit. The financial account is balanced when the stock of gold money is M. If the stock of gold exceeds M, the interest rate is lower than i^*, capital flows out, gold is shipped abroad and the money supply contracts back to the equilibrium level M.

Overall, starting at point A in all three panels, where the money stock M' exceeds the long-run equilibrium level M, both components of the balance of payments – the current and the financial accounts – are in deficit. The overall deficit means that gold is flowing out. As the money supply shrinks, over time the price level declines and the interest rate rises. The capital flow route is very fast while the trade route is slower. Panel (b) of Fig. 14.6 accounts for both channels. The key result is that they both work towards eliminating the external deficit. Likewise, they would eliminate a surplus if it arose.

Chapter 15

Optimum currency areas

The European countries could agree on a common piece of paper, . . . they could then set up a European monetary authority or central bank. . . . This is a possible solution, perhaps it is even an ideal solution. But it is politically very complicated, almost utopian.

Robert Mundell (1973)

I know very well that the Stability Pact is stupid, like all decisions which are rigid.

Romano Prodi (EU Commission President), *Le Monde*, 17 October 2002

Chapter Contents

Introduction

This chapter presents the optimum currency area theory, a systematic way of trying to decide whether it makes sense for a group of countries to abandon their national currencies. The theory develops a battery of economic and political criteria that recognize that the real economic cost of giving up the exchange rate instrument arises in the presence of asymmetric shocks – shocks that do not affect all currency union member countries. The chapter then examines whether Europe passes these tests. The conclusion is that Europe is not really an optimum currency area, but it does not fail all the tests either. A further consideration is that the adoption of the euro may change the situation. Over time, Europe may eventually satisfy all or most of the criteria.

15.1 The question, the problem and the short answer

It is usually taken for granted that each country has its own currency. After all, like the flag or the national anthem, a currency is a symbol of statehood. National heroes or rulers are proudly displayed on coins and banknotes, much as kings, emperors and feudal lords had their faces stamped on gold and silver coins. And yet, it is worth asking whether it makes good economic sense for each country to have its own currency.

The chapter provides answers to a simple question: If we forget about nations and focus purely on economic relations, how would we redraw the map of the world? To start with, does the world need more than one currency? Could Zimbabwe, Peru and China share the same currency? Most likely not. At the other extreme, should each city have its own currency, as was sometimes the case just a few centuries ago? No, of course not. These answers seem obvious, but exactly why? Box 15.1 presents an example that is suggestive of the issues involved.

Box 15.1   The case for a Californian dollar

The sunny state is host to some of the most glamorous industries, including entertainment, computer hardware and software, advanced weapons and much more. Yet, its economy is pretty unstable, as can be seen in Fig. 15.1, which displays the annual growth rate of its real GDP alongside the GDP of the rest of the USA. We can see that in the late 1990s, the years of the information technology (IT) revolution, the Californian economy grew at break-neck speed. Firms were desperately looking for staff as they were trying to seize on apparently unbounded opportunities. In 2001, the IT bubble burst and California was hit much more severely than the rest of the country. Unemployment soared.

The Californian economy bounced back in the early 2000s and again grew faster than the rest of the USA until the housing price bubble started to be deflated. This painful process, which eventually engulfed the whole world, in fact started in California, several years before it seriously affected the USA. Once again, the Californian economy sank deeper than the US economy, sending millions of people into unemployment.

Now imagine that the state of California had its own currency. An appreciation in the late 1990s would have moderated the cyclical peak, much as a depreciation in 2001 would have limited the depth of the trough by enhancing the battered state's competitiveness. A strong Californian dollar in the early 2000s would have slowed the expansion, maybe moderating the rush to buy houses. This would have limited the housing price bubble and the subsequent crisis. A depreciation in the mid-2000s could have limited the ensuing blow. But, although its economy differs from that of most other US states, California cannot use the exchange rate to insulate itself from disturbances.

Yet, no one in California has seriously proposed a monetary secession. It is not because the Californian economy is too small to justify a separate currency. Its GDP is about the same as that of Italy, larger than those of India, Russia and Spain. Somehow, all Californians consider that belonging to the US dollar currency area provides benefits that far outweigh the costs. Or, maybe, no one really asks the question because most assume that one country means one currency.

Figure 15.1 Growth rates in California and the USA, 1998–2010

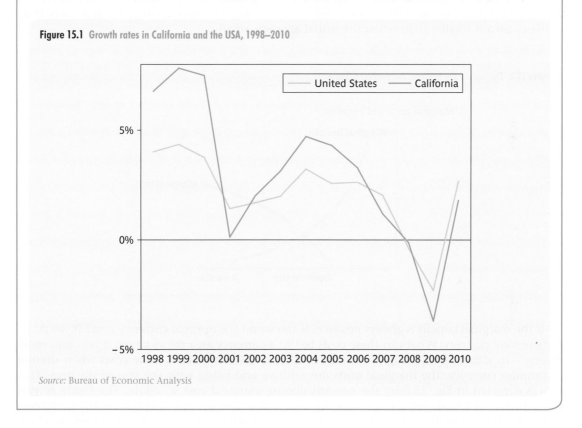

Source: Bureau of Economic Analysis

15.1.1 Why is a large currency area desirable?

Money is one of humanity's great inventions. Economics textbooks tell you that its key feature is to avoid achieving the 'double coincidence of wants', i.e. barter. With money you buy what you want without bothering about simultaneously selling something. Money is useful because it makes commercial and financial transactions immensely easier than barter and also because it is immediately recognized. The more people accept a currency, the more useful it is.[1]

In that sense, the world would benefit from having just one currency. There would be no need to exchange money when travelling, exporting or importing. Exchanging currency is not

---

[1] Technically, money is said to generate network externalities. Network externalities are studied in Chapter 18.

just bothersome – how many unspent foreign coins lie in one of your drawers? – it is also costly. Indeed, if you buy a foreign currency and re-sell it immediately, you are likely to lose 10 per cent or much more. This is how currency dealers and credit card companies get paid for the service that they provide, but this service would be unnecessary if there existed just one currency. In addition, currency transactions are risky as exchange rates fluctuate and seem always to go against you! This is why small currency areas – geographic zones that share the same currency – are clearly not optimal. A currency that is used in a small area is just not very useful.

The marginal benefit curve in Fig. 15.2 symbolically represents this idea. To recall, the marginal benefit measures the added advantage of increasing a currency area by one unit, for example one unit of GDP or one more country. Since the usefulness of a currency grows with the size of the area over which it is being used, its marginal benefit is positive. Yet, it is declining as the area expands because the extra benefit from adding one more country to an already large currency area is smaller than when the initial area was small.

Figure 15.2 The logic of the optimum currency area theory

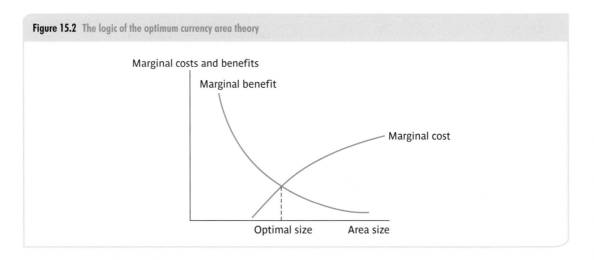

If the marginal benefit is always positive, is the world the optimal currency area? It would be if there were no costs. What can these costs be? As a currency area grows larger, it becomes more diverse – in standards of living, for instance. If more diversity means more costs when sharing a common currency, the marginal costs are positive and rising with the size of the area. This idea is depicted in Fig. 15.2 by the upward-sloping marginal cost schedule. The figure reveals the existence of a trade-off: a large currency area is desirable because it enhances the usefulness of money, but it has drawbacks. The optimal currency area corresponds to the situation where the marginal costs and benefits from sharing the same currency balance each other, as shown in Fig. 15.2. The figure is highly symbolic and there should be no pretence that we can actually draw these schedules. Yet, it summarizes what this chapter is about.

15.2 Benefits of a currency area

15.2.1 Transaction costs

With the creation of the euro, Austrian exporters can ship goods to Finland and be paid in their own currency, because that is also the currency of their customers. Before the euro, the exporters and their customers had to negotiate which currency would be used. The exporter much preferred the Austrian schilling, because that is what she uses every day and she would not have to pay a fee to her bank to exchange Finnish markkas for schillings. Of course, the Finnish customer had the exact opposite preference. No matter what, in the end someone would have to bear the transaction costs. This may seem trivial, but it is not. In a famous example, the European Commission looked at what happened when one started with one EU currency – say 100 worth of it – and exchanged it successively in all the currencies of the EU before getting back into the initial currency. The result was that less than 50 of the initial 100 would be left. Of course, no one would ever do that – except maybe teenagers roaming Europe with a Eurail pass – but the point was that transaction costs are not trivial.

Another important benefit is that goods prices become directly comparable across countries which are part of a monetary union. Along with reduced transaction costs, this allows for more competition. Stronger competition in turn is expected to benefit consumers and to encourage producers to keep improving their offerings. There is evidence that the adoption of the euro has led small and medium size firms to engage in exporting throughout the area.

15.2.2 Uncertainty

Another benefit is the elimination of exchange rate risk. When exports are priced in the currency of the exporter, the importer does not know precisely what the exchange rate will be when the time comes to settle the purchase. If the price is set in the importer's currency, it is the exporter that faces the risk. Alternatively, the party facing the risk may purchase financial insurance (through forward contracts), which adds to the cost of converting currencies. This may deter trade across currency boundaries.

Another area likely to be affected by uncertainty concerns foreign direct investments (FDI), that is, investors acquiring firms, partially or completely. Benefits from FDI include transfers of technology, returns to scale, better production structures and more. Exchange rate fluctuations deter FDI because investors may suffer losses over the long horizons over which they intend to be present in foreign countries.

15.2.3 Quality of monetary policy

Joining a monetary union implies a complete loss of national monetary policy autonomy. We will see that this is an important cost. On the other hand, swapping a domestic central bank for a collectively run central bank may bring benefits. This is the case if the domestic central bank lacks a tradition of quality in carrying out its policies and if the collective central bank stands to do a better job.

This is likely to be the case in countries where the central bank has long been controlled, directly or indirectly, by shortsighted politicians who tend to abuse the possibility of creating money to pay for budget deficits. The collective central bank is more likely to extract itself from government pressure simply because each government will not want to see the central bank financing other governments. We will see that, at least up until the sovereign debt crisis, the European Central Bank enjoyed considerable independence and delivered lower inflation than was the norm previously recorded in all member countries.

15.3 Costs of a currency area

Intuitively, it seems obvious that bringing together very diverse countries into a currency area raises difficulties. The intuition is right. Diversity is costly because a common currency requires a single central bank, and a single monetary authority is unable to react to each and every local particularity. The optimum currency area (OCA) aims at identifying these costs more precisely.

The basic idea is that diversity translates into asymmetric shocks and that the exchange rate is very useful for dealing with these shocks.

We proceed in three steps:

1 First, we define and examine the effects of asymmetric shocks.
2 Second, we study the problems that arise in the presence of asymmetric shocks in a currency area.
3 Finally, we ask how the effects of asymmetric shocks can be mitigated when national exchange rates are no longer available.

15.3.1 Shocks and the exchange rate

Imagine that the world demand for a country's exports declines because tastes change or because cheaper alternatives are developed elsewhere. This opens up a hole in the balance of trade. To re-establish its external balance, the country needs to make its exports cheaper. This calls for enhancing competitiveness. One solution would be for prices and wages to decline; but what if they do not? In this case, a depreciation will do the trick if the country has its own currency. If, however, the country is part of a wider currency area, there is no alternative to lowering prices. Macroeconomic principles, chiefly the Phillips curve, tell us that this requires that the economy slows down, deeply enough for long enough.

In order to examine the situation, we turn to the standard aggregate demand–aggregate supply diagram.[2] World demand for our goods depends on their prices relative to those of competing goods. At the aggregate level, competitiveness is captured by the real exchange rate $EP/P*$, as defined in Chapter 13. This is why, in Fig. 15.3, the vertical axis represents the real exchange rate, denoted λ, rather than just the domestic price level P (or inflation) used for closed economies. Starting from point A, where GDP is assumed to be on its trend, an adverse demand shock is represented by the leftward shift of the AD curve, from AD to AD'. If the nominal exchange rate is allowed to depreciate, or if prices are flexible, the short-run effect will be a shift from point A to point B: the real exchange rate depreciates from λ to λ'. This is a painful move, of course, but an unavoidable one given the adverse shock.

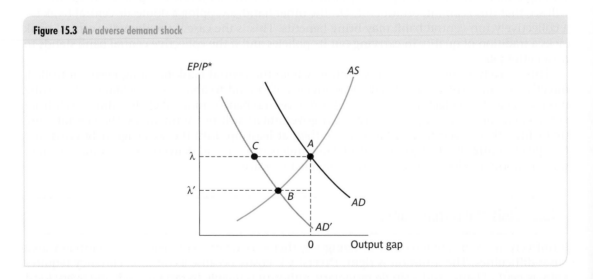

Figure 15.3 An adverse demand shock

The outcome is more painful if the exchange rate is fixed and prices are rigid. In that case, the economy moves to point C, where the output decline is even deeper. At the unchanged real exchange rate λ, domestic producers continue to supply the output corresponding to point A, but point C represents the new, lower, demand. The distance AC represents unsold goods. Obviously, domestic firms will not accumulate unsold goods for ever. Something has to give and production will fall. The recession generates incentives to gradually cut prices, eventually bringing the economy to point B. But this is likely to be the outcome of a painful and protracted process.

The example illustrates why exchange rate fixity, when combined with sticky prices, makes an already bad situation worse. In a monetary union, instead of a simple once-and-for-all change in the nominal exchange rate, a real exchange rate adjustment can only come from changes in prices and wages. If prices and wages are sticky, the adjustment can take time, creating hardship along the way. Box 15.2 tells the story of Germany.

Box 15.2   Early pain for Germany

Germany joined the Eurozone in 1999 at an overvalued exchange rate. Figure 15.4, patterned after Fig. 15.3, shows the evolution of the German real exchange rate and output gap. For a while, until 2001, Germany benefited from a worldwide expansion. Once this expansion was over, it went through several years during which GDP remained below trend. This is when the magazine *The Economist* dubbed Germany 'the sick man in Europe'. With an inflation rate lower than in the rest of the Eurozone, Germany gradually recovered competitiveness until it was pronounced healthy again in 2007. This remarkable recovery created frustrations in other euro area countries when the crisis developed in 2008 and Germany fared better.

Figure 15.4 Germany: the real exchange rate and the output gap, 1997–2008

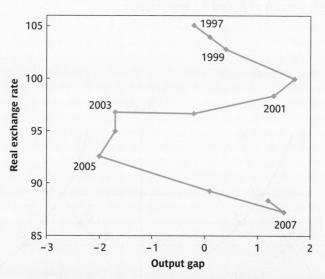

Note: The real exchange rate is the German price level relative to the average price level in the EU15 countries. The index takes the value 100 in 2000. The output gap, actual less trend GDP, is expressed in percent of trend GDP

Source: AMECO, European Commission

15.3.2 Asymmetric shocks

So far we have thought of a country in isolation to set the stage. Diversity means that different countries face different shocks. The simplest case is a currency area with two member countries. We call these countries A and B and examine what difference it makes to share or not the same currency. Note carefully that country A has two (nominal and real) exchange rates: one vis-à-vis country B and one vis-à-vis the rest of the world. The same applies to country B, of course.

If countries A and B are hit by the same adverse shock, we know from the previous section that both have to undergo a real depreciation vis-à-vis the rest of the world. If they are similar enough, to a first approximation, there is no need for their bilateral (nominal and real) exchange rate to change. They are in the same boat facing the same headwinds. This reasoning shows that the loss of the exchange rate within a currency union is of no consequence as long as all member countries face the same shocks. In that case, the union simply adjusts its common exchange rate vis-à-vis the rest of the world and its member countries are as well off as if they had each independently changed their own exchange rate.

The situation is very different, however, in the presence of an asymmetric shock. Assume, for instance, that country A is hit by an adverse shock, but not country B.

What happens then? The situation is examined in Fig. 15.5. The vertical axis measures each country's real exchange rate vis-à-vis the rest of the world: EP_A/P^* and EP_B/P^*, where P_A and P_B are the price indices in country A and country B, respectively, P^* the price level in the rest of the world, and E is the common currency's exchange rate, initially equal to E_0. Points A in both panels represent the initially balanced situation, with the same real exchange rate λ_0 in both countries: $\lambda_0 = E_0 P_A/P^* = E_0 P_B/P^*$. (Prices are assumed to be sticky – otherwise, the exchange rate regime does not matter, as we already noted above.)

The adverse shock that affects country A alone is represented in the left-hand chart, which describes country A, as the shift of the demand schedule from AD to AD'. If country A is not part of a monetary union and can change its own nominal exchange rate, its best course of action is to let it depreciate to E_1 such that the real exchange rate depreciates to $\lambda_1 = E_1 P_A/P^*$, which allows for a new equilibrium at point B. Country B has no reason to change its nominal and real exchange rates, which remain at E_0 and λ_0, respectively.

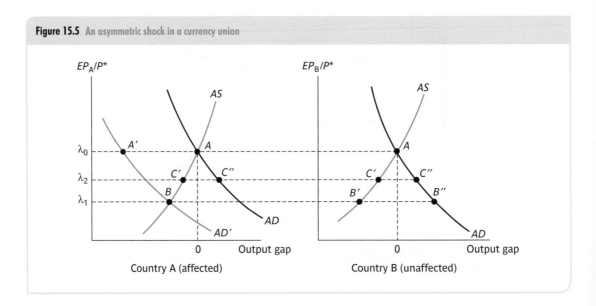

Figure 15.5 An asymmetric shock in a currency union

Things are very different when countries A and B belong to a monetary union. They cannot have different nominal exchange rates, as they would like to in this circumstance. The now-common central bank must make a choice on their behalf. If it cares only about country A, it depreciates the common exchange rate to E_1. With sticky prices, both countries must share the same real exchange rate λ_1. Figure 15.5 shows that this is not good for country B, which now faces a situation of potentially inflationary excess demand (represented by the distance $B'B''$). If the central bank favours country B, it will keep the common exchange rate unchanged. Both countries retain the initial real exchange rate λ_0, and stay at the initial point A. This suits country B well, as it does not face any disturbance, but it means excess supply for country A (represented by the distance $A'A$). Clearly, in the presence of an asymmetric shock, what suits one country hurts the other.

If the union's common external exchange rate floats freely, it will depreciate because of the adverse shock in one part of the area, but not all the way to E_1. It will decline to an intermediate level such as E_2, which corresponds to a real exchange rate $\lambda_2 = E_2 P_A/P^* = E_2 P_B/P^*$.[3] The outcome is a combination of excess supply in country A and excess demand in country B (both represented by $C'C''$). Both countries are in disequilibrium. The new exchange rate level is 'correct' on average, but it is too strong for country A, which is in recession, and too weak for country B, which is overheating.

This is the fundamental and unavoidable cost of forming a monetary union. The logic is very intuitive. With sticky prices, the nominal exchange rate is the only way of adjusting a country's competitiveness to changing conditions. If an asymmetric shock occurs, the common exchange rate cannot insulate all countries that belong to a monetary union.

Disequilibria cannot last for ever. Over time, prices are flexible and will do what they are expected to do. Consider the latest case, when the common exchange rate vis-à-vis the rest of the world is E_2. It has no reason to change any more since it has already done its job of taking into account the average situation in the union. Country A cannot sell all of its production, so its price level must eventually decline until the real exchange rate depreciates to λ_1 and country A will reach its equilibrium at point B. This will require a recession – remember, country A's goods are in excess supply – and unemployment will rise, putting downward pressure on prices. The price of country A's goods will decline until it reaches level P'_A such that $\lambda_1 = E_2 P'_A/P^*$. Country B is in the opposite situation: facing buoyant demand, the price of its goods will rise to P'_B such that its real exchange rate appreciates back to its equilibrium level, which is the original level $\lambda_0 = E_2 P'_B/P^*$. Recession and disinflation in country A, boom and inflation in country B: these are the costs of operating a monetary union when an asymmetric shock occurs.

15.3.3 Symmetric shocks with asymmetric effects

The analysis has focused on asymmetric shocks, but it applies also to the case of symmetric shocks that produce asymmetric effects. There are many reasons why no two countries react in exactly the same way to the same shock: different socio-economic structures, including labour market regulations and traditions, the relative importance of industrial sectors, the role of the financial and banking sectors, the country's external indebtedness, the ability to strike agreements between firms, trade unions and the government, and so on. A good example is the case of a sudden increase in the price of oil and gas. This shock hurts oil- and gas-importing countries but benefits – or, at least, hurts less – oil- or gas-producing countries, such as the Netherlands, Norway and the UK. It is one reason why the two latter countries have not joined the European monetary union.

---

[3] Where exactly E_2 lies depends on a host of factors, such as the relative size of the two countries and how sensitive is their trade to changes in the real exchange rate.

Another asymmetry concerns the way monetary policy operates. When a common central bank reacts to a symmetric shock, it is not a foregone conclusion that the effect of its action will be the same throughout the currency union. Differences in the structure of banking and financial markets or in the size of firms – and their ability to borrow – may result in asymmetric effects. Chapter 18 examines this aspect.

The bottom line is that symmetric shocks can have asymmetric effects. Then the analysis carried out in the previous section fully applies. The situation is similar to the one described in Fig. 15.5.

15.3.4 Policy preferences

A particular case of national differences that matter concerns policy preferences. Countries may disagree on how to deal with each and every possible shock. In practice, there rarely exists a 'best way' to deal with a shock. For example, should we be more concerned about inflation or about unemployment? Should we favour the exporters – who wish to have weak exchange rates to buttress competitiveness – or the consumers – who wish to have strong exchange rates to raise their purchasing power? These are trade-offs, which generate the confrontation of opposing interests and are dealt with through the respective influence of political parties, trade unions and lobbies. There is no reason for the resulting decision to be the same across different countries because national preferences are not necessarily homogeneous.

The result is that, traditionally, some countries have less tolerance towards inflation, towards budget deficits or towards unemployment than others. In Germany for instance, where the hyperinflation of the 1920s is still painfully remembered, price stability is widely seen as a top policy priority. In contrast, high unemployment and social unrest in France in the 1930s have left a lingering distaste for recessions, with relatively little concern for inflation.

This means that shocks, even if symmetric, will elicit different policy responses. When monetary policy is no longer carried out at the national level, the common central bank will be asked to act differently and its managers, drawn from different countries, may find it difficult to agree. It also means that the other macroeconomic instrument, fiscal policy, may be used in different directions. These issues, long latent, have surfaced in the euro area during the crisis, as explained in Chapter 19.

15.4 The optimum currency area criteria

The optimum currency area (OCA) theory brings together the benefits (Section 15.2) and the costs (Section 15.3) to derive practical criteria that can help us answer the question asked at the outset: which countries should share the same currency? In a way, the name OCA is a misnomer, for two reasons. First, because the theory does not really deal about optimality (what is best?) as it simply balances costs and benefits. Second, the theory does not even provide yes or no answers to the central question asked above. Rather it derives criteria that make a common currency acceptable, not optimal; and the criteria are never black or white, they are more or less fulfilled. Box 15.3 provides an example of the OCA criteria at work.

There are three classic economic criteria and an additional three that are political.[4] The first criterion asks what characteristics make it easier to deal with asymmetric shocks within a currency area. The next two economic criteria take a different approach: they aim at identifying which economic areas are less likely to be hit by asymmetric shocks or to face shocks moderate enough to be of limited concern. The last three criteria deal with political aspects; they ask

---

[4] The three 'political' criteria are not part of classic OCA theory. They were introduced in earlier editions of this textbook. The crisis offers a powerful demonstration of their relevance.

> Box 15.3   Should Sweden adopt the euro?

Sweden has carefully debated whether to adopt the euro. The debate ended in 2003 with a referendum that rejected membership. As recalled by Jonung and Vlachos (2007):

> *A Government Commission Report [...] set the stage for the ensuing discussions, both within as well as outside the economics profession. The Commission consisted of economists and political scientists, and was headed by Lars Calmfors, Professor of Economics at Stockholm University and at that time Chairman of the Economic Council of Sweden (Ekonomiska rådet), the scientific advisory body of the Ministry of Finance. In short, the economic analysis of the report was based on the traditional theory of optimum currency areas (OCA) listing the expected benefits and costs of Swedish membership of the euro area. The main benefits were identified as the efficiency gains from a common currency, in other words the reduction in costs concerning international transactions and the elimination of uncertainty concerning fluctuating exchange rates within the monetary union, which would generate more foreign trade and more competition. The loss of monetary policy autonomy was deemed to be the main cost of full EMU membership. [...] The surrendering of monetary policy autonomy was believed to be associated with high costs for Sweden in the event of asymmetric shocks to the domestic economy. Thus, a Swedish currency with a floating exchange rate was viewed as an insurance device. [...] In its conclusions, the Commission recommended Swedish membership in the long run, but proposed that Sweden should not enter [...] in the short run.*

whether different countries are likely to help each other when faced with asymmetric shocks. This section lists and explains the logic of the OCA criteria; Section 15.5 will examine whether they are satisfied in Europe.

15.4.1 Labour mobility (Mundell)

The first criterion was proposed by Robert Mundell (Box 15.4) when he first formulated the notion of an OCA. The idea is that the cost of sharing the same currency would be eliminated if the factors of production, capital and labour, were fully mobile across borders. Since it is conventionally assumed that capital is mobile, the real hurdle comes from the lack of labour mobility.

Mundell criterion

Optimum currency areas are those within which people move easily.

The reasoning is illustrated in Fig. 15.6, which is based on Fig. 15.5. Remember that the adversely affected country A undergoes unemployment while non-affected country B faces inflationary pressure. Both problems could be solved by a shift of the production factors (labour and capital), which are idle in country A, to country B, where they are in short supply. This reallocation is shown as a shift of both countries' supply schedules to AS', leftward for country A, rightward for country B. This reallocation changes trend – or potential – GDPs so that the output gap is zero at both equilibrium points C. What is remarkable is that there is no need for prices and wages to change in either country. Once the factors of production have moved, the currency area's nominal exchange rate E_2 delivers the real exchange rate λ_2 that is best for each country.

Box 15.4 Founders of the optimum currency area theory

Robert A. Mundell, a Canadian-born economist at Columbia University, won the Nobel Prize in part for having created the OCA theory, in part for having started the field of open economy macroeconomics. Most students are familiar with the Mundell–Fleming model. He now advocates a single worldwide currency.

Source: www.columbia.edu/~ram15/portraits.html

Ronald McKinnon, from Stanford University, has made major contributions to the international monetary literature. He is known for his critical appraisal of European monetary union.

Source: www.stanford.edu/~mckinnon/

Peter Kenen, from Princeton University, is a leading contributor to our understanding of the international monetary system and a keen observer of European monetary integration.

Source: www.princeton.edu/~pbkenen/

The Mundell criterion makes good sense: why should unemployment rise in some part of a currency area while, in other parts, firms cannot produce enough to satisfy demand? Let people and their equipment simply move!

Criticism

Yet, as always, things are less simple than they look. A few words of caution are warranted. We need to think a bit harder about what shifting production factors really means. First, it is no wonder that actual currency areas generally coincide with nation-states. Common culture and language, right and ease of resettling, etc. make labour mobility easier within a country than across borders. A national currency is not just a symbol of statehood, it is usually justified by labour mobility. Across borders, not only do cultural and linguistic differences restrain migration, but also institutional barriers further discourage labour mobility, as explained

Figure 15.6 The labour mobility criterion

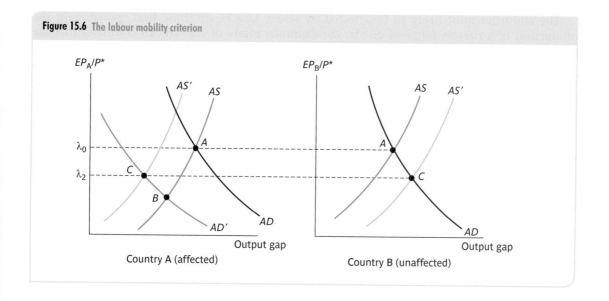

Country A (affected)   Country B (unaffected)

in Chapter 8. A response is to change legislation to make cross-border labour mobility easier and thus enlarge the size of optimum currency areas. Indeed, this is part of Europe's quest for closer integration.

Second, the goods produced in country A may differ from those produced in country B. It may take quite some time to retrain workers from country A to produce the goods of country B, if at all possible. If the shocks are temporary, it may not be worth the trouble of moving, retraining, etc. Labour mobility is not a panacea, just a factor that mitigates the costs of an asymmetric shock in a currency union.

Finally, labour needs equipment to be productive. What if all equipment is already in use in country B? The usual answer is that capital is mobile, but this view needs to be qualified. Financial capital can move freely and quickly, unless impeded by exchange controls. Installed physical capital (means of production such as plant and equipment) is not mobile. It takes time to build plants and shift the location of economic activities. Closing plants in country A can be done quickly – although social–political resistance may create stumbling blocks – but creating new production facilities in country B may take months, if not years. Even if labour were highly mobile, which it is not, shifting the supply curves as described in Fig. 15.6 may take many years. By then, the asymmetric shock may well have evaporated or even reversed.

15.4.2 Production diversification (Kenen)

Asymmetric shocks are the problem within a currency area, but how frequent are they, really? If substantial asymmetric shocks happen only rarely, the costs are episodic while the benefits accrue every day. The Kenen criterion takes a first look at this question by asking what the most likely sources of substantial and long-lasting shocks are. Most of the shocks likely to be permanent are associated with shifts in spending patterns, which may be a consequence of changing tastes (e.g. the German beer consumers find it fashionable to drink wine) or of new technology that brings about new products and makes older ones obsolete (e.g. the internet displaces faxes). Such shocks actually occur continuously, but most of them are hardly noticed outside the affected industries. To create a problem for a monetary union, a shock must be large and asymmetric.

The countries most likely to be affected by severe shocks are those that specialize in the production of a narrow range of goods. For example, many of the African countries that are part of the CFA franc zone primarily export a single agricultural product such as coffee or cacao. A decline in the demand for coffee – which may occur because new producers emerge from elsewhere in the world – is an asymmetric shock because it affects some countries in the CFA franc zone and not others. Conversely, a country that produces a wide range of products will be little affected by shocks that concern any particular good because that good weighs relatively little in total production.

This explains the second criterion for an optimum currency area, initially stated by Kenen (Box 15.4): in order to reduce the likelihood of asymmetric shocks, currency area member countries ought to be well diversified and to produce similar goods. In that case, good-specific shocks are likely to be either symmetric or of little aggregate consequence, thus lessening the need for frequent exchange rate adjustments.

Kenen criterion

Countries whose production and exports are widely diversified and of similar structure form an optimum currency area.

15.4.3 Openness (McKinnon)

The next relevant question is whether the exchange rate is at all helpful in the presence of an asymmetric shock. If not, little is lost by giving it up. In the analysis so far, the distinction between 'domestic' and 'foreign' goods refers to where the goods are produced and priced. However, many standard goods, such as paper sheets or electric bulbs, are produced in different countries but they are virtually identical. In that case, trade competition will ensure that their prices are the same everywhere, or nearly so, and therefore largely independent of the exchange rate.

Consider the example of electric bulbs produced in Sweden and think of the German market. Competition forces the competing producers to set the same price in euros, say €2.5. Pricing to market, as this is called, means that if the krona's exchange rate vis-à-vis the euro changes, Swedish bulbs will still sell for €2.5 in Germany. If the krona depreciates from 9 to 9.5, the Swedish manufacturer will see it as an increase from SKR 22.5 to SKR 23.75. If the krona appreciates from 9 to 8.5, the Swedish manufacturer will have to absorb the difference as the selling price declines from SKR 22.5 to SKR 21.25. Note that this assumes that the Swedish bulb manufacturer is too small to affect prices in Germany. Presumably, the same applies to German goods exported to Sweden. Losing the exchange rate, therefore, is of little consequence and the two countries can form a currency area without suffering much hardship in the presence of asymmetric shocks.

McKinnon criterion

Countries that are very open to trade and trade heavily with each other form an optimum currency area.

The criterion can be made more precise, as follows. When two countries A and B do not share the same currency, they each have their own exchange rate vis-à-vis the rest of the world, E_A and E_B. If they are very open and trade intensively with each other, the distinction between domestic and foreign goods loses much of its significance, as competition will equalize the prices of most goods when expressed in the same currency.

For example, if the price of country A's domestic goods in domestic currency is P_A, expressed in the rest of the world's currency it is $E_A P_A$, and similarly country B's price is $E_B P_B$. Competition ensures that $E_A P_A = E_B P_B$. Any change of one country's nominal exchange rate, say E_A, must be immediately followed by a change in local currency prices P_A such that the world price level $E_A P_A$ remains unchanged. In effect, P_A and P_B are not sticky any more. In that case, the real exchange rates of both countries vis-à-vis the rest of the world are also equal: $E_A/P_A/P^* = E_B P_B/P^*$. When prices are flexible, creating a currency union by giving up the exchange rate entails no serious loss of policy independence.

Criticism

Again, the criterion can be deceptively simple. The exchange rate does not affect competitiveness in the sense that competition forces prices to be the same. Still, the fact that the domestic price of exports (like bulbs) changes with the exchange rate may still have an impact on competitiveness, but in a different way, through profits. When the exchange rate depreciates, for instance, higher domestic-currency export prices (from SKR 22.5 to SKR 23.75 in the previous example) translate into higher profits for exporters. This may induce firms to shift their activities towards exports. Conversely an appreciation eats into the profit margin of exporters. In that case, exchange rate changes would affect the economy.

There is an answer to this objection. Nowadays, most goods have little national specificity. They are made out of imported parts, themselves made of imported parts, etc. A depreciation, then, may raise profits because of higher domestic-currency prices but it also means that imported components could become more expensive because their prices are set internationally. Some gain here, some loss there; once again we find that exchange rate changes have little or no effect.

15.4.4 Fiscal transfers

An important aspect of the analysis of Section 15.3 is that country B suffers – some inflationary pressure – from the adverse shock that hits country A if they share the same currency. It is therefore in the interest of country B to help alleviate the impact of the shock. One possibility is for country B to compensate country A financially. Such a transfer mitigates both the recession in country A, which receives the transfer, and the boom in country B, which pays out the transfer. This gives time for the shock to disappear if it is temporary, or to work its effects through prices if it is longer lasting. If shocks occur randomly, the country that pays out a transfer today will be tomorrow's beneficiary. In effect, such transfers work like a common insurance against bad shocks.

Transfer criterion

Countries that agree to compensate each other for adverse shocks form an optimum currency area.

Transfer schemes of this kind exist across regions in every country. Sometimes they are explicit; most often they are implicit. For example, if a particular region suffers an asymmetric shock, then, as income declines, so do tax payments, while welfare support – chiefly unemployment benefits – rises. This how the region receives transfers from the rest of the country. These transfers are often implicit, part-and-parcel of the redistributive mechanism at work in the country. Some federal countries, such as Germany and Switzerland, operate explicit transfer systems.

Criticism

The debt crisis has brought forward the issue of transfers. Insurance as described works if indeed shocks are random. If it is always the same countries that suffer from adverse shocks, the other countries might see it as a costly undertaking. Why could that be the case? Because any insurance involves a moral hazard. A car driver may be more reckless if he knows that his insurance will pay for all the accidents that he provokes than if he were not insured. This is why car insurance involves deductibles – you pay for some part of the costs – and experience-rated – you pay a higher premium if you are often involved in accidents. Applied to a currency union, countries may take fewer precautions to avoid frequent shocks if they expect transfers. For instance, they may remain too specialized, or too dependent on imports, or they may nurture rigid labour markets that make adjustments long and painful. We will see the importance of this criticism in Chapter 19.

15.4.5 Homogeneous preferences

Political conditions matter even for symmetric shocks. Section 15.3.2 shows that symmetric shocks do not pose any problem as long as each country reacts in the same way to the shock. But Section 15.3.4 explains how symmetric shocks can have polarizing effects akin to asymmetric shocks

---

Box 15.5 Germany and Italy: a difficult relationship

The OCA theory starts and ends with the idea that, once a country joins a monetary union, external competitiveness must be maintained the hard way – keeping costs and prices low – rather through recurrent devaluations. Figure 15.7 makes it clear that Germany worked hard on that (it started with an overvalued exchange rate) while Italy, well, let its competitiveness slip away. Unsurprisingly, Germany's current account swung into a strong surplus while Italy's went into increasing deficits. German public opinion did not conceal its annoyance with Italy, insisting that a strong euro is what the monetary union is all about. Italians called upon the ECB to adopt a policy stance that would prevent the euro from being overvalued.

Figure 15.7 External competitiveness of Germany and Italy, 1999–2012

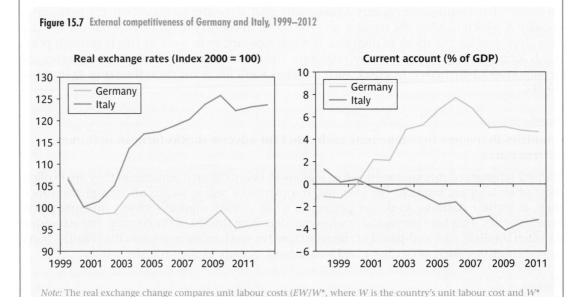

Note: The real exchange change compares unit labour costs (EW/W^*, where W is the country's unit labour cost and W^* is the average of unit labour costs in 35 industrial countries).

Source: AMECO, European Commission

when currency area member countries do not share the same preferences over policy responses. Under such circumstances, whatever the central bank chooses to do will be controversial and will leave some, possibly all, countries unhappy. At best, there will be resentment, at worst the currency union may not survive. Box 15.5 provides a classic example of this kind of tension.

Homogeneity of preferences criterion
Currency union member countries must share a wide consensus on the way to deal with shocks.

15.4.6 Solidarity vs. nationalism

The final criterion goes deeper into political considerations. Since none of the previous criteria are likely to be fully satisfied, no currency area is ever optimum. This is even true for individual countries, which unknowingly operate as currency areas. One consequence is that shocks generate political disagreements as to what the proper response should be. Such disagreements are a familiar feature in any country. They may be more delicate if asymmetric shocks generate disagreements across regions. In individual countries, the eventual resolution of such debates is usually accepted as the cost of living together – the natural consequence of statehood. The outcome is ultimately seen as acceptable because citizens of the same country readily accept some degree of solidarity with one another.

When separate countries contemplate the formation of a currency area, they need to realize that unavoidably there will be times when there will be disagreements and that these disagreements may follow national lines, especially if the shocks are asymmetric or produce asymmetric effects. For such disagreements to be tolerated, the people that form the currency union must accept that they will be living together and extend their sense of solidarity to the whole union. In short, they must have a shared sense of common destiny that outweighs the nationalist tendencies that would otherwise call for intransigent reactions.

Solidarity criterion
When the common monetary policy gives rise to conflicts of national interests, the countries that form a currency area need to accept the costs in the name of a common destiny.

15.5 Is Europe an optimum currency area?

In principle, the OCA theory should tell us whether it did make sense to establish a monetary union in Europe. As already noted, the answer is unlikely to be black and white. The benefits are hard to quantify, as are the six OCA criteria, which may be only partly fulfilled. This section distils that rich and unending debate. Box 15.6 reports on the conclusions reached in May 2003 by the British Chancellor of the Exchequer on the basis of five tests inspired by the OCA theory.

15.5.1 Labour mobility

There are always people who move, but do they move enough and as the Mundell criterion wants them to, in response to asymmetric shocks? Do they promptly take advantage of any difference in earnings, and move to where they can earn more? Is moving better than being unemployed? There are many impediments to migration.

Box 15.6 Why Britain is not yet ready for the euro

When he was appointed Chancellor of the Exchequer in 1997, Gordon Brown awarded himself the right to veto the highly political decision of British Eurozone membership. He announced that he would reach a verdict on the basis of five economic tests:

1. *Convergence.* Are business cycles and economic structures compatible so that we and others could live comfortably with euro interest rates on a permanent basis?
2. *Flexibility.* If problems emerge, is there sufficient flexibility to deal with them?
3. *Investment.* Would joining the EMU create better conditions for firms making long-term decisions to invest in the UK?
4. *Financial services.* What impact would entry into the EMU have on the competitive position of the UK's financial services industry, particularly the City's wholesale markets?
5. *Growth, stability and employment.* In summary, will joining the EMU promote higher growth, stability and a lasting increase in jobs?

In May 2003, the Chancellor finally released his first assessment. He found that the convergence and flexibility tests were not met, that the investment and financial services tests were met, and the fifth test would be met when the first two were met. From this he concluded that the UK was not yet ready, adding: 'We will report on progress in the Budget next year. We can then consider the extent of progress and determine whether on the basis of it we make a further Treasury assessment of the five tests which – if positive next year – would allow us at that time to put the issue before the British people in a referendum.'[1] There has been no further assessment of this sort.

Two characteristics of this procedure are striking. First, the heavy and explicit use of OCA economic principles. Test 1 deals with the presence of asymmetric shocks, test 2 with the ability to cope with asymmetric shocks, with heavy emphasis on labour markets, while test 3 looks at capital mobility. Test 5 summarizes the OCA approach. Test 4 is specific to the UK's specialization in financial services. Second, the tests are specified in an obviously intended vague way, leaving the Chancellor free to implicitly weigh the political aspects of the undertaking.

---

[1] The various documents are available on www.hm-treasury.gov.uk/. They include a large number of specially commissioned studies that are well worth reading.

Migrants have to consider many economic issues, such as:

- the cost of moving, possibly including the selling and buying of dwellings;
- the prospect of becoming unemployed, both in the country of origin and in the country of immigration;
- career opportunities, which means not only current but also future earnings;
- family career prospects, including the spouse and children and sometimes even more distant relatives;
- social benefits, including unemployment, health and retirement;
- taxation of earnings from both labour and savings.

Labour mobility is also subject to non-economic incentives, such as:

- cultural differences (language, religion, traditions, possibly racism and xenophobia) in the country considered for immigration;
- family and friendship links that can be weakened;
- commitment to one's country of origin (nationalism).

For these reasons, labour mobility can only be limited. A natural approach is to compare Europe with existing, well-functioning currency areas, such as the USA. Figure 15.8 shows that mobility across countries is considerably lower in Europe than in the USA. This is not really surprising; moving across countries entails many of the difficulties listed above. What is more telling is to observe that mobility within countries remains much smaller in Europe.

Why do Europeans move so little? Across countries, there are many reasons, some obvious ones like language and traditions, others less well appreciated, such as health insurance, retirement pension systems or the fact that housing tends to be more expensive and the housing market less fluid in Europe than in the USA. But within countries? Cultural aspects and welfare protection – which alleviates the pain of unemployment – seem to matter.

Low migration by European nationals could be compensated by immigration from outside the EU.[5] If immigrant workers were to move to where job offers exceed supply, some of the costs of a monetary union would be reduced. Even viewed this way, immigration – a big political issue in Europe – is relatively limited in Europe, as shown in Chapter 8.

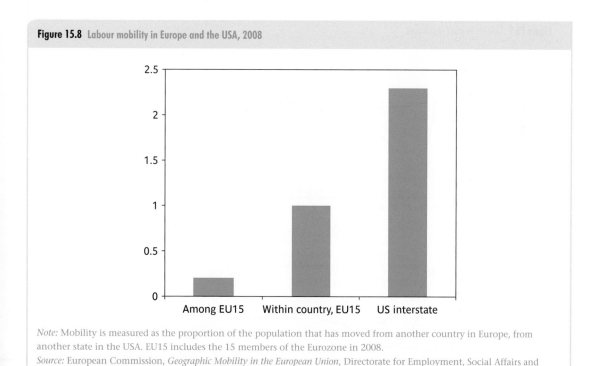

Figure 15.8 Labour mobility in Europe and the USA, 2008

Note: Mobility is measured as the proportion of the population that has moved from another country in Europe, from another state in the USA. EU15 includes the 15 members of the Eurozone in 2008.
Source: European Commission, *Geographic Mobility in the European Union*, Directorate for Employment, Social Affairs and Equal Opportunities, April 2008

---

5   See Chapter 8 for an analysis of immigration.

In summary, Europe is far from fulfilling the labour mobility criterion. An important implication is that asymmetric shocks, when they occur, are likely to be met by unemployment in countries facing loss of competitiveness. Box 15.7 reports that, indeed, when asymmetric shocks occur, migration plays a smaller role in Europe than in the USA, with the unfortunate result that employment takes most of the burden.

How does Europe's low labour mobility affect the response to an asymmetric shock? A study by Fatás (2000) compares Europe and the USA. Fatás looks at 51 regions in the USA (the 50 states and the District of Columbia) and at 54 regions in Europe (a decomposition of 14 countries, all EU countries with the exception of Luxembourg). He asks what happens when an adverse asymmetric shock occurs, i.e. when it affects just one region. Figure 15.9 shows the result. The figure depicts the joint behaviour of total employment, unemployment and the participation rate in each region (all compared with the overall situation in the USA and Europe, respectively).[1] Obviously, employment declines and, for the same shock size, the effect is quantitatively similar in Europe and in the USA. The difference lies elsewhere. In the USA, most of the drop in employment is met by regional emigration; people move to more fortunate parts of the country. In Europe, instead, most of the drop in employment is met by a fall in the participation rate; people withdraw from the labour force and stay at home. Interestingly, in the long run, in the USA those who leave do not return, and in Europe those who stop working remain inactive.

Figure 15.9 Labour market responses

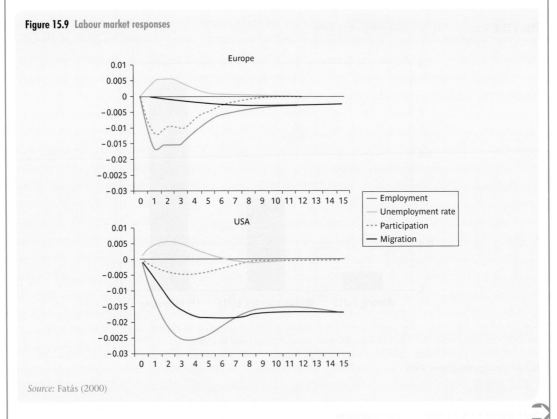

Source: Fatás (2000)

This study corroborates a key element of OCA theory: labour mobility crucially affects the response to asymmetric shocks. The twist is that, with low European labour mobility, following an adverse shock, people become unemployed and many others simply give up the hope of working.

[1] Box 8.1 provides the definitions of employment, unemployment and participation rates.

15.5.2 Diversification and trade dissimilarity

The Kenen criterion rests on the idea that asymmetric shocks are less likely among countries that share similar production patterns and whose trade is diversified. Figure 15.10 presents an index of dissimilarity of European trade. The index looks at how each country's trade structure differs from the situation in Germany (old members) or the Eurozone (new members). The index is based on the decomposition of trade into three classes of goods: agriculture, minerals and manufacturing.

Dissimilarity is highest for Latvia and Denmark, two countries that have not joined the Eurozone, but it is also low for non-member countries such as the Czech Republic, the UK and Hungary. Of interest is the case of the Netherlands, a natural gas exporter that sets it apart and yet it is an enthusiastic member of the Eurozone. The Dutch authorities must believe that the costs are outweighed by the benefits since their economy is deeply integrated with the European economy and they wish to be deeply involved in European integration.

Figure 15.10 Trade dissimilarity index

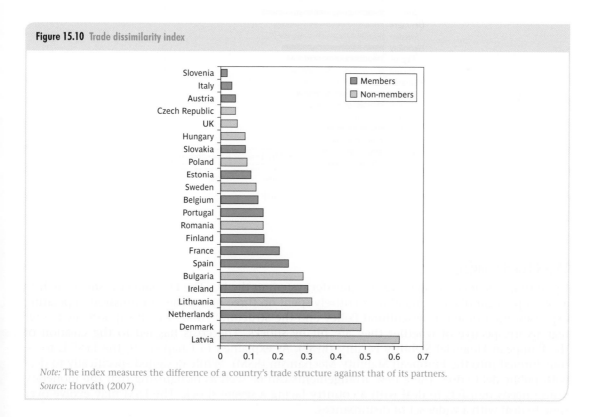

Note: The index measures the difference of a country's trade structure against that of its partners.
Source: Horváth (2007)

15.5.3 Openness

Openness, which may reduce the usefulness of an independent exchange rate, is usually defined as the share of economic activity devoted to international trade. The ratio of exports to GDP measures the proportion of domestic production that is exported. The ratio of imports to GDP measures the proportion of domestic spending that falls on imports. The openness index presented in Fig. 15.11 sums up both (and can go beyond 100 per cent). Most European countries are very open, the more so the smaller they are, which explains why the smaller countries have traditionally been the most enthusiastic supporters of the monetary union. This applies to both old and new EU member countries.

As far as the McKinnon criterion is concerned, most EU economies qualify for joining a monetary union. They are very open and well integrated within Europe.

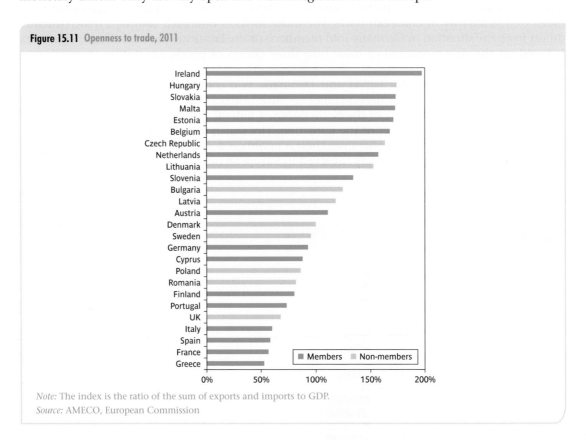

Figure 15.11 Openness to trade, 2011

Note: The index is the ratio of the sum of exports and imports to GDP.
Source: AMECO, European Commission

15.5.4 Fiscal transfers

Up until the debt crisis, there was no transfer system in the EU. The EU budget is small, slightly above 1 per cent of GDP, and almost entirely spent on three items: the Commission's operating expenses, the Common Agricultural Policy and the Structural Funds which support the poorer regions irrespective of whether they are hit by shocks. The crisis has led to the creation of the European Financial Stability Facility (EFSF). As explained in Chapter 19, the EFSF is to be transformed into the European Stability Mechanism (ESM). While designed specifically to deal with public debt crises, these new arrangements can be seen as recognizing that the monetary union needs transfers to deal with a country facing a severe shock. The ESM may evolve over time to deal with a wider set of disturbances.

On this criterion, Europe is definitely not an optimum monetary union, although a step has been taken.

15.5.5 Homogeneous preferences

Do all countries share similar views about the use of monetary policy? On the basis of past inflation rates, this does not seem to be the case. Low-inflation Germany and formerly high-inflation Italy or Greece have very little in common. Similarly, looking at public debts (Chapter 18), a gulf separates European countries' approaches to fiscal policy. So, is the verdict negative? It may be too early to tell but the crisis shows that these concerns are real.

Why has the quality of macroeconomic policies been so diverse in Europe? Is it in the genes? Medical research has not yet turned up any clue! But economic research has a lot to say about incentives that policy makers face. Broadly defined, political institutions shape their reactions to various events, and policy-making institutions differ from one country to another. This includes the respective roles of the executive and the parliament, the number of political parties and trade unions, the role of ideology and much more.

The solution has been to accompany integration steps with the setting up of common institutions. In fact, one reason why the inflation-prone countries have been eager to join the monetary union is that it provides for a degree of monetary policy discipline that has been elusive in the past. As far as the single currency is concerned, Chapter 17 shows that a key preoccupation has been to guarantee macroeconomic stability. The European Central Bank is strongly independent and constitutionally committed to price stability. National deficits are bound by an excessive deficit procedure. Still, although all countries are increasingly operating under common institutions, they do not fully share the same views on each and every issue that arises.

The result is occasional frictions among governments and a sense of estrangement among some public opinions, which was particularly visible when the Constitution was rejected in the spring of 2005. More seriously, these divergences have been on public display during the debt crisis. As recounted in Chapter 19, they explain the inadequacy of policy responses.

We can conclude that there remains some heterogeneity among national preferences. This criterion is only partly fulfilled.

15.5.6 Solidarity vs. nationalism

How deep is the European sentiment of solidarity? Put differently, how far are the citizens willing to give up parts of national sovereignty in the pursuit of common interest? There is no simple, uncontroversial way to measure the willingness of European citizens. An indication is given in Fig. 15.12 by a public opinion poll, which asked respondents whether they felt European.[6] On average, 16 per cent said they do so 'often', as opposed to 43 per cent who said 'never' and 38 per cent who said 'sometimes'. The figure shows the 'often' answer for each country. Clearly, European citizenship is not a widely held feeling. On the other hand, less than half of Europeans never feel European, although this is the case for two-thirds of British citizens! Clearly, the glass is half full, or half empty, depending on what you expect!

The European debt crisis offers a real-life test of this question. As Chapter 19 explains, the initial reaction to the Greek debt crisis was to extend collective support, very explicitly in the name of solidarity. As the crisis deepened, however, nationalistic sentiments started to rise. Reuter reports that the German newspaper *Bild* 'has lambasted Greece as a nation of lazy cheats who should be thrown out of the euro on their ear'. To which some Greek deputies responded: 'By their statements, German politicians and German financial institutions play a leading role in a wretched game of profiteering at the expense of the Greek people.'[7]

All in all, Europe is not scoring very highly on this criterion, but nor is it failing badly.

---

[6] This is the latest poll available on this question.

[7] http://www.reuters.com/article/2010/02/18/greece-germany-idUSLDE61H1IZ20100218.

Figure 15.12 Feeling European? (2006)

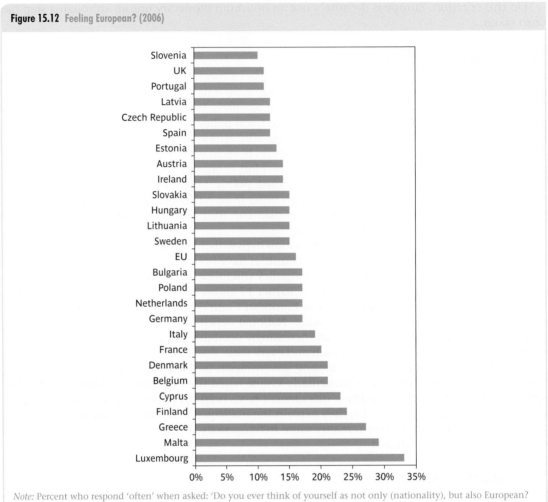

Note: Percent who respond 'often' when asked: 'Do you ever think of yourself as not only (nationality), but also European? Does this happen often, sometimes or never?'

Source: Eurobarometer (http://ec.europa.eu/public_opinion/cf/index.cfm)

15.5.7 So, is Europe an optimum currency area?

In the end, most European countries do well on openness and diversification, two of the three classic economic OCA criteria, and fail on the third one, labour mobility. Europe also fails on fiscal transfers, with an unclear verdict on the remaining two political criteria. Table 15.1 summarizes this appraisal. The mixed performance that it reveals can be interpreted in two ways.

First, it explains why the single currency project has been and remains controversial. Neither the supporters nor the opponents have been able to produce an overwhelming case. After all, that was only to be expected. A monetary union entails costs and benefits, neither of which can be measured or even compared. The OCA criteria are rarely black and white, entirely satisfied or entirely violated. In the end, the economic case is undecided, and the decision to create the monetary union must rest on political considerations.

Table 15.1 OCA scorecard

Criterion	Satisfied?
Labour mobility	No
Trade openness	Yes
Product diversification	Yes
Fiscal transfers	No
Homogeneity of preferences	Partly
Commonality of destiny	?

Second, the partial fulfilment of the OCA criteria implies that, given that the decision to go ahead has been taken, there will be costs. The OCA theory identifies these costs and suggests two main conclusions: the costs will mainly arise in the labour markets and fiscal transfers will have to be rethought.

15.6 Will Europe become an optimum currency area?

The extent to which OCA criteria are fulfilled in part reflects history, but the very fact that the single currency exists can change the situation. Will the existence of the monetary union make Europe increasingly an optimum currency area? Four main questions arise. First, does a common currency promote further trade integration, the McKinnon criterion? Second, does trade integration lead to more diversification and similarity, the Kenen criterion? Third, how do labour market conditions respond to the loss of the exchange rate, affecting the Mundell criterion? Finally, can Europe-wide transfers be envisioned? We consider these questions in turn.

15.6.1 Effects on trade

Many European policy makers strongly believe that stable exchange rates promote trade integration, which enhances fulfilment of the McKinnon criterion. This is indeed one of the benefits expected from a currency union. As time passes by, we can start evaluating this effect. Box 5.8 tells the story as it unfolds. In a nutshell, there is evidence that the adoption of the euro has encouraged trade within the area.

15.6.2 Effects on specialization

More trade integration within the Eurozone may have a disquieting effect, though. If trade leads to more specialization as each country or region focuses on its comparative advantage, then the Kenen diversification criterion may become less fulfilled as time goes by. If, instead, trade integration takes the form of intra-industry trade, then diversification will increase. This would occur if exports and imports include increasingly similar goods. In that case, every country produces the whole range of goods, simply with different brands, offering customers more choice. The jury is still out, but the evidence accumulated so far seems to support the view that diversification increases with trade integration. In that case, the Eurozone is becoming more of an OCA.

Box 15.8 The Rose and border effects

Andrew Rose, from the University of California at Berkeley, initially found that trade within a pair of countries that belong to a currency area is three times larger than trade within otherwise similar countries (Rose, 2000). Another approach has been to look at trade in border areas. Engel and Rogers (1996) focused on the border between the USA and Canada. They observe that the prices of the same goods in different cities become more different the further apart are the cities. Their calculations imply that just crossing the border has the same effect as travelling 3000 km within the same country. Further work has shown that, among the various reasons why borders matter, the fact that currencies differ plays a powerful role.

These effects are huge, so huge that they are unbelievable. A large literature has explored the robustness of these results. Reviewing the Rose effect, Baldwin et al. (2008) conclude that, so far, the euro has probably increased trade by some 5 per cent. This is much smaller than initially found, yet it remains a significant effect and the process is likely not to be complete. The same study also attributes to the common currency an increase in cross-border investments and mergers and acquisitions. This means that firms increasingly operate by assembling parts manufactured in different countries.

15.6.3 Effects on labour markets

European labour mobility is low and few expect it to increase dramatically in the near future. An alternative to mobility is flexibility; the argument runs as follows. European labour markets are noticeably less flexible than their US counterparts. For example, in the USA, firms are quite free to fire workers when economic conditions worsen, whereas in Europe firing is costly because of heavy severance pay and numerous regulations. In addition, US unemployed workers receive less generous welfare support, which encourages them to find and accept another job as soon as possible, sometimes elsewhere in the country, possibly less well paid and in a different activity. Can the loss of the exchange rate encourage reforms?

One possibility is that the single currency increases the costs of the 'European way' and reduces opposition to measures that aim at flexing the labour markets. When each country had its own currency, workers were advocating using monetary policy and the exchange rate to boost the economy. This is now impossible, at least at the national level, and to date there are no pan-European trade unions. In addition, the increasing transparency in goods prices should benefit countries where labour markets are more flexible. Thus, it is believed, economic competition will indirectly lead to competition among the welfare programmes and this will shift the trade-off between economic performance and labour protection. The opposite, a hardening of labour market rigidities, is possible as well. This possibility is based on increasing emphasis on a 'Social Europe'. Advocates of a high degree of labour protection well understand the risk of competition among the welfare programmes and they have successfully called for the adoption of Union-wide minimum standards.

There is no clear evidence yet where things are going. The European crisis may act as a trigger. Under heavy pressure, the Greek and Irish governments have pushed forward wage cuts in the public sector. If this is confirmed, it would be an illustration of how OCA principles operate. Non-fulfilment of a criterion makes the common currency difficult and costly, possibly leading to a crisis situation. The crisis in turn breaks down barriers to reforms. Of course, an alternative scenario is that it is the common currency that breaks down. At the time of writing, both outcomes are plausible.

15.6.4 Fiscal transfers

Much the same applies to fiscal transfers. In the previous edition of this text we wrote: 'There is at present no political support for established extensive and automatic intra-European transfers, but proposals regularly surface. [. . .] It is reasonably certain that, in the not-too-distant future, Europe will have adopted some form of transfer scheme.' Some schemes are currently being hotly debated. They are examined in Chapter 19.

15.6.5 Beyond the OCA criteria: politics

We have reached two important conclusions. First, Europe is not exactly an optimum currency area; it does well on some but not all of the criteria. Second, it is not just labour mobility that is insufficient but, more generally, the labour markets that display significant rigidity, especially in the large countries. In these countries, the monetary union may worsen an already painful situation of high unemployment.

It is natural therefore to ask why the European heads of state and governments who gathered in Maastricht in 1991 still decided to take the risk and set up a monetary union. The answer is: politics.[8] Interestingly enough, Harvard economist Martin Feldstein, a sharp critic of the single currency, sees it as a source of conflict:

> *Political leaders in Europe seem to be prepared to ignore these adverse consequences because they see EMU as a way of furthering the political agenda of a federalist European political union. . . . The adverse economic effects of EMU and the broader political disagreements will nevertheless induce some countries to ask whether they have made a mistake in joining. Although a sovereign country could in principle withdraw from the EMU, the potential trade sanctions and other pressures on such a country are likely to make membership in EMU irreversible unless there is widespread economic dislocation in Europe or, more generally, a collapse of peaceful coexistence within Europe.*

(Feldstein, 1997, pp. 41–2)

In Feldstein's view, the euro is not only unjustified on economic grounds (it is not an OCA) but its survival will require a major step towards a federal Europe, including common defence and foreign policies as well as a generalized harmonization of taxation and labour market regulations. In every member country of the Union, a large number of people share this view and adamantly want to preserve the nation-state.

Indeed, political considerations have been paramount in launching the euro. It is fair to say that the political leaders who agreed on the monetary union did not think at all in terms of the OCA theory (see Box 15.9). They were largely focusing on the symbolic nature of the undertaking. Precisely because money and statehood are intertwined, their intention was to move one step further in the direction of an 'ever-closer union'.

Box 15.9   The return of the OCA theory

The negotiators who prepared the Maastricht Treaty did not pay attention to the OCA theory. They were first and foremost heeding the impossible trinity principle, focusing on the need to preserve exchange rate stability in the wake of full capital movement liberalization. They were also concerned that the new currency should be as strong as the Deutschmark, hence the tough entry conditions detailed in Chapter 16. Overall they believed that, if the countries

---

[8] For a detailed discussion, see the exchange between Feldstein and Wyplosz in the symposium published in the *Journal of Economic Perspectives*, 11(4): 3–42, 1997.

European Central Bank, 17 June 2005. Left to right: Charles Wyplosz, Adam Posen (IIE, Washington), Robert Mundell, Ronald McKinnon, Vitor Gaspar (Bank of Portugal) and Otmar Issing (Chief Economist of the ECB)

allowed into the monetary union had sufficiently converged, and if the new central bank was well protected from political interference, then the undertaking would work.

This view was at variance with many economists' opinion that the OCA criteria were more important and that due account should be paid to the difficulties that would inevitably arise because the Mundell criterion was not satisfied. The authorities are now rediscovering the importance of the OCA theory. In June 2005, for instance, the European Central Bank convened a conference – where both authors of this text were asked to present their views – which paid tribute to the OCA theory and its inventors. The picture shows the panel of the concluding session.

15.7 Summary

The OCA theory seeks to determine over what geographic area it is desirable to establish a single currency. The key insight is that the usefulness of money grows with the size of the area but that costs arise when the area becomes too diverse.

Diversity matters mostly because it is a source of asymmetric shocks. In the presence of price and wage rigidity, however, the exchange rate can be a powerful instrument to deal with shocks. This is why giving up the exchange rate can be costly. The OCA theory asks what characteristics may either reduce the incidence of asymmetric shocks or take the edge off asymmetric shocks.

The logic of OCA theory is summarized in Fig. 15.13. The first question is whether asymmetric shocks are likely to occur often enough, and strongly enough, to be a serious concern. If the answer is negative, the cost of adopting a common currency is low. The McKinnon and Kenen criteria provide the answer. The McKinnon criterion says that the exchange rate is of limited use if the countries are very open. The Kenen criterion concludes that countries that produce and trade a wide range of similar goods are unlikely frequently to face asymmetric shocks.

If these criteria are not well satisfied, asymmetric shocks should be expected and the next question is whether the area is well equipped to deal with them. The Mundell criterion says that, in the absence of wage and price flexibility, labour mobility provides a way of cushioning the impact of asymmetric shocks. In the absence of labour mobility, asymmetric shocks will be costly.

The next question is whether there is a way of compensating for these shocks. It takes us to the political criteria. An obvious compensation takes the form of financial transfers. Transfers offer an insurance mechanism; a country will receive transfers when adversely hit, and will support other member countries when they face a shock. These transfers can be automatic, via taxes and welfare payments, or explicit, based on formal sharing rules.

Figure 15.13 The logic of OCA theory

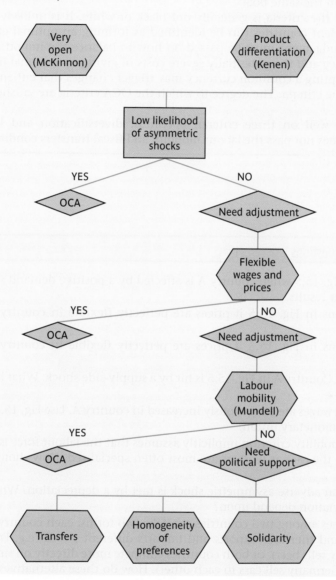

In the presence of asymmetric shocks, the common central bank will have to make hard choices. It must decide how it caters to the varied needs of individual member countries. This is bound to be a controversial decision, which can sap support for the currency area unless a common ground can be designed. Support for the central bank will be more likely if there is broad agreement on its aims, i.e. if policy preferences are reasonably homogeneous, and if there is a sense of solidarity across the currency area, i.e. if the costs are accepted because 'we are in the same boat'.

Fulfilment of the criteria is generally not black or white. It is unlikely, therefore, that several independent countries can be identified as forming an optimal currency area. In the end, some judgement must be passed on how to balance the important benefits of a common currency and the potentially severe costs of giving up national monetary policy. In addition, adopting a common currency may trigger changes that enhance the degree of satisfaction of the criteria. The degree to which the OCA criteria are satisfied could well be endogenous.

Europe does well on three criteria: openness, diversification and homogeneity of preferences. It does not pass the labour mobility and fiscal transfers conditions.

Self-assessment questions

1 Reconsider Fig. 15.5 when country A is affected by a positive demand shock. Carefully interpret your results.

2 What happens in Fig. 15.5 if prices are perfectly flexible in country A but rigid in country B?

3 What happens in Fig. 15.5 if prices are perfectly flexible in country B but rigid in country A?

4 Imagine that Country A in Fig. 15.5 is hit by a supply-side shock. What happens in each country?

5 Imagine that wages are exogenously increased in country A. Use Fig. 15.5 to explore the impact on a monetary union.

6 The labour mobility criterion implicitly assumes that the labour force is homogeneous, which is not the case as workers are most often specialized. How should this criterion be refined?

7 In Fig. 15.3 an adverse asymmetric shock is met by a depreciation. What does the size of the depreciation depend upon?

8 Trade increases among two countries can take two forms: each country becomes more specialized and therefore exports and imports different goods (e.g. France sells wine and Germany sells beer), or both countries compete more directly on similar goods (e.g. France and Germany sell cars to each other). How do these alternatives affect the OCA criteria?

9 The new Member States are likely to be affected by the Balassa–Samuelson effect presented in Chapter 13. What does this imply for their inflation rates once they join the Eurozone?

Essay questions

1 Could immigration be a solution to the labour immobility problem?

2 Can you imagine other regions in the world that could also adopt a common currency?

3 You are given the task of designing a transfer system to cope with asymmetric shocks within the Eurozone. Consider both how to collect and how to spend these resources.

4 'Admission of more countries into the Eurozone is likely to increase the risk of asymmetric shocks.' Comment.

5 In 1997, Gordon Brown, then the UK Chancellor of the Exchequer, stated that the UK would join the EMU when five economic tests were passed. These five tests are:

- Are business cycles and economic structures compatible so that we and others could live comfortably with euro interest rates on a permanent basis?
- If problems emerge, is there sufficient flexibility to deal with them?
- Would joining the EMU create better conditions for firms making long-term decisions to invest in the UK?
- What impact would entry into the EMU have on the competitive position of the UK's financial services industry, particularly the City's wholesale markets?
- In summary, will joining the EMU promote higher growth, stability and a lasting increase in jobs?

  Evaluate these tests.

6 Would the European Monetary Union benefit from British or Swedish membership?

7 Write a science fiction story: a severe asymmetric shock occurs and leads to such economic hardship that the European monetary union is dissolved. Carefully explain each step in the process.

8 Imagine that you are the governor of the central bank of Poland (or Hungary, or the Czech Republic). Would you be for or against your country adopting the euro?

Further reading: the aficionado's corner

Is Europe an OCA?
In May 2003, the UK government undertook a study on EMU membership, in fact closely following the OCA criteria. This study represents an excellent way of putting to work the material presented in this chapter:
HM Treasury (2003) *UK Membership of the Single Currency*, HMSO, Norwich. Also available, with additional detailed studies, at www.hm-treasury.gov.uk.

The central bank of Poland went through a similar exercise:
National Bank of Poland (2004) *A Report on the Costs and Benefits of Poland's Adoption of the Euro*, http://www.nbp.pl/en/publikacje/e_a/euro_adoption.pdf.

A concise summary of the debates throughout Europe before the adoption of the euro can be found in:
Wyplosz, C. (1997) 'EMU: why and how it might happen', *Journal of Economic Perspectives*, 11(4): 3–22.

The three classic OCA criteria:
Kenen, P. (1969) 'The theory of optimum currency areas', in R. Mundell and A. Swoboda (eds) *Monetary Problems of the International Economy*, Chicago University Press, Chicago.
McKinnon, R. (1962) 'Optimum currency areas', *American Economic Review*, 53: 717–25.
Mundell, R. (1961) 'A theory of optimum currency areas', *American Economic Review*, 51: 657–65.

An advanced treatment of the OCA theory:

De Grauwe, P. (2009) *Economics of Monetary Union*, Oxford University Press, Oxford.

A detailed review of OCA theory and evidence:

Mongeli, F.P. (2002) *New Views on the Optimum Currency Area Theory: What is EMU Telling Us?*, Working Paper 138, ECB, April, www.ecb.int.

References

Baldwin, R., V. DiNino, L. Fontagné, R. De Santis and D. Taglioni (2008) *Study on the Impact of the Euro on Trade and Foreign Direct Investment*, European Economy – Economic Papers 321, European Commission.

Engel, C. and J. Rogers (1996) 'How wide is the border?', *American Economic Review*, 86 (December): 1112–25.

Fatás, A. (2000) 'Intranational migration: business cycles and growth', in E. van Wincoop and G. Hess (eds) *Intranational Macroeconomics*, Cambridge University Press, Cambridge.

Feldstein, M. (1997) 'The political economy of the European Economic and Monetary Union: political sources of an economic liability', *Journal of Economic Perspectives*, 11(4): 23–42.

Horváth, R. (2007) 'Ready for Euro? Evidence on EU new member states', *Applied Economics Letters*, 14(14): 1083–6.

Jonung, L. and J. Vlachos (2007) *The Euro – What's in it for me? An Economic Analysis of the Swedish Euro Referendum of 2003*, European Economy – Economic Papers 296, Directorate General Economic and Monetary Affairs, European Commission.

Mundell, R. (1973) 'A plan for a European currency', in H. Johnson and A. Swoboda (eds) *The Economics of Common Currencies*, George Allen & Unwin, London.

Rose, A. (2000) 'One money, one market: the effects of common currencies on trade', *Economic Policy*, 30: 7–46.

Part V

EU Monetary and Fiscal Policies

Chapter 16

The European monetary union

A normal central bank is a monopolist. Today's Eurosystem is, instead, an archipelago of monopolists.

Tommaso Padoa-Schioppa (Former Executive Board member of the ECB)

Chapter Contents

Introduction

The story of the Maastricht Treaty is recounted in Chapter 14. In a nutshell, the monetary union is the outcome of a deal between Germany, which agreed to abandon its strong currency, and the other countries, which wished to move from the mark-dominated and unstable EMS while keeping exchange rates stable. Germany was highly concerned that the new currency would not be as strong as the mark. It requested guarantees. These guarantees form the backbone of the Maastricht Treaty.

The Treaty describes in great detail how the monetary union operates, as explained in Section 16.2. It includes the conditions under which countries are admitted into the Eurozone, presented in Section 16.1. The Treaty also prescribes the essential elements of the monetary policy doctrine; Section 16.3 explains how these principles are implemented to guarantee price stability. Section 16.4 explains why price stability can only be preserved if the central bank enjoys a high degree of independence and describes how this is done; it also examines the related issue of democratic accountability. The last section reviews the first years of the single currency up to the sovereign debt crisis that started in 2010 and which is the subject of Chapter 19.

16.1 The five entry conditions

In the early 1990s, the macroeconomic situation differed widely from one country to another. Germany, deeply attached to price stability, was concerned that some countries were not quite ready to adopt the required monetary discipline. It insisted that admission to the monetary union would not be automatic. A selection process was designed to certify which countries had adopted a 'culture of price stability', meaning that they had durably achieved German-style low inflation. In order to join the monetary union, a country has to fulfil five convergence criteria. At the start, all but one of the candidate countries satisfied the criteria. Greece's entry was delayed by two years. Later on, with the enlargement of the EU, the criteria effectively slowed down new Eurozone membership.

16.1.1 Inflation

The first criterion deals directly with inflation. To be eligible for monetary union membership, a country's inflation rate should not exceed the average of the three lowest inflation rates achieved by the EU Member States by more than 1.5 percentage points. Figure 16.1 shows how the 'Club Med' countries of southern Europe managed to bring their inflation rates to below the acceptable limit by 1998. Greece (not shown) failed on that criterion.

16.1.2 Long-term nominal interest rate

An inflation-prone country could possibly squeeze prices temporarily, on the last year before admission – for example, by freezing administered prices (electricity, transports) – only to relax the effort afterwards. In order to weed out potential cheaters, a second criterion requires that the long-term interest rate should not exceed the average rates observed in the three lowest-inflation-rate countries by more than two percentage points. The reasoning is shrewd. Long-term interest rates mostly reflect markets' assessment of long-term inflation.[1] Achieving a low long-term interest rate therefore requires convincing naturally sceptical financial markets that inflation would remain low 'for ever'.

16.1.3 ERM membership

The same concern about a superficial conversion to price stability lies behind the third criterion. Here, the idea is that a country must have demonstrated its ability to keep its exchange rate tied

---

[1] This is based on the Fisher principle: nominal interest rate = real interest rate + expected inflation. Since the real interest rate is reasonably constant and set worldwide, the main driving force determining the long-term interest rate is the expected long-term inflation rate.

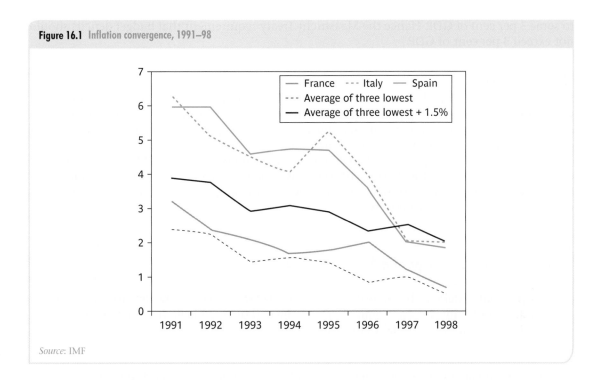

Figure 16.1 Inflation convergence, 1991–98

Source: IMF

to its future monetary union partner currencies. The requirement is therefore that every country must have taken part in the ERM for at least two years without having to devalue its currency.[2]

16.1.4 Budget deficit

The three previous criteria aim at demonstrating a country's acceptance of, and ability to achieve, permanently low inflation, but it makes sense to eradicate the incentives to tolerate high inflation. Why do some countries end up with high inflation? Inflation is not really desirable, so its acceptance must reflect some deeper problem. Indeed, inflation is typically the result of large budget deficits. The process is well known. As a government borrows to finance its budget deficits, its debt rises. If the process goes on unchecked, eventually the financial markets are likely to ask themselves whether the debts will ever be repaid. Their normal reaction, then, is to stop lending to a highly indebted government. The only alternative to borrowing to finance the deficit is to ask the central bank to run its printing press. This is how continuing budget deficits eventually translate into fast money growth, which ultimately delivers high inflation.

This is why the fourth convergence criterion sets a limit on acceptable budget deficits. But what limit? Here again, German influence prevailed. Germany had long operated a 'golden rule', which specifies that budget deficits are only acceptable if they correspond to public investment spending (on roads, telecommunications and other infrastructures). The idea is that public investment is a source of growth, which eventually generates the resources needed to pay for the initial borrowing. The German 'golden rule' considers that public investment typically amounts

---

[2] The Exchange Rate Mechanism is presented in detail in Chapter 14.

to some 3 per cent of GDP. Hence the Maastricht Treaty requirement that budget deficits should not exceed 3 per cent of GDP.[3]

16.1.5 Public debt

Much as inflation can be lowered temporarily, deficits can be made to look good in any given year (for example, by shifting public spending and taxes from one year to another). Thus it was decided that a more permanent feature of fiscal discipline ought to be added. The fifth and last criterion mandates a maximum level for the public debt. Here again, the question was: which ceiling? Unimaginatively perhaps, the ceiling was set at 60 per cent of GDP because it was the average debt level when the Maastricht Treaty was being negotiated in 1991. An additional reason was that the 60 per cent debt limit can be seen as compatible with a deficit debt ceiling of 3 per cent, as explained in Box 16.1.

Box 16.1   The arithmetic of deficits and debts

Debts grow out of deficits, but how does the debt/GDP ratio relate to the deficit/GDP ratio? A little arithmetic helps. If total nominal debt at the end of year t is Bt, its increase during the year is $B_t - B_{t-1}$, and this is equal to the annual deficit D_t:

$$B_t - B_{t-1} = D_t \qquad (1)$$

The two fiscal convergence criteria refer not to the debt and deficit levels, but to their ratios to nominal GDP Y, denoted as b_t and d_t, respectively. Divide the previous accounting equality by the current year GDP to get:

$$\frac{B_t - B_{t-1}}{Y_t} = \frac{D_t}{Y_t} \quad \text{or} \quad b_t - \frac{B_{t-1}}{Y_t} = d_t \qquad (2)$$

Then note that

$$\frac{B_{t-1}}{Y_t} = \frac{B_{t-1}}{Y_{t-1}} \frac{Y_{t-1}}{Y_t} = \frac{b_{t-1}}{1 + g_t}$$

where

$$g_t = \frac{Y_t - Y_{t-1}}{Y_{t-1}} = \frac{Y_t}{Y_{t-1}} - 1$$

is the growth rate of GDP in year t. We can rewrite the debt growth eqn (2) as:

$$b_t - b_{t-1} = (1 + g_t)d_t - g_t b_t \qquad (3)$$

If the debt-to-GDP ratio b is to remain constant, we need to have $b_t = b_{t-1}$, which from eqn (3) implies:

$$d_t = \frac{g_t}{1 + g_t} b_t \qquad (4)$$

---

[3] This entry condition is formally distinct from the same limit prescribed by the Stability and Growth Pact, which is studied in Chapter 17. There is a logical link between the two limits, though: having joined the monetary union, a country is not allowed to let its budget deficits rise again.

The fiscal convergence criteria set $d_t = 3$ per cent and $b_t = 60$ per cent. If nominal GDP grows by 5 per cent, eqn (4) is approximately satisfied. The implicit assumption is therefore that real GDP annual growth is about 3 per cent and inflation is 2 per cent, hence a nominal GDP growth rate of 5 per cent.

If the debt level is constant, the debt/GDP ratio declines as the result of GDP growth, the more so the faster nominal GDP grows. This means that some debt increase, and therefore some deficit, is compatible with a constant debt/GDP ratio, and the tolerable deficit is larger the faster nominal GDP grows.

However, by definition of what is an average, some countries had debts in excess of 60 per cent of GDP, and some much larger. In particular, Belgium's public debt stood at some 120 per cent of GDP. Yet, by 1991, Belgium had overhauled its public finances and was adamant that it was now committed to adhering to a strict budgetary discipline. Even so, it would take a long time to bring its debt to below 60 per cent.[4] As a founding member of the Common Market in 1957, an enthusiastic European country and a long-time advocate of monetary union, Belgium argued that it could not be left out because of past sins now firmly repudiated. At its request, the criterion was couched in prudent terms, requiring that the debt-to-GDP ratio be either less than 60 per cent or 'moving in that direction'.

For the countries then members of the EU, Fig. 16.2 shows the deficits and debts in 1998, the last year before the launch of the monetary union, which is when it was decided whether the

Figure 16.2 Deficits and debts in 1998

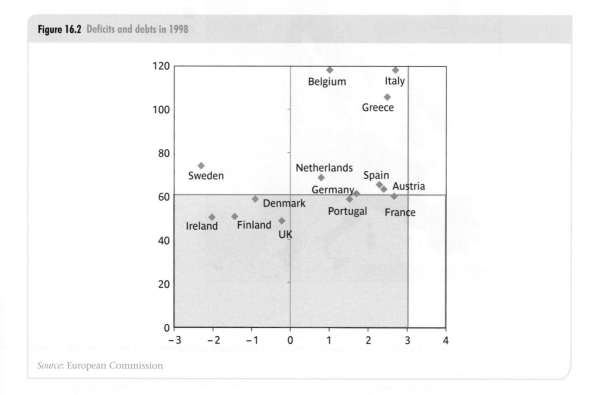

Source: European Commission

---

[4] Indeed, by 2008 before the collapse of Wall Street, the Belgian debt had been reduced to 82.6 per cent of GDP.

entry criteria were being fulfilled. All countries managed to bring their deficits below the 3 per cent threshold, sometimes thanks to accounting tricks.[5] Few, however, could report debts below 60 per cent of GDP. In the end, all were saved by the 'Belgian clause'. The shaded rectangle shows where countries should have been to strictly fulfil the two budget criteria.

16.1.6 Two-speed Europe

An important aspect of the Maastricht Treaty is that it introduced, for the first time, the idea that a major integration move could leave some countries out. The Treaty specifies that all EU member countries are expected to join as soon as practical. In 2011, 17 of the 27 EU member countries have adopted the euro, see Fig. 16.3. These countries include the 11 original members, which were joined by Greece in 2001, Slovenia in 2007, Cyprus and Malta in 2008, Slovakia in 2009 and Estonia in 2011. Denmark and the UK were given an exemption from the 'obligation' to join as part of the Maastricht Treaty. Sweden does not have an exemption but acts as if it did.[6] A number of countries that joined the EU in the 2000s are either waiting to satisfy the convergence criteria (Lithuania, Latvia) or following the Swedish example.

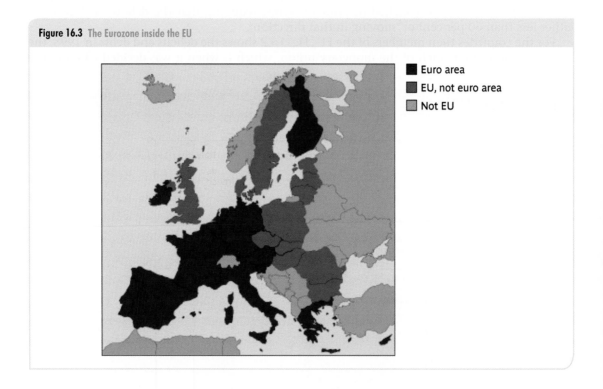

Figure 16.3 The Eurozone inside the EU

- ■ Euro area
- ■ EU, not euro area
- □ Not EU

---

[5] France privatized part of its state-owned telecommunications corporation, which provided the revenues needed to achieve the deficit target. Italy collected at the end of 1998 some taxes which would normally have been due in early 1999. Even the German government considered selling gold to pay back its debt but backed off as the Bundesbank publicly attacked the idea.

[6] When it joined the EU in 1995, Sweden asked for an exemption, which was denied. The diplomatic solution was a gentleman's agreement whereby Sweden did not enter the ERM and was therefore disqualified for monetary union membership. De facto, Sweden is treated as Denmark, with the right to decide when to apply for membership to the Eurozone.

16.2 The Eurosystem

16.2.1 *N* countries, *N* + 1 central banks

With a single currency there can be only one interest rate, one exchange rate vis-à-vis the rest of the world, and therefore one monetary policy. Normally this implies a single central bank, but this is not quite the way the euro area was set up! Each member still comes equipped with its own central bank, the last remaining vestige of lost monetary sovereignty. No matter how daring the founding fathers were, they stopped short of merging the national central banks into a single institution, partly for fear of having to dismiss thousands of employees.

The solution was inspired by federal states like Germany and the USA where regional central banks coexist with the federal central bank. But the EU is not a federation, and the word 'federation' is highly politically incorrect in Europe. Inevitably, therefore, the chosen structure is complicated. The newly created European Central Bank (ECB) coexists with the national central banks, one of which did not even exist prior to 1999 since Luxembourg, long part of a monetary union with Belgium, only established its own central bank to conform to the new arrangement.

16.2.2 The system

The European System of Central Banks (ESCB) is composed of the new, specially created European Central Bank (ECB) and the national central banks (NCBs) of all EU Member States. Since not all EU countries have joined the monetary union, a different term, Eurosystem, has been coined to refer to the ECB and the participating NCBs.[7] The Eurosystem implements the monetary policy of the Eurozone, as described below. If needed, it also conducts foreign exchange operations, in agreement with the Finance Ministers of the member countries. It holds and manages the official foreign reserves of the EMU Member States. It monitors the payment systems and it is involved in the prudential supervision of credit institutions and the financial system.

As shown in Fig. 16.4, the ECB is run by an Executive Board of six members, appointed by the heads of state or governments of the countries that have joined the monetary union, following consultation of the European Parliament. The Eurosystem is run by the Governing Council of the ESCB. It comprises the six members of the Executive Board and the governors of the NCBs of monetary union Member States. The Governing Council is the key authority deciding on monetary policy. Its decisions are, in principle, taken by majority voting, with each member holding one vote, although it seems to operate by consensus. A transitory body, the General Council, includes the members of the Governing Council and the governors of the NCBs of the countries that have not joined the monetary union. The General Council is in essence fulfilling a liaison role and has no authority.

While decisions are taken by the Governing Council, the ECB plays an important role. Its president presides over the meetings of the Governing Council and reports its decisions at press conferences. The ECB prepares the meetings of the Governing Council and implements its decisions. It also gives instructions to the NCBs to carry out the common monetary policy. An important characteristic of the ECB is that its Executive Board members are not representing any country: they are appointed as individuals, even though the large countries (France, Germany, Italy and Spain) all have a national sitting on the first Board. The first president was Dutch, Wim Duisenberg, his successor was French, Jean-Claude Trichet, and the third president is Mario Draghi from Italy. All three have previously served as governors of their own NCBs (see Box 16.2). Thus the ECB is of a federal nature while the Eurosystem is a hybrid, partly federal (the ECB) and partly including national institutions (the NCBs).

---

[7] For a full and formal description, see ECB website at http://www.ecb.int/ecb/html/index.en.html.

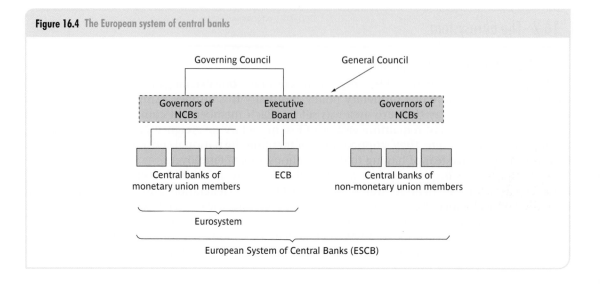

Figure 16.4 The European system of central banks

Box 16.2   ECB presidents

Source: www.ecb.int

Wim Duisenberg (1998–2003)

Wim Duisenberg, the first president of the ECB, was born in 1932. He held a PhD in economics, worked at the IMF and was professor of macroeconomics at the University of Amsterdam before entering politics in the Labour Party and serving as Minister of Finance. Later on, he joined De Netherlandsche Bank and became its governor in 1982. In 1997, he was appointed President of the European Monetary Institute, in charge of preparing the introduction of the single currency.

Source: www.banque-france-fr

Jean-Claude Trichet (2003–11)

His successor, Jean-Claude Trichet, was also a central bank governor prior to taking over the ECB. Born in 1942, he studied economics and civil engineering before attending the elite Ecole Nationale d'Administration. He capped a distinguished career in the French Finance Ministry by becoming head of the Treasury and, in 1993, Governor of the Banque de France. While at the Treasury, he designed the 'franc fort' policy of disinflation.

Mario Draghi (2011–19)

The third president is Mario Draghi, who was Governor of the Bank of Italy from 2005 to 2011. He graduated from the University of Rome and received a PhD in economics from the Massachusetts Institute of Technology. His career was mostly in the Italian Treasury, where he rose to be director general, with a stint in the private sector at Goldman Sachs International. He also taught economics at the University of Florence.

Source: http://www.bancaditalia.it

Many external observers see the size of the Governing Council as a source of difficulty. With $6 + N$ members, where N is the number of countries in the monetary union, the Council is large. It will become even larger as new members join the union, although some changes will be introduced when the euro area expands further (see Box 16.3).

Box 16.3   Changing voting rights in the Eurosystem

Monetary policy choices are often delicate, with many pros and cons to be balanced. For this kind of decision, smaller committees are more efficient than larger ones. The expansion of the EU challenges the Eurosystem decision-making process as the size of the Governing Council could eventually grow to 30 or more members – a small parliament. According to agreement reached in 2003, the size of the Council will grow until there are 15 countries in the Eurozone. Afterwards, while all Council members will be attending the meetings, only 15 NCB governors will exercise a voting right on the basis of a rotation system. The frequency at which every NCB governor will rotate will depend on the country size. A clause allowed the implementation of this arrangement to be suspended until there are 18 members. This clause was invoked in December 2008. The rotation system will therefore start with the next admission in the Eurozone.

The rotation system is complex and will evolve as the Eurozone expands beyond 21 members. An index is computed for each country, based on its GDP (5/6 of the weight) and the size of its financial sector (remaining 1/6). The resulting ranking allows classing all countries into two groups:

- The 5 largest form the first group, 4 of which will have voting rights.
- The remaining countries will make up the second group and will rotate for the remaining 11 voting rights.

When there are 22 or more members, there will be three groups, the result of splitting the second group. The corresponding voting rights are shown in Fig. 16.5. More details are available in the *Monthly Bulletin* of the ECB, May 2003.

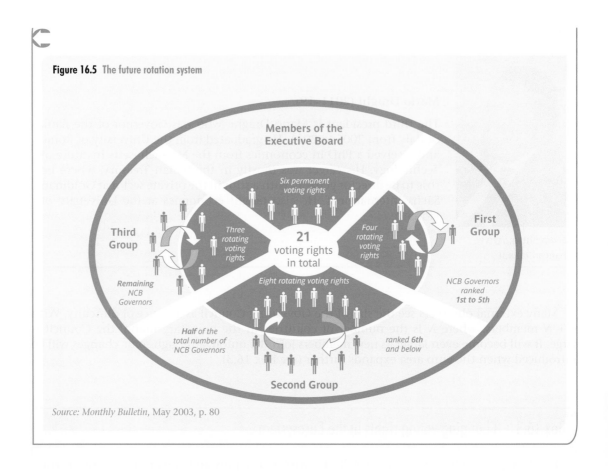

Figure 16.5 The future rotation system

Source: *Monthly Bulletin*, May 2003, p. 80

16.3 Objectives, instruments and strategy

16.3.1 Objectives

The Maastricht Treaty specifies that the main task of the Eurosystem is to deliver price stability:

> *The primary objective of the ESCB shall be to maintain price stability. Without prejudice to that objective, it shall support the general economic policies in the Union in order to contribute to the achievement of the latter's objectives.*

(Article 282-2)

The Treaty does not give an exact definition of price stability. The Eurosystem has chosen to interpret it as follows: 'Price stability is defined as a year-on-year increase in the Harmonized Index of Consumer Prices (HICP)[8] for the Eurozone of below 2 per cent. Price stability is to be maintained over the medium term.' In 2003, with fears of deflation rising, 'the Governing Council agreed that in the pursuit of price stability it will aim to maintain inflation rates close to 2 per cent over the medium term'. Many central banks typically announce an admissible range for inflation; the Eurosystem's target is not set as precisely but it is commonly understood

---

[8] The Harmonized Index of Consumer Prices is an area-wide consumer price index. The same method is also used to compute national HICPs.

that the implicit objective is to keep inflation between 1.5 and 2 per cent. The meaning of 'the medium term' is also imprecise; but is is understood to refer to a 2–3 year horizon.

The Treaty considers price stability a 'primary objective'. Secondary objectives are described in Delphic terms. The 'general economic policies in the Union' refers to Article 3, which lists many objectives, including 'the sustainable development of Europe based on balanced economic growth and price stability' and more. This leaves the Eurosystem with quite some leeway to decide its strategy. Over its first ten years, the Eurosystem has displayed flexibility; while it has emphasized price stability, it has shown itself quite sensitive to growth.

The hierarchy between price stability and other objectives has become standard among many central banks, with the notable exception of the US. It is directly related to the widely accepted macroeconomic principles that underpin Chapter 13. In particular, the standard *AD–AS* framework interprets monetary policy as shifting the *AD* (aggregate demand) curve along the *AS* (aggregate supply) curve. A key result is that, in the short run, the *AS* (or Phillips) curve says that faster growth brings about higher inflation or, conversely, inflation declines when economic growth slows down. The other result is that, in the long run, the *AS* curve is 'vertical', meaning that the trade-off between inflation and growth vanishes. This means that monetary policy cannot have a durable impact on growth and employment. This is the monetary neutrality principle (presented in Chapter 13). In the long run, instead, monetary policy determines the inflation rate. This is why central banks are typically given, as their primary duty, responsibility for inflation, which they are asked to keep low. The short-run trade-off means that central banks are also expected to take into account the state of the economy as they choose how forcefully to keep inflation low. In many respects, this is more art than science.

16.3.2 Instruments

In order to meet its objectives, any central bank must use some instrument to affect aggregate demand. They universally seek to influence the cost of credit. Like most other central banks, the Eurosystem uses the short-term interest rate. The reason is that central banks have a monopoly on the supply of cash. Very short-term assets – 24 hours or less – are very close to cash, so central banks can control very short-term rates with a high degree of precision. Changes in the short-term interest rate have a knock-on effect on longer-term interest rates (and thus on the cost of credit), on asset prices (and thus on capital costs of firms) and on the exchange rate (and thus on foreign demand for domestic goods and services). These effects, however, are not very precise as they depend on market expectations of future inflation and future policy actions. These expectations are beyond the control of the central bank but being clear about longer-run aims and intentions is part of the art of central banking.

The Eurosystem focuses on the overnight rate EONIA (European Over Night Index Average), a weighted average of overnight lending transactions in the Eurozone's interbank market). Control over EONIA is achieved in two ways:

1 The Eurosystem creates a ceiling and a floor for EONIA by maintaining open lending and deposit facilities at pre-announced interest rates. The marginal lending facility means that banks can always borrow directly from the ECB (more precisely, from the NCBs) at the corresponding rate; they would never pay more on the overnight market, so the marginal lending rate is in effect a ceiling. Similarly, since banks can always deposit cash at the ECB's deposit rate, they would never agree to lend at a lower rate, and this rate is the floor. Figure 16.6 shows that, indeed, EONIA moves within the corridor thus established.[9]

---

[9] Note that in 2009–10, EONIA was kept close to the floor. This was intended, see Chapter 19.

2 The Eurosystem conducts, usually weekly, auctions at a rate that it chooses. These auctions, called main refinancing operations, are the means by which the ECB provides liquidity to the banking system and the chosen interest rate serves as a precise guide for EONIA.

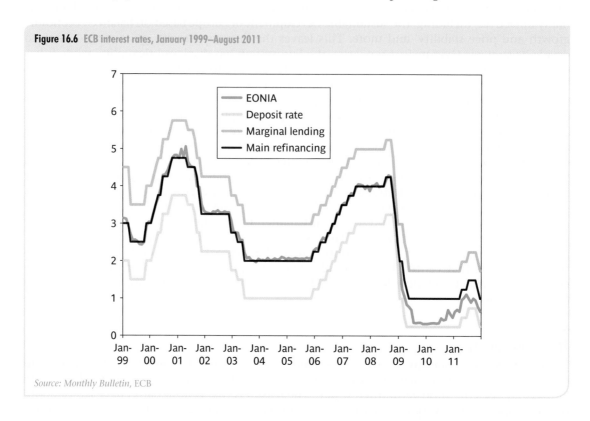

Figure 16.6 ECB interest rates, January 1999–August 2011

Source: Monthly Bulletin, ECB

How does liquidity flow from the Eurosystem to all the corners of the Eurozone banking system? As noted above, the Eurosystem organizes auctions on a regular basis. Each NCB collects bids from its commercial banks and passes the information to the ECB. The ECB then decides which proportion of bids will be accepted and instructs the NCBs accordingly. The commercial banks can then disseminate the liquidity on the interbank market. It does not matter where the initial injection is made: since there is a single interest rate throughout the Eurozone, the area-wide interbank market ensures that money is available where needed.

16.3.3 Strategy

How does the Eurosystem go about using its instrument (the short-term interest rate) to achieve its objective (inflation close to 2 per cent)? It announced its strategy in October 1998, a few months before starting its operation. In spring 2003, it conducted a strategy review to take stock of the experience accumulated so far. As stated, the strategy relies on three main elements: the definition of price stability, already presented in Section 16.3.1, and two 'pillars' used to identify risks to price stability.

The first pillar is what the Eurosystem calls 'economic analysis'. It consists of a broad review of the recent evolution and likely prospects of economic conditions (including growth, employment, prices, exchange rates and foreign conditions). The second pillar, the 'monetary analysis', studies the evolution of monetary aggregates (M3, in particular) and credit which, in the medium to long term, moves in proportion to inflation, in line with the neutrality principle. In the Eurosystem's words, 'these two perspectives offer complementary analytical frameworks to support the Governing Council's overall assessment of risks to price stability. In this respect, the monetary analysis mainly serves as a means of cross-checking, from a medium- to long-term perspective, the short- to medium-term indications coming from economic analysis' (ECB, 2003).

What does this mean in practice? At the monthly policy meeting, the Chief Economist presents to the Governing Council a broad analysis of the situation, including forecasts of inflation and growth. Monetary conditions are then used to qualify the forecasts and allow the Council to form a view of where inflation is heading. Then the real debate starts: What should happen to the interest rate? Should it be raised because inflation is perceived as excessive? How much weight should be attached to other considerations, such as growth and employment, or the exchange rate and stock markets? Importantly, the Eurosystem does not take any responsibility for the exchange rate, which is freely floating.

Is the Eurosystem's strategy special? Over the past decade, many central banks have adopted the inflation-targeting strategy. In Europe, this is the case of most non-monetary union member central banks (including the Czech Republic, Hungary, Norway, Poland, Sweden and the UK). Inflation targeting comprises announcing a target, publishing an inflation forecast at the relevant policy horizon (usually one to two years ahead), and adjusting the interest rate according to the difference between the forecast and the target. For example, if the forecast exceeds the target, the presumption is that monetary policy is tightened, i.e. that the interest rate is raised.

The Eurosystem has resisted this approach, along with the US Federal Reserve and the Bank of Japan. One reason is that the Eurosystem wants to claim the Bundesbank heritage, and the Bundesbank did not target inflation; it targeted money growth, which explains the second pillar. On the other hand, the Eurosystem's strategy resembles inflation targeting: there is an implicit target (the 2 per cent definition of price stability) and an inflation forecast is published twice a year. What the Eurosystem seems to reject is giving the impression that it acts mechanically. Box 16.4 examines this question in more detail.

Box 16.4   How different is the ECB?

Inflation-targeting central banks set the short-term interest rate with one eye on inflation forecasts and the other eye on the expected activity level, measured as the deviation from actual GDP from its 'normal' level. The Eurosystem too tries to steer inflation in the medium run towards 'close but less than 2 per cent' but does not ignore the output gap.[1] So, beyond the rhetoric, does the Eurosystem really act differently from inflation-targeting central banks? A simple way to check is to ask whether the actual interest rate is indeed driven by the deviation of inflation from its (implicit or explicit target) and by the output gap. This representation of interest rate decisions is called the Taylor rule. It involves choosing weights to be applied to the inflation and output gaps; these weights reflect the relative importance attached by the central bank to its two objectives. Figure 16.7 looks at the record of the Eurosystem (and its predecessor, the Bundesbank), of the Swedish Riksbank and of the Bank of England. It displays two short-term interest rates: the actual one and the one that would have been chosen if the central banks had followed the same Taylor rule.[2] We see that central bank behaviour has increasingly conformed to the Taylor rule formulation. This applies to the Bundesbank until 1999. Despite all of its tough rhetoric, it was an early practitioner of the Taylor rule. We also see that the Eurosystem followed suit and that its actions do not differ from those of the Riksbank or the Bank of England.

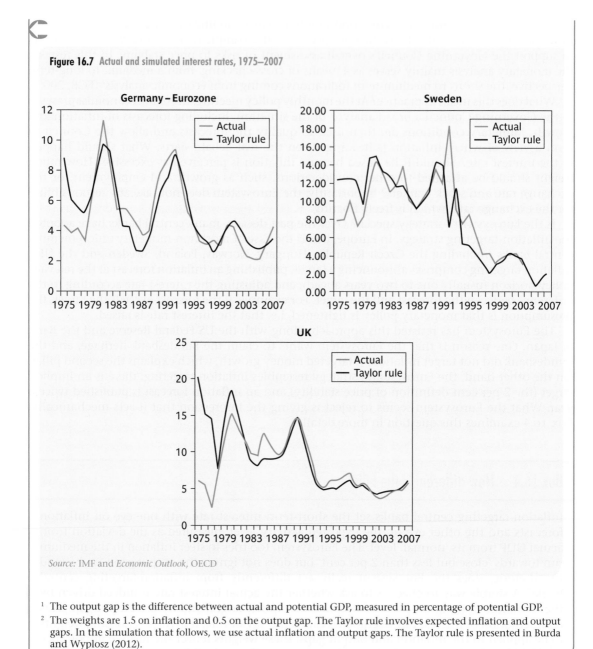

Figure 16.7 *Actual and simulated interest rates, 1975–2007*

Source: IMF and *Economic Outlook*, OECD

[1] The output gap is the difference between actual and potential GDP, measured in percentage of potential GDP.

[2] The weights are 1.5 on inflation and 0.5 on the output gap. The Taylor rule involves expected inflation and output gaps. In the simulation that follows, we use actual inflation and output gaps. The Taylor rule is presented in Burda and Wyplosz (2012).

16.4 Independence and accountability

In order to fulfil its main task of delivering price stability, a central bank must be free to operate without outside interference. While, in principle, everyone approves of price stability, some important actors occasionally have second thoughts. In particular, financially stressed governments may come to see the printing press as the least bad option. Likewise exporting firms, whose competitiveness depends on the exchange rate, frequently ask their central banks to relax monetary policy, and they are supported by trade unions, which are concerned with employment. Debtors like inflation for it erases the value of their (non-indexed) liabilities. Financial institutions often make larger profits when liquidity is plentiful. In any democracy, these are formidable coalitions. Experience with high inflation has shown that these effects are temporary – another manifestation of long-term monetary neutrality – while inflation is in fact painful, unfair to the poorer and its elimination involves long periods of slow growth and high unemployment. This is why the modern trend of focusing monetary policy on price stability also argues in favour of central bank independence from all segments of society and, in particular, from the political powers.

On the other hand, monetary policy affects citizens of the monetary union in a number of ways. The interest rate directly impacts on the cost of borrowing and on the returns from saving; the exchange rate, which is affected by the interest rate (see Chapter 13), directly impacts on the competitiveness of firms and on the purchasing power of citizens. In effect, by granting independence to their central bank, the citizens delegate a very important task to a group of individuals who are appointed, not elected, and who cannot be removed unless they commit grave illegal acts. In a democratic society, delegation to unelected officials needs to be counterbalanced by democratic accountability. This section examines how these two goals are dealt with in the EMU.

16.4.1 Independence

The Eurosystem is characterized by a great degree of independence; it is probably the world's most independent central bank because the Treaty explicitly states that both the ECB and the NCBs are strictly protected from political influence. Before joining the Eurozone, each country must adapt the statutes of its NCB to match a number of common requirements. In particular, the EU Treaty explicitly rules out any interference by national or European authorities in the deliberations of the Eurosystem:

> *When exercising the powers and carrying out the tasks and duties conferred upon them by this Treaty and the Statute of the ESCB, neither the ECB, nor a national central bank, nor any member of their decision-making bodies shall seek or take instructions from Community institutions or bodies, from any government of a Member State or from any other body. The Community institutions and bodies and the governments of the Member States undertake to respect this principle and not to seek to influence the members of the decision-making bodies of the ECB or of the national central banks in the performance of their tasks.*

(Article 107)

In addition, to guarantee their personal independence, the members of the Executive Board are appointed for a long period (eight years) and cannot be reappointed, which reduces the opportunity for pressures. Similar conditions apply to the NCB governors, although they differ slightly from one country to another, but their mandates must be for a minimum of five years. No central bank official can be removed from office unless he or she becomes incapacitated or is found guilty of serious misconduct, with the Court of Justice of the European Communities competent to settle disputes.

The independence of the Eurosystem applies to the choice of both policy objectives and instruments. The Treaty sets the objectives in terms vague enough to allow the Eurosystem to decide what it tries to achieve, as explained in Section 16.3.1. The Treaty further leaves the

Eurosystem completely free to decide which instruments it uses, and how. Other central banks sometimes have only instrument independence. This is the case of the Bank of England, which is instructed to pursue an inflation target set by the Chancellor of the Exchequer.

Finally, the ECB is financially independent. It has its own budget, independent from that of the EU. Its accounts are not audited by the European Court of Auditors, which monitors the European Commission, but by independent external auditors.

16.4.2 Accountability

Democratic accountability is typically exercised in two ways: reporting and transparency. Formally, the Eurosystem operates under the control of the European Parliament. Its statutes require that an annual report be sent to the Parliament, as well as to the Council and the Commission. This report is debated by the Parliament. In addition, the Parliament may request that the President of the ECB and the other members of the Executive Board testify to the Parliament's Economic and Monetary Affairs Committee. In practice, the President appears before the committee every quarter and the members of the Executive Board also do so quite often. In addition, the President of the EU Council and a member of the European Commission may participate in the meetings of the Governing Council without voting rights.

Transparency contributes powerfully to accountability. By revealing the contents of its deliberations, a central bank conveys to the public (the media, the financial markets and independent observers) the rationale and difficulties of its decisions. The Eurosystem does not provide detailed reports of the meetings of its Governing Council. Instead the President of the ECB holds a press conference immediately after the monthly policy-setting meeting to present its decisions in highly standardized terms. Table 16.1 shows how major central banks reveal the work of their decision-making committee meetings. Several of them publish the committee meeting's minutes within a month, but since they can be heavily edited, minutes are not necessarily very informative. Very few (the US Federal Reserve and the Bank of Japan) publish extensive records of the discussion, but with very long delays, which makes the publication irrelevant except for historical purposes. Many central banks report on individual votes, which is a clear way of indicating how certain policy makers feel about their collective decisions. The Eurosystem is nearly alone in doing none of that. It considers that revealing individual votes could be interpreted in a nationalistic manner that does not, in fact, correspond to the thinking of members of the Governing Council who are duty-bound to look only at the Eurozone as a whole.

16.5 The first years, until the Great Crisis

This section looks at how the Eurozone has operated since its creation. Because the crisis has been so unusual, we defer its study until Chapter 19. Here we just look at normal years.

16.5.1 Inflation and growth

When the euro was launched in January 1999, inflation was very low, partly because all member countries had been working hard at meeting the Maastricht entry criteria presented in Section 16.1. Soon thereafter, oil prices rose threefold in 2000. An oil shock means both more inflation and less growth, a classic dilemma that all central banks fear. Simultaneously, stock markets fell worldwide, marking the end of a long-lasting financial bubble fed by unrealistic expectations of what the information technology revolution could deliver. Within months, the US economy went into recession, and Europe's economy also slowed down. Then, the terrorist attacks of 11 September 2001 shook the world economy. There followed a mellower period until oil prices

Table 16.1 Provision of information on monetary policy meetings

	Federal Reserve	ESCB	Bank of Japan	Bank of England	Bank of Canada	Swedish Riksbank
Interest-rate decision immediately announced	Yes (after 1994)	Yes	Yes	Yes	Yes	Yes
Supporting statement giving some rationale for a change	Yes	Yes	Yes	Sometimes	Yes	Yes
Release of minutes	5–8 weeks[a]	No	1 month	13 days	n.a.	2–4 weeks
Official minutes provide full details of:						
Internal debate	Yes	No	Yes	Yes	n.a.	No
Individuals' views	Yes	No	No	Yes	No	No
Verbatim records of MP meetings are kept	No	Yes	No	No	No	Yes
Verbatim records released to the public after:	5 years	n.a.	10 years	n.a.	n.a.	n.a.

[a] The minutes are released after the following FOMC meeting.

Source: Blinder et al. (2001)

rose again to record levels, shortly before the onslaught of the crisis that erupted in the USA in mid-2007 and culminated with the Wall Street meltdown of September 2008.

It is no surprise, therefore, that the inflation rate has almost always been above the 2 per cent ceiling, as Fig. 16.9 shows. Yet, it would be wrong to conclude that the Eurosystem has failed to deliver price stability. Until late 2007, the inflation rate remained close enough to 2 per cent for comfort. An interesting observation is that professional forecasters have systematically anticipated that inflation would remain close but below 2 per cent, even though they could see that it was not the case. Anyway, no member country – including Germany – has enjoyed such a long period of low inflation since the Second World War. It is surprising, therefore, that in nearly every country a large number of people are convinced of the opposite, namely that the adoption of the euro has brought inflation. This phenomenon is discussed in Box 16.6. On the other hand, the euro area is not unique in having experienced low inflation. This general feature of the early 2000s is sometimes referred to as the Great Moderation.

Growth, on the other hand, has been generally slow in the Eurozone, prompting criticism of the ECB, including by some member governments. The criticism may be unfair. To start with, growth has been slow on average, but not in every Eurozone country. Some countries have even grown very fast, as Fig. 16.10 shows, although many of these countries were those

Box 16.5   Independence and transparency

In principle, the more independent is a central bank, the more accountable it should be, and transparency is one key element of accountability. Since there is mounting evidence that inflation tends to be lower where central banks are more independent, a good central bank should be very independent and very transparent.

A recent study has constructed scores for central bank independence and transparency. The numbers are inevitably arbitrary but Fig. 16.8, which looks at 29 countries around the world, suggests that the ECB is indeed very independent but only ranks 17th as far as transparency is concerned.

Figure 16.8 Independence and transparency indices

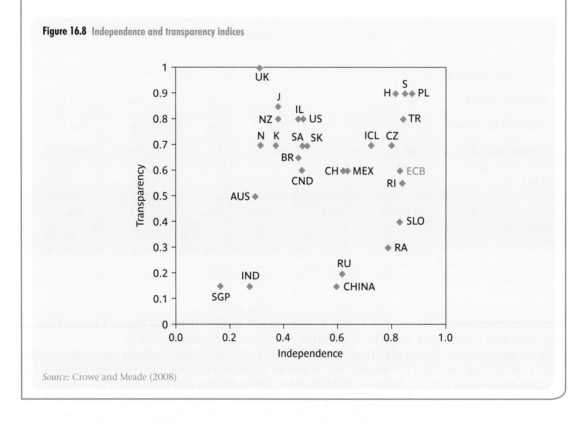

Source: Crowe and Meade (2008)

worst hit by the crisis after 2008. The overall Eurozone's growth rate is low because some of the largest members – chiefly Germany and Italy, with France only slighter better – have achieved a disappointing performance. The Eurosystem has argued that this is not due to an over-restrictive monetary policy stance. It has a point. The neutrality principle asserts that long-run growth is independent of monetary policy.

16.5.2 The exchange rate

The Eurosystem has faced another vexing issue. Just when the euro was launched in early 1999, the dollar started to rise vis-à-vis all major currencies, including the euro and, to a lesser

Figure 16.9 Inflation in the Eurozone (%), 1999Q1–2008Q4

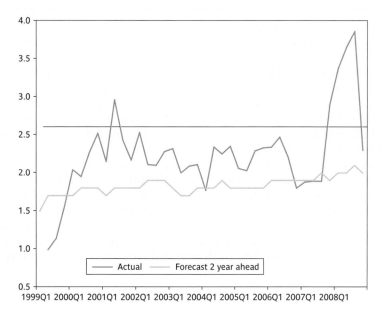

Note: The figure shows for each quarter the actual inflation rate (over the previous four quarters) and the forecast of inflation over a two-year horizon, computed by the ECB as the average of forecasts produced by professional forecasters.
Source: *Monthly Bulletin* and *Survey of Professional Forecasters*, ECB

Figure 16.10 Average annual GDP growth rate (%), 1999–2008

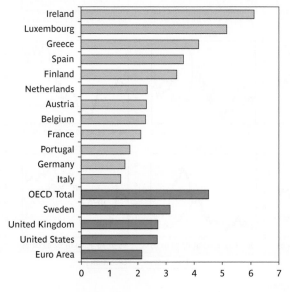

Source: *Economic Outlook*, OECD

Box 16.6   For the public, inflation is up

When euro coins and banknotes were introduced in early 2002, a number of retailers rounded up prices. This created a perception of a jump in the price level. The jump has been confirmed by HICP measures but its amount – about 0.5 per cent – is trivially small in comparison with public perceptions. Figure 16.11 shows actual inflation as measured by the HICP and an estimate of perceived inflation by citizens. Not only is the gap large in the months following the introduction of euro notes and coins, but it has not disappeared. Public opinion polls keep revealing that Eurozone citizens believe that the euro has been a major source of high and enduring inflation. In fact, many people believe that the official measure of inflation is deeply flawed since it is much lower than what 'they see'.

Many studies have been conducted to ascertain that the official index is not flawed and to try to explain why perceptions can systematically differ from 'facts'. One explanation is that rounding up has mostly affected cheap goods (an increase in €0.5 for a cup of coffee that costs €1.5 is indeed a 33 per cent increase) that people purchase frequently, which keeps reminding them of the jump. Another explanation is that people still evaluate prices by computing their value in the old currency (liras, francs, pesetas, etc.) but make their own rounding up errors as they do so. The truth is that there is still no satisfactory explanation of the phenomenon.

Figure 16.11 Inflation in the Eurozone: measured vs. perceived

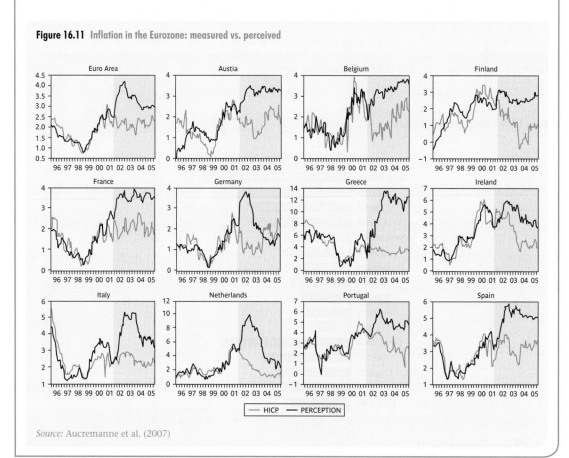

Source: Aucremanne et al. (2007)

extent, the pound sterling. Given that the US dollar has long been the world's standard, the general interpretation was that the euro was weak. This left the impression that the Eurosystem was unable to deliver the strong currency that had been predicated upon its price-stability commitment, following the PPP logic presented in Chapter 13. Then, from late 2002 onwards, the dollar started to fall. Instead of praising the Eurosystem for having finally delivered a strong currency, critics complained that the euro was overvalued and hurting European exporters. Yet, as Fig. 16.12 shows, the movements of the dollar/euro exchange rate have not been particularly out of step with the past, at least until 2007.

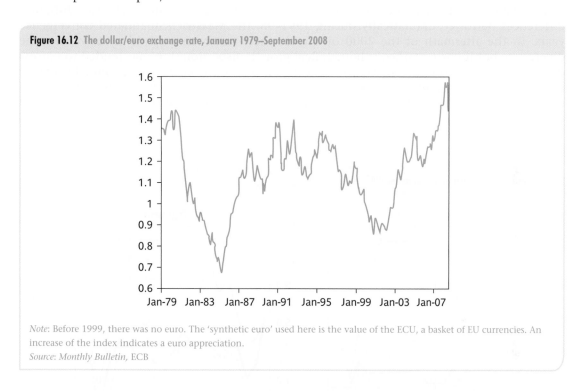

Figure 16.12 The dollar/euro exchange rate, January 1979–September 2008

Note: Before 1999, there was no euro. The 'synthetic euro' used here is the value of the ECU, a basket of EU currencies. An increase of the index indicates a euro appreciation.
Source: *Monthly Bulletin*, ECB

From the start, the Eurosystem clearly announced that it would take no responsibility for the exchange rate. Its view is that the euro is a freely floating currency. Since capital movements are completely free, this position accords well with the impossible trinity principle. The discussion of exchange rate regimes in Chapter 13 suggests that very large and closed economies, like the Eurozone, have little interest in stabilizing their exchange rates; the freely floating 'corner' is likely to be its best option, and this is where the Eurosystem has chosen to stand. 'Best option' does not mean that it does not have some unpleasant implications, however, and critics have seized on these adverse effects to blame the Eurosystem.

It is also true that the exchange rate between the euro and the dollar is as much driven by US as by European events. In that sense, it is not the euro that is too strong but the dollar that is too weak. Undoubtedly, this debate will go on for many years to come.

16.5.3 One money, one policy

Asymmetries

How about the much-feared asymmetric shocks emphasized by the optimum currency area (OCA) theory? Sure enough, there is no lack of complaints that the Eurosystem does not pay attention to economic conditions in this or that country. The fact is that with one money there can exist only one central bank, and therefore one monetary policy. The Eurosystem can only deal with the Eurozone as a whole. It would open a Pandora's Box should it ever attempt to bend its policy to a particular country. After all, a key implication of the OCA theory is that joining a monetary union implies the acceptance that member countries will occasionally have to bear some costs.

Figure 16.13 documents how different economic conditions have been throughout the Eurozone, before and after monetary union (the figure displays the Eurozone inflation and real GDP growth rates, along with the highest and lowest national rates each year). Inflation differences narrowed dramatically during 1991–98, the Maastricht-mandated convergence years. In the aftermath of the 2000 oil shock, there has been a tendency towards some divergence but it has remained subdued. Real growth dispersion, too, has tended to narrow down and has stayed that way. Of course, this was before the crisis, when some divergence reappeared, but not dramatically so. At any rate, pre-crisis evidence indicates that inflation rates do not differ any more among the Eurozone member countries than across broad regions in the USA.

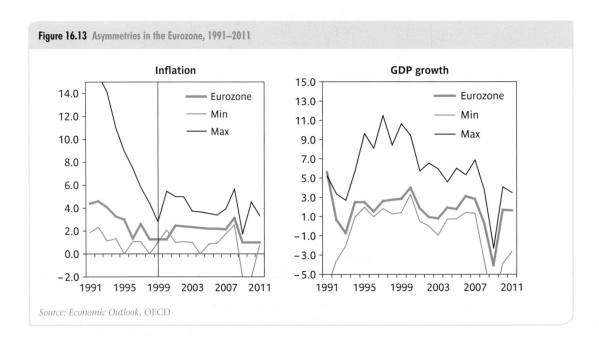

Figure 16.13 Asymmetries in the Eurozone, 1991–2011

Source: Economic Outlook, OECD

Lasting inflation differentials

No one would expect to see the same inflation rate everywhere every year. The asymmetry issue concerns the possibility that, year after year, a particular country faces systematically higher (or lower) inflation. For instance, a country that faces continuously higher inflation than others is bound to face a loss in competitiveness. If this process persists, the country would then have to undergo several years of lower inflation to restore competitiveness. As the Eurosystem strives to achieve and maintain price stability, this could require deflation – negative inflation – which is usually only achieved under severe pressure in the form of a protracted recession accompanied by high unemployment. This is an implication of the self-equilibrating Hume mechanism presented in Chapter 14. Conceivably, this ugly scenario could make leaving the Eurozone an attractive option.[10]

Figure 16.14 shows that large inflation differentials have occurred. Inflation has been lower than average in Germany, Finland and France, and higher than average in Ireland, Spain, Portugal, the Netherlands and Italy. Ominously, the four countries with the highest inflation rates are those that eventually faced the debt crisis first. What are the reasons for such a divergence? The potential explanations are:

- The Balassa–Samuelson effect. This effect, presented in Chapter 13, predicts that the real exchange rates of catching-up countries appreciate. Within a currency area, real appreciation can only be achieved through higher than average inflation.[11] This higher inflation rate does not imply a loss of competitiveness. Quite to the contrary, it is a consequence of rising productivity. This effect could be part of the explanation for the cases of Ireland, Spain and Portugal.

- Wrong initial conversion rates. Each currency was converted into euros at the ERM parity that prevailed in 1998, but there was no certainty that these conversion rates were fully adequate. For instance, it is now generally accepted that Germany's conversion rate was overvalued; this may explain why, from 1999 to 2008, its consumer price index declined by 4.5 per cent relative to the Eurozone's HICP. Similarly, Greece may have used an undervalued rate for the conversion of drachmas into euros.

- Autonomous wage and price pressure. Wage increases in excess of labour productivity gains eat into competitiveness. This basic truth may be lost when factors other than economics drive wage negotiations. For example, minimum wages can be raised to reduce inequality; civil servants – who do not face directly any foreign competition – may be well organized to extract wage increases; administered prices – electricity, transports – may be pushed up to avoid losses in state-owned companies. Such price increases next filter down to all wages and prices because they raise production costs and the general price level. These factors seem to have played a role in Greece, Italy, the Netherlands, Spain and Portugal.

- Policy mistakes. Through excessively expansionary fiscal policies or public sector price and wage increases, mentioned above, governments may, temporarily at least, contribute to inflationary pressure. Once prices are up, it is difficult to bring them down.

- Asymmetric shocks. This is the scenario that lies at the centre of the OCA theory. Oil shocks have not affected all Eurozone member countries to the same extent. Many other factors may have played a role, even though none has been identified so far.

Asymmetric monetary policy effects

Different rates of inflation have another, more subtle effect. The single monetary policy implies a common nominal interest rate throughout the Eurozone. Yet, monetary policy does not affect the economy through the nominal interest rate. What matters is the real interest rate, i.e. the nominal rate less expected inflation. Take the case of a country where inflation is, and is expected to remain, higher than average. Its real interest rate is lower than average, which means that monetary policy is comparatively expansionary. Conversely, a country with low growth and low inflation faces a relatively high real interest rate, which exerts a contractionary effect.

---

[10] From 1991 to 2001, Argentina operated a currency board arrangement vis-à-vis the US dollar (see Chapter 13 for an explanation of currency boards). For many years, however, its inflation rate exceeded the US rate. Eventually inflation turned negative, but the pain of a deep recession triggered a popular revolt that led to the end of the currency board.

[11] A Eurozone country's real exchange rate vis-à-vis the zone is EP/P^*. With a common currency the nominal exchange rate is $E = 1$, so the real exchange rate is P/P^*. A real appreciation requires that the domestic price level P increases faster than the foreign price level P^*.

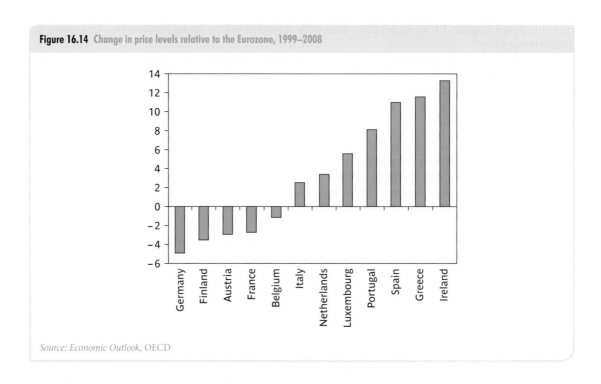

Figure 16.14 Change in price levels relative to the Eurozone, 1999–2008

Source: Economic Outlook, OECD

Is the single monetary policy systematically destabilizing, therefore? It all depends on the source of the inflation differential. If higher inflation is driven by productivity gains, e.g. the Balassa–Samuelson effect, the real exchange rate must appreciate through wage and price increases. In that case, the low real interest rate encourages investment, which is needed to implement the productivity gains, and its expansionary impact speeds up the rise of prices to their new equilibrium level.

If the higher inflation is due to national policy mistakes or unwarranted wage increases, possibly encouraged by a cyclical expansion, the low real interest rate adds fuel to an already overheated economy and monetary policy appears indeed to be destabilizing. How worrisome is this effect? One view is that there is no risk that things will get out of hand. Hume's mechanism ensures that excesses will eventually be corrected. Another view, however, is that the correction may be painful.

The debt crisis has now settled this debate. Countries with budget deficits and higher inflation rates have all been caught by financial market defiance. Lenders have started to worry about their ability to serve their debts. Chapter 19 examines this issue in greater detail. Here, we just note that there is nothing that the Eurosystem can do to prevent such a development. Member countries must avoid falling into the trap of inflation and, if it happens, they must adopt contractionary fiscal policies – which remain a national prerogative – to try to contain the expansionary pressure before the situation has deteriorated. As noted above, correcting large slippages is bound to be enormously painful, to the point where it may one day lead a country caught in this process to reconsider its continuing monetary union membership.

16.5.4 More members?

The new EU members do not have an opt-out so they are formally required to join the Eurozone 'as soon as possible'. Officially, they are out of the Eurozone because they benefit from a derogation. In order to join they must meet the five convergence criteria described in Section 16.1. The earliest that a country can become a Eurozone member is two years after having joined the ERM.

Compliance with the five entry conditions is assessed by two *Convergence Reports* prepared by European Commission and the ECB. The latest extensive report was issued in May 2008; it included the ten Member States with a derogation – Bulgaria, the Czech Republic, Estonia, Latvia, Lithuania, Hungary, Poland, Romania, Slovakia and Sweden. The report concluded that Slovakia met the conditions to join the euro area in January 2009. In 2010, a report concerned just Estonia, which was found to meet the requirements for joining the euro area. The Commission's next *Convergence Report* is expected to be produced in 2012, and it will cover all Member States with a derogation. Table 16.2 summarizes the 2008 assessment by the European Commission.[12]

Table 16.2   Non-Eurozone members: the convergence criteria in 2008

Country	Inflation	Long-term interest rate	ERM membership	Budget deficit	Public debt
Bulgaria	9.4	4.7	No	−3.4	18.0
Czech Republic	4.4	4.5	No	1.6	28.1
Estonia	8.3	n.a.	June 2004	−2.8	3.4
Hungary	7.5	No	No	5.5	66.0
Latvia	12.3	5.4	May 2005	0.0	9.7
Lithuania	7.4	4.6	June 2004	1.2	17.3
Poland	3.2	5.7	No	2.0	45.2
Romania	5.9	7.1	No	2.5	13.0
Sweden	2.4	4.2	No	−3.5	46.0
Convergence limits	3.2	6.5	> 2 years	3	60.0

Note: The countries with a derogation (Denmark and the UK) are not subject to official convergence reports.
Source: Convergence Report, European Commission, 2008

None of these nine countries were deemed fit for euro area membership. In one case, this is intentional: by not joining the ERM, Sweden does not have to join the Eurozone, which it clearly does not want to do. All the other countries missed the inflation condition, which often means that the long-term interest rate is too high, as noted in Section 16.1.2. This is a vicious circle. If the markets believe that a country will not join the Eurozone, they may keep the interest rate high, which indeed leads to the country being kept outside. Conversely, adopting the euro provides a country with a credible central bank and the promise of price stability, which immediately translates into lower interest rates. Lower interest rates, in turn, mean a significant reduction in the cost of servicing the public debt. Box 16.7 recalls how Italy benefited from this effect.

---

[12] The results for Slovakia are not reported since that country passed the test.

Box 16.7   Italy's windfall gain from Eurozone membership

Italy joined the Eurozone with a very large public debt (see Fig. 16.2). At the time when the Maastricht Treaty was agreed upon, its government was spending some 12 per cent of GDP on debt service, about one-quarter of its total expenditures. Debt service is approximately equal to the product of the interest rate and the debt value (iB, where i is the interest rate and B the debt). This means that part of the debt burden was associated with a high interest rate. Figure 16.15 shows how the Italian interest rate steadily declined in the years following the Maastricht agreement. The decline is explained by the disinflation process, as Italy strived to meet the convergence criteria. It is also explained by the credibility associated with Eurozone membership and its price-stability-oriented central bank. The remarkable feature of this evolution is the parallel decline in debt service, which has declined to about 40 per cent of what it used to be. Most of this huge windfall gain, worth 7.5 per cent of GDP, has been used by the Italian authorities to increase spending in many areas, not to reduce the debt.

Figure 16.15 The interest rate and net debt service as a percentage of GDP in Italy, 1992–2011

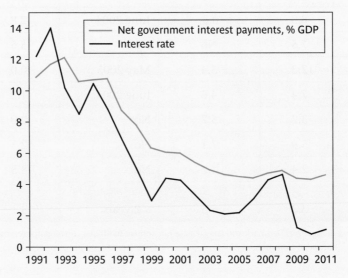

Source: Economic Outlook, OECD

16.6 Summary

The monetary union is an elaborate construction carefully mapped out in the Maastricht Treaty. The Treaty was signed in 1991 and the single currency started to operate, as planned, in 1999, even though the new currency was not issued until 2002. This long process was part of a careful approach that recognized the unique nature of the undertaking. It rested on a number of provisions:

* The adoption of a common currency had to be the final step – the 'coronation' – of a convergence process. All member countries would have to demonstrate their acceptance of price stability and of the discipline that goes with it.

* Monetary union membership would not be automatic. Admission is to be assessed on the basis of five convergence criteria: low inflation, low long-term interest rates, ERM membership, low budget deficits and a declining public debt.

* While all EU members are expected to join the currency area, two countries (Denmark and the UK) were given opt-out clauses. This was the first time that the possibility of a 'two-speed Europe' was accepted.

A monetary union implies the delegation of monetary policy to a single authority. Yet, the EU is not a federal system, so it was decided to maintain the national central banks. The resulting Eurosystem formally brings together the newly created ECB and the national central banks of all Eurozone countries. Decisions are taken by the Governing Council, chaired by the President of the ECB, which includes the ECB's Executive Committee and the governors of the central banks of the Eurozone countries. The Governing Council is very large, and is getting larger as new members join the Eurozone. It has been agreed to cap its size eventually through a rotation procedure that will take into account country size.

The Eurosystem has been given the primary goal of price stability, but it is free to decide what that means and how to go about it. It considers that price stability is achieved when the Eurozone's inflation rate is close to and below 2 per cent over the 'medium term'. It has also adopted the common practice of steering the euro short-term interest rate through three channels: the marginal refinancing facility sets a ceiling, the deposit facility sets a floor, and the interest rate is kept close to the middle of that range through regular auctions that establish the main refinancing rate.

The logic of this procedure is that the short-term interest rate affects the economy through a number of channels that operate via credit availability and the money supply, the long-term real interest rate, asset prices and the exchange rate. Thus, the effect of monetary policy on the economy, and on inflation in particular, is indirect and the Eurosystem must factor in these various effects, all of which take time to produce results.

This requires a strategy. The Eurosystem's approach is to rely on two pillars: economic analysis (the medium-term impact of current conditions on inflation) and monetary analysis (the longer-term impact of monetary aggregates on inflation). In addition, the strategy recognizes that in a monetary union, there can only be one monetary policy. This is why the Eurosystem explicitly cares only about the whole Eurozone, not about individual member countries. In addition, it takes no responsibility for the exchange rate that is freely floating.

The Eurosystem constitutionally enjoys considerable independence, both in defining its objectives and in deciding how to conduct monetary policy. It is not allowed to take instructions from any other authority, be it European or national. This independence is a condition for guaranteeing price stability, but it raises an important issue: in a democracy, every authority has to be accountable to its citizens for its actions. The solution adopted by the Maastricht Treaty is to make the Eurosystem formally accountable to the European Parliament. Accountability takes the form of an annual report and of regular hearings of the ECB president and members of the Executive Board by the Parliament's Committee on Economic and Monetary Affairs. A number of observers feel that this is too weak a form of accountability and consider that the monetary union suffers from a 'democratic deficit'.

Self-assessment questions

1 What are the five convergence criteria and what is the logic behind each of them?
2 'With one money there can exist only one central bank, and therefore one monetary policy.' What, then, is the role of national central banks in the EMU?
3 Why can inflation rates differ across the EMU member countries? What are the consequences?
4 What is the difference between Denmark and Sweden regarding monetary union membership? Which one, if any, is likely to adopt the euro first?
5 What happens to a country's interest rate when it joins the Eurozone?
6 The Eurosystem sets the money supply in the Eurozone, but what drives the money stock in each country? How does this relate to Hume's mechanism and the gold standard?
7 What is the Eurosystem's definition of price stability? What would be your own definition?
8 Why cannot the Eurosystem take responsibility for national inflation rates?
9 Compare the objectives of the Eurosystem (price stability first and foremost) and of the US Federal Reserve (price stability and low unemployment).
10 What is the rationale of the Taylor rule?

Essay questions

1 The Eurosystem asserts that, in its deliberations, it never pays attention to local (i.e. national) economic conditions. The reason is that there is a single monetary policy and that 'one size fits all'. Discuss this approach and imagine alternative approaches.
2 Find on www.ecb.int the latest press conference on monetary policy decisions and interpret the text in the light of the stated strategy.
3 The Maastricht Treaty describes in minute detail the creation of the Eurozone but is silent on a possible break-up. Imagine that a country is suffering from a severe adverse shock. Could it leave? How? What could the other countries do to try to keep it in?
4 Voting rights within the Eurosystem will change as more countries join the Eurozone. Evaluate this mechanism and imagine alternative arrangements.
5 Why are transparency and accountability so important for the Eurosystem? What kind of difficulties can you envision if the system is perceived as not sufficiently accountable? Not sufficiently transparent?
6 The convergence criteria concern nominal conditions (inflation, deficits and debts) but not real conditions (GDP per capita, growth). This was understandable for the original founders but what does it mean for the upcoming wave of accession of the ten new EU members? Should the same criteria apply? Why or why not? Is the lack of real convergence problematic?
7 Make the case for and against Eurozone membership of Poland or Hungary or the Czech Republic.
8 'The crisis that started in 2007 has shown that central banks cannot just focus on price stability. Financial stability is as important.' Comment.
9 The ECB has almost never brought its inflation rate below 2 per cent as intended. Should it raise its target or allow for a symmetric margin around 2 per cent?
10 Evaluate the democratic deficit issue and propose ways to deal with it.

Further reading: the aficionado's corner

The first decade of the euro as reviewed by the ECB:

ECB, www.ecb.int/pub/pdf/other/10thanniversaryoftheecbmb200806en.pdf?a2a06e7f1ee81c0d42249ee63d0ce0e8.

And by independent observers:

Aghion, P., A. Ahearne, M. Belka, J. Pisani-Ferry, J. von Hagen and L. Heikesten (2008) *Coming of Age, Report on the Eurozone*, BRUEGEL, Brussels. Download from www.bruegel.org.

Fatás, A., H. Flam, S. Holden, T. Japelli, I. Mihov, M. Pagano and C. Wyplosz (2009) *EMU at Ten: Should Denmark, Sweden and the U.K. Join?*, Stockholm: SNS-Centre for Business and Policy Studies. Download from www.sns.se.

Mongelli, F.P. and C. Wyplosz (2009) 'The euro at ten: unfulfilled threats and unexpected challenges', in B. Mackowiak, F.P. Mongelli, G. Noblet and F. Smets (eds), *The Euro at Ten – Lessons and Challenges*, European Central Bank, Frankfurt am Main.

Wyplosz, C. (2010) 'Ten years of EMU: successes and puzzles', in J.F. Jimeno (ed.), *Spain and the Euro: The First Ten Years*, Banco de España, Madrid.

For presentations of the Eurosystem, see:

European Central Bank (2011) *The Monetary Policy of the ECB.*

European Commission, http://ec.europa.eu/economy_finance/the_euro/index_en.htm?cs_mid=2946.

Padoa-Schioppa, T. (former member of the Executive Board of the ECB) An Institutional Glossary of the Eurosystem. Download from www.ecb.int/press/key/date/2000/html/sp000308_1.en.html.

On Taylor rules, see:

The Economist (2005) 'Monetary policy in the Eurozone has been looser than critics think', 14 July. Download from www.economist.com/finance/displayStory.cfm?story_id_4174785.

On diverging inflation rates in the Eurozone, see:

ECB (2005) 'Monetary policy and inflation differentials in a heterogeneous currency area', *Monthly Bulletin*, May, 61–78.

Useful websites

The ECB website: www.ecb.int.

The Treaty of Maastricht: http://europa.eu.int/eurlex/en/treaties/index.html.

The President of the ECB reports every quarter to the Committee of Economic and Monetary Affairs of the European Parliament. The transcripts of the meetings, politely called 'Monetary Dialogue', as well as background reports can be found at: http://www.europarl.europa.eu/activities/committees/editoDisplay.do?language=EN&id=3&body=ECON.

A website dedicated to EONIA and interest rates in the Eurozone: www.euribor.org/default.htm.

References

Aucremanne, L., M. Collin and T. Stragier (2007) *Assessing the Gap between Observed and Perceived Inflation in the Eurozone: Is the Credibility of the HICP at Stake?* Working Paper No. 112 , National Bank of Belgium.

Blinder, A., C. Goodhart, P. Hildebrand, D. Lipton and C. Wyplosz (2001) 'How do central banks talk?', *Geneva Reports on the World Economy* 3, Centre for Economic Policy Research, London.

Burda, M. and C. Wyplosz (2012) *Macroeconomics*, 6th edition, Oxford University Press, Oxford.

Crowe, C. and E. Meade (2008) 'Central bank independence and transparency: evolution and effectiveness', *European Journal of Political Economy*, 24(4): 763–77.

ECB (2003) 'The ECB's monetary policy strategy', Press release, 8 May. Download from www.ecb.int.

Chapter 17

Fiscal policy and the Stability Pact

Over the last months, Europe has gone through a serious financial crisis. Although economic recovery in Europe is now on track, risks remain and we must continue our determined action. We adopted today a comprehensive package of measures which should allow us to turn the corner of the financial crisis and continue our path towards sustainable growth.

Conclusions of European Council of March 24–25, 2011

I know very well that the Stability Pact is stupid, like all decisions which are rigid.

Romano Prodi (EU Commission President), *Le Monde*, 17 October 2002

Chapter Contents

Introduction

With the loss of monetary policy as a macroeconomic stabilization instrument, fiscal policy may assume greater importance in a monetary union. However, national fiscal policies affect other countries in a number of different ways. Do these spillover effects also call for sharing the fiscal policy instrument? This chapter first reviews how fiscal policy operates across national boundaries and presents the principles that can help to decide whether some limits on national decisions are in order. This lays the ground for an understanding of the Stability and Growth Pact. The chapter next examines the Pact's impact on policy choices and the controversies that have arisen as its shortcomings become more evident. It concludes with a presentation of a new pact, the Euro Plus Pact.

17.1 Fiscal policy in the monetary union

17.1.1 An ever more important instrument?

When joining a monetary union a country gives up one of its two macroeconomic instruments – monetary policy – but retains full control of the other – fiscal policy. Fiscal policy seems to be the way to deal with asymmetric shocks when they arise, in effect substituting for the lost monetary instrument. In this view, in the Eurozone fiscal policy becomes more important and should be used to stabilize national output and employment fluctuations and, via the Phillips curve, inflation as well. Unfortunately, fiscal policy is unlikely to be a good substitute for monetary policy. It is a very different instrument, more difficult to activate and less reliable than monetary policy. Importantly, it can be misused, and it often is misused when governments ignore the need to eventually balance their budgets.

A common problem with both instruments is that they affect spending largely through expectations. For monetary policy, as explained in Chapter 14, the central bank can only control very short-term interest rates while private spending is mostly financed through long-term borrowing. For fiscal policy, changes in public spending and/or taxes impact on the budget balance, which immediately raises the question of the financing of the public debt. Consider, for instance, a cut in income taxes designed to raise private spending. A tax cut creates a budget deficit. The government will have to borrow and increase the public debt, but how will this new debt be reimbursed? If, as is plausible, taxes are eventually raised, the policy action is properly seen as the combination of a tax reduction today and a tax increase later. This is an action unlikely to boost private consumption.[1]

Fiscal policy faces a major additional drawback: it is very slow to implement. A central bank can decide to change the interest rate whenever it deems it necessary, and can do so in a matter of seconds. Not so for fiscal policy. Establishing the budget is a long and complicated process. The government must first agree on the budget, with lots of heavy-handed negotiations among ministers. The budget must then be approved by the parliament, a time-consuming and highly political process. Then spending decisions must be enacted through the bureaucracy, and taxes can only be changed gradually as they are never retroactive. For example, income taxes can only affect future incomes, implying long delays, even though, once implemented, fiscal policy actions tend to have a more rapid effect on the economy (6 to 12 months) than does monetary policy (12 to 24 months). In the end, fiscal policy is like a tanker; it changes course very slowly.

---

[1] The extreme case where consumers save all of the tax reduction to pay for future tax increases is called Ricardian equivalence. It is explained, and its empirical validity assessed, in, for example, Burda and Wyplosz (2012).

The delay may even be such that, when fiscal policy finally affects the economy, the problem that it was meant to solve has disappeared.

In much the same way as unrestrained monetary policy eventually delivers inflation, undisciplined fiscal policy results in high public indebtedness. The crisis has shown that allowing debts to grow can destabilize a country and that the phenomenon may be contagious within the Eurozone. The inflation bias, the tendency to use monetary policy unwisely, has been reduced by making central banks independent from governments that tend to favour short-term gains (revenue from inflation) at the expense of long-term pain (getting rid of inflation once it has been unleashed). The same political instincts are the source of a deficit bias, which is examined in Section 17.2.4. The deficit bias remains a feature of several Eurozone countries, which calls for remedial action. This is the raison d'être of the Stability and Growth Pact, presented in Section 17.4.

17.1.2 Borrowing instead of transfers

Another way of looking at fiscal policy is that the government borrows and pays back on behalf of its citizens. During a slowdown, the government opens up a budget deficit that is financed through public borrowing. In an upswing, the government runs a budget surplus, which allows it to pay back its debt. A government that borrows to reduce taxes now and raises taxes later to pay back its debt is, in effect, lending to its citizens now and making them pay back later. Individual citizens and firms could, in principle, do it on their own, borrowing in bad years and paying back in good years. This would have the same stabilizing effect as fiscal policy. Is fiscal policy a futile exercise or, worse, a bad political trick? Not quite.

To start with, in the previous example the government simply acts as a bank vis-à-vis its citizens. The reason why it may make sense is that, when the economy slows down, lending becomes generally riskier and banks become very cautious. Many citizens and firms cannot borrow in bad times, or can only borrow at high cost. Indeed, their banks consider workers who lose their jobs as a bad risk, and so are firms that face sagging profits or even losses. When governments are considered a good risk, they can borrow at all times at reasonably low cost. This is why countercyclical fiscal policies can be effective.

An additional reason is related to one of the optimum currency area criteria examined in Chapter 15, the desirability of substantial inter-country transfers. In that dimension, Europe was found to do very poorly. Using fiscal policy can alleviate this problem. When a country faces an adverse asymmetric shock, its government can borrow from countries that are not affected by the shock. This is the equivalent of a transfer: instead of receiving a loan or a grant[2] from other Eurozone governments or from 'Brussels', the adversely affected country's government borrows. In this way fiscal policy makes up for the absence of 'federal' transfers in a monetary union.

17.1.3 Automatic stabilizers and discretionary policy actions

Automatic stabilizers

Fiscal policy has one important advantage: it tends to be spontaneously countercyclical. When the economy slows down, individual incomes are disappointingly low, corporate profits decline and spending is rather weak. This all means that tax collection declines: income taxes, profit taxes, VAT, etc. are less than they would be in normal conditions. At the same time, spending on unemployment benefits and on other subsidies rises. All in all, the budget worsens and fiscal policy is automatically expansionary. These various

---

[2] A grant is not to be reimbursed, but a collective system of grants implies that any country is supposed to be alternately giving and receiving, the total averaging zero over the long run. This is no different from long-term borrowing – receiving now, paying back later.

effects are called the automatic stabilizers of fiscal policy. Table 17.1 shows how much the budget balance deteriorates when the economy slows down. Roughly, on average, a 1 per cent decline in growth leads to a deterioration of the budget balance of about 0.5 per cent of GDP. There are some differences from one country to another, which reflect the structure of taxation and of welfare payments.[3] This, in turn, represents an automatic fiscal expansion.

Table 17.1   Sensitivity of government budget balances to a 1 per cent decline in economic growth

Country	%	Country	%	Country	%	Country	%
Germany	0.5	Austria	–0.5	Greece	–0.6	Portugal	–0.4
France	–0.5	Belgium	–0.5	Ireland	–0.4	Spain	–0.5
Italy	–0.4	Denmark	–0.7	Netherlands	–0.6	Sweden	–0.5
UK	–0.6	Finland	–0.5				

Source: Economic Outlook, OECD, 1997

Discretionary fiscal policy

The automatic stabilizers just happen. Discretionary fiscal policy, on the contrary, requires explicit decisions to change taxes or spending. As noted above, such decisions are slow to be made and implemented. This is why, in some countries, the budget law sets aside some funds – called rainy day funds – that can be quickly mobilized by the government if discretionary action is needed. Even then, the amounts are small and their use is often politically controversial.

An implication of the existence of automatic stabilizers is that the budget figures do not reveal what the government is doing with its fiscal policy. The budget can change for two reasons. It can improve, for example, because the government is cutting spending or raising taxes – this is called discretionary policy – or because the economy is booming – the automatic stabilizers. In order to disentangle these two factors, it is convenient to look at the cyclically adjusted budget. This procedure is based on the output gap concept. A negative gap, for instance, indicates that the economy is underperforming, that it operates below its potential. The cyclically adjusted budget balance is an estimate of what the balance would be in a given year if the output gap were zero. When output is below potential, i.e. when the output gap is negative, the actual budget balance is lower than the cyclically adjusted budget balance and conversely when the output gap is positive. The difference between the evolution of the actual and cyclically adjusted budget balances is the footprint of the automatic stabilizers.

The cyclically adjusted budget balance is a reliable gauge of the stance of fiscal policy since it separates discretionary government actions from the cyclical effects of the automatic stabilizers. An improvement indicates that the government tightens fiscal policy whereas an expansionary fiscal policy worsens the cyclically adjusted budget balance. If the government never changed its fiscal policy, the cyclically adjusted budget balance would remain constant, at least to a first approximation.[4] Box 17.1 illustrates this point in the case of the Netherlands. These two issues – the role of the automatic stabilizers and the distinction between the actual and cyclically adjusted budgets – play a crucial role in what follows.

---

[3] For example, the more progressive are income taxes, the more tax collection declines during a slowdown, hence the greater the stabilization effect. Similarly, the automatic stabilizers are stronger the larger are the unemployment benefits.

[4] Why to a first approximation? Because as the economy grows, more people climb the income ladder and face higher tax rates. Also, the structure of the economy changes, possibly changing the way taxes are collected.

Box 17.1   The automatic stabilizers in the Netherlands

Figure 17.1 displays the output gap along with the actual and cyclically adjusted budget balance of the Netherlands. We can see that the actual balance generally moves in tandem with the output gap, an indication that the automatic stabilizers are at work. Note also the steady improvement in the budget that occurred during the convergence years 1995–99. It is due partly to government efforts to meet the Maastricht conditions, as shown by the reduction of the cyclically adjusted deficit, and partly to a rising output gap that made it easier to meet the Maastricht entry condition. It is also interesting to observe that the sharp deterioration of the budget over 2001–05 – which brought the Netherlands into violation of the Stability and Growth Pact – is the consequence of a serious slowdown, and occurred in spite of visible government efforts to avoid this outcome. Then, with the financial crisis that started in 2007, the Dutch economy went into a sharp contraction; its actual deficit swung into a large deficit, most of it due to discrete action that pushed the cyclically adjusted balance sharply down, with a modest additional contribution from the automatic stabilizers.

Note that the cyclically adjusted budget, which is a measure of discretionary actions, also tends to move in the same direction as the output gap. In good years, when the output gap rises, the government conducts restrictive fiscal policies, while its policy is expansionary when the output gap declines. Put differently, fiscal policy tends to be used in a countercyclical way, which dampens the business cycle. Looking carefully at the figure shows numerous exceptions, however.

Figure 17.1 Actual and cyclically adjusted budgets in the Netherlands, 1972–2011

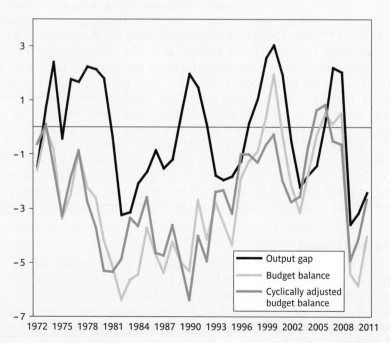

Note: All variables are measured as per cent of GDP.
Source: Economic Outlook, OECD

17.2 Fiscal policy externalities

17.2.1 Spillovers: a case for policy coordination

So far, the discussion has concerned individual countries. But fiscal policy actions by one country may spill over to other countries through a variety of channels such as income and spending, inflation, borrowing costs and financial distress. Such spillovers, called externalities, mean that one country's fiscal policy actions can help or hurt other countries. Countries subject to each other's spillovers stand to benefit from coordinating their fiscal policies. In principle, all concerned countries could agree on each other's fiscal policy to achieve a situation that befits them all. This is what policy coordination is about.

While, formally, fiscal policy remains a national prerogative, it is natural to ask whether the deepening economic integration among Eurozone countries calls for some degree of coordination. On the one hand, the setting up of a monetary union strengthens the case for fiscal policy coordination as it promotes deeper ties. On the other hand, fiscal policy coordination requires binding agreements on who does what and when. Such detailed arrangements would limit each country's sovereignty, precisely at a time when the fiscal policy instrument assumes greater importance. The question is whether sharing the same currency increases the spillovers to the point where some new limits on sovereignty are desirable and justified. To answer this question, we review the channels through which spillovers occur and examine what difference the Eurozone makes.

17.2.2 Cyclical income spillovers

Business cycles are transmitted through exports and imports. When Germany enters an expansion phase, for instance, it imports more from its partner countries. For these partner countries, the German expansion means more exports and more incomes. This is how the expansion tends to be transmitted across borders. Figure 17.2, which displays output gaps for a number of countries, confirms that business cycles are highly synchronized in Europe, and were so long before the adoption of the euro. Quite obviously, the spillover is stronger the more the countries trade with each other.

What does this mean for fiscal policy? Consider, first, the case when two monetary union member countries undergo synchronized cycles, for example both suffer from a recession. Each government will want to adopt an expansionary fiscal policy, but to what extent? If each government ignores the other's action, their combined action may be too strong as each economy pulls the other one from the recession – an effect of the Keynesian multiplier. If, instead, each government relies on the other to do most of the work, too little might be done. Consider next the case when the cycles are asynchronized. An expansionary fiscal policy in the country undergoing a slowdown stands to boost spending in the already booming country. Conversely, a contractionary fiscal policy move in the booming country stands to deepen the recession in the other country.

17.2.3 Borrowing cost spillovers

A fiscal expansion increases public borrowing or reduces public saving. As the government is usually the country's biggest borrower, large budget deficits may push interest rates up. Once they share the same currency, Eurozone member countries share the same interest rate. One country's deficits, especially if the country is large and its deficits sizeable, may impose higher interest rates throughout the Eurozone.[5] As high interest rates deter investment, they affect long-term growth. This is another spillover channel.

---

[5] Jürgen Stark, a high-level German official who was influential in designing the Stability and Growth Pact, writes: 'The state's absorption of resources which would otherwise have found their way into private investments results in higher long-term interest rates' (Stark, 2001, p. 79).

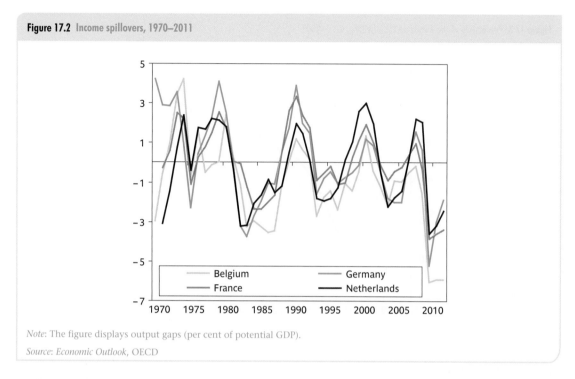

Figure 17.2 Income spillovers, 1970–2011

Note: The figure displays output gaps (per cent of potential GDP).

Source: *Economic Outlook*, OECD

As stated, the argument is weak. Since Europe is fully integrated in the world's financial markets, any one country's borrowing is unlikely to make much of an impression on world and European interest rates. On the other hand, heavy borrowing may elicit capital inflows. This could result in an appreciation of the euro, which would hurt the area's competitiveness and cut into growth. Borrowing costs thus represent another channel for spillovers.

17.2.4 Excessive deficits and the no-bailout clause

Even before the crisis, it was clear that debt sustainability could not be taken for granted in Europe. As a share of GDP, overall public indebtedness in the Eurozone had nearly tripled since 1970, as Fig. 17.3 shows.[6] In the distant past, public debts had occasionally risen but only in difficult situations, mostly during wars. The post-war debt build-up, partly related to the oil shocks of the 1970s and 1980s, illustrates what is sometimes called the 'deficit bias'. This bias reflects a disquieting tendency for governments to run budget deficits for no other reason than political expediency. Does it call for a specific collective measure?

In principle, it is in each country's interest to resist the deficit bias and there is no need for collective measures, unless spillovers can be identified. The founding fathers of the euro identified four spillovers. The first one concerns the tendency of financially hard-pressed governments to call upon the central bank to finance their deficits. Debt monetization, as this is called, is the traditional route to inflation. Central bank independence from government is the proper response and, as noted in Chapter 16, the Eurosystem enjoys very strong independence.

Second, heavy public borrowing by one country is a sign of fiscal indiscipline that could trouble the international financial markets. If markets believe that one country's public debt is unsustainable, they could view the whole Eurozone with suspicion. The result would be sizeable capital outflows and euro weakness. This potential source of spillover has not (yet?) materialized in the Eurozone.

---

[6] This is the debt for the whole zone. The situation differs from country to country.

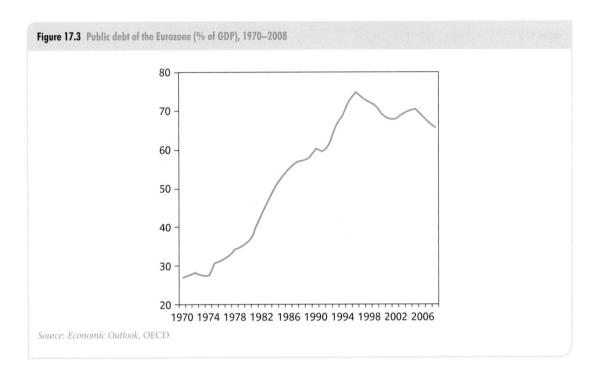

Figure 17.3 Public debt of the Eurozone (% of GDP), 1970–2008

Source: Economic Outlook, OECD

There is a third potential spillover. If a government accumulates such a debt that it can no longer service it, it must default. The experience with public debt defaults is that the immediate reaction is a massive capital outflow, a collapse of the exchange rate and of the stock markets, and a prolonged crisis complete with a deep recession and skyrocketing unemployment. Being part of a monetary union changes things radically. It is now the common exchange rate that is the object of the market reaction. The spillover can further extend to stock markets throughout the whole monetary union.

A further fear is that the mere threat of one member country's default would so concern all other member governments that they would feel obliged to bail out the nearly bankrupt government. This last risk has been clearly identified in the Maastricht Treaty, which included a 'no-bailout' clause. Article 125 of the European Treaty forbids the Eurosystem – and all other public institutions, including governments – from providing direct support to other Eurozone governments. Yet, it always was an open question whether, in the midst of an emergency, some arrangement could still be found to bail out a bankrupt government. For example, the ECB could be 'informally' pressed to relax its monetary policy to make general credit more abundant at a lower cost, which would result in inflation. More generally, it was feared that a sovereign default would badly affect the Eurozone and undermine its credibility. We will see in Chapter 19 that the no-bailout clause was ignored in May 2010.

17.2.5 The deficit bias and collective discipline

Why do governments seem to have a deficit bias, and why does this bias seem to differ from country to country, as can be seen in Table 17.2? Deficits allow governments to deliver goods and services today without facing the costs, passing the burden of debt service to future governments or even to future generations. It is tempting to do so, especially when elections are near; but adequate democratic accountability should prevent governments from indulging. Even though future generations are not here to weigh in, the current generation may reasonably expect to be called upon to service the debt, and anyway most people care about the next generation. So a debt build-up often reflects a failure of democratic control over governments. Why has this been happening in Europe's democracies?

Table 17.2   Public debts in Europe (% of GDP), 2011

Austria 73.8	Belgium 97.0	Bulgaria 18.0	Cyprus 62.3	Czech Rep. 41.3	Denmark 45.3
Estonia 6.1	Finland 50.6	France 84.7	Germany 82.4	Greece 157.7	Hungary 75.2
Ireland 112.0	Italy 120.3	Latvia 48.2	Lithuania 40.7	Luxembourg 17.2	Malta 68.0
Netherlands 63.9	Poland 55.4	Portugal 101.7	Romania 33.7	Slovakia 44.8	Slovenia 42.8
Spain 68.1	Sweden 36.5	UK 84.2		EU27 82.3	Eurozone 87.7

Source: AMECO, European Commission

Public spending is an important source of income for all sorts of citizens, organizations and firms. Taxpayers, current or future, must pay for it. Those who receive money from the government hope that they will not pay the corresponding taxes, or not fully. It is in the interest of every recipient of public spending to ask for more. In fact, they often form well-organized and influential interest groups. Democratically elected governments are naturally inclined to please the interest groups without raising taxes. The result is a widespread bias towards deficits. The importance of the bias depends on the electoral process. For instance, parliamentary regimes that involve large coalitions seem to be doing less well at keeping deficits in check.

Changing the democratic regime (the form of democracy, how elections are organized) could help, but it is a rather intractable endeavour. This is why some governments find it appealing to seek external restraint and to invoke 'Brussels' as a scapegoat that can be blamed when resisting interest groups and political friends. Collective discipline, even if not necessarily justified by spillovers, can be used as a substitute for adequate domestic institutions.

17.3 Principles

The existence of spillovers is one argument for sharing policy responsibilities among independent countries. It is not the only argument, however, and there are powerful counter-arguments. The broader question is, at which level of government – regional, national, supranational – should policies be conducted? The theory of fiscal federalism deals with this question. The principle of subsidiarity is another way of approaching the issue. Both approaches were presented earlier, in Chapter 3, and are briefly recalled in this section.

17.3.1 Fiscal federalism

The theory of fiscal federalism asks how, in one country, fiscal responsibilities should be assigned between the various levels (national, regional, municipal) of government. It can be transposed to Europe's case, even though Europe is not a federation, by asking which tasks should remain in national – possibly regional in federal states – hands and which ones should be a shared responsibility, i.e. delegated to Brussels. There are two good reasons to transfer responsibility to Brussels and two good reasons to keep it at the national level. An additional concern is the quality of government at the national and supranational level.

Two arguments for sharing responsibilities: externalities and increasing returns to scale

As noted before, spillovers, also called externalities – when one country's actions affect other countries – lead to inefficient outcomes when each country is free to act as it wishes. Sometimes too much action is taken, sometimes not enough. This is the case of tariffs (see Chapter 4) and it concerns fiscal policy as well. The other argument is that some policies are more efficient when carried out on a large scale. Increasing returns to scale can be found in the use of money,[7] in the design of commercial law or in defence (army, weapons development and production), among others.

One solution is coordination, which preserves sovereignty but calls for repeated and often-piecemeal negotiations, with no guarantee of success. Another solution is to give up sovereignty, partly or completely, and delegate a task to a supranational institution. In Europe, some important tasks have already been delegated to the European Commission (the internal market and trade negotiations) and to the Eurosystem (monetary policy).

Two arguments for retaining sovereignty: heterogeneity of preferences and information asymmetries

Consider the example of common law concerning family life (marriage and divorce, raising children, dealing with ageing parents, etc.). Practices and traditions differ across countries, sometimes to a considerable extent. In this domain, preferences are heterogeneous and a supranational arrangement is bound to create much dissatisfaction.

Now consider the decisions of where to build roads, how large to make them, where to set up traffic lights, etc. These require a good understanding of how people move, or wish to move, in a geographic area. It is a case of information asymmetry: the information is more readily available at the local level than at a more global level.

Heterogeneity of preferences and information asymmetries imply that, in these matters, it would be inefficient to share competence at a supranational level. Much of the criticism levelled at 'Brussels' concerns cases where either heterogeneity or information asymmetries are important: deciding on the appropriate size of cheese or the way to brew beer is best left to national governments, even to local authorities, no matter how important the externalities or increasing returns to scale.

The quality of government

An implicit assumption so far is that governments always act in the best interest of their citizens. While this may generally be the case, there are numerous instances when governments either pursue their own agendas or are captured by interest groups. In addition, like any institution, governments often wish to extend their domain of action, possibly in order to increase their own power or because they genuinely believe that they do a better job than lower-level jurisdictions. One can question whether there is such a thing as 'the best interest of citizens': some citizens favour some actions, others do not. Governments exist in part to deal with such conflicts and do so under democratic control, but elections cannot sanction every one of the millions of decisions that favour well-connected interests. In spite of all the good things that can be said about democracy, it is not a perfect system.

---

[7] Chapter 15 explains why this is a key benefit from forming a currency area.

What to conclude?

There are good reasons for centralizing some tasks and other good reasons for decentralizing other tasks. The theory of fiscal federalism does not provide a general answer; rather it argues in favour of a case-by-case approach and suggests that, often, we face trade-offs with no compelling answer. To make things even murkier, the observation that governments are not perfect, just human, means that we need always to keep in mind that a good solution may turn out to be bad if the government is misbehaving. In particular, the quality of government and of democratic control ought to be brought into the picture. The practical question here is whether Brussels performs better than the national governments.

17.3.2 The principle of subsidiarity

It should be clear by now that the four arguments for and against centralization at the EU level are unlikely to lead to many clear-cut conclusions, and the warning about the quality of government further complicates the issue. Weighing the various arguments and trading off the pros and cons is often mission impossible, hence another question: where should the burden of proof lie? The EU has taken the view that the burden of proof lies with those who argue in favour of sharing sovereign tasks. This is the principle of subsidiarity (presented in Chapter 3) and it is enshrined in the European Treaty:

> *In areas which do not fall within its exclusive competence, the Community shall take action, in accordance with the principle of subsidiarity, only if and insofar as the objectives of the proposed action cannot be sufficiently achieved by the Member States and can therefore, by reason of the scale or effects of the proposed action, be better achieved by the Community.*

(Article 5)

In other words: unless there is a strong case of increasing returns to scale or of externality, the presumption is that decisions remain at the national level.

17.3.3 Implications for fiscal policy

A key distinction: micro- vs. macroeconomic aspects of fiscal policy

It is helpful to separate two aspects of fiscal policy. The first aspect is structural, that is, mainly microeconomic. It concerns the size of the budget, what public money is spent on, how taxes are raised, i.e. who pays what. It also concerns income redistribution, designed to reduce inequalities or to provide incentives to particular individuals or groups. The second aspect is macroeconomic. This is the income stabilization role of fiscal policy, the idea that it can be used as a countercyclical instrument.

Here, we focus on the macroeconomic stabilization component of fiscal policy, ignoring the structural aspects, which clearly are a matter for national politics, with very limited macroeconomic impact. To simplify, we look at the budget balance and ignore the size and structure of the budget and the resulting evolution of the public debt. We apply the principles of fiscal federalism to ask whether there is a case for limiting the free exercise of sovereignty on national budget balances and debts.

The case for collective restraint

Section 17.2 identifies a number of spillovers: income flows, borrowing costs and the risk of difficulties in financing runaway deficits, possibly leading to debt default. Some of these spillovers can have serious effects across the Eurozone, as the crisis has shown. In addition, some countries have not established political institutions that are conducive to fiscal discipline so it may be in their own best interest to use Brussels as an external agent of restraint. On the other hand, it is difficult to detect any scale economy.

These externalities call for some limits on national fiscal policies, and such limits can take various forms, ranging from coordination and peer pressure to mandatory limits on deficits and debts.

The case against collective restraint

Working in the opposite direction are important heterogeneities and information asymmetries. Macroeconomic heterogeneity occurs in the presence of asymmetric shocks. A common fiscal policy, on top of a common monetary policy, would leave each country without any countercyclical macroeconomic tool. Heterogeneity can also be the consequence of differences of opinions regarding the effectiveness of the instrument. Some countries (e.g. France and Italy) have long been active users of fiscal policy whereas others (e.g. Germany) have a tradition of scepticism towards Keynesian policies. Finally, national political processes are another source of heterogeneity. In some countries, the government has quite some leeway to adapt the budget to changing economic conditions, whereas in others the process is cumbersome and politically difficult.

Information asymmetries chiefly concern the perception of the political implications of fiscal policies. Each government faces elections, and economics is often an important factor shaping voter preferences. Whether and how to use fiscal policy at a particular juncture is part of a complex political game, which makes national politics highly idiosyncratic. While governments have a lot of understanding for each other's electoral plight, they have a hard time absorbing all the fine details of foreign national politics.

Overall

It is far from clear that the macroeconomic component of fiscal policy should be subject to common limits. Quite clearly, a single common fiscal policy is ruled out, but what about some degree of cooperation? The debate is ongoing and is unlikely to be settled in the near future. The subsidiarity principle implies that, as long as the case is not strong, fiscal policy should remain fully a national prerogative. On the other hand, the spillover that could result from *excessive* deficits is important, and it forms the logical basis for the Stability and Growth Pact.

17.3.4 What does it all mean for fiscal policy in the Eurozone?

In true federal states, there is a powerful federal level of government and sub-federal governments are restrained in their ability to run deficits and hence to use fiscal policy as a macroeconomic instrument. In the Eurozone, instead, the Commission budget is far too small (1 per cent of GDP) to play any macroeconomic role. This is why a number of proposals aim at an 'economic government for Europe', including a European Finance Minister. The idea is that decentralized fiscal policies would be subject to overall coherence objectives. There is a strong logic to it, but how does it deal with sovereignty in fiscal matters?

Applying the principles of fiscal federalism to the Eurozone leaves us with few uncontroversial conclusions. There always were valid reasons for imposing fiscal discipline, and the debt crisis has made it clear that it is a survival condition for the euro. The case for policy coordination is also convincing but there are equally valid arguments in the opposite direction. All in all, the case for further transfers of sovereignty is weak.

Start with fiscal discipline. Since one country's lack of fiscal discipline may create havoc throughout the Eurozone, as has happened, a natural reaction is to seek to limit the sovereignty of member countries, at least during periods of instability. At the same time, parliamentary control over budgetary matters is a very fundamental principle of democracies ('no taxation without representation'). Challenging this principle can be justified only if there is no other way of imposing fiscal discipline through member countries. But, as explained in Box 17.2, a number of countries have alleviated their own deficit biases by reforming their budgetary processes. This indicates that national solutions can deliver fiscal discipline.

There is no doubt that policy coordination is desirable, but it is also very difficult to implement. Ideally, all governments would discuss their macroeconomic needs and the Eurosystem would indicate its contribution to overall inflation and output stabilization. Then the governments would agree on what each one would do both to deal with domestic conditions and to achieve the collective best. This is a tall order. First, because assessing each country's needs and identifying the collective best is largely beyond current knowledge. Second, because in each country the politics of fiscal policy are often conflictual. Often the outcome of the budgetary process is unpredictable until the parliament has finished voting. Finally, governments are likely to be highly reluctant to give up an important political tool.

A step has been taken in 2011 with the adoption of a 'European semester'. In January of each year, the European Commission presents its Annual Growth Survey, which includes forecasts and an evaluation of member countries' economic situation. This triggers discussions among governments and in the European Parliament. Following recommendations by the Council in March, in April every government submits to the Commission their Stability and Convergence Programmes. Along with other policy objectives, the programmes include 'medium-term budgetary strategies', essentially a statement of intentions that cover the next three years. The Commission then assesses the national programmes and submits its conclusions and recommendations in time for a June Council. The Council's own assessment is meant to shape the next steps, when budgetary proceedings revert back to the national level. Time will tell whether the European Semester succeeds in injecting some degree of coordination effective enough to take into account the spillovers described in Section 17.2. Since this new coordination mechanism does not limit national sovereignty in any way, it is hard to imagine that much will be gained.

Box 17.2   The deficit bias and the common pool effect

The deficit bias is a frequently observed feature of otherwise well-functioning democracies. Is there a systematic reason for this tendency? The common pool effect provides a convincing interpretation. It refers to a medieval practice: villages included a publicly owned field – the commons – where peasants could freely bring their cows and sheep to pasture. Each peasant had an incentive to bring as many animals as possible since grass was free. The (possibly inaccurate) result was that the commons could not feed all the animals that were grazing. Collectively, the peasants should limit the number of animals that anyone could bring but individually each peasant wanted the others to take the first step. Herds were decimated and the peasants starved.

Much the same applies to taxation: let the others pay more! It also applies to government spending: I want more public spending that is a benefit to me, so cut spending elsewhere if need be. In a democracy, voters require governments to do things for them and to pay for them with taxes paid by the others. They often get organized in powerful pressure groups that lobby the government. In that way, many spending items become political sacred cows and tax increases are known to be politically dangerous. Budget deficits emerge as a natural outcome.

Once the source of the problem is identified, a solution can be envisioned. At the heart of the common pool effect lies the budget process; the governments are politically unable to resist pressures by interest groups. The solution is to straighten up the budget process. Some countries legally limit the size of deficits; in others the government is required to decide on the deficit first, and only then to decide on spending and taxes, yet other approaches request a high degree of transparency, which undermines the influence of lobbies. This is why the deficit bias is not a universal feature.

Table 17.3 documents the track record among developed countries. For each country, it provides two pieces of evidence: in the first row, the proportion of years when the budget was in deficit over more than half a century and, in the second row, which year the budget was last seen in surplus, if that happened after 1960. The deficit bias is widely confirmed as most countries have experienced deficits for at least four years out of five. The exceptions are Norway (which benefits from huge oil and gas income), Denmark, Finland, New Zealand and Sweden, countries that display a high degree of transparency and of collective responsibility. It is also interesting to note that some countries have recently adopted some of the anti-bias solutions mentioned above; while their track record is poor, it is improving as indicated by recent surpluses.

Table 17.3 Per cent years of deficit over 1960–2011 in the OECD area

	Australia	Austria	Belgium	Canada	Germany
Percent	80%	82%	96%	76%	78%
Last surplus	2008	1974	2006	2007	2008
	Denmark	Spain	Finland	France	UK
Percent	48%	78%	20%	90%	84%
Last surplus	2008	2007	2008	1974	2001
	Greece	Ireland	Italy	Japan	Netherlands
Percent	80%	80%	100%	68%	88%
Last surplus	1972	2007		1992	2008
	Norway	New Zealand	Portugal	Sweden	USA
Percent	4%	46%	100%	42%	92%
Last surplus	2011	2008		2008	2000

Note: Sample starts later for Australia (1962), Canada (1961), Spain (1962) and Portugal (1977).

Source: Economic Outlook, OECD and Eichengreen and Wyplosz (1993) for older data

In the end, the debate has been around for a decade and is not likely to disappear for some time.[8] It pits those who attach much importance to spillovers and think that macroeconomic coordination is both promising and relatively easy to implement against those who see coordination as a collusion of self-interested governments.

17.4 The Stability and Growth Pact

17.4.1 From convergence to the quest for a permanent regime

As explained in Chapter 16, admission to the monetary union requires a budget deficit of less than 3 per cent of GDP and a public debt of less than 60 per cent of GDP, or declining towards this benchmark. But what about afterwards, in the permanent monetary union regime? Could countries achieve the two fiscal criteria, join the monetary union and then freely relapse into unbridled indiscipline? This would be against the spirit of convergence. The founding fathers of the Maastricht Treaty were keenly aware of this risk and, indeed, Article 126 unambiguously

---

[8] Some references are provided in the further reading section at the end of this chapter.

states that 'Member States shall avoid excessive government deficits' and goes on to outline a detailed 'excessive deficit procedure'. The Treaty left the practical details of the procedure to be settled later – and this is the task fulfilled by the Stability and Growth Pact (SGP).[9]

Adopted in 1997, the SGP was meant to be strictly enforced. However, because fiscal policy remains a national competence, the final say was given to ECOFIN, the council of Finance Ministers of the Eurozone, acting on proposals from the Commission. The Commission has assumed the responsibility of being the Pact's 'tough cop', but ECOFIN has been loath to make decisions that would strongly antagonize its members, especially the Finance Ministers from the large countries. In November 2003, France and Germany were to be sanctioned. Under pressure from the French and German Finance Ministers, ECOFIN recanted and put the SGP 'in abeyance'. The Commission took ECOFIN to the Court of Justice of the European Communities for violation of the Pact, an unprecedented action. In June 2004, the Court decided that ECOFIN had indeed breached the law but only because of the phrasing of its decision (the SGP cannot be put in abeyance). A new resolution quickly corrected the error, without changing the fact that France and Germany had not been sanctioned. This episode confirmed the view that the SGP was not well designed. Recognizing that it was too rigid to be enforceable, governments and the Commission prepared a reformulation of the Pact. The new version was adopted in June 2005.

Then came the great financial crisis. At the time of writing, 15 of the 17 Eurozone Member States have been found to be in excessive deficit. Obviously, this was not the time to insist on a strict application of the SGP. The Commission issued a European Economic Recovery Programme, which implicitly accepted that it would take time to revert to the 3 per cent deficit limit. It explicitly set 2013 as the target date for the limit to be enforced again. At the same time, the Commission proposed to strengthen and expand the Pact, acknowledging that it had not delivered its promises before the crisis. The proposal, informally adopted in 2011, is presented in Section 17.4.4.

17.4.2 The Pact

The SGP consists of four elements:

1. A definition of what constitutes an 'excessive deficit'.
2. A preventive arm, designed to encourage governments to avoid excessive deficits.
3. A corrective arm, which prescribes how governments should react to a breach of the deficit limit.
4. Sanctions.

The SGP applies to all EU member countries but only the Eurozone countries are subject to the corrective arm.

Excessive deficits

The SGP considers that deficits are excessive when they are above 3 per cent of GDP. The Pact also stipulates that participants in the monetary union commit themselves to a medium-term budgetary stance 'close to balance or in surplus'. The medium term is understood to represent about three years. The SGP recognizes that serious recessions, beyond any government control, can quickly lead to deepening deficits. Trying to close down deficits during a recession implies

---

[9] The initiative was taken by Germany in 1995 and the Pact adopted in June 1997 by the European Council. Informed by its own inter-war history, Germany was always concerned that fiscal indiscipline could lead to inflation. This is why it insisted on a clear and automatic procedure. It wanted to make full use of the provisions of the Maastricht Treaty, which allowed for fines in the case of excessive deficits. The other countries were less enthusiastic but Germany was holding the key to the Eurozone. France, in particular, was unhappy with the German proposal. It obtained the symbolic addition of the word 'growth' to what Germany had initially called the Stability Pact.

adopting a contractionary policy, which may deepen the recession, with potentially disastrous consequences. Consequently, the Pact defines exceptional circumstances when its provisions are automatically suspended. A deficit in excess of 3 per cent is considered exceptional if the country's GDP declines by at least 2 per cent in the year in question. The SGP also identifies an intermediate situation, when the real GDP declines by less than 2 per cent but by more than 0.75 per cent. In that case, if the country can demonstrate that its recession is exceptional in terms of its abruptness or in relation to past output trends, the situation can also be deemed exceptional. When output declines by less than 0.75 per cent, no exceptional circumstance can be claimed.

The experience of 2001–03 showed that shallow but long-lasting slowdowns, not qualifying as exceptional, could gradually seriously deepen the deficit. In such a situation, respecting the pact would require that the automatic stabilizers be prevented from operating; this could turn a shallow slowdown into a serious recession. Deepening an ongoing recession is not attractive for real-life governments, which started to complain that the SGP was too rigid.

This is why the 2005 version of the SGP introduced two elements of flexibility. First, it admitted that a negative growth rate or an accumulated loss of output during a protracted period of very low growth might be considered as exceptional. Second, it suggested taking account of 'all other relevant factors'. In contrast to the 3 per cent limit and the –2 and –0.75 per cent definition of exceptional circumstances, these new elements are vaguely specified. In particular, the notion of 'all other relevant factors' opened the door to a flexible interpretation of the SGP.

The preventive arm

As explained in Section 17.2.4, many governments exhibit a deficit bias because of domestic pressure and political expediency. The SGP can exert counter-pressure in the form of peer pressure, called mutual surveillance. The preventive arm is designed to submit Finance Ministers to a collective discussion of one another's fiscal policy in the hope that this will help with budgetary discipline. This preventive arm is meant to prevent the need for the use of the corrective arm and its politically sensitive sanctions.

In practice, each Eurozone government submits a Stability Programme early each year. The document presents the government's budget forecast for the current year and the next three years. If the deficit is expected to exceed 3 per cent of GDP, the programme also explains what actions will be taken to correct this violation of the SGP. The Commission examines each programme, including its detailed technical aspects, and submits its individual assessments to ECOFIN. Each assessment must include an evaluation of whether the planned budgets are consistent with the SGP and whether previous commitments have been honoured. The Commission may also point out technical errors, for instance overoptimistic forecasts. ECOFIN then delivers an opinion, adopted by qualified majority. The opinion can include the recommendations prescribed by the corrective arm. All these documents are made public.[10]

EU member countries that are not part of the Eurozone must still submit their fiscal plans as part of the so-called Convergence Programmes. The content of these programmes and the procedure is the same as in the case of the Stability Programmes, with the difference that ECOFIN cannot impose sanctions; it can only issue recommendations. However, for the countries that are aiming to join the monetary union, failure to comply with the SGP implies a violation of the budgetary entry criteria.

The corrective arm

When a country does not meet the requirements of the SGP, ECOFIN applies gradually increasing peer pressure. The process starts with an 'early warning'. Early warnings are issued when ECOFIN

---

[10] The stability programmes are available at: http://ec.europa.eu/economy_finance/sgp/convergence/index_en.htm.

concludes that a country is likely to see its deficit become excessive. A country given an early warning is also presented with recommendations – which may or may not be made public. The forewarned country is expected to follow these recommendations. An early warning clearly puts a country on the spot, which is bound to be deeply politically embarrassing, especially as the recommendations are unavoidably perceived as an infringement of national sovereignty. This is why an early warning can be described as a political hand grenade.

The next step is the excessive deficit procedure (EDP). The procedure is triggered by an ECOFIN opinion formally stating that a country's budget is in excessive deficit. ECOFIN simultaneously issues recommendations – following suggestions from the Commission – which the country must follow. The country is expected to prepare corrective measures promptly, which are examined by the Commission. The Commission submits its assessment to ECOFIN, which may or may not be satisfied with the proposed measures. Clearly, in this situation, the government loses some autonomy. A mandatory recommendation can be seen as a political conventional bomb.

If the deficit does not diminish below the 3 per cent limit, more recommendations, increasingly pressing and tight, can be issued. In the end, if the country remains in excessive deficit, sanctions are to be imposed by ECOFIN, as explained below. Whereas the initial SGP established a precise set of deadlines, the 2005 revision allowed for quite some flexibility, at the discretion of ECOFIN.

Sanctions

If a country fails to take corrective action and bring its deficit below 3 per cent by the deadline set by the Council, it is sanctioned. A sanction can be seen as a political nuclear bomb. The sanction takes the form of a non-remunerated deposit at the Commission. The deposit starts at 0.2 per cent of GDP and rises by 0.1 of the excess deficit up to a maximum of 0.5 per cent of GDP, as shown in Table 17.4. Deposits are imposed each year until the excessive deficit is corrected. If the excess is not corrected within two years, the deposit is converted into a fine, otherwise it is returned.

Table 17.4   Schedule of fines

Size of deficit (% of GDP)	Amount of fine (% of GDP)
3	0.2
4	0.3
5	0.4
6+	0.5

Several aspects of the SGP are noteworthy. First, formally, it does not remove fiscal policy sovereignty. Governments are in full control; they only agree to bear the consequences of their actions. Second, the intent is clearly pre-emptive since there is a lengthy procedure between the time a deficit is deemed excessive and the time when a deposit is imposed, with two more years before the deposit is transformed into a fine. Third, while a fine is politically a nuclear bombshell, the declaration that a country is in violation of the Pact is a conventional bombshell, meant to elicit prompt corrective action. Finally, all decisions are in the hands of the Council, a highly political body that can exploit many of the 'ifs' included in the Pact.

17.4.3 The Pact and countercyclical fiscal policies: how much room to manoeuvre?

The automatic stabilizers

The automatic response of budget balances to cyclical fluctuations, recalled in Section 17.1.3, is a source of difficulty for the SGP because much of its machinery, including the sanction mechanism, focuses on the 3 per cent deficit limit. The logic is that, in normal years, budgets should be balanced to leave enough room for the automatic stabilizers come into play in bad years without breaching the 3 per cent limit. Box 17.3 provides an idea of what this entails.

Discretionary policy

Countercyclical fiscal policy – the use of the budget to cushion business cycles – does not have to be confined to the automatic stabilizers. Governments can avail themselves of much more room to carry out discretionary policy by running a budget surplus, possibly a large one, in normal years. This is also shown in Box 17.3. The conclusion is that surpluses have to be even larger in good years if fiscal policy is to be used energetically in bad years. The preventive arm is to be used to that effect.

Bringing budgets to the safe zone? Staying there?

The SGP is intentionally designed to provide a strong incentive for each government to bring its budget to a position of balance, or even surplus in good years. According to its promoters, when this is achieved, monetary union member countries will have recovered almost all the required

---

Box 17.3   Good years, bad years, and the 3 per cent deficit limit

How to avoid using fiscal policy at cross-purposes and yet respect the SGP? When the economy slows down, the budget worsens. In order to avoid breaching the 3 per cent limit, the government could have to cut spending or raise taxes, which means adopting a contractionary policy stance when the opposite is needed to dampen the slowdown. The Pact's response is the preventive arm, the idea that the budget should be brought into surplus in good years in order to allow for a fiscal expansion in bad years without trespassing the limit. A simple example illustrates the idea. Table 17.1 shows that, on average, a 1 per cent decline in GDP growth tends to worsen the budget deficit by 0.5 per cent of GDP. Using this rough estimate, the left-hand panel of Fig. 17.4 shows how much, depending on the initial budget position, the GDP can decline before the automatic stabilizers bring the budget to a deficit of 3 per cent. Obviously, if the budget is already at the 3 per cent limit (the leftmost point on the horizontal axis), there is no room available and the stabilizers must be blocked – fiscal policy becomes pro-cyclical – independently of the size of the slowdown (the zero on the vertical axis). If, instead, the budget were initially balanced (the zero on the horizontal axis), it would take a fall of 6 per cent of GDP (read off the vertical axis) to reach a deficit of 3 per cent. In comparison, the GDP decline that has led France and Germany to breach the limit in 2003 was about 2 per cent.

Figure 17.4 also illustrates the discrete use of fiscal policy. The right-hand chart asks the following question: Suppose that GDP declines by 2 per cent, what is left for a further discretionary fiscal expansion over and above the automatic stabilizers? Using the same rule of thumb as in the left-hand panel, we know that the stabilizers worsen the budget by 1 per cent of GDP. The remaining room for manoeuvre depends again on the initial budget position. The graph shows that if the budget was, for instance, in a surplus of 1 per cent (to be read off the horizontal axis), the government can voluntarily increase spending, or cut taxes, to the tune of 3 per cent of GDP (the top reading on the vertical axis).

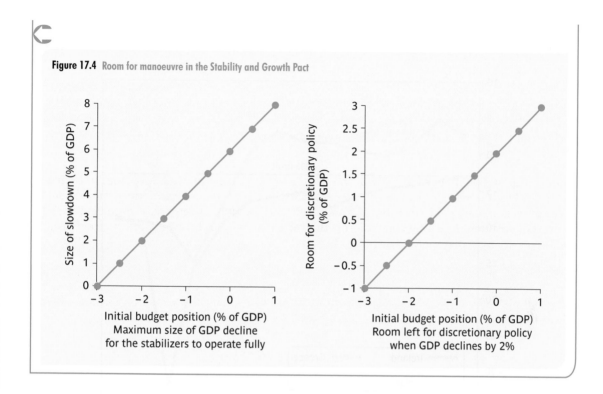

Figure 17.4 Room for manoeuvre in the Stability and Growth Pact

room for manoeuvre. Only deep recessions will prevent the countercyclical use of fiscal policy, and deep recessions will qualify as exceptional.

As it turned out, the early years of the euro were characterized by a moderate slowdown, followed after 2003 by the years of the Great Moderation, a period of continuous growth and low inflation. Three cases are presented in Fig. 17.5. Finland offers an example of a successful application of the SGP strategy. It started with a budget surplus, which shrank with the slowdown but expanded in the good years. In 2006, just before the crisis, the surplus amounted to 5.3 per cent of GDP. This left ample space for a deterioration without crossing the 3 per cent deficit line. Ireland did about as well, but the bursting of its housing bubble forced a whopping deficit of more than 30 per cent of GDP in 2010 as the government scrambled to prevent a collapse of the banking system. This is a clear case of an exceptional circumstance. Greece, on the other hand, started with a large deficit – having hidden its true situation to gain entry into the euro area – and did not use the good years to correct the situation. By 2006, the deficit stood at 6 per cent of GDP and plunged deeply when the crisis provoked a deep recession.

Controversies

The public debt crisis sweeping through the Eurozone provides ammunition to those who have been arguing that the SGP is not likely to achieve its aim of firmly establishing fiscal discipline in each and every member country. Yet, the debt crisis can be seen as the consequence of the preceding exceptional financial crisis, a one-in-a-lifetime event. The Pact was not designed for such circumstances; indeed it includes an 'exceptional circumstance' clause. Still, the Pact's history is disturbing.

The difficulties met in trying to enforce the SGP are in line with the observations presented above in Section 17.3.4. The benefits from coordination are limited, the collective need for discipline is high, but collectively enforced discipline clashes with national sovereignty. This conflict is unavoidable. Discipline cannot be enforced without the threat of sanctions. In the

Figure 17.5 Budget balances since 1999 (% of GDP)

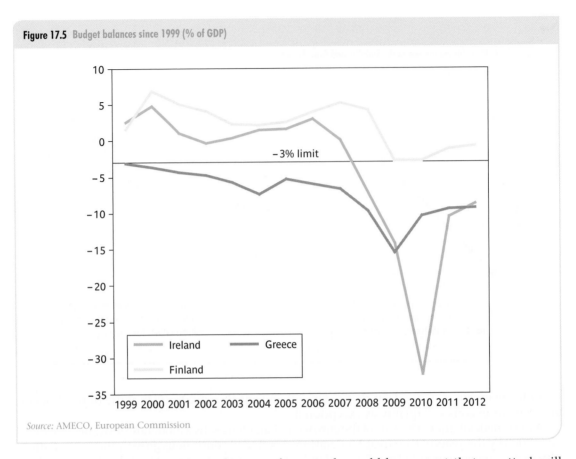

Source: AMECO, European Commission

same spirit as nuclear deterrence – the cost of an attack would be so great that no attack will be undertaken – the initial version of the SGP sought to make sanctions automatic, precisely to avoid a situation where sanctions would actually be imposed. Some small countries were put on the spot, as is explained further below, but the two largest countries called its bluff and the Pact caved in. These events exposed a latent rift between large and small countries, which complicated subsequent negotiations. The SGP was reformed in 2005 but without resolving the logical conflict that lies at its heart. While the revision upheld the principle of sanctions, it clearly sought to avoid a situation where sanctions would have to be applied. The next version, mooted in 2011, seeks to make sanctions as automatic as possible. It is presented in Section 17.4.4.

17.4.4 Euro Plus: a strengthened Stability and Growth Pact

As the debt crisis was developing and the limits of the SGP came to be officially recognized, a new reform was informally adopted in 2011 under the name of Euro Plus Pact. It remains to be made precise and definitely adopted.[11] The aim is to strengthen and expand the Pact, in effect reversing the 2005 reform, which instead tried to make it less rigid because at that time it was found politically too difficult to implement. Interestingly, the newly proposed arrangement makes no reference to the no-bailout clause; overlooking this clause during the crisis has removed a key instrument to collectively impose fiscal discipline within the Eurozone.

---

[11] The Pact has been agreed by the Eurozone member countries, joined by Bulgaria, Denmark, Latvia, Lithuania, Poland and Romania. Its precise formulation has not been finalized at the time of writing; what follows is therefore likely to depart from the end result.

The deficit target

The 3 per cent limit is artificial: Why 3 per cent and not 2 or 3.5 per cent? In addition, targeting the budget balance is like shooting at a moving duck: it changes all the time as economic conditions evolve, and it is therefore beyond government control. The answer, already sketched in the 2005 reform, is to target instead the cyclically adjusted primary budget balance, also called the structural budget balance, which captures discretionary actions. The structural budget involves two adjustments. The primary budget excludes interest payments on the existing debt. The actual budget deficit exceeds the primary budget by the amount of interest payments; when the primary budget is balanced, the actual budget exhibits a 3 per cent deficit if interest payments amount to 3 per cent of GDP, which is the case on average within the Eurozone. The second adjustment concerns cyclical fluctuations, which increase (during bad years) or decrease (in good years) the actual deficit.

The new pact requires that cyclically adjusted primary budgets be balanced. The intention is to achieve a primary budget that is balanced on average over a business cycle, thus allowing the countercyclical discretionary use of fiscal policy. Even if this is achieved, however, the debt may not be reduced over time, as explained in Box 16.1. This is why the new pact also looks at the public debt.

The debt target

Let us take a step back and ask: Why do we care about fiscal discipline in the first place? The answer is that a prolonged lack of discipline eventually leads to a debt default (see Section 17.2.4). The natural implication is that the SGP should target the debt-to-GDP ratio. As long as this ratio declines or remains at a moderate level, there is no threat of default. A debt that keeps increasing, year in, year out, is unsustainable. To be sustainable the debt, measured as a proportion of GDP, must either be stabilized at a comfortable level or eventually brought down to a comfortable level. Why should it be measured as a proportion of GDP and what is a comfortable level? First, a public debt is guaranteed by the ability of the government to raise adequate taxes; national taxable income is approximated by the GDP. Second, we do not know what is a comfortable debt level, nor is there any generally accepted prescription for a desirable debt level. A large debt carries two serious drawbacks: (1) taxes must be raised to serve the debt; (2) any slippage – as was unavoidable during the crisis – means that the debt can rise to worrying heights, which can make it difficult to borrow from nervous financial markets. A low debt level is clearly preferable to a high debt level, but there is no clear boundary between 'too big' and 'small enough'.

The EDP, as described in the Maastricht Treaty, refers to both the annual deficit (limit set at 3 per cent of GDP) and the public debt (limit set at 60 per cent of GDP). The SGP so far has made only a passing reference to the debt; it focused instead on the deficit figure. The initial intention was to require that debts do not exceed 60 per cent of GDP, which was then the European average. By end 2011, the debt average is close to 90 per cent and the old target is beyond reach for many years to come. The new pact does not pretend to make the 60 per cent mark an objective. Instead, reasonably, it states that the evolution of the debt will be one criterion used to evaluate policies.

Sanctions

If the SGP is to have any influence on governments subject to the deficit bias, it must be backed by credible sanctions. When the SGP was under discussion, one view was that it should be entirely automatic, with each step, including sanctions, to be decided by the Commission on the basis of a transparent and unambiguous roadmap. On the other hand, fiscal policy remains an element of national sovereignty. In every democracy, deciding who will pay taxes and how much, and how public money is to be spent, is in the hands of elected officials. An automatic application of the SGP, including detailed mandatory recommendations, would clearly violate this basic principle of democracy. This is why, in the end, enforcement of the SGP was entrusted to ECOFIN, the Council of Economic and Finance Ministers.

Acting on recommendations from the European Commission, ECOFIN decides by a majority of its members whether to apply the measures provided for by the Pact: early warnings, policy recommendations, application of the EDP and, in the end, the imposition of fines. But Finance Ministers are, by definition, politicians. As such, they make elaborate calculations involving tactical considerations often far away from the principles discussed here, as the various cases described in Box 17.4 illustrate. The Euro Plus Pact intends to make the decision procedure much more certain and automatic. If the pact is put into place, the Commission recommendations will be automatically accepted unless a qualified majority (two-thirds of the vote) decides to the contrary.

Box 17.4   Ten years of the Stability and Growth Pact

Over the first ten years of monetary union, the excessive deficit procedure (EDP) has been triggered 22 times for Eurozone members, which are subject to sanctions, and an additional 12 times for other EU countries, which cannot be fined (see Table 17.5). Yet, sanctions have never been imposed. This can be seen as proof that the SGP has been effective at restraining fiscal indiscipline, with a soft touch. Alternatively, it can be that ECOFIN, which makes decisions, has never been ready to sanction a fellow government. A few odd episodes, which spurred considerable controversies, are recalled here.

Table 17.5   Excessive deficit procedures since 1999

Country			
Austria	2009		
Belgium	2009		
Cyprus	2010		
France	2003	2009	
Germany	2003	2009	
Greece	2004	2009	
Ireland	2009		
Italy	2004	2005	2009
Malta	2009		
Netherlands	2004	2009	
Portugal	2002	2005	2009
Slovakia	2009		
Slovenia	2009		
Spain	2009		

Source: http://ec.europa.eu/economy_finance/sgp/index_en.htm

Ireland

In early 2001, Ireland was the first country to be formally warned. Strangely enough, its 2000 budget sported a surplus of 4.7 per cent of GDP and the Commission recognized that its debt level was low. The problem was that its 2001 budget ended up with a surplus of only 1.7 per cent of GDP, while the 2000 Stability Programme had announced a surplus of 4.3 per cent. The year 2001 was an election year and the outgoing government relaxed its virtuous stance. The Irish government and citizens were infuriated and saw the heavy hand of Brussels invading their national sovereignty. The warning was not followed up with any measure.

Germany

The Stability Programme presented by Germany at the end of 2000 anticipated a deficit of 1.5 per cent of GDP for 2001; the final figure was 2.7 per cent of GDP. Following pledges from the German government, ECOFIN decided not to follow the Commission's recommendation of an early warning. But then, contrary to the government's previous promises, the 2002 budget deficit stood at 3.8 per cent of GDP. The German government argued that this was the result of an unforeseeable exceptional event, floods in eastern Germany. This explanation did not cut much ice with the Commission and ECOFIN, and Germany, the promoter of the SGP, became the second country to be put under the EDP in January 2003.

France

For 2001, France had announced a deficit of 1.4 per cent of GDP, but the outcome was 2.7 per cent. In 2002, the deficit reached 3.2 per cent of GDP. The Commission recommended issuing an early warning, which was done by ECOFIN in January 2003. By June 2003, a further deterioration was visible, partly because President Chirac reduced income taxes in both years following an election campaign promise. ECOFIN accepted the Commission recommendation to trigger the EDP.

France and Germany escape the SGP

By November 2003, it had become clear that France and Germany were not heeding the recommendations made earlier by ECOFIN. Their 2003 deficits, not yet known, both turned out to reach 3.7 per cent of GDP, and forecasts for 2004 and 2005 did not envision a return to below 3 per cent. This led the Commission to issue mandatory recommendations, the last step before sanctions. After intense lobbying by France and Germany, ECOFIN decided by qualified majority to 'hold the excessive deficit procedure for France and Germany in abeyance for the time being'. The Court of Justice of the European Communities subsequently annulled this decision, mostly on legal technical grounds.

The Netherlands

In 2003, the Dutch deficit stood at 3.2 per cent, the result of a long slowdown (see Fig. 17.1). As it was expected to fall below 3 per cent in 2004 and afterwards, no action should have been taken. But the Dutch government, which had led the resistance against the French and German whitewash in November 2003 and was keen to restore credibility to the SGP, asked to be put under the EDP.

Implicit liabilities

Another difficult issue is related to the ageing phenomenon. It is currently expected that the share of people aged 65 years and above will rise to 30 per cent of the total population by 2060, up from 17.2 per cent in 2009. This evolution will have profound budgetary implications. Spending on health and retirement is expected to increase very significantly. At the same time, the burden of caring for more elderly people will fall on a smaller proportion of the population. The old-age dependency ratio (the number of those aged 65 and over divided by those of working age (15 to 64 years)) will increase from 25.6 per cent in 2009 to 53.5 per cent in 2060.

These expenditures represent entitlements, sometimes called implicit liabilities. They are true liabilities of the governments because they are enshrined in existing welfare programmes. They are implicit because they appear nowhere in current budgets. They are a source of concern for fiscal discipline because they will eventually increase public expenditures while the corresponding revenues are not provided for. The eventual solution will have to combine a delaying of the age at which people retire, a reduction of pension payments and possibly of health provision, and higher taxes and contributions to the welfare system. Needless to say, each solution is enormously controversial. Some countries have already taken important steps in that direction, others prefer to ignore the issue. The Euro Plus Pact requires that member governments start planning for the ageing phenomenon.

17.5 Summary

The loss of national monetary policy leaves fiscal policy as the only macroeconomic instrument. Budgets can be seen as a substitute for the absence of intra-Eurozone transfers, one of the OCA criteria not satisfied in Europe.

Fiscal policy operates in two ways:

* The automatic stabilizers come into play without any policy action because deficits increase when the economy slows down, and decline or turn into surpluses when growth is rapid.
* Discretionary policy results from willing actions taken by the government.

The main arguments in favour of some collective influence on national fiscal policies are:

* The presence of spillovers, the fact that one country's fiscal policy affects economic conditions in other Eurozone countries. The main spillover channels are: income flows via exports and imports; and the cost of borrowing, as there is a single interest rate.
* The fear that a default by a government on its public debt would hurt the union's credibility.

The theory of fiscal federalism provides arguments for and against the sharing of policy instruments. The presence of spillovers and of increasing returns to scale argues for policy sharing. The existence of national differences in economic conditions and preferences, and of asymmetries of information, argues against policy sharing. The quality of government also matters.

The Stability and Growth Pact (SGP), an application of the excessive deficit procedure (EDP) envisioned in the Maastricht Treaty, is based on four organizing principles:

* A definition of excessive deficits. In principle, deficits should not exceed 3 per cent of GDP. Special circumstances correspond to deep recessions. The 2005 revision allows for a number of 'other factors', a step designed to introduce flexibility.
* A preventive arm, which is designed to encourage governments, through peer pressure, to resist the deficit bias. Prevention rests on annual Stability Programmes. These

programmes are evaluated by the Commission, which issues a recommendation to ECOFIN. ECOFIN, in turn, expresses an opinion.

* A corrective arm, which is triggered when a country is found to have an excessive deficit. This triggers increasingly binding recommendations by ECOFIN, based on suggestions from the Commission. A milder procedure, called early warning, can be triggered when ECOFIN determines, on the basis of a recommendation from the Commission, that a country may soon run an excessive deficit.

* When a country has not followed the recommendations and remains in excessive deficit, sanctions may apply. Sanctions take the form of fines.

The difficulties encountered in the implementation of the SGP can be traced to both economic and political considerations:

* From an economic viewpoint, targeting the annual budget deficit can lead to pro-cyclical policies, i.e. policies that reinforce either a slowdown or a boom. The revised SGP intends to encourage countercyclical policies in good times.

* From a political viewpoint, the SGP faces a formidable contradiction. Fiscal policy is a matter of national sovereignty, in the hands of democratically elected governments and parliaments. At the same time, fiscal policy is recognized as a matter of common concern.

The public debt crisis has shown the danger posed by one country's lack of fiscal discipline. One response is the Euro Plus Pact, which intends to strengthen the SGP. A key feature of the newly proposed pact is the adoption of a reverse voting procedure that would imply that the European Commission's recommendations are automatically accepted unless a super-majority of countries vote against.

Self-assessment questions

1 What is the difference between actual and cyclically adjusted budgets? Why are discretionary actions visible only in changes of the cyclically adjusted budget balance?
2 In Fig. 17.1, identify years when fiscal policy is pro-cyclical, and years when it is countercyclical.
3 What are externalities or spillovers? How do they operate in the case of fiscal policy?
4 Explain the no-bailout clause.
5 What is the intended purpose of the Stability and Growth Pact?
6 How has the Stability and Growth Pact evolved since its inception?
7 When can ECOFIN impose fines in the framework of the Stability and Growth Pact?
8 If the SGP required the cyclically adjusted budget to be balanced every year, explain why fiscal policy would be strictly confined to the automatic stabilizers. What difference would it make if the cyclically adjusted budget had to be balanced on average over business cycles?
9 Why are fines under the Stability and Growth Pact sometimes described as pro-cyclical fiscal policy?
10 Why is there a contradiction between the Stability and Growth Pact and sovereignty in the matter of budgets?

Essay questions

1 How would you reform the Stability and Growth Pact?

2 Does a debt default by a member country make it impossible for this country to remain in the Eurozone?

3 When the Stability and Growth Pact was being negotiated, some countries wanted it to be a fully automatic procedure, others wanted decisions to be interpreted by the Finance Ministers. Why is this distinction important? How does the reverse voting procedure envisioned now change the procedure? Will it work?

4 Some countries argue that the monetary union needs a common fiscal policy to match the common monetary policy. Evaluate this view.

5 With the Stability and Growth Pact and its limits on fiscal policy, what is left for governments to do in the monetary union?

6 As part of its decision on whether to join the Eurozone, the UK Treasury has studied the Stability and Growth Pact and states:

Where debt is low and there is a high degree of long-term fiscal sustainability, the case for adopting a tighter fiscal stance to allow room for governments to use fiscal policy more actively is not convincing. Provided that arrangements are put in place to ensure that discretionary policy is conducted symmetrically, then long-term sustainability would not in any way be put at risk.

(Fiscal Stabilization and Eurozone, HM Treasury, May 2003)

Interpret and comment.

Further reading: the aficionado's corner

For a presentation and a defence of the Stability and Growth Pact, see:
Brunila, A., M. Buti and D. Franco (eds) (2001) *The Stability and Growth Pact*, Palgrave, Basingstoke.

For a detailed and critical presentation of the Stability and Growth Pact, see:
Eichengreen, B. and C. Wyplosz (1998) 'The Stability Pact: more than a minor nuisance?', *Economic Policy*, 26: 65–104.

On the tendency of governments not always to serve their citizens' interests and what it means for the EU, see:
Persson, T. and G. Tabellini (2000) *Political Economics*, MIT Press, Cambridge, MA.
Vaubel, R. (1997) 'The constitutional reform of the European Union', *European Economic Review*, 41(3–5): 443–50.

On the role of the SGP during the crisis:
M. Larch, P. van den Noord and L. Jonung (2010) *The Stability and Growth Pact: Lessons from the Great Recession*, European Economy – Economic Papers 429, European Commission.

On ways to reform the Pact:
Wyplosz, C. (2011) 'Fiscal discipline: rules rather than institutions', *National Institute Economic Review* 217, August.

A defence of the Pact, by one of its creators (J. Stark):
Schuknecht, L., P. Moutot, P. Rother and J. Stark (2011) *The Stability and Growth Pact: Crisis and Reform*, Occasional Paper No. 129, European Central Bank.

Fiscal policy

On the cyclical behaviour of fiscal policy, see:

European Commission (2001) 'Fiscal policy and cyclical stabilization in Eurozone', *European Economy*, 3: 57– 80.
Hallerberg, M. and R. Strauch (2002) 'On the cyclicality of public finances in Europe', *Empirica*, 29: 183–207.
Melitz, J. (2000) 'Some cross-country evidence about fiscal policy behaviour and consequences for Eurozone', *European Economy*, 2: 3–21.

For analyses on the politico-economic aspects of fiscal policy, see:

Alesina, A. and R. Perotti (1995) 'The political economy of budget deficits', *IMF Staff Papers*, 42(1): 1–37.
Persson, T., G. Roland and G. Tabellini (2000) 'Comparative politics and public finance', *Journal of Political Economy*, 108(6): 1121– 61.
von Hagen, J. and I.J. Harden (1994) 'National budget processes and fiscal performance', *European Economy Reports and Studies*, 3: 311–408.

For an introduction to the theory of fiscal federalism, see:

Oates, W. (1999) 'An essay in fiscal federalism', *Journal of Economic Literature*, 37(3): 1120–49.

European semester

On reform of the Stability and Growth Pact, see:

The view of the Commission: http://ec.europa.eu/economy_finance/publications/publication_summary7558_en.htm.
The view of the ECB: www.ecb.int/press/key/date/2005/html/sp051013.en.html.

Academic analyses and alternative proposals:

Calmfors, L. (2003) 'Fiscal policy to stabilise the domestic economy in the EMU: What can we learn from monetary policy?', *CESifo Economic Studies*, 49(3): 319–53.
Wolff, G. (2007) 'Budget institutions to counteract fiscal indiscipline in Europe?' Download from www.uni-bonn.de/ ~guntram/paperspercent5CPittsburghNewsletter022007.pdf.

Useful websites

The official texts can be found on the Commission's website at http://ec.europa.eu/economy_finance/other_pages/ other_pages12638_en.htm.

Euractiv's overview of the SGP, with many references, is at www.euractiv.com/Article?tcmuri=tcm:29-133199 -16&type=LinksDossier.

References

Burda, M. and C. Wyplosz (2012) *Macroeconomics: A European Test*, 6th edition, Oxford University Press, Oxford.
Eichengreen, B. and Wyplosz, C. (1993) 'Unstable EMS', *Brookings Papers on Economic Activity*, 1: 51–144.
OECD (1997) *Economic Outlook*, OECD, Paris.
Stark, J. (2001) 'Genesis of a pact', in A. Brunila, M. Buti and D. Franco (eds) *The Stability and Growth Pact*, Palgrave, Basingstoke.

Chapter 18

The financial markets and the euro

The big payoff on the Euro is, of course, in the capital markets. [. . .] It will move from the dull bank-based financing structure to big-time debt markets and markets for corporate equities that offer transparency for the mismanaged or sleepy European companies. Capital markets are good at kicking butt.

Rudi Dornbusch (2000), p. 242

Chapter Contents

Introduction

This chapter looks at the integration of European financial markets. Following the Single Market, adoption of the euro was expected to encourage further integration of Europe's capital markets, providing savers and borrowers alike with more and better opportunities. This, in turn, was expected to improve the overall productivity of the European economy.

The chapter starts by outlining what is special about the financial services industry, distinguishing between banks and financial markets. It shows that financial markets can be at the same time very efficient and yet subject to some important failures, which have been dramatically illustrated by the financial crisis.

Section 18.2 presents a microeconomic analysis of capital market integration. It establishes the basic result that capital market integration raises economic efficiency and welfare. The assumptions to reach this conclusion, however, are far from realistic. We mention a number of reasons why financial markets do not conform to the perfect competition paradigm and show why financial instability is unavoidable. This establishes the need for regulation and supervision.

Section 18.3 provides a review of the evolution of financial markets since the adoption of the single currency. It looks at the bond markets, at the stock markets and at banks. The Single Market (presented in Chapter 4) has already deeply modified the financial markets, but important differences remain. In particular, national resistance to Eurozone-level regulation and supervision has proven to be dangerous during the financial crisis. Newly adopted arrangements are presented.

Finally comes the question of whether the euro will become a currency used worldwide alongside the US dollar, why it matters and what has happened so far.

18.1 The capital markets

18.1.1 What are financial institutions and markets?

The capital markets are central to long-term growth, as explained in Chapter 7. Their task is to collect savings and to provide producers with the financial means that they need to invest in productive equipment and new operations. There are many different forms of capital markets and institutions that cater to different customers with varied and sometimes complex requirements. At a very general level, the capital market performs three main functions:

1 *It transforms maturity.* Savers typically do not like to part with their 'money' – we call it their assets, because money is just one type of asset – for too long. Borrowers, on the other hand, typically prefer to obtain stable resources. The markets therefore mostly borrow short and lend long.

2 *It performs intermediation.* Savers and borrowers do not meet face to face. Savers deposit their funds in financial institutions that re-lend them to borrowers. The trip may be long, going through many financial institutions and across many national borders.

3 *It deals with inherent risk.* A loan implies giving out money against the promise of future repayment. In the meantime, the borrower may face difficulties that make repayment partly or totally impossible, and some borrowers may simply be dishonest.

The best-known financial institutions are banks: they receive deposits, in effect borrowing from their customers; they offer loans; and they often provide assistance with managing portfolios. In contrast to these universal banks, investment banks specialize in managing portfolios; they do not accept deposits and sometimes cater only to wealthy customers. Many fund management firms do not even deal with individuals; they offer 'wholesale' services to banks and insurance companies. Insurance companies are also considered to be financial institutions. Part of their activity is to provide insurance, which, strictly speaking, is not a financial service. Yet, in order to face potentially high payments, they accumulate large reserves, which they want to manage in order to obtain returns as high as possible. In effect, they take 'deposits' – the insurance premia paid by their customers – that they use to 'make loans' as they invest in financial assets. In addition, many insurance companies propose pension schemes and life insurance, which can be seen as deposits with very long maturities. In fact, recent years have seen the emergence of financial conglomerates that combine classic universal banking, investment banking and insurance.

The bond and stock markets represent the other component of the financial system. Like banks, they are designed to collect savings and lend them back to borrowers, with the crucial difference that the end users – lenders and borrowers – 'meet' each other on the markets. Bonds are debts issued by firms and governments for a set maturity at an explicit interest rate, which sometimes is indexed and therefore variable. Stocks (also called shares) are ownership titles to firms: they have no maturity since they last as long as the firm itself and the returns are determined by the firm's performance. Lenders (also called investors) usually operate through intermediaries – brokers, investment banks – which they instruct to buy or sell assets on their behalf on the markets. Most small investors, and many large ones too, in fact purchase funds, which are ready-made baskets of shares and bonds managed by financial intermediaries. Each fund has particular characteristics: the relative importance of bonds and stocks, the industry or country where they invest, the degree of risk and associated guarantees, as explained in the next section.

Financial institutions come in all shapes and sizes. A few huge international banks coexist with small, strictly local ones. Some financial markets attract lenders and borrowers from all over the world (New York's Wall Street and the City of London are the two largest), whereas others deal in a very narrow range of local assets. As will be explained below, financial markets are more efficient the larger they are.

18.1.2 What do financial markets do?

Matching lending and borrowing needs: maturity

The function of financial markets is to make savers and borrowers meet and to offer each saver and each borrower the best possible deal. This not only includes returns but also the available menu of size and maturity of assets, as well as the ability to sell or buy any amount at any time.

Imagine an individual who wants to put aside a given amount. She can always deposit this amount with her bank on a chequing account and withdraw whatever she wants whenever she wants, but the interest rate offered is quite low. She can do better by choosing term deposits; in that case she will have to pay a penalty if she needs to withdraw before maturity is reached. On the other hand, term deposits offer more attractive interest, which grows with maturity. The bank thus encourages its customers to choose longer-term deposits. Why? Because the bank will re-lend the deposit to another customer who will be ready to pay a higher interest for loans of longer maturity. Time has a value, and the market sets its price.

Bank deposits are not the only way to save. She could buy bonds, with various maturities, or stocks, which are of unlimited duration. In that case, she would lend directly – albeit via her broker and the market – to the borrowers who issue bonds and stocks. The returns will be higher than bank deposits of the same maturity because these bonds and stocks are riskier than bank deposits. Risk is another issue that we now examine.

Matching lending and borrowing needs: risk

Governments, banks and firms issue bonds as a counterpart to borrowing. Their maturities range from the very short term – 24 hours or less – to the very long term – 10, 20 years or more. Firms issue stocks; the holder owns a share of the firm and is entitled to the corresponding portion of profits. Bonds and shares are risky: if the issuer goes bankrupt, they are probably worth nothing, at best a fraction of their face value.[1] How do financial markets deal with risk?

Consider the return to investing in a particular project, say a new factory. When the investment is made, there is usually no way of knowing for certain whether the project will yield profits. Even if the venture proves profitable, the future profit level is uncertain. Tastes, exchange rates, prices and the level of competition can change unexpectedly, thereby altering profits. Of course, one can make a reasonable guess as to what the profit will be, on average, but the investor is also concerned with risk. Two projects may have the same expected return, but the profit flow may be more variable (i.e. riskier) for one than for the other. Investors typically prefer the less risky project. 'A bird in the hand is worth two in the bush' is the colloquial way of expressing the commonsense principle that people tend to discount the expected value of a risky project more than that of a risk-free project.

Bonds and shares are issued by firms that plan new investments. Bondholders and shareholders thus bear the investment risk. For them to be willing to buy a risky asset, there must be a reward. This is why the rate of return is adjusted for risk by incorporating a risk premium. The premium is set so that borrowers can convince savers to bear the risk. Savers obviously prefer no or little risk, but they may be attracted by a higher return. The interest offered on each asset typically rises with the risk of the asset, as shown in Fig. 18.1. The curve describes the trade-off faced by investors between the return and the safety of an asset. Depending on her appetite for risk and return, the saver will choose where on the curve she would like to be.

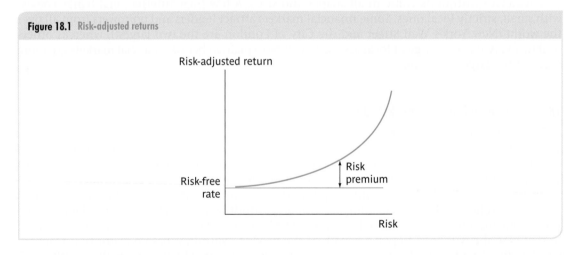

Figure 18.1 Risk-adjusted returns

Different savers will pick different points on the risk–return trade-off schedule because they have different degrees of aversion to risk. Financial markets allow every saver to find an asset that meets its preference and therefore every borrower to find the resources that he needs.[2] Markets set the risk premium on each asset by balancing demand and supply. Put differently, the markets put a price tag on risk; all assets fit nicely on the same risk–return schedule shown in Fig. 18.1, which reflects the preferences of investors and borrowers The risk–return schedule reveals the price of risk, and financial markets allow everyone to trade off a higher return for more risk, or the converse, depending on personal preferences.

Diversification

Markets do not just price risk, they also allow for diversification. The basic issue can be illustrated by an example. Ask yourself, 'How risky is it to bet on red at the roulette table?' You might answer that you win almost half the time since on a roulette wheel all numbers, except 0 and 00, are either red or black. This is the correct answer if you consider the bet-on-red 'project' in isolation. But there is a more complete answer. For instance, suppose you add a bet-on-black 'project' to your 'portfolio' of projects. That is, in addition to betting on red with each roll of the ball, you also bet on black with each roll. Now the effective risk of this betting venture is much reduced. You almost always win, except for when the ball lands on 0 or 00, in which case you lose both bets to the house.[3]

The point to note here is that the average loss from either 'portfolio' – the only-on-red portfolio and the only-on-black portfolio – is the same. In both cases, you lose on average 20 out of every 38 rolls of the ball (there are 38 numbers on the wheel – 18 red numbers, 18 black and the two zeros). However, the more 'diversified' portfolio (the both-red-and-black portfolio) is less risky because one element of the portfolio does well when the other does badly. Clearly, the both-red-and-black betting strategy would take all the fun out of betting, but when we apply the same reasoning to a more serious investment – say a worker's pension fund – then the reduced volatility is highly valued.

The lesson to be learned from this example is that the risk of a particular project must be evaluated from the perspective of the investor's total portfolio of projects. Typically, some projects will do well when others do badly, so the average return to the portfolio is less risky than any individual project. Or, to put it in terms of the 'risk-adjusted rate of return' phraseology, the risk-adjusted return on a diversified portfolio is higher than that on an undiversified portfolio of investment projects.

Financial markets can offer almost unbounded possibilities for diversification, the more so the bigger they are. By increasing the variety of projects, i.e. assets, large financial markets allow savers to hold relatively riskless portfolios composed of very risky assets. Both savers and borrowers stand to benefit from the situation. Because well-diversified portfolios bear little risk, the risk premium is reduced and this reduction is shared among savers, who receive higher returns, and borrowers, who face lower borrowing costs.

18.1.3 Characteristics of financial markets

Financial markets are shaped to deal with the functions previously described, that is, matching the needs and preferences of borrowers and lenders, pricing risk and allowing for risk diversification. A number of characteristics follow.

Scale economies

Matching and risk diversification are both easier when there are a large number of borrowers and lenders. The finance industry is subject to massive scale economies, which affect banks and financial markets. Where small banks and markets survive, it is not difficult to find some barriers to competition. The existence of different currencies is one such barrier. Indeed, before the advent of the euro, an Irish saver who purchased Portuguese assets faced currency risk in addition to the normal lending risk, and this made Irish assets more attractive to her. The creation of a single currency removes this particular barrier to competition.

Networks

Financial institutions and markets can be seen as a network of borrowers and lenders. This is another reason why financial markets tend to get ever larger. When a financial firm receives

---

[3] In finance jargon, the red and black 'projects' are perfectly negatively correlated (their correlation coefficient is −1). More generally, risk diversification is higher the more negatively correlated are the assets that make up a portfolio.

funds from a saver, it needs to re-lend these funds as soon as possible since 'time is money'. With some luck, it will find among its customers a borrower with matching needs and preferences, but more often not. The solution is to re-lend the saver's money to another financial firm that may have spotted a borrower or identified another financial firm that may have spotted a borrower, etc. This is why financial markets may be described as networks. Indeed, money passes quickly from financial firm to financial firm until it finds a house – a suitable borrower – somewhere in the network, quite possibly in a very different corner of the world.

A financial firm is like a telephone hook-up: if you are the only one with a hook-up, it is of no use. A telephone is more useful the more people are connected to the network. This effect is called a network externality. A financial firm can offer better deals when it is in contact with a large number of other firms that deal with many customers, savers and borrowers alike. Network externalities exploit increasing returns to scale: the larger the network, the better it works. The best network could well be the whole world, hence the tendency towards the globalization of financial services.

Asymmetric information

A fundamental characteristic of financial activities is that the borrower always knows more about his own riskiness than the lender. This information asymmetry carries profound implications. Borrowers may intentionally attempt to conceal some damning information for the sake of obtaining a badly needed loan. As a consequence, lenders are very careful, not to say suspicious. They may simply refuse to lend rather than take unknown risks. Alternatively, they may set the price of risk very high, i.e. they ask for very large risk premia. This, in turn, may discourage low-risk borrowers who cannot convincingly signal their true riskiness, while desperate borrowers are willing to pay any premium. If this process goes unchecked, only bad risks are present in the market and, knowing that, lenders withdraw.[4] At best, the price of risk is excessive, at worst the financial market dries up. Box 18.1 illustrates this phenomenon.

Asymmetric information is unavoidable and widespread. It tends to undermine the development of financial institutions and markets. This phenomenon explains many features of the financial services industry presented below. One general response is regulation, i.e. legislative measures that aim at reducing the overall riskiness of financial markets and institutions.

Box 18.1   Asymmetric information at its worst: the Great Crisis of 2007–08

House prices started to fall in the USA in late 2006. Why should that destroy, a year or two later, some well-established banks in New York, London and Frankfurt? Because a bank that lent money to a homeowner in Nebraska had resold this loan to a bank in, say, New York, which resold it to another bank in, say, Frankfurt, which could have resold it to a bank in New York. In the end, many banks were indirectly lending a little bit to the Nebraskan homeowner. This is risk-diversification at its best: if the homeowner defaults on his loan, every bank will suffer a minute loss. This is also information asymmetry at its worst: what does a big international bank in Paris know about the small Nebraskan borrower? Worse, these loans were not just cut into small pieces; the small pieces were repackaged together. So a bank in Brussels could hold

---

[4] This phenomenon is called adverse selection. Borrowing in a desperate situation is sometimes called 'gambling for resurrection'.

a package of portions of loans to tens of thousands of totally unknown American homeowners. It would not really know, or even care to know, who the borrowers were. In fact, it could not investigate the long chain of slicing and repackaging that had produced the assets that it had bought. When the housing market turned down and tens of thousands of homeowners stopped paying for houses that were worth less than the loans they owed, banks around the world abruptly discovered that these packages had become toxic. Too late.

Then a new information asymmetry hit the markets. Bank A knew that it had a pack of toxic assets. It would suspect that Bank B was in the same, possibly even worse, situation. Not knowing for sure, and already worried about its own situation, Bank A stopped doing business with Bank B, which anyway would not lend anything to Bank A or Bank C, or any bank. The interbank markets, where banks lend to each other, seized up. The interbank markets are often referred to as the mother of all financial markets, since this is where liquidity is redistributed. With liquidity frozen, the crisis was on its way.

18.2 Microeconomics of capital market integration

18.2.1 EU policy on capital market integration

Until the 1986 Single European Act and a 1988 directive that ruled out any remaining restriction on capital movements among EU residents, EU capital markets were not very integrated. Although the Treaty of Rome explicitly provides for the free movement of capital, several loopholes allowed EU member countries to impede capital mobility. Many EU nations just did not believe that unrestricted capital mobility was a good idea. They saw capital flows as responsible for repeated balance-of-payment and banking crises.

In the early 1960s, the European Commission promoted a partial liberalization but included numerous opt-out and safeguard clauses, which were in fact extensively used by EU members. The emphasis was on facilitating cross-border business activity, for example international transfers of capital or the repatriation of profits or wage earnings. The Single European Act 1986 went further: it established the principle that all forms of capital mobility should be allowed inside the EU. Liberalization was implemented by a series of directives, including the 1988 interdiction of all remaining restrictions on capital movements among EU residents. Article 56 of the Maastricht Treaty bans all national restrictions on the movement of capital except those required for law enforcement and national security reasons.

While there exist some macroeconomic reasons to be cautious – the impossible trinity principle, introduced in Chapter 13, implies that capital mobility makes it impossible to retain both monetary policy independence and fixed exchange rates – the benefits from capital mobility are microeconomic. They fall into two categories: allocation efficiency and diversification, which we consider in turn.

18.2.2 Economics of capital mobility: allocation efficiency

Allocation efficiency requires capital to be invested in the activities that yield the highest rewards. Capital market barriers inhibit this efficient allocation. To see how and why, imagine that there are only two nations (Home and Foreign) and that, initially, capital is not allowed to move from one country to the other. To keep things simple, we suppose that there is only one good and that it is produced by both nations using capital and labour.

The *MPK* curve in Fig. 18.2 shows that the 'marginal product of capital' (the amount of output produced by an extra unit of capital) declines as the total amount of capital employed increases. The reason is exactly the same as reason as the *MPL* curve in Fig. 8.12. Holding constant the amount of labour employed in Home, the addition of more capital increases the overall output, but each additional unit of capital adds less output than the previous one.

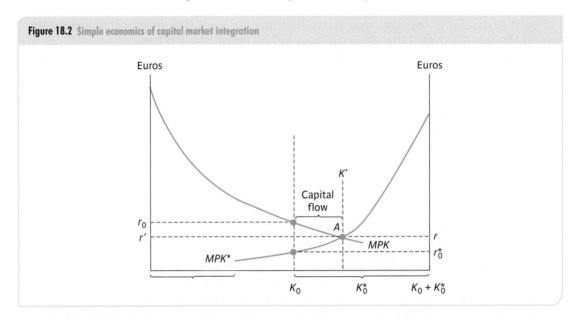

Figure 18.2 Simple economics of capital market integration

If the capital stock in Home is given by K_0, then the corresponding marginal product of capital r_0 is the rate of return earned on capital at Home, assuming that the capital market is competitive. The idea is that firms competing for Home's capital supply force the 'price' of capital, r, up to the point where the price they pay for capital just equals its marginal product. By the usual logic of competition, the outcome is that competitive firms pay r_0 and all capital is employed.

Next consider the situation in the other nation, Foreign. To keep everything in one diagram, we add the Foreign capital stock to that of Home's to get the total two-nation supply of capital. This is shown as $K_0 + K_0^*$ on the horizontal axis. We also draw the marginal product curve for foreign capital, but we reverse it since we measure the amount of capital employed in Foreign from right to left (Home employment of capital is measured from left to right). Following the same competitive logic as for Home, we see that the Foreign return to capital will be r_0^* since this is the *MPK** where all of the capital is employed in Foreign. (This way of depicting the Home plus Foreign capital stock makes it easy to study partitions of the total between the two nations; each point on the horizontal axis between zero and $K_0 + K_0^*$ shows a different partition.)

Analysis of capital market integration

As the diagram is drawn, capital earns a higher return in Home than it does in Foreign. If we now allow international capital flows and, for the sake of simplicity, assume that such flows are costless, it is clear that capital will leave Foreign and move to Home in search of a higher reward. Such capital flows raise the level of capital employed in Home and lower it in Foreign, thus narrowing the gap between r_0 and r_0^*. Indeed, under our assumption that capital flows are costless, capital moves from Foreign to Home until the returns are equalized. This occurs at point A, where the two *MPK* curves intersect. The resulting capital flow and the common reward, r, are illustrated in the diagram. Notice that the capital movement has raised the return in the sending nation and lowered it in the receiving nation.

Winners, losers and net welfare effects

Who wins and who loses from this capital movement? What are the overall effects on native workers and capital owners? To answer these questions, we need to show how one determines the impact of capital movements on the earnings of labour (we have already seen the impact on the reward to capital). Looking at Fig. 18.3, we note that the area under the *MPK* curve gives total Home output. The reason follows directly from the definition of the marginal product of capital. The first unit of capital employed produces output equal to the height of the *MPK* curve at the point where $K = 1$; just imagine a vertical bar with a width of one unit of capital. The amount produced by the second unit of capital is a new bar of the same unit width and height given by the level of *MPK* at the point where $K = 2$, and so on. Adding up all these bars of declining heights, we simply follow the *MPK* curve and map out the area under the curve.

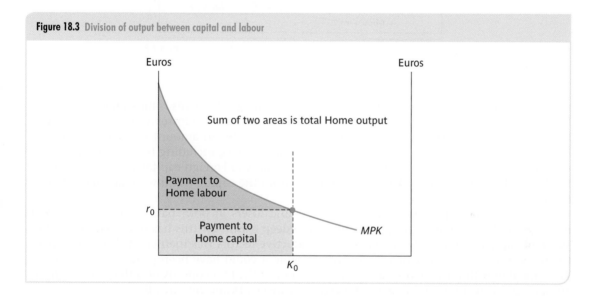

Figure 18.3 Division of output between capital and labour

The remuneration of Home capital is just the rate of return r_0, times the amount of capital, K_0. And, since we are assuming that capital and labour are the only two factors of production in this simple world, labour receives all the output that is not paid to capital. Graphically, this means that capital's income is the grey rectangle shown in the diagram, while labour's income is the blue area between the *MPK* curve and the r_0 line. With this in hand, we turn now to the welfare effects of capital flows.

In our simple, no-capital-mobility-to-free-capital-mobility policy experiment, the 'native' capital owners in Home lose since their reward has fallen from r_0 to r (see Fig. 18.2). The amount of the loss is measured by the rectangle A in Fig. 18.4 (the A in this diagram is unrelated to the A in Fig. 18.2). Home labour increases its earnings by area A plus the triangle B. Thus the total economic impact on Home citizens is positive and equal to the triangle B. Another way of seeing that Home gains from capital mobility is to note that the extra capital that flows in raises total output in Home by the areas B + C + D + E, but the payments to the new capital only equal the areas C + D + E (i.e. r' times the capital flow).

Correspondingly, Foreign output drops by D + E, while the capital remaining in Foreign sees its reward rise from r_0^* to r. The size of this gain is shown by rectangle F, which is the change in

Figure 18.4 Welfare effects of capital 'migration'

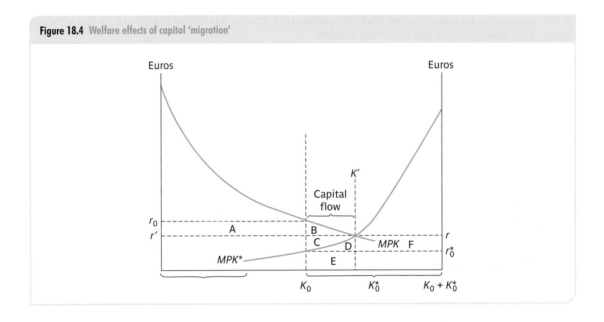

r times the amount of capital left in Foreign after the integration (this is illustrated by point *A*). Foreign labour sees its earnings drop by D + F. Combining all these losses and gains, the Foreign factors of production that remain in Foreign lose overall by an amount measured by triangle D. However, if we count the welfare of Foreign factor owners, including the capital that is now working in Home, the conclusion is reversed. Total gains to Foreign capital are C + D + F, while the loss to Foreign labour is D + F. Foreign gains from the capital outflow by an amount equal to the triangle C.

In short, while capital flows create winners and losers in both nations, collectively both nations gain from the movement of capital. The deep reason for this has to do with efficiency. Without capital mobility, the allocation of productive factors was inefficient. For example, on the margin, Foreign capital was producing r_0^*, while it could have been producing r_0 in Home. The capital flow thus improves the overall efficiency of the EU economy and the gains from this are split between Home and Foreign. Foreign gets area C; Home gets area B.

The result that both countries benefit from capital market integration is the basis for the Single Market and the Commission directive. It underpins the view that, by further encouraging capital mobility, adoption of the euro will raise economic efficiency and welfare.[5] It is important, however, to remember the assumptions that were made in reaching this result, in particular that the capital market itself is functioning perfectly well. This assumption is not warranted. Section 18.1.3 explains the many specificities of this market, including asymmetric information, which makes it difficult to deal with inherent risk, and network externalities, which skew competition. When the perfect market assumption is removed, the result no longer holds: capital market integration may or may not be beneficial; it depends on the details of the deviations from perfection and on a host of other features.

Does it mean that capital market integration is a bad idea? Probably not. The presumption is that, as long as competition is strong enough, integration is beneficial. Yet, things can go wrong and this is why the authorities have to be vigilant and, when needed – and only when needed – regulate the markets to ensure that the expected benefits from integration are reaped. This issue is taken up in Section 18.3.4.

---

[5] It is also the rationale for financial globalization, but that is another story.

18.2.3 Economics of capital mobility: the diversification effect

Section 18.1.3 explains how financial markets facilitate investment by matching borrowers and savers and by pricing risk. Capital market integration (and the exchange rate stability that comes with the euro – see next section) reduce the risk premium and therefore lower the borrowing costs of firms while offering better returns to savers. This makes Europe a better place to invest. In this way, financial market integration can raise the investment rate and growth, as explained in Chapter 7.

Since European integration is rather gradual and since many things affect the risk-adjusted rate of return, it can be difficult to figure out exactly how financial market integration affects the investment climate in Europe as a whole. The same logic, however, applies to individual nations joining the EU. Since the financial markets in some nations – for example, a small nation like Estonia – are relatively undeveloped, getting access to the European financial markets by joining may have a big impact on their risk-adjusted rate of return and thus a big impact on their investment rate.

18.2.4 Effects of the single currency on financial markets

The adoption of the euro eliminates the currency risk within the Eurozone. In principle, therefore, savers do not have to worry about where the asset is issued as long as it is denominated in euros, and borrowers can tap the whole area by taking on euro-denominated debt. There is no longer any reason for financial markets to be Finnish, Greek or German.

A single financial market first means more competition as national currencies that used to act as non-tariff barriers are eliminated.[6] Rents associated with dominating positions should disappear and the need to retain and attract new customers should push financial institutions to constantly improve their performance. A unified financial market should also allow a better exploitation of scale economies, with the emergence of large financial institutions and markets. Table 18.1 shows a ranking by the magazine *The Banker* of the largest banks in the world, according to their total assets. In 2005, there were only three Eurozone banks in the top ten league.[7] In 2011, the situation has not changed much in this respect, although these banks have climbed up the ladder. The 2007–08 crisis has taken its toll of US banks, and some Eurozone and British banks are, for the time being, the great winners; but the situation remains highly volatile. The situation mirrors the situation of stock markets: Eurozone stock markets (Frankfurt, Paris, Milan, etc.) are small in comparison with Wall Street and the City of London.

One possible negative aspect of the euro, however, is that the potential for diversification shrinks. Before the advent of the euro, a Belgian saver could diversify her portfolio by acquiring German, Italian and other European assets. Now these assets are less diverse since they all share the same currency and as cyclical conditions become more homogeneous. To achieve a high degree of diversification, these assets may have to move further, to less well-known parts of the world.[8] All in all, however, the positive effects of scale economies in a wider unified market are likely to outweigh the negative effects of reduced diversification.

Finally, the fact that the US dollar is a world currency gives US citizens and firms some advantages. The potential emergence of the euro as another world currency, and the expected benefits, are examined in Section 18.4.

---

[6] Chapter 3 presents non-tariff barriers, i.e. restrictions to trade that are designed to protect local firms by such means as specific regulation, standards, administrative authorizations and controls, etc.

[7] The situation was similar in 2005 and in the first edition of this book in 2002, except that the top ten list included one French and two German banks.

[8] This is not a serious concern. As globalization develops, so do the possibilities of diversification. Over the past few years, Chinese and Indian assets have joined Brazilian and Korean assets in well-diversified portfolios.

Table 18.1   The top ten commercial banks in 2005 and 2011 (ranked by total assets)

2005			2011		
Rank	Bank	Country	Rank	Bank	Country
1	UBS	Switzerland	1	BNP Paribas	France
2	Citigroup	USA	2	HSBC	UK
3	Mizuho	Japan	3	Deutsche Bank	Germany
4	HSBC	UK	4	Mitsubichi	Japan
5	Crédit Agricole	France	5	Barclays Bank	UK
6	BNP Paribas	France	6	Royal Bank of Scotland	UK
7	JP Morgan Chase	USA	7	Industrial and Commercial Bank of China	China
8	Deutsche Bank	Germany	8	Bank of America	USA
9	Royal Bank of Scotland	UK	9	JP Morgan Chase	USA
10	Bank of America	USA	10	Crédit Agricole	France

Source: *The Banker*, July 2005 and July 2011

18.3 Financial institutions and markets

18.3.1 Banking: What is special about banking?

The banking industry is special in three respects. First, banks are naturally fragile, and bank failures can be systemic, as explained in Section 18.3.4 below. As a consequence, banks are highly regulated and supervised.[9] Second, the information asymmetry problem is acute since banks earn profits primarily from their lending activities. Banking does not conform to the perfect market model.

One implication is that long-term relationships are important as they provide banks with track records of their customers and help to build up confidence, breaking somewhat the information asymmetry. The downside is that well-established customers have little incentive to quit their banks. While this attachment alleviates the information asymmetry problem, it also reduces competition.

That aspect is further reinforced by the fact that it is plainly painful to change bank. Many payment orders are automated, some payments and receipts are always under way, and so it is never the right time to shift to another bank. Proximity of the branch also often discourages switching. For these reasons, most banking relationships tend to be long lasting, much longer than in most other service industries, and competition is less severe.

The starting point

These features explain why banks started to develop at the local level, where they could know their customers reasonably well, thus minimizing information asymmetries. Scale economies

---

[9] The financial crisis has exposed serious gaps in regulation, see Chapter 19.

next led to a process of growth and mergers as banks sought to become ever bigger, but so far this process has generally taken place within national boundaries. Figure 18.5 shows that the number of banks has declined in the Eurozone recently, and a large part of this decline is explained by mergers and acquisitions.[10] However, a vast majority (77 per cent for the Eurozone as a whole) of these mergers and acquisitions take place within countries, especially in the larger countries.

Figure 18.5 Number of banks in the Eurozone

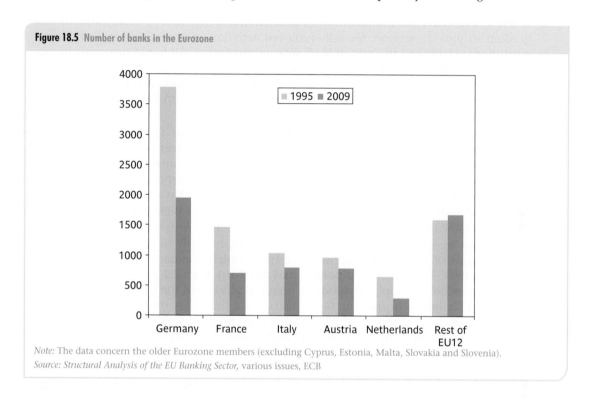

Note: The data concern the older Eurozone members (excluding Cyprus, Estonia, Malta, Slovakia and Slovenia).

Source: Structural Analysis of the EU Banking Sector, various issues, ECB

National or pan-European concentration

The fact that each country had its own currency – the exception being the Belgium–Luxembourg currency union – and that many restrictions to capital movements were in place until the late 1980s, explains why the concentration process initially took place within, and not across, countries. The advent of the euro could change all that, but little has happened so far. Several reasons have been advanced to explain the continuing apparent parochialism of banks in contrast with other industries.

First, local regulations still differ. This has long been recognized and has led to a succession of harmonization efforts, described in Box 18.2. In addition, while in theory a 'single banking market' is now in place, several non-regulatory hurdles remain. They operate like non-tariff barriers and are used by national authorities to protect homegrown banks and, in effect, stifle competition.

The 'single banking market' is not limited to the EU members. When the EFTA countries, with the exception of Switzerland, joined the European Economic Area (EEA) in 1992, they accepted the European banking legislation.

---

[10] The increase in the number of banks in the rest of the EU is entirely due to a massive increase in Ireland (from 56 to 498 banks!), a symptom of its housing price bubble. Further editions of this book will undoubtedly show a return to normal.

Box 18.2   Harmonization of banking regulation in Europe

Efforts at building a unified banking market in Europe go far back in history. The main steps are as follows:

- In 1973, a directive on the abolition of restrictions on freedom of establishment and freedom to provide services for self-employed activities of banks and other financial institutions established the principle of national treatment. All banks operating in one country are subject to the same non-discriminatory regulations and supervision as local banks. Yet, widespread capital controls limited competition and, in the absence of any coordination of banking supervision, banks were deterred from operating in different countries.

- In 1977, the First Banking Directive on the Coordination of Laws, Regulations and Administrative Provisions Relating to the Taking Up and Pursuit of Credit Institutions established a gradual phasing in of the principle of home country control. Under this principle, it is the home country of the parent bank that is responsible for supervising the bank's activities in other EU countries. The directive left open a number of loopholes, including the need to obtain authorization from the local supervision authorities to establish subsidiaries and continuing restrictions on capital movements.

- In 1989, the Second Banking Directive was designed to apply to the banking industry the provisions of the Single European Act 1986, which mandated the elimination of capital controls. The directive stipulates that any bank licensed in an EU country can establish branches or supply cross-border financial services in the other countries of the EU without further authorization. It can also open a subsidiary on the same conditions as nationals of the host state. The parent bank must now consolidate all its accounts for supervision by its own authority. Yet, the host country can impose specific regulations if they are deemed to be 'in the public interest'.

- Facing a lack of progress, a Financial Services Action Plan (FSAP) was adopted in 1999. This plan called for the harmonization of prudential rules, the establishment of a single market in wholesale financial services and efforts to unify the retail market.

- Limited results led to the adoption in 2001 of the Lamfalussy process.[1] The process involves four steps: (1) the adoption of common core legal values; (2) the adoption of detailed proposals at the national level: (3) the consolidation of these measures at the European level, including the creation of a Committee of European Securities Regulators (CESR), which brings together a new created regulator, the European Securities Committee (ESC), and the national regulators; (4) enforcement of the agreements by the European Commission.

- The financial crisis has accelerated the process. New institutions have been created; see Section 18.3.4.

---

[1] After Alexander Lamfalussy, former Chairman of the European Monetary Institute (the predecessor of the ECB), in his capacity as Chairman of a Committee of Wise Men.

Second, for several centuries, banks have developed along diverse lines, leading to different traditions in banking. While acquiring a foreign bank could be the easiest way of adjusting to that country's practices, problems with integrating personnel seem to deter mergers and acquisitions.

Third, the tax treatment of savings differs from country to country. Thus the choice of where to bank may be driven by tax purposes rather than by the quality of banking services. Tax evasion may well have become as strong an incentive to scout the European banking scene as the search for better service or risk diversification, thus undermining the very purpose of financial integration. In 2005, a new agreement came into effect to combat tax evasion; all EU-based banks must now report their foreign customers to their tax authorities.

Finally, protectionism is suspected. The fact that mergers and acquisitions in the large countries are mainly within-borders may be the result of subtly concealed protectionism.

Trade in services

Even though banks do not consolidate at the pan-European level, they could still offer services across borders. This form of competition is exactly what the Second Banking Directive was meant to promote, and the elimination of exchange risk should reinforce it. They can open new branches and move close to their customers to circumvent the information asymmetry. Figure 18.6 shows that, until the crisis, banks considerably increased their own relationships with one another across borders within the Eurozone. Deposits by foreign customers have not changed much since the adoption of the euro. One possible reason is that the costs of bank transfers from one country to another have long been dissuasive (some €17 on average for a €100 transfer in 2000, about ten times the cost of a domestic transfer). Since 2011, new legislation prohibits banks from charging a different fee for within-Eurozone transfers from the one they apply to domestic transfers. This may change the situation.

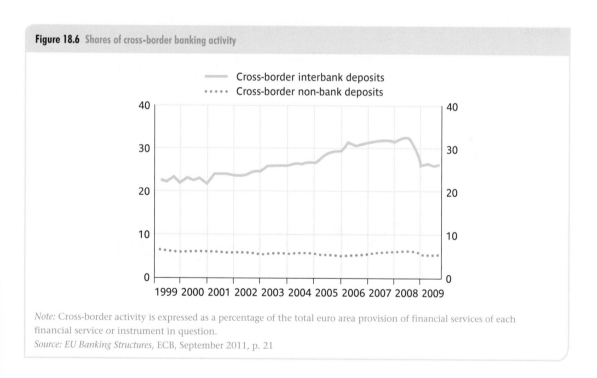

Figure 18.6 Shares of cross-border banking activity

Note: Cross-border activity is expressed as a percentage of the total euro area provision of financial services of each financial service or instrument in question.

Source: EU Banking Structures, ECB, September 2011, p. 21

18.3.2 Bond markets

We first look at the market for bonds issued by national governments, where the evolution is well documented and spectacular. Remember from Chapter 13 that the interest parity principle asserts that, when markets are well integrated, interest rates between two assets issued in different currencies differ by: (1) the expected change in the exchange rate, and (2) a premium reflecting different risks. Up until the crisis, rightly or wrongly, EU governments were believed to be highly trustworthy, financially at least. As a result, there was no significant risk premium and the only difference should have been expected exchange rate changes. With adoption of the common currency and the disappearance of exchange rates, the currency risk was eliminated and financial integration should have resulted in identical rates across the Eurozone.

This conjecture has been fully verified, as can be seen from Fig. 18.7, which displays the evolution of interest rates on government long-term bonds. For decades, interest rates had been lowest on German bonds, because of the strong currency status of the Deutschmark. As the date of launching the single currency drew nearer and more certain, the currency risk declined and gradually became irrelevant. The figure shows an impressive convergence of the French and Italian rates towards the German level by January 1999. Note the evolution of the Greek interest rate since Greece joined the Eurozone later, in January 2001. Much the same happens in the case of Slovenia. It is also interesting to observe that the UK rate does not converge since the UK has decided not to adopt the euro.

Yet a keen eye will detect that convergence is not complete. This may reflect differences in the perceived quality of governments as borrowers or less than full integration because of remaining institutional differences. As we see in Chapter 19, there probably were lingering doubts about the fiscal rectitude of some countries, captured by a small risk premium, which grew gigantic as the debt crisis started to unfold.

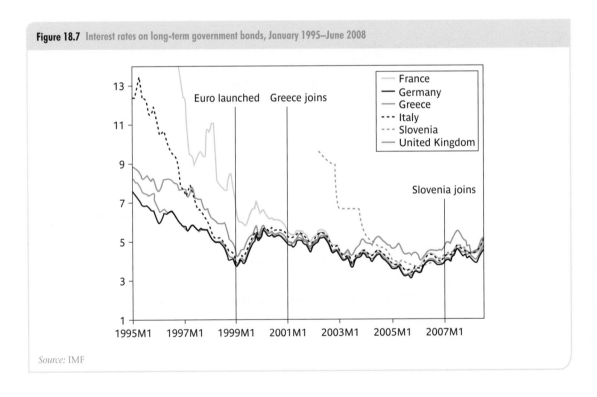

Figure 18.7 Interest rates on long-term government bonds, January 1995–June 2008

Source: IMF

18.3.3 Stock markets

The stock market is where large – and some medium-sized – firms raise the financial resources that they need to acquire capital and generally develop their activities. They issue shares, which are held by individuals or by large institutional investors, such as pension funds and insurance companies. Increasingly, individuals buy shares from collective funds designed to offer good risk–return trade-offs through extensive diversification, as explained in Section 18.1.2. Yet, for all the hype about globalization, it is striking that stock markets are characterized by a strong 'home bias': borrowers and savers alike tend to deal mostly on domestic markets and to hold domestic assets.

One reason for the home bias is information asymmetry: investors know more about domestic firms. This is unlikely to change.

Another reason is currency risk. This obstacle to capital mobility has been eliminated within the Eurozone, so we would expect less of a home bias. Is it happening? Apparently, yes. Figure 18.8 shows that Eurozone residents have acquired increasingly more shares issued in other Eurozone countries. This stands in sharp contrast to the continuing home bias affecting shares issued elsewhere.

Figure 18.8 Cross-border holdings of equity issued by euro area residents

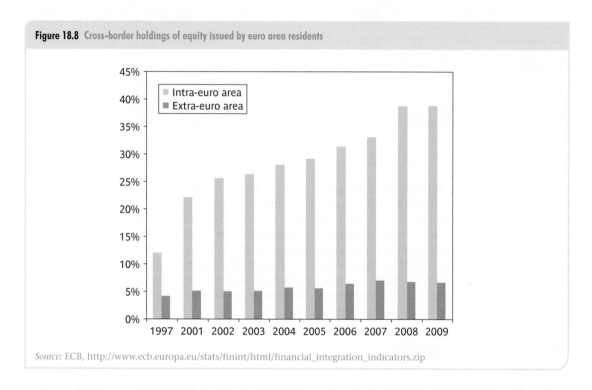

Source: ECB, http://www.ecb.europa.eu/stats/finint/html/financial_integration_indicators.zip

Another piece of evidence is provided by the evolution of stock exchanges, the marketplace where shares are traded. Most European countries long had one stock exchange, or more. This was natural when currency risk was segmenting the various national markets. Are things changing with the advent of the euro? Table 18.2 displays the sizes of stock markets in the Eurozone and in a few large financial centres. Size is measured by market capitalization, i.e. the total valuation of all the firms listed on the exchange. In comparison to the USA, Eurozone exchanges remain small, and therefore likely to suffer from limited scale economies. Even London, which hosts the largest European stock market, pales in comparison with the USA.

In the USA, which is similar to the Eurozone in economic and geographic size, there are 15 stock exchanges, but only two or three significant ones and the New York Stock Exchange (NYSE) dominates. In the Eurozone, each country insists on having its own exchange. Because stock markets display strong scale economies, the perception is that the Eurozone should be evolving towards one major centre and a handful of secondary exchanges. The question is where will they be? Each country seems to be keen to retain its stock exchange, for reasons of prestige and because it can be a major activity.

Table 18.2   Size of stock markets (total capitalization), 2010

	$ bn	% GDP		$ bn	% GDP		$ bn	% GDP
France	967	38	Ireland	60	29	United States	30,455	209
Germany	686	21	Portugal	43	19	Japan	2,126	39
Italy	477	23	Austria	32	8	United Kingdom	1,864	83
Spain	462	33	Slovenia	5	10	Switzerland	554	106
Netherlands	402	51	Estonia	2	13	Hong Kong	463	206
Finland	139	58	Slovakia	2	2			
Belgium	128	27	Cyprus	2	6			
Greece	69	23	Malta	1	13			

Source: US Census Bureau

For a while, it was thought that Frankfurt would benefit from the location of the ECB, but this has not happened. In fact, London and Frankfurt tried to merge in 1998, but this attempt failed for reasons explained in Box 18.3. In order to challenge both London and Frankfurt, a number of exchanges have merged. Euronext was created in 2000 by the exchanges of Paris, Brussels and Amsterdam, keeping physical operations in each city. Then, in 2007, Euronext merged with NYSE, but activities remain on both sides of the Atlantic. In 2003, Stockholm and Helsinki merged into OMX, which has since linked up with Copenhagen and the Baltic States (Riga, Tallinn and Vilnius), also keeping physical operations in each of these cities. Clearly, the currency issue is not driving market consolidation.

18.3.4 Regulation and supervision

The rationale

Section 18.1 identifies a number of characteristics specific to financial markets: these markets display important scale economies, they operate as networks and they suffer from information asymmetries. These characteristics imply that financial markets suffer from 'market failures', i.e. deviations from the textbook description of perfect markets. In the presence of failures, markets may malfunction, which justifies interventions by the authorities. Indeed, in every country, financial markets are regulated and the financial institutions are closely supervised.

The presence of scale economies implies that a few large firms eventually dominate the market. The tendency for competition to become monopolistic challenges the perfect competition assumption.[11] It also means that financial markets are vulnerable to difficulties suffered by one or two of these important players. This vulnerability is sharpened by the two other characteristics. The network feature means that all large financial institutions are continuously dealing with each other, and routinely borrow and lend huge amounts among each other. If one of these institutions fails, all the others may be pulled down. Failures tend to be systemic.

---

[11] As explained in Chapter 6, monopolistic competition describes the situation where a small number of large firms dominate the market.

Box 18.3   Consolidation of stock markets

Some consolidation is taking place among traditional stock markets. The most noticeable example has been the creation of Euronext in September 2000, the result of a merger of the Amsterdam, Brussels and Paris stock exchanges. Euronext is subject to Dutch legislation and has a subsidiary in each of the participating countries. Each subsidiary holds a local stock market licence that gives access to trading in all the participating countries. Euronext has integrated many market functions, but the local markets are not legally merged, which implies, for example, that the regulatory body in each of the participating countries retains its prerogatives. From the beginning, Euronext was not intended to be a closed structure and was eager to finalize agreements with other stock exchanges. In 2001, this resulted in the acquisition of Liffe, the London derivatives trading platform, and the agreement to integrate also the Portuguese exchanges of Lisbon and Porto.

Before Euronext, another, even larger merger between stock exchanges was tried. In 1998, the Deutsche Börse (DB) and the London Stock Exchange (LSE) were planning to merge in an attempt to gain a leadership position in Europe. The creation of iX ('international Exchange') was officially announced in May 2000. The DB and the LSE planned to participate in equal measure as shareholders of the new exchange, which would be subject to British legislation. It was envisaged to quote the 'blue chips' of both exchanges in London and the technology stocks in Frankfurt. The trading system would have been the German one (Xetra). While the negotiations between the two stock exchanges were still in process, the OM Gruppen, owner of the Stockholm stock exchange, made an unexpected public offer and tried to take over the LSE. This event critically affected the projected merger between DB and LSE, which was subsequently rejected by the LSE board. Yet, now and then, rumours of negotiations between the LSE and DB resurface.

Source: Adapted from Hartmann et al. (2003)

The third characteristic, the presence of information asymmetries, means that all financial firms routinely take risks. Every asset represents the right to receive payments in the future, be it 24 hours or 15 years. It is trivial to observe that the future is unknown, but this feature has deep implications for financial markets. Today's value of an asset represents the best collective judgement by financial market participants of the likely payments that the asset holder may expect to receive upon maturity. But one thing is sure: the future will differ from today's expectations. The asset may yield better returns than expected, but its value can deeply deteriorate. When this happens, asset holders see their wealth decline, and the decline is typically sudden. This is why financial systems are inherently fragile and prone to panics and crises.

As financial institutions are central to modern economies, systemic failures immediately provoke severe disruptions that leave no firm or citizen unharmed. When declines in asset values are widespread, those who hold large amounts of assets can become insolvent. Many financial institutions (banks, pension funds, insurance companies) that hold large amounts of assets may then fail, spreading the hardship to the whole economy, as numerous examples – from the Wall Street crashes of 1929 and 2007–08 to Korea in 1998 and Argentina in 2002, and the Great Crisis of 2008 – remind us.

Regulation and supervision

To reduce the incidence of such catastrophic events, and possibly even eliminate them, financial institutions are regulated. Over the years, regulation has changed and become more sophisticated. The general thrust is to ensure that financial institutions adopt prudent strategies. They are required to hold enough high-quality assets, for example bonds issued by respectable governments or by solid corporations. But the collapse in 2008 of Lehman Brothers, one of the most highly reputed banks on Wall Street, and the sovereign debt crisis in the Eurozone show that 'respectable' and 'solid' are fragile attributes.

Regulation, in turn, requires supervision. It is not enough to adopt good rules; it is essential to make sure that they are respected. Since financial conditions can quickly deteriorate, supervision must be continuous. Given the complexity of modern finance, and the possibility of hiding emerging problems, supervisors must be as sophisticated as the financiers themselves, and they need to exercise their duties with great diligence and firmness. Over 2007–08, it emerged that supervisors were ill informed, ill prepared or technically unable to cope with the crisis.

Adapting regulation and supervision to the single currency

Regulation – the establishment of rules – is largely designed at the EU level[12] whereas supervision – the implementation and enforcement of regulation – continues to be carried out at the national level. This assignment of tasks is understandable. The EU's central aim is often described as 'the four freedoms': free mobility of goods, services, assets and people. For financial services to be freely traded, financial institutions need to be allowed to operate throughout the EU if they so wish. If national regulations differed too much, financial institutions would have to register in each and every country where they wished to operate. This would greatly hamper the mobility of financial services. Savers, unsure about the quality of foreign regulations, would prefer to keep their money at home.

What about supervision? One argument for keeping supervision at the national level is the existence of another kind of information asymmetry, this time between supervisor and supervisee. Obviously each financial firm knows more about its business, and the risks that it is taking, than its supervisor. Quite likely, most firms wish to hide their difficulties, especially if their disclosure would lead to fines or outright closure. It is argued that these information asymmetries are lower at the national than at the union level. National supervisors know their financial institutions well, and over the years have developed a relationship that allows for a smooth process. Another argument is subsidiarity: unless proved impossible or inefficient, supervision should remain at the national level.

When the euro was created, the solution was therefore some common minimum regulation and decentralized supervision. The financial crisis that hit Europe in 2008 showed that this system was not adequate. Box 18.4 recalls two bank crises that illustrated the problem with different national supervisors when a bank with significant cross-border activities fails. Another development was the late September 2008 decision by Ireland to offer a full guarantee to deposits and liabilities of six Irish banks. The other countries, which offered limited guarantees, became concerned that their own banks would be at a disadvantage at a crucial moment. Following harsh declarations, one by one and each in its own way, all countries ended up offering unlimited guarantees to deposits at their own banks.

These events led to the appointment of a task force. The ensuing De Larosière Report (2009) dutifully noted that national supervisors did not share information with one another, leaving governments in the dark when emergency decisions had to be made. The report also revealed that the ECB, tasked with the function of lender of last resort, was not any better informed of the true situation of stressed banks. Following proposals of the De Larosière Report, it has been decided to create the European System of Financial Supervision (ESFS), which includes four new institutions:

■ The European Banking Authority (EBA), which is charged with collecting detailed information on all EU banks.

---

[12] More precisely, EU-level regulation sets minimum standards, leaving individual countries free to establish more stringent – but not more lenient – rules. Within this principle, national-level rules are subject to the principle of mutual recognition, i.e. foreign rules are recognized as substitutes for domestic ones.

- The European Systemic Risk Board (ESRB), which looks at the overall picture, especially the cross-border links among financial institutions that so far were unknown. The ESRB, which is chaired by the President of the ECB, can issue binding recommendations.

- The European Insurance and Occupational Pensions Authority (EIOPA), which is like the ESRB but with a focus on insurance companies and pension funds.

- The Joint Committee of the European Supervisory Authorities (ESAs), which brings the national supervisors together with a view to improving transparency.

These institutions come on top of existing national regulators and supervisors. As far as banking regulation is concerned, the European Commission is expected to issue new directives that would aim at making banks safer (but less profitable).

Box 18.4   Fortis and Dexia

Fortis Bank was a bank owned by a Belgian and a Dutch parent, with a significant presence in Luxembourg. Like many other European banks, it had accumulated large amounts of assets made of subprime loans. In 2007, it acquired part of a major Dutch Bank, ABN-AMRO, which strained its resources. To make things worse, it had large loans outstanding to Lehman Brothers. By late September 2008, following the demise of Lehman, Fortis came under extreme stress and required emergency support. The Belgian, Dutch and Luxembourg supervisory authorities sharply disagreed and each one went its own way. The Dutch authorities nationalized the Dutch part of Fortis and ABN-AMRO. The Belgian authorities nationalized the rest, i.e. the non-Dutch part of Fortis, and sold most of it to French bank BNP-Paribas. Why was Fortis thus split? According to Claessens et al. (2010), 'Belgian and Dutch authorities have had a long tradition of cooperation, but Fortis was systemically important in both Belgium and the Netherlands. The Belgian authorities wanted to rescue Fortis as a whole, keeping the home base in Brussels while the Dutch authorities wanted to return ABN-AMRO, which had just been acquired by Fortis, to Dutch control.'

Dexia is a Belgian bank, the outcome of the merger of a Belgium and a French bank, both specializing in lending to local authorities. Dexia bought a US financial institution that was exposed to both Lehman and the subprime market and faced acute losses in late September 2008. Days after Fortis, Dexia was in need of being rescued. This time, the Belgian and French authorities cooperated and injected funds to save Dexia and keep it intact.

These two almost simultaneous events show that there is no Eurozone doctrine on how to deal with failed banks, which makes these traumatic events even more perilous. The difference of treatment is explained by Pisani-Ferry and Sapir (2010) as follows: 'First, Dexia was (and still is) owned by a single holding company headquartered in a single country whereas Fortis was owned by two parent companies located in two separate countries. Second, the shareholders of Dexia were closely connected to governments.' In other words, truly European banks die more easily than national banks, especially if they do not have well-connected friends.

18.4 The international role of the euro

The classic attributes of money apply to its international role. Externally, a currency can be a medium of exchange used for international trade, a unit of account used to price other currencies or widely traded commodities, and a store of value used by foreign individuals and authorities.

Domestically, these attributes are underpinned by the legal status of money; internationally, they have to be earned.

In the nineteenth century, sterling was the undisputed international currency. It was displaced by the US dollar in the twentieth century. Clearly, only large economies can expect their currency to achieve an international status, a condition that the Eurozone fulfils. Currently, some 330 million people live in the Eurozone, and new membership could eventually bring this number to 480 million, to be compared with 310 million people living in the USA. The EU's GDP is 75 per cent of that of the USA. Another condition is that the currency must be stable. The Eurosystem's commitment to price stability further suggests that, eventually, the euro can aspire to playing a large international role. Will it, and if so, when? Would it be a good thing? These are the issues that we consider in this final section.

18.4.1 Medium of exchange: trade invoicing

Whenever an export takes place, there must be an agreement on the currency that will be used to set the price and then carry out the payment. Will it be the exporter's, the importer's or a third currency? Each side of the trade would rather use its own currency to avoid exchange costs and uncertainty. In that sense, the Eurozone stands to benefit from a wider acceptability of its currency.

There is some evidence that European firms are increasingly able to invoice trade in euros, as shown in Fig. 18.9. Yet the bulk of primary commodities (oil, gas, raw materials) are priced in US dollars in specialized markets, and this is unlikely to change in the foreseeable future. Even if European firms can now more often avoid exposure to currency risk by using the euro, the dollar is and will remain the currency of choice among countries that are in neither the US nor the euro currency areas. The exception seems to be countries on the periphery of the EU, mostly those in Europe that will join the Eurozone in the coming years.

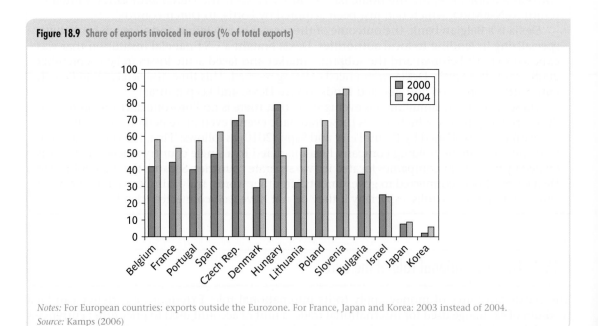

Figure 18.9 Share of exports invoiced in euros (% of total exports)

Notes: For European countries: exports outside the Eurozone. For France, Japan and Korea: 2003 instead of 2004.
Source: Kamps (2006)

18.4.2 Unit of account: vehicle currencies on foreign exchange markets

The foreign exchange market is a network of financial institutions that trade currencies among themselves. This is a huge market where, on any average day, some US$3000 billion worth of exchanges take place (this amounts to almost a quarter of US GDP). Most of the world currencies are not really traded, as explained in Box 18.5. The bulk of transactions involve a vehicle currency. Table 18.3 reports the percentage of trades that involve, on one side or another, the three main world currencies (the sum for all currencies would be 200 per cent since each transaction involves a pair of currencies). The share of the euro in 2010 is much smaller than the sum of the shares of its constituent currencies. This simply reflects the elimination of exchange rate transactions among the currencies that joined the Eurozone. Overall, the table reveals considerable stability. The pre-eminence of the dollar remains unchallenged.

Table 18.3 Currency composition of exchange trading volume (%)

	US dollar	Euro	Yen	Deutsch-mark	French franc	ECU and other ERM currencies	Pound sterling	Swiss franc
1992	82.0		23.4	39.6	3.8	11.8	13.6	8.4
1998	87.3		20.2	30.1	5.1	17.3	11.0	7.1
2010	84.9	39.1	19.0				12.9	6.4

Note: If all currencies were listed, the sum would be 200 per cent since each exchange involves two currencies.
Source: Triennial Central Bank Surveys, BIS

18.4.3 Store of value: bond markets

Large firms and governments borrow on the international markets by issuing long-term debt, i.e. bonds. This is an enormous market. Figure 18.11 shows that the share of bonds issued in euros has taken off following the launch of the euro. This is not very surprising in view of the market integration that has taken place, as explained in Section 18.3.2. Given the recent turmoil, however, it is not surprising either that the share of euro-denominated bonds has declined. Interestingly, the City of London has become the leading marketplace for this instrument whereas New York seems uninterested.

18.4.4 Store of value: international reserves

All national central banks hold foreign exchange reserves to underpin trust in their currencies and, if need be, to intervene on foreign exchange markets. Currencies appropriate for this role of store of value must be widely traded; they must also be perceived as having long-term stability. Figure 18.12 shows that the euro has made some progress since its creation, but the dollar seems firmly entrenched as the leading currency.

European countries at the periphery of the Eurozone (including the UK) are gradually replacing dollars with euros. A number of developing countries have also announced their intention to do so, largely for political reasons. Recently, various Asian authorities, including China, who accumulated vast reserves in dollars, have diversified into the euro.

Why should the euro eat into the dollar's market share? Besides politics, central banks are traditionally unwilling to change the currency composition of their reserves. In particular, large-scale sales of dollars could precipitate a depreciation of the US currency with two adverse effects: the depreciation would alter international competition in trade and it would create losses for

---

Box 18.5   Vehicle currencies

Each transaction must involve two currencies. Since there exist more than 180 currencies in the world, there are about 16,000 bilateral exchange rates.[1] If all these bilateral rates were traded, most of them (think of the exchange rate between the Samoan tala and the Honduran lempira) would involve very few trades, resulting in a host of shallow, hence inefficient and volatile, markets. This is why foreign exchange markets use the property of triangular arbitrage to considerably reduce the number of currency pairs that are traded.

The idea is simple and illustrated in Fig. 18.10. Consider two currencies, A and B, and their bilateral exchange rate, e_{AB}. Currency A has an exchange rate vis-à-vis the dollar, $e_{A\$}$, and so does currency B, $e_{B\$}$. Once these two rates are known, the bilateral rate can be found as $e_{AB} = e_{A\$} / e_{B\$}$. In this example, the dollar is used as a currency vehicle and the implied bilateral rate e_{AB} is called a cross-rate. In practice, cross-rates are rarely traded and very few currencies are used internationally.

Figure 18.10 Triangular arbitrage

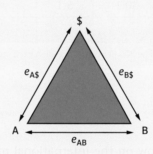

[1] With n currencies, there exist $n(n-1)/2$ bilateral exchange rates. Here, $16,110 = (180 \times 179)/2$.

---

dollar-holders, including for the central banks themselves. This is why, even if the euro may be an attractive store of value, a major shift would require a serious deterioration in the dollar's own quality as a store of value. For example, Fig. 18.12 shows that the dollar's share dropped in the late 1970s when inflation rose in the USA. The financial crisis that originated in 2007 in the USA seems somehow to have dented the dollar's supremacy.

18.4.5 The euro as an anchor

When a country does not let its exchange rate float freely, it must adopt an anchor, a foreign currency to which its own currency is more or less rigidly tied. The anchor, which works as a unit of account, can be a single currency or a basket of currencies. The link can be deliberately vague – known as a managed float – or quite explicit, ranging from wide crawling bands to the wholesale adoption of a foreign currency (for details, see Chapter 14).

In 2007, out of some 100 currencies not classified as freely floating, 18 used the euro as an anchor in one way or another. Adding the countries of French-speaking countries that form their own currency unions and countries that use as anchor currency baskets that include the

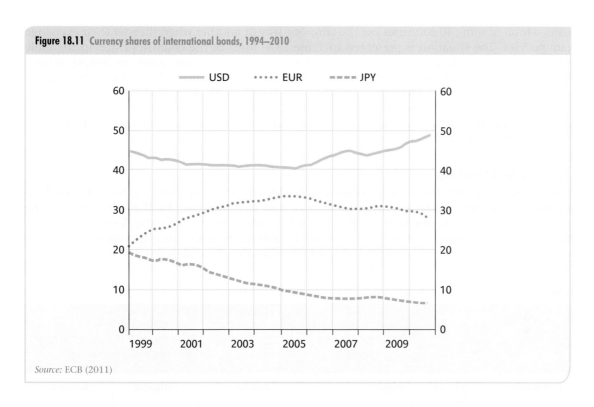

Figure 18.11 Currency shares of international bonds, 1994–2010

Source: ECB (2011)

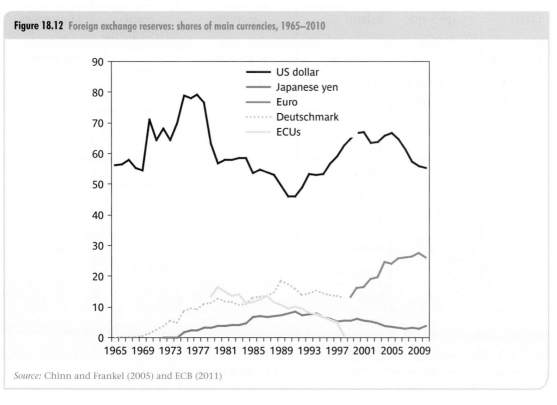

Figure 18.12 Foreign exchange reserves: shares of main currencies, 1965–2010

Source: Chinn and Frankel (2005) and ECB (2011)

euro, a total of some 40 countries use the euro one way or another when they set their exchange rate policies. The situation is presented in Table 18.4. Most of the countries listed in the table are geographically close to the Eurozone (central and eastern Europe, northern Africa) or have historical ties to one of its constituent legacy currencies (e.g. French-speaking Africa). Two former members of the Yugoslav Federation, Kosovo and Montenegro, have 'euroized', i.e. they have unilaterally adopted the euro as their own currency but are not part of the Eurosystem. Three countries operate a currency board tied to the euro, including two Baltic States (Latvia and Lithuania) that are ERM members.

18.4.6 Parallel currencies

Foreign currencies are also sometimes used alongside the domestic currency, fulfilling all three functions of means of payment, unit of account and store of value. Parallel currencies, as the phenomenon is called, emerge in troubled countries where the value of the domestic currency is eroded by very rapid inflation or political instability. In most cases, the parallel currency circulates in cash form, but a number of countries also allow bank deposits.

Table 18.4   Countries using the euro as an anchor (as of May 2011)

ERM 2	Peg to euro	Peg to basket including the euro	Managed floating with euro as referemce currency	Euro-based currency boards	Unilateral euroization
Denmark	CFA Franc Zone	Algeria	Croatia	Bulgaria	Kosovo
Latvia	Cape Verde	Belarus	Czech Rep.	Bosnia-Herzegovina	Montenegro
Lithuania	Comoros	Botswana	Macedonia		Micro states
	São Tomé e Principe	Fiji	Romania		
		Iran			
		Kuwait			
		Libya			
		Morocco			
		Russia			
		Samoa			
		Singapore			
		Syria			
		Tunisia			
		Vanuatu			

Note: The micro states are: Republic of San Marino, Vatican City, Principality of Monaco, Andorra.
Source: ECB (2011)

The dollar is the universal parallel currency of choice, but the Deutschmark circulated widely in central and eastern Europe and in Turkey, and the French franc used to circulate widely in northern Africa and parts of sub-Saharan Africa. In all these countries the euro has replaced the Deutschmark and the franc. The problem with the use of parallel currencies is that little is known about it, if only because this is highly informal and not captured by official statistics. The ECB estimates that some 107 billion euros – 13 per cent of all bank euro bank notes in circulation – are outside the Eurozone. As a comparison, the Federal Reserve estimates that 450 billion dollars are circulating outside the USA.

Another 'parallel' use of banknotes concerns illegal activities, both within and outside the country. A distinguishing feature of euros is that they exist in very large denominations, which makes it easy to pack vast amounts of money in a small suitcase. Figure 18.13 shows the use of available denominations of euros and dollars. The banknote of choice in the Eurozone (e.g. in ATMs) is the €50 denomination, larger than the $20 denomination that dominates in the USA. The figure also shows that large denominations represent a large share of total currency denomination in both the Eurozone and the USA.

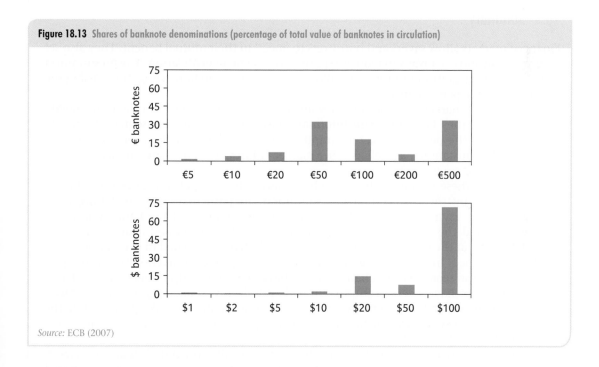

Figure 18.13 Shares of banknote denominations (percentage of total value of banknotes in circulation)

Source: ECB (2007)

18.4.7 Does it matter?

In the minds of some Europeans, the euro is challenging the supremacy of the dollar. Indeed, the dollar reigns supreme: it is the currency of choice for international trade; it is the first foreign currency that is held by individuals, corporations and central banks; and it is also the currency most widely used to denominate financial assets. The wish to displace the dollar is no doubt driven by political sentiment, but what about the economic advantages?

When international trade is invoiced in a foreign currency, importers and exporters face an exchange risk. Many months can elapse between the moment a commercial contract is undertaken and payment is made. In the intervening period, the exchange rate may change, imposing a risk on traders. They can purchase insurance (in the form of forward exchange contracts), but at a cost. US firms, which mostly carry out international transactions in dollars, thus enjoy some advantage.

In addition, 'greenbacks' are conspicuous all over the world. It is estimated that half of the dollars printed by the USA circulate outside its borders. Paper money is virtually costless to produce but, of course, it is not freely provided, being exchanged against goods, services or assets. The profit earned by the central bank, known as seigniorage, is a form of tax. When it is levied on residents, it is just one form of domestic taxation, but when levied on foreigners, it represents a real transfer of resources. The value of expatriate dollars is about 3 per cent of the US GDP – a nice sum. However, once we realize that it has been accumulated over several decades, it is not really a significant source of revenue.

All in all, the economic benefits of having a world currency are quite modest. This explains why the ECB considers that a possible international role for the euro is something that it should neither encourage nor discourage. Beyond some legitimate pride, it does not really care.

18.5 Summary

Financial markets allow savers and borrowers to 'meet' to their mutual benefit. They also set a price on risk and offer ways to reduce exposure to risk via diversification. The presumption is that market integration improves the allocation of saving and borrowing, thus raising the overall economic performance.

The financial markets are special. They are subject to economies of scale, they operate as networks and they face important information asymmetries. As a consequence, they do not conform to the perfect market assumption. In particular, they are prone to systemic instability. This instability, as well as other market failures, explains why financial systems are regulated and supervised.

Banks share these characteristics, which explains why competition does not take the form predicted by the perfect market assumption. In particular, large switching costs and information asymmetries explain why a deep restructuring of the banking industry has not followed the adoption of the euro. So far, bank mergers and acquisitions have occurred mostly at the national level; only a few banks have succeeded in expanding across borders. Differences in national regulations and some degree of protectionism on the part of supervisors also seem to limit changes. Plans have been drawn up to break this logjam.

Bond markets have been promptly unified, yet deeply shaken by the crisis. Stock markets, on the other hand, remain small. Some consolidation is taking place, but the largest European exchanges, including Europe's largest – London – remain undersized relative to New York or Tokyo.

The Eurozone, which has every reason to become a fully integrated financial market, remains broken along national barriers. Regulation and supervision remain a national prerogative, which has proven to be highly problematic during the crisis. While EU directives impose minimum standards for national regulation, supervisors have not shared crucial information and have intervened with a view to protect national institutions. This has led to an overhaul of regulation and supervision, partly strengthening collective oversight.

The effects of the launch of the euro are still under way, and depend on which market segment is considered. The euro has the potential to challenge the US dollar as an international currency, but old habits die hard and, despite some changes, the dollar's supremacy has not been seriously dented. The euro has made some progress in trade invoicing and bond issuance. At the periphery of the Eurozone, it plays a dominant role as anchor for local currencies and, possibly, parallel currency.

Self-assessment questions

1 What is depth in financial markets? What is breadth? What are network externalities?
2 What is the phenomenon of information asymmetry? How can it explain why banks refuse credit to some customers? How can it contribute to systemic risk in financial markets?
3 List the reasons why banks are subject to increasing returns to scale. Why do fixed switching costs matter for competition among banks?
4 How do we know that bond markets were unified in the Eurozone upon the launch of the euro? Why has this not happened for stock markets?
5 Explain how the three functions of money apply at the international level.
6 What is the phenomenon of gambling for resurrection? Why can it be lethal to financial markets?
7 What is the difference between regulation and supervision? What are the dangers of decentralized supervision in the Eurozone? Why is centralization resisted?
8 What are the changes to regulation and supervision put in place after the crisis?
9 In what sense is the euro slow in challenging the dollar supremacy?
10 What is the difference between a parallel and a vehicle currency?

Essay questions

1 Banks can expand through either organic growth (winning new customers) or mergers and acquisitions. How does this distinction matter for the single European banking market?
2 'The real reason why Eurozone countries can't agree on a single supervising agency is that each one wants to protect its own financial institutions.' Evaluate this view.
3 'The Great Crisis of 2007–08 has exposed the high degree of coordination of central banks and the division of governments.' Evaluate and comment.
4 Has the crisis clearly demonstrated that the Eurozone's system of regulation and supervision is ill adapted?
5 The largest dollar banknote denomination is $100, the largest euro denomination is €500. This has led some to suspect that Europe wants to capture the market of currencies used for illegal transactions. What is your view of this motive?
6 Comment on the quote from Rudi Dornbusch at the head of this chapter.
7 Finance is a major industry in the UK, accounting for some 5 per cent of its GDP. Does this characteristic make membership of the Eurozone rather more or less appealing?
8 'Will the euro displace the dollar as the world's leading currency over the next twenty years? Nah, the Chinese currency (the yuan) will.' Comment.

Further reading: the aficionado's corner

The De Larosière Report (2009) on the supervisory architecture of the Eurozone after the financial crisis, http://ec.europa.eu/internal_market/finances/docs/de_larosiere_report_en.pdf

The Lamfalussy Report (a 2001 report on measures to take to support further integration of European financial markets). Download from http://europa.eu.int/comm/internal_market/en/finances/general/lamfalussyen.pdf.

On the evolution of financial markets:

Baltzer, M., L. Cappiello, R. De Santis and S. Manganelli (2008) *Measuring Financial Integration in New EU Member States*, Occasional Paper No. 81, ECB.

Coeurdacier, N. and P. Martin (2007) *The Geography of Asset Trade and the Euro: Insiders and Outsiders*, Discussion Paper No. 6032, CEPR, London.

Lane, P. (2009) 'EMU and financial integration', in B. Mackowiak, F.P. Mongelli, G. Noblet and F. Smets (eds) *The Euro at Ten – Lessons and Challenges*, ECB.

Kalmli-Ozcan, S., S. Manganelli, E. Papaioannou and J.L.Peydro (2009) 'Financial integration, macroeconomic volaitility and risk-sharing – the role of the monetary union', in B. Mackowiak, F.P. Mongelli, G. Noblet and F. Smets (eds) *The Euro at Ten – Lessons and Challenges*, ECB.

On the international role of the euro, see:

Chinn, M. and J. Frankel (2005) *Will the Euro Eventually Surpass the Dollar as Leading International Reserve Currency?*, NBER Working Paper 11510. Download from www.nber.org/papers/w11510.

Lim, E.-G. (2006) *The Euro's Challenge to the Dollar: Different Views from Economists and Evidence from COFER (Currency Composition of Foreign Exchange Reserves) and Other Data*, Working Paper 06/153, International Monetary Fund.

Portes, R. (2008) *The International Role of the Euro: A Status Report*, European Economy – Economic Papers 317, European Commission.

Useful websites

Websites concerned with regulation and supervision:

Basel Committee on Banking Supervision: www.bis.org/bcbs/aboutbcbs.htm.

ECB–CFS research network: www.eu-financialsystem.org.

Financial Services Action Plan website, full of reports and legal texts: http://europa.eu.int/comm/internal_market/en/finances/actionplan/.

Financial Stability Institute (FSI): www.bis.org/fsi/index.htm.

References

Chinn, M. and J. Frankel (2005) *Will the Euro Eventually Surpass the Dollar as Leading International Reserve Currency?*, NBER Working Paper 11510. Download from www.nber.org/papers/w11510.

Claessens, S., R.J. Herring and D. Schoenmaker (2010) *A Safer World Financial System: Improving the Resolution of Systemic Institutions*, Geneva Reports on the World Economy 12, ICMB and CEPR.

Dornbusch, R. (2000) *Keys to Prosperity, Free Markets, Sound Money and a Bit of Luck*, MIT Press, Cambridge, MA.

ECB (2011) *Review of the International Role of the Euro*, European Central Bank, Frankfurt am Main.

Hartmann, P., A. Maddaloni and S. Manganelli (2003) 'The Eurozone financial system: structure, integration and policy initiatives', *Oxford Review of Economic Policy*, 19(1): 180–213.

Kamps, A. (2006) *The Euro as Invoicing Currency in International Trade*, Working Paper No. 665, ECB.

Pisani-Ferry, J and A. Sapir (2010) 'Banking crisis management in the EU: an early assessment', *Economic Policy* 62: 341–73.

Chapter 19

The Eurozone in crisis

> We knew that a storm was brewing but, admittedly, we did not know exactly where. Neither did we know what would trigger it, or when it would come.
>
> Jean-Claude Trichet, President of the ECB. Keynote address in Mackowiak et al. (2009)

Chapter Contents

Introduction

The Eurozone was just celebrating its first decade of existence when the global financial crisis that had started in 2007 morphed into a public debt crisis concentrated on the area. The second stage of the great crisis has not just marred the early achievements of the single currency. It has also revealed deep flaws in the construction of the Eurozone – described in earlier chapters. This concluding chapter looks at the crisis, which is bound to leave a profound imprint on the history of the monetary integration in Europe. Some expect the Eurozone to emerge tighter and stronger while others foresee a breakup, and possibly the end of the euro.

This chapter is being completed in October 2011, at a time of considerable uncertainty. New decisions are being announced every week and financial markets continuously bounce in various directions. The book will be published in mid-2012, and hopefully studied for a few years afterwards. We are keenly aware that 'the only sure thing about the future is that there is no sure thing', as the saying goes. The events of the past two years are most unlikely to be the end of the crisis. We know that we stand to be proven wrong unless we stick to just a list of what has happened so far. Yet, we believe that good economic analysis is useful to see through the foam of day-by-day news, so we venture some interpretations and we even try to decipher the likely course of events. We try to be careful, but we ask for the reader's understanding should many of the statements that we put forward prove to be incorrect.[1]

The first two sections describe and interpret, respectively, the two crises that have hit the Eurozone since 2007: the US-born financial crisis and the European sovereign debt crisis. Section 19.3 examines the efforts by the Eurozone authorities to end the sovereign debt crisis. So far at least, these efforts have not been successful; we explain why. Then, in Section 19.4 we look at the long run. The crisis has revealed a number of weaknesses in the construction of the Eurozone. We review various options to address these weaknesses.

19.1 Stage one: the global financial crisis

Between 2001, the year of the high-tech crisis, and 2007, the year of the financial crisis, the USA and much of the rest of the world enjoyed an unprecedented period of prosperity, the combination of sustained growth and declining inflation. The Great Moderation lasted longer and was more widespread than any previous cyclical upswing. Policy makers were quick to claim responsibility for this achievement, ignoring the silent build-up of tensions that have led to the worst economic crisis since the Great Depression. Knowledge of what had caused the Great Depression helped to contain the crisis that originated in the USA, but it led to rapid increases in public debts. This, in turn, set the stage for the second phase of the crisis, which has so far been concentrated in the Eurozone.

19.1.1 Financial deregulation

Following the Great Depression, for which US financial markets were blamed, strict regulation was designed to limit risk-taking by banks and financial institutions. The deregulation phase started in the 1980s and culminated in 1999 with the repeal of the Glass–Steagall Act of 1933. There followed a rapid expansion of the financial sector in the USA, and Europe soon followed with its own deregulation process associated with the Single European Act adopted in 1986 (although deregulation in Europe never went as far as in the USA).

---

[1] Debates since the crisis erupted have been intense. A good place to follow ongoing views and suggestions is the website VoxEU, which is run by Richard Baldwin and where we both write regularly, alongside some of the world's best economists (http://www.voxeu.org/).

A first result of deregulation was that banks developed activities not directly related to their traditional role of collecting deposits and making loans. Increasingly, banks became active investors themselves. In order to expand this lucrative activity, they borrowed globally and short-term to invest globally in long-term financial instruments. This created two mismatches. The maturity mismatch, between their short-term borrowings and long-term investments, meant that they had to continuously renew their borrowings; they became vitally dependent on their ability to do so. The currency mismatch, with borrowing and lending in different currencies, meant that they could run into difficulty should the value of their lending decline relative to the value of their borrowing because of exchange rate movements. Because ordinary customer deposits are crucial to everyday economic life, banks cannot just go bankrupt; if they fail, they must be bailed out. Banks were taking major risks but these risks were implicitly borne by their governments (and taxpayers). Avoiding this socialization of losses had been a key motivation of the Glass–Steagall Act, including restricting the banks to the dull – and not very profitable – business of deposit taking.

19.1.2 The subprimes and all that

Another aspect of this profound change concerned house mortgages in the USA. Keen to encourage individual homeownership, the US authorities adopted measures that made it possible and lucrative to lend to people long considered as a bad risk. As the Great Moderation was taking hold, and with it the perception that growth was sure to persist, bankers became less sensitive to risk. They approached people who until then could never hope to borrow[2] and offered the now-infamous subprime loans. These loans were very special.

They usually included an initially low interest rate that would be significantly increased after two or three years. This reassured low-income people, especially as the loans could be easily refinanced: when the interest rate was stepped up, a new loan would be granted to pay back the previous loan. Assuming that the price of the house had increased, the borrower could borrow even more, again at the initially low rate, and keep some cash after repaying the previous loan. Borrowers were led to expect that they could borrow again before the next step-up kicked in. Thus subprime mortgage lenders offered ever bigger loans to highly risky borrowers. Everyone loved this system, especially the US consumers who used houses like ATMs.[3]

This was possible as long as house prices kept increasing. Almost miraculously, prices did keep increasing. Abundant mortgage loans – both subprimes and others – fed strong purchases. House prices grew fast, doubling in five years as Fig. 19.1 shows. By the mid-2000s, a (very small) number of experts started to talk about a housing bubble, meaning that prices had gone far too high and would have to decline, quite a lot in fact.[4] The figure shows that, indeed, prices reached a plateau in April 2006 and started a rapid decline one year later. It then took two years for prices to find a floor.

Meanwhile, subprime borrowers became trapped. With houses worth less, they could not borrow as much as before, and certainly not enough to pay back the previous loan before interest rates rose. These higher interest payments proved impossible to honour for more and more people. The loans became 'delinquent', meaning that the lenders could not expect full repayment. The best that they could do was to foreclose the houses and sell them quickly. But prices were declining fast and sales were becoming difficult; in fact, foreclosures pushed prices further down. The lenders started to lose money.

---

[2] These people have been mischievously characterized as NINJAs (No Income, No Job or Address).

[3] A number of mortgage companies have since been prosecuted for deceptive selling practices. Some of them actually remunerated people who were bringing new clients, irrespective of their borrowing ability.

[4] Yale economist and co-author of *Irrational Exuberance*, Robert Shiller famously earned the nickname Mr Bubble in 2005: 'It's worthwhile to reflect that although home prices have gone up a lot in the recent years, they are just the same houses, right? There's no change in the services they provide. It's just the value we put on them. And so a house's value can just evaporate overnight, too. If people suddenly get very wary of investing in houses because they don't think the prices are going to go up or if they think they're going to fall, then that will cause home prices to fall.' http://www.npr.org/templates/story/story.php?storyId=4679264.

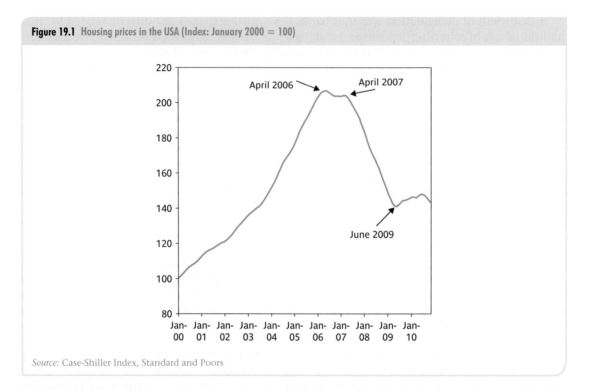

Figure 19.1 Housing prices in the USA (Index: January 2000 = 100)

Source: Case-Shiller Index, Standard and Poors

But who where the lenders? This is where things become complicated but interesting. Specialized mortgage companies sprang up during the years of the Great Moderation. They borrowed money, granted loans and promptly sold the loans to banks: the banks paid for the right to receive interest and capital as agreed in the loan contracts. This allowed the mortgage companies to lend again, and again, making a small profit each time. Banks that accumulated the loans, in turn, sold them to other banks; they enhanced their profits thanks to a process called securitization, which is presented in Box 19.1. The result of this process was that large banks, mostly in the USA and in Europe, ended up owning very many subprime mortgages in the form of securities. Many of these securities were attributed high ratings on the basis of the fact that, so far, very few subprime borrowers had defaulted on their loans, which is not surprising because house prices were rising.

Box 19.1   Securitization, or how to turn lead into gold

The securitization process consists in lumping together large amounts of individual mortgage loans, which are collectively less risky than any one taken separately, and then subdividing the package into 'tranches' that are organized hierarchically in such a way that some can be considered less risky than others. The process is illustrated in Fig. 19.2. The first box on the left represents a bank, typically a large one, which has bought a large number of loans from primary mortgage lenders. It will turn these loans into securities, (mistakenly) using the principle of risk diversification, according to which a large portfolio of loans is reasonably safer than the individual loans that it contains.

Figure 19.2 Securitization

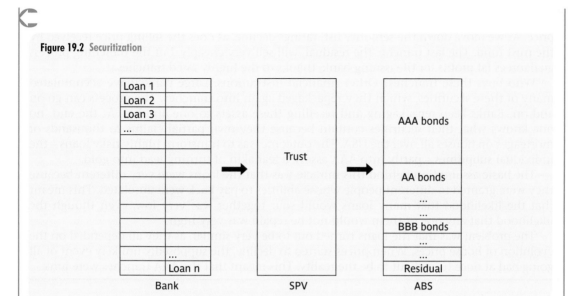

The process is managed by a trust fund, called a special purpose vehicle (SPV), which is a subsidiary of the bank. This fund owns the loans, each of which is a mortgage secured by a house. The fund then issues so-called asset-backed securities (ABS), which are titles of ownership to the loans. These ABS are structured in a very special way, called tranching. The overall process can be described in five steps:

1. Put together a large number of subprimes with the same maturity, worth a total of, say, $1 million. This is the trust fund. The value of the fund is backed by all the houses of all the borrowers.

2. Create a first security – i.e. a partial ownership of the trust find – worth $100,000. Call it Security One, and sell it with a promise that the total amount (capital and interest) will be paid back on maturity unless the total value of the fund drops to less than $900,000. This is called a senior tranche, because it is that part of the trust fund that will be reimbursed as a priority.

3. Now take another $100,000 and call it Security Two. Sell with the promise that it will be reimbursed after Security One and as long as the value of the fund exceeds $800,000. Security Two is junior to Security One and senior to all the rest.

4. Keep going on until you have issued securities that amount to $950,000.

5. Issue the last security, a claim to the last $50,000 in the trust fund. This is the most junior ABS, which will be fully paid only if the trust fund has made no loss. Any loss will be borne first by this last tranche. If the loss is exactly $50,000, the last ABS will be worth nothing. If the loss exceeds $50,000, say $70,000, the last security is worth nothing and the penultimate security will bear the remaining $20,000. And so on.

If one believes that most subprime loans will be paid back, the upper tranche can be considered as perfectly safe and it receives an AAA rating. It sells well, for a high price. The next tranche is also quite safe but its junior position justifies only an AA rating, still with a good selling price. As we move down the seniority list, ratings decline, as does the selling price received by the trust fund. The last tranche, the residual, will sell very cheaply, but the tranching process guarantees fat profits for the issuing bank, thanks to the highly rated tranches.

Who buys these tranches? Other financial institutions. Large banks have accumulated many of these securities, which they repackaged again into tranches. The process can go on and on. Banks keep repackaging and reselling these assets to one another. At the end, no one knows what their securities contain because they own partial claims to thousands of mortgages on houses all over the USA. The outcome was to transform highly risky loans – the individual subprimes – partly into AAA assets, a feat akin of turning lead into gold.

The basic assumption behind this miracle was that the loans were very different because they were granted to different people whose abilities to pay back were unrelated. This meant that the likelihood that many loans would sour together was very low, even though the likelihood that any one of them would not be repaid was very high.

The problem was that the loans turned out to be very similar, as they all depended on the evolution of house prices. When prices started to decline, the supposedly unlikely event of all going bad at once turned out to be the reality. This meant that the AAA tranches were junk.

19.1.3 Banks: meltdown and rescues

Once house prices stopped rising, things changed drastically. The diversification principle – each loan is special – turned into a hellish mechanism. Suddenly it was realized that a great many subprimes were likely to sour together. The best securities quickly lost their superb ratings. Many of the world's largest banks had eagerly played the subprime game; now they faced heavy losses and looked alarmingly fragile. These banks were mainly from the USA, the UK, France and Germany, because banks in other countries (Spain and Italy, for instance, as well as in Asia and Latin America) were instructed by their supervisors not to wade into such unknown business.

In April 2007, one of the largest US mortgage lenders, New Century Financial Corporation, declared bankruptcy. In July, one of the jewels of Wall Street, bank Bears Stearns, announced that it would stop honouring the commitments of one of its SPVs. When BNP Paribas did the same in August 2007, banks grew suspicious of one another and stopped their mutual lending that makes up the interbank market. The interbank market lies at the heart of the monetary system; it assures fluidity as it continuously moves around huge amounts of cash from one bank to another. Interbank markets froze in the USA and in other major financial centres around the world where large banks were active. Many banks could not find the cash that they needed for routine daily operations. Central banks scrambled to provide liquidity directly to their banks in the hope of maintaining normal banking operations.

For a while, things seemed to quieten down, but just below the surface trouble was brewing. As house prices quickly fell, loan delinquency rose and banks were facing losses. These losses were moderate – the US mortgage market is small relative to the world of finance – but banks were increasingly unable to operate. The world global banks are tightly linked to each other by myriads of mutual loans so that the chain is as weak as its weakest link. Between September 2007 and the spring of 2008, several major banks failed, including Britain's Northern Rock and Wall Street's Bears Stearns, which was taken over by JP Morgan Chase with the help of the US Treasury.

The failure of Lehman Brothers on 15 September 2008 triggered the worst financial crisis since 1929. The US authorities refused to bail this prestigious bank out because they considered that Lehman had taken huge but highly profitable risks, and they did not want taxpayers to pay for the consequences. It took a few hours to realize that Lehman owed considerable sums to nearly every financial institution that matters, both in the USA and in Europe.

Actively cooperating, central banks around the world scrambled to support their banks. They offered cash, they bought tons of securities – now called toxic assets – derived from mortgage loans, and they experimented with various innovative rescue measures. Within a few months, the US Federal Reserve Bank more than doubled the size of its balance sheet, while the ECB's own balance sheet increased by more than 50 per cent (Fig. 19.3), something never done before.

The contagion from the obscure subprime market, largely in the hands of hardly known, local mortgage-lending companies, to the largest financial establishments in both the USA and Europe is striking. As explained above, these large banks had been deeply involved in the securitization process, then seen as the apex of financial engineering. When the US housing market tumbled, they suffered moderate losses at first. But the subprime rout triggered chain effects largely because of a massive information asymmetry.[5] Because each major financial institution suspected that the others were suffering losses, they stopped trading with each other. Access to short-term borrowings, crucial to post Glass–Steagall banks as explained above (Section 19.1.1), dried up. Banks found themselves unable to honour their maturing borrowings. They were forced to sell some of their assets, quickly and at whatever price they could fetch. Fire sales, as this panic strategy is called, meant that a wide range of financial assets lost value, which triggered losses several times bigger than those directly linked to the subprime-backed securities. Interestingly,

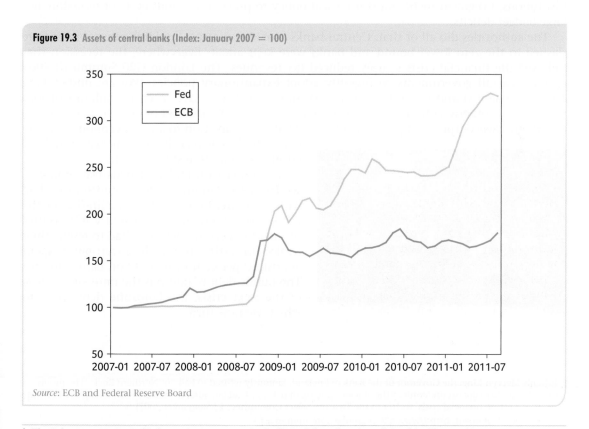

Figure 19.3 Assets of central banks (Index: January 2007 = 100)

Source: ECB and Federal Reserve Board

---

[5] The inherent presence of information asymmetries in financial markets is explained in Chapter 18.

Asian and Latin American banks, badly burnt in previous financial crises, had stayed out of the subprime business. This allowed them to ride the crisis relatively unscathed. This was a stunning turn of fortune.

Another channel of contagion affected some European countries. As in the USA, house price bubbles also occurred in Europe, including in Ireland, Spain and the UK. House prices stabilized and then started to decline at about the same time as in the USA. Although subprime-like mortgages are unlawful in Europe, many banks or mortgage lenders found themselves overextended and faced mounting losses. Lenders like Northern Rock in the UK, Allied-Irish in Ireland and numerous Spanish Cajas (regional saving and loan banks) in Spain had to be rescued.

19.1.4 Avoiding a new Great Depression

When house prices peaked in the USA and it emerged that the subprime construction would crumble, the authorities – governments and central banks – were more exasperated than concerned. They resented what they saw as reckless risk taking and, above all, market statements that the crisis would get deeper until troubled banks were bailed out.[6] Yet, they soon remembered the lessons learned from the Great Depression: (1) large financial institutions – called systemic, because their failures can drag the whole financial system and the economy into a tailspin – must be rescued; (2) deep distress in the financial system is soon followed by a profound and long-lasting recession; (3) central banks must provide liquidity to the financial system and adopt sharply expansionary policies; (4) governments must bail out banks and other financial institutions; (5) governments must use fiscal policy to prevent a vicious cycle of recession and large budget deficits.

The authorities did all of that. Central banks provided massive liquidity, interest rates were slashed to the zero lower bound and banks were kept afloat. Everywhere, the recession that followed the financial crisis sharply reduced tax revenues. The London G20 Summit in 2009 called upon all governments to urgently adopt expansionary policies: 'We are undertaking an unprecedented and concerted fiscal expansion, which will save or create millions of jobs which would otherwise have been destroyed, and that will, by the end of next year, amount to $5 trillion, raise output by 4 per cent, and accelerate the transition to a green economy. We are committed to deliver the scale of sustained fiscal effort necessary to restore growth.'[7]

The impact on budget deficits was dramatic, see Fig. 19.4. Among the few countries that had paid great attention to fiscal discipline before the crisis, Ireland and Spain apparently lost control of their budgets. In fact, they had to rescue their banks; in 2010, the Irish government spent almost 30 per cent of its GDP on bank bailouts. The public debt build-up is the immediate cause of the next crisis, the Eurozone debt crisis, to which we now turn.

---

[6] Initially Mervyn King, the Governor of the Bank of England, famously refused to bail out Northern Rock: 'The provision of such liquidity support undermines the efficient pricing of risk. . . . That encourages excessive risk-taking and sows the seeds of a future financial crisis' (Letter to the Treasury Select Committee, 12 September 2007).

[7] G20 Leaders Statement. http://www.g20.org/pubcommuniques.aspx.

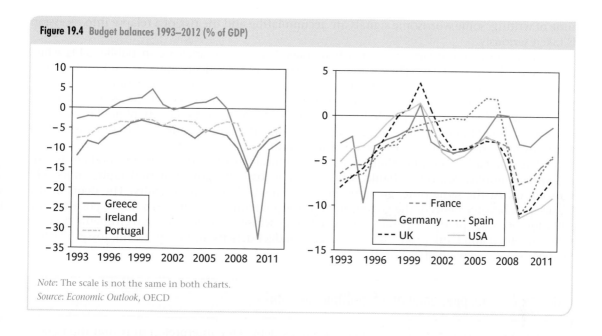

Figure 19.4 Budget balances 1993–2012 (% of GDP)

Note: The scale is not the same in both charts.
Source: *Economic Outlook*, OECD

19.2 Stage two: the public debt crisis in the Eurozone

19.2.1 The legacy of the financial crisis: the Great Paradox

If the goal was to return quickly to positive growth, by mid-2011 things looked good, as Fig. 19.5 shows. The recession has been deep but relatively short-lived by previous standards. Yet, at the

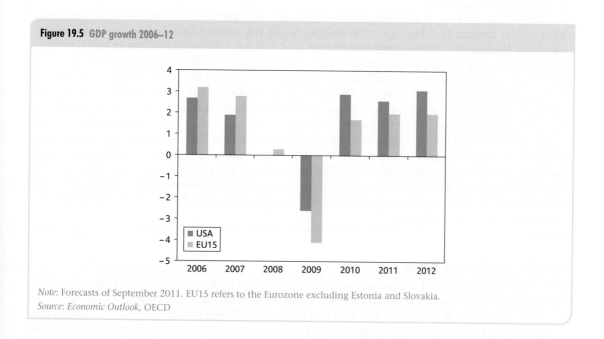

Figure 19.5 GDP growth 2006–12

Note: Forecasts of September 2011. EU15 refers to the Eurozone excluding Estonia and Slovakia.
Source: *Economic Outlook*, OECD

time of writing, some worrisome signals are accumulating and the risk of a relapse into recession is taken seriously.

Negative growth and large budget deficits have led to a fast increase in public debts when measured as a ratio to GDP. (This is the right measure, because debts must be paid for by taxes, and taxes are essentially levied on the incomes that make up the GDP.) The result is an amazing paradox: the financial crisis has led governments to run considerable budget deficits, but the deficits have led financial markets to become worried about the sustainability of public finances.

In fact, governments and banks are tied in a very deep way. Banks hold bonds issued by their governments because, traditionally, these bonds are considered as safe. They are used on the interbank market and in exchanges with the central bank because they are 'good assets'. An unexpected implication is that banks will suffer large losses if a government defaults on its debt obligations. At the same time, governments must rescue banks in difficulty. The debts of the banks then become debts of the government. If the government itself is in a fragile position, the situation becomes pretty desperate. To make things worse, in a recession governments become more indebted and bank profits decline. Bigger budget deficits and deeper bank losses create a vicious cycle, as explained in Box 19.2.

Box 19.2   The phenomenon of multiple equilibria

Why did markets start to worry about the Greek debt? One interpretation is that the rapid deterioration of public finances, after decades of neglect, convinced the markets that Greece could not honour its public debt. In addition, the 'discovery' by the new government of debts hidden by its predecessor contributed to market alarm.

An alternative interpretation is that market participants started to worry about what could happen if other market participants were worried. They realized that the Greek government could have to pay a higher interest rate to keep borrowing and the cost of servicing the debt could rise quickly, adding to the deficit. This would trigger further interest rate increases, larger deficits, and so on.

The subtle, but crucial difference between the two interpretations is that the first considers that a debt default had become unavoidable while the second one implies that the crisis occurred because the markets worried that it could occur, not really because it had become unavoidable. The second interpretation thus involves a self-fulfilling prophecy. It recognizes that there are (at least) two possibilities: (1) markets worry and the crisis occurs; (2) markets remain sedate and the debt level is not considered as lethal. This is referred to as a case of multiple equilibria: a crisis may or may not occur, depending on what markets worry about.

Multiple equilibria cannot be proven or disproven because they happen only when there is a reason for markets to worry. There is always a cause, but the cause may not be serious enough to make the crisis unavoidable. Multiple equilibria reflect the fact that the financial markets are driven by expectations of the future. They are suspected in numerous crises. Perhaps Lehman did not have to fail? It may be that it failed because other banks refused to lend cash to Lehman, because they feared that Lehman could fail. Ex post, Lehman was surely bankrupt, but beforehand?

19.2.2 Greece: crisis and bailout

By late 2007, the public debt of Greece stood at 105 per cent of GDP, more or less the same as in 2000. It was a large amount, but for a long time markets did not express particular concern about it, at least if we look at Fig. 13.2. By late 2009, the debt had jumped to 127 per cent of GDP. This is when views among financial market participants shifted. Figure 13.2 shows that this is when the interest rate faced by the Greek government, long quasi-identical to the German bond rate, started to rise. While one may quibble whether the Greek government could honour its debt at the pre-crisis interest rate, there is little doubt that borrowing at a 10 per cent rate, then 15 and 20 per cent, imposes an unbearable debt burden. By early 2010, the Greek government was facing a desperate situation.

When a government finds itself unable to borrow, or only at punitive rates, the normal solution is to apply to the International Monetary Fund (IMF) for emergency assistance. The IMF provides loans under conditions that require the government to take remedial action. Promptly reducing a budget deficit under IMF monitoring is painful, but the alternative, to completely stop the deficit for lack of any financing, is even more painful. A particularity of IMF lending is that it is arranged through the central bank, following a letter of agreement signed by the Finance Minister. Greece's central bank is part of the Eurosystem (see Chapter 16) and the ECB publicly voiced opposition to an IMF intervention in Eurozone affairs. In line with Eurozone governments, the ECB promoted a purely European solution. After several announcements of increasingly larger financial packages failed to sway the markets, in May 2010 the European Council decided a joint IMF–EU–ECB (called Troika) rescue operation. It also created a new institution, the European Financial Stability Facility (EFSF), designed to deal with other similar cases should they arise.

Greece was offered a €110 billion loan under conditions set and monitored by the Troika. The conditions emphasized public spending cuts and enhanced tax revenues, as well as a bevy of structural – i.e. supply side – reforms aiming at boosting competitiveness. But a fiscal contraction acts fast while supply-side reforms take years to produce their effects. Unsurprisingly, one year later the Greek economy was gripped in a severe recession, its tax revenues were falling, the deficit situation was not seriously improved and Greece needed fresh money. The Troika declared itself disappointed and requested stronger measures in exchange for a new €100 billion loan. Many expect that Greece will have to restructure its debt anyway, meaning that it will default partially.

19.2.3 Contagion inside the Eurozone

The bailout of Greece in May 2010 was a turning point. The official reason for a decision that may be incompatible with the Treaty (see Box 19.3) was that it would avoid highly dangerous contagious effects. This goal proved elusive. Ireland received its own loan of €85 billion from the EFSF and the IMF in November 2010. Portugal followed suit with a €78 billion loan in May 2011. As indicated above, Greece came back for a fresh new loan in the summer of 2011.

Box 19.3   Do the country bailouts violate the Treaty?

Two articles of the European Treaty were interpreted as making it impossible for the ECB and governments ever to lend directly to Eurozone governments. The idea was to buttress fiscal discipline and warn governments that they would have to fend for themselves (e.g. by applying to the IMF for emergency assistance) if they found themselves unable to borrow from financial markets, banks and individuals. The first article concerns the ECB:

> *Article 123(1): Overdraft facilities or any other type of credit facility with the European Central Bank or with the central banks of the Member States (hereinafter referred to as 'national central banks') in favour of Union institutions, bodies, offices or agencies, central governments, regional, local or other public authorities, other bodies governed by public law, or public undertakings of Member States shall be prohibited, as shall the purchase directly from them by the European Central Bank or national central banks of debt instruments.*

The second article concerns governments and the Commission:

"Article 125(1): The Union shall not be liable for or assume the commitments of central governments, regional, local or other public authorities, other bodies governed by public law, or public undertakings of any Member State, without prejudice to mutual financial guarantees for the joint execution of a specific project. A Member State shall not be liable for or assume the commitments of central governments, regional, local or other public authorities, other bodies governed by public law, or public undertakings of another Member State, without prejudice to mutual financial guarantees for the joint execution of a specific project."

This prescription was widely called the no-bailout clause. The official answer was to invoke the solidarity principle from yet another article:

"Article 122
1. Without prejudice to any other procedures provided for in the Treaties, the Council, on a proposal from the Commission, may decide, in a spirit of solidarity between Member States, upon the measures appropriate to the economic situation, in particular if severe difficulties arise in the supply of certain products, notably in the area of energy.
2. Where a Member State is in difficulties or is seriously threatened with severe difficulties caused by natural disasters or exceptional occurrences beyond its control, the Council, on a proposal from the Commission, may grant, under certain conditions, Union financial assistance to the Member State concerned. The President of the Council shall inform the European Parliament of the decision taken."

The other official argument is that the ECB has not lent directly to governments but only bought existing debt on financial markets, as authorized by Article 123. Neither have governments become 'liable for or assume(d) commitments' of other governments as forbidden by Article 125; they only offered loans. Yet large ECB bond purchases are not in the spirit of the no-bailout clause and, by lending to governments that may default, the lenders have made some commitments.

The German Constitutional Court has been asked to rule on the decision. In September 2011, it formally stated that the bailouts were not violating the German constitution but asked for more parliamentary control. It did not specifically address the case of the European Treaty. French ministers have offered their own evaluation. Europe Minister Pierre Lellouche stated: 'It is expressly forbidden in the treaties by the famous no bail-out clause. De facto, we have changed the treaty',[1] while Finance Minister Christine Lagarde (a professional lawyer) said: 'We violated all the rules because we wanted to close ranks and really rescue the euro zone. . . . The Treaty of Lisbon was very straightforward. No bailout.'[2]

[1] *Financial Times*, 27 May 2010.
[2] Reuters, http://www.reuters.com/article/2010/12/18/us-france-lagarde-idUSTRE6BH0V020101218.

19.2.4 Why contagion within the Eurozone?

The contagion within the Eurozone is highly troubling. Figure 19.6, which looks at the OECD countries, shows that public indebtedness is not enough to explain why these countries, and not others, have faced the wrath of the financial markets. Ireland, for instance, has been one of the most fiscally disciplined countries in the EU (see Fig. 19.4). As explained above, its public finances deteriorated suddenly when a massive banking crisis was met with a government rescue.

Portugal was seen as a country with a poor fiscal discipline record and low growth prospects, suggesting that it would be difficult to reduce its public indebtedness soon. Greece, Ireland and Portugal clearly suffer from serious weaknesses, but many other developed countries are in a delicate situation too. The multiple equilibria interpretation of crises, presented in Box 19.2, suggests that it just so happened that markets focused their attention on these three countries; given their weaknesses, they were unable to turn the tide.

But why did the crisis spread only to Eurozone countries? One answer is that the crisis is not over and could well spread outside the area. Another answer is that, in this kind of situation, membership of a monetary union may be a weakness. Countries with their own currencies have a national central bank that may help their governments. For instance, the US Federal Reserve has acquired a large amount of the Federal debt as part of its efforts to restart growth. Financial markets may have been reassured that the Fed would not stand idle if the debt crisis were to

Figure 19.6 Public debts in 2009 (% of GDP)

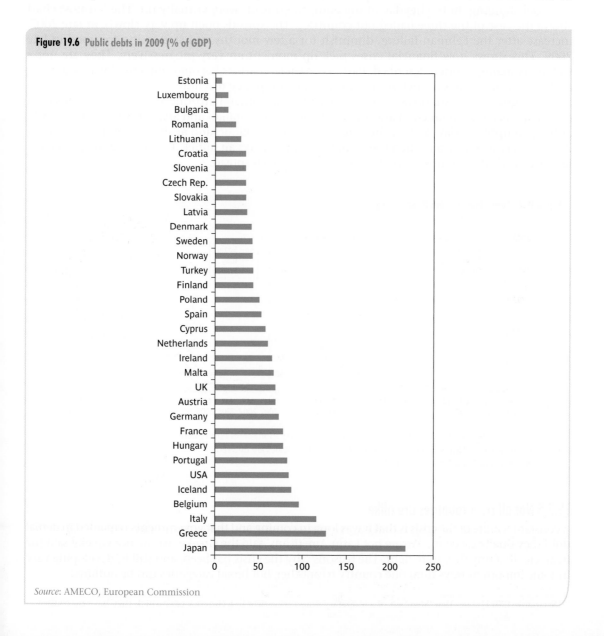

Source: AMECO, European Commission

cross the Atlantic. In the Eurozone, the ECB is admittedly more distant from any member country and has repeatedly stated that it has no inclination towards helping out governments – or their successors – that it considers guilty of fiscal indiscipline.[8] Yet another answer is that the creation of the EFSF, intended to prevent contagion, has had the exact opposite effect. By indicating a willingness to bail out countries subject to market pressure, the authorities may have inadvertently encouraged the markets to focus attention on the Eurozone. Finally, it could be that the situation has been made worse because of mistaken policy choices, as discussed in Section 19.3.

At the time of writing, other Eurozone countries already face some disquieting market pressure. Figure 19.7 displays the spreads of various government bond rates over the German bond rate. In order to interpret this figure, note that markets demand higher interest rates the more they feel a government might not fully honour its borrowing commitments. Under the assumption that German bonds are perfectly safe, the spreads are a good measure of a country's financial standing. In the heyday of the euro, the spreads were virtually nil. The leftmost chart shows the case of the three bailed-out countries. The spreads open up very slowly in late 2007, increase after the Lehman failure, diminish for a few months and start rising for good in late 2009. This shows how financial crises pick up momentum very progressively. They are not a sudden tsunami, as often described. Rather, financial markets become concerned very gradually and their concern rises as they see no, or insufficient, policy reaction.

The rightmost chart shows the spreads of some other Eurozone countries, which could eventually become engulfed in another contagious wave. Italian and Spanish spreads rise slowly at first, abruptly in May 2010 at the time of the Greek bailout, and again during the summer of 2011. This is also the time when the French spread displays an uptick. Comparing the two charts leaves us with the impression that contagion could well spread.

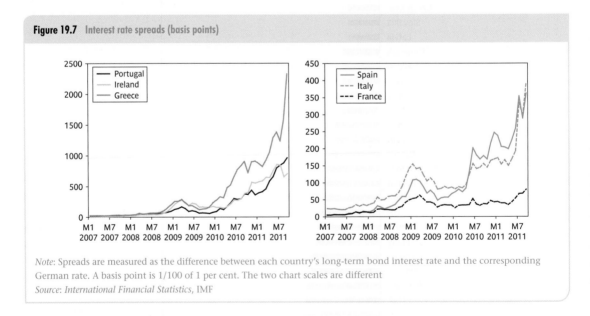

Figure 19.7 Interest rate spreads (basis points)

Note: Spreads are measured as the difference between each country's long-term bond interest rate and the corresponding German rate. A basis point is 1/100 of 1 per cent. The two chart scales are different

Source: *International Financial Statistics*, IMF

19.2.5 Not all crisis countries are alike

A constant feature of the crisis is that it was long in coming and that governments remained in denial until they finally caved in. 'We are not Latin Americans' said the Greeks; 'we are not Greeks' said the Irish, etc. In a way they were right. The reasons why the crisis has been, and still is, developing vary in some important ways from one country to another, but broad categories can be outlined.

---

[8] De Grauwe (2011) states that 'Members of a monetary union issue debt in a currency over which they have no control.'

Some countries have a poor history of fiscal discipline, as illustrated in Fig. 17.3. Markets doubted that Greece and Portugal could still add debt to an already high mountain without eventually defaulting. Greece came first probably because a new government promptly revealed that the accounts of its predecessor were not truthful.

Ireland and Spain, on the other hand, had displayed an impressive degree of fiscal discipline. The problem came from the banking systems. Both countries had allowed fast bank credit expansion to feed a house price bubble. When the bubble burst, the bank loans quickly soured. All large Irish banks needed a bailout, leading the government to inject 30 per cent of GDP in 2010. Markets may have trusted the Irish government to roll back this sudden debt increase, but they were worried that this could not be the end of the story. Indeed, in a now-classic erroneous move, the Irish government did not just guarantee all bank deposits, it also guaranteed all bank liabilities. The potential costs of this guarantee were unknown, in fact immeasurable. The resulting massive uncertainty triggered the crisis. The size of the eventual cost of bank bailouts is also the reason why Spain is on the endangered list.

Some other countries exhibit some of these features to a lesser extent. For a decade, Italy had managed to stabilize its public debt at about 110 per cent of GDP. It did not let it grow much during the crisis, in fact relying on expansionary fiscal policies elsewhere to contain the recession. Was this a sign of fiscal discipline? Not quite, because the debt remains very large and has not been reduced in better years. Italian banks have not accumulated subprime-based assets – they were not allowed to by the central bank – nor has there been any house price bubble. But Italy is not growing, which is a source of fragility for banks and makes debt reduction difficult. This is why Italy is also in the danger zone.

France has a poor record of fiscal discipline (Table 17.3) but its debt is comparatively moderate. It has undergone a house price bubble, but the bubble has not (yet?) burst. Its banks have accumulated toxic assets and the clean-up is far from complete. Germany shares with France the problem of banks badly hit as a result of the US subprime crisis and not thoroughly cleaned up. Its reputation as a fiscally disciplined country may not be fully justified by the history of the past two decades, but it is buttressed by the adoption in 2009 of a constitutional zero-budget rule (see Section 19.4.1). Belgium too has a problem with its banks and, like Italy, it has a lingering huge public debt. These are in-between countries, which could be pushed into the danger zone if their circumstances deteriorate.

19.3 Dealing with the crisis: short-term policy responses

The financial markets have continuously warned policy makers that determined action was needed to stop the debt crisis. Much like before the eventual collapse of Lehman Brothers, they have asked for a comprehensive solution. Policy responses have been partial and half-hearted, with a growing rift within the Eurozone. Market doubts concern the strategy of imposing fiscal restraints in the midst of a severe recession, the limited resources and tools of the EFSF, the situation of European banks and the role of the ECB.

19.3.1 Why do financial markets fret?

The financial markets worry that some governments might be led to partly repudiate their public debts, imposing losses on investors. They also worry about wider repercussions, including bank failures and a possible breakup of the Eurozone. More than anything, however, markets hate uncertainty. In that respect, the policy responses have had a deleterious effect on financial markets, which in return have increased the pressure on governments. Many of the step increases in interest spreads (Fig. 19.7) can be traced back to policy decisions that markets perceived as 'too little, too late'. A good example is the creation of the EFSF in May 2010, which was meant to 'shock and awe' the financial markets. Governments announced that they had put together a package worth €750 billion. In addition to the €440 billion of the EFSF, they included €60 billion to come from the European Commission and €250 billion from the IMF. It quickly transpired that the €440 billion really meant €250 billion (see Section 19.3.3), that the Commission could not really provide €60 billion (about half of its annual budget) and that the IMF makes no ex ante commitment. The markets interpreted this as an indication that governments were either not aware of the risks ahead or that they were unwilling to recognize them. They concluded that crisis would be left to fester.

19.3.2 Fiscal policy strategy

The response to the Greek crisis has become a template for the other countries. In cooperation with the IMF – which so far has never co-organized emergency lending – the EU has provided a loan to cover about one year of budgetary needs. As with all IMF loans, stiff conditions have been attached; the innovation is that these conditions were negotiated with the Troika, not the IMF alone. The conditions call for cuts in public expenditures, tax increases and a host of structural requirements designed to improve the performance of the economy: a reduction of the size of the civil service along with wage reductions, the privatization of state-owned companies, improvement of tax collection, elimination of closed-shop professions, pension reform and much more.

The wisdom of requiring fiscal austerity when the economy is in recession, however, was met with some scepticism. Would not fiscal austerity prevent a return to positive growth? Table 19.1 presents the standard multi-year forecasts produced by the IMF at the time of the May 2010 agreement and those from July 2011, following the annual review of the situation. Also included are new forecasts for GDP growth produced in September 2011. Each time, growth is revised downward. Unsurprisingly, the expected worsening of the situation feeds into a disappointing outcome for the budget. Further disappointments are likely in the case of Portugal, exposing a tendency to ignore the contractionary impact of the policies requested from these countries. This is an additional reason for markets to fret and for the crisis to deepen and spread.

Table 19.1   IMF forecasts for Greece

	Real GDP growth				
	2009	2010	2011	2012	2013
May 2010	−2	−4	−2.6	1.1	2.1
July 2011		−4.5	−3.9	0.6	2.1
September 2011		−4.5	−5	−2	
	Budget balance				
	2009	2010	2011	2012	2013
May 2010	−13.6	−8.1	−7.6	−6.5	−4.9
July 2011		−10.4	−7.6	−6.5	−4.8

Source: IMF

19.3.3 The European Financial Stability Facility

The creation of the EFSF was meant to provide policy makers with readily available resources in case of contagion. Initially, the EFSF was allowed to borrow and lend €440 billion. The borrowing is guaranteed by all Eurozone member countries, some of which are perceived as healthy while others are likely candidates for a rescue at some point down the road. As a confidence-building instrument, it was decided that the EFSF should be rated AAA. Concerned by the threat of contagion among the facility's guarantors, the rating agencies requested that only €250 billion of the €440 billion borrowed be available for lending, the remaining being kept as a guarantee. Once Ireland and Portugal were granted EFSF assistance, this amount proved to be insufficient to meet possible needs by large countries like Italy and Spain. In addition, the EFSF was restricted initially to lending directly to countries, excluding the purchase of existing debts.

These limitations led to a July 2011 decision to increase the lending power up to €440 billion and to give the EFSF more flexibility, allowing purchases of existing public debts as well as contributions to bank bailouts. Even so, the resources are still seen by critics as short of potential needs, prompting new discussions under way at the time of writing. In addition, in September 2011, Germany's Constitutional Court ruled that the Bundestag must first approve any new loan by Germany to the EFSF; this may seriously restrict the facility's newly won flexibility.

The EFSF's bumpy road reflects a number of difficulties. It does not make grants – it only lends with interest – but the fact that some loan recipients are seen as potential defaulters means that the EFSF is taking risks. These risks are fundamentally borne by all the countries that contribute to the facility. Fiscally disciplined countries are reluctant to take on these risks. This is important, because the scale of the EFSF is small in comparison with the public debts of potential borrowers: Italy's debt, for instance, amounts to some €1900 billion. This is why increasing the size of the EFSF significantly faces mounting opposition in some countries. The result is growing anxiety on the financial markets.

19.3.4 European banks

It is normal for banks to hold sizeable amounts of their government's debt. These bonds are used as collateral to present to the central bank to obtain the cash needed for everyday business. As a result, Greek banks hold large amounts of Greek government debt, German banks hold German public debt, Italian banks hold Italian public debt, etc. The result is that doubts about any government's ability to service its debt instantly translate into doubts about the health of national banks. This is a channel of crisis contagion from public debts to banks, as already mentioned.

Chapter 18 presents evidence of the increasing integration of European bond markets following the creation of the euro. As a result, banks have acquired the public debts of other Eurozone countries, quite naturally since these bonds are in euros and they are accepted by the ECB. The unintended result is that doubts about a Eurozone government's ability to service its debt instantly translate into doubts about the health of banks across the monetary union. This is a channel for crisis contagion across countries.

The public debt crisis has therefore instilled doubts about banks. Governments have reacted by denying the link. Facing deep market scepticism, they have resorted to stress tests, following similar tests carried out in the USA, which identified a few weak banks but cleared concerns about most others. In Europe, the newly created European Banking Authority (EBA) was tasked with carrying out the tests.[9]

Stress tests are simulations carried out by banks under the control of their supervising authority. The banks are asked to report the effect on their books of various stressing events, which are bound to imply losses. A first wave of stress tests was carried out in 2010. The results identified six banks as failing the test and therefore in need of recapitalization. Importantly, the stress did not include any risk of sovereign default. If anything, these tests raised the level of market anxiety because they were seen as proof that the governments, which specified the events to be simulated, were first and foremost interested in 'proving' that banks are healthy. A second wave was carried out a year later and released in July 2011, just when the public debt crisis was worsening, as illustrated in Fig. 19.7. This time, the risk of a sovereign default was

---

[9] The EBA is presented in Chapter 18.

included in the simulations, but the size of the default (15 per cent) was seen as much too small at a time when Greek debt was selling at half its value. Again, most banks were deemed in good health, including Dexia, which failed for the second time in early October.

The perception that governments have been overly protective of their national banks has raised the spectre of Japan's 'lost decade'. As explained in Box 19.4, the protective attitude of Japanese authorities following a house price bubble in the early 1990s has cost the country two decades of low growth. In August 2011, Christine Lagarde, the new Managing Director of the IMF and former French Finance Minister – presumably well aware of the situation of French banks – stated that 'banks need urgent recapitalization. They must be strong enough to withstand the risks of sovereigns and weak growth. This is key to cutting the chains of contagion. If it is not addressed, we could easily see the further spread of economic weakness to core countries, or

---

Box 19.4 Japan's lost decade(s)

Much like China today, Japan achieved impressively high growth rates in the 1950s and 1960s, as a poor and war-torn country became a rich economic powerhouse that established brand names like Toyota, Sony and Matsushita. Much like China in the future, growth remained high but slowed down in the 1970s and 1980s as Japan was catching up with the most advanced countries in terms of technology and productive equipment. This is the normal growth catch-up process. What the Japanese called the lost decade of the 1990s has now become two decades of near-zero growth over the 1990s and 2000s, as Table 19.2 shows.

Table 19.2 GDP growth and inflation rates in Japan (average percent per annum)

	Growth	Inflation
1960–69	10.1	5.4
1970–79	5.2	9.0
1980–89	4.4	2.6
1990–99	1.5	1.2
2000–09	0.7	–0.3

Source: Economic Outlook, OECD

This did not have to happen. Following the bursting of a house price bubble fed by reckless mortgage loans, the Japanese authorities reacted by bringing the interest rate to zero and by adopting strongly expansionary fiscal policies. It did not work because a string of weak governments did not force near-bankrupt banks to restructure. 'Zombie banks', as they were called, were unable and unwilling to lend. As a result, monetary policy was unable to restart the economy, since it mostly operates through bank credit. Anyway, with a negative inflation rate, even a zero interest rate is not expansionary. More surprising is the ineffectiveness of fiscal policy; maybe it was not expansionary enough to counteract the paucity of bank credit. The result is that the Japanese public debt, above 200 per cent of GDP by 2011, is the world's highest.

even a debilitating liquidity crisis.'[10] The initial reaction in Europe was one of outrage. By early October 2011 (at the time of writing), Eurozone governments are reportedly preparing a bank recapitalization process.

19.3.5 Will the Eurozone break up?

Having observed the weaknesses of the euro construction, a number of people have concluded that the Eurozone is doomed. Several arguments have been presented to back up this claim. First, the failure to establish fiscal discipline throughout the monetary union – both the ineffectiveness of the Stability and Growth Pact and the loss of the no-bailout clause – means that countries with strong positions have good reasons to leave in order to avoid having to pay for those that have let their debts grow to the point where they can no longer honour them. Second, the countries with high debts need to grow fast to generate tax revenues. In general, defaulting countries undergo a sharp exchange rate depreciation, which provides the demand boost that they need to recover and grow. Third, the crisis has exposed a gap between a well-functioning North and a badly wounded South. Solidarity between these groups has been strained. Fourth, many international investors do not believe that the euro can survive. Whether they are right or not, this is a self-fulfilling process that will not stop, as explained in Box 19.2. Finally, Europe is not an optimum currency area (see Chapter 15). It was an experiment doomed to failure.

Arguments in the opposite direction are also powerful. First, a breakup of the Eurozone would have catastrophic implications. Some countries would face a deep depreciation which would make it difficult or even impossible to honour public and private debts contracted in euros. The precedent of Argentina (see Box 19.5), illustrates how disturbing the situation can become. The other countries would face a strong appreciation, which would severely hurt their international competitiveness and trigger similar uncertainty regarding debts in euros. Second, a new currency would have to be printed and reintroduced. It took three years to introduce the euro in 2002; it is likely that a long time would be needed before national currencies could be reintroduced. How would transactions be carried out in the meantime? Third, it may well be that some countries will have to default, but that does not require an exit from the Eurozone. By being part of the Eurozone, a country is protected from a simultaneous currency crisis with serious risks for its banking system. Fourth, there is no legal procedure for a country to leave – or to be expelled from – the Eurozone; adopting the euro was meant to be a one-way street. Fifth, the crisis has made it clear that the euro construction needs to be improved, and solutions exist. Finally, the Eurozone may not be an optimum currency area, but neither is it hugely ill-suited to operating a common currency. Arguably, the deeper problem has been political mishandling of the crisis.

In the end, the creation of the euro was partly justified by economic reasons, partly promoted for political reasons (see Chapter 15). Leaving the Eurozone would not represent a clear-cut economic gain and would have deep drawbacks in the short run, which is why no government is likely to do so for economic reasons. Political developments, on the other hand, may decide otherwise.

19.3.6 Short-run solutions: how to stop the crisis?

The crisis has two related components: a public debt crisis and a looming banking crisis. Both must be dealt with together. Governments with large, or merely suspicious-looking, debts must bring them down, at least as a share of GDP. This calls for contractionary fiscal policies, which hurt growth and make it very difficult to close the deficit. In addition, countries under market pressure face large interest rates, which makes further borrowing hard, perhaps impossible, to service.

---

[10] http://www.imf.org/external/np/speeches/2011/082711.htm.

Box 19.5   Giving up a currency: Argentina in 2001

In 1991 Argentina adopted a currency board arrangement, declaring that the peso would be worth US$1 and that this parity would never be changed. The convertibility law, as the arrangement was called, was solid because it required that the central bank hold as many dollars as it issued pesos. Full coverage of domestic currency, a characteristic of currency boards, makes the arrangement unassailable, in theory at least. Over the next few years, inflation – Argentina's scourge for decades – disappeared and the economy grew quite fast. People came to see the peso and the dollar as equivalent currencies. However, because inflation did not quite decline to the US rate, Argentine goods became gradually too expensive and the economy started to suffer, as Fig. 19.8 shows. Without the ability to depreciate and restore competitiveness, the situation became increasingly desperate. A political crisis set in and, in the midst of intense social turmoil, Argentina abandoned the convertibility law in late 2001.

The peso instantly lost half of its value. Millions of contracts set in dollars, from loans to rents and sales, were into total disarray. If they remained in dollars, borrowers, people with house rentals and large industrial producers would become bankrupt. If they were switched into pesos, the losses to lenders, house owners and sellers would be immense. It took months, and a devastating banking crisis, to sort the situation out. GDP contracted by more than 10 per cent in 2002, after having declined by nearly 20 per cent over the previous five years. Yet, the depreciation of the peso boosted Argentina's competitiveness and the economy turned around in 2003. From there on, it has grown very fast.

In many respects, the Argentine case is similar to an exit from a monetary union. It shows how difficult it is to abandon a currency but also how helpful a depreciation can be. One difference with a monetary union is that, during the currency board years, the peso continued to circulate alongside the dollar: not all contracts were in dollars, vending machines accepted mostly pesos, and the peso did not have to be reintroduced from scratch.

Figure 19.8 The real GDP of Argentina (US$ billion)

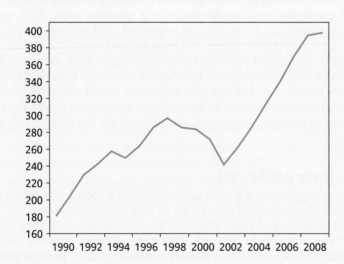

Source: World Development Indicators, World Bank

The Troika hopes that the combination of loans and deficit-reducing measures will still succeed, if only because it will favourably impress the financial markets. This would make it possible for governments currently under pressure to borrow again at low interest rates. Rightly or wrongly, the financial markets believe that this strategy will not work and that countries already in trouble, and some others as well, will have no choice but to repudiate their debts, at least partly. This is why these countries cannot borrow on the markets or, if they can, only at punitive interest rates.

A comprehensive solution is likely to involve two elements. First, some countries will have to repudiate some of their public debts to alleviate their burden. Second, as a consequence, banks will have to be rescued. A likely scenario is that the pattern observed since the beginning of the crisis will continue. Alarms will flare up on the markets, prompting the authorities to address the latest concern. This will bring about a lull, but markets will again focus on unresolved weaknesses and tensions will rise again. At the present time, the list of unresolved issues is the following.

Public debt restructuring

A number of countries are unlikely to stem the tide of their rising public debts. After more than a year of denial, the July 2011 Council accepted that Greece will need to restructure its debt. This has led to an arrangement for Private Sector Involvement (PSI) whereby the banks that hold Greek bonds will voluntarily refinance them when they mature, thus giving Greece a longer time horizon to sort itself out. The PSI programme has been arranged at the suggestion of banks and, unsurprisingly, it will not reduce the size of the debt burden significantly. It may help but it does not offer a lasting solution to the excessive size of the Greek debt.

Indeed, debt restructuring can either provide temporary relief but without reducing the value of the debt, or involve the cancellation of some fraction of the debt. The latter is probably unavoidable in a number of cases. Debt reduction is most unlikely to be voluntary, because creditors almost never agree collectively to take a loss. Even if some creditors are willing to reduce their claims, it is in the interest of the others to hold out and hope to be repaid in full once the debt burden has been brought down to a manageable level. For this reason, debt reductions are usually messy. Defaulting countries must negotiate agreements with a host of creditors who are upset in the first place, and who individually try to achieve special arrangements. Debt negotiations usually take quite some time – months or years.

The likely outcome is muddling through, with the following features. A small, insufficient, debt cancellation will be accepted by the EU, leading to painful negotiations between the defaulting government and banks, with considerable interference by the other governments keen to protect their own banks. It will then take some time to realize that the size of the default was insufficient, triggering another one, and another one, until the debts of a few countries have been reduced sufficiently.

Bank recapitalization

As explained in Section 19.3, debt cancellations are bound to put a number of banks under stress and to require bailouts by the authorities. Here again, after a period of denial – linked to the denial that defaults are inevitable – Eurozone governments are gradually recognizing that many banks are in a precarious situation. The failure of Dexia in October 2011 has been an important wake-up call.

Short of subjecting banks to a rigorous stress test, and drawing the implications, the authorities can try to muddle through. This will involve punctual bailouts when banks fail because they are unable to raise funds from the markets, their customers and their shareholders. It will also involve requests that banks raise more capital, which many may be unable to do. This will then force their governments to provide cash, possibly through partial or complete nationalization, possibly through other schemes that involve financing by state-owned institutions, which may be created to that effect, for example following the Swiss approach to the bailout of UBS presented in Box 19.6.

Box 19.6   The bailout of UBS

UBS was Switzerland's (and the world's – see Table 18.1) largest bank, with global operations and assets worth close to four times the country's GDP. UBS had acquired vast amounts of assets based on US mortgages, including the infamous subprimes. Following the collapse of Lehman Brothers, UBS appeared to be in serious difficulty. Since it was too big to fail, the Swiss authorities promptly decided to bail it out. Yet, they did not want to offer a gift to UBS. Quite to the contrary, they imagined a clever arrangement that would protect taxpayers and, possibly, be profitable. The November 2008 bailout of UBS included two steps.

First, the Swiss federal government recapitalized UBS. This took the form of a loan that could be transformed into shares at the discretion of the government. Thus, either UBS would reimburse the government, including interest on the loan, or the government would become a shareholder – and then sell its shares to make a profit – whichever was better for taxpayers. In fact, the government sold its loan to UBS to private investors in August 2009 and made a 20 per cent profit out of that transaction.

Second, the central bank, the Swiss National Bank (SNB), created a subsidiary called the Stabfund. The construction is rather complicated but it is designed to limit potential losses to the SNB, with the possibility of profits. It works as follows. The fund bought much of UBS toxic assets at market price, at a time when the market was depressed. The Stabfund received 90 per cent of its resources from a loan by the SNB, the remaining 10 per cent being provided by UBS. The Stabfund, under direct SNB control, is asked to sell its portfolio of assets – acquired at a low price – at its discretion over several years, with the objective of protecting the SNB. If the Stabfund suffers losses, the first 10 per cent are to be borne by UBS. If losses exceed 10 per cent, the SNB will not be fully reimbursed. If the sales turn out to be profitable, the SNB will receive back the full amount of its loan, including interest, plus 50 percent of the profits. Recent valuation indicates that the SNB is making a profit, but it will take a few years to know the end of the story.

19.4 Long-run solutions: how to avoid another Eurozone crisis?

The crisis has exposed some key weaknesses of the Eurozone construction.[11] First and foremost is the absence of a mechanism that enforces fiscal discipline in each and every member country. Second is the fragmentation of banking regulation and supervision among national authorities that protect their institutions and fail to internalize the overall effects of bank failures. Third is the ECB's reluctance, fed by internal divisions, to take on a determined leadership role. Fourth is the politicization of the rescue efforts, illustrated by the limited role played by the European Commission throughout the crisis. In the long run, after the crisis, these weaknesses will have to be addressed.

19.4.1 Fiscal discipline
As discussed at length in Chapter 17, existing arrangements have failed to deliver fiscal discipline throughout the Eurozone and the new Stability and Growth Pact is unlikely to be more effective until a new treaty reduces the sovereignty of national governments and their parliaments. With

---

[11] These weaknesses did not come as a surprise. Previous editions of the present textbook described them.

the no-bailout rule more in doubt than ever, this key weakness of the Eurozone remains. A number of better possibilities exist and some have been under consideration since the beginning of the crisis. One view is that the Eurozone must be strengthened and that more integration is needed. Another view is that the problem can be fixed without (much) more integration.

Less sovereignty and Eurobonds

The pro-integration camp considers that many governments have misused their fiscal sovereignty, to the point of endangering the euro. The response must be to reduce the room for fiscal policy manoeuvre that Member States have retained. Several solutions have been put forward, most of which require a Treaty change. One solution is to establish a 'federal' authority that would have the means to follow fiscal policies in Member States closely and the power to issue 'mandatory recommendations'. This idea comes in various guises (for example, an economic government for Europe or a Eurozone Finance Minister), all of which raise difficult questions about the role of the Commission, which is the EU's executive branch but has no specific Eurozone role.

Another pro-integration approach is the creation of Eurobonds, collectively issued by Eurozone governments. Eurobonds have several appealing features. They would cement solidarity. A single market for Eurobonds would develop, allowing Eurobonds to compete effectively with US Treasury bonds as the instrument of choice for other countries to accumulate foreign exchange reserves. Importantly, this would avoid the current situation where some countries are under heavy market pressure to the point where they might default. In effect, through these bonds, the governments would guarantee each other's borrowing. Obviously, no government would accept to underwrite another one's debt unless it is given an unbreakable guarantee that fiscal profligacy will no longer occur. Thus the Eurobonds idea cannot really be divorced from the fundamental issue of how to control fiscal discipline in each and every Eurozone member country.[12]

These pro-integration proposals involve a reduction in national sovereignty over fiscal policies. They echo the view that a monetary union cannot last long without a political union. No one really knows whether this assessment is correct or not. The Eurozone crisis has certainly shown the limits of a monetary union not backed by deep political integration.

Better national institutions

Yet another view instead blames bad institutions. It accepts that a monetary union cannot last long if fiscal discipline is not guaranteed in every Member State. It notes that the existing arrangements did not, and could not, work. The Stability and Growth Pact suffers from structural flaws (Chapter 17) and the no-bailout clause was meant to be a deterrent, which proved of no value as it was ignored the first time it became binding. This view notes that sovereignty in fiscal affairs does not preclude discipline at the national level. After all, it is in the interest of each country to limit the deficit bias and achieve fiscal discipline and many countries have adopted national institutional arrangements that work.

Various state-level fiscal discipline arrangements already exist. They include the Dutch procedure that binds governments for the duration of the legislature, independent councils that are influential whistle-blowers as in Sweden, the Swiss debt brake, a constitutional requirement that the budget be balanced over the long run, which has been adopted by Germany, or mandatory budget surpluses as in Chile and Brazil. Rather than aiming at deeper political integration, which

---

[12] One creative proposal differs. It suggests that countries would be allowed to issue Eurobonds – called 'blue bonds' – up to 60 per cent of their GDP. The rest, the 'red bonds', would remain purely national, with no collective protection and junior to the 'blue bonds'. Thus the collective signature would only guarantee the first tranche, which is reasonably safe and there is no need for sovereignty transfers. The proposal by Jacques Delpla and Jakob von Weizsacker is available at: http://www.bruegel.org/publications/publication-detail/publication/403-the-blue-bond-proposal/.

may face widespread opposition by public opinion, the idea is to formally require that Eurozone membership be subject to the adoption of adequate fiscal institutions tailored to each country's own political traditions.

The Commission has suggested making such arrangements a requirement, but this again requires a Treaty as it impinges on sovereign matters. Since the beginning of the crisis, a number of countries – following Germany, Ireland, Portugal, Spain and Italy – have adopted, or are considering adopting, various versions of the debt brake presented in Box 19.7.

Box 19.7   The Swiss debt brake

In 2009, Germany adopted a constitutional rule closely patterned after the Swiss 'debt brake'. The rule will be implemented in Germany in 2016.[1] The original Swiss arrangement was adopted and written into the constitution in 2000 and came into force in 2003. Figure 19.9 shows that the rule has been effective, including during the crisis.

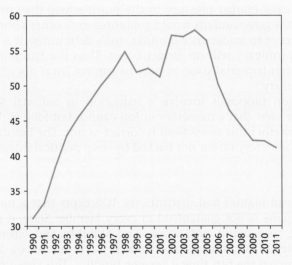

Figure 19.9 Swiss public debt (% of GDP)

Source: Economic Outlook, OECD

The Swiss debt brake requires that the overall federal budget be balanced over the cycle (in Germany the target is a deficit of less than 0.35 per cent of GDP). To that effect, any imbalance, whether positive or negative, is credited into a control account. The government must return this account to balance 'over the next few years' whenever it is negative. No requirement applies when the cumulated amount is positive. The rule combines clarity with flexibility, since it does not rule out temporary deficits while giving the government discretion on how quickly deficits are compensated for by surpluses. A further element of flexibility concerns exceptional circumstances (deep recession, natural disasters and the like).

[1] The implementation date has been delayed because of the crisis. A variant will apply to the Länder as of 2020.

19.4.2 Bank regulation and supervision

Chapter 18 explains that a number of institutions have been created following the crisis: the European Banking Authority (EBA), the European Systemic Risk Board (ESRB), the European Insurance and Occupational Pensions Authority (EIOPA) and the Joint Committee of the European Supervisory Authorities (ESAs). A common feature of these institutions is that they do not replace comparable pre-existing state-level institutions. The exception is the ESRB, which deals with a newly identified risk that was not monitored previously: the possibility that the failure of one institution brings down the whole financial system, as happened following the collapse of Lehman Brothers. While each country is now sensitive to the issue of systemic risk, the ESRB is clearly tasked with this responsibility.

In principle, the other Eurozone-level institutions must work hand in hand with their national counterparts. At a time of crisis, however, with a large amount of losses at stake, supervisors have a tendency to minimize the risk. Complete information may be slow to emerge precisely when rapid action is required. The objective of a single financial market, part of the agreed-upon Single Market requirement, is at odds with a decentralized system of supervision. Eventually, state-level regulation and supervision will have to be replaced by – or put under the authority of – Eurozone authorities.

19.4.3 ECB as lender of last resort

Central banks are lenders of last resort, because they can instantly create as much money as needed for emergency interventions. Governments, in contrast, must borrow to acquire emergency funds. As explained in Chapter 16, the ECB is primarily tasked with achieving low inflation. Yet, like all central banks, it must also maintain stability in occasionally disturbed financial markets, if necessary by lending to failing institutions. As a 'federal' institution, the ECB faces a difficulty: who should pay for its emergency interventions? The usual procedure is that the central bank provides instant cash for a bank bailout but the relevant government provides a formal guarantee that it will eventually cover the cost. This is an explicit feature of the Eurozone as well.[13] But what happens when governments are financially too weak to assume the costs? Worse, what happens when it is the governments themselves that are in need of bailout?

These questions have no formal answer, if only because the no-bailout clause ruled out ECB interventions when the states are unable to pay. As explained in Section 19.2.3, the no-bailout clause has been largely ignored and the ECB has waded into a legal and practical no-man's-land. In its first definition, the EFSF was only allowed to lend fresh money to governments unable to borrow at reasonable costs. It was barred from buying existing public debts. As a result, the ECB was the only Eurozone institution that could stabilize the bond markets. Its Securities Market Programme (SMP) has been used first to support the value of public debts of the three countries receiving EU–IMF support, and next to buy bonds issued by the Italian and Spanish governments, when these two countries came under market pressure in the summer of 2011.

While it is not uncommon for central banks to support government bonds, the SMP has raised many eyebrows. First, the ECB stands to suffer losses if it buys bonds from a country that subsequently defaults. Who will pay for these losses? Second, a long-held view is that central bank support of failing governments eventually leads to inflation. Inflation is not an issue as the Eurozone is undergoing low growth, but what will happen to the hundreds of billions of euros created by the ECB as part of its SMP purchases? Third, by bailing out governments, the ECB is creating a serious moral hazard. Will the SMP not provide incentives for governments to overspend if they may assume that any shortfall will be paid for by the ECB? Finally, as the residual buyer of public debts, the ECB is drawn into being part of national fiscal policies.

---

[13] In practice, the Eurosystem authorizes the relevant national central bank to carry out the emergency intervention.

On the other hand, the crisis is creating severe disturbances in financial markets, and financial stability is a responsibility of central banks. A contagion of state defaults, followed by bank distress and a deep recession, could sap political support for the euro. It is difficult to imagine that the ECB would remain idle when faced with a threat to the very existence of the euro. There is no simple answer to these questions either. They were not even asked when the euro was being set up, but the crisis has shown that more thinking and some action are needed.

19.4.4 Governance of the Eurozone

A spectacular feature of the crisis is that de facto management has been in the hands of the Eurozone's two largest countries, France and Germany. The Commission has been largely passive. There has always been a tension between the community principle and intergovernmentalism. In principle, the Commission assumes the executive role and Member States jointly hold the ultimate authority as the Council acts as the legislative branch of European government. The community principle is that the Commission takes initiatives and member governments approve or disapprove. Intergovernmentalism instead relies on governments to take and negotiate initiatives. The crisis has witnessed a shift to intergovernmentalism and a dominating role by the two largest countries.

The obvious reason for this shift is that a crisis requires prompt decision making and that the 17 Eurozone countries cannot collectively deliberate in this situation. In addition, the Commission's mandate is not limited to the Eurozone, so it has no particular authority for Eurozone affairs. In order to improve effectiveness, the Lisbon Treaty has created the post of President of the Council, currently held by Herman van Rompuy, but his brief also extends to the whole EU.

The crisis, therefore, has made it clear that the Eurozone needs its own system of governance. For a while, this role has been assumed by the Eurogroup, which brings together the Finance Ministers of the Eurozone. The Eurogroup is a subgroup of the ECOFIN Council, which includes all the Finance Ministers of the EU. Yet, given the importance of the issues treated during the crisis, it has been decided that the Heads of State and Governments of the Eurozone will meet twice a year. This is not a structure that can handle emergency situations, because of both its size and the episodic frequency of the meetings. Yet, it represents a symbolic step given the reluctance of formalizing a 'two-speed Europe'.

A number of other propositions have been advanced and the debate is sure to continue. For instance, the ECB President, Jean Claude Trichet, has suggested that a new position be created: the Economic and Finance Minister of Europe. This person would have some, as yet undefined, authority to enforce fiscal discipline in Member States, which may require a new Treaty.

19.5 Summary

Bank deregulation in the 1980s and 1990s changed the US financial industry. One of these changes implied the development of house mortgage companies. Easy credit resulted in the emergence of a house price bubble. The apparently unending rise of real estate prices, in turn, opened up home ownership to people hitherto considered too risky to lend to. The subprime loans allowed them to borrow temporarily at relatively low interest rates; rising housing prices allowed them to borrow again and again to pay back the original loans before interest rates stepped up.

The subprime loans were then disseminated throughout the banking systems in both the USA and Europe through the process of securitization. This processed lumped loans

into 'tranches'. The more senior securities were given top ratings and found their way into the books of subsidiaries of the world's largest and most highly reputed banks. When house prices turned down, this construction started to unravel. Stuck with 'toxic assets', banks became suspicious of one another. Interbank markets froze. Cut off from their cash lifeline, banks started to wobble until Lehman Brothers failed.

The ensuing crisis has shown how tightly linked large banks are. A relatively small accident has mushroomed into a global financial meltdown. European banks have been particularly affected because some held large quantities of securities backed by subprimes but also because the freezing of the interbank markets cut essential access to short-term financing. Central banks vigorously stepped in to provide banks with liquidity.

Governments too intervened quite forcefully. They used fiscal policy to avoid a protracted recession, deepening budget deficits above and beyond the cyclical effects. In many countries, they also bailed out banks, sometimes at great cost. The result has been a rapid increase in public debts. This, in turn, worried the financial markets, paving the way for the second stage of the crisis.

Greece was the first country to face mounting financial market concerns. As it became clear that the Greek government could not borrow from the financial markets, an extraordinary rescue was coordinated between the IMF, the ECB and the other Eurozone countries. At the same time, it was decided to create the European Financial Stability Facility (EFSF) to cope with possible future needs of Eurozone governments. The EFSF and the IMF then provided assistance to Ireland and Portugal.

A condition for these loans is that the borrowing countries close their budget deficits quite soon. With the economy in recession, fiscal stabilization measures produce disappointing results while they prevent the economies from recovering. This reinforces financial market fears that some countries will have to restructure their public debts. Debt restructuring, in turn, threatens banks, which hold large amounts of public debts. This is why the Eurozone now faces a combination of sovereign debt and bank crises. Contagion to more countries is a distinct possibility, further raising the stakes for the Eurozone and making solutions increasingly difficult, both economically and politically.

The crisis has shown that the Eurozone construction suffered from important weaknesses. These weaknesses include the lack of fiscal discipline in some member countries, the absence of Eurozone-wide banking regulation and supervision, the ECB's difficult position as lender of last resort, and the lack of economic governance. These are issues for longer-run reforms, some of which may require a new Treaty.

Self-assessment questions

1 What is the EFSF? How is it financed and what actions can it undertake?
2 What is the phenomenon of information asymmetry? How can it explain why banks refuse credit to some customers? How can it contribute to systemic risk in financial markets?
3 Why are some countries under market pressure?
4 Explain why banks and governments are caught in a situation where they can weaken each other.
5 What are interest spreads? What do they tell us? Use Fig. 19.7 to show that the Greek bailout did not achieve its aim.

Essay questions

1 Why is the sovereign debt crisis spreading only within the Eurozone?
2 Should subprime lending have been subject to rigorous consumer protection and, if so, what would you propose?
3 Imagine a breakup of the Eurozone.
4 How would you set up a European government for the Eurozone?
5 If you were the President of the ECB, what would you have done since early 2010?

Further reading: the aficionado's corner

As the crisis is ongoing, most writings are not yet published. An excellent source of high-quality comments and analyses is the website VoxEU (http://www.voxeu.org/).

On financial crises in general:
Reinhart, C. and K. Rogoff (2009) *This Time is Different*, Princeton University Press, Princeton, NJ.

On the origins of the crisis in the Eurozone:
Eichengreen, B. (2009) 'Ireland's Rescue Package: Disaster for Ireland, Bad Omen for the Eurozone', VoxEU, http://www.voxeu.org/index.php?q=node/5887.

On the ECB policies:
De Grauwe, P. (2011) 'The European Central Bank as a Lender of Last Resort', VoxEU, http://www.voxeu.org/index.php?q=node/6884.

On fiscal discipline in the Eurozone:
Bordo, M., L. Jonung and A. Marliewicz (2011) 'A Fiscal Union for the Euro: Some Lessons from History', VoxEU, http://www.voxeu.org/index.php?q=node/7007.
Cooley, T. and R. Marimon (2011) 'A Credible Commitment for the Eurozone', VoxEU, http://www.voxeu.org/index.php?q=node/6772.
IMF (2009) 'Fiscal Rules – Anchoring Expectations for Sustainable Public Finances', http://www.imf.org/external/np/pp/eng/2009/121609.pdf.
Wyplosz, C. (2011) 'Fiscal discipline: rules rather than institutions', *National Institute Economic Review* 217: R19–R30.

On the banking crisis:
Hau, H. (2011) 'Bank Recapitalisation is the Best Euro Rescue Strategy', VoxEU, http://www.voxeu.org/index.php?q=node/6923.

On governance of the Eurozone:
De Grauwe, P. (2011) 'The Governance of a Fragile Eurozone', unpublished paper, University of Leuven, http://www.econ.kuleuven.be/ew/academic/intecon/Degrauwe/PDG-papers/Discussion_papers/Governance-fragile-eurozone_s.pdf.

On a breakup of the Eurozone:
Eichengreen, B. (2010) 'The Euro: Love it or Leave it?', VoxEU, http://www.voxeu.org/index.php?q=node/729.
Levy Yeyati (2011) 'How Argentina left its Eurozone', VoxEU, http://www.voxeu.org/index.php?q=node/7055.

References
Mackowiak, B., F.P. Mongelli, G. Noblet and F. Smets (eds) (2009) *The Euro at Ten – Lessons and Challenges*, ECB.

Index